Richmond County, Virginia
MARRIAGE RECORDS
1854–1890
Annotated

Wesley E. Pippenger

HERITAGE BOOKS
2018

HERITAGE BOOKS

AN IMPRINT OF HERITAGE BOOKS, INC.

Books, CDs, and more—Worldwide

For our listing of thousands of titles see our website
at
www.HeritageBooks.com

Published 2018 by
HERITAGE BOOKS, INC.
Publishing Division
5810 Ruatan Street
Berwyn Heights, Md. 20740

Cover Photo: "Busy Day in Warsaw, Around 1907." This photograph depicts the courthouse bounds at the turn of the 20th century. The buildings shown in the picture are as follows, from left to right: the L.E. Mumford Bank, Coleman's Store, and the Wallace Hotel. Across the road are a small frame building thought to be Shackleford's Store, the Colonial courthouse, and the 1816 clerk's office. Doubtless it is court day, and some of the people are heading to the Wallace Hotel dining room for lunch. [Courtesy: Richmond County Museum, Warner Collection]

International Standard Book Number
Paperbound: 978-0-7884-5813-2

TABLE OF CONTENTS

INTRODUCTION

This work is a compilation of data found in 1,702 marriage records of Richmond County, Virginia, for the years 1854 through 1890. The number of marriages greatly increased after the War of the Rebellion. The data are derived from multiple sources, including: marriage licenses or applications, minister returns of marriage, consents by guardian or parent, or entries in either of two bound marriage registers, and supplemented with family Bible records, cemetery records, military records, and other publications. The index contains an entry heading for C.S.A. to list 160 Confederate soldiers identified. Please note that a considerable amount of information about cemetery burials can be found on the Internet at the website known as *Findagrave.com*, and may be consulted for accuracy and thoroughness.

Original records have been microfilmed by the Library of Virginia, and each of the items used are listed below along with the reel number of the film found at the Library. Not all recorded parts of a marriage are necessarily found together on a microfilm copy. The parties are presumed to be residents of Richmond County at the time of the record unless otherwise stated. Also, the place of marriage and residence is presumed to be Richmond County unless otherwise noted.

With respect to consents or other notes in the file at the courthouse in Warsaw, Virginia, the name of the bride or groom is not repeated unless the signature is different from the clerk's recording of the names. If either party did not sign their name completely, it is noted, i.e. Sally [her X mark] Smith. Some difficulty is found with surnames being spelled differently between multiple, or within the same, record. For instance, it is difficult to determine between Clark or Clarke, Morris or Morriss, Sanders or Saunders, Sanford or Sandford, Venie or Veney, etc. The spelling found on a person's tombstone may be used when found.

Data have been presented as found in the original records by considering all individual pieces found. Oddly, the date of marriage on the minister return and in either of the two marriage registers (state and local copy) differs frequently. In these cases, the date found on the minister return portion of the marriage license is used. Also, the compiler has inserted information from outside sources in brackets, i.e. "[ ]", or in over 1,400 footnotes. These additional sources include a range of published marriage records from surrounding counties as well as the well-respected work of the late George Harrison Sanford King, in his *Marriages of Richmond County, Virginia, 1668-1853*, which contains much additional data in appendices, addenda and corrigenda. Additional publications used are found in the Bibliography. Specific sources are listed at the end of each item. The index contains over 12,000 entries.

I thank Rosa S. Forrester, Clerk of Richmond County Circuit Court for her assistance and support.

Wesley E. Pippenger
Little Egypt
Tappahannock, Virginia

ABBREVIATIONS AND SOURCE CODES

Abbreviations

B	Black		FB	Free Blacks
a.	Born		LVA	Library of Virginia
bur.	Buried		M.G.	Minister of [the] Gospel
C.S.A.	Confederate States Army		q.v.	Latin for *quod vide*, meaning to see
C	Consent			elsewhere
Co.	County		res.	residence of or resided in
Col.	Colored		Rev.	Reverend
d.	Died		s/o	son of
d/o	daughter of		w/o	Wife of
Dr.	Doctor		wid/o	Widow of

Old style abbreviations are used for states, i.e. Va. for Virginia, or Mass. for Massachusetts.

Source Codes

C	Marriage Certificates, Consents, Licenses and Ministers Returns, 1850-1854 [LVA Reel 202]
C1	Marriage Certificates, Consents and Licenses, 1854-1858 [LVA Reel 203]
C2	Marriage Certificates, Consents and Licenses, 1858-1860 [LVA Reel 204]
C3	Marriage Certificates, Consents and Licenses, 1861-1867 [LVA Reel 205]
C4	Marriage Certificates, Consents and Licenses, 1866-1868 [LVA Reel 206]
C5	Marriage Certificates, Consents and Licenses, 1868-1871 [LVA Reel 207]
C6	Marriage Certificates, Consents and Licenses, 1871-1873 [LVA Reel 208]
C7	Marriage Certificates, Consents and Licenses, 187[4]-1876 [LVA Reel 209]
C8	Marriage Certificates, Consents and Licenses, 1877-1879 [LVA Reel 210]
C9	Marriage Certificates, Consents and Licenses, 1879-1882 [LVA Reel 211]
C10	Marriage Certificates, Consents and Licenses, 1882-1885 [LVA Reel 212]
C11	Marriage Certificates, Consents and Licenses, 1885-1888 [LVA Reel 213]
C12	Marriage Certificates, Consents and Licenses, 1888-1891 [LVA Reel 214]
NN	The *Northern Neck News* (Warsaw, Va.). Some entries are found for the period 1879-1886.
R	Register of Marriages, 1853-1935, copy of Virginia Bureau of Vital Statistics at The Library of Virginia, varying content, with page number when found [LVA Reel 42 Vital Statistics].
R1	Register of Marriages, 1853-1906, in the clerk's office, with page number; however, due to deteriorating condition it is not served to researchers. [LVA Reel 53]

ACTS
of the
GENERAL ASSEMBLY
of the
STATE OF VIRGINIA

ACT REQUIRING VITAL STATISTICS

Chapter 25
An Act Concerning the Registration of Births, Marriages and Deaths,
Passed April 11, 1853

*Three registers
to be kept by
clerk.*

1. Be it enacted by the general assembly, that from and after the first day of January eighteen hundred and fifty-four, the clerk of every county and corporation court shall keep three books, to be called, respectively, the register of marriages, the register of births, and the register of deaths.

*Duty of minis-
ters.*

2. Henceforth it shall be the duty of every minister or other person celebrating a marriage, and of the clerk or keeper of the records of any religious society which solemnizes marriages by the consent of the parties in open congregation, at once to make a record of every marriage between white persons solemnized by or before him, and within two months after such marriage to return a certificate thereof, signed by him, to the clerk of the court of the county or corporation in which the same is solemnized. Such record and certificate shall set forth, as far

*What set forth
in his record.*

as the same can be ascertained, the date and place of the marriage, the full names of both the parties, their ages and condition before the marriage (whether single or widowed), the places of their birth and residence, the names of their parents and the occupation of the husband.

*Abstract by
clerk.*

3. The clerk to whom such certificate shall be returned, shall file and preserve the same in his office, and within twenty days after receiving the same, record a full abstract thereof in his register of marriages, setting out, in convenient tabular form, all the circumstances therein stated and the name of the person signing the certificate, and make an index of the names of both the parties married.

*If marriage out
of state.*

4. If at the time of celebrating any marriage out of this state, either or both of the parties thereto be a resident or residents of this state, a certificate or statement thereof, verified by the affidavit of any person present at such celebration, may be returned to the clerk of the court of the county or corporation in which the husband resides, if he be such resident, and otherwise, of the county or corporation in which the wife resides, and an abstract thereof shall be recorded by him in the manner prescribed in the third section.

*Penalty on min-
ister for noncom-
pliance.*

5. If any minister who shall give bond in order to his being authorized to celebrate marriage in this state, shall fail to comply with the second section, the condition of such bond shall be deemed to be thereby broken, and he shall be subject to the penalty hereinafter prescribed for such failure.

6. Every such clerk of a court shall, on or before the first day of the next November term of his court, post at the front door of his courthouse a copy of the second section, with a statement of the penalties for violations thereof.

7. Every commissioner of the revenue shall make an annual registration of the births and deaths in his district. When he ascertains the personal property subject to taxation, he shall ascertain the births and deaths that have occurred in the year ending on the thirty-first day of December preceding, and such circumstances as he is hereinafter required to record. He shall ascertain the births and deaths in each family from the head of such family, if practicable.

8. He shall record in a book to be kept by him for that purpose, so far as can be ascertained, the date and place of every such birth; the full name of the child, (if it has a name;) the sex and color thereof; and if colored, whether free or slave; also whether the child was born alive or stillborn; the full name of the mother; and if the child be free and born in wedlock, the full name, occupation and residence of the father; if the child be a slave, the name of the owner; if there be more than one child born at one birth, the fact and number shall be stated; and any other circumstances of interest relating to any birth.

9. Every such commissioner shall in like manner record in a book to be kept by him for that purpose, the place and date of every death in his district during the year ending on the preceding thirty-first day of December; the full name, sex, age, condition (whether married or not,) and color of the deceased; and if colored, whether free or slave; also the occupation, if any, of the deceased, and his or her place of birth, the names of his or her parents, and (if the deceased was married) the name of the husband or wife; and if the deceased was a slave, the name of the owner; also the disease or cause of the death, so far as such facts can be ascertained.

10. The commissioner shall make and subscribe an affidavit, upon each of the books so to be kept by him, to the effect that he has pursued the directions in this act, according to the best of his skill; and he shall return his said books to the clerk of the court of his county or corporation on or before the first day of June.

11. Such clerk shall thereupon record a full abstract of the contents of the said book, containing a record of births, in his said register of births, setting forth, in convenient tabular form, all the circumstances hereinbefore required to be recorded, with references to the commissioners' books, and making an alphabetical index of the names of the free children born, and (when they have no names) of the names of the parents, and also of the names of the owners of the slaves born, placing in the index the dates of the births.

12. He shall in like manner record a full abstract of the contents of the said book, containing a record of deaths, in his said register of deaths, setting forth, in convenient tabular form, all the circumstances hereinbefore required to be recorded, with reference to the commissioners' book, and making an alphabetical index of the names of the deceased and the names of the owners of deceased slaves, and placing in the index the dates of the deaths.

13. Every such clerk of a court shall file and preserve in his office the books so deposited with him by the commissioners.

14. He shall transmit to the auditor of public accounts a copy of his register of marriages during the preceding year, on or before the first day of March in each year, and a copy of his

register of births and register of deaths during the preceding year, on or before the first day of August in each year.

15.   Such copies shall be filed and preserved in the said auditor's office, and from them the auditor shall prepare an abstract annually of marriages, births and deaths in each county and corporation, and make a report upon said registrations once in every period of two years, to be laid before the general assembly.

16.   The said books to be kept by the clerks, and copies, (or of any part thereof,) certified by the clerk lawfully having custody thereof, shall be prima facie evidence of the facts therein set forth in all cases.

17.   A clerk shall be entitled to ten cents for every copy of an entry in said books relating to a marriage, birth or death, to be paid by the party requiring the copy.

18.   If a commissioner in any case cannot obtain the requisite information concerning any birth or death from the head of the family, as before required, he shall obtain the same from such persons as are hereinafter required to give it; or if that cannot be done, from any other persons, always recording the name of the person giving the information.

19.   Every physician and surgeon shall, in a book to be kept by him, make a record at once of the death of every person dying in this state, upon whom he has attended at the time of such death, setting out as far as practicable the circumstances herein required to be recorded by a commissioner respecting deaths. He shall give to a commissioner of the revenue, whenever called on by him for that purpose, annually, a copy of such record, so far as the same relates to deaths in such commissioner's district.

20.   Every coroner shall keep a like record of the deaths in relation to which he acts officially, and give a copy thereof to any commissioner of the revenue, whenever called on by him for that purpose, annually, so far as the same relates to deaths in such commissioner's district. For every neglect or failure to perform any duty required of him by this section, a coroner shall forfeit twenty dollars.

21.   The commissioner shall make such entries or corrections in his record of deaths as may be supplied or warranted by the copies so to be furnished to him by physicians, surgeons and coroners, noting the source of the information.

22.   The head of any family, if he be not at his residence when the commissioner calls there to obtain the information required by this act to be obtained of him, shall give the same information to the proper commissioner of the revenue on or before the first day of June in the same year; and for a failure or neglect to do so, shall forfeit one dollar. If any head of a family, being lawfully requested to give any such information, shall refuse to give the same, he shall forfeit ten dollars.

23.   If any commissioner of the revenue fail to obtain any information respecting a birth or death, which he is by this act authorized or required to obtain, and which he can produce, he shall for every such failure and for every failure to record the information acquired by him respecting a birth or death, according to this act, forfeit five dollars.

For failure to
perform duties
in 10th section.

24.   If any commissioner of the revenue fail to perform the duties required of him by the tenth section of this act, he shall forfeit fifty dollars.

Penalty of clerk
for failure of
duty.

25.   If any clerk of a court fail to perform the any duty required of him by the third section of this act, he shall forfeit ten dollars for every such offence; and if he fail to perform any duty required of him by the eleventh, twelfth, thirteenth or fourteenth section, he shall, for every such offence, forfeit fifty dollars.

Fine for making
false returns.

26.   If any clerk of a court, commissioner of the revenue, physician, surgeon, coroner or minister celebrating a marriage, or clerk or keeper of the records of any religious society, shall, in any book, register or record, which such officer or person is by this act required to keep or make, or in any copy or certificate which by this act he is required to make or give, knowingly make any false, erroneous or fraudulent entry, record, registration or written statement, he shall for every such offence forfeit not less than one hundred nor more than five hundred dollars.

Fine for false
information.

27.   If any person, upon whose information or statement any record or registration may lawfully be made under this act, shall knowingly give any false information, or make any false statement to be used for the purpose of making any such record or registration, he shall forfeit not less than fifty nor more than three hundred dollars for every such offence.

Forms and in-
structions, how
finished.

28.   The auditor of public accounts shall furnish the clerk of every county and corporation court and every commissioner of the revenue with all forms and instructions which he may deem necessary or proper for carrying this act into effect.

Commencement.

29.   This act shall take effect **the first day of July eighteen hundred and fifty three**.

MINISTERS

Ainslie, Peter, Jr. Minister of the Gospel. Disciples of Christ. Died 22 MAR 1887 of tuberculosis in Essex Co., age 70y2m25d, s/o Rev. Peter Ainslie of Richmond Co., probably buried at *Cottage Hill* in Essex Co. Records 1863-1880.

Bain, William F. Served King George Circuit, Methodist Episcopal Church South. Born 20 JUL 1831 in Williamsburg, Va., d. 20 JAN 1902 in Charlottesville, Va., bur. Cedar Grove Cemetery of Fauquier Co., s/o Rev. George A. and Frances M. Bain. Records 1864-1869.

Battaile, B.R. Records 1873.

Baynham, William Armistead (1813-1887).[1] Minister of the Gospel. Baptist. Records 1855.

Beale, Frank Brown. Born 11 APR 1852 at Hague, Westmoreland Co., d. 31 JUL 1908 at Helmet, King and Queen Co., bur. Upper King and Queen Baptist Church, s/o Gen. Richard Lee Turberville Beale[2] and Lucy Maria Brown. Served Nomini Baptist, 1856-1857; Menokin Baptist, 1872, m. 6 DEC 1883 in King and Queen Co. to Susie M.H. Garnett. Records 1879-1888.

Beale, George William (1842-1921). Records 1873-1874.

Berry, J. Dorsey. No information.

Betts, Charles Nelms. Born 15 MAR 1837, died 7 JUN 1902, bur. Smithfield Baptist Church cemetery. Served Coan and Fairfield Baptist, Totuskey Baptist, 1888-1889. Records 1886-1888.

Blackwell, Peter (Col.). Served Mount Zion Baptist to 1883. Records 1777-1882.

Brannin, James F. (1826-1912). Methodist Episcopal Church South. Records 1861-1880.

Brown, Allen (Col.). Records 1868-1882.

Carter, Walker (Col.). Records 1879-1888.

Claybrook, Frederick William. Born 3 AUG 1844, d. 14 AUG 1914 in Kilmarnock, Lancaster Co., s/o Richard A. Claybrook and Charlotte T. Brown. Served Lebanon Baptist, then Farnham Baptist, 1880-1886. He was married twice. Records 1878-1885.

Coffin, William H. Died in NOV 1884. Served North Farnham Episcopal, 1854-1856. Records 1854-1856.

Connelly, George Matthew. Served Welcome Grove Baptist from 1888. Records 1888-1890. Also as George M. Conley.

Corbin, Travis (Col.). Records 1866-1874.

Crocker, William Andrew. Born 4 NOV 1827 in Isle of Wight Co., d. 27 JUN 1901 in Farnham, Va., bur. Calvary United Methodist Church cemetery, s/o James Crocker and Frances Hiles Woodley. Served the Methodist Episcopal Church South in Warsaw in 1874; Heathsville Circuit. He married Frances Keaton Jennings, b. 5 APR 1827, d. 13 DEC 1898. Records 1872-1890.

DeBerry, Junius B., pastor Richmond Circuit, Methodist Church. Died FEB 1909 in his 74th year. Records 1877-1878.

Dodson, Bartholomew. Records 1847-1870.

Dunaway, Elder A.B. Served Lebanon Baptist; Farnham Baptist, 1871-1879. Records 1873-1878.

Dunaway, J. Manning. Served Farnham Baptist, 1889-1892; Totuskey Baptist, 1890-1892. Records 1889-1890.

Fisher, Andrew. Served North Farnham Episcopal, 1859-1860. Wife Margaret Poe. Records 1859-1871.

---

[1] There is a tablet to the memory of Rev. William A. Baynham (b. 13 OCT 1813, d. 16 JUN 1887) at Enon Baptist Church at Supply, Va., just within Essex Co. and its boundary with Caroline Co. His wife Virginia Baynham (d. 8 FEB 1853 age 67) and son John M. Baynham (1811-1856) are bur. at *Springfield*, located just south of Loretto in Essex Co., Va.

[2] Richard Lee Turberville Beale (b. 24 MAY 1819, d. 18 APR 1893) and his wife Lucy Maria Brown (d. 15 JAN 1894 age 74) are bur. in the Beale Family Cemetery at *Hickory Hill* near Hague, Va.

Fones, Henry Harrison, M.G. Served Rappahannock Baptist up to 1887 and again 1888-1894; Farnham Baptist, 1887-1888, and other locations. Born 16 MAR 1840 in Westmoreland Co., d. 24 JUN 1922 in Washington, D.C., bur. Rappahannock Baptist Church cemetery. Served in several military companies, and Chaplin in the 55th Va. Inf., C.S.A. Married to Susan Ann Pullen. Records 1866-1890.

Goodwin, John. Minister of the Gospel. Records 1854-1855.

Graham, Jeremiah. Records 1869-1877.

Hankinson, Isaiah. Served Mulberry Chapel. Records 1867.

Johnson, B.H. Served the Methodist Episcopal Church South. Records 1855.

Johnson, Martin. Served North Farnham Episcopal, 1883-1885. Records 1884-1886.

Kinsolving, Arthur Barksdale. Died 1951 in Fisher's Island, N.Y., bur. St. Thomas Episcopal Church cemetery, Owings Mills, Baltimore Co., Md. Married in 1896 to Sally Archer Bruce. Served North Farnham Episcopal, 1886-1889. Records 1887-1889.

King, Henry P.F. Methodist Episcopal Church. Records 1857.

Kirk, William Heath. Born 18 AUG 1804, d. 15 MAR 1884, bur. Coan Baptist Church cemetery, Heathsville, Va. Served Farnham Baptist up to 1848; Coan and Morattico Baptist Churches in Northumberland County. Records 1854-1876.

Laws, George (Col.). Served New Zion Baptist from 1867. Records 1866-1890.

Leonard, Chauncey (Col.). Records 1871.

Lewis, Robert (Col.). Served Clarksville Baptist. Records 1880-1890.

Moore, Lloyd. Records 1857-1860.

Nash, Bushrod W. No information.

Northam, George H. Son of George R. Northam who was pastor of Nomini Baptist; served Menokin Baptist, 1848-1854 and was succeeded by his son George H. Northam, Jr. for 17 years. The father, born 1793, died 1854, and his wife Elizabeth Sanford Walker (b. 1827, d. 18 AUG 1856) are probably buried in the Sanford Family Cemetery located at *Springfield*, near Montross, Va. Records 1853-1890.

Payne, Daniel. Records 1872-1886.

Porter, James S., M.G. Methodist Episcopal Church South. Records 1862-1863.

Pullen, John, M.G. Served Rappahannock Baptist, 1842-1867, and Nomini Baptist. Born 7 JUL 1804, d. 30 DEC 1869, bur. Rappahannock Baptist Church cemetery. Records 1847-1866.

Reamy, Adoniram Judson. Born 19 APR 1853 at Foneswood, Va., d. 21 OCT 1935 in Edwardsville, Northumberland Co., bur. Warsaw Baptist Church cemetery. Married Mattie Ramsdell, b. 1 AUG 1857 in Georgia, d. 22 MAR 1938 in Edwardsville, Va.

Reamy, Robert Neale. Served Rappahannock Baptist in 1867, assisted at Welcome Baptist. Born 1 FEB 1817, d. 27 AUG 1894, bur. in Reamy Family cemetery at Foneswood, Va. He was married to Virginia Jane Owens, b. 1 FEB 1822 at Shiloh, King George Co., d. 12 APR 1900 in Northumberland Co. Records 1875-1890.

Reynolds, Albert D. Born 1844, d. 12 FEB 1912. Served in Co. D, 9th Va. Cav., C.S.A. Served Coan Church, and Totuskey Baptist, 1892-1896. He was married twice. Records 1883-1887.

Rich, Edmond (Col.). Records 1878-1890.

Robinson, Jacob (Col.). Served Mount Zion Baptist, 1884-1902; Mulberry Baptist. Served 1887-1890.

Rowe, John Gallatin. Born 27 FEB 1827 in Fredericksburg, Va., d. 16 APR 1891 of cancer, s/o George Rowe and Lucy Leitch. Founded Bowling Green Methodist Church in Bowling Green, Va. Married Margaret Ann Purcell. Records 1857-1859.

Sanford, R.J. Born c.1825, also a physician in Westmoreland Co. Records 1871-1887.

Sparks, Charles (Col.). Served Mount Zion Baptist Church. Records 1882-1887.

Thomas, Thomas G. (Col.). Founding pastor of Clarksville Baptist c.1868. Records 1866-1890.

Tucker, Beverley Dandridge. Born 9 NOV 1846, d. 17 JAN 1930, bur. Zion Episcopal Church, Charles Town, W.Va. Episcopal Bishop, served St. John's Episcopal Church at Warsaw, Va., 1873-1882. Married to Anna Maria Washington (1851-1927).

Veney, David "Davy," Sr. (Col.). Served Jerusalem Baptist at Emmerton, Va. to 1867, then Mulberry Baptist.

Walker, W.W. Methodist Episcopal Church South; prisoner in 1864 at Point Lookout. Records 1857-1888.

Ward, William Norvell. Protestant Episcopal clergyman, b. 19 APR 1805 in Lynchburg, Va., graduated 1834 from the Theological Seminary in Alexandria, first served in Spotsylvania Co., m. 9 AUG 1836 in Leesburg, Va. to Mary Smith Blincoe. Served North Farnham Episcopal from 1840-1853. Instrumental in organizing the 55th Virginia Infantry of the C.S.A. He died 25 FEB 1881[1] at *Bladensfield* near Warsaw, Va. and was buried in Hollywood Cemetery of Richmond, Va. See Evelyn D. Ward, *The Children of Bladensfield* (New York, N.Y.: The Viking Press, 1978) for story of the Ward Family.

Weaver, James A. Elder (1810-1895). Served Nomini Baptist Church. Records 1857-1877.

Wharton, Dabney Miller (1804-1887). Memorialized at St. James Episcopal Church, Montross, Va. Rector, Montross Parish. Records 1866-1887.

Wilkinson, John (Col.). Served Ebenezer Baptist and Mulberry Baptist. Records 1880.

Williams, Elijah L. Served Farnham Baptist, 1849-1852. Records 1845-1866.

Williamson, Robert. Minister of the Gospel. Served Farnham Baptist, 1856-1870, and founded the Farnham Male Institute. Born 10 DEC 1828 in Princess Anne Co., d. 2 OCT 1910. He was married first to Matoaca Dickenson, b. 25 NOV 1842 in King and Queen Co., d. 27 JUL 1890. His second wife was Sarah James Dickenson, b. 2 NOV 1854, d. 28 JAN 1933. All were bur. in Farnham Baptist Church cemetery.

---

[1] Also see *Northern Neck News*, 4 MAR 1881 and 1 APR 1881. Hereafter abbreviated NN:.

MARRIAGE LICENSE.

VIRGINIA, *Richmond County*   to wit:

To any Person Licensed to Celebrate Marriages:

You are hereby authorized to join together in the Holy State of Matrimony, according to the rites and ceremonies of your Church, or religious denomination, and the laws of the Commonwealth of Virginia, *Richard L Belfield* and *Mary P. Crabb*

Given under my hand, as Clerk of the *County* Court of *Richmond County* this *27* day of *May* 186*8*

Ro Hall CLERK.

CERTIFICATE TO OBTAIN A MARRIAGE LICENSE.

To be annexed to the License, required by Act passed 15th March, 1861.

Time of Marriage, *May 28th 1868*

Place of Marriage, *Richmond County, Va.*

Full names of Parties Married, *Richard L Belfield & Mary P Crabb*

Age of Husband, *21 years*

Age of Wife, *21 years*

Condition of Husband, (widowed or single,) *single*

Condition of Wife, (widowed or single,) *single*

Place of Husband's Birth, *Richmond County*

Place of Wife's Birth, *Same*

Place of Husband's Residence, *same*

Place of Wife's Residence, *same*

Names of Husband's Parents, *John D. & Elizabeth Belfield*

Names of Wife's Parents, *William M. M. & Ann T Crabb*

Occupation of Husband, *Farmer*

Given under my hand this *27* day of *May* 186*8*

Ro Hall CLERK.

MINISTER'S RETURN OF MARRIAGE.

I CERTIFY, that on the *28* day of *May* 1868, at *Pittsville*
Richmond Co. Va, *the residence of Bride's father*, I united in marriage the above named and described parties, under authority of the annexed License.

Peter Ainslie

☞ The Minister celebrating a Marriage is required, within TEN days thereafter, to return the License to the Office of the Clerk who issued the same, with an endorsement thereon of the FACT of such marriage, and of the TIME and PLACE of celebrating the same.

Figure 3 - Marriage License Sample 1

MARRIAGE LICENSE.

Virginia, _Richmond County_ **to-wit:**

TO ANY PERSON LICENSED TO CELEBRATE MARRIAGES:

You are hereby authorized to join together in the Holy State of Matrimony, according to the rites and ceremonies of your Church, or Religious Denomination, and the laws of the Commonwealth of Virginia, _James Homes_ and _Cealia Gordon_

GIVEN under my hand, as Clerk of the _____ _County_ Court of _Richmond County_, this _8th_ day of _April_, 18_79_.

L. D. Warner, Clerk.

CERTIFICATE TO OBTAIN A MARRIAGE LICENSE.

To be Annexed to the License, required by Acts passed 15th March, 1861, and February 27th, 1866.

Time of Marriage _Apr. 10th 1879_

Place of Marriage _Richmond Co._

Full Names of Parties Married _James Homes & Cealia Gordon_

Color _colored_

Age of Husband _54 years_

Age of Wife _28 years_

Condition of Husband (widowed or single) _Widowed_

Condition of Wife (widowed or single) _Single_

Place of Husband's Birth _Richmond Co._

Place of Wife's Birth _Richmond Co._

Place of Husband's Residence _Richmond Co._

Place of Wife's Residence _Richmond Co._

Names of Husband's Parents _Phil Homes & Daphne Homes_

Names of Wife's Parents _Ellic Gordon & Maria Gordon_

Occupation of Husband _Farming_

Given under my hand this _8th_ day of _April_, 18_79_.

L. D. Warner, Clerk.

MINISTER'S RETURN OF MARRIAGE.

I CERTIFY, That on the _10_ day of _Apr_, 18_79_, at _the house of james homes_ I united in Marriage the above-named and described parties, under authority of the annexed License.

J G Thomas

☞ The Minister celebrating a Marriage is required, within TEN days thereafter, to return the License to the Office of the Clerk who issued the same, with an endorsement thereon of the FACT of such Marriage, and of the TIME and PLACE of celebrating the same.

Figure 4 - Marriage License Sample 2

Marriage License

Virginia, *Richmond County* to wit:

TO ANY PERSON LICENSED TO CELEBRATE MARRIAGES:

You are hereby authorized to join together in the Holy State of Matrimony, according to the rites and ceremonies of your Church, or religious denomination, and the laws of the Commonwealth of Virginia, *Alfred H. Belfield* and *Susan Ann Saunders*

Given under my hand, as Clerk of the *County* Court of *Richmond County* this *22nd* day *December 1879*

L. D. Warner Clerk.

CERTIFICATE TO OBTAIN A MARRIAGE LICENSE.

To be annexed to the License, required by Acts passed 16th March 1861, and February 27th, 1866.

Time of Marriage,	*Dec. 25. 1879*	Condition of Wife, (widowed or single)	*Single*
Place of Marriage.	*Richmond Co.*	Place of Husband's Birth,	*Richmond Co.*
Full Names of Parties Married.	*Alfred H. Belfield & Susan Ann Saunders*	Place of Wife's Birth,	*Richmond Co.*
		Place of Husband's Residence,	*Richmond Co.*
Color,	*White*	Place of Wife's Residence,	*Richmond Co.*
Age of Husband,	*26 years*	Names of Husband's Parents,	*Jn. A. Belfield Mary F. Belfield*
Age of Wife,	*36 years*	Names of Wife's Parents,	*Edw. d. & Maria Saunders*
Condition of Husband, (widowed or single)	*Single*	Occupation of Husband,	*Dpy. Sheriff*

Given under my hand this *22nd* day of *December 1879*

L. D. Warner Clerk.

MINISTER'S RETURN OF MARRIAGE.

I Certify, That on the *25th* day of *December 1879* at *Chestnut Hill, Richmond Co.* I united in Marriage the above-named and described parties, under authority of the annexed License.

F. B. Beale

The Minister celebrating a marriage, is required, within TEN days thereafter, to return the license to the Office of the Clerk who issued the same, with an endorsement thereon of the FACT of such marriage, and of the TIME and PLACE of celebrating the same.

Figure 5 - Marriage License Sample 3

Sir

I herewith transmit to you a list of Marriages Celebrated by virtue of License issued by you as Clerk of Richmond County Court. Up to February 24 1848.

Reuben Kelly	to	Elizabeth Sanderse	Jan. 20 1847
Vincent Marks	to	Susan France	Jan. 21 1847
Edward P. Bolderson	to	Louisa Jones	Jan. 21 1847
William Marks	to	Julia Hall	Feb. 17 1847
James Jones	to	Mary Hall	Mar. 10. 1847
Ritchard C. Belfield	to	Mary Francis Harwood	Mar. 31 1847
Clinton Jones	to	Catherine Brown	June. 23 1847
Salathial G. Bolderson	to	Elizabeth M. Oliff	Sept. 29. 1847
Henry Reverton	to	Fidelia Ann Drake	Dec. 28 1847
Thomas Stickers	to	Elizabeth Morriss	Dec. 30 1847
Robert Jones	to	Lucy Ann Carter	Dec 30 1847
John Sanderse	to	Frances Jinkins	Jan 13. 1848

yours respectfully

John Pullen

Figure 6 - Minister Return Sample

The Clerk of Richmond County Court is hereby authorized to issue a License for the Marriage of Middleton C. Lewis and my daughter Sarah Ann Clark. Given under my hand this 20th day of March 1854.

Witness

John Harrison

Elizabeth her + mark Clark. (Seal)

Figure 7 - Consent Sample

A

Alderson, Thomas L. to Georgeanna Headley.[1] THOMAS L. ALDERSON, farmer, age 28, widowed, b. and res. Northumberland Co., s/o John D. and Alice [Wilkins] Alderson,[2] to GEORGEANNA HEADLEY, age 17y8m, single, b. Richmond Co., d/o Joseph T. and Eliza Ann Headley. Consent 22 JUL 1878 unsigned by the bride's parent, no wit. J.B. DeBerry, Pastor Richmond Circuit. 23 JUL 1878 at the parsonage. [C8, R:311, R1:45]

Alexander, Beverly (Col.) to Hannah Rich (Col.). BEVERLY ALEXANDER, laborer, age 26, single, b. Richmond Co., s/o Peggy Reese, to HANNAH RICH, age 25, single, b. Richmond Co., d/o John and Lucy Hudland. Consent 7 OCT 1879 by bride Hannah [her X mark] Rich, wit. John R. Hudland. Peter Blackwell. 8 OCT 1879 at B. Harrison's. [C8, R:308, R1:47]

Alexander, James F.[3] to Martha E. Packett. JAMES F. ALEXANDER, farmer, age 25, single, b. King and Queen Co., s/o Richard and Martha Alexander, to MARTHA E. PACKETT, age 18, single, b. Richmond Co., d/o John and Maria [Courtney] Packett.[4] Andrew Fisher. 5 SEP 1861 at Wm. H. Packett's. [C3, R:123, R1:10]

Allen, John (Col.) to Letty Yerby (Col.). JOHN ALLEN, farmer, age 22, single, b. Richmond Co., s/o Thomas and Mary K. Allen, to LETTY YERBY, age 22, single, b. Richmond Co., d/o Reuben and Lavinia Yerby. Consent 18 FEB 1871 by bride Letty [her X mark] Yerby, wit. Rob. Newsom. E.A. Gibbs. 5 MAR 1871 at Mrs. Hill's. [C5, R:244, R1:29]

Allison, George William to Anna Augusta Mullen.[5] GEORGE WILLIAM ALLISON, oyster planter, age 28, single, b. Richmond Co., s/o William and Margaret Ann [Jones] Allison,[6] to ANNA AUGUSTA MULLEN, age 18, single, b. Richmond Co., d/o Francis William and Mary Jane [Miskell] Mullen.[7] Consent 18 APR 1887 by father F.W. Mullen, wit. G.A. Carter. G.H. Northam. 19 APR 1887 at *Plain View*. [C11, R:291, R1:69]

Allison, James Waters[8] to Clarissa Kirkpatrick. JAMES ALLISON, farming, age 56, widowed, b. Ireland, res. Richmond Co., s/o James and Mary Allison, to CLARISSA KIRKPATRICK, age 48, widow, b. Pennsylvania, d/o James and Martha Kirkpatrick. G.H. Northam. 26 NOV 1889 at res. of J. Kirkpatrick. [C12, R:328, R1:75]

---

[1] Thomas Alderson (b. 1869, d. 1 JUN 1909 of cancer at Rainswood, Va.) and his wife Georgeanna Alderson (d. 1931 age 70) were bur. in Oakland United Methodist Church cemetery, Farnham, Va.
[2] John D. Alderson, widower, and Alice Wilkins, widow, were married by bond 29 APR 1845 in Northumberland Co.
[3] James F. Alexander enlisted at Tappahannock, Va. in Co. G, 15th Va. Cav., C.S.A.
[4] John Packett and Maria Courtney were married by bond 4 FEB 1841 in Richmond Co.
[5] George William Allison (b. 16 OCT 1858, d. 31 JAN 1918) and wife Anna Augusta Mullen (b. 6 JUN 1867, d. 11 JAN 1901) are bur. in Jerusalem Baptist Church cemetery.
[6] William Allison (1 JUN 1824, d. 7 JUL 1901) and wife Margaret Ann Jones (b. 1 NOV 1832, d. 11 OCT 1894) are bur. in North Farnham Church cemetery. William Allison and Margaret Ann Jones were married by bond 1 MAY 1850 in Richmond Co.
[7] Francis William Mullen (b. 21 MAY 1834, d. 10 JAN 1917) and wife Mary Jane Miskell (b. 15 AUG 1846, d. 12 JUL 1928) are bur. at Jerusalem Baptist Church cemetery.
[8] James W. Allison (b. 15 DEC 1833, d. 8 MAR 1898), bur. in Hollywood Cemetery, Richmond, Va.

Allison, William to Betty Dameril. WILLIAM ALLISON, farmer, age 37, widowed, b. Ireland, s/o James and Mary Allison, to BETTY DAMERIL, age 22, single, b. Richmond Co., d/o John and Heffy Dameril. Elder James A. Weaver. 11 MAR 1869 at the res. of the bride. [C5, R, R1:26]

Ambrose, Elijah[1] to Cordelia A. Moss. ELIJAH AMBROSE, farmer, age 36, widowed, b. Richmond Co., s/o Elijah and Katy Ambrose, to CORDELIA MOSS, age 31, single, b. Richmond Co., d/o Thomas and Mary Moss. Consent 6 JUN 1862 by bride Codelia [her X mark] Moss, wit. Wm. R. Balderson. John Pullen. 11 JUN 1862 at John Pullen's house. [C3, R:140, R1:12]

Ambrose, Joseph to Frances Jenkins. JOSEPH AMBROSE,[2] farmer, age 20y3½m, single, b. Richmond Co., s/o Elijah and Caroline [Pratt] Ambrose,[3] to FRANCES JENKINS, age 22, single, b. Richmond Co., d/o James and Ann [Jenkins] Jenkins.[4] Consent 30 DEC 1873 by bride, wits. John Oliff, Eliza [Ambrose]. B.R. Battaile. 2 JAN 1874 in Westmoreland Co. [C7, R:230, R1:36]

Ambrose, Redman B., Jr. to Julia Ann Balderson. REDMAN B. AMBROSE, farmer, age 20y6m, single, b. Richmond Co., s/o R.B. [Redman] and Apphia [C. Gutridge] Ambrose,[5] to JULIA ANN BALDERSON, age 19, single, b. Richmond Co., d/o Leonard and Mahala [Ambrose] Balderson.[6] Consent 18 DEC 1871 by father R.B. Ambrose, wit. J.E. [his X mark] Barrett; consent 14 DEC 1871 by father Leonard [his X mark] Balderson, wits. M.A. Carter, J.E. [his X mark] Barrett. H.H. Fones. 21 DEC 1871 at the house of Leonard Balderson. [C6, R:245, R1:30]

Anadale, John W. to Linnie F. Reamy. JOHN W. ANIDALE [sic],[7] farmer, age 30, single, b. and res. Westmoreland Co., s/o Thomas and Nancy [Ann Carpenter] Anadale, to LINNIE F. REAMY, age 16, single, b. Richmond Co., d/o James O. and Mary J. [Jane Norris] Reamy.[8] Consent 29 JAN 1878 by mother Mary J. Reamy, wit. W.T. Coats. F.W. Claybrook. 2 FEB 1878 at Mary J. Reamy's. [C8, R:310, R1:44]

Anadale, William[9] to Mary Florence Eugenia Belfield. WILLIAM ANADALE, merchant, age 40, single, b. and res. Westmoreland Co., s/o Thomas and Nancy [Ann Carpenter] Anadale, to FLORENCE E. BELFIELD, age 16y8m, single, b. Richmond Co., d/o John W. and Mary E. [Payton] Belfield.[10] Consent 12 DEC 1879 by bride, wits. Mary E. Belfield, Walter J. Belfield. F.B. Beale. 14 DEC 1879. [C9, R:309, R1:48]

Anthony, James H. to Cordelia Delano. JAMES H. ANTHONY, farmer, age 27y7m20d, single, b. Richmond Co., s/o James and Hanie [Hinson] Anthony,[11] to CORDELIA DELANO, age 19, single, b. Richmond Co., d/o Joseph P. [Peterson] and Lucinda [Lyell Self] Delano.[12] Consent

---

[1] Elijah Ambrose [also Ambers] served in Co. G, 15th Va. Cav., and Co. E, 41st Mil., C.S.A.
[2] Surname is found as Ambers in the Register but is correct at Ambrose.
[3] Elijah Ambrose and Caroline Pratt were married 20 AUG 1849 in Richmond Co. by Rev. William Balderson.
[4] James Jenkins and Ann Jenkins were married 31 MAR 1853 in Richmond Co. by Rev. John Pullen.
[5] Redman B. Ambrose and Apphia C. Gutridge were married by bond 20 APR 1832 in Richmond Co.
[6] Leonard Balderson and Mahala Balderson were married 22 MAR 1842 in Richmond Co. by Rev. William Balderson.
[7] The surname also appears as Annadale or Annandale.
[8] James O. Reamy and Mary Jane Morris were married by bond 14 SEP 1843 in Richmond Co.
[9] William Annadale, b. 20 AUG 1837, d. 29 APR 1910 at Potomac Mills, Westmoreland Co., is bur. in the Annadale Family Cemetery off of Route 3 near Lerty, Va.
[10] John W. Belfield, Jr. and Mary E. Payton were married 16 AUG 1849 in Richmond Co. by Rev. John Pullen.
[11] James Anthony and Haney Hinson were married 21 DEC 1840 in Richmond Co. by Rev. John M. Waddey.
[12] Joseph Delano and Lucinda Self were married by bond 25 AUG 1847 in Richmond Co.

undated by bride and father J.P. Delano, wit. R.D. Clark. G.H. Northam. 23 MAY 1877. [C8, R:307, R1:43]

Anthony, James H. to Catharine Jones. JAMES H. ANTHONY, farming, age 34, widowed, b. Richmond Co., s/o James and Hannah Anthony, to CATHARINE JONES, age 21y6m5d, single, b. Richmond Co., d/o Thomas Jones. Consent 13 MAY 1881 by bride Catharine [her X mark] Jones, wit. W.D. Garland. G.H. Northam. 12 MAY 1881. [C9, R:336, R1:53]

Anthony, Richard Henry to Mrs. Georgeanna Beverton, widow of John Roe. RICHARD HENRY ANTHONY, farming, age 23, single, b. Richmond Co., res. Essex Co., s/o Vincent and Hester Ann Anthony, to GEORGEANNA ROE, age 25, widow, b. Richmond Co., d/o Henry and Fidelia [Ann Drake] [Beverton].[1] G.H. Northam. 25 NOV 1879. [C8, NN:5 DEC 1884, R:309, R1:48]

Anthony, Vincent[2] to Henrietta Beverton. VINCENT ANTHONY, farming, age 31, single, b. Richmond Co., s/o James Anthony [and Hanie Hinson], to HENRIETTA BEVERTON, age 35, single, b. Richmond Co., d/o Henry Davis and Elizabeth. Consent 26 APR 1854 by Jennetta Beverton and Robert Beverton, wit. Redman B. Ambrose. License issued 26 APR 1854. John Pullen. 26 APR 1854. [C1, R, R1:1]

Arnold, Frank J. to Mina M. Harris. FRANK J. ARNOLD, farming, age 21y7m22d, single, b. Redhouse, N.Y., s/o Joseph Arnold and wife now Sarah C. Kelley, to MINA M. HARRIS, age 17, single, b. Richmond Co., d/o John P. [Patphry] and Susan E. [Cowen] Harris. W.H. Gregory. 24 SEP 1884 at the Warsaw church. [C10, NN:26 SEP 1884, R:355, R1:62]

Arnold, Dr. Thomas Thornton to Mary Randolph Brockenbrough.[3] THOMAS THORNTON ARNOLD, physician, age 34, single, b. and res. King George Co., s/o John and Frances [Price] Arnold, to MARY RANDOLPH BROCKENBROUGH, age 22, single, b. Richmond Co., d/o Wm. [Austin] and Mary [Carter Gray] Brockenbrough. Andrew Fisher. 14 JUN 1870 at *The Cottage*. [C5, R:233, R1:28]

Ashton, James (Col.) to Louisa Thompson (Col.). JAMES ASHTON, oystering, age 20y8m, single, b. and res. Westmoreland Co., s/o Frances Ashton, to LOUISA THOMPSON, age 17, single, b. Richmond Co., d/o Jane Thompson. Consent 23 DEC 1885 from groom's mother Frances [her X mark] Ashton, wit. Wm. Newman; consent 23 DEC 1885 from bride's mother Jane [her X mark] Thompson, wit. Wm. Newman. M.F. Sanford. [C11, R:319, R1:66]

Atwell, Thomas O. to Bettie J. Tiffey. THOMAS O. ATWELL, carpenter, age 26, single, b. and res. Westmoreland Co., s/o Thomas F. and Bettie Atwell, to BETTIE J. TIFFEY, age 19, single, b. Richmond Co., d/o Robert B. [Bispham] and [Elizabeth] Betty S. Tiffey.[4] Consent 20 FEB 1889 by mother Betty S. Tiffey. J.B. Askew. 20 FEB 1889 at Andrew Chapel, Montross, Va. [C12, R:327, R1:74]

---

[1] Henry Beverton and Fidelia Ann Drake were married 28 DEC 1847 in Richmond Co. by Rev. John Pullen.
[2] Vincent Anthony served in Co. K, 9th Va. Cav., and Co. D, 40th Va. Inf., C.S.A.
[3] Dr. Thomas T. Arnold (b. 23 SEP 1835, d. 25 APR 1917) and wife Mary R. Brockenbrough (b. 19 JUL 1848) are bur. in the Arnold Family Cemetery at *Willow Hill*, King George Co. First served in Co. E, 15th Va. Cav., and other units, C.S.A.
[4] Robert B. Tiffey (b. 23 MAR 1830, d. 26 JUN 1881) and wife Elizabeth "Bettie" S. are buried in Andrew Chapel United Methodist Church cemetery, Montross, Va. There is a marriage record 8 JAN 1857 in Westmoreland Co. for Robert B. Tiffey to Bell S. Harvey. He served in Co. A, 15th Va. Cav., C.S.A.

Atwell, William R. to Elizabeth "Bettie" Chinn Rockwell.[1] WILLIAM R. ATWELL, printer, age 30, single, b. and res. Alexandria, Va., s/o W.E. [William] and M.J. [Mary Jane Higdon] Atwell,[2] to BETTIE CHINN ROCKWELL, age 22, single, b. Richmond Co., d/o William and Mary [B. Jeffries] Rockwell.[3] Consent 28 NOV 1872 by bride, wit. Wm. Rockwell, [E.O.] Rockwell. W.W. Walker. 28 NOV 1872 at *Oakley*. [C6, R:238, R1:32]

Aylett, William R., to Alice R. Brockenbrough. WILLIAM R. AYLETT, lawyer, age 27, single, b. and res. King William Co., s/o Philip and Judith P. [Page Waller] Aylett, to ALICE R. BROCKENBROUGH, age 22, single, b. Richmond Co., d/o Moore F. [Fauntleroy] and Sarah [Smith] Brockenbrough.[4] Andrew Fisher. 31 JUL 1860. [C2, R:153, R1:9]

B

Bachelor, John S. to Bettie A. Hanks. JOHN S. BACHELOR, oysterman, age 27, single, b. Kent Co., Md., s/o John Henry and Mary A. Bachelor, to BETTIE A. HANKS, age 25, single, b. Richmond Co., d/o William E. and Virginia A. [Dunaway] Hanks. Consent 17 FEB 1887 by bride, wit. William E. Hanks. Robert Williamson. 23 FEB 1887 in Farnham Parish. [C11, R:290, R1:69]

Bailey, James (Col.) to Martha Newton (Col.). JAMES BAILEY, ditcher, age 38, single, b. Richmond Co., s/o William and Franky Bailey, to MARTHA NEWTON, age 36, single, b. Richmond Co., d/o Jupiter and Fanny Newton. Elijah L. Williams. 27 SEP 1866 at *Durrett's Hill*. [C4, R:272, R1:18]

Bailey, James (Col.) to Sophronia Rich (Col.). JAMES BAILEY, timber cutter, age 26, single, b. Richmond Co., s/o William and Winny Bailey, to SOPHRONIA RICH, age 23, single, b. Richmond Co., d/o Betty Rich, father unknown. Daniel R. Payne. Consent 30 MAY 1873 by bride, wit. Thomas Rich. 1 JUN 1873 at the res. of Lucy Rich. [C6, R:235, R1:34]

Bailey, James W. to Mary C. Middleton. Consent 17 APR 1856 by bride, wit. Ro. R. Middleton. No return. [C1]

Bailey, Stephen C. (Col.) to Nancy Thompson (Col.). STEPHEN C. BAILEY, farmer, age 44, widowed, b. Richmond Co., s/o Robert and Maria Bailey, to NANCY THOMPSON, age 30, widow, b. Richmond Co., d/o Moses and Peggy Thompson. Edmond Rich. 4 DEC 1890 at the res. of Nancy Thompson. [C12, R:324, R1:77]

Bailor, Hazzard (Col.) to Cheney Saunders (Col.). HAZZARD BAILOR, cooper, age 23y7m, single, b. Essex Co., res. Westmoreland Co., s/o Hilliard and Sally Bailor, to CHENEY SAUNDERS, age 18, single, b. Richmond Co., d/o George and Cloria Ann Saunders. Rev. T.G. Thomas. 26 DEC 1882 at the house of George Sa[u]nders. [C10, R:314, R1:57]

---

[1] Williiam R. Atwell (b. 17 JAN 1842, d. 28 FEB 1884) and wife Elizabeth C. Rockwell (b. 1849, d. 29 JAN 1942 in D.C.) are bur. at Methodist Protestant Cemetery in Alexandria, Va. His parents, William E. Atwell (1812-1899), a tailor, and Mary Jane Higdon (1817-1910), d/o John Higdon, are bur. there as well.
[2] William Atwell and wife Mary Jane Higdon were married by bond 3 MAY 1837 in Alexandria, Va.
[3] William Rockwell and Mary B. Jeffries were married 22 APR 1846 in Richmond Co. by Rev. Elijah L. Williams.
[4] Col. Moore Fauntleroy Brockenbrough was married 12 NOV 1823 at the res. of Robert Weir in Tappahannock, Va. to Sarah Smith.

Bailor, Moore (Col.) to Winny Saunders (Col.). MOORE BAILOR, laborer, age 23, single, b. Richmond Co., s/o Ralph and Mary Bailor, to WINNY SAUNDERS, age 25, single, b. Richmond Co., d/o Alexander and Mollie Saunders. Thomas G. Thomas. 12 APR 1867 at res. of Wm. H. McKenny. [C4, R:286, R1:21]

Bailor, Moore (Col.) to Clarissa Saunders (Col.). MOORE BAILOR, farmer, age 25, widowed, b. Richmond Co., s/o Ralph and Mary Bailor, to CLARISSA SAUNDERS, age 22, single, b. Richmond Co., d/o Solomon and Maria Saunders. Thomas G. Thomas. 2 JAN 1876 near Zion Church. [C7, R:304, R1:39]

Bailor, Washington (Col.) to Mary Jane Barber (Col.). WASHINGTON BAILOR, laboring, age 51y6m, widowed, b. Richmond Co., s/o Thomas and Penny Bailor, to MARY JANE BARBER, age 22, single, b. Richmond Co., d/o John and Mary Barber. Rev. Robert Lewis. 5 JAN 1886 at Clarksville [Church]. [C11, R:315, R1:67]

Baily, Jesse (Col.) to Rosella Hobbs (Col.). JESSE BAILEY,[1] farming, age 21y3m, single, b. Richmond Co., s/o Stephen Baily and Maria Veney now Kelly, to ROSELLA HOBBS, age 18, single, b. Richmond Co., d/o Elizabeth Morgan (name of father not given). Consent 30 JUL 1883 by bride Rosella [her X mark] Hobbs, Elizabeth [her X mark] Morgan, wit. R.H. [his X mark] Thrift. Rev. John Wilkerson. 31 JUL 1883 at res. of Henry Palmer, Farnham, Va.[2] [C10, R:357, R1:59]

Balderson, Arthur[3] to Mildred Booker. ARTHUR BALDERSON, farming, age about 25, single, b. Richmond Co., Upper Dist., s/o Gilbert [Hardwick] Balderson and Rebecca [Bailey Laycock], to MILDRED BOOKER, age about 21, single, b. Richmond Co., Farnham Parish, [parents not given]. Consent 14 JUN 1854 by bride, wit. William H. Sandy. 15 JUN 1854 at Miskeal Cates's in Richmond Co., Upper Dist. John Pullen, M.G. 15 JUN 1854. [C1, R, R1:1]

Balderson, Charles Clifton to Ida E. Scates.[4] C.C. BALDERSON, farming, age 30, single, b. Richmond Co., s/o Charles H. [Hiram] and Virginia [J. Coates] Balderson, to IDA E. SCATES, age 18, single, b. Richmond Co., d/o James A. and Virginia Scates. G.M. Conley. 7 FEB 1889 at Oak Row.[5] [C12, R:327, R1:74]

Balderson, Charles Hiram to Virginia J. Coates.[6] CHARLES H. BALDERSON, shoe and boot maker, age about 27, single, b. Richmond Co., s/o James B. [Bailey] Balderson and wife Pheson [Feisin F. Franklin],[7] to VIRGINIA COATES, age about 22, single, b. Richmond Co., d/o James B. Coates and wife Elizabeth [Carpenter]. Consent 2 AUG 1856 by bride [C1], wits. James H. Jinkins, John Morriss. John Pullen. 7 AUG 1856 at Mrs. Susan Carter's. [C1, R, R1:3]

---

[1] Surname is also found spelled Bayley as in the Register.
[2] Farnham, Va. is located on Highway 3 at the junction of Routes 602 and 607.
[3] Arthur Balderson served as a private in Co. G, 17th Reg. Va. Inf., C.S.A., was illiterate, and living in Newland, Va. in 1890.
[4] Charles Clifton Balderson (b. 31 OCT 1859, d. 29 NOV 1927) and wife Ida E. Scates (b. JUN 1870, d. 10 JUL 1917) are bur. in Balderson Family Cemetery near Newland, Va.
[5] Oak Row, Va. is a locality in the north end of the County at the junction of Routes 624 and 638.
[6] Charles H. Balderson (d. 22 SEP 1890) and wife Virginia J. Coates (b. 1834, d. 21 AUG 1896) are bur. in Rappahannock Baptist Church cemetery. He served in Co. D, 40th Va. Inf., C.S.A. He may be the same who was musician in Co. B, 40th Va. Inf.
[7] James B. Balderson and Feisin F. Franklin were married by bond 17 OCT 1826 in Westmoreland Co.

Balderson, Charles Worthington to Alice J.J. Saunders.[1] CHARLES W. BALDERSON, farming, age 23, single, b. Richmond Co., s/o T.N. [Theoderick Noel] and Dorothea L. [Lane Sanders] Balderson, to ALICE J.J. SAUNDERS, age 19, single, b. Richmond Co., d/o Allen J. Saunders and Alice D.C. [Newman] his wife now Jenkins. Consent 13 MAR 1879 by mother Alice D.C. Jenkins, sworn by James M. Scates. R.N. Reamy. 20 MAR 1879 at T.N. Balderson's. [C8, R:307, R1:46]

Balderson, Ezekiel and Artemissia A. Payton. EZEKIEL BALDERSON, age about 28, single, b. in district No. 2, Richmond Co., s/o James P. Balderson and wife Elizabeth [Evans],[2] to ARTEMISSIA A. PAYTON,[3] age about 19, single, b. district No. 1, Richmond Co., d/o John A. Payton and wife Elizabeth [Norris].[4] Consent 22 MAY 1856 by mother Elizabeth Peyton [sic], wit. Frances E. Peyton and Wm. Carter. John Pullen, M.G. 4 JUN 1856 at T.N. Balderson's. [C1, R, R1:3]

Balderson, George Graham[5] to Elizabeth Ann Newman. GRAYHAM BALDERSON [sic], farming, age 21 on 8 DEC 1856, single, b. Richmond Co., s/o Gilbert H. [Hardwick] Balderson and wife Elizabeth [Pope], to ELIZABETH ANN NEWMAN, age 21 on 9 NOV 1856, single, b. Richmond Co., d/o Joseph Newman and wife Sophiah [Hinson].[6] Consent 22 SEP 1856 by Daniel Hinson, guardian of bride, wits. Charles H. Balderson, Zachariah Sanders. Consent 22 SEP 1856 by T.N. Balderson, guardian of groom, wits. Charles H. Balderson, Zachariah Sanders. John Pullen, M.G. 25 SEP 1856 at Elizabeth Balderson's. [C1, R:148, R1:4]

Balderson, Henry Addison to Mrs. Georgie Etta Edmonds Sanders.[7] HENRY A. BALDERSON, farming, age 25, single, b. Richmond Co., s/o Graham G. and Elizabeth Balderson, to GEORGIE E. SANDERS, age 23, widow, b. Richmond Co., d/o George and Sally E. Edmonds. Consent 10 MAY 1890 by bride. H.H. Fones. 14 MAY 1890. [C12, R:323a, R1:77]

Balderson, James B. to Cornelia Bulger. JAMES B. BALDERSON, mechanic, age 75, widowed, b. Richmond Co., [names of parents incomplete], to CORNELIA BULGER, age 22y8m, single, b. Richmond Co., d/o John Bulger and Julia A. Bowen.[8] Consent undated by bride Cornelia [her X mark] Bulger, wit. G.M. Conley. R.N. Reamy. 22 JAN 1880. [C9, R:314, R1:49]

Balderson, James Franklin to Mary Susan Carter.[9] JAMES F. BALDERSON, shoemaker, age 24, single, b. Richmond Co., s/o James B. and Felicia Balderson, to MARY S. CARTER, age 19, single, b. Richmond Co., d/o James Carter and Susan Oliff. Consent 3 OCT 1860 by bride's mother Susan [her X mark] Olliff [sic], wit. Wm. T. Reamy. John Pullen. 14 OCT 1860. [C2, R:154, R1:9]

---

[1] Charles W. Balderson (b. 3 MAR 1854, d. 24 JUN 1914) and wife Alice J.J. Saunders (b. 9 SEP 1862, d. 25 JUN 1954) are bur. in Rappahannock Baptist Church cemetery.
[2] James P. Balderson and Elizabeth Evans, widow, were married by bond 21 JAN 1818 in Richmond Co.
[3] License reads Artimetion A. Payton.
[4] John A. Payton and Elizabeth Morris were married by bond 11 NOV 1828 in Richmond Co.
[5] Graham [or Grayham] Balderson served in Co. K, 9th Va. Cav., C.S.A., and was wounded at Malvern Hill, Va.
[6] Joseph Newman and Sophia Hinson were married by bond 1 FEB 1830 in Richmond Co.
[7] Henry A. Balderson (b. 27 JUN 1866, d. 4 FEB 1940) is bur. in Rappahannock Baptist Church cemetery.
[8] John Bulger and Julia Ann Hinson were married 24 JAN 1850 in Richmond Co. by Rev. John Pullen.
[9] James F. Balderson (b. 30 APR 1836, d. 10 OCT 1905) and wife Mary S. Carter (b. 16 AUG 1941, d. 30 DEC 1911 in D.C.) are bur. in Rappahannock Baptist Church cemetery.

Balderson, James Henry to Sarah Margaret Dodson.[1] JAMES H. BALDERSON, house carpenter, age 25y1m23d, single, b. Richmond Co., s/o John W. [William] Balderson and Elizabeth [Lewis Hudson] Balderson (dec'd.), to SARAH M. DODSON, age 19, single, b. Northumberland Co., d/o Presley M. and Eliza E. Dodson. Consent 16 MAR 1888 by Eliza E. [her X mark] Dodson, wit. J.C. [his X mark] Thrift. Charles N. Betts. 18 MAR 1888 at the res. of J.C. Thrift. [C11, R:315, R1:72]

Balderson, James Manoah to Frances Ellen Mealey.[2] JAMES M. BALDERSON, farming, age 28, single, b. Richmond Co., s/o David and Susan [Mothershead] Balderson,[3] to FANNIE E. MEALEY,[4] age 18, single, b. Richmond Co., d/o William E. and Mary E. Mealley [sic]. Consent 26 JAN 1885 by mother Mary E. Mealey, wit. L.R. Harris. G.H. Northam. 23 JAN 1885 at *West View*. [C10, NN:6 FEB 1885, R:316, R1:64]

Balderson, John to Alice S. Scates. JOHN BALDERSON, farmer, age 21, single, b. Richmond Co., s/o David and Susan [Mothershead] Balderson,[5] to ALICE S. SCATES, age 22, single, b. Richmond Co., d/o Thomas and Susan [Sanders] Scates.[6] Consent by bride Allice [her X mark] Scates, wit. T.N. Balderson. Age of bride sworn to by Braxton Reynolds. H.H. Fones. 22 DEC 1870 at Mrs. S. Scates'. [C5, R:234, R1:28]

Balderson, John Andrew to Mary Jane Hall.[7] JOHN A. BALDERSON, farmer, age 25, single, b. Richmond Co., s/o Leonard and Mahala [Ambrose] Balderson,[8] to MARY J. HALL, age 18, single, b. Richmond Co., d/o Bladen and Frances [Morris] Hall.[9] Robert N. Reamy. 9 JUL 1868 at Bladen Hall's. [C5, R:254, R1:24]

Balderson, John Andrew[10] to Ida Elizabeth Bowen. JOHN A. BALDERSON, farming, age 42, widowed, b. Richmond Co., s/o Leonard and Mahala [Ambrose] Balderson, to IDA ELIZABETH BOWEN, age 30, single, b. Richmond Co., d/o John and Maria Bowen. G.H. Northam. 26 AUG 1885 at H. Brown's. [C10, R:317, R1:65]

Balderson, John L. to Mrs. Lucy A. Newman. JOHN L. BALDERSON, farming, age 38, widowed, b. Richmond Co., s/o David and Susan [Mothershead] Balderson, to LUCY A. NEWMAN, age 26, widow, b. Richmond Co., d/o Thomas A. and Martha [Brewer Sanford] Jenkins. Consent 14 JAN 1890 by bride Lucy A. [her X mark] Newman, no wit. Geo. M. Conley. 15 JAN 1890 near Newland, Va.[11] [C12, R:323, R1:76]

---

[1] James H. Balderson (b. 10 MAY 1864, d. 31 MAY 1948) and wife Sarah M. Dodson (b. 22 FEB 1872, d. 24 DEC 1940) are bur. in Smithland Baptist Church Cemetery, Coan, Va.
[2] James Manoah Balderson (1857-1916) and his wife Frances Ellen Mealey (1867-1946) are bur. in Milden Cemetery.
[3] David Balderson and Susan Mothershead were married by bond 27 DEC 1849 in Westmoreland Co.
[4] Surname appears also as Mealley.
[5] David Balderson and Susan Mothershead were married by bond 27 DEC 1849 in Westmoreland Co.
[6] Thomas Scates and Susan Sanders were married 5 FEB 1838 in Richmond Co. by Rev. Thomas M. Washington.
[7] John Andrew Balderson (b. 8 JAN 1843, d. 30 OCT 1920) is bur. at Cobham Park Baptist Church cemetery. He served in Co. G, 15th Va. Cav., C.S.A., and first enlisted in Tappahannock, Va.
[8] Leonard Balderson and Mahala Ambrose were married 22 MAR 1842 in Richmond Co. by Rev. William Balderson.
[9] Bladen Hall and Frances Morris had bond 27 JUL 1848, were married 8 FEB 1849 in Richmond Co. by Rev. John Pullen.
[10] John A. Balderson (b. 8 JAN 1843, d. 30 OCT 1920) is bur. at Cobham Park Baptist Church cemetery. He served in Co. G, 15th Va. Cav., C.S.A.
[11] Newland, Va. is a locality in the northern part of the County at the south junction of Routes 624 and 638.

Balderson, John William[1] to Mrs. Elizabeth Lewis Hudson. JOHN W. BALDERSON, farmer, age 24, single, b. Richmond Co., s/o John [Lee] and Lucy [Pearce Tune] Balderson, to ELIZABETH HUDSON, age 28, widow, b. Richmond Co., d/o Thomas P. and Betsy [Elizabeth Dameron] Lewis.[2] Consent 11 JAN 1860 by bride Elizabeth [her X mark] Hudson, wit. Presley J. Hudson. Elder James A. Weaver. 12 JAN 1860.[3] [C2, R1:8]

Balderson, John William[4] to Maria S. Sydnor. JOHN W. BALDERSON, farmer, age 32, widowed, b. Richmond Co., s/o John [Lee] and Lucy [Pearce Tune] Balderson,[5] to MARIA S. SYDNOR, age 24, single, b. Richmond Co., d/o Fortunatus and Martha [Hale] Sydnor.[6] Elder James A. Weaver. 13 MAR 1867 at the res. of Fortunatus Sydnor. [C4, R:286, R1:20]

Balderson, Joseph Hardwick to Jane Elizabeth Edmonds.[7] JOSEPH H. BALDERSON, farming, age 23, single, b. Richmond Co., s/o Graham [G.] and Elizabeth Balderson, to JANIE E. EDMONDS, age 19, single, b. Richmond Co., d/o George A. and Sallie [Sarah Ann Hall] Edmonds. Consent 13 DEC 1880 by mother Sallie [her X mark] Edmonds, wit. T.A. [his X mark] Jenkins. R.N. Reamy. 15 DEC 1880. [C9, R:317, R1:52]

Balderson, Joseph [Melvin] to Lucy Ann Bowen.[8] JOSEPH M. BALDERSON, farmer, age 28, single, b. Richmond Co., s/o Henry and Fanny [Balderson] Balderson,[9] to LUCY A. BOWEN, age 22, single, b. Richmond Co., d/o Joseph H. and Sarah A. [Marshall] Bowen.[10] H.H. Fones. 8 JAN 1868 at Joseph H. Bowen's. [C4, R:253, R1:23]

Balderson, Presley Carter to Mary Ann Coates.[11] PRESLEY C. BALDERSON, farmer (at present a soldier), age 24, single, b. Richmond Co., s/o James B. [Bailey] and Fezon F. [Feisin F. Franklin] Balderson, to MARY ANN COATS [sic], age 20, single, b. Richmond Co., d/o John A. and Elizabeth [Balderson] Coats. Consent 29 AUG 1863 by father John A. Coats, wit. Joseph Scates. John Pullen. 2 SEP 1863 at John A. Coats'. [C3, R:160, R1:13]

Balderson, Ransdell S. to Jemima Lewis.[12] RANSDELL BALDERSON, carpenter, age 26, widowed, b. Richmond Co., s/o Berryman Balderson[13] and wife Betty [Elizabeth Fones], to JEMIMA LEWIS, age 20, single, b. Richmond Co., d/o Thomas P. [Parker] Lewis and wife Elizabeth [Dameron].[14] Consent 5 JAN 1860 by parents Thomas P. [his X mark] Lewis, and

---

[1] John W. Balderson (b. 1835, d. 12 JAN 1903) is bur. at Gibeon Baptist Church cemetery in an unmarked grave. He served in Co. K, 9th Va. Cav., C.S.A.

[2] Thomas P. Lewis and Elizabeth Dameron were married by bond 23 OCT 1822 in Richmond Co.

[3] Minister return gives date of marriage 12 JAN 1860, while the license notes date 11 JAN 1860.

[4] John W. Balderson (b. 1835, d. 12 JAN 1903) is bur. in Gibeon Baptist Church cemetery in an unmarked grave. He served in Co. K, 9th Va. Cav., C.S.A., and was discharged on the account of physical disability.

[5] John Balderson and Lucy Tune were married by bond 1 JAN 1831 in Richmond Co.

[6] Fortunatus Sydnor and Martha Hale were married by bond 21 JUL 1841 in Northumberland Co.

[7] Joseph H. Balderson (b. 21 JUN 1857, d. 1 MAR 1939) and wife Jane E. Edmonds (b. 28 NOV 1861, d. 18 APR 1921) are bur. at Rappahannock Baptist Church cemetery.

[8] Joseph M. Balderson (b. 24 SEP 1838, d. 20 NOV 1917) and wife Lucy A. Bowen (b. 24 JUN 1843, d. 30 DEC 1922) are bur. in Rappahannock Baptist Church cemetery. He is recorded as Joseph Madison Balderson in Co. D, 40th Va. Inf., C.S.A.

[9] Henry Balderson and Frances Balderson were married by bond 18 DEC 1838 in Richmond Co.

[10] Joseph Bowing and Sarah A. Marshall were married 26 DEC 1838 in Richmond Co. by Rev. Lovell Marders.

[11] Presley Carter Balderson (b. 14 MAR 1837 or 8, d. 27 DEC 1925 in Washington, D.C.) and his wife Mary Ann Coates (b. 10 MAR 1840, d. 14 MAY 1904) are bur. at Andrew Chapel United Methodist Church cemetery. He served in Co. D, 40th Va. Inf., C.S.A. His tombstone gives birth year 1837.

[12] Ransdell S. Balderson and wife Jemima Lewis (1838-1873) are bur. in Gibeon Baptist Church cemetery. He served in Co. K, 9th Va. Inf., C.S.A.

[13] Berryman Balderson (1781-1832) is s/o Gilbert Balderson and Nancy Hardwick.

[14] Thomas P. Lewis, Sr. (b. 18 JUN 1791, d. 1 MAR 1885 in Northumberland Co.) and wife Elizabeth Dameron (b. 24 OCT 1796, d. 22 APR 1894) are bur. in Gibeon Baptist Church cemetery.

Elizabeth Lewis, wit. Richard L. Falter. Elder James A. Weaver. 8 JAN 1860. [C2, R:153, R1:8]

Balderson, Ransdell S. to Mary Ann Harper. RANSEL BALDERSON [sic], farmer, age 40, widowed, b. Richmond Co., s/o Berryman and Elizabeth [Fones] Balderson, to MARY ANN HARPER, age 2[2], single, b. Richmond Co., d/o Benjamin and Elizabeth Harper. Consent by mother Elizabeth [her X mark] Harper, wit. William Allison. James A. Weaver. 30 SEP 1877 at the res. of the bride's mother. [C8, R:307, R1:43]

Balderson, Robert B. to Adeline Beacham. ROBERT B. BALDERSON, farmer, age 27, single, b. Richmond Co., s/o Berryman and Elizabeth [Fones] Balderson, to ADELINE BEACHAM, age 14, single, b. Richmond Co., d/o Samuel Beacham. Elder James A. Weaver. 3 JAN 1860. [C2, R:153, R1:8]

Balderson, Robert W. to Susan Ann Pullen. ROBERT W. BALDERSON, farmer, age 31, single, b. Richmond Co., s/o James P. and Elizabeth [Evans] Balderson, to SUSAN ANN PULLEN, age 18, single, b. Richmond Co., d/o John and Henrietta Pullen. Consent 23 MAY 1859 from father John Pullen, wits. Thos. E. Pullen, William H. Mothershead. 25 MAY 1859. [C2, R:165, R1:7]

Balderson, Selathiel George William[1] to Aremitta C. "Mitty" Balderson. SELATHIEL BALDERSON, farming, age 28, widowed, b. Richmond Co., s/o Arthur and Milly [Mildred Booker] Balderson, to MITTY BALDERSON, age 21, single, b. Richmond Co., d/o William [S.] and Mary [Mary Jane Scott] Balderson. Consent 2 MAR 1886 by Millie A. Balderson, Hardridge Balderson. R.N. Reamy. 31 MAR 1886 at P.B. Balderson's. [C11, R:315, R1:67]

Balderson, Silas Noel to Alice Ann Balderson[2]. SILAS N. BALDERSON, farmer, age 23, single, b. Richmond Co., s/o T.N. [Theoderick Noel] and Sarah E. Balderson, to ALICE ANN BALDERSON, age 20y7m25d, single, b. Richmond Co., d/o G.G. [George Graham] and Elizabeth [Ann Newman] Balderson. Consent 27 OCT 1879 by father G.G. Balderson, wit. R.W. Hinson. R.N. Reamy. 30 OCT 1879. [C8, R:308, R1:48]

Balderson, Theophilus C. to Willie Ann Ambrose. THEOPHILUS C. BALDERSON, farmer, age 21, single, b. Richmond Co., s/o Leonard and Mahala [Ambrose] Balderson, to WILLIE ANN AMBROSE, age 19, single, b. Richmond Co., d/o Elijah and Delie [Cordelia A. Moss] Ambrose. Consent 1 DEC 1880 by father Elijah [his X mark] Ambrose, wit. Hutson [his X mark] Oliff. R.N. Reamy. 5 DEC 1880. [C9, R:316, R1:51]

Balderson, Thomas Gilbert to Mary Frances Davis.[3] THOMAS G. BALDERSON, farmer, age 29, widowed, b. Richmond Co., s/o Gilbert H. [Hardwick] and Elizabeth [Pope] Balderson, to MARY F. DAVIS, age 25, single, b. King George Co., d/o Addison J. and Mary Davis. Consent 21 NOV 1874 by bride, wits. Thomas E. Pullen, James F. Balderson. Robert N. Reamy. 26 NOV 1874 at James Balderson's. [C7, R1:38]

---

[1] Salathiel G. Balderson (b. 15 FEB 1859, d. 24 AUG 1924) is bur. at Nomini Baptist Church cemetery. He was divorced from Aremitta.
[2] Silas Noel Balderson (b. 22 MAR 1856, d. 14 JUL 1940) and wife Alice Ann Balderson (b. 5 MAR 1859, d. 17 NOV 1919) are bur. at Newland Church of Christ cemetery.
[3] Thomas G. Balderson (1849-1884) and wife Mary F. Davis (1847-1917) are bur. at Welcome Grove Baptist Church cemetery.

Balderson, Thomas Gilbert[1] to Mrs. Susan M. Spilman Quisenbury. THOMAS G. BALDERSON, farmer, age 23, single, b. Richmond Co., s/o Gilbert H. [Hardwick] and Elizabeth [Pope] Balderson, to SUSAN M. QUISENBURY, age 28, widow, b. Westmoreland Co., d/o John and Thursey [Thirza Hoult] Spilman.[2] Consent 19 FEB 1866 by bride, wit. James A. Jenkins. John Pullen. 21 FEB 1866 at Susan Quisenbury's. [C4, R:270, R1:16]

Balderson, William S.[3] to Mary Jane Scott. WILLIAM S. BALDERSON, plasterer, age 24, single, b. Richmond Co., s/o James P. and E. [Elizabeth Evans] Balderson, to MARY JANE SCOTT, age 23, single, b. Richmond Co., d/o Thomas and Mary Scott. Consent 2 NOV 1857 by bride Miss Mary Jane [her X mark] Scott, wit. Lewis H. Sisson. G.H. Northam, Baptist minister. 4 NOV 1857 at James Scott's. [C1, R:159, R1:5]

Balderson, William Tasker[4] to Willie Ann R. Balderson. WILLIAM T. BALDERSON, farmer, age 21, single, b. Richmond Co., s/o William O. [Octavius] and Julia Ann [Sanders] Balderson,[5] to WILLIE A.R. BALDERSON, age 20, single, b. Richmond Co., d/o T.N. [Theoderick Noel] and Dorothea L. [Lane Sanders] Balderson. Consent by father T.N. Balderson, wits. William DeCon, Edward Middleton. J.W. Williams. 6 DEC 1872 at the res. of the bride's father. [C6, R:238, R1:32]

Ball, Armistead to Susan Henry. ARMISTEAD BALL, painter, age 21, single, b. Westmoreland Co., s/o Clarissa Ball (father's name not given), to SUSAN HENRY, age 24, single, b. Richmond Co., d/o Sally Henry (father's name not given). Consent 30 DEC 1860 by bride Susan [her X mark] [Henry], wit. Henry [his X mark] [Fosset]. John Pullen. 10 JAN 1861. [C3, R:123, R1:10]

Ball, Edmund (Col.) to Chamomile Veney (Col.). EDMUND BALL, farming, age 37, widowed, b. Richmond Co., res. Westmoreland Co., s/o Martin and Nancy Williams, to CHAMOMILE VENEY, age 20, single, b. Richmond Co., d/o Jesse and Felicia Veney. Consent 28 DEC 1881 by father Jesse [his X mark] Veney, wits. O.M. [Oscar Mitchell] Lemoine, M.J. Veney. David Veney. 29 DEC 1881 at Emmerton, Va. [C9, R:337, R1:55]

Ball, Garrett (Col.) to Lucinda Hall (Col.). GARRETT[6] BALL, farmer, age 63, single, b. Westmoreland Co., s/o Ned and Clara Ball, to LUCINDA HALL, age 32, single, b. Richmond Co., d/o Hannibal Thompson and Celie Hall. Consent 9 OCT 1878 by bride Lucinda [her X mark] Hall, no wit. Edmond Rich. 10 OCT 1878 at the res. of Harriet Ball. [C8, R:311, R1:45]

Ball, Harris (Col.) to Lettie Gaskins (Col.). HARRIS BALL, oystering, age 28y[2]m2d, single, b. Lancaster Co., s/o Butler and Easter Ball, to LETTIE GASKINS, age 22y11m, single, b. Richmond Co., d/o Robert Gaskins and Lucy Gaskins (dec'd.). Consent 20 MAR 1888 by bride, wit. Israel Oakley. Rev. W. Carter. 22 MAR 1888 at the residence. [C11, R:315, R1:72]

---

[1] Thomas G. Balderson (1849-1884) is bur. at Welcome Grove Baptist Church cemetery.
[2] John Spilman (c.1788-1872) and Thirza Hoult (b. 1 SEP 1799, d. 1870) were married by bond 3 MAY 1815 in Westmoreland Co., and she is d/o John Hoult and Jane Balderson.
[3] William S. Balderson served in Co. D, 40th Va. Inf., C.S.A.
[4] According to an obituary, William Tasker Balderson (b. 4 JUN 1851, d. 14 JUN 1910) is buried in an unmarked grave at Menokin Baptist Church cemetery.
[5] William O. Balderson and Julia Ann Sanders were married 11 SEP 1849 in Richmond Co. by Rev. William N. Ward.
[6] The given name also appears as Garriet.

Ball, Peter (Col.) to Emma Maiden (Col.). PETER BALL, farmer, age 23, single, b. Richmond Co., s/o Mary Ball, to EMMA MAIDEN, age 18, single, b. Richmond Co., d/o Hannah Maiden. Consent 3 MAY 1872 by mother Hannah Maiden, wit. Thos. R. Maiden. H.H. Fones. 26 MAY 1872. [C6, R:237, R1:31]

Ball, Robert (Col.) to Mary Ann Thompson (Col.). ROBERT BALL, laborer, age 26, single, b. Richmond Co., s/o Robert and Clarissa Ball, to MARY ANN THOMPSON, age 21, single, b. Westmoreland Co., d/o Tena Thompson. Consent 16 APR 1878 by bride, wit. Moses Thompson. Edmond Rich. 17 APR 1878 at the house of Robert Thompson. [C8, R:311, R1:44]

Ball, William (Col.) to Elizabeth Chatmon (Col.). WILLIAM BALL, farmer, age 21y6m, single, b. Richmond Co., s/o George Weathers and Lucy Ball, to ELIZABETH CHATMON, age 21, single, b. Richmond Co., d/o James and ~~Elizebeth~~ Fanny Chatmon. Consent 3 JUN 1874 by Edmond Spence. Jeremiah Graham. 4 JUN 1874 at Savern Field. [C7, R:230, R1:36]

Ball, William (Col.) to Margaret E. Johnson (Col.). WILLIAM BALL, age 28, single, b . Richmond Co., s/o Jarret and Betsey Ball, to MARGARET E. JOHNSON, age 27, single, b. Westmoreland Co., d/o Billy and Phebe Johnson. Consent 13 AUG 1881 from Farnham by bride Margarett E. [her X mark] Johnson, wit. H.B. [Henry] Scott.[1] G.H. Northam. 18 AUG 1881 at *Glenmore*. [C9, R:338, R1:54]

Ball, William (Col.) to Mrs. Lucy Burton (Col.). WILLIAM BALL, farming, age 55, widowed, b. and res. Westmoreland Co., s/o Martin Williams and Nancy Ball, to LUCY BURTON, age 44, widow, b. Richmond Co., d/o Vincent Brann and Jennie Jenkins. Consent 5 JAN 1885 by bride Lucie Burton. [Edmond] Rich. 8 JAN 1885 at the place where the bride boards. [C10, R:316, R1:64]

Barber, Thomas (Col.) to Winnie Bryant (Col.). THOMAS BARBER, laborer, age 23y10m, single, b. Richmond Co., s/o John and Mary Barber, to WINNIE BRYANT, age 22, single, b. Westmoreland Co., d/o Charles and Louisa Bryant. Consent 15 JUL 1880 and oath by Mrs. Louisa Bryant. Rev. T.G. Thomas. 15 JUL 1880. [C9, R:316, R1:51]

Barnes, John W. to Sarah E. Haynie. JOHN W. BARNES, farmer, age 31, single, b. Richmond Co., res. Lancaster Co., s/o Samuel and Frances Barnes, to SARAH E. HAYNIE, age 18, single, b. Richmond Co., d/o Joseph H. and Sarah I. Haynie. Consent 2 JAN 1871 signed by Sarah Isabela Haynie, Elizabeth Haynie. Wm. H. Kirk. 11 JAN 1871 at the res. of Mrs. Haynie. [C5, R:244, R1:29]

Barnes, Joseph (Col.) to Richardanna Carrington (Col.). JOSEPH BARNES, laborer, age 22y9m, single, b. Richmond Co., s/o Thomas and Chania Barnes, to RICHARDANNA CARRINGTON, age 22y8m, single, b. Richmond Co., d/o Israel and Isadoria Carrington. Rev. T.G. Thomas. 7 DEC 1881. [C9, R:338, R1:54]

Barnes, Thomas William Keane[2] to Harriet A. Elmore. THOMAS W. BARNES, farmer, no age, single, b. Richmond Co., [names of parents left blank], to HARRIET A. ELMORE, no age,

---

[1] Henry B. Scott (b. 1819 in Essex Co., d. 13 MAY 1889 in Baltimore, Md.), practiced medicine near Farnham, Va.
[2] Thomas W. Barnes served in Co. E, 40th Reg., Va. Inf., C.S.A.

single, b. Richmond Co., d/o John W. Elmore. Consent 16 JUN 1870 by bride, wit. Joseph Patterson. Charles E. Watts. 19 JUN 1870 at Joe Waller's. [C5, R:233, R:28]

Barrack, Alfonso to Tebedore Eudora [Flowers] Barrack.[1] ALFONSO BARRACK, farmer, age 24, b. Richmond Co., s/o Charles and Martha Barrack, to TEBIEDO BARRACK, age 17y1m24d, single, b. Lancaster Co., d/o David and Jane Barrack. Consent 24 FEB 1877 by Alfonso and Charles Barrack, guardian of bride. A.B. Dunaway. 28 FEB 1877 at the house of Charles Barrack. [C8, R:306a, R1:42]

Barrack, Joseph to Maria Augusta Bryant. JOSEPH BARRACK, farmer, age 24, single, b. Richmond Co., s/o Charles and Margaret Barrack,[2] to MARIA AUGUSTA BRYANT, age 17, single, b. Richmond Co., d/o Joseph W. and Catharine Bryant. William H. Kirk. 25 APR 1872. [C6, R:237, R1:31]

Barrett, James to Mary Jenkins. JAMES BARRETT, farmer, age 50, widower, b. Westmoreland Co., s/o William and Felicia Barrett, to MARY JENKINS, age 45, single, b. Richmond Co., d/o Reuben Jenkins. Consent 25 FEB 1873 by bride, wit. B.B. Smoot. H.H. Fones. 2 MAR 1873. [C6, R:235, R1:33]

Barrett, James to Mrs. Susan B. Ambrose, widow of Richard T. Fones. JAMES BARRETT, farmer, age 56, widowed, b. Westmoreland Co., s/o William and Felicia Barrett, to SUSAN B. FONES, age 45, widow, b. Richmond Co., d/o R.B. [Redman] and Sofiah Ambrose. Consent 28 DEC 1880 by bride. R.N. Reamy. 12 JAN 1881. [C9, R:335, R1:52]

Barrett, James R. to Louisa Reynolds. JAMES R. BARRETT, farming, age 20, single, b. Richmond Co., s/o James E. and Alphire [Affire J. Ambrose] Barrett,[3] to LOUISA REYNOLDS, age 22, single, b. Richmond Co., d/o John and Mary Reynolds. G.M. Conley. 26 DEC 1889 at *Millview*. [C12, R:329, R1:75]

Barrett, John M. to Allice R. Barrett. JOHN M. BARRETT, farming, age 22y10m9d, single, b. Richmond Co., s/o James E. and Amelia Barrett, to ALLICE R. BARRETT, age 17, single, b. Richmond Co., d/o James and Martha E. Barrett. Consent 27 DEC 1887 by bride and Martha E. Barrett, wit. Albert Bowen. M.F. Sanford. 29 DEC 1887 at the home of the bride. [C11, R1:71]

Barrett, Robert E. to Rebecca Mozingo. ROBERT E. BARRETT, laborer, age 27, single, b. Richmond Co., s/o John and Mary Barrett, to REBECCA MOZINGO, age 21, single, b. Richmond Co., d/o John and Ruth Mozingo. Consent 3 FEB 1874 by bride Rebecca [her X mark] Mozingo, and father [John] [his X mark] Mozingo, wit. Pierce [his X mark] Mozingo. D.M. Wharton. 5 FEB 1874 at the minister's res. [C7, R:230, R1:36]

---

[1] Alfonso Barrack (b. 10 MAR 1854, d. 11 APR 1931) and wife Tebedore Eudora [Flowers] (1861-1936) are bur. at Farnham Baptist Church cemetery.
[2] Charles Barrack (b. 23 MAY 1819, d. 1 SEP 1877) and his wife Margaret (b. 6 SEP 1826, d. 8 DEC 1875) are bur. in Farnham Baptist Church cemetery.
[3] James E. Barrett (b. 22 OCT 1838, d. 6 SEP 1916), and his wife Affire J. Ambrose (b. 14 DEC 1844, d. 31 MAY 1897) are bur. in the Barrett Family Cemetery off Route 645. He served in Co. D, 40th Va. Inf., C.S.A. She is a d/o Redman B. Ambrose and Apphia C. Gutridge.

Barrett, Tunstill C. to Mary Susan Marks.[1] TUNSTILL C. BARRETT, sawyer, age 25, single, b. Richmond Co., s/o Mary A. Barrett (name of father not given[2]), to MARY S. MARKS, age 25, single, b. Richmond Co., d/o Vincent and Mary Marks. D.M. Wharton. 17 MAY 1883 at the white public school house No. 4. [C10, R:356, R1:59]

Barrett, Washington Dangerfield to Sophronia Nash. WASHINGTON DANGERFIELD BARRETT, farmer, age 20y6m, single, b. Westmoreland Co., s/o James and Amelia [Wafel] Barrett,[3] to SOPHRONIA NASH, age 21, single, b. Richmond Co., d/o Zachariah and Mary [Marks] Nash.[4] Consent 8 MAR 1872 by bride, wit. James Barrett, P.M. Saunders. H.H. Fones. 10 MAR 1872 at *Mulberry Island*.[5] [C6, R:237, R1:31]

Barron, Samuel, Jr., Capt. in the Confederate States Navy, to Agnes M. Smith.[6] SAMUEL BARRON, JR., merchant, age 32, single, b. Norfolk, Va., s/o Samuel [Sr.] and Imogen Barron, to AGNES M. SMITH, age 23, single, b. Northumberland Co., d/o James M. and Agnes Smith. Andrew Fisher. 11 MAY 1869 at Warsaw, Va. [C5, R, R1:26]

Barrott, James E. to Apphia Ambrose. JAMES E. BARROTT, farmer, age 28, single, b. Richmond Co., s/o John and Mary Barrott, to AFPHIRE AMBERS [sic],[7] age 22, single, b. Richmond Co., d/o Redman [B.] and Afphire [Apphia C. Gutridge] Ambers [Ambrose]. D.M. Wharton. 28 FEB 1867 at the res. of the minister. [C4, R:286, R1:20]

Bartlett, Charles E. to Martha F. Courtney. CHARLES E. BARTLETT, farmer, age 25, single, b. Westmoreland Co., s/o James and Sarah Ann [Sacra] Bartlett,[8] to MARTHA F. COURTNEY, age 18, single, b. Richmond Co., d/o Jeremiah and Ann [Alderson] Courtney. Consent undated [c.1869] from father Jeremiah Courtney, and consent in 1870 from bride. Elder James A. Weaver. 4 JAN 1870 at res. of Mr. Lee. [C5, R:233, R1:27]

Bartlett, Charles Henry to Salinia Olliff. CHARLES HENRY BARTLETT, farmer, age 21y10m, single, b. Westmoreland Co., s/o William and Myra Bartlett, to SALINIA OLLIFF, age 21y3m, single, b. Richmond Co., d/o Jesse and Bethuel [Jenkins] Olliff.[9] Consent 22 DEC 1876 by father Jesse Olliff, wit. W.H. Balderson. R.N. Reamy. 26 DEC 1876. [C7, R:306, R1:41]

Bartlett, Henry to Mary Ann Hall. HENRY BARTLETT, age about 26, single, b. upper district of Richmond Co., s/o Isaac Bartlett and wife Winny [Winifred Crask],[10] to MARY ANN HALL, age about 16, single, b. upper district of Richmond Co., d/o Stephen Hell [sic] and wife Mary Ann Hall.[11] Consent 14 JAN 1856 by Mary An [her X mark] Hall, and Mary Ann Jones, wit. John [his X mark] Hall, gives bride as Marian Hall. John Pullen, M.G. 17 JAN 1856 at James Jones' in upper district. [C1, R, R1:3]

---

[1] Tuncil or Tunstill C. Barrett and wife Mary Susan Marks (d. 1943) are bur. at Welcome Grove Baptist Church cemetery.

[2] The Register provides no name of the mother, rather the father as Henry A. Barrett.

[3] James Barrott and Amelia Wafel were married by bond 25 MAY 1850 in Richmond Co.

[4] Zachariah Nash and Mary Marks were married by bond 12 MAR 1833 in Richmond Co.

[5] *Mulberry Island* is an old plantation that fronted the Rappahannock River between Wilna and Garland Creeks. It was named by the Bernard Family.

[6] Samuel Barron (b. 1836, d. 29 NOV 1892) and wife Agnes M. Smith (b. JAN 1848, d. 14 OCT 1914) are bur. in St. John's Episcopal Church Cemetery.

[7] The surname is likely Ambrose.

[8] James Bartlett and Sarah Ann Sacra were married by bond 18 DEC 1837 in Richmond Co.

[9] Jesse Oliff and Bethuel Jenkins were married by bond 17 MAY 1842 in Westmoreland Co.

[10] Isaac Bartlett and Winifred Crask were married by bond 5 NOV 1798 in Richmond Co.

[11] Stephen Hall and Mary Ann Hall were married by bond 5 OCT 1829 in Richmond Co.

Bartlett, James (Col.) to Patsey Fauntleroy (Col.). JAMES BARTLETT, farmer, age 40, widowed, b. Richmond Co., s/o Ralph and Fanny Bartlett, to PATSEY FAUNTLEROY, age 40, widow, b. Richmond Co., d/o George Fauntleroy. Consent 16 MAY 1869 by bride Patsey [her X mark] Fauntleroy, wit. W.M. Elmore. Davy Veney. 19 MAY 1869 at Mulberry Chapel.[1] [C5, R, R1:26]

Bartlett, James to Mrs. Martha S. Bowen, widow of Thomas Allen Scates. JAMES BARTLETT, farmer, age 50, widowed, b. and res. Westmoreland Co., [names of parents not completed], to MARTHA S. BOWEN, age 46, widow, b. Richmond Co., d/o [Richard and Polly Bowen].[2] Consent 8 DEC 1887 by bride and Willey [her X mark] Bowen. M.F. Sanford. 11 DEC 1887 at the home of the bride. [C11, R1:71]

Bartlett, John to Willie Ann Balderson. JOHN BARTLETT, farmer, age 65, widowed, b. Richmond Co., [names of parents not completed], to WILLIE ANN BALDERSON, age 19, single, b. Richmond Co., d/o Harriet F. Balderson. Consent 21 MAR 1876 by mother Harritt [sic] [her X mark] Balderson, wit. Richard [his X mark] Bartlett. H.H. Fones. 28 MAR 1876. [C7, R:304, R1:40]

Bartlett, John A.[3] to Willie A. Sisson. JOHN A. BARTLETT, farmer, age 24, bachelor, b. Richmond Co., s/o John and Laurinda [Balderson] Bartlett,[4] to WILLIE A. SISSON, age 16, single, b. Richmond Co., d/o Robert and Amanda [Ann Sanders] Sisson.[5] Consent 19 SEP 1870 by father Robert Sisson, wit. A.L. Saunders, also signed Willie Sisson. H.H. Fones. 22 SEP 1870 at R. Sisson's near *Stony Hill*.[6] [C5, R:233, R1:28]

Bartlett, John P.[7] to Emily C. Sandy. JOHN P. BARTLETT, blacksmith, age 26, single, b. Richmond Co., s/o Thomas and Polly Bartlett, to ELIZA C. SANDY, age 22, single, b. Richmond Co., d/o Samuel and Elizabeth [Pullen] Sandy. Consent 21 FEB 1862 by bride, wit. William H. Sandy. John Pullen. 25 FEB 1862 at Samuel Sandy's. [C3, R:140, R1:11]

Bartlett, Joseph to Frances Ambrose. JOSEPH BARTLETT, farmer, age 22, single, b. Richmond Co., s/o Samuel and Mahala [Carter] Bartlett, to FRANCES AMBROSE, age 18, single, b. Richmond Co., d/o Elijah and Caroline [Pratt] Ambrose. Consent 14 OCT 1873 by father Elijah Ambrose, no wit. B.R. Battaile. 22 OCT 1873 at *Mulen Hill* in Westmoreland Co. [C6, R:235, R1:34]

Bartlett, Robert B. to Emma J. Sanders.[8] ROBERT B. BARTLETT, farmer, age 25, single, b. Richmond Co., s/o John and Lorinda [Balderson] Bartlett, to EMMA J. SANDERS, age 21, single, b. Richmond Co., d/o George W. [Washington] and Charlotte [Scates] Sanders. Consent 24 DEC 1873 by bride Emma J. [her X mark] Sanders, wit. J.W. Bartlett. H.H. Fones. 28 DEC 1873. [C6, R:236, R1:35]

---

[1] Mulberry Church is located about a mile and a quarter east of Emmerton, Va. on Route 619.
[2] The parents names for the bride and groom seem to be messed up, as the marriage in 1865 for Martha S. Bowen to Thomas A. Scates clears up any confusion.
[3] John A. Bartlett received a pension from service in Co. D, 40th Va. Inf., C.S.A.
[4] John Bartlett and Lorinda [also Lawienda, Lourinda] Balderson were married by bond 10 FEB 1836 in Richmond Co.
[5] Robert Sisson and Amanda Ann Sanders were married by bond 5 AUG 1847 in Richmond Co.
[6] Stony Hill is a locality in the north end of the County at the junction of Routes 622 and 624 near Rappahannock Church.
[7] John P. Bartlett served in Co. G, 15th Va. Cav., C.S.A. and is listed in Co. D, 40th Va. Inf. as well.
[8] Robert B. Bartlett and wife Emma J. Sanders (b. 1852, d. 10 NOV 1905) are bur. at Welcome Grove Baptist Church cemetery.

Bartlett, Samuel James[1] to Emily Jane Balderson. SAMUEL BARTLETT, farmer, age 37, widowed, b. Richmond Co., s/o John and Lorinda [Balderson] Bartlett, to EMILY JANE BALDERSON, age 21y8m, single, b. Richmond Co., d/o Arthur and Millie [Mildred Booker] Balderson. Consent 23 JAN 1882 by bride, wit. Arthur Balderson. Rev. M.T. Sanford. 26 JAN 1882 at the home of the bride. [C9, R:312, R1:55]

Bartlett, Samuel to Virginia A.S. Scates. SAMUEL BARTLETT, farmer, age 21y5m, single, b. Richmond Co., s/o John and Laurinda [Balderson] Bartlett, to VIRGINIA A.S. SCATES, age 18, single, b. Richmond Co., d/o Elijah and Louisa A. [Bartlett] Scates.[2] John Pullen. 28 JAN 1864 at Elijah Scates'. [C3, R:139, R1:14]

Bartlett, Samuel to L.A.D. Scates. SAMUEL BARTLETT, farmer, age 28, widowed, b. Richmond Co., s/o John and Myranda Bartlett, to L.A.D. SCATES, age 25, single, b. Richmond Co., d/o Elijah and Louisa [A. Bartlett] Scates. Consent 27 DEC 1875 by bride L.A.D. [her X mark] Scates, wit. J.W. Bartlett. H.H. Fones. 29 DEC 1875. [C7, R:262, R1:39]

Bartlett, William Joseph to Virginia M. Scates.[3] WILLIAM J. BARTLETT, farmer, age 25, single, b. Richmond Co., s/o John [H.] and Laurinda [Lorinda Balderson] Bartlett, to VIRGINIA M. SCATES, age 21, single, b. Richmond Co., d/o John B. and Elizabeth [Marks] Scates.[4] Consent 2 OCT 1863 by bride, wits. Elisebeth Scates, Oscar P. Morriss. Robert N. Reamy. 6 OCT 1863 at the res. of Mrs. Elizabeth Scates. [C3, R:160, R1:13]

Baynham, Joseph (Col.) to Mrs. Judy Gouldman (Col.). JOSEPH BAYNHAM, farmer, age 21y11m, single, b. Essex Co., s/o Thomas and Happy Baynham, to JUDY GOULDMAN, age 21, widow, b. Westmoreland Co., parents unknown. Consent 4 APR 1874 by bride Judy [her X mark] Gouldman, wit. J.W. Chinn. Allen Brown, minister. 2 MAY 1874 at the bride's home. [C7, R:230, R1:36]

Beacham,[5] Dandridge C. to Margaret Ann Hynson. Consent undated c.1857 by father John Hynson, wits. Fauntleroy W. Mozingo, B.H. Hynson. No license or minister return. [C1]

Beacham, Joseph Harding[6] to Paulina W. Dunaway. JOSEPH H. BEACHAM, age 25, single, b. Northumberland Co., s/o Joseph H. [Hudnall] and Sarah M.C. [Mary Catharine Gresham] Beacham, to PAULINA W. DUNAWAY,[7] age 19, single, b. Richmond Co., d/o R.W. [Rawleigh] and Amanda [Critcher] Dunaway.[8] Consent 17 APR 1865 by mother Amanda Dunaway, wit. Thos. N. Oldham. Robert Williamson, M.G. 20 APR 1865 at Mrs. Dunaway's in Farnham Parish. [C3[9], R:204, R1:14]

---

[1] Samuel J. Bartlett served in Co. I, 40th Reg. Va. Inf., C.S.A.

[2] Elijah Scates and Louisa A. Bartlett were married by bond 5 FEB 1827 in Richmond Co.

[3] William J. Bartlett (b. 6 OCT 1838 in Lancaster Co., d. 3 JUN 1925) and wife Sarah A. Scates are bur. at Welcome Grove Baptist Church cemetery. He initially served as a private in Co. I, 40th Va. Inf., C.S.A. and thereafter other units. He operated a general store and grocery near Newland, Va.

[4] John B. Scates and Betsy Marks were married by bond 10 MAR 1830 in Richmond Co.

[5] The surname also appears as Beauchamp. He is likely the Dandridge C. Beauchamp who served in Co. D, 40th Va. Inf., C.S.A.

[6] Joseph H. Beacham (b. 1808, d. 27 MAY 1858) is bur. with his parents at Melrose United Methodist Church cemetery, Lewisetta, Va.

[7] Surname also appears as Dunnaway.

[8] Rawleigh W. Dunaway and Amanda Critcher were married by bond 5 JAN 1842 in Richmond Co.

[9] The certificate is signed by George W. Sydnor as clerk *pro tem* during the Civil War.

Beal, Fleet M. to Ann Gordon. Consent 25 JUN 1855 by mother Fanny Gordon, signed by parties and Fanny Gordon, wit. John C. [his X mark] Brann. No license or minister return. [C1]

Beardsley, Jay W. to Mrs. Susan R. Lewis. JAY W. BEARDSLEY, farmer, age 53, widowed, b. New Brunswick, son John H. and Rebecca Beardsley, to SUSAN R. LEWIS, age 43, widow, b. Baltimore, Md., d/o Charles Lawrence and Eleanor Windsor. Consent 4 MAR 1880 by bride, no wit. W.A. Crocker. 9 MAR 1880. [C9, R:314, R1:50]

Beardsley, Jay W. to Elizabeth A. Purssell. JAY W. BEARDLEY [sic], carpenter, age 46, widower, b. New Brunswick, s/o John [H.] and Rebecca Beardley, to ELIZABETH A. PURSSELL, age 32, single, b. Richmond Co., d/o V.R. and Ann B. Purssell. Consent 11 JAN 1878 by bride. G.H. Northam. 20 JAN 1878. [C8, R:310, R1:44]

Bearl, William (Col.) to Mary Elizabeth Tate (Col.). WILLIAM BEARL, farming, age 22, single, b. and res. Westmoreland Co., s/o Thomas and Judy Bearl, to MARY ELIZABETH TATE, age 21, single, b. Richmond Co., d/o Lucinda Tate, [name of father not given]. Consent 22 DEC 1883 by mother Lucinda Tate, wits. G.E. Omohundro, P. Tate. Rev. Robert Lewis. 27 DEC 1883 at the minister's residence. [C10, R:358, R1:60]

Beazley, Thomas to Olly Martin Douglass. THOMAS BEAZELEY [sic], farmer, age 28, single, b. Caroline Co., s/o Richard and C. Beazeley [sic], to OLLY MARTIN DOUGLASS, age 22, single, b. Richmond Co., d/o Samuel and Ann Douglass. Consent 20 DEC 1879 at Farnham Church[1] by father Samuel [his X mark] Douglass, wit. S.G. Bryant. W.A. Crocker. 23 DEC 1879 at the res. of the bride's father. [C9, R:309, R1:49]

Belfield, Alfred Harwood to Susan Ann Saunders.[2] ALFRED H. BELFIELD, deputy sheriff, age 26, single, b. Richmond Co., s/o Richard C. and Mary F. [Frances Harwood] Belfield,[3] to SUSAN ANN SAUNDERS, age 36, single, b. Richmond Co., d/o Edward [S.] and Maria [Belfield] Saunders.[4] F.B. Beale. 25 DEC 1879 at *Chestnut Hill*.[5] [C9, NN:2 JAN 1880, R:309, R1:49]

Belfield, Benjamin B. to Elizabeth M. Jennings. BENJAMIN B. BELFIELD, farmer, age 26, widowed, b. Richmond Co., s/o Thomas and Jane Belfield, to ELIZABETH M. JENNINGS, age 28, single, b. Richmond Co., d/o James and Mary Jennings. G.M. Connelley. 4 APR 1889 near *Farmer's Fork*.[6] [C12, R:327, R1:74]

Belfield, Edwin Daingerfield to Lucy A. Moss Omohundro.[7] EDWIN D. BELFIELD, farmer, age 22, single, b. Richmond Co., res. Westmoreland Co., s/o John D. [Daingerfield] and Elizabeth [Belfield] Belfield,[8] to L.A.M. OMOHUNDRO, age 18, single, b. Westmoreland Co., d/o Edward

---

[1] Farnham Episcopal Church is located at the junction of Routes 607 and 602.
[2] Alfred Harwood Belfield (b. 9 APR 1854, d. 18 DEC 1935), and his wife Susan Ann Saunders (b. 10 AUG 1841, d. 14 JUN 1931) are bur. at Menokin Baptist Church cemetery.
[3] Richard C. Belfield and Mary Frances Harwood were married by bond 31 MAR 1847 in Richmond Co. by Rev. John Pullen.
[4] Edward S. Saunders and Maria Belfield were married by bond 5 DEC 1825 in Richmond Co.
[5] *Chestnut Hill* is located on the north side of Route 621 and just west of Route 690. It was the early home of Col. Thomas Beale. The house was taken down in the early 21st century.
[6] *Farmer's Fork* is located north of Warsaw, Va. at the junction of Routes 690 and 637.
[7] Edwin Daingerfield Belfield (1851-1947) and his wife Lucy Moss Omohundro (1856-1932) are bur. in the Belfield Family Cemetery on *Belle Mount Farm*.
[8] John D. Belfield and Elizabeth Belfield were married by bond 22 DEC 1845 in Richmond Co.

B. and Sally A.F. [Reamy] Omohundro.[1] Consent 26 AUG 1874 by Sally A.F. Omohundro, wit. G.E. Omohundro. G.W. Beale. 27 AUG 1874 at res. of Mrs. Omohundro. [C7, R:230, R1:36]

Belfield, George W. to Catherine Hazzard. GEORGE W. BELFIELD, farming, age 22, single, b. Northumberland Co., res. Lancaster Co., s/o George T. and Alice Belfield, to CATHERINE HAZZARD, age 22, single, b. Richmond Co., d/o William and Susan Hazzard. Consent 20 JAN 1890 from Ottoman, Va. by bride, wit. George E. Lewis. Rev. Jas. T. Eubank. 21 JAN 1890 at the bride's mother's. [C12, R:323, R1:76]

Belfield, John Augustine to Mary Frances Omohundro.[2] JOHN AUGUSTINE BELFIELD, farming, age 21y4m, single, b. Richmond Co., res. Westmoreland Co., s/o Dr. R.A. [Richard Alexander][3] and Fanny S. [Southall Daingerfield] Belfield, to MARY F. OMOHUNDRO, age 29, single, b. Westmoreland Co., d/o Edward B. and S.A.F. [Sarah Ann F. Reamy] Omohundro. Consent 23 NOV 1881 by bride. F.B. Beale. 24 NOV 1881 at Farmer's Fork. [C9, R:338, R1:54]

Belfield, John W. to Mary A. Settle. JOHN W. BELFIELD, farmer, age 20, single, b. Richmond Co., s/o J. [John] Daingerfield and Elizabeth [Belfield] Belfield, to MARY A. SETTLE, age 21, single, b. Richmond Co., d/o Frederick and Diana [T. Claughton] Settle. G.H. Northam. 7 MAY 1868 at *Pleasant Valley*. [C4, R:253, R1:23]

Belfield, Richard Lawrence to Mary Peake "Mollie" Crabb.[4] RICHARD L. BELFIELD, farmer, age 21, single, b. Richmond Co., s/o John D. [Daingerfield] and Elizabeth [Belfield] Belfield, to MARY P. CRABB, age 21, single, b. Richmond Co., d/o William M.M. and Ann T. [Peck] Crabb.[5] Peter Ainslie. 28 MAY 1868 at *Pittsville*, the res. of the bride's father. [C4, R:254, R1:24]

Belfield, Thomas Jones to Mary Jane Yeatman. THOMAS JONES BELFIELD, farming, age 38, single, b. Richmond Co., s/o Thos. M. and Eliza Jane [McClannahan] Belfield,[6] to MARY JANE YEATMAN, age 30, single, b. Richmond Co., d/o Jas. H. and Alice J. [Belfield] Yeatman, *q.v.* Consent 4 MAR 1890 by bride, wit. R.H. Yeatman. Rev. J.B. Askew. 5 MAR 1890 at the res. of Mrs. Alice J. Yeatman. [C12, R:323a, R1:76]

Bell, Bartholomew Ewell to Alpharetta Virginia Clark.[7] BARTHOLOMEW E. BELL, farmer, age 21y6m25d, single, b. Northumberland Co.,s/o William D. [Dew] and Charlotte M. [McAdam Nutt] Bell, to ALPHARETTA V. CLARK, age 17y2m16d, single, b. Richmond Co., d/o John N. and Lucinda Clark. Consent 30 APR 1877 by mother Lucinda [her X mark] Clark, wit. bride. G.H. Northam. 1 MAY 1877. [C8, R:307, R1:42]

Bell, Charles David to Mrs. Alice V. Harrison, widow of John A. Gordon. CHARLES DAVID BELL, farmer, age 21, single, b. Richmond Co., s/o Vincent R. and Mary A. [Ann Rock] Bell,[8] to ALICE

---

[1] Edward B. Omohundro and Sarah A. Reamy were married by bond 1 JUL 1839 in Westmoreland Co.

[2] John A. Belfield (b. 24 JUL 1860, d. 22 FEB 1922) and wife Mary F. Omohundro (b. 24 MAY 1857, d. 1 DEC 1943) are bur. at a large monument in Menokin Baptist Church cemetery.

[3] Dr. Richard Alexander Belfield (b. 1 MAY 1832 at *Belle Mount Farm*, d. 25 APR 1885) is bur. at Menokin Baptist Church cemetery. He was s/o Col. John Wright Belfield and Mary Daingerfield. He practiced at his home *Rock Spring*.

[4] Richard Lawrence Belfield (b. c.OCT 1846, d. 16 JUL 1910) and wife Mary Peake Crabbe Belfield (b. c.JUL 1845, d. 18 MAR 1918), were bur. at *Belmont* in Stonewall District.

[5] William M.M. Crabb and Ann T. Peck were married 22 FEB 1838 in Richmond Co. by Rev. Lovell Marders.

[6] Thomas M. Belfield and Eliza Jane McClannahan were married by bond 22 NOV 1841 in Westmoreland Co.

[7] Bartholomew E. Bell (b. 5 OCT 1856, d. 19 NOV 1897 in Warsaw, Va.) and wife Alphretta V. Clark (b. 14 FEB 1858, d. 3 MAR 1928) are bur. at Totuskey Baptist Church cemetery.

[8] Vincent R. Bell and Mary Ann Rock were married by bond 22 JUN 1848 in Northumberland Co.

V. GORDON, age 25, widow, b. Richmond Co., d/o John A. and Margaret Harrison. H.H. Fones. 30 AUG 1877. [C8, R:307, R1:43]

Bell, Joseph McAdam to Eliza Jane Self.[1] JOSEPH M. BELL, farmer, age 22, single, b. Northumberland Co., s/o William D. and Charlotte M. [Nutt] Bell, to ELIZA JANE SELF, age 18, single, b. Richmond Co., d/o Moses and Mary [S. Smith] Self.[2] Consent 19 DEC 1860 by bride and Moses Self, wit. James C. Northwood. Elder O.M.T. Samuels. 19 DEC 1860. [C2, R:154, R1:9]

Bell, Robert Lewis to Mary S. Self.[3] ROBERT L. BELL, sailor, age 32, single, b. Northumberland Co., s/o William D. and Charlotte M. [Nutt] Bell, to MARY S. SELF, age 31, single, b. Richmond Co., d/o Moses and Mary S. [Smith] Self. Consent 23 FEB 1874 from *Locust Lane* by bride, no wit. Elder James A. Weaver. 23 FEB 1874 at the res. of the bride. [C7, R:230, R1:36]

Bell, William D. to Ida M. Northen.[4] WILLIAM D. BELL, farming, age 25, single, b. Northumberland Co., s/o William D. and Charlotte M. [Nutt] Bell, to IDA NORTHEN, age 18, single, b. Richmond Co., d/o Charles A. [Alexander] and Sarah R. [Rebecca Bell] Northen, *q.v.* Consent in FEB 1886 by father Charles A. Northen, wit. William D. Bell. G.H. Northam. 17 FEB 1886 at C.A. Northen's. [C11, NN:5 MAR 1886, R:315, R1:67]

Benson, George H.[5] to Elizabeth Wilson. GEORGE H. BENSON, farmer, age 22, single, b. Massachusetts, s/o Isaac Benson and wife Sarah, to ELIZABETH WIL[L]SON, age 16, single, b. Richmond Co., d/o Elizabeth, [father unknown]. Consent 17 MAR 1856 by mother Elizabeth [her X mark] Conley, wit. Jas. A. McKnight. William H. Coffin, M.G. 20 MAR 1856. [C1]

Berkley, Charles (Col.) to Fannie Boyd (Col.). CHARLES BERKLEY, farming, age 22, single, b. Essex Co., s/o Charles and Hanna Berkley, to FANNIE BOYD, age 21, single, b. Essex Co., s/o George and Winnie Boyd. Peter Blackwell. 6 FEB 1879 at Mount Zion Church. [C8, R:307, R1:49]

Beverley, William A. (Col.) to Ellenora Greggs (Col.). WILLIAM A. BEVERLEY, laborer, age 23, single, b. Essex Co., s/o Dangerfield and Julia Beverley, to ELLENORA GREGGS, age 22, single, b. Richmond Co., d/o Malinda Greggs. Consent 14 JAN 1873 by bride Ellenora [her X mark] Greggs, no wit. Thomas G. Thomas. 19 JAN 1873. [C6, R:235, R1:33]

Bevis, Thomas to Catharine Alice Purcell.[6] THOMAS BEVIS, farmer, age 38, divorced, b. Gloucester Co., N.J., s/o Abraham and Sarah A. [Moore] Bevis, to CATHARINE A. PURSSELL [sic], age 27, single, b. Richmond Co., d/o V.R. and Ann B. Purssell. Consent 2 NOV 1877 by bride. W.A. Crocker. 4 NOV 1877. [C8, R:307, R1:43]

---

[1] Joseph McAdam Bell (b. 16 APR 1838, d. 12 JUL 1912) and wife Eliza J. Self (b. 3 MAR 1842, d. 12 DEC 1908) are bur. at Totuskey Baptist Church cemetery. He served in Co. K, 9th Va. Cav., C.S.A., and was wounded in the shoulder with a musket ball at Hanover Courthouse.

[2] Moses Self and Mary S. Smith were married by bond 5 JAN 1826 in Westmoreland Co.

[3] Capt. Robert L. Bell (1842-1886) and wife Mary S. Self (1839-1910) are bur. at Totuskey Baptist Church cemetery. As Captain of the *S.S. Acadia*, he was lost at sea.

[4] William D. Bell (b. 8 AUG 1860, d. 25 JAN 1940) and his wife Ida M. Northen (b. 26 DEC 1870, d. 24 SEP 1952) are bur. at Totuskey Baptist Church cemetery.

[5] George H. Benson served in Co. E, 40th Rev., Va. Inf., C.S.A. as a wagoner.

[6] Thomas Bevis (b. 26 SEP 1839, d. 4 MAY 1919), whose second wife was Catharine Alice Purcell, was bur. Corinth Methodist Episcopal Church cemetery, Avalon, Va. NN:14 JAN 1881 announced the death of Catharine Alice Bevis, wife of Thomas Bevis.

Bird, William (Col.) to Catharine Phillips (Col.). WILLIAM BIRD, oysterman, age 23, single, b. Richmond Co., s/o Edward and Betty Bird, to CATHARINE PHILLIPS, age 20, single, b. Richmond Co., d/o Baylor Christopher and Carter Columbus Phillips. Rev. W. Carter. 4 JAN 1883 at the bride's home. [C10, R:355, R1:58]

Biscoe, Melville to Isabella Frances "Belle" Pearson.[1] MELVILLE BISCOE, farming, age 20, single, b. Lancaster Co., s/o Henry L. [Lawson] and Sarah C. [Chowning Blakemore] Biscoe,[2] to ISABELLA F. PEARSON, age 19, single, b. Richmond Co., d/o Lawson [T.] Pearson [and Alice M. Saunders].[3] Consent by Th. Oldham, guardian of groom, and I.F. Pearson, wit. G.H. Northam. Robert Williamson, M.G. 10 NOV 1857 at Farnham house. [C1, R:160, R1:5]

Bispham, Robert to Mary Jane Jenkins. ROBERT BISPHAM, farming, age about 32, single, b. upper district of Richmond Co., s/o William Bispham and wife Mary [Asbury],[4] to MARY JANE JENKINS, age about 22, single, b. Westmoreland Co., d/o William B. and Felatia Jenkins. Consent 2 FEB 1856 by bride Mary Jane [her X mark] Jinkins [sic], wit. James H. Jennings. John Pullen, M.G. 7 FEB 1856 at Wm. Jenkins' in upper district. [C1, R, R1:3]

Blair, Moses (Col.) to Belinda Gatewood (Col.). MOSES BLAIR, farmer, age 45, single, b. Richmond Co., s/o Joseph and Hannah Blair, to BELINDA GATEWOOD, age 18, single, b. Richmond Co., d/o Allen and Celia Gatewood. Andrew Fisher. 18 MAR 1866 at Warsaw, Va. [C4, R:271, R1:17]

Blue, James (Col.) to Mrs. Julia Ann Ford (Col.). JAMES BLUE, laborer, age 32, widowed, b. Richmond Co., s/o Henrietta Thompson, to JULIA ANN FORD, age 30, widow, b. Richmond Co., [parents unknown]. Thomas G. Thomas. 11 MAR 1877 at Clarksville Baptist Church. [C8, R:306a, R1:42]

Blue, James (Col.) to Mrs. Mary Bramham (Col.). JAMES BLUE, farmer, age 25, single, b. Richmond Co., s/o Hannah Blue, to MARY BRAMHAM, age 22, widow, b. Westmoreland Co., d/o Julia Ann Minor. Jeremiah Graham. 28 NOV 1869 at res. of Armistead Jackson. [C5, R, R1:26]

Blueford, Robert G.[5] to Elizabeth Ann Beacham. Consent 19 MAY 1854 by Elizabeth Ann Beacham to marry Robt. G. Bluford [sic], wit. John Harrison. No license or minister return. [C1]

Bolden, Charles T. to Susan A. Scates. CHARLES T. BOLDEN, laborer, age 34, widowed, b. Fredericksburg, Va., s/o Elijah and Mary Bolden, to SUSAN A. SCATES, age 27, single, b. Richmond Co., d/o Thomas and Susan [Sanders] Scates.[6] Consent 17 DEC 1883 from Stonewall, Va. by bride, wits. James A.B. Sanders, J.W. Carter. R.N. Reamy. 27 DEC 1883. [C10, R:358, R1:60]

---

[1] Melville Biscoe (1838-1883) and his wife Isabella Frances Pearson (b. 26 SEP 1839, d. 4 JUL 1911) are bur. in Jerusalem Baptist Church cemetery, as well as Lawson T. Pearson (1811-1891) who was a captain in the Richmond Co. Reserves, C.S.A., and his wife Alice Chilton (1809-1891). Also see NN:23 FEB 1883.

[2] Henry Lawson Biscoe (1815-1947), of *Pleasant View Farm*, and wife Sarah Chowning Blakemore (b. 13 OCT 1812, d. 23 DEC 1880) are bur. in Jerusalem Baptist Church cemetery. She married second to Thomas C. Oldham.

[3] Capt. Lawson T. Pearson and Alice M. Saunders were married by bond 26 NOV 1842 in Richmond Co.

[4] William Bispham and Mary Asbury, widow, were married by bond 19 JUL 1820 in Richmond Co.

[5] He served in the 41st Va. Mil., C.S.A. We also find Robert Blewford in Co. K, 9th Va. Cav., C.S.A.

[6] Thomas Scates and Susan Sanders were married by bond 5 FEB 1838 in Richmond Co. by Rev. Thomas M. Washington.

Booker, John (Col.) to Maria J. Burrel (Col.). JOHN BOOKER, blacksmith, age 21, single, b. Henrico Co., s/o Julius and Hardinia Booker, to MARIA J. BURREL, age 20, single, b. Richmond Co., d/o William and Ellen Burrel. Andrew Fisher. 8 MAR 1866 at the res. of Wm. Burrel. [C4, R:270, R1:16]

Boothe, James J. to Mrs. Frances A. Douglass Lankford. JAMES J. BOOTHE, farming, age 50, single, b. Westmoreland Co., s/o Samuel D. and Mary Boothe, to FRANCES A. LANKFORD, age 42, widow, b. Northumberland Co., d/o Thomas and Patsy Douglass. Consent 14 DEC 1886 by bride, wit. L.L. Headley. Rev. A.D. Reynolds. 14 DEC 1886 at the res. of the bride. [C11, R1:68]

Bosman, George W. to Bettie Emma Luckum. GEORGE W. BOSMAN, waterman, age 24, single, b. Maryland, s/o Isaac and Maria Bosman, to BETTIE EMMA LUCKUM, age 21, single, b. Richmond Co., d/o Joseph D. and Lucinda [S. Harrison] Luckum.[1] Consent undated by father Joseph D. [his X mark] Luckum, wit. [R.]H. Lyell. A.B. Dunaway. 19 MAR 1876 at the house of Joseph Luckum. [C7, R:304, R1:40]

Boswell, Augustus C.[2] to Lucy A.C. Booker. AUGUSTUS C. BOSWELL, blacksmith, age 26, single, b. Northumberland Co., s/o Henry and Elizabeth [F. Booth] Boswell,[3] to LUCY A.C. BOOKER, age 22, single, b. Richmond Co., d/o George and Maria Booker.[4] Consent 26 DEC 1865 by bride Lucy A.C. [her X mark] Booker, wit. W.E. Hill. Robert Williamson, M.G. 28 DEC 1865 at Durrettsville, Va. [C3, R:205, R1:15]

Bowen, Charles to Josephine F. Vickers. CHARLES BOWEN, merchant, age 22, single, b. Richmond Co., s/o William Bowen and Annie [Bowen] Bowen,[5] *q.v.*, to JOSEPHINE F. VICKERS, age 21, single, b. Essex Co., d/o Thomas and Elizabeth [Morris] Vickers.[6] Consent 20 MAY 1890 by bride, no wit. G.M. Connelly. 22 MAY 1890 near Oak Row. [C12, R:323a, R1:77]

Bowen, Frederick to Mrs. Mary F. Yeatman, widow of Levi Yeatman. FREDERICK BOWEN, house carpenter, age 24, single, res. Richmond Co., s/o William and Nancy A. [Bowen] Bowen, *q.v.*, to MARY F. YEATMAN, age 26, widow, res. Richmond Co., d/o Henry and Elizabeth Davis. Consent 23 DEC 1857 from mother Elizabeth [her X mark] Davis, Mary [her X mark] Yeatman, wit. John H. Yeatman. 24 DEC 1857 at res. of Henry P.F. King in Westmoreland Co. Rev. Henry P.F. King, M.E. Church. [C1, R:160, R1:5]

Bowen, James to Mrs. Virginia Peyton Jones. JAMES BOWEN, farmer, age 24, single, b. Richmond Co., s/o James and Susan Bowen, to VIRGINIA JONES, age 25, widow, b. Richmond Co., d/o John [A.] and Elizabeth [Morris] Peyton.[7] Robert N. Reamy. Consent 27 MAR 1866 by bride, wit. J.W. Belfield. 29 MAR 1866 at the res. of John W. Belfield. [C3, C4, R:271, R1:17]

---

[1] Joseph Luckum and Lucinda S. Harrison were married by bond 18 DEC 1849 in Richmond Co.
[2] Augustus C. Boswell served in Co. E, 40th Reg., Va. Inf., C.S.A.
[3] Henry Boswell, widower, and Elizabeth F. Booth were married by bond 26 SEP 1838 in Richmond Co.
[4] There is a marriage bond 29 JUN 1836 in Richmond, Va. for George W. Booker and Mary W. Davis.
[5] William Bowen (b. 26 JAN 1837, d. 17 MAR 1910) and his wife Annie Bowen (b. 17 MAR 1850, d. 1925) are bur. in Rappahannock Baptist Church cemetery. He served in Co. D, 40th Va. Inf., C.S.A.
[6] Thomas Vickers and Elizabeth Morris were married by bond 29 DEC 1847 in Richmond Co., with consent of her parents John and Elizabeth Morris.
[7] John A. Payton, of Westmoreland Co., and Elizabeth Morris were married by bond 11 NOV 1828 in Richmond Co.

Bowen, James, to Eliza Reynolds. JAMES BOWEN, miller, age 50, widowed, b. Richmond Co., s/o John and Milly Bowen, to ELIZA REYNOLDS, age 18, single, b. Richmond Co., d/o William and Hannah Reynolds. Consent 10 DEC 1862 by mother Hannah [her X mark] Reynolds, wit. R.C. Belfield. G.H. Northam. 11 DEC 1862. [C3, R:140, R1:12]

Bowen, John to Cornelia Carter Scott. JOHN BOWEN, farmer, age 28, single, b. Richmond Co., s/o John Bowen (dec'd.) and Maria Bowen, to CORNELIA CARTER SCOTT, age 21, single, b. Richmond Co., d/o James and Matilda Ann [Scott] Scott.[1] Consent 20 DEC 1878 by James Scott and R.C. Mozingo. F.B. Beale. 22 DEC 1878 near *Piney Grove*.[2] [C8, R:312, R1:46]

Bowen, Joseph to Martha S. Scates. JOSEPH BOWEN, farmer, age 23, single, b. Richmond Co., s/o James S. and Susan [Wilson] Bowen,[3] to MARTHA S. SCATES, age 21, single, b. Richmond Co., d/o Thomas and Susan [Sanders] Scates.[4] No minister return. 27 DEC 1860. [C2, R:154, R1:9]

Bowen, Joseph A. to Ella J. Sanders. JOSEPH A. BOWEN, sailor, age 25, single, b. Richmond Co., s/o Joseph and Sarah Bowen, to ELLA J. SAUNDERS [sic], age 21y8m, single, b. Richmond Co., d/o Griffin and Maria [A. Sanders] Sanders.[5] Consent 26 JAN 1882 by bride, wit. C.C. Balderson. H.H. Fones. 28 DEC 1882. [C10, R:314, R1:57]

Bowen, Joseph M. to Ann Weaver. JOSEPH M. BOWEN, farmer, age about 22, single, b. Richmond Co., s/o William H. Bowen and wife Rebecca, to ANN WEAVER, age about 17, single, b. Richmond Co., d/o Henry Weaver and wife Nancy. Consent 10 JUN 1857 from mother Nancy [her X mark] Weaver, wit. Joseph Bowen. John Pullen, M.G. 14 JUN 1857 at Joseph Bowen's. [C1, R:159, R1:4]

Bowen, Joseph Pompey[6] to Annie Virginia Scates. JOSEPH P. BOWEN, farming, age 20, single, b. Richmond Co., s/o James and Virginia H. Bowen, to ANNIE V. SCATES, age 19, single, b. Richmond Co., d/o James A. and Virginia [A. Hinson] Scates, *q.v.* Consent 15 MAR 1887 by groom's parents, wit. J.G. Sanders; consent 15 MAR 1887 by bride's parents. Geo. M. Conley. 17 MAR 1887 at *Pleasant View*. [C11, R:290, R1:69]

Bowen, Kelly H. to Mrs. Julia Ann Hinson Bulger. KELLY H. BOWEN, farmer, age 58, widowed, b. Richmond Co., s/o Thomas and Mary Bowen, to JULIA A. BULGER, age 35, widow, b. Richmond Co., d/o William [F.] and Mary [Ann Neale] Hinson.[7] Consent 16 APR 1863 by bride, wit. William D. Olliff. John Pullen. 21 APR 1863 at George Newman's. [C3, R:160, R1:12]

Bowen, Samuel to Alice Nash.[8] SAMUEL BOWEN, farmer, age 25, single, b. Richmond Co., s/o Richard and Mary Bowen, to ALICE NASH, age 20, single, b. Richmond Co., d/o Emily Nash. R.N. Reamy. 8 AUG 1878 at the house of the minister. [C8, R:311, R1:45]

---

[1] James Scott and Matilda A. Scott were married 9 NOV 1853 by Rev. George H. Northam.
[2] Piney Grove is a locality at the south junction of Route 600 and 637, and was also the name of a farm there that was owned by William Settle.
[3] James S. Bowen and Susan Wilson were married by bond 5 JAN 1837 in Westmoreland Co.
[4] Thomas Scates and Susan Sanders were married by bond 3 FEB 1838 in Richmond Co.
[5] Griffin Sanders and Maria A. Sanders were married 12 JAN 1843 by Rev. R.N. Herndon.
[6] Joseph P. Bowen (b. 12 OCT 1867, d. 4 JUL 1928) is bur. at Providence United Methodist Church cemetery, Chiltons, Va.
[7] William F. Hinson and Mary Ann Neale were married by bond 23 JAN 1826 in Westmoreland Co.
[8] Samuel Bowen (1853-1936) and wife Alice Nash (1861-1939) are bur. in Rappahannock Baptist Church cemetery.

Bowen, Thomas to Martha Scates. THOMAS BOWEN, farming, age about 24, single, b. Richmond Co., s/o Wm. Bowen and wife Rebecca, to MARTHA SCATES, age about 19, single, b. Richmond Co., d/o Joseph Scates and wife Lucy [Sanders].[1] Consent 23 MAR 1857 by J.C. Mitchell, guardian of bride, wit. Richard Scates. John Pullen, M.G. 2 APR 1857 at John Pullen's. [C1, R:159, R1:4]

Bowen, Thomas W. to Adaline G. Gouldman. THOMAS W. BOWEN, farming, age 33y4m, single, b. Richmond Co., s/o Joseph H. and Sarah A. [Marshall] Bowen,[2] to ADALINE G. GOULDMAN, age [2]7, single, b. Essex Co., d/o Hiram and Sarah A. [Ann Gray] Gouldman.[3] Consent in MAR 1883 by bride, no wit. H.H. Fones. 29 MAR 1883. [C10, NN:13 APR 1883, R:356, R1:58]

Bowen, William, to Nancy A. Bowen. WILLIAM BOWEN, farmer, age 30, single, b. Richmond Co., s/o Kelly H. and Maria [Fegget] Bowen,[4] to NANCY A. BOWEN, age 22, single, b. Richmond Co., d/o Richard and Mary Bowen. John Pullen. 30 DEC 1866 at Bladen Jenkins'. [C4, R:273, R1:19]

Bowen, William D. to Mrs. Mary Scates, widow of Joseph Scates. WILLIAM D. BOWEN, farming and laboring, age 28, single, b. Richmond Co., s/o Joseph and Jane Bowen, to MARY SCATES, age 25, widow, b. Westmoreland Co., d/o Eliza Matthews. Consent signed by Mrs. Mary [her X mark] Scates, Mr. [Dorsey] [his X mark] Bowen. Geo. M. Conley. 5 OCT 1887 at *Welcome Grove*.[5] [C11, R:292, R1:70]

Bowen, William H. to Lizzie H. Jones. WILLIAM H. BOWEN, fisherman, age 28, single, b. Richmond Co., s/o James and Ann Bowen, to LIZZIE H. JONES, age 20y10m, single, b. Stafford Co., d/o Clinton Jones and Catherine [Brown] Jones[6] now Mozingo. Consent 2 NOV 1875 by mother Catherine Mozingo, signed by Lizzie H. Jones, wit. A.L. Saunders. D.M. Wharton. 4 NOV 1875 at the res. of the minister in Westmoreland Co. [C7, R:262, R1:38]

Bowlar, Charles (Col.) to Flary Willie Deleever (Col.). CHARLES BOWLAR, farming, age 35, single, b. Baltimore, Md., d/o Cupid Bowlar and Mary Campbell (formerly his wife), to FLARY WILLIE DELEEVER, age 24, single, b. Middlesex Co., d/o Elizabeth Deleever. Consent 13 JUL 1887 by mother Liza Deleever. Rev. Jacob Robinson, Pastor of Mt. Zion Church. [C11, R:292, R1:70 twice]

Bowzer, James to Miami Nelson. JAMES BOWZER, blacksmith, age 38, single, b. City Point, Va., s/o Thomas and Amy Bowzer, to MIAMI NELSON, age 35, single, b. Westmoreland Co., d/o James and Lavinia Nelson. William F. Bain. 29 DEC 1865 at the Methodist Parsonage. [C3, R:205, R1:15]

Boyd, Jerry (Col.) to Mary Johnson (Col.). JERRY BOYD, farming, age 58, widowed, b. Richmond Co., s/o Spencer and Lucy Boyd, to MARY JOHNSON, age 38, single, b. Richmond Co., d/o Carter Maden and Nancy Grey née Johnson. George Laws. 27 DEC 1883 at *Lansdown*. [C10, R:358, R1:60]

---

[1] Joseph Scates and Lucy Sanders were married by bond 15 FEB 1826 in Richmond Co.
[2] Joseph Bowing [sic] and Sarah A. Marshall were married 26 DEC 1838 in Richmond Co. by Rev. Lovell Marders.
[3] Hiram Gouldman and Sarah Ann Gray were married 8 MAY 1840 in Essex Co.
[4] Kelly H. Bowen and Mariah Fegget were married by bond 17 DEC 1827 in Westmoreland Co.
[5] Presumably Welcome Grove Baptist Church, which is located on the west side of Route 624 and about 9 miles north of Warsaw, Va.
[6] Clinton Jones and Catharine Brown were married by bond 19 JUN 1842 in Richmond Co., by consent of her father John Brown.

Boyd, Robert (Col.) to Alcey Douglas (Col.). ROBERT BOYD, oysterman, age 21, single, b. King and Queen Co., s/o Thomas Boyd and Louisa Stewart, to ALCEY DOUGLAS, age 17, single, b. Westmoreland Co., d/o [Booker Boyd], Willis and Judy Douglas. Consent by mother Judy [her X mark] Gouldin, wit. J.W. Chinn. Robert Williamson, M.G. 8 JUN 1872 at *Wilna*.[1] [C6, R:237, R1:31]

Bragg, Robert M. to Sarah F. Pursell. ROBERT M. BRAGG, farming, age 24 on 3 APR 1854, single, b. Westmoreland Co., s/o T.M. [Thomas Moore] Bragg and Margaret [Bispham] his wife,[2] to SARAH F. PURSELL, age 18 in June 1854, single, b. Richmond Co., d/o S.D. [Stephen] Purcell and Catharine [Payton].[3] Consent 10 MAR 1854 by Catharine Brinham, guardian of bride, wit. John C. Atzerodt, John L. Smith. Rev. John Pullen. 12 MAR 1854. [C, R, R1:1]

Brann, James to Keturah L. Efford. JAMES BRANN, farmer, age 21, single, b. Richmond Co., s/o Reuben G. and Frances E. [Elizabeth] Brann, to KETURAH L. EFFORD, age 23, single, b. Richmond Co., d/o George W. and Betsey [Elizabeth W. Thrift] Efford.[4] Robert Williamson, M.G. 31 DEC 1867 at G.W. Efford's. [C4, R:287, R1:22]

Brann, James P. to Priscilla S. Jones. JAMES P. BRANN, farmer, age 28, widowed, b. Richmond Co., s/o Reuben [G.] and [Frances] Elizabeth Brann, to PRISCILLA S. JONES, age 26, single, b. Richmond Co., d/o Jesse and Apphia [Lewis] Jones.[5] Consent 16 NOV 1874 by bride. G.H. Northam. 17 NOV 1874. [C7, R:230, R1:37]

Brann, James P. to Lena L. Dunaway. JAMES P. BRANN, farming, age 43, widowed, b. Richmond Co., s/o Reuben G. and Frances Elizabeth Brann, to LENA L. DUNAWAY, age 17, single, b. Richmond Co., d/o Robert R. and Mary Jane Dunaway. Rev. J. Manning Dunaway. 10 NOV 1889 at *Woodford*.[6] [C12, R:328, R1:75]

Brasse, Charles W. to Rosa Lewis. CHARLES W. BRASSE, oystering &c., age 27, single, b. Madison Co., [N.Y.], res. Northumberland Co., s/o John W. and Sarah Brasse, to ROSA LEWIS, age 21y4m29d, single, b. Northumberland Co., d/o Samuel and Lutitia Lewis. Consent 3 JAN 1890 by bride Rossie Lewis, wit. C.Willie Brasse. G.H. Northam. 3 JAN 1890 at *Glenmore*. [C12, R:323, R1:76]

Bray, John (Col.) to Fannie Parrot (Col.). JOHN BRAY, oysterman, age 28, single, b. Richmond Co., s/o Adam Bray and Fannie Stowel, to FANNIE PARROT, age 28, single, b. Richmond Co., d/o Nelson Parrot and Ellen Drake. Consent 28 MAY 1879 by Fannie [her X mark] Parrot, no wit. Walker Carter, minister. 29 MAY 1879 at the res. of the bride. [C8, R:307, R1:47]

Brewer, Jackson to Mrs. Sallie Saunders. JACKSON BREWER, farming, age 21y2m, single, b. Richmond Co., s/o Richard [Ellett] and Frances Jane [Hinson] Brewer, *q.v.*, to SALLIE SAUNDERS, age 23, widow, b. Richmond Co., d/o George W. and Frances Saunders.

---

[1] There are two properties called *Wilna* in Richmond Co. One is a noted ante-bellum home of the Joseph William Chinn Family on the bank of the Rappahannock River and below Sharps, Va., and the other is a home of the Carter Mitchell Family.
[2] Thomas Moore Bragg and Margaret Bispham were married 13 MAY 1813 in Richmond Co.
[3] Stephen D. Pursell [sic] and Catharine Payton, widow, were married by bond 20 MAY 1831 in Richmond Co.
[4] George W. Efford and Elizabeth W. Thrift were married by bond 24 DEC 1836 in Richmond Co.
[5] John Jones and Apphia Lewis were married by bond 25 APR 1837 in Richmond Co.
[6] *Woodford* was an old estate northeast of Sharps, Va. and was owned by the McCarty Family.

Consent 27 DEC 1883 by bride Sallie [her X mark] Saunders, wit. J.H. Jett. R.N. Reamy. 30 DEC 1883. [C10, R:358, R1:60]

Brewer, Richard Ellett[1] to Frances Jane Hinson. RICHARD ELLIOTT BROWN, age 30, single, b. Richmond Co., s/o Thomas and Mary [Hinson] Brewer,[2] to FRANCES JANE HINSON, age 20, single, b. Richmond Co., d/o Meredith and Nelly [Coates] Hinson.[3] Consent 17 DEC 1861 by mother Nelly [her X mark] Hinson, signed Frances Jane [her X mark] Hinson, wits. Ritchard Ellett [his X mark] Brewer, sworn by Thomas A. Carter. John Pullen. 19 DEC 1861. [C3, R:124, R1:11]

Broaddus, William H. to Frances E. Payton. WILLIAM H. BROADDUS, carpenter, age about 25, single, b. King and Queen Co., s/o John B. Broaddus and wife Sophiah, to FRANCES E. PAYTON, age about 18, single, b. Richmond Co., d/o John [A.] Payton and wife Elizabeth [Morris].[4] Consent 11 NOV 1856 by mother Elizabeth [her X mark] Payton, wits. T.N. Balderson, R.T. Reamy. John Pullen, M.G. 12 NOV 1856 at Elizabeth Payton's. [C1, R:148, R1:4]

Broaddus, William T. to Martha J. Saunders. WILLIAM T. BROADUS [sic], farming, age 22, single, b. Richmond Co., s/o William H. and Frances E. [Payton] Broadus, to MARTHA J. SAUNDERS, age 18, single, b. Richmond Co., d/o William O. and Catharine [Jennings] Saunders, *q.v.* Consent 22 DEC 1879 by father W.O. Saunders, wit. William C. Carpenter. R.N. Reamy. 23 DEC 1879 at O. Vt. Saunders'. [C9, NN:2 JAN 1880, R:309, R1:48]

Bronner, Charles J. to Emma P. Sisson. CHARLES J. BRONNER, farmer, age 19, single, b. Westfield, N.J., s/o Joseph P. [Prosper] and Abby [Cory] Bronner,[5] to EMMA P. SISSON, age 17, single, b. Richmond Co., d/o J.T. [John Taliaferro] and A.E. [Anna Elizabeth Clarke] Sisson. Consent undated by J.T. Sisson, wit. Jos. P. Bronner. G.H. Northam. 21 OCT 1873. [C6, R:235, R1:34]

Brooke, William W. to Mary Bettie Balderson. WILLIAM W. BROOKE, merchant, age 28, single, b. Richmond Co., s/o William and Ann [Belfield] Brooke,[6] to MARY BETTIE BALDERSON, age 17, single, b. Richmond Co., d/o Charles H. [Hiram] and Virginia [J. Coates] Balderson, *q.v.* Consent 3 NOV 1879 by father Charles H. Balderson, wit C.C. Balderson and T.N. Balderson. H.H. Fones. 6 NOV 1879. [C8, R:308, R1:48]

Brooks, Reuben to Eliza C. Thrift. REUBEN BROOKS, farmer, age 23, single, b. Middlesex Co., s/o Richard and Caty Brooks, to ELIZA C. THRIFT, age 21, single, b. Lancaster Co., d/o Fenton and Eliza Thrift. Consent 18 SEP 1860 by bride, attested to by Jas. Dickinson that she is over age 21. Robert Williamson, M.G. 20 SEP 1860 at Farnham Baptist Church.[7] [C2, R:153, R1:9]

---

[1] Middle name also appears as Elliott. Richard E. Brewer served in Co. D, 40th Va. Inf., C.S.A.
[2] Thomas Brewer and Mary Hinson were married by bond 4 JAN 1821 in Westmoreland Co.
[3] Meredith Hinson and Nelly Coates were married by bond 7 MAY 1839 in Westmoreland Co.
[4] John A. Payton and Elizabeth Morris were married by bond 11 NOV 1828 in Richmond Co.
[5] Joseph Prosper Bronner (b. 15 NOV 1823 in France, d. 13 OCT 1901) and his wife Abby Cory (b. 9 AUG 1815, d. 8 DEC 1885) are bur. at Totuskey Baptist Church cemetery.
[6] William Broocke and Nancy Belfield were married by bond 7 SEP 1846 in Richmond Co.
[7] The license gives place of marriage as Old Farnham Church. Farnham Baptist Church is located 3 miles south of Farnham, Va. on the south side of Route 608.

Brooks, Richard M. to Elizabeth E. Johnson.[1] RICHARD M. BROOKS, farmer, age 22, single, b. Richmond Co., s/o Richard H. and Mary J. [Harrison] Brooks,[2] to ELIZABETH E. JOHNSON, age 18, single, b. Richmond Co., d/o James and Mary Johnson. Robert Williamson, M.G. 31 JAN 1866 at Jas. Johnson's. [C4, R:270, R1:16]

Brooks, Robert (Col.) to Hannah Jordan (Col.). ROBERT BROOKS, farmer, age 26, widowed, b. Northumberland Co., s/o [Andrew] and Betsey Brooks, to HANNAH JORDAN, age 18, single, b. Richmond Co., d/o Ned and Lina Jordan. Robert Haynie. 30 NOV 1871 at the res. of Ned Jordan. [C6, R:245, R1:30]

Brooks, Sedwic Walter to Elmira Ingraham. SEDWIC WALTER BROOKS, farmer, age 22, single, b. Richmond Co., s/o Richard H. and Mary Jane Brooks, to ELMIRA INGRAHAM, age 18, single, b. Richmond Co., d/o William and Mary Ingraham. Andrew Fisher. 1 DEC 1870 at Mrs. Ingraham's. [C5, R:234, R1:28]

Brooks, Stephen (Col.) to Marina Veney (Col.). STEPHEN BROOKS, ditcher, age 51, single, b. Northumberland Co., s/o Stephen and Sarah Brooks, to MARINA VENEY, age 27, single, b. Richmond Co., d/o Jerry and Charlotte Veney. Travis Corbin. 20 APR 1867 at Hill's Store. [C4, R:286, R1:21]

Brooks, Stephen (Col.) to Mrs. Betsey Plaiter (Col.). STEPHEN BROOKS, farmer and ditcher, age 63, widowed, b. Northumberland Co., s/o Stephen and Sarah Brooks, to BETSEY PLAITER, age 45, widow, b. Richmond Co., [names of parents not completed]. Allen Brown, minister. 5 NOV 1876 at the bride's home. [C7, R:305, R1:41]

Brown, Allen (Col.) to Frances Tate (Col.). ALLEN BROWN, farmer, age 30, single, b. Richmond Co., s/o John and Mary A. Brown, to FRANCES TATE, age 18, single, b. Richmond Co., d/o Joseph and Betsy Tate. Travis Corbin. 11 JUL 1867 at Joseph Tate's. [C4, R:286, R1:21]

Brown, Anthony (Col.) to Nancy Ball. ANTHONY BROWN, farmer, age 2[4], bachelor, b. Lancaster Co., s/o Wm. and Mary Brown, to NANCY BALL, age 17, single, b. Richmond Co., d/o Sarah Ann Johnson [father's name obliterated]. Consent 11 JUN 1870 by father George [his X mark] Johnson, wit. B.W. Brockenbrough. David Veany. 11 JUN 1870 at Gardy's Mill.[3] [C5, R:233, R1:28]

Brown, Benjamin L. to Amanda Ann Sandford. BENJAMIN L. BROWN, farmer, age 22, single, b. and res. Lancaster Co., s/o Robert and Nancy Brown, to AMANDA A. SANDFORD, age 21, single, b. Westmoreland Co., d/o Henry and Mary A. Sandford. Consent 17 JUL 1860 by bride Amandy Ann [her X mark] Sandford, wit. Mary A. [her X mark] Sandford. No minister return. 25 JUL 1860. [C2, R:153, R1:9]

Brown, Charles Lewis to Rutha Elizabeth Mozingo. CHARLES LEWIS BROWN, oystering and fishing, age 24, single, b. and res. Westmoreland Co., s/o William Brown and Sally Foxabell,

---

[1] Richard M. Brooks (1840-1933) and wife Elizabeth H. Johnson [sic] (1847-1929) are bur. in Jerusalem Baptist Church cemetery. He served as corporal in Co. D, 47th Va. Inf., C.S.A.
[2] Richard Brooks and Mary Harrison were married by bond 15 DEC 1834 in Richmond Co.
[3] Gardy's Millpond is located about a half mile above Garland's Millpond in the central part of the county on Marshy Swamp, and was where Jacob Gardy operated a mill.

to RUTHA ELIZABETH MOZINGO, age 19, single, b. Richmond Co., d/o Pierce and Sally Elizabeth Mozingo. Consent 21 MAR 1883 by father Pierce [his X mark] Mozingo, wits. William R. Mozingo, Charles H. Sargent. D.M. Wharton at the res. of the bride's father. 22 MAR 1883. [C10, R:355, R1:58]

Brown, Emanuel (Col.) to Sarah A. Newman (Col.). EMANUEL BROWN, farmer, age 23, single, b. Richmond Co., s/o Joseph and Sophia Brown, to SARAH A. NEWMAN, age 22, single, b. Westmoreland Co., d/o Eliza Newman. Davy Veney, Pastor. 11[1] SEP 1867 at Mulberry Church. [C4, R:287, R1:21]

Brown, George (Col.) to Josephine Rich (Col.). GEORGE BROWN, stevedore, age 26, single, b. Westmoreland Co., res. Baltimore, Md., s/o George and Winnie Brown, to JOSEPHINE RICH, age 24y6m, single, b. Richmond Co., d/o Lindsey and Phirlishia Rich [sic]. Consent by bride 21 JUN 1881, no wit. John Wilkerson. 23 JUN 1881 at *Level Green*. [C9, R:336, R1:53]

Brown, Jacob (Col.) to Betty Alice Darby (Col.). JACOB BROWN, farmer, age 21, single, b. Richmond Co., s/o Tom and Fanny Brown, to BETTY ALICE DARBY, age 13, single, b. Richmond Co., d/o Emily Darby. Consent 5 DEC 1878 by mother, wit. John W. [his X mark] Darby. Allen Brown, minister. 6 DEC 1878 at the bride's home. [C8, R:312, R1:46]

Brown, James Hudson to Sarah Bowen.[2] HUDSON BROWN, farmer, age 23, single, b. Richmond Co., s/o William W. and Mary [Reynolds] Brown,[3] to SARAH BOWEN, age 21, single, b. Richmond Co., d/o John and Maria Bowen. G.H. Northam. 20 DEC 1865. [C3, R:204, R1:15]

Brown, James W. to Sarah C. Connellee. JAMES W. BROWN, farmer, age 64, widowed, b. Richmond Co., s/o John and Elizabeth Brown, to SARAH C. CONNELLEE, age 21, single, b. Richmond Co., d/o Autumn and Juliann [Mazuro] Connellee.[4] Consent 21 SEP 1864 from [mother] Sarah J. Connellee, signed by Juliann Connellee, wit. H.M. Pursell. Robert Williamson, M.G. 25 SEP 1864 at res. of H. Clarke. [C3, R:139, R1:14]

Brown, John to Mary Ann Packett. JOHN BROWN, farmer, age 23, single, b. Richmond Co., s/o William and Mary Brown, to MARY ANN PACKETT, age 27, single, b. Richmond Co., d/o John and Maria [Courtney] Packett.[5] G.H. Northam. 19 DEC 1872. [C6, R:238, R1:33]

Brown, John C.[6] to Martha France. JOHN C. BROWN,[7] farmer and carpenter, age 32, single, b. Richmond Co., s/o Hudson and Polly [France] Brown,[8] to MARTHA FRANCE, age 21, single, b. Richmond Co., d/o John and Betsy [Elizabeth Hall] France.[9] John Pullen. 4 AUG 1859 at John France's. [C2, R:165, R1:7]

---

[1] The license gives date of marriage 11 SEP 1867, while the return notes 4 SEP 1867.
[2] James Hudson Brown (b. 15 SEP 1843, d. 28 OCT 1910 of heart disease) and his wife Sarah Bowen (b. 27 SEP 1845, d. 28 MAY 1911) are bur. in Cobham Park Baptist Church cemetery.
[3] William W.H. Browne and Mary Reynolds were married by bond 22 JAN 1838 in Richmond Co. by Rev. Thomas M. Washington.
[4] Autumn Connellee and Juliann Mazuro were married by bond 23 JUL 1842 in Richmond Co.
[5] John Packett and Maria Courtney were married 4 FEB 1841 in Richmond Co. by Rev. William N. Ward.
[6] John C. Brown served in Co. K, 9th Va. Cav., C.S.A.
[7] The Register has this recorded as Bowens.
[8] Hudson Brown and Polly France were married by bond 1 NOV 1813 in Richmond Co. She was b. 11 JUL 1793, d/o John France and Catherine Fones. The groom was s/o Thomas Brown and Ann Morris.
[9] John France, widower, and Elizabeth Hall were married by bond 16 MAY 1829 in Richmond Co.

Brown, Lewin Randolph[1] to Sarah Anne Brown. LEWIN R. BROWN, farming, age 22, single, b. Richmond Co., s/o J. [James] Hudson and Sarah [Bowen] Brown, *q.v.*, to ANNIE BROWN, age 22, single, b. Richmond Co., d/o Robert and Sallie A. [Sarah Ann Scates] Brown, *q.v.* Geo. M. [Conley] Connelley. 23 DEC 1888 near *Cobham Park*.[2] [C12, R:317, R1:73]

Brown, Richard (Col.) to Willie Ann Bailey (Col.). RICHARD BROWN, farming, age 23, single, b. Richmond Co., res. Northumberland Co., s/o William and Rachel Brown, to WILLIE ANN BAILEY, age 20, single, b. Richmond Co., d/o John Bell and Eliza Bailey. Consent 23 DEC 1879 by Eliza Bailey, wits. Jos. T. Headley, Thos. L. Alderson. G.H. Northam. 25 DEC 1879 at the res. of the bride. [C9, R:309, R1:49]

Brown, Richard H. to Mary Bowen. RICHARD H. BROWN, farming, age 25y7d, single, b. Westmoreland Co., s/o William Brown and Martha Sutton, to MARY BOWEN, age 22, single, b. Richmond Co., d/o Kelley [H.] and Julia Ann [Hinson Bulger] Bowen, *q.v.* Consent undated by bride Mary [her X mark] Bowen. Geo. M. Conley. 19 DEC 1888 near *Millview*. [C12, R:317, R1:73]

Brown, Robert[3] to Sarah Ann Scates. ROBERT BROWN, farming, age about 24, single, b. Richmond Co., s/o Hudson Brown and wife Mary [Polly France], to SARAH ANN SCATES, age about 17, single, b. Richmond Co., d/o J.B. [John B.] Scates and wife Elizabeth [Marks].[4] Consent 17 MAR 1856 by father John B. Scates, also signed by Elizabeth Scates, Mary Ann Scates, wit. Samuel [his X mark] Marks. John Pullen, M.G. 18 MAR 1856 at J. Bartlett Scates' in upper district. [C1, R, R1:3]

Brown, Samuel to Juliet Thompson. SAMUEL[5] BROWN, farmer, age 21, single, b. Northumberland Co., s/o Sampson and Martha Brown, to JULIET THOMPSON,[6] age 21, single, b. Richmond Co., d/o James and Eliza Thompson. Consent 1 APR 1861 by bride Juliet [her X mark] Tompson [sic], wit. Henry [his X mark] Thomson [sic]. Barth. Dodson, Baptist parson. 6 APR 1861. [C3, R:123, R1:10]

Brown, Thomas to Martha Marks. THOMAS BROWN, laborer, age 27, single, b. Richmond Co., s/o William and Mary Brown, to MARTHA MARKS, age 21, single, b. Richmond Co., d/o Vincent and Mary [France] Marks. Consent by bride's parents, wit. by bride. G.H. Northam. 9 OCT 1879 at Mr. Marks'. [C8, R:308, R1:48]

Brown, Thomas to Fannie Cash. THOMAS BROWN, laborer, age 38, widowed, b. Richmond Co., s/o William and Mary Brown, to FANNIE CASH, age 37, single, b. Richmond Co., [names of parents not completed]. G.H. Northam. 22 OCT 1890 at *Glenmore*. [C12, R:324, R1:77]

Brown, William C. to Emma E. Hall. WILLIAM C. BROWN, sawyer, age 23, single, b. and res. Westmoreland Co., s/o Patterson and Julia A. Brown, to EMMA E. HALL, age 20, single, b. Richmond Co., d/o William H. and Mary Jane Hall. Consent 16 NOV 1887 by bride and W.J.

---

[1] Lewin Randolph Brown (b. 28 NOV 1867, d. 21 OCT 1948) is bur. in Cobham Park Baptist Church cemetery.
[2] *Cobham Park* is located ad the junction of Highway 3 and Route 360.
[3] Robert Brown served in Co. K, 90th Va. Cav., C.S.A.
[4] John B. Scates and Betsy Marks were married by bond 10 MAR 1830 in Richmond Co.
[5] The license shows signature of the groom as Saml. Brown; however, the application and return gives Samson Brown.
[6] The surname appears as Thomson, Tompson, and Thompson.

[his X mark] Hall, wit. T.W. Howell. No minister return. Planned for 17 NOV 1887. [C11, R:293, R1:70]

Brown, William F. to Eleanor Douglas McClanahan. WILLIAM F. BROWN, engineer, age 28, single, b. in the District of Columbia, res. Baltimore, Md., [names of parents not completed], to ELEANOR DOUGLAS McCLANAHAN, age 24, single, b. Richmond Co., d/o Meredith M.[1] and Jane M. McClanahan. A.B. Kinsolving. 27 APR 1887 at the house of Mrs. Jane M. McClanahan. [C11, R:291, R1:71]

Brown, William H. to Frances E. Scates. WILLIAM H. BROWN, farmer, age 28, single, b. Richmond Co., s/o Thomas and Sally Brown, to FRANCES E. SCATES, age 20, single, b. Richmond Co., d/o Washington and Betsy Scates. John Pullen. 21 DEC 1864 at Washington Scates'. [C3, R:139, R1:14]

Bryant, Caleb Litchfield to Luetta J. Lusby.[2] CALEB L. BRYANT, farming, age 25y3m13d, single, b. Richmond Co., s/o Richard P. Bryant and Alsey [Alice C. Brown] Bryant (dec'd.),[3] to LUETTA J. LUSBY, age 18y11m, single, b. Richmond Co., d/o Thomas W. [Washington] Lusby and Martha [A. Sebree Dunnaway] Lusby (dec'd.), *q.v.* Consent 1 MAY 1885 by father Thomas W. Lusby, wit. Chas. W. Barrack. F.W. Claybrook. 3 MAY 1885. [C10, R:317, R1:64]

Bryant, Charles to Mary E. Hinson. CHARLES BRYANT, farming, age about 33, widowed, b. Westmoreland Co., s/o Reuben Bryant and wife Sarah, to MARY E. HINSON, age about 21, single, b. Richmond Co., d/o Austin Hinson and wife Mahaly [Hueson].[4] Consent 21 JUL 1857 by bride Mary E. [her X mark] Hinson, wit. A.J. Hinson. John Pullen, M.G. 23 JUL 1857 at Andrew Hinson's. [C1, R:159, R1:5]

Bryant, Columbus Taylor to Laura Alice Sisson.[5] COLUMBUS T. BRYANT, farming, age 23, single, b. Richmond Co., s/o Reuben A. [Alexander] Bryant and Mary [Ann] T. Bryant née Thrift,[6] to LAURA S. SISSON, age 24, single, b. Richmond Co., d/o Richard H. [Hugh] Sisson and Eliza [Jane] Sisson née Cralle. Consent 22 FEB 1887 from Village, Va.[7] by parties. G.H. Northam. 24 FEB 1887 at res. of Richard H. Sisson. [C11, R:290, R1:69]

Bryant, Edward to Artamitia Parker Douglas. EDWARD BRYANT, farming, age 35, single, b. Richmond Co., s/o Hiram [G.] and Barbara [Burton] Bryant, to ARTAMITIA PARKER DOUGLAS, age 26, single, b. Richmond Co., d/o William Douglas and Elizabeth his wife now Waterfield. Consent 28 DEC 1886 by bride, wit. Mrs. Elizabeth Waterfield. Rev. A.D. Reynolds. 28 DEC 1886 at the res. of the bride. [C11, R1:68]

---

[1] Library of Virginia, Bible Records, Harris Family Bible Record, 1811-1982, "Meridith M.M. McClanahan Departed this life Jan. 26th 1878 in the 48 year of his age." Also, "Jane M. McClanahan his wife, Departed this life November 24th 1891 in the 62 year of her age."
[2] Caleb L. Bryant (b. 18 JAN 1859, d. 1918) and wife Etta J. Lusby (1865-1936) are bur. in Farnham Baptist Church cemetery.
[3] Richard P. Bryant and Alice C. Brown were married by bond 1 FEB 1847 in Richmond Co. He is s/o Thomas Bryant and Frances Dodson.
[4] Austin Hinson and Mahaly Hueson were married by bond 17 MAR 1829 in Westmoreland Co.
[5] Columbus T. Bryant (b. 5 JUN 1863, d. 22 JAN 1931) and his wife Laura A. Sisson (b. 5 JUN 1862, d. 18 JUL 1911) are bur. at Totuskey Baptist Church cemetery.
[6] Reuben A. Bryant, farmer, (b. 1817, d. 28 MAY 1882), son of Jesse Reuben Bryant and Barbara White, and his wife Mary Ann Thrift are bur. in the Bryant Family Cemetery at Village, Va. He served as a private in Co. C, 41st Reg. Va. Mil., C.S.A. and other units. Reuben Bryant and Mary Thrift were married 18 DEC 1845 in Richmond Co. by Rev. E.L. Williams.
[7] Village is a village that is located about 8 miles east of Warsaw, Va. on Highway 360 at its junction with Route 617.

Bryant, Elias H. to Anna A. Rock. ELIAS H. BRYANT, farmer, age 27, single, b. Richmond Co., d/o Hyram [G.] and Barbary [Burton] Bryant,[1] to ANNA A. ROCK, age 25, single, b. Northumberland Co., d/o Alexander and Nancy [Haden] Rock.[2] Consent 29 DEC 1871 by bride Anna [her X mark] Rock, wit. E.M. Raines. R.J. Sanford. 31 DEC 1871. [C6, R:245, R1:30]

Bryant, George Henry[3] to Estelle F. Rock. GEORGE H. BRYANT, age 27, single, b. Richmond Co., s/o Reuben A. [Alexander] and Mary Ann [Thrift] Bryant,[4] to ESTELLE F. ROCK, age 25, single, b. Richmond Co., d/o Griffin and Juliet [A. Davis] Rock.[5] Consent by bride and groom George [his X mark] Bryant, no wit. G.H. Northam. 10 JAN 1883. [C10, R:355, R1:58]

Bryant, James Chichester to Catharine Jane Wright.[6] JAMES C. BRYANT, age 24, single, b. Richmond Co., s/o Joseph W. and Catharine E. [Barrack] Bryant,[7] to CATHARINE J. WRIGHT, age 18, single, b. Richmond Co., d/o A.M. [Alexander] and Margaret Wright.[8] Consent 7 JAN 1867 by bride, wit. A.M. Wright, O. Bryant. Robert Williamson, M.G. 16 JAN 1867 at Alex. Wright's. [C3, C4, R:285, R1:19]

Bryant, Joseph R. to Mary S. Northen. JOSEPH R. BRYANT, farmer, age 22, single, b. Richmond Co., s/o Richard and Peggy Bryant, to MARY S. NORTHEN, age 20, single, b. Richmond Co., d/o William M. and Mary Northen. Consent 24 JUL 1880 by bride, also signed by her father Wm. M. Northen, wit. Julius M. [his X mark] Hall. W.A. Crocker. 25 JUL 1880. [C9, R:316, R1:51]

Bryant, Melville to Mrs. Elizabeth Dixon. MELVILLE BRYANT, farmer, age 18y1m, single, b. Richmond Co., s/o William C. and Martha [Ann Garland Lewis] Bryant,[9] to ELIZABETH DIXON, age 22y5m, widow, b. Richmond Co., d/o Rawleigh and Catharine [Bryant] Elmore.[10] Consent 2 APR 1872 by bride, wit. [Jas.] S. McVey; consent 2 APR 1872 by father William C. Bryant, no wit. Barth. Dodson, Baptist parson. 4 APR 1872. [C6, R:237, R1:31]

Bryant, Richard Payne, Capt. to Sarah E. Bryant.[11] RICHARD P. BRYANT, age 40, widowed, b. Richmond Co., s/o Thomas W. and Frances [Dodson] Bryant,[12] to SARAH E. BRYANT, age 20, single, b. Richmond Co., d/o Jos. W. and Catharine D. [Barrack] Bryant. Robert Williamson, M.G. 28 NOV 1865 at Beard's Store. [C3, R:205, R1:15]

---

[1] Hiram G. Bryant and Barbary Burton were married by bond 29 OCT 1834 in Northumberland Co.

[2] Alexander Rock, widower, and Mary Haden were married by bond 13 FEB 1841 in Northumberland Co.

[3] George Henry Bryant (b. 1856, d. 1 FEB 1919) was bur. in Bryant Family cemetery at Village, Va.

[4] Reuben Alexander Bryant (b. 1817, d. 28 MAY 1882) and wife Mary Ann Thrift (b. 3 MAR 1827, d. 2 FEB 1890) were bur. in Bryant Family cemetery at Village, Va.

[5] Griffin Rock and Juliet A. Davis were married 28 OCT 1852 in Richmond Co. by Rev. E.L. Williams.

[6] James C. Bryant (b. 13 JUN 1842, d. 18 MAY 1883 of consumption) and wife Catharine Jane Wright (b. 22 SEP 1848, d. 15 MAR 1922) are bur. in Farnham Baptist Church cemetery. He first served in Co. E, 40th Reg. Va. Inf., C.S.A., and was wounded and captured at Gettysburg, Pa.

[7] Joseph W. Bryant (b. c.1821, d. 23 DEC 1878, s/o Samuel Bryant and Sarah Stott) and his wife Catharine Barrack (b. c.1822, d. 28 AUG 1884, d/o Reubin Barrack and Alice Dobyns) are bur. in the Bryant Family Burial Ground near Robley, Va. Robley is located at the junction of Highway 3 and Route 61 near the south end of the County. Joseph Bryant and Catharine Barrick were married by bond 6 SEP 1841 in Lancaster Co.

[8] Alexander M. Wright and Eliza M. Mothershead were married by bond 16 AUG 1845 in Richmond Co.

[9] William C. Bryant and Martha Ann Garland Lewis were married 20 OCT 1845 in Richmond Co. by Rev. E.L. Williams.

[10] Rawleigh Elmore and Catharine Bryant were married by bond 24 FEB 1835 in Richmond Co.

[11] Capt. Richard P. Bryant (b. 30 AUG 1824, d. 22 APR 1905) and his second wife Sarah E. Bryant (b. 14 AUG 1843, d. 30 MAR 1916) are bur. in Farnham Baptist Church cemetery. He was sheriff of Richmond Co. from 2 AUG 1869 to 1 JUL 1875.

[12] Thomas Bryant (b. 1 JUL 1783, d. 4 JAN 1853) and Fanny Dodson (b. 30 OCT 1785, d. 1 DEC 1857) were married by bond 23 SEP 1803 in Richmond Co. See King, p. 29 for the Bible record of the Thomas Bryant Family. Richard P. Bryant was b. 30 AUG 1824.

Bryant, Synico George to Mrs. Flavor Ann Douglas Dodson.[1] SYMCO G. BRYANT, age 24, single, b. Richmond Co., s/o R.D. [Rawleigh] and Winnie [Winny B . Haydon] Bryant,[2] to FLAVOR A. DODSON [sic], age 25, widow, b. Richmond Co., d/o S.H. [Samuel] and [Lucy] Ann [Doggett] Douglas.[3] Consent 11 OCT 1879 by bride, wit. G.B. [George Bernard] Dungan. W.A. Crocker. 15 OCT 1879 at the res. of the bride's father. [C8, R:308, R1:48]

Bryant, Thomas (Col.) to Bettie Ann Lewis (Col.). THOMAS BRYANT, laborer, age 35, single, b. Richmond Co., s/o James C. Bryant and Charlotte Bryant now Veney, to BETTIE ANN LEWIS, age 22, single, b. King George Co., d/o Maria Jackson. Consent 17 SEP 1877 by bride Bettie Ann [her X mark] Lewis, wit. Jas. B. McCarty. Allen Brown, minister. 20 SEP 1877 at the bride's home. [C8, R:307, R1:43]

Bryant, William Alexander to Madora Ann Ficklin.[4] WILLIAM A. BRYANT, farmer, age 25, single, b. Richmond Co., s/o A. [Alexander] and Jane M. [Burch] Bryant,[5] to MEDORA A. FICKLIN [sic], age 20, single, b. Richmond Co., d/o W.W. [William] and Mary [B. Rockwell] Ficklin.[6] Consent 7 DEC 1874 by G.H. Northam, guardian of Medora, wit. B.W. Brockenbrough. W.A. Crocker. 10 DEC 1874 at Calvary Church.[7] [C7, R:230, R1:37]

Buffington, Edward Stanard, Dr. to Nannie M. Lyell.[8] EDWARD S. BUFFINGTON, doctor, age 26, single, b. and res. Huntington, W.Va., s/o Peter and Eliza Buffington, to NANNIE M. LYELL, age 22, single, b. Richmond Co., d/o Richard H. and Elizabeth [T. Tapscott] Lyell.[9] Consent 15 NOV 1873 by father R.H. Lyell, wit. Edwin Lyell. W.A. Crocker. 19 NOV 1873 at the res. of the bride's father. [C6, R:235, R1:34]

Buffington, Peter Cline to Louisa J. Garland.[10] PETER C. BUFFINGTON, farmer, age 50, widowed, b. and res. Cabell Co., s/o William and Nancy [Scales] Buffington, to LOUISA J. GARLAND, age 23, single, b. Richmond Co., d/o James V. and Juliet [F.J. Lyell] Garland.[11] William F. Bain. 22 SEP 1864 at res. of James V. Garland [*Plain View*]. [C3, R:139, R1:14]

Bulger, James H. to Willie A. Hall. JAMES H. BULGER, sailor, age 34y8m, single, b. Alexandria, Va., s/o John Bulger and Julia Ann Bowen [Hinson?],[12] to WILLIE A. HALL, age 23, single, b. Richmond Co., d/o John and Martha Hall. Consent 5 AUG 1885 by bride, wit. Robert France. H.H. Fones. 9 AUG 1885. [C10, R:317, R1:65]

Bundy, Robert (Col.) to Malinda Washington (Col.). ROBERT BUNDY, farming, age 23y8m, single, b. Richmond Co., s/o Henry Bundy and Nancy Laws, to MALINDA WASHINGTON, age 22,

---

[1] Synico G. Bryant (b. 27 JAN 1851, d. 6 JAN 1917) and wife "Flava" A. Douglas Bryant (b. 2 MAR 1854, d. 28 NOV 1916) are bur. in Oakland United Methodist Church cemetery.

[2] Rawleigh D. Bryant and Winny B. Haydon were married by bond 22 JAN 1849 in Richmond Co.

[3] Samuel H. Douglass and Lucy Ann Doggett were married 1 JUN 1850 in Richmond Co. by Rev. John Godwin.

[4] William Alexander Bryant (b. 20 JUL 1849, d. 12 APR 1912 at Emmerton, Va.) and wife Madora Ann Ficklin (b. 2 SEP 1854, d. 22 JUL 1931) are bur. at Calvary United Methodist Church cemetery.

[5] Alexander Bryant and Jane M. Burch were married by bond 19 OCT 1847 in Richmond Co.

[6] William W. Ficklin and Mary B. Rockwell were married 8 NOV 1853 in Richmond Co. by Rev. John Godwin.

[7] Calvary Church is located on the south side of Highway 3 about 2½ miles west of Farnham, Va.

[8] Edward S. Buffington, former mayor of Huntington, W.Va. (b. 11 AUG 1847, d. 24 FEB 1929) and wife Nannie M. Lyell (b. 8 OCT 1851, d. 23 DEC 1925) are bur. in Spring Hill Cemetery of Huntington, W.Va.

[9] Richard H. Lyelll and Elizabeth T. Tapscott were married by bond 5 OCT 1840 in Richmond Co.

[10] Peter C. Buffington (b. 22 SEP 1814, d. 18 APR 1875) and his wife Louisa J. Garland (b. 28 NOV 1841, d. 1918) are bur. in Spring Hill Cemetery, Huntington, W.Va. He was the first elected mayor of Huntington, W.Va.

[11] James V. Garland and Juliet F.J. Lyell were married by bond 3 FEB 1834 in Richmond Co.

[12] John Bulger and Julia Ann Hinson were married 24 JAN 1850 in Richmond Co. by Rev. John Pullen.

single, b. Richmond Co., d/o John and Martha Washington. Thomas G. Thomas. 30 DEC 1879 at the house of the minister. [C9, R:309, R1:49]

Bunting, William Carlton Wheeler to Elizabeth Muir.[1] WILLIAM C.W. BUNTING, farmer, age 18y11m, single, b. Baltimore, Md., s/o John and Margaret Bunting, to ELIZABETH MUIR, age 2[8]y2m, single, b. Scotland, s/o William M. and Grace Muir.[2] Consent undated by Jno. J. Bunting. F.B. Beale. 21 NOV 1888 at *[C]abin Ford*, Westmoreland Co. [C11, R:316, R1:73]

Burch, Robert C. to Mary Fleet Wright. ROBERT C. BURCH, farmer, age 48, widowed, b. Richmond Co., s/o Gibson [B.] and Sarah [S. Northen] Burch,[3] to MARY FLEET WRIGHT, age 31, single, b. Richmond Co., d/o Alexander [M.] and Eliza [M. Mothershead] Wright.[4] G.H. Northam. 16 JAN 1877. [C8, R:306a, R1:42]

Burr, Fleet (Col.) to Rose Blair (Col.). FLEET BURR, farming, age 25, single, b. Richmond Co., s/o Henry and Haney Burr, to ROSE BLAIR, age 21, single, b. Richmond Co., d/o Joseph and Malinda Blair. Rev. Davey Veaney. 29 DEC 1889 at F.F. Kemp's farm. [C12, R:329, R1:75]

Burrell, Dandridge to Eliza Newman, "free persons of color." DANDRIDGE BURRELL,[5] farming, age 23, single, b. Richmond Co., s/o George and Mary Burrell, to ELIZA NEWMAN, age 21, single, b. Richmond Co., d/o John and Milly Newman. Consent 1 MAY 1861 by bride Eliza [her X mark] Newman and Jno. [his X mark] Newman, wit. Wm. H. Newman. Andrew Fisher. 2 MAY 1861 at the rectory of Farnham Parish. [C3[6], R:123, R1:10]

Burrell, Henry to Martha Ball. HENRY BURREL,[7] farmer, age 35, widowed, b. Richmond Co., s/o Maria Burrel, to MARTHA BALL, age 21y8m, single, b. Richmond Co., d/o Sarah Ann Ball. Consent 22 JAN 1873 by bride Martha [her X mark] Ball, wit. C.A. Pursell. Elder James A. Weaver. 23 JAN 1873 at the res. of Steven Bayles. [C6, R:235, R1:33]

Burrell, James Andrew (Col.) to Laurena Burton (Col.). JAMES ANDREW BURRELL, oystering, age 23y4m17d, single, b. Westmoreland Co., s/o Thomas and Alice Burrell, to LAURENA BURTON, age 19y5m17d, single, b. Richmond Co., d/o Thomas and Lucy Burton. Consent 23 AUG 1884 by Lucy [her X mark] [Pullin], John W. Thompson. Edmond Rich. 24 AUG 1884 at the res. of the minister. [C10, R:355, R1:62]

Burrell, Richard Adolphus (Col.) to Anna Jenkins (Col.). RICHARD ADOLPHUS BURRELL, day laborer, age 22, single, b. Richmond Co., s/o Henry and Mary Burrell, to ANNA JENKINS, age 20, single, b. Richmond Co., d/o David and Polly Jenkins. G.H. Northam. 5 OCT 1882. [C9, R:313, R1:56]

Burril, Fleet (Col.) to Harriet Ann Wallace (Col.). FLEET BURRIL, farmer, age 21, single, b. Richmond Co., s/o William Burril and Hannah Williams, to HARRIET ANN WALLACE, age 19,

---

[1] Elizabeth Muir (b. 3 SEP 1860, d. 12 MAY 1931), wife of William C. Bunting, is bur. in St. John's Episcopal Church Cemetery.
[2] William M. Muir (b. MAR 1825, d. 8 AUG 1907) and wife Grace R. Muir (b. 16 SEP 1824, d. 1 MAR 1928) are bur. in St. John's Episcopal Church cemetery.
[3] Gilson B. Burch and Susan S. Northen were married by bond 17 DEC 1833 in Richmond Co.
[4] Alexander M. Wright and Eliza M. Mothershead were married by bond 16 AUG 1845 in Richmond Co.
[5] The surname appears in Register 1 as Burwell.
[6] Chronologically, this is the first record on a new form, with the license on top, certificate in the middle, and return at the bottom.
[7] The surname also appears as Burrell as in Register 1.

single, b. Maryland, d/o William and Rachel Wallace. Consent 15 MAY 1866 by mother Rachel [her X mark] Wallace, wit. George [his X mark] Johnson. Elder James A. Weaver. 17 MAY 1866 at the res. of Nat. Morer. [C4, R:271, R1:17]

Burroughs, Jesse to Ann S. McKenney. JESSE BURROUGHS, merchant, age 36, widowed, b. and res. Northumberland Co., s/o Jesse and Rebecca Burroughs, to ANN S. McKENNEY, age 22, single, b. Richmond Co., d/o Jared A. and Elizabeth McKenney. Consent 2 MAY 1859 by bride, wits. Richard P. Forester, Joseph [his X mark] Tomas [sic]. No minister return. 11 MAY 1859. [C2, R:165, R1:7]

Burton, James to Mrs. Nancy Rock. JAMES BURTON, farmer, age 63, widowed, b. Richmond Co., s/o Thomas and Mary Burton,[1] to NANCY ROCK, b. 50, widow, b. Northumberland Co., d/o Winny Hayden [father's name not known]. Barth. Dodson, parson. 30 MAY 1861 at house of Nancy Rock. [C3, R:123, R1:10]

Burton, Jesse (Col.) to Judy Rankins (Col.). JESSE BURTON, age 72, widowed, b. Westmoreland Co., s/o Daniel and Dina Burton, to JUDY RANKINS, age 60, widow, b. Richmond Co., d/o Moses Rankins and Darkey Venie. David Veney. 28 APR 1872 at Henry Palmer's. [C6, R:237, R1:31]

Butler, Samuel C.F. to Mrs. Susan Hoosencraft Hinson. SAMUEL C.F. BUTLER, farmer, age 46, widowed, b. Westmoreland Co., s/o Wesley and Frances T. [Crask] Butler,[2] to SUSAN HINSON, age 40, widow, b. Richmond Co., d/o Meredith and Hannah Hoosencraft. Consent 26 DEC 1865 by bride Susan [her X mark] Hinson, wits. T.N. Balderson and Geo. W. Balderson who proves certificate. 28 DEC 1865 at the res. of Cordelia Jett. [C3, R:205, R1:15]

C

Callahan, Thomas R. to Mary A. Mothershead. THOMAS R. CALLAHAN, merchant, age 22, single, b. Westmoreland Co., s/o William C. and Mary R. [Rice] Callahan,[3] to MARY A. MOTHERSHEAD, age 20, single, b. Richmond Co., d/o Richard H. and Fanny [Frances S. McKenney] Mothershead.[4] G.H. Northam. 12 MAY 1867 at Lyells, Va.[5] [C4, R:286, R1:21]

Callahan, William C. to Mrs. Frances T. Hart. WILLIAM C. CALLAHAN, tailor, in 36th year, widower, b. Lancaster Co., s/o William and Elizabeth Callahan, to FRANCES T. HART, in 41st year, widow, b. Essex Co., d/o Baylor and Rachel [Eubank] Carlton. William N. Ward, M.G. 7 JAN 1856 in Warsaw, Va. [C1, R, R1:3]

Callahan, William C., Jr. to Victoria B. Rock.[6] WILLIAM C. CALLAHAN, JR., carpenter, age 20y10m, single, b. Westmoreland Co., s/o William C. [Sr.] and ~~Elizabeth~~ Mary [R. Rice] Callahan, to VICTORIA[7] B. ROCK, age 18, single, b. Northumberland Co., d/o Thomas C. and

---

[1] Thomas Burton and Molly White were married by bond 14 MAY 1791 in Richmond Co.
[2] Wesley Butler and Frances T. Crask were married by bond 24 NOV 1813 in Westmoreland Co.
[3] William C. Callahan and Mary R. Rice were married 25 MAR 1844 in Richmond Co.
[4] Richard H. Mothershead and Frances S. McKenney were married 1 JAN 1846 in Richmond Co. by Rev. John Pullen.
[5] Lyells, Va. is a locality at the junction of Highway 3 and Route 203 very near the northern boundary of the County. The name stems from when Samuel Lyell opened a post office at his store there in 1836.
[6] William C. Callahan (1848-1902) and wife Victoria B. Rock (1851-1918) are bur. at Calvary United Methodist Church cemetery.
[7] Spelling of the bride's name also appears as Vicktorien B. Rock, or in the Register as Victoria B. Rock.

Ann [Fulks] Rock.[1] Consent 12 DEC 1871 by W.C. Callahan, and 20 DEC 1871 by Thomas C. [his X mark] Rock, wit. Dandridge C. [his X mark] Winstead. G.H. Northam. 20 DEC 1871 at the res. of the bride's father. [C6, R:245, R1:30]

Campbell, Elijah (Col.) to Delie Johnson (Col.). ELIJAH CAMPBELL, farmer, age 60, single, b. Richmond Co., res. Lancaster Co., s/o Robin and Letty Campbell, to DELIE JOHNSON, age 45, single, b. Northumberland Co., [parents unknown]. Consent 7 OCT 1872 by bride Delie [his X mark] Johnson, wit. [L.] G. Williams. Daniel Payne. 12 OCT 1872 at Mount Zion Church. [C6, R:238, R1:32]

Campbell, John to Ella McCummings. JOHN CAMPBELL, merchant, age 35, single, b. King and Queen Co., s/o Robert and Eliza Campbell, to ELLA McCUMMINGS, age 21, single, b. Richmond Co., d/o Samuel and Maria McCummings. Consent undated [c.1866] by bride, wit. Sally Yates. No minister return. 1 MAR 1866. [C4, R:271, R1:17]

Campbell, John to Sarah Scates. Consent 22 JUN 1871 by bride, wits. J.B. [his X mark] Reamy. No license or minister return. [C6, R1:30]

Canan, James A. to Jane E. Stott. JAMES A. CANAN, pump maker, age 25, single, b. Cecil Co., Md., s/o William and Betsy A. Canan, to JANE E. STOTT, age 15, single, b. Richmond Co., d/o Thaddeus C. and Elizabeth [W. Dale] Stott.[2] Consent 1 OCT 1858 by James Dickenson, guardian, wit. Thos. Ball. No minister return. 5 OCT 1858. [C2, R:138, R1:6]

Carey, Edmond (Col.) to Mimia Nelson (Col.). EDMOND CAREY, farming, age 45, widowed, b. Richmond Co., s/o George and Celia Carey, to MIMIA NELSON, age 28, single, b. Westmoreland Co., d/o William and Rachel Nelson. Rev. Robert Lewis. 23 DEC 1886. [C11, R:317, R1:68]

Carpenter, Charles Benjamin to Minnie Carpenter.[3] CHARLES B. CARPENTER, farming, age 23, single, b. Richmond Co., s/o Eli [C.] and Mary [Carter] Carpenter,[4] to MINNIE CARPENTER, age 16, single, b. Richmond Co., d/o William [H.] and Eliza Jane [Jenkins] Carpenter, *q.v.* Consent from Carter's Wharf[5] on 27 AUG 1890 by father William [his X mark] Carpenter, wit. Wm. P. Pitts. Lawrence B. White, minister Baptist denomination. 28 AUG 1890 at the res. of the bride. [C12, R:324, R1:77]

Carpenter, John to Mrs. Mary Hart Douglass. JOHN CARPENTER, farming, age about 31, single, b. Richmond Co., upper district, s/o Jeremiah Carpenter and Ann,[6] to MARY DOUGLASS, age about 35, widow, b. Richmond Co., upper district, d/o Reuben Hart and Betsy. Consent 22 NOV 1854 by bride Mary [her X mark] Douglass, wit. Jane Coats. John Pullen, M.G. 24 NOV 1854. [C1, R, R1:1]

---

[1] Thomas C. Rock and Ann Fulks were married by bond 30 JUL 1838 in Richmond Co., by consent of his father Alexander Rock.
[2] Thaddus C. [sic] Stott and Elizabeth W. Dale were married by bond 31 MAY 1834 in Richmond Co.
[3] Charles B. Carpenter (b. 29 SEP 1866, d. 12 JUN 1934) and his wife Minnie Carpenter (b. 5 FEB 1873, d. 5 AUG 1946) are bur. in Rappahannock Baptist Church cemetery.
[4] Eli C. Carpenter and Mary Carter were married 30 DEC 1852 in Richmond Co. by Rev. James W. Hunnicutt.
[5] Carter's Wharf is a boat landing on the Rappahannock River at the west end of Route 622, and was named for James Carter.
[6] A marriage bond 20 MAR 1817 for Jeremiah Carpenter and Nancy Oliff is in Westmoreland Co.

Carpenter, John Thomas to Willie Ann Sanders. JOHN THOMAS CARPENTER, farmer, age 23, single, b. Richmond Co., s/o Eli [C.] and Mary [Carter] Carpenter, to WILLIE ANN SANDERS, age 22, single, b. Richmond Co., d/o George and Frances Sanders. Consent 2 JAN 1882 by George Saunders. R.N. Reamy. 7 JAN 1882 at res. of George [Sanders]. [C9, R:312, R1:55]

Carpenter, Samuel Brooks to Martha Ellen Oliff. SAMUEL BROOKS CARPENTER, farming, age 26, single, b. Richmond Co., s/o Eli [C.] and Mary E. [Carter] Carpenter, to MARTHA ELLEN OLIFF, age 18, single, b. Richmond Co., d/o Vincent and Betsy Oliff. Consent by bride, wit. B.B. Smoot. R.N. Reamy. 9 DEC 1885. [C11, R:319, R1:66]

Carpenter, William C. to Mary Ann Virginia Sanders. WILLIAM C. CARPENTER, farmer, age 21y4d, single, b. Richmond Co., s/o Ely [Eli C.] and Mary [Carter] Carpenter, to MARY ANN VIRGINIA SANDERS, age 19y7m, single, b. Richmond Co., d/o William O. and Catherine Sanders. R.N. Reamy. 26 DEC 1876. [C7, R:306, R1:41]

Carpenter, William H. to Eliza J. Jenkins. WILLIAM H. CARPENTER, waterman, age about 35, single, b. Richmond Co., s/o Elizabeth Carpenter [father not known], to ELIZA J. JENKINS, age 30, single, b. Richmond Co., d/o Henry and Selina [Crask] Jenkins.[1] Consent 3 FEB 1883 by bride, wit. George W. Balderson. R.N. Reamy. 13 FEB 1883. [C10, R:355, R1:58]

Carter, Albert (Col.) to Laura Mason (Col.). ALBERT CARTER, farmer, age 29, widowed, b. Richmond Co., res. Lancaster Co., s/o James and Mary Carter, to LAURA MASON, age 18, single, b. Richmond Co., d/o Leroy and Tabby Mason. William H. Kirk. 30 DEC 1873. [C6, R:236, R1:35]

Carter, Charles H. (Col.) to Eliza Jackson (Col.). CHARLES H. CARTER, farming, age 24, single, b. Richmond Co., s/o Edward and Lucy Carter, to ELIZA JACKSON, age 21, single, b. Richmond Co., d/o William B. Jackson. Consent 22 APR 1881 by father William B. Jackson. John Wilkerson. 24 APR 1881 at Mulberry Church. [C9, R:336, R1:53]

Carter, Daniel to Mrs. Mary Hinson Brewer. DANIEL CARTER, farmer, age 56, widower, b. Richmond Co., s/o John and Mary Carter, to MARY BREWER, age 56, widow, b. Richmond Co., d/o John and Mary Hinson. Consent 31 DEC 1857 by bride, wits. William Hall, Ethan A. [Brewer]. James A. Weaver, minister of the Union Baptist Church. 1 JAN 1858. [C1; R:138, R1:6]

Carter, Edward H. to Elizabeth Ambrose. EDWARD H. CARTER, farmer, age 27, single, b. Essex Co., res. Westmoreland Co., s/o Landon P. Carter and Cordelia Carter,[2] to ELIZABETH AMBROSE, age [3]8, single, b. Richmond Co., d/o Redman [B.] and Apphia [C. Gutridge] Ambrose.[3] Consent 4 NOV 1872 by bride, wit. Frederick [his X mark] Hinson. H.H. Fones. 4 NOV 1872 at the house of Thomas Bowen. [C6, R:238, R1:32]

Carter, Elton (Col.) to Sally Carey (Col.). ELTON CARTER, farming, age 21, single, b. Richmond Co., s/o William and Lettie Carter, to SALLY CAREY, age 21, single, b. Richmond Co., d/o

---

[1] Henry Jenkins and Selina Crask were married 28 MAR 1845 in Richmond Co. by Rev. William Balderson.
[2] Landon Carter and Delia Carter, widow, were married by bond 17 DEC 1831 in Essex Co.
[3] Redman B. Ambrose and Apphia C. Gutridge were married by bond 20 APR 1832 in Richmond Co.

Addison and Rosetta Carey. Consent 15 JAN 1890 by William [his X mark] Carter, wit. Jas. Quillen. Rev. T.G. Thomas. 16 JAN 1890 at Clarksville Church. [C12, R:323, R1:76]

Carter, Fleet to Annor Lewis. FLEET CARTER, farmer, age 23, single, b. Richmond Co., s/o Harry Sanders and Winny Carter, to ANNA LEWIS, age 21, single, b. Northumberland Co., d/o James and Betty Lewis. Consent 23 NOV 1869 by bride Annor [her X mark] Lewis, wit. Robert Gaskins. Robert Williamson, M.G. 25 NOV 1869 at Morratico Creek, Farnham [Parish]. [C5, R, R1:26]

Carter, Franklin Landon to Bettie A. Jones. FRANKLIN LANDON CARTER, farmer, age 22, single, b. Richmond Co., s/o John and Nancy Carter, to BETTIE A. JONES, age 25, single, b. Richmond Co., d/o Robert and Lucy Jones. Consent 19 JAN 1878 by bride. R.N. Reamy. 24 JAN 1878 at Robert Jones'. [C8, R:310, R1:44]

Carter, George A.[1] to Bettie E. English. GEORGE A. CARTER, farmer, age 29, single, b. Richmond Co., s/o Charles and Margaret N. [Jesper] Carter,[2] to BETTIE E. ENGLISH, age 23, single, b. Richmond Co., d/o Thomas and Matilda [Corey] English.[3] Consent 28 APR 1870 by bride, no wit. Robert Williamson, M.G. 28 APR 1870 at res. of Thomas English. [C5, R:233, R1:27]

Carter, John A. to Mary I. Oliff. JOHN A. CARTER, farmer, age 27, single, b. Richmond Co., s/o Daniel Carter and Sarah Hinson, to MARY I. OLIFF, age 19, single, b. Richmond Co., d/o James L. Oliff and Lucinda Jones. Bushrod W. Nash, of a Baptist denomination. 27 DEC 1855. [C1, R, R1:3]

Carter, Miskel Arthur to Mary J. Fisher.[4] MISKEL A. CARTER, farmer, age 24, single, b. Richmond Co., s/o William and Mary [Ann Scrimger] Carter,[5] to MARY J. FISHER, age 21, single, b. Essex Co., d/o John and Anna Fisher. Consent 7 JAN 1863 by bride, wit. John M. Barton. John Pullen. 8 JAN 1863 at res. of Samuel G. Dishman. [C3, R:160, R1:12]

Carter, Moses (Col.) to Laura Taylor (Col.). MOSES CARTER, oysterman, age 28, widowed, b. Richmond Co., s/o Patty Carter, to LAURA TAYLOR, age 21y2m22d, single, b. Richmond Co., d/o Peter Taylor (dec'd.) and Margaret Taylor. Consent 27 MAY 1879 by Laura [her X mark] Taylor, no wit. Walker Carter. 29 MAY 1879 at the res. of the bride. [C8, R:307, R1:47]

Carter, Moses (Col.) to Louisa Jane Taylor (Col.). MOSES CARTER, oysterman, age 22y3m, single, b. Richmond Co., s/o Patsy Carter, to LOUISA JANE TAYLOR, age 17, single, b. Richmond Co., d/o Peter and Margaret Taylor. Oath to age of bride by Joseph Newton, father-in-law and guardian. Robert Williamson, M.G. 28 DEC 1871 at *Indian Banks*.[6] [C6, R1:30]

---

[1] George A. Carter (b. 17 SEP 1840, d. 22 FEB 1918), who served as a private in Co. E, 40th Va. Inf., C.S.A., wounded at Chancellorsville, is bur. in Jerusalem Baptist Church cemetery.
[2] Charles Carter and Margaret N. Jesper were married by bond 14 FEB 1838 in Richmond Co.
[3] Thomas English and Matilda Corey were married by bond 5 DEC 1831 in Richmond Co.
[4] Miskel A. Carter (b. 9 SEP 1834, d. 26 FEB 1903) and his second wife Mary J. Fisher (b. 6 JAN 1844, d. 25 JUL 1903) are bur. at Rappahannock Baptist Church cemetery. He served in the C.S.A., and was postmaster and wharf agent at Carter's, Va.
[5] Mary A. Scrimger (b. 1814, d. 23 APR 1889 at *China Hill*), wife of William Carter, is bur. at Rappahannock Baptist Church cemetery. They were married by bond 24 APR 1834 in Richmond Co.
[6] *Indian Banks* is one of the oldest homes in the Northern Neck. It is situated where Lancaster and Morattico Creeks flow into the Rappahannock River, on a site selected by Thomas Glasscock. It was the residence of Thomas Dobyns, who died there on 26 OCT 1845, aged about 66 years.

Carter, Simon (Col.) to Rose Glasgow (Col.). SIMON CARTER, laborer, age 27, single, b. Richmond Co., s/o George and Winny Carter, to ROSE GLASGOW, age 26, single, b. Richmond Co., d/o Thomas and Nancy Glasgow. Age of parties proved by oath of Simon Carter. Robert Williamson, M.G. 29 JUL 1866 at Wm. George's in Farnham Parish. [C4, R:271, R1:17]

Carter, Thomas A. to Martha Hinson. THOMAS A. CARTER, farmer, age 22, single, b. Richmond Co., s/o Daniel and Sarah Carter, to MARTHA HINSON, age 20, single, b. Richmond Co., res. Westmoreland Co., d/o Austin and Mahaley [Hudson] Hinson.[1] James A. Weaver, Baptist minister. 29 DEC 185[7]. [C2; R:138, R1:6]

Carter, William (Col.) to Mrs. Ann Ball (Col.). WILLIAM CARTER, farming, age 63, widowed, b. Richmond Co., s/o Simon and Rachel Carter, to ANN BALL, age 37, widow, b. Richmond Co., d/o Tina Thompson. Rev. T.G. Thomas. 9 JAN 1890 at the house of Charles Smith. [C12, R:323, R1:76]

Carter, William (Col.) to Isabella Burrell (Col.). WILLIAM CARTER, farmer, age 24, single, b. Richmond Co., s/o James Carter and Lucy Robb, to ISABELLA BURRELL, age 19, single, b. Richmond Co., d/o Thomas and Alcey Burrell. Consent 22 MAY 1871 by father Thomas [his X mark] Burrell, wits. William Allison, Robert [his X mark] Beverley. Jeremiah Graham, preacher. 25 MAY 1871 at house of Robert L. Proctor (dec'd.). [C5, R:244, R1:29]

Case, Joseph to Julia A. Fones. JOSEPH CASE, farmer, age 27, single, b. Ohio, res. Lancaster Co., s/o John B. and Sarah Case, to JULIA A. FONES, age 2[1]y3m, single, b. Richmond Co., d/o Thomas B. and Nancy [Richards] Fones.[2] Robert Williamson, M.G. 30 MAR 1869 at T.B. Fones'. [C5, R, R1:25]

Casey, James to Martha Ward. JAMES CASEY, clerk, age 36, single, b. and res. Baltimore, Md., s/o George and Mary E. Casey, to MARTHA WARD, age 32, single, b. Leesburg, Va., d/o William N. and Mary [Smith Blincoe] Ward. Consent 11 JUN 1869 by Wm. N. Ward. Wm. N. Ward. 16 JUN 1869 at the res of the minister. [C5, R, R1:26]

Cash, George W. to Etta M. Scates. GEORGE W. CASH, farming, age 21, single, b. Richmond Co., s/o William and Louisa [Ambrose] Cash, q.v., to ETTA M. SCATES, age 17, single, b. Richmond Co., d/o T. [Thomas] Allen Scates and Martha [S. Bowen] Scates (dec'd.), q.v. Consent 23 DEC 1889 by father T. Allen [his X mark] Scates, wits. John Campbell, R.F. Fones. G.M. Conley. 26 DEC 1889 at *Millview*. [C12, R:329, R1:75]

Cash, John[3] to Sally Marks. JOHN CASH, farming, age about 28, single, b. Richmond Co., s/o William Cash and wife Fe[lic]ia [France],[4] to SALLY MARKS, age about 29, single, b. Richmond Co., d/o Reuben Marks and wife Frances [France].[5] Consent 2 FEB 1856 by bride Sally [her

---

[1] Austin Hinson and Mahaley Hudson were married by bond 17 MAR 1829 in Westmoreland Co.

[2] Thomas B. Fones and Nancy Richards were married by bond 9 FEB 1826 in Richmond Co.

[3] John Cash served in Co. K, 9th Va. Cav., C.S.A.

[4] William Cash and Fillishsha France were married by bond 7 JAN 1829 in Richmond Co. See King, p. 34 for reference to France Family Bible record. Her parents were John France and Catharine Fones.

[5] Reuben Marks and Fanny France were married by bond 12 JAN 1819 in Richmond Co. She was b. 2 OCT 1796, d/o John France and Catharine Fones.

X mark] Marks, wits. H.M. Hellrigle, Vinson Marks, William Cash. John Pullen, M.G. 19 FEB 1856 at Mrs. Cash's in upper district. [C1, R, R1:3]

Cash, William[1] to Louisa Ambrose. WILLIAM CASH, farmer, age 24, single, b. Richmond Co., s/o William and Felicia [France] Cash, to LEVISA AMBROSE [sic], age 23, single, b. Richmond Co., d/o [Redman] B. and Apphia C. [Gutridge] Ambrose. Consent 29 DEC 1865 by bride Livisa [her X mark] Ambrose, wits. Richard T. [Jenk] and father B. Ambrose. Henry H. Fones. 2 JAN 1866 at res. of Redman[d] B. Ambrose. [C4, R:270, R1:16]

Cash, William J. to Mrs. Mary E. Bulger, widow of James Weadon. WILLIAM J. CASH, farming, age 24y9m21d, single, b. Richmond Co., s/o John and Sally [Marks] Cash, *q.v.*, to MARY E. WEADON, age 30, widow, b. Richmond Co., d/o James Bulger and Julia [Ann] Bowen. Consent 24 NOV 1887 by bride. Geo. M. Conley. 24 NOV 1887 near *Fair Side*. [C11, R:293, R1:71]

Cavell, N.M. to Nellie E. Harris. N.M. CAVELL, farmer, age 27, single, b. Fairfax Co., res. Spotsylvania Co., s/o Charles and Emma Cavell, to NELLIE E. HARRIS, age 24, single, b. Richmond Co., d/o James M. and Amanda Harris. W.H. Gregory. 5 DEC 1882. [R:314, R1:57]

Chapman, Dr. Pearson to Edmonia Kerr Ward.[2] PEARSON CHAPMAN, physician, age 36, single, b. Charles Co., Md., res. Perrymansville [sic], Harford Co., Md., s/o Pearson Chapman and Sigismunda [Mary] Alexander,[3] to E. KERR WARD, age 33, single, b. Warsaw, Va., d/o Rev. William N. Ward and Mary [Smith] Blincoe. William N. Ward, P.E. Church. 21 NOV 1876 at *Bladensfield*.[4] [C7, NN:15 DEC 1882, R:306, R1:41]

Chase, Marshall D. to Mrs. Susan Barrett. MARSHALL D. CHASE, farming, age 58y9m24d, widowed, b. Eaton, N.H., s/o William Chase and Hannah Libbey, to SUSAN BARRETT, age 48, widow, b. Richmond Co., d/o Redman B. and Apphia [C. Gutridge] Ambrose. Consent 18 MAY 1883 by D.M. Wharton; consent 10 FEB 1883 by bride. Minister return blank. [C10, R:355, R1:58]

Chiles, John to Mary Ann Pinkard. JOHN CHILES, farmer, age 35, widowed, b. Hamberg, Ger., s/o John and Sophy Chiles, to MARY ANN PINKARD, age 42, single, b. Northumberland Co., d/o Polly Pinkard [father's name not known]. Consent 29 MAR 1861 by bride Mary Ann [her X mark] Pinkard, wits. Richard P. Forester, Samuel R. Deubre. Barth. Dodson, Baptist parson. 2 APR 1861. [C3, R:123, R1:10]

Chilton, William to Eugenia Gertrude Harding.[5] WILLIAM CHILTON, treasurer of Lancaster Co., age 34, single, b. and res. Lancaster Co., s/o R.H. [Henry] and Susan F. [Glasscock] Chilton,[6]

---

[1] William Cash served in Co. D, 40th Va. Inf., C.S.A., wounded in action in his left elbow.
[2] Pearson Chapman (b. 5 AUG 1840, d. 1915) and his first wife Edmonia Kerr Ward (b. 4 NOV 1842, d. 8 DEC 1882) are bur. at St. George's Episcopal Church cemetery in Perryman, Harford Co., Md.
[3] Pearson Chapman is s/o George Chapman and Susan Pearson Alexander; Sigismunda Mary Alexander is d/o Robert Alexander and Helen Bailey Brown.
[4] *Bladensfield* was initially part of a tract acquired by Robert "King" Carter from Robert Cary. It descended to Carter's grandson Robert Carter, of *Nomini Hall*, who deeded it to his daughter Anne Tasker Carter who married John Peck. In 1842, it was the home of Rev. William Norvell Ward.
[5] William Chilton (b. 17 dEC 1845, d. 24 MAY 1922) and wife Eugenia Gertrude Harding (b. 22 SEP 1860, d. 22 APR 1898) are bur. in Farnham Baptist Church cemetery.
[6] R.H. Chilton (1811-1872) and wife Susan G. Chilton (d. 10 DEC 1866, age 52) are bur. at St. Mary's Whitechapel Episcopal Church, Lancaster Co.

to EUGENIA G. HARDING, age 20, single, b. Richmond Co., d/o Cyrus and Laura E. [Blackwell] Harding.[1] Consent 4 DEC 1880 by father Cyrus Harding, wit. F.W. Lewis. F.W. Claybrook. 7 DEC 1880 at Farnham Baptist Church. [C9, R:316, R1:51]

Chinn, Henry (Col.) to Liza Ann Palmer (Col.). HENRY CHINN, farmer, age 20, single, b. Lancaster Co., s/o Matilda Pinn [sic], to LIZA ANN PALMER, age 21, single, b. Richmond Co., d/o Mary Beverton. Consent 25 DEC 1873 by bride, wit. William [his X mark] Beve[r]ton. Elder James A. Weaver. 26 DEC 1873 at the res. of the bride's parents. [C6, R:236, R1:35]

Christopher, James Eubank to Mary Leanna Lowery.[2] JAMES E. CHRISTOPHER, farming, age 28, single, b. Richmond Co., res. Lancaster Co., s/o William and Jane D. Christopher, to LELA M. LOWRY [sic], age 16, single, b. Richmond Co., d/o James and Julia A.[French] Lowery, *q.v.* Consent 16 DEC 1890 by Julie A. Lowry, wit. Robert W. France. G.H. Northam. 18 DEC 1890 at Mrs. Lowry's. [C12, R:324, R1:78]

Churchill, Henry (Col.) to Sarah Smith (Col.). HENRY CHURCHILL, farmer, age 21, single, b. Richmond Co., res. Lancaster Co., s/o Alfred and Matilda Churchill, to SARAH SMITH, age 17, single, b. Lancaster Co., names of parents omitted "for good cause." Travis Corbin. 9 FEB 1867 at *Willow Grove*. [C4, R:285, R1:20]

Churchwell, Charles H. (Col.) to Ann Taylor (Col.). CHARLES H. CHURCHWELL, farming, age 24, b. Lancaster Co., s/o Eliza Churchwell née Carter, to ANN TAYLOR, age 15y7m, single, b. Richmond Co., d/o Letty Connelley and her former husband Shadrack Taylor (dec'd.). Consent 26 JAN 1887 from Ivanhoe, Va. by bride Ann [her X mark] Taylor, wits. Lety [sic] Conalley, W. Connellee. Rev. W. Carter. 28 JAN 1887 at the res. of the bride. [C11, R:290, R1:69]

Churchwell, Samuel (Col.) to Mrs. Geogeanna Newton (Col.). SAMUEL CHURCHWELL, mechanic, age 40, widowed, b. Richmond Co., s/o Samuel and Jane [Day] Churchwell, to GEORGEANNA NEWTON, age 39, widow, b. Richmond Co., d/o Lindsay and Felicia Rich. Consent 31 MAR 1879, form unsigned. Thomas G. Thomas. 3 APR 1879 at the minister's house. [C8, R:307, R1:47]

Churchwell, Samuel (Col.) to Jane Jenkins (Col.). SAMUEL CHURCHWELL, bricklayer, age 24, single, b. Richmond Co., s/o Samuel Churchwell [FB] and Jane Day [FB],[3] to JANE JENKINS, age 18, single, b. Richmond Co., d/o Frances Jenkins, father unknown. Consent 3 JUL 1855 from mother Frances [her X mark] Jenkins, wit. William L. Lee. Howard W. Montague, M.G. 4 JUL 1855 in Essex Co., Va. [C1, R:153, R1:2]

Clarke, Cyrus to Mrs. Sarah J. Brann Beazley. CYRUS CLARKE, farmer, age 39, single, b. Richmond Co., s/o David and Drusilla [R. Woollard] Clarke,[4] to SARAH J. BEAZLEY, age 28, widow, b. Richmond Co., d/o Reuben [G.] and Frances [D. Efford] Brann.[5] No minister return. 9 JUN 1864. [R:139, R1:13]

---

[1] Cyrus Harding and L.E. Blackwell were married 14 NOV 1857 in Northumberland Co.
[2] James E. Christopher (1862-1929) and wife Mary L. Lowery (1874-1920) are bur. in Providence Baptist Church cemetery, Miskimon, Va.
[3] Samuel Churchwell and Jane Day, both free persons of color, were married by bond 8 APR 1819 in Richmond Co.
[4] David Clarke and Drucilla R. Woollard were married by bond 4 JUN 1816 in Richmond Co.
[5] Reuben G. Brann and Frances D. Efford were married by bond 5 MAY 1830 in Richmond Co.

Clark, Dandridge C. to Sarah Ann Waterfield.[1] DANDRIDGE CLARK, farmer, age 34, single, b. Richmond Co., s/o Joseph Clark and Sally [Haydon] Clark (dec'd.), to SARAH A. WATERFIELD, age 21y2m6d, single, b. Richmond Co., d/o John Waterfield and Rachel Ann [Clark] Waterfield (dec'd.), *q.v.* Consent 26 JAN 1878 by bride Sarah A. [her X mark] Waterfield, wit. [R.]D. Clark. G.H. Northam. 27 JAN 1878. [C8, R:310, R1:44]

Clark, Elijah to Asenath Ada Fallen. ELIJAH CLARK, farming, age 19y5m24d, single, b. Richmond Co., s/o Hiram [James] and Ann [T. Lewis] Clark,[2] to ASENATH ADA FALLEN, age 21y18d, single, b. Richmond Co., d/o Richard L. and Martha Fallen. Consent 10 JAN 1886 by father Richard L. Fallen, wits. bride and Ann Clark. R.N. Reamy. 13 JAN 1886. [C11, R:315, R1:67]

Clark, Francis C. to Martha E. Pullen. FRANCIS C. CLARK, farmer, age 24, single, b. and res. King George Co., s/o Overton and Ann Clark, to MARTHA E. PULLEN, age 22, single, b. Richmond Co., d/o John and Henrietta Pullen. Robert N. Reamy. 20 AUG 1868 at Mrs. Pullen's. [C5, R:254, R1:24]

Clarke, George W. to Elizabeth C. Elmore. GEORGE W. CLARKE, farmer, age 38, single, b. Richmond Co., s/o Washington and Elizabeth Clarke, to ELIZABETH C. ELMORE, age 30, single, b. Richmond Co., d/o Henry and Harriet Elmore. Consent 20 DEC 1870 by bride, wit. Wm. H. Clark. Wm. H. Kirk. 22 DEC 1870 at the house of Elizabeth Dixon. [C5, R:234, R1:28]

Clark, George W. to Adlener Lewis.[3] GEORGE W. CLARK, farmer, age 46, widowed, b. Richmond Co., s/o Washington and Elizabeth Clark, to ADLENER LEWIS, age 16, single, b. Richmond Co., d/o John T. and Rachel Lewis. Consent 17 JUN 1881 by bride, signed by John T. Lewis, wit. John T. [her X mark] Waterfield. F.W. Claybrook. 19 JUN 1881 at [Mayon] Baptist Church. [C9, R:336, R1:53]

Clark, James H. to Annie V. Bell. JAMES H. CLARK, farming, age 22, single, b. Richmond Co., res. Northumberland Co., s/o Hiram J. [James] Clark and Ann T. Clark (née Lewis),[4] to ANNIE V. BELL, age 19, single, b. Richmond Co., d/o Vincent R. and Mary A. [Ann Rock] Bell.[5] Consent by bride 11 AUG 1882, wit. Mary A. Bell, Charles Thrift. G.H. Northam. 27 AUG 1882 at res. of J. Middleton. [C9, R:313, R1:56]

Clark, John to Mrs. Julia Ann Maslin. JOHN CLARK, laborer, age 33, single, b. Ireland, s/o Robert and Margaret Clark, to JULIA ANN MASLIN, age 36, widow, b. Richmond Co., "names of parents omitted for good cause." Elder James A. Weaver. 7 AUG 1866 at the res. of the bride's mother. [C4, R:271, R1:17]

Clark, John R. to Mrs. Mary Lewis Brann. JOHN R. CLARK, farmer, age 21, widowed, b. Richmond Co., s/o William and Elizabeth Clark, to MARY BRANN, age 40, widow, b. Richmond Co., d/o Thomas and Elizabeth Lewis. Consent 8 SEP 1866 by bride Mary [her X mark] Brann, wits.

---

[1] Dandridge C. Clark (b. 1841, d. 17 SEP 1912) and his wife Sarah Ann Waterfield (b. 20 NOV 1856, d. 23 JAN 1915) are bur. at Totuskey Baptist Church cemetery. He served in Co. D, 47th Va. Inf., C.S.A.
[2] Hiram Clarke and Ann Lewis were married 18 FEB 1852 in Richmond Co. by Rev. Elijah L. Williams.
[3] Adlener Lewis (b. 20 DEC 1865, d. 11 AUG 1942), wife of George W. Clark, is bur. at Oakland United Methodist Church cemetery.
[4] Hiram James Clark (b. 5 MAY 1828, d. 25 MAR 1882 in Heathsville, Va.) and wife Ann T. Lewis (b. 10 FEB 1831, d. 11 AUG 1893) are bur. in Gibeon Baptist Church cemetery.
[5] Vincent R. Bell and Mary Ann Rock were married by bond 22 JUN 1848 in Northumberland Co.

Hiram Clark, William J. Clark. Elder James A. Weaver. 9 SEP 1866 at the res. of the bride. [C3, R:272, R1:18]

Clarke, John W. to Elizabeth Lambert. JOHN W. CLARKE, farmer, age 22, single, b. Richmond Co., s/o John R. and Sarah [Kent] Clarke,[1] to ELIZABETH LAMBERT, age 25, single, b. Richmond Co., d/o William and Frances [Clarke] Lambert.[2] Consent 22 AUG 1873 by bride. Elder James A. Weaver. 24 AUG 1873 at the res. of the widow [Mrs.] King. [C6, R:235, R1:34]

Clarke, Joseph to Nancy Weathers. JOSEPH CLARKE, farmer, age 40, widower, b. Richmond Co., s/o Landon Clarke and Nancy, to NANCY WEATHERS, age about 30, single, b. Richmond Co., d/o William Weathers and wife Frances [A. Hardwick].[3] Consent 28 MAY 1855 by bride Nancy [her X mark] Weathers, wit. Joseph Weathers. William N. Ward, M.G. 29 MAY 1855. [C1, R:153, R1:2]

Clarke, Joseph W. to Willeyann C. Hudson. JOSEPH W. CLARKE, farmer, age 22, single, b. Richmond Co., s/o Joseph Clarke, to WILLIEANN C. HUDSON, age 18, single, b. Richmond Co., d/o Meredith and Elizabeth [F. Lewis] Hudson.[4] Consent 10 NOV 1873 by parties, wit. Jeremiah S. Lewis. Elder James A. Weaver. 13 NOV 1873 at the res. of the bride. [C6, R:235, R1:34]

Clarke, Randall Davis to Emma Delano.[5] R.D. CLARKE, farmer, age 22, single, b. Richmond Co., s/o John H. [Henry] and Lucinda [Jane Bryant] Clarke,[6] to EMMA DELANO, age 19, single, b. Richmond Co., d/o J.P. [Joseph Peterson] and Lucinda [Lyell Self] Delano.[7] Elder James A. Weaver. 23 JAN 1873 at the res. of the bride's father. [C6, R:235, R1:33]

Clark, Spilman B.[8] to Margaret Hale. SPILMAN B. CLARK, farmer, age 23, single, b. Richmond Co., s/o Meshack and Eliza [Elizabeth B. Clark] Clark,[9] to MARGARET HALE, age 21, single, b. Richmond Co., d/o Moses and Nancy [Sydnor] Hale. Consent 9 MAY 1861 by bride Margaret [her X mark] Hale and Moses Hale, wits. Benjn. Tucker, Rostin [his X mark] Hale. James A. Weaver. 9 MAY 1861 at Moses Hale's. [C3, R:123, R1:10]

Clarke, Vincent R.[10] to Winney Clarke. VINCENT R. CLARKE, farmer, age 20, single, b. Richmond Co., res. Westmoreland Co., s/o Shadrack and Sally Clarke, to WINNEY CLARKE, age 18, single, b. Richmond Co., d/o William and Elizabeth Clarke. Consent 11 JUN 1859 by bride Winney [her X mark] Clarke, and mother of bride Elizabeth [her X mark] Clarke, and mother of groom Sarah [her X mark], wits. Middleton Lewis, Benjamin Tucker. James A. Weaver. 12 JUN 1859. [C2, R:165, R1:7]

---

[1] John R. Clarke and Sarah Kent were married 21 OCT 1852 in Richmond Co. by Rev. William C. Haynes.
[2] William Lambert and Frances Clarke were married by bond 16 FEB 1846 in Richmond Co.
[3] William Weathers and Frances A. Hardwick were married by bond 9 FEB 1809 in Richmond Co.
[4] Meredith Hudson and Elizabeth F. Lewis were married 10 MAR 1852 in Richmond Co. by Rev. John Godwin.
[5] Randall Davis Clarke (b. 8 DEC 1850, d. 8 APR 1911) and his wife Emma Delano (b. 9 SEP 1853, d. 24 APR 1925, unmarked) are bur. in the Clarke Family Burial Ground, located off of Route 620.
[6] John H. Clarke and Lucy Bryant were married by bond 24 FEB 1835 in Richmond Co.
[7] Joseph Delano and Lucinda Self were married by bond 25 AUG 1847 in Richmond Co.
[8] Spilman Clark served in Co. G, 15th Va. Cav., C.S.A.
[9] Meshack Clark and Elizabeth B. Clark were married by bond 2 JAN 1824 in Richmond Co.
[10] A Vincent R. Clark, who served in Co. E, 40th Va. Inf., C.S.A., was killed at the Battle of 2nd Manassas in 1862.

Clarke, William to Jane Lewis. WILLIAM CLARKE, farmer, age 24, single, b. Richmond Co., s/o Elizabeth Clarke, to JANE LEWIS, age 21, single, b. Richmond Co., d/o Thomas Lewis and Elizabeth. Consent 17 JAN 1856 by bride Jane [her X mark] Lewis, wit. William King. A. Dulaney, minister. 22 JAN 1856 at E. Clarke's. [C1, R:159, R1:4]

Claughton, Joseph (Col.) to Rosa S. Jessup (Col.). JOSEPH F. CLAUGHTON,[1] oysterman, age 28, single, b. Richmond Co., s/o Samuel and Harriet Claughton, to ROSA S. JESSUP, age 27, single, b. Richmond Co., d/o Marcus and Adaline Jessup. Consent 5 FEB 1883 by bride, wit. John [his X mark] Phillips; consent 5 FEB 1883 by sister of bride Georgianna [her X mark] Fitzue [sic]. Charles Sparks. 7 FEB 1883 at Mount Zion Church. [C10, R:355, R1:58]

Coates, Alfred to Ann Coates. ALFRED COATES, farmer, age 41, single, b. Richmond Co., s/o Samuel and Ann Coates, to ANN COATES, age 40, single, b. Richmond Co., d/o James and Betsy Coates. John Pullen. 5 SEP 1866 at res. of Charles Balderson. [C4, R:272, R1:18]

Coats, Cornelius (Col.) to Precilla Thompson (Col.). CORNELIUS COATS, laboring, age 27, widowed, b. Richmond Co., s/o Sandy and Lucinda Coats, to PRECILLA THOMPSON, age 26, single, b. Richmond Co., d/o Harry and Jane Thompson. Consent 2 DEC 1885 by Jane [her X mark] Thompson, wit. John [his X mark] Corbin. Robert Lewis. 3 DEC 1885. [C10, R:318, R1:65]

Coats, Edward T. to Sarah Ann Morriss.[2] EDWARD T. COAT[E]S, farmer, age about 25, single, b. upper part of Richmond Co., s/o James Coats and wife Elizabeth, to SARAH MORRISS, age about 19, single, b. in the upper part of Richmond Co., d/o John Morriss and wife Elizabeth. Consent 28 DEC 1855 by Sarah [her X mark] Morriss, wits. William A.H. Saunders, John Morriss, Charles H. Balderson. John Pullen, M.G. 2 JAN 1856 at the residence of John Morriss in upper district. [C1, R, R1:3]

Coates, Ezekiel H. to Ella A. Morriss. EZEKIEL H. COATES, shoemaker, age 23, single, b. Richmond Co., s/o Miskell and Elizabeth [Hall] Coates,[3] to ELLA A. MORRISS, age 21, single, b. Richmond Co., d/o Robert and Ann Morriss. Consent in JUL 1872 by bride, wit. Hiram [his X mark] Saunders. H.H. Fones. 21 JUL 1872 at house of G.W. Balderson. [C6, R:238, R1:32]

Coats, Henry R. to Mary Ferrall. HENRY R. COATS, farmer, age 45, widower, b. Richmond Co., s/o Thomas and Mary Coats, to MARY FERRALL,[4] age 30, single, b. Essex Co., parents unknown. Consent 20 JUL 1860 [sic] by bride, wits. James Saunders, J.W. Scrimger. E.L. Williams. 20 FEB 1860. [C2, R:153, R1:8]

Coats, Henry R. to Mrs. Mary C. Thrift Headley. HENRY R. COATS, farmer, age 51, widowed, b. Richmond Co., s/o Thomas and Mary Coats, to MARY C. HEADLEY, age 40, widow, b. Richmond Co., d/o William and Jane [Northen] Thrift. Elijah L. Williams. 18 SEP 1862 at the bride's house. [C3, R:140, R1:12]

---

[1] Surname also appears as Clayton.
[2] Sarah A. Morris [Jenkins] (b. 17 SEP 1836, d. 28 SEP 1819), wife of Edward T. Coates, is bur. at Welcome Grove Baptist Church cemetery. She was later married to Robert Arthur Jenkins in Essex Co.
[3] Miskell Coats and Elizabeth Hall were married by bond 20 NOV 1848 in Richmond Co.
[4] Spelling Ferrall based on her signature, but also appears as Ferrell.

Coates, John A. to Mrs. Elizabeth Sanders Oliff. JOHN A. COATES, farming, age about 48, widower, b. Richmond Co., s/o Samuel Coates and wife Leucy, to ELIZABETH OLIFF, age 38, widow, b. Richmond Co., d/o Robert Sanders. Consent undated by bride, wit. Loretty Sanders. John Pullen, M.G. 30 JUL 1857 at Zachariah Sanders'. [C1, R:159, R1:5]

Coats, Miskell[1] and Mary Saunders. Consent 29 NOV 1856 by bride Mary [her X mark] Sanders, wits. John Morriss, Bladen Hall. No license or minister return. [C1]

Coates, Richard to Mrs. Frances A. Pew, widow of James P. Parr. RICHARD COATES, white, farmer, age 35, widowed, b. Richmond Co., s/o Henry and Elizabeth [R. Woollard] Coates, to FRANCES A. PARR, age 37, widow, b. Richmond Co., d/o Martin [Lewis] and Nancy [Habron] Pugh [Pew].[2] G.H. Northam. 5 APR 1871 at *North Bend*. [C5, R:244, R1:29]

Coats, Richard A. to Lucy L. Balderson. RICHARD A. COATS, farmer, age 23, single, b. Richmond Co., s/o Samuel and Ann Coats, to LUCY L. BALDERSON, age 18, single, b. Richmond Co., d/o John and Hannah [Dameron] Balderson.[3] Consent 12 NOV 1860 by mother Hanner [her X mark] Balderson, wit. James W. Balderson. Elder James A. Weaver. 14 NOV 1860. [C2, R:154, R1:9]

Coates, Richard A.[4] to Mrs. Adeline Beacham, widow of Robert B. Balderson. RICHARD A. COATES, farmer, age 35, widowed, b. Richmond Co., names of parents blank [Samuel and Ann Coats], to ADELINE BALDERSON, age 30, widow, b. Richmond Co., d/o Samuel Beacham. Consent 7 DEC 1871 by bride Adline [sic] [her X mark] Balderson, wit. Thomas [his X mark] Lewis. Elder James A. Weaver. 7 DEC 1871 at the res. of Rich. Volis. [C6, R:245, R1:30]

Coats, Richard H. to Doelissa Hahn. RICHARD H. COATS, age 24, single, b. Richmond Co., s/o Henry R. and Elizabeth Coats, to DOELISSA HAHN, age 22, single, b. Richmond Co., d/o Benjamin and Rainey Hahn. E.L. Williams, 27 DEC 1860. [C2, R:153 and 154, R1:9]

Coats, Richard H. to Elizabeth Schools. RICHARD H. COATS, farmer, age 33, widowed, b. Richmond Co., s/o Richard H. and Elizabeth Coats, to ELIZABETH SCHOOLS, age 22, single, b. King and Queen Co., d/o Alexander and Laura C. Schools. G.H. Northam. 23 MAY 1872. [C6, R:237, R1:31]

Coates, Robert Leslie to Susan A. Jenkins.[5] ROBERT L. COATES, farming, age 22y7m5d, single, b. Richmond Co., s/o Edward [T.] and Sally [Sarah Ann Morris] Coates, to SUSAN JENKINS, age 21, single, b. Richmond Co., d/o Thomas [A.] and Martha [Brewer Sandford] Jenkins, *q.v.* Consent 24 OCT 1882 from Newland, Va. by bride, wits. James Jenkins and Henry A. Balderson. H.H. Fones. 26 OCT 1882. [C9, R:313, R1:56]

Coates, Samuel B. to Bettie A. Elmore. SAMUEL B. COATES, carpenter, age 41, single, b. Richmond Co., s/o Zachariah and Mary [Woollard] Coates,[6] to BETTIE A. ELMORE, age 25,

---

[1] Miskell Coates served in Co. G, 15th Va. Cav., C.S.A. His age is 38 in 1861.
[2] Martin Pew and Nancy Habron were married by bond 26 FEB 1824 in Richmond Co. He is s/o Lewis Pugh and Nancy Richards.
[3] John Balderson and Hannah Dameron were married by bond 2 JAN 1839 in Richmond Co.
[4] A Richard A. Coats enlisted in Co. K, 9th Va. Cav., C.S.A.
[5] Robert L. Coates (b. 9 AUG 1857, d. 1939), was first married to Susan A. Jenkins.
[6] Zachariah Coats and Mary Woollard were married by bond 6 JUN 1846 in Richmond Co.

single, b. Richmond Co., d/o William and Virginia Elmore. Consent 3 JUN 1889 by bride, wit. Jos. [his X mark] Schools. Robert Williamson. 5 JUN 1889 at Farnham. [C12, R:327, R1:74]

Coats, Smith to Ida Hinson. SMITH COATS, farming, age 25, single, b. Richmond Co., s/o Carter S. Coats (dec'd.) and Maria Coats, to IDA HINSON, age 22, single, b. Richmond Co., d/o John and Virginia Hinson. Consent 18 FEB 1887 by bride. R.N. Reamy. 24 FEB 1887. [C11, R:290, R1:69]

Coates, Thomas J., d. 29 AUG 1917, to Virginia C. Beacham, d. 22 DEC 1938. THOMAS J. COATES, oystering, age 30, single, b. Richmond Co., s/o Henry R. and Elizabeth Coates, to VIRGINIA C. BEACHAM, age 22, single, b. Richmond Co., d/o Hiram P. and Virginia [A. Lewis] Beacham.[1] Consent 19 JAN 1886 by father Hiram P. Beacham. G.H. Northam. 21[2] JAN 1886 at Mr. [Hiram P.] Beacham's. [C11, NN:29 JAN 1886, R:315, R1:67]

Coats, Warren T. to Mary C. Reamy. WARREN T. COATS, farmer, age 22, single, b. Richmond Co., s/o James C. and Martha [Ann Gutridge] Coats, to MARY C. REAMY, age 18, single, b. Richmond Co., d/o James O. and Mary J. [Jane Morris] Reamy. Consent 22 DEC 1873 by bride, wit. Mary J. Reamy. Robert N. Reamy. 25 DEC 1873 at M.J. Reamy's. [C6, R:236, R1:35]

Coats, William H. to Priscilla Saunders. WILLIAM H. COATS, farmer, age 22y10m, single, b. Westmoreland Co., s/o James C. and Ann Coats, to PRISCILLA SAUNDERS, age 23, single, b. Richmond Co., d/o Griffin and Maria Sanders [sic]. Consent 15 JAN 1872 by bride Prisciller [sic] Saunders, wit. Griffin Sanders. Robert N. Reamy. 18 JAN 1872 at res. of Griffin Saunders. [C6, R:237, R1:31]

Coats, Zachariah C. to Lealia W. Franklin. ZACHARIAH C. COATS, farming, age 24, single, b. Richmond Co., res. Westmoreland Co., s/o Alexander and Elizabeth Coats, to LEALIA W. FRANKLIN, age 19, single, b. Richmond Co., d/o Philip M. and Mary S. [Webb] Franklin, *q.v.* Consent 5 OCT 1885 by bride's parents. G.H. Northam. 8 OCT 1885 at *Glenmore*. [C10, R:317, R1:65]

Coleman, James W. to Narcis A. Rock. JAMES W. COLEMAN, carpenter, age 21y4m, single, b. Lancaster Co., s/o James H. and Tamza S. [Callahan] Coleman,[3] to NARCIS A. ROCK, age 17, single, b. Richmond Co., d/o Thomas C. and Ann [Fulks] Rock.[4] G.H. Northam. 30 DEC 1873. [C6, R:236, R1:35]

Coleman, William E. to Bessie Augusta Johnson.[5] WILLIAM E. COLEMAN, merchant, age 30, single, b. Richmond Co., s/o Wilson and Elizabeth [Richards] Coleman,[6] to BESSIE AUGUSTA JOHNSON, age 21, single, b. Richmond Co., d/o Thomas E. [Edwin] and Mary E. [Ellen

---

[1] Hiram P. Beacham (b. 27 FEB 1833, d. 10 JUL 1910) and wife Virginia A. Lewis (b. 1 FEB 1833, d. 18 AUG 1920) are bur. in Farnham Baptist Church cemetery.
[2] Library of Virginia, Bible Records, Beacham Family Bible Record, 1856-1938, gives date of marriage 22 JAN 1886.
[3] James H. Coleman and Tomza Callahan were married by bond 7 SEP 1850 in Lancaster Co.
[4] Thomas C. Rock (b. 15 DEC 1819, d. 8 MAR 1906) and wife Ann Fulks (b. 16 JUN 1821, d. 29 MAR 1907) are bur. in Calvary United Methodist Church cemetery. Thomas C. Rock and Ann Fulks were married by bond 30 JUL 1838 in Richmond Co.
[5] William E. Coleman (b. 24 FEB 1851, d. 9 JUN 1904) and his wife Bessie A. Johnson (b. 18 JUL 1859, d. in FEB 1928) are bur. in St. John's Episcopal Church cemetery.
[6] Wilson Coleman and Elizabeth C. Thrift Richards, wid/o Reuben S. Richards, were married by bond 26 FEB 1846 in Richmond Co.

Bramham] Johnson, *q.v.* Consent 20 MAY 1881 from *Rose Hill* by bride, wit. T.E. Johnson. G.H. Northam. 24 MAY 1881 at Jerusalem Church.[1] [C9, NN:27 MAY 1881, R:336, R1:53]

Comodore, Thomas J. (Col.) to Eliza E. Mason (Col.). THOMAS J. COMODORE, teacher, age 30, single, b. Washington, D.C., res. Lancaster Co., s/o Holdsworth and Magdalene Comodore, to ELIZA E. MASON, age 17, single, b. Richmond Co., d/o Leroy and Tabitha Mason. Consent by bride 29 OCT 1883 at Ivanhoe, Va., and Tabitha [her X mark] Mason, wit. J.E. Blakemore. Charles Sparks. [C10, R:357, R1:59]

Compton, Key, d. 5 MAY 1927 in Baltimore, Md. to Sally Tayloe, b. 29 DEC 1865, d. 25 SEP 1947. KEY COMPTON, transportation, age 25 on May 21st, single, b. Charles Co., Md., res. Norfolk, Va., s/o Barnes and Margaret H. [Holliday Sothoron] Compton,[2] to SALLY TAYLOE, age 22, single, b. Richmond Co., d/o Henry A. [Augustine] and C.N. [Courtenay Norton Chinn] Tayloe. Arthur B. Kinsolving. 18 OCT 1888 at *Mt. Airy*.[3] [C11, R:316, R1:73]

Conars, Lawrence to Elizabeth Hinson. LAWRENCE CONARS, laborer, age 22, single, b. Ireland, s/o Patrick Conars and wife Bettie, to ELIZABETH HINSON, age 25, single, b. Richmond Co., d/o Thornton and Betharia [Sandford] Hinson.[4] Consent 9 AUG 1856 by Elizabeth [her X mark] Henson, wit. John Packett. E.L. Williams, minister. 9 AUG 1856 at Durrettsville, Va. [C1, R, R1:3]

Conley, Addison to Melinda Clark. ADDISON CONLEY, farmer, age 19, single, b. Westmoreland Co., s/o Autum and Julia A. [Mazuro] Conley,[5] to MELINDA CLARK, age 23, single, b. Richmond Co., d/o Meshack and Eliza Clark. James A. Weaver. 4 JUN 1868. [C4, R:254, R1:24]

Conley, George M. to Julia A.E. Sanders. GEORGE M. CONLEY, farmer, age 25, single, b. Richmond Co., s/o James and Elizabeth Conley, to JULIA A.E. SANDERS, age 20, single, b. Richmond Co., d/o George W. and Charlotte [Scates] Sanders.[6] Consent 3 JAN 1877 by George B. Sanders [sic], Julia A.E. Saunders [sic], wit. A.L. Saunders. H.H. Fones. 7 JAN 1877. [C8, R:306a, R1:42]

Conley, George M. to Ira D. France. GEORGE M. CONLEY, minister, age 33, widowed, b. Richmond Co., s/o James and Elizabeth Conley, to IRA D. FRANCE, age 17, single, b. Richmond Co., d/o John and Catharine [Sanders] France, *q.v.* R.N. Reamy. 3 FEB 1886. [C11, R:315, R1:67]

Conley, Richard H. to Eliza J. Sandford. RICHARD H. CONLEY, mechanic, age 57y11m16d, widowed, b. Gloucester Co., s/o Edward and Betsey Conley, to ELIZA J. SANDFORD, age 35, single, b. Westmoreland Co., d/o William and Nancy Sandford. Consent 25 MAY 1885 by bride, wit. Richard P. Forester. G.H. Northam. 28 MAY 1885 at the Sanford's [sic]. [C10, NN:5 JUN 1885, R:317, R1:64]

---

[1] Jerusalem Church is located at Emmerton, Va.
[2] Barnes Compton (b. 6 NOV 1830, d. 2 DEC 1898), a U.S. Congressman, and wife Margaret Holliday Sothoron (b. 21 APR 1838, d. 12 JUN 1900 in Laurel, Md.) are bur. in Loudon Park Cemetery of Baltimore, Md.
[3] *Mount Airy* was established by William Tayloe, the younger, and is located on the north side of Route 360 at Warsaw, Va.
[4] Thornton Hinson and Bethiah Sandford were married by bond 25 JUL 1816 in Westmoreland Co.
[5] Autumn Connellee and Juliann Mazuro were married by bond 23 JUL 1842 in Richmond Co.
[6] George W. Sanders and Charlotte Scates were married 27 MAR 1851 in Richmond Co. by Rev. John Pullen.

Conley, Robert L. to Emma Frances Lewis.[1] ROBERT L. CONLEY, mechanic, age 23, single, b. Richmond Co., s/o R.H. and Rebecca M. Conley, to FRANCES M. LEWIS [sic], age 18, single, b. Richmond Co., d/o Richard Lewis (dec'd.) and Elizabeth M. Lewis. Consent 20 MAR 1880 by bride and her mother Elizabeth M. Lewis, wit. C.H. Jones. W.A. Crocker. 23 MAR 1880 at Oakland Church.[2] [C9, R:315, R1:50]

Conley, Washington (Col.) to Mrs. Lettie Taylor (Col.). WASHINGTON CONLEY, farming, age 52y8m, widowed, b. and res. Northumberland Co., s/o Williamson and Martha Conley, to LETTIE TAYLOR, age 47, widow, b. Richmond Co., d/o Willis and Winnie Mason. Consent 22 JAN 1884 from Ivanhoe, Va. by bride, wit. C.B. Lyell. Rev. W. Carter. 24 JAN 1884 at the bride's home. [C10, R:353, R1:61]

Connellee, James D. to Willie Ann A. Beverton.[3] JAMES D. CONNELLEE, farmer, age 22, single, b. Richmond Co., s/o James and Mary Connellee, to WILLIANN A. BEVERTON, age 19, single, b. Richmond Co., d/o Henry and Fidelia [Ann Drake] Beverton.[4] G.H. Northam. 8 FEB 1866 at Austin Richards'. [C4, R:270, R1:16]

Connellee, James H. to Mrs. Sarah J. Brann, widow of Cyrus Clarke, *q.v.* JAMES H. CONNELLEE, farmer, age 20y7m, single, b. Richmond Co., s/o Richard H. and Rebecca [M. Clarke] Connellee,[5] to SARAH J. CLARKE, age 35y10m, widow, b. Richmond Co., d/o Reuben [G.] and Frances [D. Efford] Brann.[6] Consent 23 OCT 1872 by parties, wit. Dandridge [Winstead]. G.H. Northam. 24 OCT 1872. [C6, R:238, R1:32]

Connollee, John R. to Ann S. Douglass. JOHN R. CONNELLEE,[7] farmer, age 23, single, b. Richmond Co., s/o Wm. H. Conely and Emeline Whittle, to ANN S. DOUGLASS, age 18, single, b. Northumberland Co., res. Richmond Co., d/o Wm. Douglass and Nancy Walker. Consent 7 JAN 1858 by Thomas Oldham, guardian of Ann, wits. R.S. Bryant, Richard Dawson; also signed by Ann [her X mark] Douglass. Barth. Dodson, Baptist parson. 11 JAN 1858 at *Belle Mount.* [C1, R:138, R1:6]

Connellee, Joseph D. to Anna Davis. JOSEPH D. CONNELLEE, farmer and mechanic, age 31, single, b. Westmoreland Co., s/o Autum and Julia A. [Mazuro] Connellee,[8] to ANNA DAVIS, age 20, single, b. Richmond Co., d/o William L. and Eliza [A. Fidler] Davis, *q.v.* Consent undated by bride, wit. by her parents. Robert Williamson. 17 OCT 1888 at res. of Wm. Davis near Farnham, Va. [C11, R:316, R1:73]

Connellee, Robert to Mrs. Frances B. Balderson. ROBERT CONNELLEE, farmer, age about 66, widower, b. Richmond Co., s/o Lewis and Elizabeth Connellee, to FRANCES B. BALDERSON, age about 45, widow, b. Richmond Co., d/o William Balderson and wife Frances. Consent 18

---

[1] Robert L. Conley (1857-1928) and wife Emma Frances Lewis (b. 16 MAY 1862, d. 7 FEB 1932) are bur. in Farnham Baptist Church cemetery.
[2] Oakland Church is located near the east border of the County on Route 612 at Mulch, Va.
[3] Willie Ann Beverton (b. 1851, d. 24 JUN 1930), wife of James D. Connellee, and d/o Henry Beverton and Fidelia Ann Drake, is bur. in St. John's Episcopal Church cemetery. James D. Connellee served in Co. K, 9th Va. Cav., C.S.A.
[4] Henry Beverton and Fidelia Ann Drake were married 28 DEC 1847 in Richmond Co. by Rev. John Pullen.
[5] Richard H. Connelly and Rebecca M. Clarke were married 30 DEC 1850 in Richmond Co. by Rev. Elijah L. Williams.
[6] Reuben G. Brann and Frances D. Efford were married by bond 5 MAY 1830 in Richmond Co.
[7] Spelling varies, Conely, Connelly, Connellee, etc.
[8] Autumn Connellee and Juliann Mazuro were married by bond 23 JUL 1842 in Richmond Co.

AUG 1856 by bride, wits. James C. Mothershead, Joseph Bowen. John Pullen, M.G. 19 AUG 1856 at Frances Balderson's. [C1, R:148, R1:3]

Connelly, Andrew to Mary C. French. ANDREW CONNELLY, farmer, age 26, single, b. Richmond Co., s/o Washington [T.] and Elizabeth [G. Hundley] Connelly,[1] to MARY C. FRENCH, age 29, single, b. Richmond Co., d/o [Rodham] and Hannah [Haydon] French.[2] Consent 17 JUL 1876 by bride, wit. Hannah French. A.B. Dunaway. 20 JUL 1876. [C7, R:305, R1:40]

Conley, Elias L. to Mary C. Bryant.[3] ELIAS L. CONNELLY [sic], farmer, age 30, widowed, b. Richmond Co., res. Lancaster Co., s/o Washington T. and Elizabeth [G. Hundley] Connelly, to MARY C. BRYANT, age 20, single, b. Richmond Co., d/o R.P. [Richard] and Alice C. [Brown] Bryant. Consent 18 MAR 1874 from *Selma Farm* by father R.P. Bryant, wit. James W. Bryant. William H. Kirk. 19 MAR 1874 at the res. of R.P. Bryant. [C7, R:230, R1:36]

Connelly, Richard Andrew to Charlotte W. Sanders.[4] R.A. CONLY [sic], farmer, age 22, single, b. Richmond Co., [names of parents not completed], to CHARLOTTE W. SANDERS, age 19, single, b. Richmond Co., d/o George W. and Charlotte [Scates] Sanders. H.H. Fones. 13 APR 1879. [C8, R:308, R1:47]

Connelly, Thomas M. to Sarah Ann Scrimger. THOMAS M. CONNELLY, farmer, age 35, single, b. Richmond Co., s/o James and Mary Connelly, to SARAH ANN SCRIMGER, age 22, single, b. Richmond Co., d/o George B. and Susan [Ann Hill] Scrimger.[5] G.H. Northam. 24 JAN 1877. [C8, R:306a, R1:42]

Conness, James R. to Anna Clarke. JAMES R. CONNESS, farming, age 22, single, b. Richmond Co., s/o Elias and Betsy Conness née Hinson, to ANNA CLARK [sic], age 21, single, b. Richmond Co., d/o Joseph and Nancy [Weathers] Clark[e], *q.v.* G.H. Northam. 29 APR 1883. [original, R:356, R1:59]

Conoley, Jacob (Col.) to Lettie Monroe (Col.). JACOB CONOLEY, hostler, age 22, single, b. Northumberland Co., res. New Jersey, s/o John and Jennie Conoley, to LETTIE MONROE, age 18, single, b. Richmond Co., d/o James and Fanny Monroe. Consent 14 AUG 1873 by father James Monroe. Travis Corbin, minister. 17 AUG 1873 at Ebenezer Baptist Church. [C6, R:235, R1:34]

Conors, Larry to Novella Keiser. LARRY CONORS, well digger, age 45, widowed, b. Ireland, s/o Patrick and Elizabeth Conors, to LOVELLA KEISER, age 20, single, b. Northumberland Co., d/o James A. and Nancy [Vanlandingham] Keiser.[6] Consent by parties, undated, no wit. G.H. Northam. 25 AUG 1881 at the res. of James A. Keiser. [C9, R:338, R1:54]

---

[1] Washington T. Connelly and Elizabeth G. Hundley, widow, were married by bond 17 DEC 1833 in Richmond Co.

[2] Rodham French and Hannah Haydon were married by bond 16 OCT 1830 in Northumberland Co.

[3] Elias L. Conley (b. 7 AUG 1839, d. 26 APR 1917) and wife Mary C. Bryant (b. 19 NOV 1853, d. 19 MAY 1937) are bur. in Farnham Baptist Church cemetery. The Conley spelling is used as is found on the tombstones.

[4] Richard A. Connelly (1855-1928) and wife Charlotte W. Sanders (b. 1861, d. 5 JUL 1926) are bur. at Welcome Grove Baptist Church cemetery. In Register 1 as R.A. Conley.

[5] George B. Scrimger and Sarah Ann Hill were married 15 NOV 1847 in Richmond Co. by Rev. William N. Ward.

[6] James Keiser and Nancy Vanlandingham were married by bond 8 JUL 1856 in Northumberland Co.

Constable, Clifford Hamilton to Frances Daingerfield Douglas.[1] CLIFFORD H. CONSTABLE, farming, age 38y4m, single, b. Ashton, Ireland, s/o Joshua Constable and Sarah Timberlake,[2] to FRANCES DAINGERFIELD DOUGLAS, age 32, single, b. King William Co., d/o Dr. W.W. [William Walter] and Georgina Douglas. R.A. Castleman. 16 JAN 1890 in Warsaw, Va. [C12, R:323, R1:76]

Cook, Alexander B.[3] to Sarah Ann Johnson. ALEXANDER B. COOK, carpenter, age 27, single, b. King and Queen Co., s/o Baylor and Patsy Cook, to SARAH ANN JOHNSON, age 17, single, b. Richmond Co., d/o James and Mary Johnson. A. Dulaney, minister. 7 NOV 1858 at bride's father. [C2, two versions, R:138, R1:6]

Cooke, George W.[4] to Frances A. Clarke. GEORGE W. COOKE, farmer, age 30, single, b. Richmond Co., s/o John and Tabitha [Suttle] Cooke,[5] to FRANCES A. CLARKE, age 21, single, b. Richmond Co., d/o Atterson and Caroline Clarke. Consent 17 FEB 1859 by bride, wit. W.R. Doggins. George H. Northam. 24 FEB 1859 at Warsaw, Va. [C2, R:165, R1:7]

Cookman, Charles L. to Josephine E. Hudson. CHARLES L. COOKMAN, mechanic, age 23, single, b. and res. Northumberland Co., s/o Jerry [Jeremiah] and Betsy [Elizabeth J. Headley] Cookman,[6] to JOSEPHINE E. HUDSON, age 27, single, b. Northumberland Co., d/o Robert M. and Mary Hudson. Consent 28 DEC 1885 by parent of bride (unsigned), wit. R.M. Hudson. R.N. Reamy. 29 DEC 1885. [C11, R:319, R1:66]

Cookman, Filmore Ezekiah[7] to Frances Madora Dodson. FILMORE COOKMAN, farmer, age 21y3m8d, single, b. and res. Northumberland Co., s/o William [George] and Mary [Magdalene Lewis] Cookman, *q.v.*, to FANNIE DODSON, age 16y6m5d, single, b. Richmond Co., d/o Edward L. and Martha A. [Ann Pope] Dodson.[8] Consent 22 DEC 1876 by Edward L. Dodson, Dandridge Winstead. W.A. Crocker. 25 DEC 1876 at the house of the bride's father. [C7, NN:30 JAN 1885, R:306, R1:41]

Cookman, William Andrew[9] to Alpharetta A. Hudson. WILLIAM A. COOKMAN, farming, age 25, single, b. and res. Northumberland Co., s/o Jeremiah and Elizabeth [J. Headley] Cookman, to ALPHARETTA A. HUDSON, age 22, single, b. Richmond Co., d/o Robert M. and Mary Hudson. Consent in MAY 1883 by parties. R.N. Reamy. 23 MAY 1883. [C10, R:356, R1:59]

---

[1] Clifford Hamilton Constable (b. 20 SEP 1855 in Kent, Eng., d. 28 FEB 1931 in Warsaw, Va.) and his wife Frances Daingerfield Douglas (b. 17 AUG 1857 in Williamsburg, Va., d. 22 FEB 1925 in Warsaw, Va.) are bur. in St. John's Episcopal Church cemetery.

[2] Joshua Constable (1822-1884) and his wife Sarah Timberlake (1830-1904) are bur. in St. John's Episcopal Church cemetery.

[3] A.B. Cook served in Co. D, 47th Reg., Va. Inf., C.S.A.

[4] George W. Cooke served as captain in Co. G, 15th Va. Cav., C.S.A.

[5] John Cooke and Tabitha Suttle were married by bond 11 OCT 1819 in Caroline Co.

[6] Jeremiah Cookman and Elizabeth J. Headley were married by bond 13 JAN 1834 in Northumberland Co.

[7] Filmore E. Cookman (b. 13 SEP 1855, d. 15 JAN 1885) is bur. in Oakland United Methodist Church cemetery. After his death widow Fanny (b. 24 MAY 1860, d. 18 JAN 1926) was married to Cornelius Andrew Jackson Gill, and was bur. in Roseland Cemetery in Northumberland Co.

[8] Edward L. Dodson (b. 1 DEC 1823, d. 3 JAN 1898) and wife Martha Ann Pope (b. 3 SEP 1831, d. 8 JAN 1909) are bur. in Oakland United Methodist Church cemetery. Edward L. Dodson and Martha Ann Pope were married 18 FEB 1852 in Richmond Co. by Rev. Bartholomew Dodson.

[9] William A. Cookman (b. 1857, d. 26 OCT 1926 in D.C.) is bur. at Rock Creek Cemetery in Washington, D.C.

Cookman, William George[1] to Mary Magdalene Lewis. WILLIAM COOK,[2] farmer, age 21, single, b. Northumberland Co., s/o John and Polly Cook, to MARY LEWIS, age 21, single, b. Northumberland Co., d/o Valentine and Milly [Stott] Lewis.[3] John Goodwin, M.G. 10 AUG 1854. [C1, R, R1:1]

Cookman, William George to Judith Elizabeth Dodson.[4] WILLIAM A. [sic] COOKMAN, farming, age 19y9m, single, b. and res. Northumberland Co., s/o William [George] Cookman and Mary M. [Magdalene Lewis] his wife now Douglass, *q.v.*, to JUDITH E. DODSON, age 20y7m, single, b. Richmond Co., d/o Edward L. and Martha A. [Ann Pope] Dodson. Consent 24 DEC 1878 by bride, Mary M. Douglass, Edward T. Dodson. W.A. Crocker. 26 DEC 1878 at the res. of the bride's father. [C8, R:312, R1:46]

Corbin, Benjamin H. (Col.) to Bettie Allen Lyell (Col.). BENJAMIN H. CORBIN, oystering, age 21, single, b. Richmond Co., s/o Stephen and Mary Corbin, to BETTIE ALLEN LYELL, age 20, single, b. Richmond Co., d/o Margaret Lyell [name of father not provided]. Consent 31 OCT 1884 by mother Margaret [her X mark] Lyell, and bride Bettie A. [her X mark] Lyell, wits. H.M. Hutt, R.L. Reynolds, Stephen Corbin. Rev. W. Carter. 6 NOV 1884 at the bride's home. [C10, R:355, R1:63]

Corbin, Charles (Col.) to Tebie Phillips (Col.). CHARLES CORBIN, oysterman, age 22, single, b. Richmond Co., s/o Travers and Virginia Corbin, to TEBIE PHILLIPS, age 26, single, b. Richmond Co., d/o Jack and Mary Phillips. Allan [sic] Brown. 4 MAY 1882. [C9, R:313, R1:56]

Corbin, Cornelius James (Col.), to Maria Henry (Col.). CORNELIUS JAMES CORBIN, oystering, age 25, single, b. Richmond Co., s/o Travers and Virginia Corbin, to MARIA HENRY, age 28, single, b. Caroline Co., d/o Edmond and Milly Henry. Consent 28 FEB 1882 from Milton Wharf by bride. Charles Sparks. 2 MAR 1882 at Motley's farm. [C9, R:312, R1:55]

Corbin, Frederick (Col.) to Nancy W. Parris (Col.). FREDERICK CORBIN, farming, age 28, single, b. and res. Westmoreland Co., s/o John and Jane Corbin, to NANCY W. PARRIS, age 21y5m, single, b. Richmond Co., d/o William and Lucetta Parris. Rev. Robert Lewis. 20 AUG 1890 at the res. of the minister in Westmoreland Co. [C12, R:324, R1:77]

Corbin, George (Col.) to Mary Stewart (Col.). GEORGE CORBIN, oysterman, age 21, single, b. Richmond Co., s/o Travers and Virginia Corbin, to MARY STEWART, age 21, single, b. Richmond Co., d/o Henry and Hannah Stewart. Allen Brown, minister. 29 FEB 1874 at the res. of the bride. [C7, R:230, R1:36]

Corbin, Goen (Col.) to Georgeanna Veney (Col.). GOEN CORBIN, farmer, age 50, widowed, b. Richmond Co., s/o Goen and Matilda Corbin, to GEORGEANNA VENEY, age 23, single, b. Richmond Co., d/o George and Millie Veney. Rev. L. Harrod, Pastor of Ebenezer and Mulberry Baptist Churches. 10 JUL 1890 at the res. of the parents. [C12, R:323a, R1:77]

---

[1] William G. Cookman (b. 20 JUN 1831, d. 20 APR 1862 of camp disease in Richmond, Va.), s/o John Cookman and Mary Rock, is bur. in Roseland Cemetery, Reedville, Va. He served in Co. C, 40th Va. Inf., C.S.A.
[2] The Register version gives surname Cookman.
[3] Valentine Lewis and Milly Stott were married 5 FEB 1824 in Westmoreland Co.
[4] William George Cookman (b. 17 MAR 1860, d. 30 SEP 1936) and his first wife Judith Elizabeth Dodson are bur. in Oakland United Methodist Church cemetery.

Corbin, Gowen (Col.) to Amy Johnson (Col.). GOWEN CORBIN, laborer, age 22, single, b. Richmond Co., s/o Henry and Betsey Corbin, to AMY JOHNSON, age 19, single, b. Essex Co., d/o Henry Johnson and Mary Johnson now Richie. Consent 16 NOV 1876 by mother Mary [her X mark] Richie, wit. Belle Wright. Thomas G. Thomas. 16 NOV 1876 at the house of Mary Richie. [C7, R:305, R1:41]

Corbin, Jesse (Col.) to Evelina Cox (Col.). JESSE CORBIN, laborer, age 19y11m5d, single, b. Richmond Co., s/o Henry and Betsey Corbin, to EVELINA COX, age 19, single, b. Richmond Co., d/o Adam and Maria Cox. Rev. Robert Lewis. 9 JUN 1881. [C9, R:336, R1:53]

Corbin, William (Col.) to Rachel Gains (Col.). WILLIAM CORBIN, farmer, age 26, single, b. Richmond Co., s/o Gowen and Rose Corbin, to RACHEL GAINS, age 27, single, b. Richmond Co., d/o Harry and Fanny Gains. Thomas G. Thomas. 25 JUL 1874 at house of Gowen Corbin. [C7, R:230, R1:36]

Courtney, Henry[1] to Sarah F. Brann. HENRY COURTNEY, farmer, age 27, widowed, b. Richmond Co., s/o John and Nancy [Moore] Courtney,[2] to SARAH F. BRANN, age 22, single, b. Richmond Co., d/o William and Angella [Morris] Brann.[3] Consent 7 JUL 1859 by Sarah [her X mark] Brann, wit. Henry Packett. Lloyd Moore. 7 JUL 1859. [C2, R:165, R1:7]

Courtney, James to Elizabeth Carter. JAMES COURTNEY, farmer, age 22, single, b. Richmond Co., s/o Leonard and Mary [Alderson] Courtney, to ELIZABETH CARTER, age 21, single, b. Westmoreland Co., d/o Fenner Carter and wife Rebecca [Sanders].[4] Consent 30 SEP 1857 by bride Elizabeth [her X mark] Carter, wit. James L. Packett. William N. Ward, M.G. 1 OCT 1857. [C1, R:159, R1:5]

Courtney, James to Sophia Yeatman. JAMES COURTNEY, farmer, age 30, widower, b. Richmond Co., s/o Leonard and Mary [Alderson] Courtney,[5] to SOPHIA YEATMAN, age 30, single, b. Westmoreland Co., parents names omitted "for good cause." Consent 2 JAN 1866 by bride, wit. R.H. Mothershead. Elder James A. Weaver. 2 JAN 1866 at the res. of R.H. Mothershead. [C4, R:270, R1:16]

Courtney, James Henry to Mrs. Margaret Brown Bunting. JAMES HENRY COURTNEY, farmer, age 25, single, b. Richmond Co., s/o Addison and Catherine E. Courtney, to MARGARET BUNTING, age 44, widow, b. Ireland, d/o James and Jane Brown. Consent undated by bride. W.F. Robins. 26 FEB 1890 at the res. of Mrs. Bunting. [C12, R:323a, R1:76]

Courtney, Jeremiah to Lizzie Salzig. JEREMIAH COURTNEY, sailor and farmer, age 22y5m18d, single, b. Richmond Co., s/o Jere. Courtney and Ann Courtney née Alderson,[6] to LIZZIE SALZIG, age 18y8d, single, b. Richmond Co., d/o Peter and Catharine Salzig. G.H. Northam. 27 APR 1886 at *Glenmore*. [C11, R:316, R1:67]

---

[1] Henry Courtney served in Co. G, 15th Va. Cav., C.S.A.
[2] John Courtney and Nancy Moore were married by bond 25 APR 1816 in Richmond Co.
[3] William Brann and Angilla Morris were married by bond 31 JAN 1828 in Westmoreland Co.
[4] Fenner Sanders and Rebeckah Sanders were married by bond 14 DEC 1825 in Richmond Co.
[5] Leonard Courtney and Mary Alderson were married by bond 4 NOV 1812 in Richmond Co.
[6] Jeremiah Courtney and Ann Alderson were married 7 DEC 1848 in Richmond Co. by Rev. William N. Ward.

Courtney, Jerry to Mrs. Mary Elizabeth Holloway Pritchard. JERRY COURTNEY, farmer, age 49, widower, b. Richmond Co., s/o Leonard and Mary [Alderson] Courtney, to MARY E. PRITCHARD, age 32, widow, b. Richmond Co., d/o Jerry and Kittie Holloway. Consent 27 OCT 1866 by bride. Elder James A. Weaver. 31 OCT 1866 at the res. of the bride. [C4, R:272, R1:18]

Courtney, Littleton Gordon to Kate Watson. LITTLETON GORDON COURTNEY, farming, age 31, single, b. Richmond Co., res. Westmoreland Co., s/o William and Mary Courtney, to KATE WATSON, age 26, single, b. Westmoreland Co., res. Richmond Co., parents unknown. Consent 18 MAR 1885 by bride. A.D. Reynolds. 18 MAR 1885 at the res. of the minister. [C10, R:316, R1:64]

Courtney, Richard to Mrs. Mary Brann Courtney. RICHARD COURTNEY, farmer, age 35, widowed, b. Richmond Co., s/o Leonard and Mary [Alderson] Courtney, to MARY COURTNEY, age 35, widow, b. Richmond Co., d/o William Brann. Elder James A. Weaver. 14 FEB 1867 at the res. of the bride. [C4, R:285, R1:20]

Courtney, Richard, to Ann Hardwick. Consent 21 DEC 1854 by bride, wit. Henry Packett. No license or minister return. [C1]

Courtney, Walter[1] to Jane E. Courtney. WALTER COURTNEY, farmer, age 21, single, b. Richmond Co., s/o John and Nancy Courtney, to JANE E. COURTNEY, age 21, single, b. Richmond Co., d/o Leonard and Mary [Alderson] Courtney. William N. Ward. 25 DEC 1856. [R:148, R1:4]

Courtney, William Leonard to Mary E. Bowen. WILLIAM LEONARD COURTNEY, farming, age 24, single, b. Richmond Co., s/o Walter and Jane [E. Courtney] Courtney, to MARY E. BOWEN, age 27, single, b. Richmond Co., d/o John and Maria Bowen. Consent 11 OCT 1884 by bride. Rev. A.D. Reynolds. 1 OCT 1884 at the res. of R.C. Mozingo. [C10, R:355, R1:62]

Cox, James Landon (Col.) to Mary Diggs (Col.). JAMES LANDON COX, farmer, age 24, single, b. Richmond Co., s/o Bass and Mary Maden Cox, to MARY DIGGS, age 25, single, b. Northumberland Co., d/o William and Peggy Ball. Thomas G. Thomas. 13 NOV 1869 at Henry Martin's house. [C5, R, R1:26]

Cox, John to Mary Ellen Faucett. JOHN COX, shoemaker, age 23, single, b. Richmond Co., s/o Delarue and Charlotte Cox, to MARY ELLEN FAUCETT, age 21, single, b. Richmond Co., d/o John and Susan Faucett. Consent by bride Mary Elin [her X mark] Fosett, signed by Susen [her X mark] Josking, wit. John H. Davis. John Pullen. 26 MAR 1862 at Susan Faucett's. [C3, R:140, R1:11]

Cox, Joseph (Col.) to Mrs. Millie Maden, widow of Lewis Tate (Col.). JOSEPH COX, farming, age 23, single, b. Richmond Co., s/o Cornelius and Catharine Cox, to MILLIE TATE, age 30, widow, b. Richmond Co., d/o Del Maden and Lucy Boyd. Rev. T.G. Thomas. 13 DEC 1888 at the house of Jesse Liverpool. [C12, R:317, R1:73]

---

[1] Walter Courtney served in Co. G, 15th Va. Cav., C.S.A.

Cox, Mercer (Col.) to Fanny Carter (Col.). MERCER COX, farmer, age 36, widowed, b. Richmond Co., s/o Newman and Hannah Cox, to FANNY CARTER, age 21, single, b. Richmond Co., d/o William and Letty Carter. George Laws. 21 OCT 1869 at *The Glebe*, wit. W.B. Mitchell. [C5, R, R1:26]

Cox, Mercer (Col.) to Julia Williams (Col.). MERCER COX, laborer, age 52, widowed, b. Richmond Co., s/o Newman and Hannah Cox, to JULIA WILLIAMS, age 29, single, b. Richmond Co., d/o Stafford and Easter Williams. Rev. Robert Lewis. 14 APR 1881. [C9, R:335, R1:53]

Cox, Robert [FB] to Winney Catharine Newman [FB]. ROBERT COX, farmer and shoemaker, age about 20, single, b. Richmond C., s/o Delarue Cox, to WINNEY CATHARINE NEWMAN, age about 20, single, b. Richmond Co., d/o John and Milly Newman. Consent 9 DEC 1857 by bride's father John [his X mark] Newman, Winny [her X mark] Newman, wit. Wm. H. Newman. W.W. Walker, M.G. 10 DEC 1857 at John Newman's. [C1, R:160, R1:5]

Cox, Samuel (Col.) to Lucy Ann Thompson (Col.). SAMUEL COX, farmer, age 22y8m, single, b. Richmond Co., s/o Dell [Delarue] and Charlotte Cox, to LUCY ANN THOMPSON, age 21y10m24d, single, b. Richmond Co., d/o Daniel and Hannah Thompson. Consent 18 APR 1877 by bride, wit. Moses Thompson. George [his X mark] Laws. 19 APR 1877 at *The Hermitage*. [C8, R:306a, R1:42]

Cox, Thomas (Col.) to Bella Palmer (Col.). THOMAS COX, farmer, age 28, single, b. Richmond Co., s/o Ben and Mary Cox, to BELLA PALMER, age 21, single, b. Richmond Co., d/o Peter and Lila Palmer. Consent 3 DEC 1868 by bride Bella [her X mark] Palmer; R.F. Mitchell, J.P. attests to her age. George Laws. 3 DEC 1868 at *Cedar Grove*.[1] [C5, R1:25]

Cox, Washington (Col.) to Rachel Davis (Col.). WASHINGTON COX, farming, age 19, single, b. Richmond Co., s/o Mat and Sarah Cox, to RACHEL DAVIS, age 21, single, b. Richmond Co., d/o Eliza Dale formerly Davis. Rev. T.G. Thomas. 13 APR 1884. [C10, R:354, R1:62]

Crabb, Tasker Carter[2] to Mildred Edmonia Pendleton.[3] TASKER C. CRABB [sic], farmer, age 24, single, b. Richmond Co., s/o William M.M. [Middleton Mayo][4] and Ann T. [Tasker Carter Peck] Crabb, to MILDRED E. PENDLETON, age 23, single, b. Richmond Co., d/o Francis W. [Walker] and Sarah F. [Frances Turner] Pendleton.[5] Andrew Fisher. 22 OCT 1867 in Warsaw, Va. [C4, R:287, R1:21]

---

[1] There are two homes in Richmond Co. known as *Cedar Grove*. One was located on the bluff facing the Rappahannock River, between *Grove Mount* and *Belle Mount*. It was in early times the home of Priscilla Carter who married Robert Mitchell who first lived in a house later known as *Burnt House*. The second was the home of Dr. Erasmus Derwin Booker and was located on Route 602, 2 miles east of North Farnham Church.

[2] Tasker C. Crabbe, Sr. (b. 15 FEB 1844 at *Pittsville*, d. 25 JAN 1918 at *Carville*, near Oldhams, Westmoreland Co., Va.), lived at *Oak Hill* and *Sunnyside*, is bur. at Menokin Baptist Church cemetery. He served in Co. C, 9th Va. Cav., C.S.A.

[3] Mildred Edmonia Pendleton (b. 1844, d. 19 OCT 1872 in Warsaw, Va.), first wife of Tasker Carter Crabb, is bur. in St. John's Episcopal Church cemetery.

[4] William M.M. Crabb was sheriff of Richmond Co. from 5 JUL 1852 to 7 JUL 1856.

[5] Francis W. Pendleton and Sarah F. Turner were married by bond 27 JAN 1833 in Caroline Co. He was clerk of Richmond County Court from 1849 to 1865.

Crabb, Tasker Carter to Julia B. McCarty.[1] TASKER CRABB, farmer, age 30, widowed, b. Richmond Co., s/o William M.M. [Middleton Mayo] and Ann [Tasker Carter Peck] Crabb,[2] to JULIA B. McCARTY, age 24, single, b. Richmond Co., d/o Madison P. and Olivia [Ann Mitchell] McCarty.[3] Edmund Murdaugh, Presbyter. 15 DEC 1874 at Peter P. Burr's in Fredericksburg, Va. [C7, R:230, R1:37]

Crabb, Tasker Carter to Mrs. Sarah Alpha France, widow of Addison J. Hall. TASKER C. CRABBE, farming, age 43, widowed, b. Richmond Co., s/o William M.M. and Ann T. [Tasker Carter Peck] Crabb, to SARAH A. HALL, age 24, widow, b. Richmond Co., d/o John and Catharine [Sanders] France, *q.v.* Geo. M. Conley. 9 OCT 1887 near Newland, Va. [C11, R:292, R1:70]

Cralle, Andrew Broaddus to Martha Luemma Winstead.[4] ANDREW B. CRALLE, farmer, age 22, single, b. and res. Northumberland Co., s/o [Darius] Griffin and Maria [Gatewood Gordon] Cralle,[5] to LUEMMA WINSTEAD, age 25, single, b. Richmond Co., d/o George [Lunsford] and Martha [Hall Beachum Headley] Winstead.[6] W.W. Walker. 11 FEB 1874 at the res. of George Winstead. [C7, R:230, R1:36]

Cralle, Charles Richard to Sarah "Sally" E. Allison.[7] CHARLES RICHARD CRALLE, oystering, age 32, single, b. Richmond Co., s/o Kenner R. [Richard] and Margaret [H. Saunders] Cralle, *q.v.*, to SALLY E. ALLISON, age 22, single, b. Richmond Co., d/o William and Margaret [Ann Jones] Allison. Robert Williamson. 21 DEC 1887 at Farnham, Va. [C11, R:293, R1:71]

Cralle, Gabriel (Col.) to Martha Rollins (Col.). GABRIEL CRALLE, oysterman, age 21y8m21d, single, b. Richmond Co., s/o William and Julia Cralle, to MARTHA ROLLINS, age 21y8m, single, b. Richmond Co., d/o Michael and Daphne Rollins. Charles Sparks. 24 NOV 1881 at the bride's house on Dr. Motley's farm. [C9, R:338, R1:54]

Cralle, Gabriel (Col.) to Georgia E. Williams (Col.). GABRIEL CRALLEY [sic], oystering, age 30, widowed,[8] b. Richmond Co., s/o William and Julia Cralley [sic], to GEORGIA E. WILLIAMS, age 20, single, b. Richmond Co., d/o Elijah and Susan A. Williams. Consent 2 JUN 1890 by parties, wit. Mrs. Susan [her X mark] Williams, Grant Yates. Nelson A. Atkins. 5 JUN 1890 at Ebenezer Baptist Church. [C12, R:323a, R1:77]

Cralle, James Walter to Susannah "Minnie" Hyland Lamkin.[9] JAMES W. CRALLE, farming, age 24y3m, single, b. Richmond Co., s/o Kenner R. [Richard] and Margaret H. [Saunders] Cralle, *q.v.*, to MINNIE H. LAMKIN, age 17y6m, single, b. Richmond Co., d/o Robert J. [James] and

---

[1] Tasker C. Crabbe (b. 15 FEB 1844, d. 25 JAN 1918 near Oldhams, Va.) and second wife Julia B. McCarty (b. 1847, d. 10 SEP 1886) are bur. in Menokin Baptist Church cemetery. He served in Co. B, 40th Va. Inf., then transferred to Co. C, 9th Va. Cav., C.S.A.
[2] William M.M. Crabb and Ann T. Peck were married 22 FEB 1838 in Richmond Co. by Rev. Lovell Marders.
[3] Madison P. McCarty and Olivia Ann Mitchell were married by bond 10 JAN 1838 in Richmond Co.
[4] Andrew B. Cralle (b. 24 MAR 1841, d. 20 FEB 1900) and wife Martha L. Winstead (b. 27 DEC 1848, d. 28 JUL 1928) are bur. in Gibeon Baptist Church cemetery.
[5] D. Griffin Cralle (b. 1801, d. 7 JUL 1848) and wife Mariah G. Gordon (1805-1873) are bur. in Gibeon Baptist Church cemetery.
[6] George Lunsford Winstead (b. 27 OCT 1813, d. 22 MAR 1898) and wife Martha Hall Beacham Headley (b. 19 DEC 1813, d. 16 MAY 1916) are bur. in Henderson United Methodist Church cemetery. George L. Winstead and Martha H.B. Headley ywere married by bond 8 NOV 1836 in Richmond Co.
[7] Charles R. Cralle (b. 13 SEP 1855, d. 19 SEP 1930) and wife Sarah E. Allison (b. 27 OCT 1865, d. 12 OCT 1939) are bur. in Farnham Baptist Church cemetery.
[8] Gabriel Cralle was previously married 24 NOV 1881 in Richmond Co. to Martha Rollins.
[9] James Walter Cralle (b. 29 DEC 1860, d. 2 JAN 1899) and wife Minnie Hyland Lamkin (b. 20 SEP 1867, d. 5 DEC 1948) are bur. at Calvary United Methodist Church cemetery. Also see Library of Virginia, Bible Records, Lamkin Family Bible Record.

Annie M. [Maria George] Lamkin, *q.v.* Consent 30 MAR 1885 by bride, wit. Annie M. Lamkin, J.W. Cralle, W.A. Crocker. 30 MAR 1885 at *Retreat.* [C10, R:316, R1:64]

Cralle, Joseph S. to Mrs. Sarah E. Omohundro, widow of Samuel Spilman Cralle. JOSEPH S. CRALLE, age 25, single, b. Richmond Co., s/o Samuel and Fanny [M. Belfield] Cralle,[1] to SARAH E. CRALLE, age 24, widow, b. Richmond Co., d/o Thomas and Sarah [P. Hunter] Omohundro.[2] G.H. Northam. 7 JAN 1868. [C4, R:287, R1:22]

Cralle, Kenner Richard, to Margaret H. Saunders.[3] KENNER R. CRALLE, farmer, age 21, single, b. Richmond Co., s/o Kenner R. Cralle and Susan [Mickelberry Street],[4] to MARGARET H. SAUNDERS, age 17, single, b. Richmond Co., d/o Richard and Alice [M. Chilton] Saunders.[5] William H. Kirk. 19 OCT 1854 at Farnham house. [C1, R, R1:1]

Cralle, Kenner Richard, to Bettie Frances Rice.[6] KENNER RICHARD CRALLE, farmer, age 35, widowed, b. Richmond Co., s/o Kenner R. and Susan [Mickelberry Street] Cralle,[7] to BETTIE F. RICE, age 25, single, b. Richmond Co., d/o Peter W. [Webb] and Judith [C. Boothe] Rice.[8] Robert Williamson, M.G. 2 DEC 1868 at *Locust Hill.* [C5, R:254, R1:24]

Cralle, Mott (Col.) to Dinkey Webb (Col.). MOTT CRALLE, oysterman, age 24y8m12d, single, b. Richmond Co., s/o William Cralle and Judy Cralle now Haynie, to DINKEY WEBB, age 19, single, b. Richmond Co., d/o Ned and Molly Webb. Consent 12 JAN 1880 at Milton Wharf by Ned [his X mark] Webb, wit. L. Reede. Allen Brown, minister. 14 JAN 1880 at the bride's home. [C9, R:314, R1:49]

Cralle, Richard Pemberton to Mary Caroline Bryant.[9] RICHARD P. CRALLE, farming, age 24, single, b. Richmond Co., s/o Samuel [Jr.] and Frances M. [Belfield] Cralle, to MARY C. BRYANT, age 27, single, b. Richmond Co., d/o Reuben and Mary [Thrift] Bryant.[10] R.N. Reamy. 7 JAN 1880. [C9; R:314, R1:49]

Cralle, Samuel Spelman[11] to Sarah E. Omohundro. SAMUEL S. CRALLE, farmer, age 27, single, b. Richmond Co., s/o Samuel Cralle, to SARAH E. OMOHUNDRO, age 18, single, b. Richmond Co., d/o Thomas Omohundro. Consent 11 JUL 1861 by father Thos. Omohundro, wit. Wm. H.

---

[1] Samuel Cralle, Jr. and Frances M. Belfield were married by bond 10 SEP 1832 in Richmond Co.

[2] Thomas Omohundro and Sary P. Hunter were married by bond 23 DEC 1824 in Westmoreland Co.

[3] Library of Virginia, Bible Records, Cralle Family Bible Record, 1813-1925. Margaret H. Saunders, b. 13 FEB 1837, d. 10 JAN 1868 at 3 o'clock.

[4] Kenner Cralle and Susan M. Street were married by bond 14 MAY 1832 in Richmond Co.

[5] Richard Saunders and Alice M. Chilton were married by bond 9 MAR 1835 in Lancaster Co.

[6] Kenner Richard Cralle (b. 11 OCT 1833, d. 3 MAR 1914) and wife Bettie F. Rice (b. 1843, d. 22 FEB 1925) are bur. in Farnham Baptist Church cemetery.

[7] Library of Virginia, Bible Records, Reynolds Family Bible Record, 1813-1927, "Susan M. Street was born Jan. 8, 1813." Also, "Susan M. Cralle died at Farnham, Va., Aug. 3, 1887 in the 75th year of her age." She is bur. in Farnham Baptist Church cemetery. Another Bible at LVA, Cralle Family Bible Record, 1813-1925, also records the death of Susan Mickelberry Cralle.

[8] Library of Virginia, Cralle Family Bible Record, 1813-1925, records the death of Judith C. Rice on 18 DEC 1889 age 78y11m23d, and Peter W. Rice, 12 MAY 1892 in his 84th year. Peter W. Rice (b. 17 JAN 1811, d. 12 MAY 1894 [sic]) and wife Judith C. Booth (b. 25 JAN 1811, d. 18 DEC 1889) are bur. in Farnham Baptist Church cemetery. A marriage bond 9 MAR 1840 is found in Northumberland Co. for Peter W. Rice and Judith C. Pursell.

[9] R.P. Cralle (b. 17 DEC 1853, d. 13 DEC 1914) and wife Mary C. Bryant (b. 9 MAY 1852, d. 10 JAN 1935) are bur. in Gibeon Baptist Church cemetery.

[10] Reuben Bryant and Mary Thrift were married 18 DEC 1845 in Richmond Co. by Rev. E.L. Williams.

[11] Samuel Spelman Cralle (d. 2 MAY 1863) was bur. in the Belfield Family cemetery. He served as captain in Co. D, 40th Va., C.S.A., killed in action at Chancellorsville.

Omohundro, sworn by Benjamin Omohundro. James F. Brannin. 11 JUL 1861 at the res. of Thos. Omohundro. [C3, R:123, R1:10]

Cralle, Zebulon (Col.) to Roberta Verne (Col.). ZEBULON[1] CRALLE, oystering, age 24y11m24d, single, b. Richmond Co., s/o William and Judy Cralle, to ROBERTA VERNE, age 16, single, b. Richmond Co., d/o George and Julia Ann Verne. Consent 24 DEC 1883 from *Milton* [sic] by George [his X mark] Vern. Bride "will be 17 years old on the 7th of Augt. 1884." Rev. W. Carter. 25 DEC 1883 at the church. [C10, R:358, R1:60]

Crump, Beverley Tucker to Henrietta Ogle Tayloe.[2] BEVERLEY T. CRUMP, attorney-at-law, age 30, single, b. Richmond City, Va., s/o William W. [Wood] and Mary T. [Susan Tabb] Crump, to ETTA O. TAYLOE, age 23, single, b. Richmond Co., d/o Henry A. [Augustine] and Courtenay N. [Norton Chinn] Tayloe.[3] Rev. Martin Johnson. 15 OCT 1884 at the res. of the bride [*Mount Airy*]. [C10, NN:17 OCT 1884, R:355, R1:62]

Cruzen, Richard (Col.) to Betty Rust (Col.). RICHARD CRUZEN, wagoner, age 21, single, b. Essex Co., s/o William and Mary Cruze[n] (now Mary Bailor), to BETTY RUST, age 24, single, b. Richmond Co., [parents names blank]. Thomas G. Thomas. 27 MAR 1869 in Warsaw, Va. [C5, R, R1:25]

Cummings, Henry to Emma L. Beauchamp. HENRY CUMMINGS, mechanic, age 23, single, b. and res. Wilmington, Del., s/o Alexander and Rebecca Cummings, to EMMA L. BEAUCHAMP,[4] age 21, single, b. Richmond Co., d/o D.C. [Dandridge C.] and Margaret A. [Ann Hynson] Beauchamp [Beacham], *q.v.* Consent 18 OCT 1880 by bride, wit. R.H. Fones, Jr. W.A. Crocker. 18 OCT 1880 at the res. of the bride's father. [C9, R:316, R1:51]

Cundiff, Henry Fleet, Rev.[5] to Elizabeth Caroline Webb. HENRY FLEET CUNDIFF, farmer and Baptist minister, age 35, widower, b. and res. Northumberland Co., s/o Thomas Cundiff and Sarah Downing,[6] to ELIZABETH CAROLINE WEBB, age 27, single, b. Richmond Co., d/o William Webb and Margaret M. Shepherd.[7] Consent 7 DEC 1857 by bride, wits. M.M. Webb, R.H. Lyell. Robert Williamson, M.G. 15 DEC 1857 at *Millwood*. [C1, R1:5]

Cupid, Denis (Col.) to Mrs. Sinah Newton Gibson (Col.). DENIS CUPID,[8] farmer, age 60, widowed, b. Richmond Co., s/o Martin and Millie Cupid, to SINAH GIBSON, age 26, widow, b. Richmond Co., d/o John and Lucy Newton. Consent 17 MAY 1872 by bride Sinah [her X mark] Gibson, wit. Willis T. Mitchell. George Laws. 18 MAY 1872 at *Cedar Grove*. [C6, R:237, R1:31]

Cupid, Nelson (Col.) to Frances Matthews (Col.). NELSON CUPID, laborer, age 32, single, b. Richmond Co., s/o Dennis and Sicily Cupid, to FRANCES MATTHEWS, age 21, single, b.

---

[1] The consent has groom as Zebulon Cralle, while the license and both registers give Zebedee Cralle.

[2] Hon. Beverley Tucker Crump (b. 10 JUN 1854, d. 29 MAR 1930 in Florida) and wife Henrietta Ogle Tayloe (b. 25 JUL 1861, d. 29 AUG 1949 in Richmond, Va.) are bur. in Hollywood Cemetery, Richmond, Va.

[3] Henry Augustine Taylor (b. 27 MAR 1836, d. 19 DEC 1908) and his wife Courtney Norton Chinn (b. 22 MAR 1840, d. 26 MAR 1908) are bur. at *Mount Airy* near Warsaw, Va.

[4] The surname also appears as Beacham.

[5] Henry Fleet Cundiff served in Co. F, 40th Va. Inf., and d. 4 NOV 1880, bur. in Fairfield Baptist Church cemetery at Burgess, Va. with his favorite Bible.

[6] Thomas Cundiff, ward of William Sydnor, and Sally Downing, d/o Betsy Downing, were married by bond 10 DEC 1821 in Richmond Co.

[7] William Webb and Margaret M.C. Shepherd were married by bond 17 NOV 1825 in Richmond Co.

[8] The surname also appears as Cupit.

Richmond Co., d/o Leroy and Adeline Matthews. Consent 20 DEC 1866 by mother Adeline [her X mark] Matthews, wit. S.E. Mitchell. George Laws. 22 DEC 1866. [C4, R:272, R1:18]

Curry, Samuel (Col.) to Henrietta Maiden (Col.). SAMUEL CURRY, oysterman, age 21y11m, single, b. Richmond Co., s/o Henry and Milly Curry, to HENRIETTA MAIDEN, age 22, single, b. Richmond Co., d/o [Powell] and Priscilla Maiden. Allen Brown, minister. 22 JAN 1873 at the bride's house. [C6, R:235, R1:33]

Curry, Samuel (Col.) to Lulie Churchwell (Col.). SAMUEL CURRY, oystering, age 37, widowed, b. Richmond Co., s/o Henry and Millie Curry, to LULIE CHURCHWELL, age 20, single, b. Richmond Co., d/o Harry and Sarah Churchwell. Consent 21 DEC 1889 from Ivanhoe, Va. by bride, wit. Lillian [illegible]. Rev. Jacob Robinson, Pastor of Zion Church. 23 DEC 1889 at Mt. Zion Church, Ivanhoe, Va. [C12, R:328, R1:75]

Curtis, Henry C. to Roberta J. Davis. HENRY C. CURTIS, farmer, age 60, widowed, b. Somerset Co., Md., s/o John B. Curtis, to ROBERTA J. DAVIS, age 30, single, b. Richmond Co., d/o Robert Davis. W.A. Crocker. 22 JUL 1880. [C9, R:316, R1:51]

D

Dale, Thomas (Col.) to Eliza Davis (Col.). THOMAS DATE, coachman, age 29, single, b. Richmond Co., s/o Henry and Jenny Dale, to ELIZA DAVIS, age 28, single, b. Richmond Co., names of parents "omitted for good cause." Thomas G. Thomas. 28 MAY 1868 at minister's house. [C4, R:254, R1:24]

Dameron, Joseph to Amelia A.V. Ambrose. JOSEPH DAMERON, farmer, age 28, single, b. Richmond Co., s/o John C. and Esther [Shelly] Dameron,[1] to AMMELIA A.V. AMBROSE, age 21, single, b. Richmond Co., d/o R.B. [Redman B.] and Aphia [Apphia C. Gutridge] Ambrose. Consent 20 DEC 1869 by bride Amealiea A.V. [her X mark] Ambrose, wits. father R.B. Ambrose, James Barrett. H.H. Fones. 22 DEC 1869 at R.B. Ambrose's. [C5, R, R1:27]

Dameron, Richard Christopher to Mildred Cleopatra "Minnie" Fallin.[2] RICHARD C. DAMERON, merchant, age 36, single, b. Richmond Co., s/o Leroy O. [Oldham] and Frances R. [Walker] Dameron,[3] to MINNIE C. FALLIN, age 19, single, b. Richmond Co., d/o Richard L. [Luke] and Martha [Dorothy Stephens] Fallin.[4] Consent in OCT 1889 by parties, wit. Richard L. Fallin. A. Judson Reamy. 15 OCT 1889 at the home of Mr. W.C. Middleton. [C12, R:328, R1:74]

Dameron, Richard L. to Alice Harper. RICHARD L. DAMERON, farmer, age 28, single, b. Richmond Co., res. Westmoreland Co., s/o John C. and Hester [Esther Shelly] Dameron, to ALICE HARPER, age 25, single, b. Richmond Co., d/o Benjamin and Betsy Harper. Consent 5 FEB 1872 by bride Alice [her X mark] Harper, wit. Rodham A. [his X mark] Douglas. Elder James A. Weaver. 8 FEB 1872 at the house of Benjamin Harper. [C6, R:237, R1:31]

---

[1] John C. Dameron and Esther Shelly were married by bond 7 APR 1837 in Richmond Co.
[2] Richard C. Dameron (b. 26 JUL 1844, d. 12 JUL 1909) and his wife Mildred C. Fallin [McKenney] (b. 7 MAR 1870, d. 25 JAN 1957), bur. Gibeon Baptist Church cemetery.
[3] Leroy Dameron and Frances Walker were married by bond 15 JUL 1820 in Northumberland Co.
[4] Richard Luke Dameron (b. 24 OCT 1836, d. 26 JUL 1915) and wife Martha Dorothy Stephens (b. 20 SEP 1840, d. 29 AUG 1924). He served in Co. G, 15th Va. Cav., C.S.A.

Dameron, Richard L. to Mary F. Bartlett. R.L. DAMERON, farming, age 45, widowed, b. Richmond Co., s/o John C. and Hester [Esther Shelly] Dameron, to MARY F. BARTLETT, age 35, single, b. Westmoreland Co., [names of parents not completed]. Consent 7 NOV 1887 by parties, wit. Th. T. Lewis. R.N. Reamy. 8 DEC 1887. [C11, R:293, R1:71]

Dandridge, Alfred (Col.) to Sallie Gillis (Col.). ALFRED DANDRIDGE, farmer, age 26, single, b. Richmond Co., s/o George and Rebecca Dandridge, to SALLIE GILLIS, age 19, single, b. Richmond Co., d/o Cyrus and Judy Gillis. Consent 23 DEC 1871 by father Cyrus [his X mark] Gillis, wits. S. Barron, Jim [his X mark] Sale. George Laws. 28 DEC 1871. [C6, R:245, R1:30]

Dandridge, Alfred (Col.) to Winnie Ann Holmes (Col.). ALFRED DANDRIDGE, farming, age 36, widowed, b. Essex Co., s/o George and Rebecca Dandridge, to WINNIE ANN HOLMES, age 22, single, b. Richmond Co., d/o James Holmes and Eve Holmes (dec'd.). Consent 17 AUG 1886 by bride's father James [his X mark] Holmes, wit. Ned L. Dandridge. Rev. George Laws. 19 AUG 1886 at *Cherry Hill*. [C11, R:316, R1:68]

Dandridge, Dennis (Col.) to Jinnie Rollins (Col.). DENNIS DANDRIDGE, farming, age 24, single, b. Richmond Co., s/o George Dandridge and Sukie Hubbard, to JINNIE ROLLINS, age 23, single, b. Essex Co., d/o Edmund and Martha Rollins. Oath by S.G. Dishman as to ages of parties. George [his X mark] Laws, wit. John D. Garland. 25 MAR 1880 at Dean's. [C9, R:315, R1:50]

Dandridge, Edward Lewis (Col.) to Isabella Coleston (Col.). EDWARD LEWIS DANDRIDGE, laborer, age 23, single, b. Richmond Co., s/o George and Rebecca Dandridge, to ISABELLA COLESTON, age 22, single, b. Richmond Co., d/o Winny Coleston [name of father not known]. George Laws. 20 APR 1867 at the res. of J.H. Barton. [C4, R:286, R1:21]

Dandridge, Robert (Col.) to Augusta Holmes (Col.). ROBERT DANDRIDGE, farmer, age 26, single, b. Richmond Co., s/o George and Rebecca Dandridge, to AUGUSTA HOLMES, age 17, single, b. Richmond Co., d/o James and Eve Holmes. Consent 16 FEB 1878 by James [his X mark] Holmes, wit. [A.]H. Burton. George Laws. 17 FEB 1878 at New Zion Church.[1] [C8, R:310, R1:44]

Daniel, John H. to Mrs. Georgianna Garland, widow of William Ryland Jeter, d. 8 JAN 1870 in Baltimore, Md. JOHN H. DANIEL, merchant, age 35, single, b. Pittsylvania Co., res. Baltimore, Md., s/o Hezekiah G. and Mary [Watkins] Daniel, to GEORGIANNA JETER, age 30, widow, b. Richmond Co., d/o James V. and Juliet F.J. [Lyell][2] Garland. Joseph H. Davis. 25 NOV 1867 at [*Plain View*] res. of J.V. Garland. [C4, R:287, R1:22]

Darby, James (Col.) to Charlotte Stewart (Col.). JAMES DARBY, oysterman, age 21y6m, single, b. Richmond Co., s/o Washington and Emily Darby, to CHARLOTTE STEWART, age 21y9m20d, single, b. Richmond Co., d/o Henry and Hannah Stewart. Consent 28 FEB 1878 by bride Charlotte [her X mark] Stewart, wit. Geo. [his X mark] Veney. Allen Brown, minister. 28 FEB 1878 at the bride's home. [C8, R:310, R1:44]

---

[1] New Zion Baptist Church is located on the east side of Route 624 ad the junction with Route 636.
[2] Library of Virginia, Bible Records, Lyell Family Bible Records, 1778-1897, "Juliet F.J. Lyell, Daughter of John Lyell & Lucy [Sandford] his Wife was born Feby. 28th 1816." Also, "John Lyell and Miss Lucy Sandford Were married Decr. 9th 1796."

Darby, James (Col.) to Mary Veney (Col.). JAMES DARBY, farming, age 30, widowed, b. Richmond Co., s/o Washington and Emily Darby, to MARY VENEY, age 23, single, b. Richmond Co., d/o Hannah Veney. Consent 30 JUN 1888 by mother Hannah [her X mark] Veney. Rev. L. Marshall. 1 JUL 1888 at Second Baptist Church. [C11, R:316, R1:72]

Darby, John W. (Col.) to Rose Roan (Col.). JOHN W. DARBY, farming, age 34, widowed, b. Richmond Co., s/o Washington and Emily Darby, to ROSE ROAN, age 26, single, b. Richmond Co., d/o Thomas and Lucy Roan. Rev. L. Harrod. 25 DEC 1890 at res. of Charles Lavere. [C12, R:324, R1:78]

Darby, Washington, Jr. (Col.) to Edmonia Williams (Col.). WASHINGTON DARBY, JR., laborer, age 21y10½m, single, b. Richmond Co., s/o Washington Darby, Sr. and Emily, to EDMONIA WILLIAMS, age 16, single, b. Richmond Co., d/o Edward and Evelina Williams. Consent 1 OCT 1873 by bride; also consent by John Mayden who notes bride is daughter of his sister Evelina Williams who is in Washington, D.C. Travis Corbin, D.D. 2 OCT 1873 at *Cabinet Hall*. [C6, R:235, R1:34]

Davenport, John T. to Fannie E. Davenport. JOHN T. DAVENPORT, farming, age 38, widowed, b. Lancaster Co., res. Northumberland Co., s/o Joseph and Maria B. Davenport, to FANNIE E. DAVENPORT, age 24, single, b. Richmond Co., d/o William E. Davenport and Ellen Barnes. Consent undated by bride. E.P. Parham, minister M.E. Church South. 23 OCT 1889 at res. of the bride's father. [C12, R:328, R1:74]

Davenport, Joseph[1] to Lavalia P. Hintin. JOSEPH DAVENPORT, farmer, age 23, widowed, b. Richmond Co., s/o Thomas [D.] and Lucy [Davenport] Davenport,[2] to LAVALIA P. HINTIN, age 20, single, b. Northumberland Co., d/o George and Catharine Hintin. No minister return. 4 OCT 1860. [C2, R:154, R1:9]

Davenport, Rufus Samuel[3] to Susan Thomas. RUFUS S. DAVENPORT, farming, age 35, single, b. Richmond Co., s/o William E. Davenport and Ellen Barnes, *q.v.*, to SUSAN THOMAS, age 17, single, b. Lancaster Co., d/o Andrew and Bettie Thomas. Consent 18 DEC 1890 by bride, wits. Mrs. Bettie Thomas, James L. Conley. J. Manning Dunaway. 19 NOV 1890 at the bride's residence. [C12, R:324, R1:77]

Davenport, William E. to Ellen Barnes. WILLIAM E. DEVENPORT [sic],[4] farmer, age 32, widower, b. Richmond Co., s/o Joseph [P.] and Lucy [T. Simmonds] Davenport,[5] to ELLEN BARNS [sic], age 22, single, b. Richmond Co., d/o Samuel and Frances [Edwards] Barnes.[6] Consent 22 APR 1854 by bride, wit. W.H. Davenport. John Goodwin, M.G. 26 APR 1854 at Joseph W. Bryant's. [C1, R, R1:1]

Davenport, William E. to Julia A. Rice. WILLIAM E. DAVENPORT, farming, age 64, widowed, b. Richmond Co., s/o Joseph [P.] and Lucy T. [Simmonds] Davenport, to JULIA A. RICE, age 45,

---

[1] Joseph Davenport served in Co. G, 40th Va. Inf., C.S.A., and died 12 AUG 1896 of typhoid fever in Lara, Va.
[2] Thomas D. Davenport and Lucy Davenport were married 4 JAN 1826 in Richmond Co. by Rev. Jeremiah B. Jeter.
[3] Rufus S. Davenport (b. 26 JAN 1856, d. 4 JAN 1935), bur. Lebanon Baptist Church cemetery, Lancaster Co.
[4] The Register version gives surname Davenport.
[5] Joseph Davenport and Lucy Simmonds were married by bond 10 DEC 1817 in Richmond Co.
[6] Samuel Barnes and Frances Edwards were married by bond 22 FEB 1831 in Northumberland Co.

single, b. Lancaster Co., d/o Thomas and Nancy [C. Hazzard] Rice.[1] Consent 23 NOV 1885 by bride, no wit. F.W. Claybrook. 26 NOV 1885 in Lancaster Co. [C10, R:318, R1:65]

Davenport, William J. to Virginia A. Haynie. WILLIAM J. DAVENPORT, farming, age 26, single, b. Richmond Co., s/o William E. Davenport and Ellen Barnes, *q.v.*, to VIRGINIA A. HAYNIE, age 22, single, b. Richmond Co., d/o Joseph and Betsey Haynie. Consent 19 DEC 1884 by bride, wit. John Hazzard. W.H. Edwards. 21 DEC 1884 at the res. of Mr. Haynie. [C10, R:356, R1:63]

Davis, Alexander to Mary French.[2] ALEXANDER DAVIS, farmer, age 33, single, b. Richmond Co., s/o Alfred and Sally [B. Self] Davis,[3] to MARY FRENCH, age 33, single, b. Richmond Co., d/o Joseph and Mary French. G.H. Northam. 19 NOV 1881 at Totusky Baptist Church. [C9; R:338, R1:54]

Davis, Andrew J. to Lucy Ann Clarke. ANDREW J. DAVIS, farmer, age 22, single, b. Richmond Co., s/o Luke W. and Mahala B. [Kennan] Davis,[4] to LUCY ANN CLARKE, age 21, single, b. Richmond Co., s/o Edwin and Rebecca Clarke. Consent 25 DEC 1866 by bride. Robert Williamson, M.G. 27 DEC 1866 at Durrettsville, Va. [C4, R:273, R1:19]

Davis, Dandridge to Alice Clarke.[5] DANDRIDGE DAVIS, farmer, age 24, single, b. Richmond Co., s/o Alfred and Sallie [B. Self] Davis,[6] to ELIS CLARK [sic], age 20, single, b. Richmond Co., d/o John H. [Henry] and Lucinda J. [Jane Bryant] Clark.[7] Elder James A. Weaver. 12 MAR 1867 at res. of J.H. Clark. [C4, R:286, R1:20]

Davis, Edward (Col.) to Ibby Harrod (Col.). EDWARD DAVIS, age 50, single, b. Richmond Co., s/o David and Maria Davis, to IBBY HARROD, age 40, single, b. Richmond Co., parents names "omitted for good cause." Thomas G. Thomas. 30 JAN 1867 at the house of J.B.C. [C4]

Davis, Floyd F. to Sufronia Clark.[8] FLOYD F. DAVIS, engineer, age 24, single, b. Richmond Co., s/o Robert and Isabella Davis, to SOPHRONIA CLARK, age 18, single, b. Richmond Co., d/o Spilman B. and Margaret [Hale] Clark, *q.v.* Consent 19 OCT 1883 by parties and Spillman B. Clark. G.H. Northam. 21 OCT 1883. [C10, R:357, R1:59]

Davis, Henry to Mrs. Elizabeth Clark Holeva. HENRY DAVIS, farming, age 32, widowed, b. Richmond Co., res. Northumberland Co., s/o William and Sarah Davis, to ELIZABETH HOLEVA, age 32, widow, b. Richmond Co., d/o Joseph Clark. Consent 12 MAY 1886 by Robert R. Middleton. G.H. Northam. 13 MAY 1886 at res. of J. Clark. [C11, R:316, R1:67]

Davis, James H. to Roselia Keyser. JAMES H. DAVIS, farming, age 24, single, b. Richmond Co., s/o Jane Davis, to ROSELIA KEYSER, age 16, single, b. Richmond Co., d/o James A. and Nancy A. Keyser. Consent 30 JUL 1889 by bride Roseler [her X mark] Keyzer, James A. [his

---

[1] Thomas Rice and Nancy C. Hazzard were married by bond 6 MAR 1838 in Lancaster Co.
[2] Alexander Davis (b. 1845, d. 15 SEP 1915) and his wife Mary French (1855-1920) are bur. at Totuskey Baptist Church cemetery.
[3] Alfred Davis and Sally B. Self were married 27 JAN 1841 in Richmond Co. by Rev. William N. Ward.
[4] Luke W. Davis and Mrs. Mahalah B. Kennan were married 13 APR 1843 in Richmond Co. by Rev. William N. Ward.
[5] Dandridge Davis (b. 1842, d. 1905) and his wife Alice Clarke (b. 1846, d. 3 JAN 1926) are bur. at Totuskey Baptist Church cemetery.
[6] Alfred Davis and Sally B. Self were married 27 JAN 1841 in Richmond Co. by Rev. William N. Ward.
[7] John H. Clarke and Lucy Bryant were married by bond 24 FEB 1835 in Richmond Co.
[8] Floyd F. Davis (1857-1912) and his wife Sufronia F. Clark (1866-1924) are bur. at Totuskey Baptist Church cemetery.

X mark] Keyzer, and Nancy A. [her X mark] Keyzer, wit. J.D. Connellee. G.H. Northam. 4 AUG 1889 at *Glenmore*. [C12, R:327, R1:74]

Davis, James L. to Eleanor G. Tucker.[1] JAMES L. DAVIS, farming, age 30, single, b. Richmond Co., s/o Joseph H. and Martha Davis, to ELEANOR G. TUCKER, age 20, single, b. Richmond Co., d/o William E. and Judith L. [Tune] Tucker.[2] Consent 19 JUN 1888 from Farnham, Va. by bride, wit. C.C. Lindon. Charles N. Betts. 20 JUN 1888 at the res. of W.E. Tucker. [C11, R:316, R1:72]

Davis, John A. to Milly Bowen. JOHN A. DAVIS, farmer, age 23, single, b. Richmond Co., s/o Henry and Elizabeth [P. English] Davis, to MILLY BOWEN, age 21, single, b. Richmond Co., d/o John and Maria Bowen. Consent 1 APR 1863 by bride Milly [her X mark] Bowen, wits. Samuel R. Franklin, V. [his X mark] Anthony. G.H. Northam. 5 APR 1863 at *Woodbine* in Westmoreland Co. [C3, R:160, R1:12]

Davis, John R. to Catharine C. Clark. JOHN R. DAVIS, farmer, age 36, widowed, b. Richmond Co., s/o John and Joanna [Jackson] Davis, to CATHARINE C. CLARK, age 21, single, b. Richmond Co., d/o Edward and Rebecca [M. Dobyns] Clark.[3] Robert Williamson, M.G. 16 JAN 1868 at Durrettsville, Va. [C4, R:253, R1:23]

Davis, John Robeson to Isabella L. Hammack. JOHN ROBESON DAVIS, farming, age 26, single, b. Richmond Co., s/o John and Jane Davis, to IZEBELL HAMMACK, age 17, single, b. Richmond Co., d/o Rhody C. and Catharine [M. Yeatman] Hammack.[4] Consent 27 JAN 1857 by father Rodham C. Hammack, wit. Thos. G. Williams. A. Dulaney, minister. 27 JAN 1857. [C1, R:159, R1:4]

Davis, Joseph (Col.) to Elizabeth Monday (Col.). JOSEPH DAVIS, farmer, age 24, single, b. Richmond Co., s/o Thomas and Julia Davis, to ELIZABETH MONDAY, age 22, single, b. Essex Co., d/o George Monday. Consent 23 JAN 1878 by bride Elizabeth [her X mark] Monday, wit. A.P. Wilson. George [his X mark] Laws. 24 JAN 1878 at *Mulberry Island*. [C8, R:310, R1:44]

Davis, Nathan N. to Susan E. Swain. NATHAN N. DAVIS, farming, age 23, single, b. Richmond Co., s/o E.J. Davis, to SUSAN E. SWAIN, age 21, single, b. Northumberland Co., d/o Richard and Betsey Swain. G.H. Northam. 7 JAN 1880. [C9, R:314, R1:49]

Davis, Richard W., to Jane Barnes. Consent 15 MAR 1855 by bride, wit. William E. Hill. No license or minister return. [C1]

Davis, Stephen (Col.) to Harriet E. Jackson (Col.). STEPHEN DAVIS, farmer, age 22, single, b. Charlotte Co., s/o Stephen and Sophia Davis, to HARRIET E. JACKSON, age 22, single, b. Richmond Co., d/o Benj. Askins and Mary Jackson. Isaiah Hankinson. 25 DEC 1867 at Mulberry Chapel. [C4, R:287, R1:22]

---

[1] James L. Davis (b. 8 FEB 1855, d. 3 NOV 1935) and wife Eleanor G. Tucker (b. 13 FEB 1868, d. 23 AUG 1931) are bur. in Calvary United Methodist Church cemetery.
[2] William E. Tucker and his wife Judith L. Tune (1842-1915) are bur. at Totuskey Baptist Church cemetery. His marker is broken and fallen. They were married 12 DEC 1866 in Northumberland Co.
[3] Edward Clarke and Rebecca M. Dobyns were married 27 JUN 1844 in Richmond Co. by Rev. William N. Ward.
[4] Rodham Hammock and Catherine M. Yeatman, d/o Ann H. Yeatman, were married by bond 8 DEC 1838 in Westmoreland Co.

Davis, Sydnor to Susan Woollard. SYDNOR DAVIS, farmer, age 53, widowed, b. Richmond Co., s/o John and Joanah [Jackson] Davis, to SUSAN WOOLLARD, age 32, single, b. Lancaster Co., d/o Lemuel and Affia [Apphia T. Tune] Woollard. James A. Weaver. 7 JUN 1870 at the res. of Lemuel Woollard. [C5, R:233, R1:28]

Davis, William L. to Eliza A. Fidler. WILLIAM L. DAVIS, farmer, age 24, single, b. Richmond Co., s/o Sydnor and Mary [Woollard] Davis,[1] to ELIZA A. FIDLER, age 21, single, b. Essex Co., d/o Joseph and Ann [Ferrill] Fidler.[2] Robert Williamson, M.G. 6 MAY 1867 at Joseph Fidler's. [C4, R:286, R1:21]

Davis, William P. to Mary S. Smith. WILLIAM P. DAVIS, farming, age 24, single, b. Richmond Co., s/o William H. and Maria Davis, to MARY S. SMITH, age 18, single, b. Richmond Co., d/o Ann Smith [name of father not given]. Rev. A.D. Reynolds. 19 JUL 1883 at the res. of J.C. Smith. [C10, R:357, R1:59]

Dawson, Branson (Col.) to Martha Carter (Col.). BRANSON DAWSON, farming, age 23, single, b. Northumberland Co., s/o Joseph Gordon and Hannah Dawson, to MARTHA CARTER, age 16, single, b Richmond Co., d/o Walter Carter and Froney Bailey. Consent 1 JAN 1880 by bride at Farnham Church, wit. G.W. Cam[p]bell. A. Brown. 7 JAN 1880. [C9, R:314, R1:49]

Dawson, Stepter (Col.) to Georgeanna Hill (Col.). STEPTER DAWSON, farming, age 22, single, b. Richmond Co., s/o John Henderson and Hannah Dawson, to GEORGEANNA HILL, age 15, single, b. Richmond Co., d/o William and Frances Ann Hill. Consent 2 APR 1881 in Washington District by mother Frances [her X mark] Ann Hill, wit. Peter [Fitzhugh]. Allen Brown, minister. 8 APR 1881 at the bride's home. [C9, R:335, R1:52]

Dawson, Steptoe Whitfield to Anna Tyler.[3] STEPTOE DAWSON, farmer, age 22, single, b. Richmond Co., s/o Spellman and Elizabeth [Littrell] Dawson, to ANNA TYLER, age 17, single, b. Richmond Co., d/o James and Frances [Keyser] Tyler, *q.v.* Consent by mother Frances [her X mark] Tyler, and bride, wits. R.G. Scates, J.H. Purcell. J.B. DeBerry, P.C. 5 DEC 1877 at the res. of the bride's father. [C8, R:307, R1:43]

Debreau, William to Addie Brooks. WILLIAM DEBREAU, fisherman, age 31, widowed, b. Philadelphia, Pa., s/o Michael and Rachel Debreau, to ADDIE BROOKS, age 21y2m, single, b. Essex Co., d/o Stableton [sic] and Rosa [Hayes] Brooks.[4] Oath by Leonard M. Sheaffer as to age of bride. Beverley D. Tucker. 7 MAY 1881 at the res. of Mr. Shaeffer. [C9, R:336, R1:53]

Delano, George Taylor [1848-1932] to Naomi Iebydo Clark. GEORGE T. DELANO, farmer, age 21, single, b. Richmond Co., s/o Joseph [Peterson] and Lucinda [Lyell Self] Delano, to NAOMA IEBYDO CLARK, age 16, single, b. Richmond Co., d/o John H. and Lucinda [Bryant] Clark.[5] Consent, undated, by parties, wit. J.P. Delano. Elder James A. Weaver. 1 DEC 1869 at the res. of the bride's father. [C5, R, R1:27]

---

[1] Sydnor Davis and Mary Woollard were married by bond 17 JAN 1840 in Richmond Co.
[2] The marriage bond 24 MAR 1840 in Essex Co. is for Joseph H. Fiddler to Jane Ferrill.
[3] Steptoe Whitfield Dawson (b. 9 FEB 1855, d. 21 SEP 1929 in Nuttsville, Va.) and his first wife Anna Tyler (b. 25 JAN 1861, d. 7 SEP 1898) are bur. in the Dawson Family Cemetery, near Nuttsville, Va.
[4] S.M. Brooks and Rosa Hayes were married by bond 21 SEP 1840 in Essex Co.
[5] John H. Clarke and Lucy Bryant were married by bond 24 FEB 1835 in Richmond Co.

Delano, George Taylor to Matilda Frances Clark.[1] GEORGE T. DELANO, farmer, age 23, widowed, b. Richmond Co., s/o Joseph P. [Peterson] and Lucinda [Lyell Self] Delano, to MATILDA FRANCES CLARK, age 24, single, b. Richmond Co., d/o John and Mary Clark. Elder James A. Weaver. 30 AUG 1871 at the res. of the bride groom. [C6, R:245, R1:30]

Delano, George Taylor to Henrietta Bowen.[2] GEORGE T. DELANO, farmer, age 41, widowed, b. Richmond Co., s/o J.P. [Joseph Peterson] and Lucinda [Lyell Self] Delano, to RETTA BOWEN [sic], age 22, single, b. Richmond Co., d/o Kelley [and Julia Ann Bulger] Bowen, *q.v.* G.M. Connelly. 9 AUG 1889 at *Pittsville*. [C12, R:328, R1:74]

Delano, Joseph Patterson [sometimes Peterson] to Mrs. Ella Susan Sisson, widow of Eli Patterson Packett.[3] JOSEPH P. DELANO, public officer and farmer, age 54, widowed, b. Westmoreland Co., s/o George and Nancy Delano, to ELLA S. PACKETT, age 24, widow, b. Richmond Co., d/o James and Susan [Crowder] Sisson.[4] Consent by bride, wit. J.F. Alexander. G.H. Northam. 8 MAY 1878. [C8, R:311, R1:45]

Delano, Moses Self to Susan Ann Packett.[5] MOSES DELANO, carpenter, age 20, single, b. Westmoreland Co., s/o Joseph [Peterson] and Lucinda [Lyell Self] Delano, to SUSAN ANN PACKETT,[6] age 17, single, b. Richmond Co., d/o James L. [Lewis][7] and Jane [sic] Packett. Consent 18 JAN 1871 by father James L. Packett, and J.P. Delano, wit. B.W. Brockenbrough. Elder James A. Weaver. 25 JAN 1871 at res. of bride's father. [C5, R:244, R1:29]

Delano, Moses Self to Harriett 'Hallie" Virginia Packett.[8] MOSES S. DELANO, carpenter, age 22, widowed, b. Westmoreland Co., s/o Joseph P. [Peterson] and Lucinda [Lyell Self] Delano, to HARRIETT V. PACKETT, age 17, single, b. Richmond Co., d/o James L. [Lewis] and Virginia [Parr] Packett.[9] Consent 28 DEC 1872 by parties. Elder James A. Weaver. 28 DEC 1872 at the res. of Joseph Delano. [C6, R:238, R1:31]

Delano, William Joseph to Virginia Elizabeth Packett.[10] JOSEPH WILLIAM [sic] DELANO, farmer, age 22, single, b. Richmond Co., s/o Joseph P. [Patterson] and Lucinda [Jane Lyell] Delano, to VIRGINIA ELIZABETH PACKETT, age 17y7m, single, b. Richmond Co., d/o Eli [Patterson] Packett and Ella S. [Susan Sisson] Packett now Delano. Consent 27 AUG 1878 by Ellen E. Delano, John S. Packett, wit. J.F. Alexander. G.H. Northam. 28 AUG 1878. [C8, R:311, R1:45]

---

[1] George T. Delano (b. 8 SEP 1848, d. 12 DEC 1932) and wife Matilda F. Clark (b. 18 JUL 1848, d. 2 DEC 1888). He is bur. at Corinth Methodist Episcopal Church cemetery at Avalon, Va. with his third wife Henrietta Bowen.

[2] George T. Delano and his third wife Henrietta Bowen (b. 3 SEP 1869, d. 11 OCT 1929) are bur. in Corinth Methodist Episcopal Church cemetery, Avalon, Va.

[3] Joseph Peterson Delano (b. 3 APR 1824, d. 9 JAN 1911) and his second wife Ella Susan Sisson (1840-1911) are bur. in the Packett-Delano Family Burial Ground near Warsaw, Va. He served in Co. G, 15th Va. Cav., C.S.A.

[4] James Sisson and Susan Crowder were married by bond 16 DEC 1828 in Richmond Co.

[5] Susan Ann Packett Delano (b. 24 SEP 1853, d. 10 SEP 1872) is bur. in the Packett-Delano Family Burial Ground, near Warsaw, Va.

[6] Surname appears as Packet and Packett.

[7] James L. Packett (b. 5 JUN 1810, d. 20 OCT 1871) and wife Virginia Jane Parr (b. 15 AUG 1830, d. 15 NOV 1913), are bur. in the Packett Family Cemetery near Warsaw, Va.

[8] Moses Self Delano (b. 9 JUL 1850, d. 17 MAR 1923) and his second wife Hallie Virginia Packett (b. 25 JUL 1855, d. 22 SEP 1906), are bur. in the Packett-Delano Family Burial Ground, near Warsaw, Va.

[9] Virginia Parr (b. 15 AUG 1830, d. 15 NOV 1913), wife of James Lewis Packett (b. 5 JUN 1810, d. 20 OCT 1871), and daughter of Henry Parr and Hallie Carter, is bur. with her husband in the Packett-Delano Family Burial Ground, near Warsaw, Va. James L. Packett and Virginia Parr were married 28 OCT 1852 in Richmond Co. by Rev. Elijah L. Williams.

[10] William Joseph Delano (b. 19 DEC 1855-d. 10 JAN 1926 at his home *Level Green* near Wellford's Wharf) and wife Virginia Elizabeth Packett (b. 4 JAN 1860, d. 2 SEP 1932) are bur. in Warsaw Baptist Church cemetery. The marriage record has Joseph William Delano, while his tombstone is William Joseph Delano.

Denson, Terry to Sophia E. Hudson. Oath by bride 4 APR 1881 regarding her birth. No license or minister return. [C9]

Dericksen, Edward to Mahaley Anne Harris, b. 1 MAR 1832. EDWARD DERICKSEN, sailor, age 37, widowed, b. Delaware, s/o Joseph and Rebecca Derrickson, to MAHALA[1] A. HARRIS, age 25, single, b. Richmond Co., d/o John and Mehaley/Mahaly Harris.[2] Consent 4 MAR 1857 by bride, wit. Jane Mc. Harris. A. Dulaney, minister. 5 MAR 1857. [C1, R:159, R1]

Dickerson, Reuben (Col.) to Judy Yeatman (Col.). REUBEN DICKERSON, farmer, age 46, single, b. Hanover Co., s/o Thomas and Virginia Dickerson, to JUDY YEATMAN, age 24, single, b. Richmond Co., d/o George and Winnie Yeatman. Thomas G. Thomas. 7 DEC 1876 at the house of George Yeatman. [C7, R:306, R1:41]

Didlake, Wilfred T. to Mary J. Gallagher. WILFRED T. DIDLAKE, sudler, age 24. single, b. and res. Baltimore, Md., s/o Henry H. and Matilda C. Didlake, to MARY J. GALLAGHER, age 20, single, b. Richmond Co., d/o James A. and Lucy Gallagher. Elder James A. Weaver. 8 NOV 1871 at James Gallagher's. [C6, R:245, R1:30]

Dixon, Robert A. to Harriet Ann Bryant.[3] ROBERT A. DIXON, farmer, age 21, single, b. Northumberland Co., s/o Thomas and Rachel [Winson] Dixon,[4] to HARRIET A. BRYANT, age 25, single, b. Richmond Co., d/o Richard [D.] and Lucy [C. Elmore] Bryant.[5] W.A. Crocker. 2 JUN 1874 at the res. of James Clarke. [C7, R:230, R1:36]

Dobyns, Augustine W. to Lavalia Lewis. AUGUSTINE W. DOBYNS, farmer, age 29, widowed, b. Richmond Co., s/o Chichester and Frances [L. Bryant] Dobyns,[6] to LAVALIA LEWIS, age 22, single, b. Northumberland Co., d/o Alfred B. and Lucinda [Lucy Booth] Lewis.[7] E.L. Williams. 6 FEB 1861. [C3, R:123, R1:10]

Dodson, Charles E.M. to Mrs. Ollif M. Beazley. CHARLES E.M. DODSON, sailing, age 27, single, b. Richmond Co., s/o Milton and Mary J. Dodson, to OLLIF M. BEAZLEY, age 28, widow, b. Richmond Co., d/o Samuel and Ann Douglas. Consent 19 FEB 1889 by parties. G.H. Northam 20 FEB 1889 at Mrs. Beazley's. [C12, R:327, R1:74]

Dodson, Farrol L. to Saphronia C. Balderson.[8] FARROL L. DODSON, mechanic, age 20y8m, single, b. and res. Northumberland Co., s/o Presley M. and Eliza Ann [Pearson] Dodson,[9] to SAPHRONIA E. BALDERSON, age 18y7m, single, b. Richmond Co., d/o John W. [William] and Elizabeth [Lewis Hudson] Balderson, *q.v.* Consent 23 MAY 1884 by parties, Presley M. Dodson, John W. [his X mark] Balderson, wit. Charles L. Thrift. R.N. Reamy. 29 MAY 1884. [C10, NN:6 JUN 1884, R:354, R1:62]

---

[1] License gives bride's name as Mehaly A. Harris, which is closer to the spelling of Mehaley found in the family Bible.
[2] Also see Library of Virginia, Bible Records, Harris Family Bible Record, 1811-1982.
[3] Robert A. Dixon (1848-1913) and wife Harriett Ann Bryant (b. 15 FEB 1854, d. 10 MAY 1929) are bur. at Henderson United Methodist Church cemetery, Hyacinth, Va.
[4] Thomas Dixon and Mrs. Rachel Winson were married by bond 29 DEC 1844 in Northumberland Co.
[5] Richard D. Bryant and Lucy C. Elmore were married by bond 3 MAR 1847 in Northumberland Co.
[6] Augustine W. Dobyns, bachelor, and Sarah J. Hale, spinster, were married 8 FEB 1853 in Richmond Co. by Rev. Elijah L. Williams. Chichester Dobyns and Fanny L. Bryant were married by bond 25 DEC 1811 in Richmond Co.
[7] Alfred Lewis and Lucy Booth were married by bond 2 DEC 1834 in Northumberland Co.
[8] Farrol L. Dodson (b. 1 SEP 1863, d. 2 JUN 1955) and wife Saphronia C. Balderson (b. 3 OCT 1866, d. 15 MAR 1915) are bur. in Roseland Cemetery, Reedville, Va. Farrol is the spelling on his tombstone, but one may find Feriol Dodson in records.
[9] Presley M. Dodson and Eliza A. Pearson were married 8 NOV 1854 in Northumberland Co.

Dodson, Ferdinand to Mary J. Hayden. FERDINAND DODSON, farming, age 23, single, b. Westmoreland Co., s/o Alex [Alexander] and Catharine [Bryant] Dodson,[1] to MARY J. HAYDEN, age 22, single, b. Richmond Co., d/o John D. and Jane Hayden. Consent 4 JAN 1881 by parties Ferdinand [his X mark] Dodson, and Mary J. [her X mark] Hayden. G.H. Northam. 6 JAN 1881 at the res. of Mr. Hayden. [C9, R:335, R1:52]

Dodson, James E. to Olive Hall. JAMES E. DODSON, farmer, age 22, single, b. Richmond Co., s/o William and Margaret Dodson, to OLIVE HALL, age 19, single, b. Richmond Co., d/o Griffin D. and Alcey [Alice Dodson] Hall.[2] Consent 18 JAN 1881 by mother Alice Hall, wit. Eppa C. Walker. W.A. Crocker. 18 JAN 1881. [C9, R:335, R1:52]

Dodson, Lawson P. to Tebado Douglass. LAWSON P. DODSON, farming, age 24, single, b. Richmond Co., s/o William and Margaret Dodson, to TEBADO DOUGLASS, age 24, single, b. Richmond Co., d/o Jere [Jeremiah] and Winnie Douglass. Consent 14 FEB 1884 by parties. G.H. Northam. 17 FEB 1884 at the res. of Mrs. Douglass. [C10, NN:22 FEB 1884, R:354, R1:61]

Dodson, Leroy B. to Julia Ann Walker.[3] LEROY B. DODSON, mechanic, age 23, single, b. Richmond Co., s/o Edward [L.] and Martha A. [Ann Pope] Dodson,[4] to JULIA ANN WALKER, age 18, single, b. Richmond Co., d/o Eppa C. and Jane [A. Dodson] Walker.[5] Consent 18 NOV 1876 by father Eppa C. Walker, wit. Edward Walker. R.J. Sanford. 22 NOV 1876. [C7, R:306, R1:41]

Dodson, Robert E. to Mellie N. Richardson.[6] ROBERT E. DODSON, farmer, age 27, single, b. and res. Northumberland Co., s/o Joseph B. and Louisa [Winstead] Dodson, to MELLIE N. RICHARDSON, age 21, single, b. Richmond Co., d/o George S. and Mary J. [Straughan] Richardson.[7] Consent 30 MAY 1881 by bride. A. Wiles, minister. 31 MAY 1881 at Salem Baptist Church. [C9, NN:10 JUN 1881 and 13 JUL 1883, R:336, R1:53]

Dodson, Warren W. to Allunie E. Winstead. WARREN W. DODSON, farmer, age 22, single, b. Richmond Co., d/o Edward L. and Martha A. [Ann Pope] Dodson, to ALLUNIE E. WINSTEAD, age 15y2m18d, single, b. Richmond Co., d/o Dandridge C. and Lillie A. [Ann Rock] Winstead.[8] Consent 19 FEB 1877 by D.C. Winstead, wit. C. Callahan, Jr. J.B. DeBerry. 21 FEB 1877 at the res. of the bride's father. [C8, R:306a, R1:42]

Dodson, William F. to Mary P. Douglass. WILLIAM F. DODSON, farming, age 22y6m, single, b. Richmond Co., s/o William J. and Margaret Dodson, to MARY P. DOUGLASS, age 20, single, b. Richmond Co., d/o Jeremiah and Winnie Douglass. Consent 1 MAY 1886 by mother Mrs.

---

[1] Alexander Dodson and Catharine Bryant were married by bond 3 FEB 1848 in Northumberland Co.
[2] Griffin D. Hall and Alice Dodson were married by bond 27 JUL 1848 in Richmond Co.
[3] Leroy B. Dodson (1855-1927) and wife Julia A. Walker are bur. at Cedar Hill Cemetery, Suitland, Md.
[4] Edward L. Dodson and Martha Ann Pope were married 18 FEB 1852 in Richmond Co. by Rev. Bartholomew Dodson.
[5] Eppa Walker and Jane A. Dodson were married 11 MAY 1847 in Richmond Co. by Rev. Bartholomew Dodson.
[6] Robert E. Dodson (b. 26 MAY 1855, d. 8 JUL 1883 by drowning) and his wife Mellie N. Richardson (b. 18 SEP 1859, d. 8 JUL 1883) are bur. in the Richardson Family Graveyard near Luttrellville, Va. Luttrellville is a locality on the northern boundary of the County at the junction of Routes 600 and 616.
[7] George S. Richardson (b. 16 SEP 1824, d. 20 JUN 1865) and his wife Mary J. Richardson (b. 26 JUL 1826, d. 13 JUL 1901) are bur. in the Richardson Family Graveyard near Luttrellville, Va. George S. Richardson and Mary J. Straughan were married by bond 2 DEC 1847 in Richmond Co.
[8] Lillie Ann Rock Winstead (b. 3 JAN 1841, d. JUL 1900), d/o Thomas C. Rock and Ann Fulks, is bur. at Oakland United Methodist Church cemetery.

Winnie [his X mark] Douglass, wit. Lawson P. [his X mark] Dodson. G.H. Northam. 2 MAY 1886 at res. of Mrs. Douglass. [C11, R:316, R1:67]

Dodson, William J. to Roberta Wilkins. WILLIAM J. DODSON, farming, age 60, widowed, b. Richmond Co., s/o Alexander Dodson, to ROBERTA WILKINS, age 22, single, b. Richmond Co., d/o Samuel and Iretta Wilkins. Consent 6 SEP 1887 by bride Roberta [her X mark] Wilkins. Rev. A.D. Reynolds. 11 SEP 1887 at the res. of John Haydon. [C11, R:292, R1:70]

Doggins, William R. to Mary W. Connellee. WILLIAM R. DOGGINS, merchant, age 39, single, b. Essex Co., s/o Samuel and Sarah [Covington] Doggins,[1] to MARY W. CONNELLEE, age 35, single, b. Richmond Co., d/o Sibby Connellee. William F. Bain. 26 MAY 1864 at Miss Sibbie Connellee's. [C3, R:139, R1:13]

Douglass, Alexander to Deania D. Dawson. ALEXANDER DOUGLASS, farming, age 21y1m7d, single, b. Richmond Co., s/o William and Elizabeth Douglass, to DEANIA D. DAWSON, age 21, single, b. Northumberland Co., d/o John Dawson and Eliza C. Dawson now Hayden. Consent 15 FEB 1881 by Elijah B. Haydon. W.A. Crocker. 15 FEB 1881. [C9, R:336, R1:53]

Douglas, Alexander Henry (Col.) to Elizabeth Rich (Col.). ALEXANDER HENRY DOUGLAS, farmer, age 24, single, b. Westmoreland Co., s/o George and Eliza Douglas, to ELIZABETH RICH, age 21, single, b. Richmond Co., d/o Beverly and Mary Rich. Consent by Betsey Rich, wit. Jarott Thompson. Rev. John Wilkerson. 23 NOV 1882 at Dr. Middleton's, Farnham. [C9, R:313, R1:57]

Douglass, Augustine P. to Mary L. Jenkins. AUGUSTINE P. DOUGLASS, farming, age 27, single, b. Richmond Co., s/o Thos. H. and Malinda [Douglass] Douglass,[2] to MARY L. JENKINS, age 21, single, b. Richmond Co., d/o Matthew [Jr.] and [Emmaline] Susan [Harper] Jenkins.[3] Consent 6 OCT 1879 by bride, wit. D.E. Douglass. G.H. Northam. 8 OCT 1879 at Mrs. Jenkins'. [C8, R:308, R1:48]

Douglass, Columbus J. to Virginia L. Beazley. COLUMBUS J. DOUGLASS, farming, age 24y5m3d, single, b. Richmond Co., s/o Jeremiah and Winefred Douglass, to VIRGINIA L. BEAZLEY, age 24y14d, single, b. Richmond Co., d/o William and Sarah Beazley. Consent 16 JAN 1884 by bride, wit. [J.]G. Bryant. G.H. Northam. 16 JAN 1884 at Mr. Beazley's. [C10, NN:25 JAN 1884, R:353, R1:61]

Douglas, Edward Emmerlas to Mary A. Davis.[4] EDWARD EMMERLAS DOUGLAS, farming, age 22, single, b. Richmond Co., s/o Samuel H. and [Lucy] Ann [Doggett] Douglas,[5] to MARY A. DAVIS, age 21, single, b. Richmond Co., d/o William L. and Eliza A. [Fidler] Davis. Consent 22 DEC 1886 by bride, wits. William L. Davis, Eliza A. Davis. G.H. Northam. 22 DEC 1886 at the res. of William L. Davis. [C11, R:317, R1:68]

---

[1] Samuel Doggins and Sarah Covington were married by bond 21 JAN 1818 in Essex Co.
[2] Thomas H. Douglass and Malindy Douglass were married 4 APR 1845 in Richmond Co. by Rev. E.L. Williams.
[3] Matthew Jenkins, Jr. and Emmaline Susan Harper were married 28 NOV 1849 in Richmond Co. by Rev. William N. Ward.
[4] Edward E. Davis (b. 1865, d. 19 JUN 1944) and wife Mary A. Davis (b. 1868, d. 18 FEB 1919) are bur. in Oakland United Methodist Church cemetery.
[5] Samuel H. Douglass and Lucy Ann Doggett were married 1 JUN 1850 in Richmond Co. by Rev. John Godwin.

Douglass, James to Mrs. Mary E. Pursell. JAMES DOUGLASS, farmer, age 36, single, b. Richmond Co., s/o William Douglass and Nancy Lewis,[1] to MARY E. PURSELL, age 24, widow, b. Richmond Co., d/o Peter McKenny and [A.] Conley. Consent 13 APR 1857 by bride, wit. Richard Dawson. William H. Kirk. 15 APR 1857. [C1, R:159, R1:4]

Douglas, James William to Susan Elizabeth Headley. JAMES WILLIAM DOUGLAS, farmer, age 24, single, b. Northumberland Co., s/o John and Elizabeth Douglas, to SUSAN ELIZABETH HEADLEY, age 28, single, b. Richmond Co., d/o Daniel [M.] and Delia [Ferdelia D. Bryant] Headley.[2] Consent 8 MAY 1871 by parties, wit. William A. Lewis. R.[J.] Sanford. 10 MAY 1871. [C5, R:244, R1:29]

Douglass, Milton W.[3] to Alice V. Harrison. MILTON W. DOUGLASS, farmer, age 25, single, b. Richmond Co., s/o John W. and Mary H. Douglass, to ALICE V. HARRISON, age 20, single, b. Richmond Co., d/o Samuel and Eliza Harrison. Consent 18 MAR 1863 by mother Eliza [her X mark] Harrison, wit. George W. Efford. Robert Williamson, M.G. 25 MAR 1863 at George Efford's in Farnham Parish. [C3, R:160, R1:12]

Douglass, Thadeus Henry to Willie A. Clark. THADEUS HENRY DOUGLASS, farmer, age 21, single, b. Richmond Co., s/o Jeremiah and Winnie Douglass, to WILLIE A. CLARK, age 16, single, b. Richmond Co., d/o James D. and Martha Ann Clark. Consent 3 MAR 1884 by bride and Martha A. Clark, wit. Octavus A. Clark. G.H. Northam. 5 MAR 1884. [C10, NN:14 MAR 1884, R:354, R1:61]

Douglass, William G. to Mary A. Hayden. WILLIAM G. DOUGLASS, farmer, age 39, widower, b. Richmond Co., s/o Edward and Elizabeth Douglass, to MARY A. HAYDEN, age 21, single, b. Richmond Co., d/o George D. and Fanny Hayden. Consent 26 NOV 1858 by bride, wit. George G. Hudson. No minister return. 30 NOV 1858 at [res. of] George D. Hayden. [C2, R:138, R1:6]

Douglass, William H. to Susanna Davis. WILLIAM H. DOUGLAS, farmer, age 30, single, b. and res. Westmoreland Co., s/o Rhodam and Nellie Douglass, to SUSANNA DAVIS, age 19, b. Richmond Co., d/o Alfred and Sarah Davis. Consent 28 FEB 1866 by bride Susanna [her X mark] Davis, Alfred Davis, wit. Thos. L. McKenney. Elder James A. Weaver. 28 FEB 1866 at the res. of Alfred Davis. [C4, R:270, R1:16]

Douglas, Dr. William Walter to Elizabeth Landon "Betty" Chinn.[4] WILLIAM W. DOUGLAS, physician, age 28, widowed, b. James City Co., s/o William R.C. and Lucy A. Douglas, to BETTY L. CHINN, age 20, single, b. Richmond Co., d/o Bartholomew C. and Cordelia B. [Ball McCarty Yerby] Chinn.[5] Andrew Fisher. 19 JUN 1860. [C2, R:153, R1:9]

Drake, Benjamin (Col.) to Harriet G. Carter (Col.). BENJAMIN DRAKE, oystering, age 30, single, b. Richmond Co., s/o Beverly Croxton and Mary Ann Mason née Drake, to HARRIET G.

---

[1] William Douglas and Nancy Lewis were married 17 OCT 1805 in Richmond Co.

[2] Daniel M. Headley and Ferdelia D. Bryant were married by bond 11 APR 1833 in Northumberland Co.

[3] M.W. Douglas served in Co. D, 47th Reg., Va. Inf., C.S.A.

[4] Dr. William W. Douglas (b. 6 FEB 1834 in New Kent Co., d. 24 JUL 1902) and his second wife Elizabeth L. Chinn of *Edge Hill* (b. 25 NOV 1839, d. 22 MAR 1896) are bur. at St. John's Episcopal Church cemetery, Warsaw, Va. He last served as surgeon in the 10th Va. Cav., C.S.A.

[5] Bartholomew Carter Chinn (b. 1802, d. 20 FEB 1852), son of Dr. John Y. Chinn, and his wife Cordelia Ball McCarty [later m. Addison Oscar Yerby] (b. 13 NOV 1819, d. 6 JAN 1890) are bur. in St. John's Episcopal Church Cemetery. Bartholomew C. Chinn, widower, and Cordelia B. McCarty were married by bond 6 MAR 1838 in Richmond Co.

CARTER, age 23, single, b. Lancaster Co., d/o Walker and Letta Carter. Consent 9 AUG 1887 from Ivanhoe, Va. by bride Hattie Carter. Jacob Robinson. 9 AUG 1887 at Mt. Zion Church, Ivanhoe, Va. [C11, R:292, R1:70]

Drake, George W.[1] to Mrs. Alice Richards Howe. GEORGE W. DRAKE, farmer, age 36, single, b. Richmond Co., s/o Richard and Nancy Drake, to ALICE HOWE, age 36, widow, b. Richmond Co., d/o William and Margaret Richards. Consent 23 JAN 1866 by bride, wit. John M. [Montague] Richards.[2] G.H. Northam. 25 JAN 1866 at Austin Richards'. [C4, R:270, R1:16]

Drake, Richard M. to Arretta A. Rust. Consent 17 MAR 1857 by S.A. Rust, wits. J.B. Mozingo, Henry Beverton. Assenting: Arretta A. Rust, wit. J.B. Mozingo, Henry Beverton. No license or minister return. [C1]

Drake, William (Col.) to Julia Thompson (Col.). WILLIAM DRAKE, oystering, age 21y11m, single, b. Richmond Co., s/o Thomas and Sophronie Drake, to JULIA THOMPSON, age 17, single, b. Richmond Co., d/o John Thompson and Harriet Davis. Rev. W. Carter. 15 FEB 1883 at the bride's house. [C10, R:355, R1:58]

Dunaway, Arthur (Col.) to Fannie Day (Col.). ARTHUR DUNAWAY, farming and oystering, age 25, single, b. Richmond Co., s/o William and Jane Dunaway, to FANNIE DAY, age 21, single, b. Richmond Co., d/o Washington and Martha Day. Consent 5 DEC 1889 by bride Fannie [her X mark] Day. Rev. W. Carter. 5 DEC 1889 at the home of the bride. [C12, R:328, R1:75]

Dunaway, Eddie Ross to Ella Frances Jackson. EDDIE ROSS DUNAWAY, farming, age 21y3m, single, b. Lancaster Co., s/o Robert R. and Mary Elizabeth Dunaway, to ELLA FRANCES JACKSON, age 23y5m, single, b. Richmond Co., d/o Daniel S. and Mildred Elizabeth Jackson. Robert Williamson, Farnham, Va. 22 JAN 1888 at *Bower Hill*.[3] [C11, R:315, R1:72]

Dunaway, Edward, Jr. (Col.) to Martha Lee (Col.). EDWARD DUNAWAY, JR., farmer, age 21, single, b. Richmond Co., s/o Ned and Mary Dunaway, to MARTHA LEE, age 21, single, b. Richmond Co., d/o Solomon and Harriet Lee. Consent 4 NOV 1874 by bride Martha [her X mark] Lee, wit. Kenner R. Cralle. Allen Brown, minister. 5 NOV 1874. [C7, R:230, R1:37]

Dunaway, George (Col.) to Susan Harris (Col.). GEORGE DUNAWAY, oysterman, age 24, single, b. Richmond Co., s/o Bill and Jennie Dunaway, to SUSAN HARRIS, age 21y5m, single, b. Westmoreland Co., d/o Walter and Binnie Harris. Consent 24 NOV 1874 by bride Susan [her X mark] Harris, wit. Kenner R. Cralle; oaths regarding age of parties. Allen Brown, minister. 26 NOV 1874 at the bride's home. [C7, R:230, R1:37]

Dunaway, George (Col.) to Celia Young (Col.). GEORGE DUNAWAY, oystering, age 32, widowed, b. Richmond Co., s/o William and Virginia Dunaway, to CELIA YOUNG, age 19, single, b. Essex Co., d/o Isaac and Handy Young. Consent 18 JAN 1882 by mother Handy [her X mark] Young, wits. T.J. Downing, Richard Lomax. Rev. W. Carter. 19 JAN 1882. [C9, R:312, R1:55]

---

[1] George W. Drake served in Co. D, 47th Rev., Va. Inf., C.S.A.
[2] John Montague Richards (b. 24 APR 1848, d. 11 OCT 1928) is bur. at Menokin Baptist Church cemetery.
[3] *Bower Hill* is located near Downings, Va. off of Route 647. It once belonged to Cyrus Harding, Sr.

Dunaway, Robert Royston[1] to Virginia Self. R.R. DUNAWAY, farming, age 44y8m27d, widowed, b. Richmond Co., s/o John and Nancy Dunaway, to VIRGINIA SELF, age 20, single, b. Northumberland Co., d/o Mary Ann Self. Consent 25 MAY 1885 by mother Mary Ann [her X mark] Self, wit. Charles E. Stephens. G.H. Northam. 28 MAY 1885 at *Laurel Grove.* [C10, NN:5 JUN 1885, R:317, R1:64]

Dunaway, William H. (Col.) to Eliza McKay (Col.). WILLIAM H. DUNAWAY, farmer, age 22, single, b. Richmond Co., s/o William and Harriet M. Dunaway, to ELIZA McKAY, age 21, single, b. Richmond Co., d/o Benjamin and Betsy McKay. Travis Corbin. 30 JAN 1868 at Potter's Field. [C4, R:253, R1:23]

---

[1] Robert Royston Dunaway (d. 1911) served in Co. E, 40th Reg., Va. Inf., C.S.A.

E

Edmonds, Ezekiel[1] to Emily J. Bowen. EZEKIEL EDMONDS, farmer, age 28, single, b. Westmoreland Co., s/o Richard and Nellie [Penelope Marks] Edmonds,[2] to EMILY J. BOWEN, age 23, single, b. Richmond Co., d/o Kelly H. and Maria [Fegget] Bowen.[3] Consent 22 JAN 1866 by bride, wits. Charles H. Balderson, James Jenkins. Robert N. Reamy. 28 JAN 1866 at res. of James Jenkins. [C4, R:270, R1:16]

Edmonds, George A. to Sarah Ann Hall. GEORGE A. EDMONDS, farmer, age 25, single, b. Westmoreland Co., s/o Richard and Penelope [Marks] Edmonds, to SARAH ANN HALL, age 22, single, b. Richmond Co., d/o Newman and Susan [Gutridge] Hall.[4] Consent 1 MAY 1860 by bride Sarah Ann [her X mark] Hall, wits. Susan Hall, T.N. Balderson. John Pullen. 2 MAY 1860.[5] [C2, R:153, R1:8]

Edwards, Richard B.[6] to Sada Cordelia Hook, merchant and farmer. RICHARD B. EDWARDS, merchandising, age 45, widowed, b. Westmoreland Co., s/o Richard L. and Ann M. [McKinney] Edwards,[7] to SADA CORDELIA HOOK, age 17, single, b. Warren, Pa., d/o Orin Hook and Sarah C. Hook now Kelly. Consent 20 DEC 1888 by S.C. Kelley, wit. J.W. Hearn. F.B. Beale. 20 DEC 1888. [C12, R:317, R1:73]

Efford, George W., Jr. to Julia Ann Harrison.[8] GEORGE W. EFFORD, farmer, age 28, single, b. Richmond Co., s/o John L. [sic] and Elizabeth [Douglas] Efford, to JULIA ANN HARRISON, age 22, single, b. Richmond Co., d/o Samuel and Eliza [Hudson] Harrison.[9] Consent 26 DEC 1859 by bride Julia [her X mark] Harrison, wit. R.W.D. Carter. Robert Williamson. 29 DEC 1859 at Farnham Baptist Church. [C2, R:165, R1:8]

Elmore, Richard D. to Lucy C. Bryant. RICHARD D. ELMORE, farmer, age 22, single, b. Richmond Co., s/o Rawleigh and Catharine [Bryant] Elmore,[10] to LUCY C. BRYANT, age 21, single, b. Richmond Co., d/o Richard D. and Lucy [C. Elmore] Bryant. Consent 13 DEC 1872 by bride, no wit. W.A. Crocker. 18 DEC 1872 at the res. of J.C. Clarke. [C6, R:238, R1:32]

Elmore, Rollow W. to Mrs. Mary J. Headley. ROLLOW W. ELMORE, farmer, age 28, single, b. Richmond Co., s/o Joseph and Betsey [Elizabeth Elmore] Elmore,[11] to MARY J. HEADLEY, age 30, widow, b. Richmond Co., d/o Samuel and Olivia Ann [Elmore] Bryant.[12] Consent 28 JUN 1872 in Farnham Township by bride, no wit. Barth. Dodson. 4 JUL 1872. [C6, R:237, R1:32]

Elmore, William McKindree to Sarah Ellen Wright. WILLIAM McKINDREE ELMORE, school teacher, age 20, batchelor, b. Northumberland Co., s/o John [H.] and Lucy [Jane Edwards] Elmore, to SARAH ELLEN WRIGHT, age 21, spinster, b. Richmond Co., d/o George and

---

[1] Ezekiel Edmonds served in Co. D, 40th Reg., Va. Inf., C.S.A.
[2] Richard Edmonds and Penelope Marks were married by bond 3 JAN 1820 in Westmoreland Co.
[3] Kelly H. Bowen and Mariah Fegget were married by bond 17 DEC 1827 in Westmoreland Co.
[4] Newman Hall and Susanna Millians [or Williams] Guttridge were married by bond 3 APR 1820 in Richmond Co.
[5] Minister return gives date of marriage 2 MAY 1860, while the license notes date 3 MAY 1860.
[6] Richard B. Edwards served in Co. A, 15th Va. Cav., C.S.A.
[7] Richard Edwards and Ann Maria McKinney, d/o Gerard McKinney, were married 22 JAN 1829 in Westmoreland Co.
[8] George W. Efford (b. 31 MAR 1826, d. 21 JUL 1881) and wife Julia M. Harrison (b. 4 JUN 1837, d. 10 NOV 1919) are bur. in Farnham Baptist Church cemetery. He served in Co. K, 9th Va. Cav., C.S.A.
[9] Samuel Harrison and Eliza Hudson were married by bond 2 JAN 1832 in Richmond Co.
[10] Rawleigh Elmore and Catharine Bryant were married by bond 24 FEB 1835 in Richmond Co.
[11] Joseph Elmore and Elizabeth Elmore were married by bond 16 JAN 1836 in Richmond Co. She is d/o George W. Elmore.
[12] Samuel Bryant and Olivia A. Elmore were married by bond 9 APR 1823 in Richmond Co.

Catharine Wright. Consent 24 JAN 1854 by John H. Elmore, wit. George L. Winstead and E.C. Elmore. Consent 25 JAN 1854 by G.M. Wright and Sarah E. Wright, wit. E.C. Elmore. License 25 JAN 1854 by F.W. Pendleton, clerk. Return by Rev. John Goodwin, at the residence of George Wright. 1 FEB 1854. [C, R, R1:1]

Elms, Joseph (Col.) to Catharine Brown (Col.). JOSEPH ELMS, farmer, age 29, single, b. Richmond Co., s/o George and Harriet Elms, to CATHARINE BROWN, age 23, single, b. Richmond Co., d/o William and Susan Brown. Allen Brown, minister. 16 JAN 1873 at the bride's house. [C6, R:235, R1:33]

Elms, Ralph (Col.) to Bettie Smith (Col.). RALPH ELMS, farmer, age 27, single, s/o Richmond Co., s/o George and Harriet Elms, to BETTIE SMITH, age 22, single, b. Richmond Co., d/o Joseph and Mollie Smith. No minister return. 11 JUL 1867. [R:286, R1:21]

Eppes, Edmund (Col.) to Sarah Venie (Col.). EDMUND EPPES, laborer, age 27, single, b. Petersburg, Va., s/o Edmund and Eliza Eppes, to SARAH VENIE, age 21, single, b. Richmond Co., d/o Joseph and Judy Venie. Travis Corbin. 27 JAN 1867 at Joseph Veney's. [C4, R:285, R1:19]

Epps, Mathew (Col.) to Mamie Thompson (Col.). MATHEW EPPS, farming, age 26, single, b. and res. Westmoreland Co., s/o John and Malinda Epps, to MAMIE THOMPSON, age 21, single, b. Richmond Co., d/o Jos. and Iretta Thompson. Rev. T.G. Thomas. 12 MAR 1888 at the house of the minister. [C11, R:315, R1:72]

Eubank, Giles F. to Florence E. Garland.[1] GILES F. EUBANK, merchant, age 39, widowed, b. Lancaster Co., res. Baltimore, Md., s/o Thomas D. and Elizabeth E. Eubank,[2] to FLORENCE E. GARLAND, age 2[1], single, b. Richmond Co., d/o James V. and Juliet F.[J. Lyell] Garland. Consent 13 MAY 1876 by bride, and oath to her age by mother Juliette F. Garland. W.A. Crocker. 16 MAY 1876. [C7, R:305, R1:40]

Eubank, Philip Cowles to Frances Matilda Dickenson.[3] PHILIP C. EUBANK, farmer, age 28, single, b. and res. Essex Co., s/o William and Mary [Hemingway] Eubank, to FANNIE M. DICKENSON, age 21, single, b. Richmond Co., d/o James M.[4] and Sarah [Motley] Dickenson.[5] Robert Williamson, M.G. 18 APR 1867 at *Sion House*.[6] [C4, R:286, R1:21]

Evans, David F. to Frances B. Oliver. DAVID F. EVANS, sailoring, age 40, widowed, b. and res. St. Mary's Co., Md., s/o Franklin and Julia Ann Evans, to FRANCES B. OLIVER, age 18, single, b. Northumberland Co., d/o Benjamin Oliver and Frances A. his wife now Lankford. Consent

---

[1] Florence E. Garland Eubank (b. 15 NOV 1854, d. 20 JUL 1886 at Huntington, W.Va.), was bur. at Coan Church in Northumberland Co.
[2] Thomas D. Eubank (b. 9 MAY 1808, d. 5 MAR 1864) and his wife Elizabeth E. Eubank (b. 12 APR 1812, d. 9 APR 1864) were buried in the Eubank-Gill Family Cemetery in Lancaster Co.
[3] Philip C. Eubank (b. 29 MAR 1837, d. 20 APR 1907) and wife Frances M. Dickenson (b. 10 AUG 1845, d. 20 MAR 1908) are bur. in Greenlawn Memorial Park.
[4] James M. Dickenson (b. 8 FEB 1819 in Essex Co., d. 5 MAY 1882) and his first wife Sarah Motley (b. 10 APR 1821 in King & Queen Co., d. 28 NOV 1863) are bur. in Farnham Baptist Church cemetery.
[5] Library of Virginia, Bible Records, Dickenson Family Bible Record, 1819-1961, "James Dickenson & Sarah Motley were married 1st Apr. 1841."
[6] *Sion House* was partly the estate of Leroy Griffin whose widow Judith married John Fauntleroy. It is located about 5 miles from Farnham Church.

22 JUN 1886 by bride and Frances A. Lankford, wit. L.S. Headley. Rev. A.D. Reynolds. 24 JUN 1886. [C11, R:316, R1:68]

Evens, James (Col.) to Mrs. Esther Taylor Davis (Col.). JAMES EVENS, farmer, age 69, widowed, b. Northumberland Co., s/o Daniel and Mary Ann Evens, to ESTHER DAVIS, age 40, widow, b. Northumberland Co., d/o Mitchell and Betsey Taylor. Thomas G. Thomas. 20 OCT 1874 at the house of Robert Ball. [C7, R:230, R1:37]

Everett, Washington B. to Mary E. Efford. Consent 14 JUL 1855 by bride Miss Mary G. [her X mark] Giford [sic], wit. R.L. Shackleford. No license or minister return. [C1]

Evins, Mac (Col.) to Virginia W. King (Col.). MAC EVINS, waterman, age 23y4m18d, single, b. Essex Co., s/o Landon and Matilda Evins, to VIRGINIA W. KING, age 16y9m21d, single, b. Richmond Co., d/o Martha King. Consent 28 DEC 1886 from *Chestnut Grove* by Martha [her X mark] King, wit. Dennis [his X mark] Taylor. George Laws. 29 DEC 1886 at *Holly Grove*. [C11, R:317, R1:68]

F

Fallin, Charles W. to Rosalie Lemoine. CHARLES W. FALLIN, farming, age 33, single, b. and res. Northumberland Co., s/o Charles W. and Elizabeth M.D. [Travers] Fallin,[1] to ROSALIE LEMOINE, age 26, single, b. Richmond Co., d/o Fereol [Jr.] and Ann [Maria Saunders] Lemoine. Consent 21 JAN 1884 by bride, wit. O.M. Lemoine. W.H. Gregory. 23 JAN 1884. [C10, NN:8 FEB 1884, R:353, R1:61]

Fauntleroy, Henry (Col.) to Mrs. Sarah Washington (Col.). HENRY FAUNTLEROY, oystering and farming, age 45, widowed, b. Richmond Co., [names of parents not completed], to SARAH WASHINGTON, age 35, widow, b. Richmond Co., [names of parents not completed]. Consent 23 APR 1887.[2] Charles Sparks. 12 MAY 1887 at Thomas Jones'. [C11, R:291, R1:71]

Fauntleroy, James (Col.) to Felicia Ann Jones (Col.). JAMES FAUNTLEROY, farming, age 39, widowed, b. and res. Westmoreland Co., s/o Emanuel and Amia Fauntleroy, to FELICIA ANN JONES, age 21, single, b. Richmond Co., d/o Hannah Jones. Consent 26 NOV 1881 by mother Hannah [her X mark] Jones, wit. William [Lewis]. Rev. Robert Lewis. 27 NOV 1881. [C9, R:338, R1:5r]

Fauntleroy, Robert J. (Col.) to Julia Mason (Col.). ROBERT J. FAUNTLEROY, farmer, age 22y9m, single, b. Richmond Co., s/o Henry Fauntleroy and Mary Veney, to JULIA MASON, age 18, single, b. Richmond Co., d/o Willis Mason and Winney Williams. Consent 9 SEP 1876 by mother Winny [her X mark] Williams, wit. Willis Mason. Allen Brown, minister. 4 SE 1876 at the bride's home. [C7, R:305, R1:41]

---

[1] Charles W. Fallin and Elizabeth M.D. Travers, ward of Robert Mayo, were married by bond 17 OCT 1845 in Northumberland Co.
[2] On microfilm at the end of the year 1887.

Ficklin, Thomas Dorsey to Ann Lyell.[1] THOMAS D. FICKLIN, merchant, age 34, widowed, b. Richmond Co., res. Lancaster Co., s/o C. [Christopher] D. and Mary [A.F. Wright] Ficklin,[2] to ANNIE LYELL, age 23, single, b. Westmoreland Co., d/o Joseph L.[3] and Susan [B. Dishman] Lyell. Consent 18 NOV 1869 by bride, no wit. W.F. Bain. 23 NOV 1869 at res. of R.H. Lyell. [C5, R, R1:26]

Ficklin, Thomas Dorsey to Euphrasia A. Garrett. THOMAS DORSEY FICKLIN, merchant, age 22, single, b. Richmond Co., s/o Christopher D. and Louisa [Franklin] Ficklin,[4] to EUPHRASIA A. GARRETT, age 20, single, b. Middlesex Co., d/o William and Margaret M. Garrett. Consent by mother of bride Margaret Critcher, wits. Wm. M. Garrett, R.H. Lyell. Robert Williamson, M.G. 20 DEC 1856 at the residence of M.M. Garrett her mother. [C1, R:159, R1:4]

Fiddler, Joseph H., d. 11 FEB 1870, to Elizabeth Coates. JOSEPH H. FIDDLER, farmer, age 55, widowed, b. Essex Co., s/o Churchwell and Susan Fiddler, to ELIZABETH COATES, age 20, single, b. Richmond Co., d/o Henry R.[5] and Elizabeth Coates. Consent 27 SEP 1864 by father Henry R. Coates, wit. Richard R. Coates. E.L. Williams. 28 SEP 1864 at res. of James Sanders. [C3, R:139, R1:14]

Fidler, James Robert to Levicie C. Harriss.[6] JAMES R. FIDDLER [sic], farmer, age 24, single, b. King and Queen Co., s/o Joseph H. and Jane Fidler, to LEVISA C. HARRISS, age 20, single, b. Richmond Co., d/o Henry M. and Fanny [Frances Mealey] Harriss.[7] Consent 7 APR 1866 by bride, also signed by Joseph H. Fiddler [sic], guardian, wit. Thomas M. [his X mark] Harris. Robert Williamson, M.G. 8 APR 1866 at George Thrift's in Farnham Parish. [C4, R:271, R1:17]

Fidler, James Robert to Martha O. Jenkins.[8] JAMES R. FIDLER,[9] oysterman or farmer, age 38, widowed, b. Richmond Co., s/o Joseph and Susan Fidler, to MARTHA JENKINS, age 21y9m, single, b. Richmond Co., d/o Matthew and Susan Jenkins. Consent 6 JUL 1880 by bride. G.H. Northam. 7 or 18 JUL 1880 at Mrs. Jenkins'. [C9[10], R:315, R1:51]

Fidler, Joseph H. to Mrs. Mary Pew Hudson. JOSEPH H. FIDLER,[11] farmer, age 46, widower, b. Essex Co., s/o Churchwell and Susan Fidler, to MARY HUDSON, age 35, widow, b. Richmond Co., d/o Martin [L.] and Nancy [Habron] Pew.[12] E.L. Williams. 20 NOV 1861 at the res. of Martin Pugh.[13] [C3]

---

[1] Thomas D. Ficklin, of *Falling Oaks* (b. 31 JAN 1835, d. 2 MAR 1888 in Litwalton, Va.) and wife Ann Lyell (b. 17 APR 1846, d. 20 AUG 1921) are bur. at Bethel United Methodist Church cemetery at Lively, Va. He served in Co. B, 40th Va. Inf., C.S.A.

[2] Christopher D. Ficklin and Mary A.F. Wright were married 3 AUG 1843 in Richmond Co. by Rev. William N. Ward. The *Richmond Enquirer*, 3 JUL 1849, notes: "Died, at Farnham, Richmond Co., Va., on Mon., the 11th of June, 1849, of Spasmodic Cholera, Mr. Christopher D. Ficklin, in the 52d year of his age ... a fond and affectionate father ... a member of the Episcopal Church."

[3] Library of Virginia, Bible Records, Lyell Family Bible Records, 1778-1897, appears to give James S. Lyell who was married to Susan B. Dishman by Rev. Samuel Templeman on 20 MAR 1830 at *Oak Grove*, Westmoreland Co.

[4] Christopher Ficklin and Louisa Franklin were married by bond 19 APR 1821 in Richmond Co. Louisa d. at Farnham Church, in Richmond Co., on Sat., 6 DEC 1841.

[5] Library of Virginia, Bible Records, Beacham-Coates Family Bible Record, 1869-1911, notes H.R. Coates d. 12 JUN 1884 at *Cabinet Hall*.

[6] James Robert Fidler (b. 13 MAR 1842, d. 4 OCT 1906) and his wife Levicie C. Fidler (b. 25 JUL 1845, d. 10 JUL 1879) are bur. in Jerusalem Baptist Church cemetery. Fidler served as a private in Co. K., 9th Va. Cav., C.S.A., wounded at Gettysburg, Pa., was absent then deserted.

[7] Henry M. Harris and Frances Mealey were married by bond 6 JUN 1835 in Richmond Co.

[8] Martha O. Jenkins (b. 24 JUL 1849, d. 1 JAN 1909), second wife of James Robert Fidler, is bur. in Jerusalem Baptist Church cemetery.

[9] Surname appears in the Register as Fiddler.

[10] There are two licenses, which are not filmed together, with differing dates of marriage.

[11] Surname appears two ways, Fidler and Fiddler.

[12] Martin Pew and Nancy Habron were married by bond 26 FEB 1824 in Richmond Co.

[13] Surname appears both as Pew and Pugh.

Fidler, William H. to Catharine A. Davis. WILLIAM H. FIDLER, age 23, single, b. Richmond Co., d/o Joseph and Jane [Ferrill] Fidler, to CATHARINE A. DAVIS, age 18, single, b. Richmond Co., d/o L.W. [Luke] and Mahala [B. Kennan] Davis. Consent 22 DEC 1873 by father L.W. Davis, wit. M.F. Lindon. G.H. Northam. 24 DEC 1873. [C6, R:236, R1:35]

Fisher, Andrew (Col.) to Mary Alice Williams (Col.). ANDREW FISHER, farmer, age 23, single, b. Richmond Co., s/o John and Winnie Fisher, to MARY ALICE WILLIAMS, age 17, single, b. St. Mary's Co., Md., d/o Elijah and Ellen Williams. Peter Blackwell. 9 MAR 1882 at res. of Elijah Williams. [C9, R:312, R1:55]

Fitzhugh, Peter (Col.) to George Anna Jessup (Col.). PETER FITZHUGH, farmer, age 27, single, b. Richmond Co., s/o Aaron and Lucinda Fitzhugh, to GEORGE ANNA JESSUP, age 23, single, b. Richmond Co., d/o Marcus and Adaline Jessup. Allen Brown, minister. 29 JAN 1874 at the bride's house. [C7, R:230, R1:36]

Fitzhugh, Philip (Col.) to Millie Cupit (Col.). PHILIP FITZHUGH, laboring, age 55, widowed, b. Loudoun Co., s/o Joshua and Jennie Fitzhugh, to MILLIE CUPIT, age 40, single, b. Richmond Co., d/o Tasker and Jane Cupit. T.G. Thomas. 10 DEC 1885. [C11, NN:18 DEC 1885, R:318, R1:65]

Fogg, Thomas J. to V.M. Lumpkin. THOMAS J. FOGG, farming, age 22, single, b. and res. Essex Co., s/o James E. and Lucy N. [Dunn] Fogg,[1] to V.M. LUMPKIN, age 21, single, b. King & Queen Co., d/o Robert Lumpkin and [blank] Lumpkin (dec'd.). H.H. Fones. 8 OCT 1885. [C10, R:317, R1:65]

Fones, Arthur Plummer to Olathea Lee Lewis.[2] ARTHUR P. FONES, mechanic, age 21y8m9d, single, b. Richmond Co., s/o William H. [Henry] and Mary E. [Elizabeth Wilson] Fones, to LEALY LEWIS, age 18, single, b. Westmoreland Co., d/o Thomas P. and Virginia Lewis. Consent 14 DEC 1879 by father Thomas P. Lewis, wit. William P. Middleton. R.N. Reamy. 18 DEC 1879 at the res. of W.P. Middleton. [C9, R:309, R1:48]

Fones, Charles H. to Mary Susan Moss. CHARLES H. FONES, farming, age 21y4m26d, single, b. Richmond Co., s/o Richard [T.] and Susan B. [Ambrose] Fones, *q.v.*, to MARY SUSAN MOSS, age 20y3m, single, b. Richmond Co., d/o William Moss and Rosey Ann Moss now Nash. Consent 17 APR 1880 by bride's mother Rosey Ann [her X mark] Nash, wit. Wm. [his X mark] Cash. D.M. Wharton. 18 APR 1880 at the minister's res. in Westmoreland Co. [C9, R:315, R1:50]

Fones, Eugene Warner to Permelia Ann Scates.[3] EUGENE WARREN FONES, farming, age 18, single, b. Richmond Co., s/o Richard [T.] Fones and Susan B. [Ambrose] his wife now Chase, to PERMELIA ANN SCATES, age 20, single, b. Richmond Co., d/o Thomas A. [Allen] and Martha [S. Bowen] Scates. Consent 29 JAN 1887 by mother Susan B. [her X mark] Chase, wit. Wm. [his X mark] Bowen; consent 29 JAN 1887 by parents of the bride Thos. A. [his X mark]

---

[1] James E. Fogg and Lucy Ann Dunn were married 11 DEC 1844 in Essex Co.
[2] Arthur Plummer Fones (b. 9 APR 1856, d. 3 JUL 1935) and his first wife Oleathea "Lealy" Lewis (b. 7 JUL 1861, d. 22 MAR 1908) are bur. in Cobham Park Baptist Church cemetery.
[3] Eugene W. Fones (b. 20 NOV 1869, d. 20 FEB 1950 in Williamsburg, Va.) and wife Permelia A. Scates (b. 6 SEP 1866, d. 17 DEC 1943) are bur. in Rappahannock Baptist Church cemetery.

Scates, Martha [her X mark] Scates, wit. Wm. [his X mark] Bowen. D.M. Wharton. 6 FEB 1887 at the public school house near the minister's residence. [C11, R:290, R1:69]

Fones, Henry H., Rev. to Mrs. Susan Ann Pullen,[1] widow of Robert B. Fones and Robert W. Balderson. HENRY H. FONES, minister of the gospel, age 31, single, b. and res. Westmoreland Co., s/o John H. and Elizabeth [Hall] Fones,[2] to SUSAN A.P. BALDERSON, age 30, widow, b. Richmond Co., d/o John and Henrietta Pullen. Consent 22 JAN 1872 by bride, wit. F.C. Clarke. Robert N. Reamy. 24 JAN 1872 at Mahaly Pullin's. [C6, R:237, R1:31]

Fones, Henry Randall[3] to Sarah Jane Hart. HENRY R. FONES, carpenter, age 23, single, b. and res. Westmoreland Co., s/o James B. and Mary A. [Ann Gutridge] Fones,[4] to SARAH JANE HART, age 18, single, b. Caroline Co., d/o Fielding Hart. Consent 21 MAY 1860 from bride, and James Reamy for the bride, wit. R.L. Reamy. Robert N. Reamy. 22 MAY 1860 at *Stony Hill*. [C2, R:153, R1:8]

Fones, Joseph W. to Mary A. Balderson. Consent 15 DEC 1856 signed with mark by both parties, wits. William H. Sandy, Jas. A.B. Sanders. No license or minister return. [C1]

Fones, Richard to Mrs. Delila Brown, widow of William Prescott. RICHARD FONES, age 45, widowed, birthplace blank, s/o Thomas [B.] and Nancy [Richards] Fones,[5] to DELILA PRESCOTT, age 30, widow, b. Richmond Co., d/o William and Mary Brown. Beverley D. Tucker. 14 JUN 1877 at St. John's Episcopal Church, Warsaw, Va. [C8, R:307, R1:43]

Fones, Richard Fairfax to Alphia J. Cash.[6] RICHARD F. FONES, farming, age 25, widowed, b. Westmoreland Co., s/o Richard T. and Susan B. [Ambrose] Fones, to ALPHIA J. CASH, age 20, single, b. Westmoreland Co., d/o William and Louisa Cash. Geo. M. Conley. 13 FEB 1890 at *Millview*. [C12, R:323, R1:76]

Fones, Richard T. to Susan B. Ambrose. RICHARD T. FONES, farming, age about 20, single, b. Westmoreland Co., s/o John H. Fones and wife Elizabeth [Hall], to SUSAN B. AMBROSE, age about 18, single, b. Richmond Co., d/o Redmond B. Ambrose and [Apphia C. Gutridge]. John Pullen, M.G. 8 JAN 1856 at Redmond B. Ambrose's. [C1, R, R1:3]

Fones, Thomas B. to Mrs. Fanny Wilcox. THOMAS B. FONES, farmer, age 66, widowed, b. Richmond Co., s/o Joseph and Jane [Drake] Fones, to FANNY WILCOX, age 48, widow, b. Richmond Co., d/o William Clarke. James A. Weaver. 21 OCT 1868. [C5]

Fones, Thomas Mathew to Sarah Elizabeth Brown.[7] THOMAS M. FONES, farmer, age 23, single, b. Richmond Co., s/o Thomas B. and Nancy [Richards] Fones, to SARAH ELIZABETH BROWN, age 20, single, b. Richmond Co., d/o William and Mary Brown. Consent 14 MAR 1877

---

[1] Susan Fones (b. 1839, d. 1917) is bur. at Rappahannock Baptist Church cemetery. Her first husband, Private Robert W. Balderson (d. 9 JUN 1862) is bur. in Hollywood Cemetery, Richmond, Va. He served in Co. K, 9th Va. Cav., C.S.A.

[2] John H. Fones and Elizabeth Hall were married by bond 11 DEC 1829 in Richmond Co.

[3] Private Henry Randall Fones (b. 12 AUG 1836, d. 27 JAN 1863 in D.C.) is bur. in Arlington National Cemetery. Served in C.S.A.

[4] James B. Fones and Mary Ann Gutridge were married by bond 19 DEC 1833 in Westmoreland Co.

[5] Thomas B. Fones and Nancy Richards were married by bond 9 FEB 1826 in Richmond Co. She is d/o R. Mitchell from *Grove Mount*.

[6] Richard F. Fones (b. 1 DEC 1864, d. 19 NOV 1923) and wife Alphia J. Cash (1879-1931) are bur. in Beulah Baptist Church cemetery.

[7] Thomas Mathew Fones (b. 20 MAY 1854, d. 30 MAY 1914, killed by lightning) and his wife Sarah Elizabeth Brown are memorialized at Jerusalem Baptist Church cemetery.

by mother Mary Brown, wit. Thomas [his X mark] Brown. G.H. Northam. 15 MAR 1877. [C8, R:306a, R1:42]

Fones, William Henry to Mary F. Hall. WILLIAM HENRY FONES, farmer, age 21y1m, single, b. Westmoreland Co., s/o Richard T. Fones (dec'd.) and Susan Bailey [Ambrose], to MARY F. HALL, age 28, single, b. Richmond Co., d/o John and Catharine [F. Butler] Hall.[1] Consent 13 FEB 1878 by bride Mary F. [her X mark] Hall, wit. R.A. Conley. H.H. Fones. 13 FEB 1878. [C8, R:310, R1:44]

Fones, William Henry[2] to Susan A. Scrimger. WILLIAM H. FONES, mechanic, age 45, widowed, b. Richmond Co., s/o Thomas [B.] and Nancy [Richards] Fones, to SUSAN A. SCRIMGER, age 23, single, b. Richmond Co., d/o George B. and Susan Ann [Hill] Scrimger.[3] G.H. Northam. 21 JUN 1883. [C10, R:356, R1:59]

Ford, Gustavus to Sarah E. Bell. GUSTAVUS FORD, merchant, age 23, single, b. Talbot Co., Md., s/o Littleton D. and Catharine Ford, to SARAH E. BELL, age 17, single, b. Northumberland Co., d/o William D. and Charlotte M. [Nutt] Bell.[4] Consent 14 MAR 1866 from *Bellfield* by mother Charlotte M. Bell, wit. R.L. Northen. Robert Williamson, M.G. 14 MAR 1866 at Joseph Bell's. [C3, C4, R:271, R1:17]

Forester, F. Bain to Julia B. Self. F. BAIN FORESTER, farming, age 23, single, b. Richmond Co., s/o Richard P. and Sally [E. Hynson] Forester, to JULIA B. SELF, age 15, single, b. Richmond Co., d/o [Steptoe T. and] Mahala Self née Lewis. G.H. Northam. 20 AUG 1890 at *Glenwood*. [C12, R:324, R1:77]

Forrester, Richard Henry L. to Rebecca J. Hynson.[5] RICHARD H.L. FORRESTER,[6] farmer, age 26, single, b. Richmond Co., s/o Richard P. and Sarah Forrester, to REBECCA J. HYNSON, age 23, single, b. Delaware, d/o John and Rebecca Hynson. Consent 16 DEC 1872 at Emmerton, Va.[7] by bride, no wit. G.H. Northam. 19 DEC 1872. [C6, R:238, R1:32]

Forester, Richard P., Col. to Sallie E. Hynson.[8] RICHARD P. FORESTER, farmer, age 45, widowed, b. Richmond Co., s/o William W. and Emma [D. Glascock] Forester,[9] to SALLIE E. HYNSON, age 20, single, b. New Castle Co., Del., d/o John and Rebecca Hynson. Consent 9 JUN 1862 by Rebecca Hynson, wit. George W. Price. Robert Williamson, M.G. 12 JUN 1862 at Farnham Church. [C3, R:140, R1:11]

Forester, William W. to Rosella F. Sydnor. WILLIAM W. FORESTER, farming, age 25y6m8d, single, b. Richmond Co., s/o Richard P. Forester and Frances Forester (dec'd.), to ROSELLA F. SYDNOR, age 22, single, b. Richmond Co., d/o John and Nancy [Lewis] Sydnor. Consent

---

[1] John Hall and Catharine P. Butler were married 13 JAN 1841 in Richmond Co. by Rev. John M. Waddey.
[2] William Henry Fones (b. 23 SEP 1839, d. 25 JAN 1916), who served in Co. K, 9th Va. Cav., C.S.A., is bur. in Cobham Park Baptist Church cemetery.
[3] George B. Scrimger and Susan Ann Hill were married 15 NOV 1847 in Richmond Co. by Rev. William N. Ward.
[4] William D. Bell and Charlotte Nutt, ward of Thomas S. Sydnor, were married by bond 24 JAN 1837 in Northumberland Co.
[5] Richard Henry Forester (1844-1930) and wife Rebecca J. Hynson (b. 14 DEC 1849, d. 17 JUL 1899) are bur. in Calvary United Methodist Church cemetery.
[6] The surname also appears as Forester.
[7] Emmerton is located between Totuskey Creek and Farnham, Va. on Highway 3 at Route 619.
[8] Col. Richard P. Forester (1817-1895) and wife Sallie E. Hynson (1842-1890) are bur. at Calvary United Methodist Church cemetery.
[9] William W. Forester and Emma D. Glascock were married by bond 3 DEC 1816 in Richmond Co.

15 NOV 1884 by parties. Robert Williamson, Farnham. 18 DEC 1884 at *Oakland*. [C10, R:356, R1:63]

Forrest, Edgar Malcolm to Lucy Tasker Mitchell.[1] EDGAR M. FORREST, farming, age 24, single, b. Washington, D.C., s/o D.C. [D. Craufurd][2] and C.S. Forrest, to LUCY T. MITCHELL, age 26, single, b. Richmond Co., d/o William B. and Julia E. Mitchell. F.B. Beale. 22 NOV 1887 at Menokin Church. [C11, R:293, R1:70]

France, John, Jr. to Catharine Sanders.[3] JOHN FRANCE, JR., farmer, age 24, single, b. Richmond Co., s/o John France and wife Elizabeth [Hall], to CATHARINE SANDERS, age 16, single, b. Richmond Co., d/o James C. Sanders and wife Sarah. Consent 17 AUG 1859 by father James C. Sanders, wit. James M. Scates. John Pullen. 18 AUG 1859 at James C. Sanders'. [C2, R:165]

France, John A. to Lydia L. Robinson. JOHN A. FRANCE, farmer, age 21, single, b. Richmond Co., [names written over], to LYDIA L. ROBINSON, age 21, single, b. Richmond Co., d/o John and Mary Robinson. Consent 14 JAN 1870 by bride, wit. E.K. [Nevitt]. Robert N. Reamy. 17 JAN 1870. [C5, R:233, R1:27]

France, Joseph to Julia Ann Antony. JOSEPH FRANCE, farmer, age 41, widowed, b. Richmond Co., s/o John and Elizabeth [Hall] France,[4] to JULIA A. ANTONY, age 26, single, b. Richmond Co., parents unknown. Consent 18 SEP 1872 by bride, wit. S.T. Reamy. Robert N. Reamy. 20 SEP 1872 at house of James C. Sanders. [C6, R:238, R1:32]

France, Joseph to Louisa Ann Scott. JOSEPH FRANCE, farming, age 52, widowed, b. Richmond Co., s/o John and Elizabeth [Hall] France, to LOUISA[5] ANN SCOTT, age 23, single, b. Richmond Co., d/o James and Matilda Ann [Scott] Scott.[6] Consent 31 OCT 1883 by father James A. Scott. F.B. Beale. 31 OCT 1883. [C10, R:357, R1:59]

France, Robert Jackson to Margaret N.A.P.F.E. Balderson.[7] ROBERT FRANCE, farmer, age 23, single, b. Richmond Co., s/o John [Jr.] and [Mary] Elizabeth [Hall] France, to MARGARET N.A.P.F.E. BALDERSON, age 22, single, b. Richmond Co., d/o James B. [Bailey] and Fezon F. [Feisin F. Franklin] Balderson. John Pullen. 21 DEC 1865 at James B. Balderson's. [C3, R:205, R1:15]

France, Thomas Rodney[8] to Catharine L. France. THOMAS R. FRANCE, farmer, age 19, single, b. Richmond Co., s/o John and Betsy France, to CATHARINE L. FRANCE, age 17, single, b. Richmond Co., d/o Caty France. Consent 15 APR 1862 by mother Caty [her X mark] France, and John [his X mark] France, wit. Richard Scates. John Pullen. 17 APR 1862 at John France's. [C3, R:140, R1:11]

---

[1] Edgar Malcom Forrest (1864-1937) and his wife Lucy Tasker Mitchell (b. 14 MAR 1861, d. 20 JAN 1914) are bur. at Menokin Baptist Church cemetery.

[2] D. Craufurd Forrest (1828-1876) is bur. in St. John's Episcopal Church cemetery.

[3] Catharine France (b. 8 NOV 1842, d. 14 JAN 1917), wife of John, is bur. in the France Family Graveyard near Newland, Va.

[4] John France, widower, and Elizabeth Hall, spinster, were married by bond 16 MAY 1829 in Richmond Co.

[5] The Register gives Levisa Ann Scott.

[6] James Scott and Matilda A. Scott were married 6 NOV 1853 in Richmond Co. by Rev. George Northam.

[7] Robert J. France (b. 1841, d. 1924) and his wife Margaret Balderson (b. 1844, d. 22 SEP 1912) are bur. at Rappahannock Baptist Church cemetery. He served in Co. D, 40th Va. Inf., C.S.A.

[8] Thomas R. France served in Co. K, 9th Va. Cav., C.S.A., and was killed in the Seven Days' Battle around Richmond, Va.

France, Vincent to Mrs. Louisa Jones. VINCENT FRANCE, miller, age 36, widowed, b. and res. Northumberland Co., s/o Presley France and Lucy Brown,[1] to LOUISA JONES, age 42, widow, b. and res. Northumberland Co., d/o Linsey Dawson and Mary Haynie. Barth. Dodson, Baptist parson. 9 FEB 1860. [C2, R:153, R1:8]

France, Vinson C. to Alice C. Douglas. VINSON C. FRANCE, miller, age 45, widowed, b. Northumberland Co., s/o Daniel and Lucy France, to ALICE C. DOUGLAS, age 28, single, b. Richmond Co., d/o Thomas H. and Rachel [Bryant] Douglas. Consent 28 JUN 1869 by bride, no wit., oath from William G. Douglas that groom is over age 21. B. Dodson, Parson. 1 JUL 1869 at William G. Douglas'. [C5, C6, R, R1:26]

France, William to Mary Jane Weeden. WILLIAM FRANCE, age 26 on 25 OCT 1864, single, b. Richmond, s/o John and Elizabeth France, to MARY JANE WEEDEN, age 19, single, b. Richmond Co., d/o [Richard] and Julia A. Weeden. John Pullen. 22 DEC 1864 at res. of Julia A. Weeden. [C3[2], R:139, R1:14]

Franklin, Philip M. to Mary S. Webb. PHILIP M. FRANKLIN, farmer, age 21, single, b. Richmond Co., s/o Samuel R. and Susan S. Franklin,[3] to MARY S. WEBB, age 17, single, b. Richmond Co., d/o William B. and Ann Webb. G.H. Northam. 18 JAN 1866 at William W. Webb's. [C4, R:270, R1:16]

Franklin, William Ryland to Aphia Judson Sisson.[4] WILLIAM R. FRANKLIN, mechanic, age 23, single, b. Richmond Co., s/o Samuel [R.] and Susan [S. Sisson] Franklin, to APHIA J. SISSON, age 18, single, b. Richmond Co., d/o J.T. and Anna E. Sisson. Consent 8 DEC 1879 by bride's parents, wit. C.J. Bronner. G.H. Northam. 11 DEC 1879 at J.T. Sisson's. [C8, R:309, R1:48]

G

Gaines, Arthur (Col.) to Mrs. Phoebe Ann Paris (Col.). ARTHUR GAINES, farming, age 47y8m, widowed, b. and res. Essex Co., s/o Page and Dolly Gaines, to PHOEBE ANN PARIS, age 40, widow, b. Essex Co., d/o Mr. and Mrs. Wood. Rev. T.G. Thomas. 9 APR 1882 at Clarksville Baptist Church. [C9, R:312, R1:56]

Gaines, Thomas (Col.) to Mrs. Mary Ward (Col.). THOMAS GAINES, farmer, age 35, single, b. Richmond Co., s/o Harry and Fanny Gaines, to MARY WARD, age 21, widow, b. Richmond Co., d/o Washington and Betsey Veney. George Laws. 17 MAR 1870 at *Cobham Park*. [C5, R:233, R1:27]

Gallagher, James to Fanny Ellen Harper. JAMES GALLAGHER, farming, age 6[?], widowed, b. Ireland, s/o Bernard and M. Jane Gallagher, to FANNY ELLEN HARPER, age 28, single, b. Richmond Co., d/o Benjamin and Elizabeth Harper. Beverley D. Tucker. 9 JUN 1881 at the res. of Mrs. E. Harper. [C9, NN:10 JUN 1881[5], R:336, R1:53]

---

[1] Presly [sic] France and Lucy Brown were married by bond 12 AUG 1811 in Northumberland Co.
[2] License is signed by William D. Garland, J.P., in absence of the clerk [F.W. Pendleton] who is in the hands of the enemy.
[3] Samuel R. Franklin (b. 1821, d. 11 OCT 1885) and his wife Susan S. (1828-1865) are bur. in the Franklin Family Cemetery near Nomini Grove, Va.
[4] William R. Franklin (1854-1933) and wife Aphia J. Sisson (1861-1947) are bur. at Totuskey Baptist Church cemetery.
[5] Announcement of the death of Lucy C. Gallagher, wife of James Gallagher.

Gallagher, John E. to Elizabeth J. Parr. JOHN E. GALLAGHER, farmer, age 23 in Oct., single, b. Richmond Co., s/o Robert and Henrietta [Sisson] Gallagher, to ELIZABETH J. PARR, age 24, single, b. Richmond Co., d/o James P. and Ann Parr. Consent 22 AUG 1882 by parties, wit. John S. Packett. G.H. Northam. 24 AUG 1882 at Mr. Packett's. [C9, R:313, R1:56]

Gallagher, Robert to Henrietta Sisson. ROBERT GALLAGHER, farmer, age 22, single, b. Ireland, s/o Barney Gallagher and wife Mary, to HENRIETTA SISSON, age 18, single, b. Richmond Co., d/o James Sisson and wife Susan [Crowder].[1] William N. Ward, M.G. 6 NOV 1856. [C1, R:159, R1:5]

Gallagher, William H. to Dorcas Virginia Lewis. WILLIAM H. GALLAGHER, teacher, age 22, single, b. Richmond Co., s/o James and Lucy Gallagher, to DORCAS VIRGINIA LEWIS, age 17, single, b. Richmond Co., d/o Parker R. and Mary F. [Cookman] Lewis.[2] Consent 2 APR 1876 by Parker R. Lewis, wit. James B. Brown. G.H. Northam. 4 APR 1876. [C7, R:304, R1:40]

Gardener, Eprim (Col.) to Martha Dandridge (Col.). EPRIM GARDANNER [sic], laborer, age 21, single, b. Essex Co., s/o Ephraim and Eliza Gardener, to MARTHA DANDRIDGE, age 21, single, b. Richmond Co., d/o John and Mary Dandridge. George Laws. 9 JUN 1867 at the res. of T. Herbert. [C4, R:286, R1:21]

Garland, Edward Wilson to Laura E. Gardy.[3] EDWARD W. GARLAND, miller, age 29, single, b. Richmond Co., s/o William D. and Maria A. [McKenney] Garland, to LAURA E. GARDY, age 18, single, b. Richmond Co., d/o Jacob and Elizabeth M. [Rheiner] Gardy.[4] A.B. Kinsolving. 13 JUL 1887 at the house of Jacob Gardy. [C11, R:292, R1:70]

Garland, George William to Ada Virginia Saunders.[5] GEORGE W. GARLAND, farming, age 33, single, b. Richmond Co., s/o W.D. [William Daniel] and Maria [A. McKenney] Garland,[6] to ADA V. SAUNDERS, age 19y2m, single, b. Richmond Co., d/o Thomas H. and Martha E. [Ella English] Saunders. Consent 17 DEC 1879 by father Thomas H. Saunders, signed by bride. G.H. Northam. 18 DEC 1879 at Mrs. Saunders. [C9, R:309, R1:48]

Garland, James Vincent, Jr. to Annie Thomas Lyell.[7] JAMES V. GARLAND, merchant, age 40, single, b. Richmond Co., res. Northumberland Co., s/o James V. Garland, Sr. and Juliet F.[J. Lyell] Garland, to [N]ANNIE T. LYELL, age 25, single, b. Spotsylvania Co., d/o Samuel Lyell, Jr. and Sarah Lyell. Consent 17 NOV 1876 by Samuel Lyell, Jr. and bride. Beverley D. Tucker. 21 NOV 1876 at Samuel Lyell's. [C7, R:306, R1:41]

---

[1] James Sisson and Susan Crowder were married by bond 16 DEC 1828 in Richmond Co.

[2] Parker Lewis and Mary F. Cookman were married by bond 11 DEC 1857 in Northumberland Co.

[3] Edward Wilson Garland (1858-1921) and wife Laura Gardy (b. 12 OCT 1868, d. 8 AUG 1951) are bur. in St.. John's Episcopal Church cemetery.

[4] Jacob Gardy (1827-1890) and his second wife Elizabeth Rheiner (1838-1894) are bur. in St. John's Episcopal Church cemetery.

[5] George W. Garland and (b. 20 JAN 1846, d. 26 AUG 1910) wife Ada V. Saunders (b. 3 OCT 1860, d. 1 JUN 1928 in D.C.) are bur. in Farnham Baptist Church cemetery.

[6] *Walnut Lawn*, the ancestral home of Col. William Daniel Garland, is located just south of Warsaw, Va., and has a family cemetery that includes burials for the Colonel (b. 16 OCT 1823-17 SEP 1896) and his wife Maria A. McKenney (b. 23 OCT 1823-14 NOV 1900).

[7] James V. Garland, Jr. (b. 27 OCT 1836, d. 13 FEB 1896) and wife Nannie W. Lyell (b. 4 SEP 1848, d. 20 NOV 1923) are bur. at Bethany Baptist Church cemetery at Callao, Va. See Library of Virginia, Bible Records, Lyell Family Bible Records, 1778-1897, which gives "James V. Garland and Annie T. Lyell were married in the morning of the 21st of November 1876 by the Rev. Beverley D. Tucker." Also, Annie Thomas Lyell was born Monday, 4th Sept. 1848 at [4] o'clock P.M. at *Cottage Green* the residence of her grandfather Wiatt. See NN:5 JAN 1883 for death notice for Juliette F. Garland. James Vincent Garland served in Co. D, 47th Rev., Va. Inf., C.S.A.

Garland, John Daniel to Bettie Blanche Garland.[1] JOHN D. GARLAND, attorney-at-law, age 30, single, b. Richmond Co., s/o William D. [Daniel] and Maria A. [McKenney] Garland, to BETTIE BLANCHE GARLAND, age 23, single, b. Richmond Co., d/o Moore F. and Elizabeth P. [Cooke] Garland.[2] W.W. Walker. 20 MAR 1879 at Warsaw Methodist Episcopal Church. [C8, R:307, R1:46]

Garner, James (Col.) to Jennie Rich (Col.). JAMES GARNER, laborer, age 22, single, b. Essex Co., s/o Dick and Hannah Garner, to JENNIE RICH, age 24, single, b. Richmond Co., d/o Sophronia Rich. Allen Brown, minister. 16 JUN 1877 at the bride's house. [C8, R:307, R1:43]

Garner, Nathaniel (Col.) to Ellen Ball (Col.). NATHANIEL GARNER, laborer, age 54, widowed, b. Westmoreland Co., s/o John and Nancy Garner, to ELLEN BALL, age 23, single, b. Richmond Co., d/o John Wood and Betsey Ball. Rev. T.G. Thomas. 3 MAY 1883. [C10, R:356, R1:59]

Gaskins, Frederick (Col.) to Catharine Johnson (Col.). FREDERICK GASKINS, farming, age 28y8m, single, b. Westmoreland Co., s/o Hiram and Julia Gaskins, to CATHARINE JOHNSON, age 30, single, b. Richmond d/o Benjamin and Fanny Johnson. Consent 16 JUN 1883 by bride Catharine [her X mark] Johnson. G.H. Northam. 17 JUN 1883. [C10, R:356, R1:59]

Gaskins, William H. (Col.) to Champain Thompson (Col.). WILLIAM H. GASKINS, merchant, age 25y1m2d, single, b. Richmond Co., s/o George Gaskins and Eliza Johnson, to CHAMPAIN THOMPSON, age 20, single, b. Richmond Co., d/o William and Julia Thompson. Consent 6 APR 1881 by William Thompson, wit. William H. Gaskins. Allen Brown, minister. 8 APR 1881 at the bride's home. [C9, R:335, R1:52]

George, Alwin to Mahele Ann Self. ALWIN GEORGE, oysterman, age 21, single, b. and res. Lancaster Co., s/o John M. and Nancy [C. Thrall] George,[3] to MAHELE ANN SELF, age 15, single, b. Richmond Co., d/o Samuel [Z.] and Martha [Luckham] Self.[4] Consent 15 SEP 1873 by mother Martha Ann [her X mark] Self, wit. Richard W. Hall who also gives oath to age of groom. A.B. Dunaway. 18 SEP 1873 at Ivanhoe, Va.[5] [C6, R:235, R1:34]

George, James to Bell Self. JAMES GEORGE, farmer, age 21, single, b. and res. Lancaster Co., s/o John M. and Nancy C. [Thrall] George,[6] to BELL SELF, age 21, single, b. Richmond Co., d/o John and Martha Self. Consent 8 OCT 1871 by bride Bell [her X mark] Self, wit. Phillip Hinson. Robert Williamson. 11 OCT 1871 at the house of James Dickinson, Farnham Crossroads. [C6, R:245, R1:30]

George, William Edward to Maria Mildred Stott.[7] WILLIAM EDWARD GEORGE, farming, age 23, single, b. Lancaster Co., s/o Thomas D. [Dobyns] George and Ann Kilpatrick,[8] and MARIA

---

[1] John Daniel Garland (b. 31 OCT 1848, d. 26 DEC 1928), and wife Bettie Blanche Garland (b. 11 JUL 1855, d. 11 APR 1922) are bur. at *Walnut Lawn*, near Warsaw, Va.
[2] Moore F. Garland and Elizabeth P. Cooke were married by bond 15 NOV 1841 in Richmond Co.
[3] John M. George and Ann C. Thrall were married by bond 21 DEC 1830 in Lancaster Co.
[4] Samuel Z. Self and Martha Luckham were married 29 APR 1845 in Richmond Co. by Rev. Elijah L. Williams, by consent of her father William Luckham.
[5] *Ivanhoe* was changed in 1889 to Downings, Va.
[6] John M. George and Ann C. Thrall were married by bond 21 DEC 1830 in Lancaster Co.
[7] William E. George (b. 24 JAN 1834, d. 13 JUL 1904) and wife Maria M. Stott (b. 31 MAY 1836, d. 18 FEB 1900) are bur. in Farnham Baptist Church cemetery. He served in Co. E, 40th Reg., C.S.A.
[8] Thomas Dobyns George and Ann K. Patrick were married by bond 19 MAY 1823 in Lancaster Co.

MILDRED STOTT, age 21, single, b. Richmond Co., d/o Thaddeus Stott and Elizabeth W. Dale.[1] Consent 15 MAR 1858 by bride, wit. Charles [his X mark] Barrick. Robert Williamson, M.G. 16 MAR 1858 at *Sion House.* [C1, R:138, R1:6]

Gibson, Archibald (Col.) to Mary Davis (Col.). ARCHIBALD GIBSON, farming, age 24, single, b. Va., s/o Randall Gibson [name of mother not given], to MARY DAVIS, age 23, single, b. Richmond Co., d/o Leson and Milie Davis. Consent 30 APR 1883 by bride Mary [her X mark] Davis. George Laws, Sr. 3 MAY 1883 at the minister's house. [C10, R:356, R1:59]

Gibson, John Henry (Col.) to Jane Jackson (Col.). JOHN HENRY GIBSON, laborer, age 21, single, b. Augusta Co., s/o Randall and Patsey Gibson, to JANE JACKSON, age 23, single, b. Richmond Co., d/o Judith Jackson. George Laws. 9 JAN 1876. [C7, R:304, R1:39]

Gillis, John (Col.) to Rachel Jackson (Col.). JOHN GILLIS, laborer, age 22, single, b. Richmond Co., s/o Cyrus and Julia Gillis, to RACHEL JACKSON, age 18, single, b. Richmond Co., d/o M. Maiden and Jane Gibson formerly Jackson. Consent 1 MAY 1878 by mother Jane [her X mark] Jackson, wit. John Henry [his X mark] Gibson. George [his X mark] Laws. 5 MAY 1878 at *Doctor's Hall.*[2] [C8, R:311, R1:45]

Gillis, Peter (Col.) to Lizzie Gordon (Col.). PETER GILLIS, farming, age 22, single, b. Richmond Co., s/o Cyrus and Julia Gillis, to LIZZIE GORDON, age 20, single, b. Richmond Co., d/o Samuel and Sarah Gordon. Consent 21 MAY 1887 by mother Sarah Gordon, wits. R.J. Pullen, Wm. Johnson. George Laws. 22 MAY 1887 in Warsaw, Va. [C11, R:291, R1:70]

Gillis, William (Col.) to Eliza Kennedy (Col.). WILLIAM GILLIS, farming, age 23, single, b. Richmond Co., s/o Cyrus and Judy Gillis, to ELIZA KENNEDY, age 25, single, b. Richmond Co., d/o Adam and Betsey Kennedy. Consent 31 OCT 1889 by bride Eliza [her X mark] Kennedy, wit. R.C. Mitchell. George Laws. 4 NOV 1889. [C12, R:328, R1:75]

Glasco, Hamilton (Col.) to Martha Roane (Col.). HAMILTON GLASCO, oysterman, age 39, single, b. Richmond Co., s/o Chichester and Polly Glasco, to MARTHA ROANE, age 24, single, b. Richmond Co., d/o Carter and Kitty Roane. Consent undated by mother Kitie [her X mark] Jackson, wit. Junius [Benson]. Allen Brown, minister. 20 DEC 1873 at the res. of the bride. [C6, R:236, R1:35]

Glasco, Henry (Col.) to Lucy McCuen (Col.). HENRY GLASCO, laborer, age 24, single, b. Richmond Co., s/o Thomas and Amy Glasco, to LUCY McCAN,[3] age 24, single, b. Essex Co., d/o Bartlett and Patty McCan. Consent 3 JUN 1866 by bride Lucy [her X mark] McCun [sic], wit. Thos. [his X mark] Glasco. Groom's father consents in person. Elijah L. Williams. 3 JUN 1866. [C4, R:271, R1:17]

Glascoe, Nacy (Col.) to Louisa J. Lewis (Col.). NACY GLASCOE, laborer, age 22, single, b. Richmond Co., s/o Thomas and Amy Glascoe, to LOUISA J. LEWIS, age 28, single, b. Richmond Co., d/o Phillip and Alice Thompson. Travis Corbin. 31 JAN 1867 at H. Curtis'. [C4, R:285, R1:20]

---

[1] Thaddus C. [sic] Stott and Elizabeth W. Dale were married by bond 31 MAY 1834 in Richmond Co.
[2] *Doctor's Hall* is located near where the Rappahannock Creek (Cat Point) empties into the Rappahannock River.
[3] Consent gives bride's surname as McCuen, while the license gives McCan.

Glasgow, Lewis (Col.) to Virginia Ann Rich (Col.). LEWIS GLASGOW, oystering, age 27, single, b. Richmond Co., s/o Thomas and Annie Glasgow, to VIRGINIA ANN RICH, age 23, single, b. Richmond Co., d/o James H. and Betsey Rich. Consent 18 DEC 1887 by parties, wit. J.H. Lemoine. N.A. Atkins. 29 DEC 1887 at res. of William Northen. [C11, R:293, R1:71]

Glassgo, Benton to Frances R. Mason. BENTON GLASSGO, farmer, age 31, single, b. Richmond Co., s/o Thomas and Nancy Glassgo, to FRANCES R. MASON, age 16, single, b. Richmond Co., d/o Leroy and Tell Mason. Consent 2 MAR 1869 by bride Frances [her X mark] Mason, wit. Leroy [his X mark] Mason. Robert Williamson, M.G. 4 MAR 1869 at Leroy Mason's. [C5, R, R1:25]

Godard, Harrison (Col.) to Hannah Carter (Col.). HARRISON GODARD, farmer, age 25, single, b. Richmond Co., s/o Stafford and Amanda Godard, to HANNAH CARTER, age 19y19d, single, b. Westmoreland Co., d/o Ben Carter and Mima Taylor. Consent by Myann [her X mark] Taylor, wit. Thomas Gordon. George Laws. 21 JAN 1883. [C10, R:355, R1:58]

Goddard, Gordon (Col.) to Mrs. Nessie Beverley (Col.). GORDON GODDARD, farmer, age 53, widower, b. Richmond Co., s/o Daniel and Becky Goddard, to NESSIE BEVERLEY, age 35, widow, b. Essex Co., d/o Easter Holmes. Consent 12 JAN 1871 by bride Nessie [her X mark], wit. Samuel Cox. George Laws. 15 JAN 1871 at New Zion Church. [C5, R:244, R1:29]

Goldman, Beverly, Jr. to Peggy Davis, free persons of color. BEVERLY GOLDMAN, JR., carpenter, age 25, single, b. Richmond Co., s/o Beverly and Jane Goldman, to PEGGY DAVIS, age 21, widow, b. Richmond Co., d/o Susan Davis [father's name not known]. Consent 7 JUL 1860 by bride Peggy [her X mark] Davis, wit. Lewis [his X mark] Thomson. No minister return. 10 JUL 1860. [C2, R:153, R1:9]

Goldman, Thornton (Col.) to Mrs. Hannah Ann Saunders (Col.). THORNTON GOLDMAN, mechanic, age 52, widowed, b. Richmond Co., s/o of Beverly and Jane Goldman, to HANNAH ANN SAUNDERS, age 45, widow, b. Richmond Co., d/o Johnson and Nellie Veney. John Wilkinson, minster. 18 NOV 1880 at *Piney Grove*. [C9, R:316, R1:51]

Gordon, Daniel (Col.) to Elizabeth Saunders (Col.). DANIEL GORDON, farmer, age 27, single, b. Richmond Co., s/o Stafford and Amanda Gordon, to ELIZABETH SAUNDERS, age 18, single, b. Richmond Co., d/o Solomon and Maria Saunders. Consent 8 DEC 1874 by father Solomon [his X mark] Saunders, wit. Samuel Cox. George Laws. 17 DEC 1874 at *Cedar Grove*. [C7, R:230, R1:37]

Gordon, Daniel (Col.) to Maria Wright (Col.). DANIEL GORDON, farmer, age 27, single, b. Westmoreland Co., s/o John A. and Mary Gordon, to MARIA WRIGHT, age 23, single, b. Richmond Co., d/o Daniel and Nelly Wright. Consent undated by bride. Rev. Robert Lewis. 14 JAN 1886 at Clarksville Church. [C11, R:315, R1:67]

Gordon, John A. to Alice V. Harrison. JOHN A. GORDON, farmer, age 50, single, b. Richmond Co., s/o John and Elizabeth Gordon, to ALICE V. HARRISON, age 17, single, b. Richmond Co., d/o John and Margaret Harrison. G.H. Northam. 14 FEB 1867. [C4, R:285, R1:20]

Gordon, Sedwick (Col.) to Isabella Johnson (Col.). SEDWICK GORDON, farming, age 25y11m23d, single, b. Richmond Co., s/o Stafford and Amanda Gordon, to ISABELLA JOHNSON, age 23y5m, single, b. Richmond Co., d/o Oliver Johnson and Tena Robb. Consent 16 JAN 1887 by bride Isabella [her X mark] Johnson. George Laws. 16 JAN 1887 at New Zion [Church]. [C11, R:290, R1:69]

Gordon, Stafford, Jr. (Col.) to Isabella Washington (Col.). STAFFORD GORDON, JR., farming, age 26, single, b. Richmond Co., s/o Stafford [Sr.] and Amanda Gordon, to ISABELLA WASHINGTON, age 24, single, b. Richmond Co., d/o Cyrus and Peggie Washington. Consent 1 FEB 1882 by bride Isabella [his X mark] Washington, wit. Thomas Gordon. George Laws. 2 FEB 1882 at *Grove Mount*.[1]   [C9, R:312, R1:55]

Gordon, Thomas (Col.) to Delilah Dickenson (Col.). THOMAS GORDON, farming, age 29, single, b. Richmond Co., so Gorgon [sic] Goddard and Mary Gordon, to DELILAH DICKENSON, age 19y8m, single, b. Richmond Co., d/o Rachel Palmer [name of father not given]. Consent 11 DEC 1883 from *Cedar Grove* by Rachel [her X mark] Palmer, wit. S.E. Mitchell, D. Gordon. George Laws. 13 DEC 1883. [C10, R:357, R1:60]

Gouldman, Alexander Baylor to Virginia Frances Gray. ALEXANDER BAYLOR GOULDMAN, farmer, age 30, widowed, b. and res. Essex Co., s/o Fendall and Lucy Gouldman, to VIRGINIA FRANCES GRAY, age 21, single, b. Caroline Co., d/o [C.C.] and P.V. Gray. Oath 30 MAY 1870 by John S. Gray as to age of the bride. H.H. Fones. 1 JUN 1870 at res. of Mr. Gray. [C5, R:233, R1:28]

Gouldman, Edmond (Col.) to Mrs. Julia Fisher Douglas (Col.). EDMOND GOULDMAN, oysterman, age 23, single, b. Essex Co., s/o Edward and Cynie Gouldman, to JULIA DOUGLAS, age 33, widow, b. Westmoreland Co., d/o William and Melvina Fisher. Travis Corbin. 13 FEB 1869 at *Riverdale*.[2] [C5, R, R1:25]

Gray, Alexander (Col.) to Margaret Dandridge (Col.). ALEXANDER GREY [sic], laborer, age 35, widowed, b. Essex Co., s/o Sally Beverley, to MARGARET DANDRIDGE, age 27, single, b. Richmond Co., d/o George and Beckey Dandridge. Oath 27 NOV 1877 to age of bride by S.G. Dishman. George Laws. 28 NOV 1877 at *Grove Mount*. [C8, R:307, R1:43]

Gray, Bates (Col.) to Mary Frances Colston (Col.). BATES GRAY, laborer, afe 22, single, b. Essex Co., s/o Alex and Caroline Gray, to MARY FRANCES COLSTON, age 25, single, b. Richmond Co., d/o Amey Colston. Consent 11 MAY 1879 by S.[S.] Dishman. George Laws. 17 MAY 1879 at *Waterview*. [C8, R:307, R1:47]

Green, Henry A. (Col.) to Celia Dandridge (Col.). HENRY A. GREEN, coach maker, age 28, single, b. Caroline Co., s/o Harriet Green [father's name not known], to CELIA DANDRIDGE, age 20, single, b. Richmond Co., d/o Juliet Cox [father's name not known]. Consent 6 MAR 1866 by

---

[1] *Grove Mount* is located on a bluff overlooking the Rappahannock River near *Cedar Grove* and *Belle Mount*. It is 4 miles west of Route 360 and is accessed from Route 624. It is an early home of the Belfield Family.
[2] *Riverdale Farm* is located on the Rappahannock River shore near Sharps, Va. It was established as a portion of property of Moore Fauntleroy. It was occupied by the Plummer Family, and at the death of Col. Alfred Plummer passed to his daughter Elizabeth who married Cornelius White Barber.

Juliet [her X mark] Cox, wit. W.E. Hill. Robert Williamson, M.G. 8 MAR 1866 at Peter Cox's (Col.). [C3, C4, R:270, R1:16]

Green, Napoleon C. to Dora M. Harris. NAPOLEON C. GREEN, mechanic, age 22, single, b. King George Co., res. Washington, D.C., s/o Lindsey and Ellen [Rollins] Green,[1] to DORA M. HARRIS, age 27, single, b. Richmond Co., d/o James M. and Amanda J. Harris. R.J. Sanford. 8 JUN 1887 at the res. of J.M. Harris. [C11, R:292, R1:70]

Gregory, James to Frances Bowin. Consent MAY 1858 by bride Frances [her X mark] Bowin, wit. Samuel G. Brown. No license or minister return. [C2]

Grey, William B. to Alice Parsons. WILLIAM B. GREY, farmer, age 25, single, b. Caroline Co., s/o P.P. [Parmenus] and Caroline Virginia [Jeter] Grey,[2] to ALICE PARSONS, age 17, single, b. Baltimore, Md., d/o Stephen P. and Eliza Parsons. Consent 22 JAN 1876 by father Stephen P. Parsons, wit. W.E. Coleman. J.H. Davis. 23 JAN 1876 at the res. of the bride. [C7, R:304, R1:39]

Griggs, William to Frances Kelly. WILLIAM GRIGGS, farmer, age 25, single, b. and res. Westmoreland Co., s/o Nancy Griggs [father unknown], to FRANCES KELLY, age 21, single, b. Richmond Co., d/o Rose Kelly [father unknown]. Consent 17 NOV 1863 by mother Rose [her X mark] Kelly, wits. M.P. McCarty, Richard Kelly. G.H. Northam. 23 DEC 1863. [C3, R:160, R1:13]

Grimes, Anthony (Col.) to Sarah Jones (Col.). ANTHONY GRIMES, fisherman, age 36, single, b. Richmond Co., s/o Frederick and Dina Grimes, to SARAH JONES, age 23, single, b. Richmond Co., d/o Charles and Onia Jones. Allen Brown, pastor of Ebenezer Baptist Church. 12 MAR 1872. [C6, R:237, R1:31]

Grissett, Andrew T. to Ann Sorell Balderson. ANDREW T. GRISSETT, waterman, age 23 on 25 MAY 1857, single, b. Westmoreland Co., s/o Thomas Grissett and wife Mary [Murry],[3] to ANN SORELL BALDERSON, age 18 on 11 JUL 1857, single, b. Richmond Co., d/o William R. Balderson and wife Amelia [Ambrose].[4] Consent 19 MAY 1857 from father Wm. R. Balderson, wits. T.N. Balderson and Lindsey Owens. John Pullen, M.G. 21 MAY 1857 at John Pullens'. [C1, R:159, R1:5]

Gundy, Benjamin (Col.) to Winney Bailor (Col.). BENJAMIN GUNDY, farmer, age 25, single, b. and res. Essex Co., s/o Solomon and Millie Gundy, to WINNEY BAILOR, age 22, single, b. Richmond Co., d/o John Bailor. Thomas G. Thomas. 3 DEC 1868 at John Baylor's. [C5, R:254, R1:24]

Gundy, Ollie (Col.) to Julia Florence Ward (Col.).[5] OLLIE GUNDY, oystering, age 26, single, b. Essex Co., s/o Ben and Ann Gundy, to FLORENCE WARD, age 18, single, b. Richmond Co.,

---

[1] Linsay Green and Ellen Rollins were married 24 OCT 1849 in King George Co. Lindsey Green (b. c.1826, d. 29 DEC 1887) was bur. in the Green Family Cemetery near Rollins Fork, King George Co.
[2] Parmenas P. Gray and Virginia Jeter were married 24 FEB 1841 in Caroline Co.
[3] Thomas Grissett and Mary Murry were married by bond 12 JAN 1825 in Westmoreland Co.
[4] William Balderson, Jr. and Amelia Ambrose were married by bond 5 FEB 1833 in Richmond Co.
[5] Julia Florence Ward Gundy (b. 27 JUL 1871, d. 20 FEB 1920) is bur. at Mount Zion Baptist Church cemetery.

d/o William and Louisa Ward.[1] Consent 26 FEB 1889 by Louisa Ward and William Ward, wit. Robert A. Yerby. Rev. Jacob Robinson, Ivanhoe, Va. 28 FEB 1889 at Mt. Zion Baptist Church. [C12, license not on film; R:327, R1:74]

Gutridge, Armistead Carter[2] to Florence B. Reamy. ARMISTEAD C. GUTRIDGE, farmer, age 25, single, b. and res. Westmoreland Co., s/o John and Elizabeth [Ann Atkins] Gutridge,[3] to FLORENCE B. REAMY, age 15, single, b. Richmond Co., d/o James O. and [Mary] Jane [Morris] Reamy. Consent 6 SEP 1878 by A.C. Gutridge, guardian. F.W. Claybrook. 15 SEP 1878 at John Gutridge's in Westmoreland Co. [C8, R:311, R1:45]

Gutridge, George W. to Lucy A. Bartlett. GEORGE M. GUTRIDGE, farmer, age 23, single, b. Richmond Co., s/o Newton and Harriet [Scates] Gutridge,[4] to LUCY A. BARTLETT, age 22, single, b. Richmond Co., d/o Samuel and Mahala [Carter] Bartlett.[5] Consent 27 DEC 1859 by bride Lucy [her X mark] Bartlett, wits. Daniel Carter, Samuel Bartlett. John Pullen. 29 DEC 1859 at John Pullen's. [C2, R:165, R1:8]

H

Habron, George to Eliza A. Habron. GEORGE HABRON,[6] farmer, age 21, single, b. Richmond Co., s/o Benjamin and Arena [Sanford] Habron,[7] to ELIZA A. HABRON, age 22, single, b. Richmond Co., d/o John and Ann Habron. Consent 21 JAN 1873 by parties, wit. George W. Efford. A.B. Dunaway. 23 JAN 1873 at the house of George Efford. [C6, R:235, R1:33]

Hale, Camarite M. to Mrs. Lydia A. Tucker, widow of Alpheus Woollard. CAMARITE M. HALE, farmer, age 21, single, b. Richmond Co., s/o Moses and Nancy [Sydnor] Hale, to LYDIA A. WOOLLARD, age 16, widow, b. Richmond Co., d/o Benjamin and Harriet R. Tucker. Consent 24 NOV 1868 by bride, wits. Moses Hale, Sh. R. [his X mark] Tucker. James A. Weaver. 24 NOV 1868. [C5, R:254, R1:24]

Hale, Charles W. to Elizabeth Dodson. CHARLES W. HALE, farming, age 24, single, b. Northumberland Co., s/o Thomas and Jane Hale, to ELIZABETH DODSON, age 22, single, b. Richmond Co., d/o Ella [sic] and Elizabeth Dodson. Consent 31 AUG 1881 by parties Charles H.[8] [his X mark] Hale, and Miss Elizabeth [her X mark] Dodson, wits. John Haydon, Fird Dodson. Robert Williamson. 1 SEP 1881 near Union Village. [C9, R:338, R1:54]

Hale, George Filmore to Richard Anna Harrison. GEORGE FILMORE HALE, sailing, age 24y3m28d, single, b. Richmond Co., s/o James W. and Sarah E. Hale, to RICHARD ANNA HARRISON, age 22, single, b. Richmond Co., d/o Richard H. and Rebecca B. [Dameron] Harrison. Consent 28 JAN 1883 by bride and Filmore Hale, wit. Lawrence W. Thrift. G.H. Northam. 31 JAN 1883. [C10, R:355, R1:58]

---

[1] Louisa Ward (b. 10 APR 1827, d. 1 DEC 1927 in Boston, Mass.), widow of William Ward, is bur. at Mount Zion Baptist Church cemetery.
[2] Armistead Carter Gutridge (b. 10 APR 1853, d. 15 JUN 1921) is bur. at Grant United Methodist Church cemetery, Lerty, Va.
[3] John Gutridge and Elizabeth Ann Atkins were married by bond 19 OCT 1844 in Westmoreland Co.
[4] Newton Gutridge and Harriet Scates were married by bond 10 JUL 1833 in Richmond Co.
[5] Samuel Bartlett and Mahala Carter were married by bond 26 SEP 1832 in Richmond Co.
[6] The surname also appears as Haybron. Also, the form blank to indicate race of the parties was not completed.
[7] Benjamin Habron and Rany Sanford were married by bond 14 SEP 1832 in Richmond Co.
[8] The license is written as Charles W. Hale; however, the groom's signature block (where he signed with an X) is for Charles H. Hale.

Hale, George W.[1] to Mrs. Elizabeth "Bettie" Frances King, widow of John Martin Sisson. GEORGE W. HALE, farmer, age 45, widowed, b. Richmond Co., s/o William B. and Elizabeth P. [Headley] Hale,[2] to ELIZABETH F. SISSON, age 35, widow, b. Richmond Co., d/o B.B. [Benedict] and Elizabeth A. [Campbell] King.[3] Consent 15 MAY 1882 by parties. G.H. Northam. 21 MAY 1882 at the res. of B.F. Sisson. [C9, NN:26 MAY 1882, R:313, R1:56]

Hale, James A.[4] to Mary S. Fallen. JAMES A. HALE, farmer, age 29, single, b. Richmond Co., s/o Thomas R. and Margaret B. [Haydon] Hale,[5] to MARY S. FALLEN. age 22, single, b. Richmond Co., d/o Jeremiah and Ann [Dameron] Fallen.[6] Consent 17 JAN 1866 by parties, proved by Presley Hudson. E.L. Williams. 17 JAN 1866 at John Balderson's. [C4. R:270, R1:16]

Hale, James A. to Lenorah L. Lewis. JAMES A. HALE, farmer, age 32, widowed, b. Richmond Co., res. Northumberland Co., s/o Thomas [R.] and Margaret B. [Haydon] Hale, to LENORAH L. LEWIS, age 22, single, b. Richmond Co., d/o Jeremiah S. and K. [Katurah Ann Thrift] Lewis.[7] R.L. Sanford. 15 JUL 1869 at the res. of John Harrison. [C5, R, R1:26]

Hale, James W.[8] to Mrs. Mary Frances Marshall, widow of James Pew. JAMES W. HALE, farmer, age 37, widowed, b. Richmond Co., s/o William S. and Elizabeth F. [King] Hale,[9] to MARY F. PUGH [sic], age 24, widow, b. Albemarle Co., d/o George and Jane Marshall. Consent 20 MAY 1874 by bride, wit. Thomas F. Hammack. Rev. William McK. Hammack of Westminster, Md. 21 MAY 1874 at the res. of R.C. Hammack. [C7, R:230, R1:36]

Hale, Lombard G. to Mrs. Malinda Condley. LOMBARD G. HALE, farming, age 30, single, b. Richmond Co., s/o Moses and Nancy [Sydnor] Hale,[10] to MALINDA CONDLEY, age 32, widow, b. Richmond Co., d/o Meshack and Eliza[zabeth] [B. Clark] Clark.[11] Consent 30 JAN 1883 by bride, wit. Robert Hall. G.H. Northam. 31 JAN 1883. [C10, NN:2 FEB 1883, R:355, R1:58]

Hale, Moses to Malissa C. Woollard. MOSES HALE, farming, age 23, single, b. Richmond Co., s/o Royston R. and Winnie [V. Clark] Hale, to MALISSA C. WOOLLARD, age 22, single, b. Richmond Co., d/o James G. and Sophia Woollard née Lewis. Consent 12 DEC 1890 by bride Malise C. [her X mark] Wollard, wit. J.D. Connellee. W.A. Crocker. 14 DEC 1890. [C12, R:324, R1:77]

Hale, Royston R. to Mrs. Winny B. Clark. ROSTEN R. HALE, farmer, age 22, single, b. Richmond Co., res. Westmoreland Co., s/o Moses and Nancy [Sydnor] Hale, to WINNY B. CLARK, age 23, widow, b. Richmond Co., d/o [Wilbert? and Elizabeth Clark[12]]. Consent 2 MAR 1866 by

---

[1] George W. Hale (1833-1908) is bur. at Totuskey Baptist Church cemetery. He served in Co. A, 41st Va. Reg., C.S.A.
[2] William B. Hale and Elizabeth P. Healey were married by bond 19 JAN 1826 in Northumberland Co.
[3] Benedict B. King and Elizabeth Campbell were married by bond 16 DEC 1830 in Northumberland Co.
[4] James A. Haile served in Co. K, 9th Va. Cav., C.S.A.
[5] Thomas Hale and Margaret Haydon were married by bond 16 AUG 1830 in Richmond Co.
[6] Jeremiah Fallin and Ann Dameron were married by bond 27 JAN 1834 in Richmond Co.
[7] Jeremiah S. Lewis (b. 23 AUG 1825, d. 19 JUN 1891) and wife Katurah Ann Thrift (b. 28 AUG 1823, d. 12 JUN 1882) are bur. in Gibeon Baptist Church cemetery. Jeremiah Lewis and Keterah Thrift were married by bond 27 APR 1847 in Richmond Co.
[8] James W. Hale served in Co. E, 40th Reg., Va. Inf., C.S.A.
[9] Bettie F. Hale (b. 11 MAY 1846, d. 26 JAN 1904), second wife of George W. Hale and widow of John Martin Sisson, is bur. at Totuskey Baptist Church cemetery. William S. [or B.] Hale and Purdelia Bisky King were married by bond 28 JAN 1837 in Richmond Co.
[10] The surname is also found as Haile. Moses Haile and Nancy Sydnor were married by bond 17 DEC 1838 in Richmond Co.
[11] Meshack Clark and Elizabeth B. Clark were married by bond 2 JAN 1824 in Richmond Co.
[12] Names of bride's parents are written over and are illegible.

bride Winny B. [her X mark] Clark, wits. Meshack Clarke and Benjn. Tucker. Elder James A. Weaver. 3 MAR 1866 at the res. of Meshack Clarke. [C4, R:270, R1:16]

Hale, Sydnor P. to Virginia Sydnor. SYDNOR P. HALE, farmer (now a soldier in 9th Cavalry), age 22, single, b. Northumberland Co., s/o Moses and Nancy [Sydnor] Hale, to VIRGINIA SYDNOR, age 22, single, b. Richmond Co., d/o Thomas and Jane [Self] Sydnor.[1] Consent 19 JUN 1863 by bride, wit. Mesack [his X mark] Clarke, Benjn. Tucker. James A. Weaver. 20 JUN 1863 at Meshack Clarke's. [C3, R:160, R1:12]

Hale, William H. to Mary J. Hudson. WILLIAM H. HALE, farmer, age 21, single, b. Richmond Co., s/o William S. and Cordelia B. [King] Hale, to MARY J. HUDSON, age 24, single, b. Richmond Co., d/o Samuel and Nancy [Lewis] Hudson.[2] Elder James A. Weaver. 13 MAR 1867 at the res. of Augt. Hale. [C4, R:286, R1:20]

Hale, William R.B. to Elizabeth A. Rock.[3] WILLIAM R.B. HALE, farmer, age 23, single, b. Richmond Co., s/o William B. and Elizabeth P. Hale, to ELIZABETH A. ROCK, age 21, single, b. Richmond Co., d/o John D. and Sophia [Hammock] Rock.[4] Robert Williamson, M.G. 24 DEC 1867 at the res. of the bride's father. [C4, R:287, R1:22]

Hall, Addison J. to Sarah Alpha France. ADDISON J. HALL, coachmaking, age 32, single, b. and res. Westmoreland Co., s/o Richard Hall and Eliza Hall (dec'd.), to SARAH ALPHA FRANCE, age 21, single, b. Richmond Co., d/o John and Catherine France. Rev. A.D. Reynolds. 29 OCT 1885 at the res. of the minster. [C10, R:318, R1:65]

Hall, Dorsey B. to Mary E. Bartlett. DORSEY B. HALL, farmer, age 23, single, b. Richmond Co., s/o John and Catharine P. [Butler] Hall,[5] to MARY E. BARTLETT, age 18, single, b. Richmond Co., d/o John and Loranda [sic] [Balderson] Bartlett.[6] R.N. Reamy. 14 JAN 1868 at the res. of John Bartlett. [C4, R:253, R1:23]

Hall, Dorsey B. to Mary J. Hall. DORSEY B. HALL, farmer, age 26, widower, b. Richmond Co., s/o John and Catharine P. [Butler] Hall, to MARY J. HALL, age 20, single, b. Richmond Co., d/o James and Nancy [Bartlett] Hall.[7] Consent 30 AUG 1870 by mother Nancy [her X mark] Hall, wit. John [his X mark] Hall. E. Bohannon, M.G. 31 AUG[8] 1870 near *Cherry Grove*. [C5, R:233, R1:28]

Hall, Henry C. to Sarah E. Saunders. HENRY C. HALL, farmer, age 36, single, b. Richmond Co., s/o Robert and Sibby Hall, to SARAH E. SAUNDERS, age 30, single, b. Richmond Co., d/o Edward S. and Maria [Belfield] Saunders.[9] G.H. Northam. 7 FEB 1867. [C4, R:285, R1:19]

---

[1] Thomas Sydnor and Jane Self were married by bond 15 AUG 1834 in Richmond Co.
[2] Samuel Hudson and Nancy Lewis were married by bond 9 AUG 1825 in Richmond Co.
[3] William B. Hale (b. 17 SEP 1845, d. 13 APR 1922 in Morattico, Lancaster Co.) and wife Elizabeth A. Rock (b. 26 AUG 1850, d. 25 FEB 1922) are bur. in Farnham Baptist Church cemetery. He served in Co. E, 40th Va. Inf., C.S.A.
[4] John D. Rock and Sophia Hammock were married by bond 22 MAR 1841 in Richmond Co.
[5] John Hall and Catharine P. Butler were married 13 JAN 1841 in Richmond Co. by Rev. John M. Waddey.
[6] John Bartlett and Lorinda Balderson were married by bond 10 FEB 1836 in Richmond Co.
[7] James Hall and Ann Bartlett were married by bond 9 APR 1834 in Richmond Co.
[8] License gives date of marriage 31 AUG 1870, while the return notes 1 SEP 1870.
[9] Edward S. Saunders and Maria Belfield were married by bond 8 MAY 1833 in Richmond Co.

Hall, John to Martha Bartlett. JOHN HALL, farmer, age 39, widowed, b. Richmond Co., s/o William and Mary Hall, to MARTHA BARTLETT, age 28, single, b. Richmond Co., d/o William and Isebella Bartlett. Statement 12 NOV 1856 by William B. Marks that bride is over age 21, wit. F.W. Pendleton,[1] clerk. S.H. Northam, minister of the Baptist denomination. 14 NOV 1856. [C1, R:159, R1:4]

Hall, Julius Bliss to Elizabeth Bagby Harwood.[2] JULIUS B. HALL, painter, age 34, single, b. and res. Westmoreland Co., s/o William B. and Mary A. [Ann Omohundro] Hall,[3] to ELIZABETH B. HARWOOD, age 21, single, b. Richmond Co., d/o Richard H. and Mary Harwood. Consent 1 DEC 1865 at Menokin P.O. by bride Bettie Harwood, wit. Wm. T. Harwood. G.H. Northam. 21 DEC 1865 at *Menokin*.[4] [C3, R:205, R1:15]

Hall, Julius M. to Frances E. Northen.[5] JULIUS M. HALL, farmer, age 22, single, b. Richmond Co., s/o Griffin D. and Alice [Dodson] Hall,[6] to FRANCES E. NORTHEN, age 15, single, b. Northumberland Co., d/o W.M. and Mary E. Northen. Consent 10 NOV 1873 by bride, wit. W.M. Northen. W.A. Crocker. 12 NOV 1873 at the res. of the bride's father. [C6, R:235, R1:34]

Hall, Kirk White[7] to Mary B. Sanders. KIRK WHITE HALL, fishing, age 21y9d, single, b. Richmond Co., s/o Bladen and Frances Ann [Morris] Hall,[8] to MARY B. SANDERS, age 15, single, b. Richmond Co., d/o Robert C. [Christian, Jr.][9] and Charlotte [Susan Hynson] Sanders. Geo. M. [Conley] Connelly. 5 SEP 1888 at B[eu]lah Church. [C11, R:316, R1:73]

Hall, Luther Fleming to Annie M. Omohundro.[10] LUTHER F. HALL, farming, age 21, single, b. Richmond Co., s/o Julius B. [Bliss] and Bettie B. [Elizabeth Bagby Harwood] Hall, to ANNIE M. OMOHUNDRO, age 28, single, b. Richmond Co., d/o William H. and Eliza A. [Ann Hutt] Omohundro.[11] Consent 15 OCT 1889 by bride. W.F. Robins. 16 OCT 1889. [C12, R:328, R1:74]

Hall, Octavus to Mrs. Susan Oliff, widow of William Wilson. OCTAVUS HALL, farmer, age 20, single, b. Richmond Co., s/o Robert and Catharine Hall, to SUSAN WILSON, age 22, widow, b. Richmond Co., d/o James and Lucy Oliff. Consent 11 MAR 1862 by father Robert [his X mark] Hall, wits. Saml. T. Reamy, and Saml. [his X mark] Hall. John Pullen. 12 MAR 1862 at Robert Hall's. [C3, R:140, R1:11]

Hall, Octavius to Mrs. Mary Jane Oliff Carter. OCTAVIUS HALL, farmer, age 24, divorced by decree of Circuit Court on 3 APR 1866, b. Richmond Co., res. Westmoreland Co., s/o Robert

---

[1] Francis Walker Pendleton (b. 7 DEC 1808, d. 25 APR 1865), was clerk of court in Richmond Co. from 1849 until his death, and is bur. in St. John's Episcopal Church cemetery, as is his wife Sarah Frances Pendleton (b. 4 NOV 1809 in Caroline Co., d. 29 APR 1872).
[2] Julius B. Hall (b. 4 NOV 1831, d. 9 DEC 1906) and his wife Elizabeth B. Harwood (b. 16 DEC 1844, d. 8 JAN 1911) are bur. in Menokin Baptist Church cemetery.
[3] William B. Hall and Mary Ann Omohundro, d/o Richard Omohundro, were married by bond 10 OCT 1825 in Westmoreland Co.
[4] The ruins of *Menokin* are located about 4 miles from Warsaw, Va. The property belonged to Col. John Tayloe of *Mount Airy*.
[5] Julius M. Hall (b. 15 DEC 1850, d. 15 APR 1931) and wife Frances E. Northen (1858-1930) are bur. in the Hall Family Cemetery at *Rainswood*, Northumberland Co.
[6] Griffin D. Hall and Alice Dodson were married by bond 27 JUL 1848 in Richmond Co.
[7] Kirk White Hall (b. 25 AUG 1867, d. 1 SEP 1893) and his parents Bladen Hall (b. 13 OCT 1822, d. 2 JUL 1898) and Frances Ann Morris (1832-1881) are bur. in Cobham Park Baptist Church cemetery.
[8] Bladen Hall and Frances Morris were married 8 FEB 1849 in Richmond Co. by Rev. John Pullen.
[9] Robert C. Sanders (b. 27 APR 1847, d. 16 JUL 1912) and his two wives are bur. in the Sanders Family Cemetery near Warsaw, Va.
[10] Luther F. Hall (b. 2 JUL 1868, d. 15 MAR 1939) and wife Annie M. Omohundro (b. 16 JAN 1857, d. 13 NOV 1926) are bur. at Cedar Hill Cemetery, Suitland, Md.
[11] Williiam H. Omohundro and Eliiza Ann Hutt were married 16 DEC 1851 in Richmond Co. by Rev. Alfred Wiles.

and Catharine [Drake] Hall,[1] to MARY JANE CARTER, age 28, widow, b. Richmond Co., d/o James and Lucy Oliff. Consent 2 MAY 1866 by bride Mary Jane [her X mark]. John Pullen. 6 MAY 1866 at house of John Pullen. [C4, R:271, R1:17]

Hall, Richard (Col.) to Ellen Ward (Col.). RICHARD HALL, farmer, age 21, single, b. Richmond Co., s/o Christopher and Matilda Hall, to ELLEN WARD, age 21, single, b. Richmond Co., d/o Ralph and Eliza Ward. Consent 30 JAN 1868 by mother Eliza [her X mark], wit. Ro. [his X mark] Bagby. Andrew Fisher. 1 FEB 1868 at Warsaw, Va. [C4, R:253, R1:23]

Hall, Richard Henry to Alice M. Tiffey.[2] RICHARD H. HALL, farming, age 24, single, b. and res. Westmoreland Co., s/o R.M. [Richard Madison] Hall (dec'd.) and Henrietta [A. Healy] Hall,[3] to ALICE M. TIFFEY, age 16y10m, single, b. Richmond Co., d/o Robert B. [Bispham] and Elizabeth [S.] Tiffey. Consent 13 DEC 1880 by father Robert B. Tiffey. F.B. Beale. 14 DEC 1880. [C9, R:316, R1:51]

Hall, Richard Wait to Catharine Alice Douglass. RICHARD WAIT HALL, farming, age 23, single, b. Richmond Co., s/o Griffin Dandridge and Alcy Hazzeltine [Alice Dodson] Hall, to CATHARINE OLIVE DOUGLAS, age 21, single, b. Richmond Co., d/o Samuel M. and Lucy Ann Douglass. Consent 11 APR 1887 by bride, wit. by her parents. G.H. Northam. 13 APR 1887 at res. of S. Douglass. [C11, R:291, R1:69]

Hall, Robert to Mary E. Webb. ROBERT HALL, teacher, age 29, single, b. Lancaster Co., s/o Addison and Susan C. [Edmonds] Hall,[4] to MARY E. WEBB, age 18, single, b. Richmond Co., d/o William and Margaret M. [Shepherd] Webb.[5] Consent 9 SEP 1859 by mother Margaret M. Webb, wit. J.D. Ficklin. Addison Hall, M.G. 13 SEP 1859 at the dwelling of Mrs. Webb. [C2, R:165, R1:7]

Hall, Robert to Mary Cordelia Jones.[6] ROBERT HALL, lawyer, age 38, widowed, b. Lancaster Co., s/o Addison and Susan [C. Edmonds] Hall, to MARY C. JONES, age 22, single, b. Richmond Co., d/o Thomas and Ann S. Jones. Andrew Fisher. 16 SEP 1868 at Warsaw, Va. [C5, R:254, R1:24]

Hall, Robert H.H. to Ella J. Scates. ROBERT H.H. HALL, farming, age 23, single, b. Richmond Co., s/o John Hall [name of mother not provided], to ELLA J. SCATES, age 22, single, b. Richmond Co., d/o James M. and Henrietta Scates. H.H. Fones. 3 JAN 1883. [C10, R:355, R1:58]

Hall, Robert J. to Jennie L. Marks. ROBERT J. HALL, farming, age 22y9m20d, single, b. Richmond Co., s/o William J. and Mary J. [Jane Conley] Hall, to JENNIE L. MARKS, age 18, single, b. Richmond Co., d/o Vincent and Mary V. [France] Marks.[7] Consent undated by mother Mary V.

---

[1] Robert Hall and Catharine Drake were married by bond 2 MAR 1842 in Westmoreland Co.
[2] Richard Henry Hall (b. 8 APR 1856, d. 3 APR 1957) and wife Alice Tiffey (b. 23 JAN 1865, d. 13 DEC 1944) are bur. at Andrew Chapel United Methodist Church cemetery.
[3] Richard Madison Hall, s/o William B. Hall, and Henrietta A. Healy, d/o Mary A. Healy, were married by bond 20 MAY 1846 in Westmoreland Co.
[4] Addison Hall and Susan Edmonds were married by bond 1 JAN 1817 in Lancaster Co.
[5] William Webb and Margaret M.C. Shepherd were married by bond 17 NOV 1825 in Richmond Co.
[6] Robert Hall (b. 27 FEB 1830, d. 19 JUL 1891) and his wife Mary Cornelia Jones (1846-1916), d/o of Thomas Jones (1811-1893) and Ann Seymour Trowbridge (d. 1877) are bur. in St. John's Episcopal Church cemetery.
[7] Vincent Marks and Mary France were married by bond 9 MAY 1850 in Richmond Co.

[her X mark] Marks, wit. R.A. Connelly, Wm. P. [his X mark] Hall. Geo. M. Conley. 23 JAN 1890 at *Millview.* [C12, R:323, R1:76]

Hall, Robert Ryland to Willie Anne Bryant.[1] ROBERT RYLAND HALL, clerking in store, age 38, single, b. Westmoreland Co., res. Northumberland Co., s/o Robert and Sibby [Sabella Templeman] Hall,[2] to WILLIE B. BRYANT [sic], age 23, single, b. Richmond Co., d/o Reuben A. and Mary A. [Thrift] Bryant.[3] Consent 29 DEC 1885 by bride. Rev. A.D. Reynolds. 30 DEC 1885 at the res. of Mary A. Bryant. [C11, R:318, R1:65]

Hall, Samuel to Olivia Crask. SAMUEL HALL, farming, age about 21, single, b. Richmond Co., s/o Newman Hall and wife Susan [Williams Gutridge],[4] to OLIVIA CRASK, age about 22, single, b. Westmoreland Co., d/o Thomas Crask and wife Elizabeth. Consent 6 APR 1858 by Wm. Carter, guardian of groom, wits. Thos. E. Pullen, B.F. Smoot. Consent 5 APR 1858 by bride Olivia [her X mark] Crask, wits. Thos. E. Pullen, James Dishman. John Pullen, M.G. 15 APR 1858 at Mrs. Susan Hall's above *Stony Hill.* [C2, R:138, R1:6]

Hall, Samuel James to Ella Susan Bulger.[5] SAMUEL J. HALL, farming, age 20, single, b. Richmond Co., s/o John Hall and Martha Hall (dec'd.), to ELLA S. BULGER, age 23, single, b. Richmond Co., d/o [Mr.] Bowen (dec'd) and Julia Bowen. Consent 19 FEB 1884 by bride; consent 19 FEB 1884 by John [his X mark] Hall, wits. Samuel J. Hall, Dorsey B. Hall. H.H. Fones. 21 FEB 1884. [C10, R:353, R1:61]

Hall, William H. to Elspeth B. "Bettie" Settle.[6] WILLIAM H. HALL, merchant, age 24, single, b. and res. Westmoreland Co., s/o William B. and Mary Ann [Omohundro] Hall, to ELSPETH B. SETTLE, age 22, single, b. Richmond Co., d/o Frederick and Diana T. [Claughton] Settle. G.H. Northam. 1 FEB 1866 at *Pleasant Valley.* [C4, R:273, R1:19]

Hall, William J. to Mary Jane Conley. WILLIAM J. HALL, farmer, age 25, single, b. Richmond Co., s/o James and Ann [Bartlett] Hall, to MARY JANE CONLEY, age 17, single, b. Richmond Co., d/o James S. and Elizabeth [Harrison] Conley.[7] Consent 28 FEB 1862 by mother Elizabeth [her X mark] Conley, wit. R.H. Harrison. Robert Williamson, M.G. 6 MAR 1862 at the res. of the bride's mother. [C3, R:140, R1:11]

Hall, William Moss to Henrietta Belfield.[8] WILLIAM M. HALL, farming, age 21, single, b. and res. Westmoreland Co., s/o Shelton M. and Julia A. [Drake] Hall,[9] to HENRIETTA BELFIELD, age 23, single, b. Richmond Co., d/o Richard C. and Mary F. [Frances Harwood] Belfield.[10] F.B. Beale. 22 DEC 1880 at *Chestnut Hill.* [C9, R:316, R1:51]

---

[1] Willie Anne Bryant Hall (b. 5 SEP 1860, d. 3 DEC 1937) is bur. in the Bryant Family cemetery at Village, Va. Robert Ryland Hall served in Co. K, 9th Va. Cav., C.S.A.

[2] Robert Hall and Sabella Templeman, d/o Samuel Templeman, were married by bond 19 JAN 1825 in Richmond Co.

[3] Reuben Bryant and Mary Thrift were married 18 DEC 1845 in Richmond C. by Rev. E.L. Williams.

[4] Newman Hall and Susanna Williams Guttridge were married by bond 3 APR 1820 in Richmond Co.

[5] Samuel J. Hall (b. 28 JAN 1864, d. 20 OCT 1920) and wife Ella S. Bulger (b. 1862, d. 30 MAR 1943) are bur. at Welcome Grove Baptist Church cemetery.

[6] William H. Hall (b. 2 MAY 1840, d. 5 JAN 1881) and wife Elspeth B. Settle (b. 7 NOV 1842, d. 23 MAY 1925) are bur. at Menokin Baptist Church cemetery.

[7] James S. Connolly and Elizabeth Harrisonn were married by bond 2 AUG 1841 in Richmond Co.

[8] William M. Hall (1859-1913) and his wife Henrietta Belfield (1856-1946) are [Her] memorialized at Menokin Baptist Church cemetery, with his burial at the Hall Family Cemetery near Nomini Grove, Va.

[9] Shelton M. Hall and Julia A. Drake were married by bond 8 APR 1857 in Westmoreland Co.

[10] Richard C. Belfield and Mary Frances Harwood were married 31 MAR 1847 in Richmonc Co. by Rev. John Pullen.

Hall, Woody N.[1] to Mary L. Beacham,[2] b. 25 NOV 1863. WOODIE [sic] N. HALL, farming, age 23, single, b. Richmond Co., s/o Bladen and Frances [Ann Morris] Hall, to MARY L. BEACHAM,[3] age 21, single, b. Richmond Co., d/o Hiram P. and Virginia A. [Lewis] Beacham.[4] Consent 23 MAR 1885 by father Hiram P. Beacham, wit. W.N. Hall. G.H. Northam. 25 MAR 1885 at res. of Mr. Beacham. [C10, NN:27 MAR 1885, R:316, R1:64]

Hamilton, Joseph (Col.) to Patsey Roane (Col.). JOSEPH HAMILTON, laborer, age 38, single, b. Smithfield, Isle of Wight Co., s/o Thomas and Mary Hamilton, to PATSEY ROANE, age 29, single, b. Richmond Co., parents unknown. Consent by bride, wit. W.A. [Jones]. Thomas G. Thomas. 25 FEB 1877 at Clarksville Baptist Church. [C8, R:306a, R1:42]

Hammack, Benedict to Mrs. Jane E. Muire. BENEDICT HAMMACK, shoemaker, age 46, widowed, b. Richmond Co., s/o Lewis and Lucy [Clarke] Hammack,[5] to JANE E. MUIRE, age 36, widow, b. Westmoreland Co., d/o Charles [S.] and Ann O. [Olive] Askins.[6] Consent undated by bride, wit. J.D. Ficklin. Lloyd Moore. 21[7] FEB 1860. [C2, R:153, R1:8]

Hammack, James L. to Mrs. Marie E. Hammack, widow of Martin L. Pew [Peugh].[8] JAMES L. HAMMACK, farmer, age 25, single, b. Richmond Co., s/o Rodham C. and Catharine [M. Yeatman] Hammack,[9] to MARIA E. PEUGH, age 24, widow, b. Richmond Co., d/o Benedict and Ellen [B. Polk] Hammack.[10] Consent 20 DEC 1868 by bride, no wit. J.H. Davis. 23 DEC 1868 at *Shandy Hall*.[11] [C4, C5, R:254, R1:24]

Hammock, Thomas F. to Sarah A.L. Winstead. THOMAS F. HAMMOCK, farmer, age 26, single, b. Richmond Co., s/o Rhodam C. and Catharine M. [Yeatman] Hammock, to SARAH A.L. WINSTEAD, age 25, single, b. Richmond Co., d/o George L. and Martha H.B. [Headley] Winstead.[12] J.B. DeBerry. 29 APR 1877 at the res. of the bride's father. [C8, R:307, R1:42]

Hanks, George Washington to Willie Ann Clark.[13] GEORGE W. HANKS, farmer, age 33, single, b. Richmond Co., s/o Ewell and Sarah [C. Stott] Hanks,[14] to WILLIE ANN CLARK,[15] age 18, b. Richmond Co., single, d/o Richard and Susan [Northen] Clark.[16] Consent 2 FEB 1861 by Richard [his X mark] Clark, Jr., wits. A. Bryant, A.J. Yeatman. E.L. Williams. 10 FEB 1861. [C3, R:123, R1:10]

---

[1] Woody N. Hall (b. 29 MAY 1861, d. 14 APR 1943) is bur. in Cobham Park Baptist Church cemetery.

[2] Mary L. Beacham Hall (b. 25 NOV 1863, d. 3 JUL 1931), wife of Woody N. Hall, is buried in Warsaw Baptist Church cemetery.

[3] The Beacham surname may also be found as Beauchamp.

[4] Hiram P. Beacham (b. 27 FEB 1833, d. 10 JUL 1910) and wife Virginia Ann Lewis (b. 1 FEB 1833, d. 18 AUG 1920) are bur. at Farnham Baptist Church cemetery.

[5] Lewis Hammack and Lucy Clarke were married by bond 26 DEC 1811 in Richmond Co.

[6] Charles S. Askins and Nancy Olive were married by bond 17 APR 1820 in Westmoreland Co.

[7] Library of Virginia, Bible Records, Hammack Family Bible Record, gives date of marriage 22 FEB 1860.

[8] James L. Hammack (1838-1919) and wife Marie E. Peugh (1840-1905) are bur. at Calvary United Methodist Church cemetery. He served in Co. M, 55th Va. Inf., C.S.A., dropped from the rolls as a deserter.

[9] Rodham Hammock and Catherine M. Yeatman, d/o Ann H. Yeatman, were married by bond 8 DEC 1838 in Westmoreland Co.

[10] Benedict Hammack and Ellen B. Polk were married by bond 23 DEC 1834 in Richmond Co.

[11] *Shandy Hall* was the seat of the Suggett Family.

[12] George L. Winstead and Martha H.B. Headley were married by bond 8 NOV 1836 in Richmond Co.

[13] George W. Hanks (b. 31 AUG 1827, d. 24 JUL 1907) and his wife Willie Anne Clark(e) (b. 21 JAN 1843, d. 6 AUG 1892) are bur. in the Hanks Family Cemetery near Emmerton, Va. He served in Co. D, 47th Rev., Va. Inf., C.S.A., but deserted in 1862.

[14] Ewell Hanks and Sally C. Stott were married by bond 4 JAN 1814 in Richmond Co.

[15] Surname also appears as Clarke.

[16] Richard Clarke and Sarah Northen were married by bond 25 FEB 1832 in Richmond Co.

Hanks, William E.[1] to Virginia Dunaway. Consent 8 DEC 1856 by bride Virginia [her X mark] Dunaway, wit. J.W. Bryant. No license or minister return. [C1]

Harding, Cyrus to Julia G. Blackwell.[2] CYRUS HARDING, farmer, age 43, widowed, b. Northumberland Co., s/o Cyrus and Juliet [Anderson] Harding,[3] to JULIA G. BLACKWELL, age 40, single, b. Northumberland Co., d/o Samuel [B.] and Ann [Nelms] Blackwell.[4] Consent by bride, wit. James B. McCarty. A.B. Dunaway. 29 OCT 1878 at *Bower Hill*. [C8, R:312, R1:45]

Harding, Milton Beauregard to Virginia P. Lemoine.[5] MILTON B. HARDING, farming, age 29y6m, single, b. and res. Northumberland Co., s/o Lucius T. and Addie [Adeline Hudnall] Harding, to VIRGINIA P. LEMOINE, age 32, single, b. Richmond Co., d/o Feriol [Jr.] and Ann Maria [Saunders] Lemoine.[6] Consent[7] 25 JAN 1886 by bride, wit. O.M. Lemoine. Rev. Martin Johnson, P.E. Church. 26 JAN 1886 at Farnham Church. [C11, NN:29 JAN 1886, R:315, R1:67]

Harper, Lucius to Lue Ellen Davis.[8] LUCIUS HARPER, farming, age 23, single, b. Richmond Co., s/o Benjamin and Elizabeth Harper,[9] to LUE ELLEN DAVIS, age 23, single, b. Richmond Co., d/o Alfred and Sally [B. Self] Davis.[10] G.H. Northam. 21 AUG 1879. [C8, R:308, R1:47]

Harper, Taliaferro to Susan Ann Courtney.[11] TALLIAFERRO HARPER [sic], farmer, age 22, single, b. Richmond Co., s/o Benjamin and Elizabeth Harper, to SUSAN ANN COURTNEY, age 21, single, b. Richmond Co., d/o Jeremiah and Ann [Alderson] Courtney.[12] G.H. Northam. 2 AUG 1881 at the res. of Mrs. Courtney. [C9, R:338, R1:54]

Harrington, Columbus to Anna Belle Yeatman.[13] COLUMBUS HARRINGTON, farmer and tanner, age 30, widowed, b. Dorchester Co., Md., s/o John and Elizabeth Harrington, to ANNA B. YEATMAN, age 24, single, b. Richmond Co., d/o H.A. [Henry Austin] and Ann W. [Reynolds] Yeatman.[14] Consent 2 JAN 1865 by bride, wit. A. Yeatman. William F. Bain. 5 JAN 1865 at H.A. Yeatman's. [C3, R:204, R1:14]

Harrington, Henry W. to Mrs. Florence L. Lowry Harris. HENRY W. HARRINGTON, farming, age 30y8m, single, b. Kent Co., Del., s/o Isaac G. and Ann E. Harrington, to FLORENCE L. HARRIS, age 24, widowed, b. Richmond Co., d/o Jordan B. and Elizabeth [Elizabeth Grant

---

[1] William E. Hanks served in Co. D, 47th Reg., Va. Inf., C.S.A., and deserted in 1862. A William E. Hanks (b. 1 DEC 1834, d. 27 NOV 1900) is bur. at Farnham Baptist Church cemetery.

[2] Major Cyrus Harding, Jr. (b. 17 AUG 1834, d. 23 MAR 1893) and his wife J.G. Blackwell (1835-1913) are bur. at Farnham Baptist Church cemetery. He served in Co. B, 40th Va. Inf., and Co. D, 15th Va. Cav., C.S.A. He lived at *Bower Hill* in Richmond Co.

[3] Cyrus Harding and Juliet Anderson, widow, were married by bond 10 OCT 1829 in Northumberland Co.

[4] Samuel B. Blackwell and Ann Blackwell, d/o Edwin and Catharine Nelms, were married by bond 3 NOV 1808 in Northumberland Co.

[5] Milton B. Harding (b. 1 JUL 1856, d. 4 OCT 1894) and wife Virginia P. Lemoine (b. 24 MAY 1852 at Emmerton, Va., d. 9 DEC 1953 at Remo, Va.) are bur. at Wicomico United Methodist Church cemetery.

[6] Feriol Lemoine, Jr. (b. 23 SEP 1804, d. 23 DEC 1857) and Ann Maria Saunders were married by bond 5 FEB 1833 in Richmond Co. He was a physician and also served as sheriff and Commissioner of the Revenue, 1849-1852.

[7] The consent gives name of groom as Millard B. Harding.

[8] Lucius Harper (b. 1856, d. 23 OCT 1913 in Warsaw, Va.) and his first wife "Louella" Davis (1858, d. 5 JUN 1894 in Warsaw, Va.) are bur. at Totuskey Baptist Church cemetery.

[9] Benedict [sic] Harper and Elizabeth Weathers were married by bond 23 AUG 1845 in Richmond Co.

[10] Alfred Davis and Sally B. Self were married 27 JAN 1841 inn Richmond Co. by Rev. William N. Ward.

[11] Taliaferro Harper (b. 28 JUL 1861, d. 28 JUL 1931) and his first wife Susan Ann Courtney (b. 8 AUG 1859, d. 22 AUG 1929) are bur. at Totuskey Baptist Church cemetery.

[12] Jeremiah Courtney and Ann Alderson were married 7 DEC 1848 in Richmond Co. by Rev. William N. Ward.

[13] Anna Belle Yeatman (b. 2 JUL 1839, d. 10 JUN 1932), wife of Columbus Harrington, is bur. in St. John's Episcopal Church cemetery.

[14] Henry A. Yeatman and Nancy W. Reynolds were married by bond 8 JUL 1833 in Richmond Co.

Marshall] Lowry, q.v. W.H. Gregory. 30 SEP 1884 at the Methodist parsonage. [C10, R:355, R1:62]

Harris, Crutcher Jackson to Henrietta Davis.[1] CRUTCHER HARRIS, farming, age 17, single, b. Richmond Co., s/o Robert M. Harris and Sarah [Jackson Mozingo] his wife now Saunders, q.v., to HENRIETTA DAVIS, age 17, single, b. Richmond Co., [names of parents not completed]. Consent 3 OCT 1887 by groom's mother Sarah [her X mark] Saunders, wit. Wm. N. Harris. G.H. Northam. 4 OCT 1887 at *Glenmore*. [C11, R:292, R1:70]

Harris, Henry (Col.) to Martha Ham (Col.). HENRY HARRIS, farmer, age 30, widowed, b. Richmond Co., s/o Hampton and Erin Harris, to MARTHA HAM, age 21, single, b. Richmond Co., d/o Moses and Mary Ham. Consent 11 DEC 1874 by bride Martha [her X mark] Ham, wit. Richard Lommat. A.B. Dunaway. 17 DEC 1874. [C7, R:230, R1:37]

Harris, J. Roane, to M. Alice Fiddler. J. ROANE HARRIS, oystering, age 22, single, b. Richmond Co., s/o James M. and Amanda [J. Quay] Harris,[2] to M. ALICE FIDDLER, age 18, single, b. Richmond Co., d/o James R. and Cornelia Fiddler. Consent 23 APR 1886 by father J.R. Fiddler. G.H. Northam. 25 APR 1886 at *Walker's Hill*. [C11, R:316, R1:67]

Harris, John Patphry, b. 7 SEP 1827, to Susan E. Cowen. JOHN P. HARRIS, farming, age 24, single, b. Richmond Co., s/o John Harris [and Mahala M. Berrick] to SUSAN E. COWEN, age 22, single, b. Stafford Co., d/o Jeferson [sic] Cowen. Consent 27 MAR 1857 by bride, wit[s]. Arabella [and/or] Isabella Bloxton. A. Dulaney, minister. 31 MAR 1857. [C1, R1:4]

Harris, Robert to Malissa Jane Bispham. ROBERT HARRIS, farming, age 28, single, b. Westmoreland Co., s/o Stephen and Mary Jane Harris, to MALISSA JANE BISPHAM, age 20y2m16d, single, b. Richmond Co., d/o Robert Bispham and Mary Jane Hinson. Consent 17 DEC 1882 by Mary Jane [her X mark] Hinson, and Malisia [her X mark] Bispham, wit. M.F. Hinson. R.N. Reamy. 20 DEC 1882. [C10, R1:57]

Harris, Robert M. to Mrs. Sarah Jackson, widow of Meredith M. Mozingo. ROBERT M. HARRISS [sic], farmer, age 42, widowed, b. Richmond Co., s/o John P. and Mahala [M. Berrick] Harriss,[3] to SARAH J. MOZINGO, age 28, widow, b. Richmond Co., d/o George and Mariah [Hale] Jackson.[4] Elder James A. Weaver. 21 OCT 1866 at the res. of Thos. Lewis. [C4, R:272, R1:18]

Harris, William Henry to Lizzie F. Lowry. WILLIAM HENRY HARRIS, mechanic, age 26, single, b. Richmond Co., s/o William N. and Elizabeth [Stubbs] Harris, to LIZZIE F. LOWRY, age 18, single, b. Richmond Co., d/o Jordan B. and Elizabeth [Grant Marshall] Lowry, q.v. Consent 27 MAR 1879 by E. Lowry, wit. Z.J. Morgan. W.A. Crocker. 27 MAR 1879 at the res. of the minister. [C8, R:307, R1:46]

---

[1] Crutcher J. Harris (1869-1941) and his wife Henrietta Davis are bur. at Totuskey Baptist Church cemetery.
[2] James M. Harris and Amanda J. Quay, d/o Sarah Ann Harris, were married 27 NOV 1851 in Richmond Co. by Rev. Alfred Wiles.
[3] John Harris and Mahala M. Berrick, d/o Caty Berrick, were married by bond 27 APR 1811 in Richmond Co.
[4] George Jackson and Maria Hale were married by bond 9 OCT 1834 in Northumberland Co.

Harris, William Muse to Mary Celeste Carter.[1] WILLIAM M. HARRIS, farmer, age 26, single, b. and res. Westmoreland Co., s/o Charles W. and Mary M. [Muse Reed] Harris,[2] to MARY C. CARTER, age 24, single, b. Richmond Co., d/o William and Mary S. [Ann Scrimger] Carter.[3] Consent 4 AUG 1873 by bride, wit. J.W. Carter. H.H. Fones. 10 AUG 1873 at *China Hill*.[4] [C6, R:235, R1:34]

Harrison, Beverly (Col.) to Annie Rich (Col.). BEVERLY HARRISON, laborer, age 40, single, b. Maryland, s/o Tom Harrison, to ANNIE RICH, age 30, single, b. Richmond Co., d/o John and Lucy Hudland. Consent 7 OCT 1879 by bride Annie [her X mark] Rich, wit. John R. [his X mark] Hudland. Peter Blackwell. 8 OCT 1879 at B. Harrison's. [C8[5], R:308, R1:47]

Harrison, Colos Augustus to Mary Jane Thrift.[6] COLOS HARRISON, age 25, single, b. Richmond Co., s/o John and Margaret Harrison, to MARY J. THRIFT, age 20, single, b. Richmond Co., d/o Richard [T.] and [Alice] Ann [Lewis] Thrift.[7] Consent 11 JAN 1871 by bride Mary J. [her X mark] Thrift, and Richard [his X mark] Thrift, wit. James W. Hale. G.H. Northam. 11 JAN 1871 at the house of Richard T. Thrift. [C5, R:244, R1:29]

Harrison, Samuel Addison[8] to Mrs. Emily A. Hanks Vanlandingham. S.A. HARRISON, farmer, age 28, bachelor, b. Richmond Co., s/o William and Lucinda [Connolley] Harrison,[9] to EMILY A. VANLANDINGHAM, age 29, widow, b. Richmond Co., d/o Turner and Elizabeth Hanks. Wm. A. Kirk. 30 OCT 1870 at *Edge Hill*.[10] [C5, R:234, R1:28]

Harrison, Samuel Addison to Augusta R. Rock.[11] S. ADDISON HARRISON, farmer, age 31, widowed, b. Richmond Co., res. Lancaster Co., s/o William and Lucinda [Connolley] Harrison, to AUGUSTA R. ROCK, age 21, single, b. Richmond Co., d/o Griffin and Juliet [A. Davis] Rock.[12] A.B. Dunaway. 15 SEP 1874 at *Edge Hill*. [C7, R1:37]

Haydon, George D. and Mrs. Catharine Headley, widow of George H. Wright. GEORGE D. HAYDON, farmer, age 64, widowed, b. Richmond Co., s/o John and Winny [Winifred Davis] Haydon,[13] to CATHARINE WRIGHT, age 53, widow, b. Northumberland Co., d/o James and Elizabeth Headley. Consent 10 OCT 1866 by bride. Barth. Dodson, Parson. 18 OCT 1866 at the house of B. Dodson. [C4, R:272, R1:18]

---

[1] William M. Harris (b. 3 JAN 1847, d. 17 JAN 1915) and wife Mary Celeste Carter (b. 15 DEC 1847, d. 29 MAY 1938) are bur. at Andrew Chapel United Methodist Church cemetery, Montross, Va. He served in Co. A, 15th Va. Cav., C.S.A.

[2] Charles W. Harris and Mary Muse Reed, d/o Joseph B. Reed, were married by bond 11 JUN 1844 in Westmoreland Co.

[3] William Carter and Mary Ann Scrimger were married by bond 24 APR 1834 in Richmond Co.

[4] *China Hill* is the highest spot in the county.

[5] Chronologically, this is the first marriage record entered on a newly-reformatted form.

[6] Colos A. Harrison (b. 1845, d. 14 FEB 1917) and wife Mary J. Thrift (b. 20 SEP 1851, d. 30 AUG 1917) are bur. unmarked in Gibeon Baptist Church cemetery.

[7] Richard T. Thrift (b. 1815, d. 10 MAY 1891) and wife Alice A. Lewis (b. 22 SEP 1821, d. 3 MAY 1915 at Village, Va.) are bur. at Totuskey Baptist Church cemetery. Richard T. Thrift and Alice Ann Lewis, d/o Jeremiah Lewis, were married by bond 14 OCT 1841 in Richmond Co.

[8] Samuel Addison Harrison served in the 40th Reg., Va. Inf., C.S.A.

[9] William Harrison and Lucinda Connolley were married by bond 21 DEC 1841 in Richmond Co.

[10] *Edge Hill* once stood on a hill overlooking Lancaster Creek and was a home of the Chinn Family.

[11] Samuel A. Harrison (1842-1924) and wife Augusta R. Rock (1853-1923) are bur. in Farnham Baptist Church cemetery.

[12] Griffin Rock and Juliet A. Davis were married 28 OCT 1852 in Richmond Co. by Rev. E.L. Williams.

[13] John Haydon and Winifred Davis were married by bond 21 NOV 1794 in Richmond Co.

Haydon, George T. to Serena A. Forester.[1] GEORGE T. HAYDON, farming, age 25, single, b. Richmond Co., s/o George B. and Elizabeth [S.] Haydon, to SERENER A. FORESTER [sic], age 22, single, b. Richmond Co., d/o George B. and Porlina Forester. Consent 15 JAN 1886 by bride. Rev. R.H. Potts. 17 JAN 1886 at res. of George B. Forester. [C11, R:315, R1:67]

Hayden, George T.B. to Elizabeth Rust. GEORGE T.B. HAYDEN, farmer, age 25, single, b. Richmond Co., s/o George D. and Frances Hayden, to ELIZABETH RUST, age 22, single, b. Richmond Co., d/o Elizabeth Rust [father's name unknown]. Consent 29 OCT 1859 by Elizabeth [her X mark] Rust, wit. Thomas B. Burris. John G. Rowe. 3 NOV 1859. [C2, R:165, R1:7]

Hayden, Samuel W. to Alice A. Efford.[2] SAMUEL W. HAYDON,[3] farmer, age 23, single, b. Richmond Co., s/o George [D.] and Frances Hayden, to ALICE A. EFFORD, age 23, single, b. Richmond Co., d/o John and Elizabeth [Douglas] Efford.[4] Consent 23 FEB 1866 by bride. Robert Williamson. 27 FEB 1866 at Richard Dawson's. [C4, R:270, R1:16]

Haynes, Franklin to Lillie Blanch Jenkins. FRANKLIN HAYNES, fishing and oystering, age 27, widower, b. Sagdahock Co., Me., s/o Marian and Martha Haynes, to LILLIE BLANCH JENKINS, age 14, single, b. Richmond Co., d/o John and Caroline [Jones] Jenkins, *q.v.* Consent 1 DEC 1884 by John [his X mark] Jenkins, wit. Thos. N. Oldham. G.H. Northam. 4 DEC 1884. [C10, NN:12 DEC 1884, R:355, R1:63]

Haynes, Richard R. to Ida F. Pullen.[5] RICHARD R. HAYNES, farmer, age 22, single, b. Richmond Co., s/o William C. and Louisa R. [Harwood] Haynes,[6] to IDA F. PULLEN, age 18, single, b. Westmoreland Co., d/o Thomas E. and Martha A. Pullen. Consent 26 OCT 1875 by father Thomas E. Pullen, wits. W.K. Reamy, R.J. Pullen. H.H. Fones. 27 OCT 1875. [C7, R:262, R1:38]

Haynes, William F. to Katie L. Jones. WILLIAM F. HAYNES, miller, age 28, single, b. Richmond Co., s/o William C. Haynes and Louisa R. [Harwood] Haynes (dec'd.), to KATIE L. JONES, age 28, single, b. Baltimore, Md., d/o John C. and Louisa Jones. Consent 11 MAY 1886 by bride, wit. F.G. Settle. H.H. Fones. 12 MAY 1886. [C11, R:316, R1:67]

Haynie, Hiram to Clementine Davenport.[7] HIRAM HAYNIE, farming, age 30, widowed, b. Richmond Co., s/o Joseph and Mary Elizabeth Haynie, to CLEMENTINE DAVENPORT, age 24, single, b. Richmond Co., d/o William E. Davenport and Ellen Barnes, *q.v.* Consent 28 MAR 1885 by bride. W.H. Edwards. 1 APR 1885 at the res. of the bride's father. [C10, R:316, R1:64]

---

[1] George T. Haydon (b. 12 JAN 1862, d. 20 AUG 1926) and wife Serena A. Forester (b. 28 MAY 1863, d. 10 FEB 1919) are bur. in Oakland United Methodist Church cemetery.
[2] Samuel E. Hayden (b. 3 SEP 1841, d. 8 JAN 1909) and wife Alice A. Efford (b. 1845, d. 6 NOV 1890) are bur. at Bethany Baptist Church cemetery, Callao, Va.
[3] Surname appears as both Hayden and Haydon.
[4] John D. Efford and Elizabeth Barrack were married by bond 19 APR 1819 in Richmond Co.
[5] Richard R. Haynes (b. 9 APR 1853, d. 6 JUL 1926) and his wife Ida F. Pullen (b. 21 MAR 1857, d. 30 JUL 1898) are bur. in Menokin Baptist Church cem.
[6] William C. Haynes (b. 25 OCT 1829, d. 5 JUN 1898) and his wife Louisa R. Harwood (b. 18 FEB 1827, d. 18 FEB 1881) are bur. in Menokin Baptist Church cem. William C. Haynes and Louisa R. Harwood were married 30 MAR 1848 in Richmond Co. by Rev. George Northam.
[7] Hiram Haynie (b. 31 OCT 1854, d. 14 MAY 1915) and wife Clementine Davenport (b. 22 SEP 1860, d. 10 APR 1934) are bur. at Lebanon Baptist Church cemetery.

Haynie, Octavus (Col.) to Mrs. Judie Cralle (Col.). OCTAVUS HAYNIE, oysterman, age 32, single, b. Westmoreland Co., s/o James and [H]yram Haynie, to JUDIE CRALLE, age 43, widow, b. Richmond Co., d/o James and Nelly Venie. Travis Corbin, minister. 12 JUN 1873 at the res. of Judie Cralle. [C6, R:235, R1:34]

Haynie, Thomas E. to Ella M. Lusby.[1] THOMAS E. HAYNIE, farming, age 24y11m9d, single, b. Northumberland Co., res. Lancaster Co., s/o Steptoe and Mary Ann Haynie, to ELLA LUSBY, age 18, single, b. Richmond Co., d/o Thomas W. and Elizabeth Lusby. Consent 27 MAR 1886 by father Thomas W. Lusby, wit. M.F. [Millard] Ficklin. R.H. Potts. 30 MAR 1886. [C11, NN:2 APR 1886, R:315, R1:67]

Headley, Alexander N. to Mrs. Lydia E. Rice Dewbry.[2] ALEXANDER N. HEADLEY, merchant, age 29, single, b. Richmond Co., s/o Lindsey Headley, to LYDIA E. DEWBRY, age 33, widow, b. Northumberland Co., d/o Isaac and Nancy [W. Dodson] Rice.[3] Consent 25 SEP 1876 by bride Lydia [her X mark] Dewbry, wit. W.M. Northen. William H. Kirk. 30 SEP 1876. [C7, R:305, R1:41]

Headley, Isaac E. to Mary S. Robinson. ISAAC E. HEADLEY, farmer, age 28y5m, single, b. and res. Northumberland Co., s/o Ezekiel H. and Elizabeth A. [Barnes] Headley,[4] to MARY S. ROBINSON, age 2[0]y5m18d, single, b. Northumberland Co., d/o Robert R. and Caroline A.B. Robinson. Consent 2 MAY 1876 by bride, wit. Jesse Bryant. G.H. Northam. 3 MAY 1876. [C7, R:305, R1:40]

Headley, John T. to Mrs. Mary J. Malone. JOHN T. HEADLEY, farmer, age 59, widowed, b. Richmond Co., s/o Griffin and Martha H. [Beacham] Headley,[5] to MARY J. MALONE, age 27, widow, b. Northumberland Co., d/o Samuel and Olivia [N. Elmore] Bryant.[6] Barth. Dodson, Parson. 4 SEP 1867 at house of Mary J. Malone. [C4, R:287, R1:22]

Headley, Joseph to Alice Shirley. JOSEPH HEADLEY, farmer, age 20, single, b. Northumberland Co., s/o Landmon Headley and Elizabeth Rock,[7] to ALICE SHIRLEY, age 16, single, b. Northumberland Co., d/o Robert Shirley and Elizabeth Ric[e].[8] Consent undated by John Hobson Follin, guardian of the bride, wit. William M. Northen. Consent 5 DEC 1855 by father Landmon Headley, wit. George B. Forester. John Goodwin, M.G. 6 DEC 1855 at Emma Forester's. [C1, R:153, R1:2]

Headley, Joseph to Mrs. Belle Thrift, widow of Daingerfield Jenkins. JOSEPH HEADLEY, farming, age 51, widowed, b. and res. Northumberland Co., s/o Landman H. and Elizabeth [Rock] Headley, to BELLE JENKINS, age 40, widow, b. Richmond Co., d/o Samuel [B.] and Mary [A.G. Webb] Thrift.[9] Consent in APR 1887 by bride. Rev. A.D. Reynolds. 14 APR 1887 at the res. of the minister. [C11, R:291, R1:71]

---

[1] Thomas E. Haynie (b. 9 APR 1858, d. 29 JUL 1931) and wife Ella M. Lusby (b. 7 SEP 1868, d. 20 APR 1920) are bur. in Farnham Baptist Church cemetery.
[2] Alexander N. Headley (1843-1915) and wife Lydia R. (1843-1915) are bur. at Coan Baptist Church cemetery.
[3] Isaac Rice and Nancy W. Dodson were married by bond 26 APR 1838 in Northumberland Co.
[4] Ezekiel H. Headley and Elizabeth Barnes were married by bond 30 DEC 1837 in Northumberland Co.
[5] Griffin Headley and Martha H. Beacham were married by bond 12 JAN 1803 in Northumberland Co.
[6] Samuel Bryant and Olivia N. Elmore were married by bond 9 APR 1823 in Richmond Co.
[7] Landmon Headley and Elizabeth Rock, d/o William Rock, were married by bond 25 JAN 1832 in Northumberland Co.
[8] Robert Shirly and Elizabeth Rice, ward of William Rice, were married by bond 8 JAN 1838 in Northumberland Co.
[9] Samuel B. Thrift and Mary A.G. Webb were married by bond 4 MAY 1844 in Richmond Co.

Headley, Judson C. to Mary E. Clark. Consent 9 MAR 1886 by bride, wit. James J. Boothe. No license or minister return. [C11]

Headley, Lindsey to Mrs. Susan Luttrell Scrimger. LINDSEY HEADLEY, farmer, age 63, widowed, b. Northumberland Co., s/o Randal[l] and Elizabeth [Jones] Headley,[1] to SUSAN SCRIMGER, age 56, widow, b. Richmond Co., d/o John and Elizabeth [Gordon] Luttrell.[2] Consent 1 DEC 1874 by parties, no wit. Elder James A. Weaver. 2 DEC 1874 at the res. of the bride. [C7, R:230, R1:37]

Headley, Louis L. to Lucy L. Sisson. LOUIS[3] L. HEADLEY, farmer, age 25, single, b. Richmond Co., s/o Lindsay and Jane [Newsom] Headley,[4] to LUCY L. SISSON, age about 19, b. Richmond Co., d/o [E]lburton [H.] and Hannah [Elizabeth Hardwick] Sisson.[5] Consent 16 APR 1872 by Lucy Sisson, wit. John T. Sisson. William H. Kirk. 18 APR 1872 at Hainesville [sic], Va. [C6, R:237, R1:31]

Headley, Napoleon B. to Julia Ann Clark.[6] NAPOLEON HEADLEY, engineer, age 24, single, b. Northumberland Co., s/o John [Henry] and Margaret [Elizabeth Blackerby] Headley,[7] to JULIA ANN CLARK, age 17, single, b. Northumberland Co., d/o Hiram and Ann T. Clark. Consent undated by Ann [her X mark] Clark and bride, wit. James W. Hale. R.N. Reamy. 15 SEP 1886. [C11, R:316, R1:68]

Headley, Samuel Andrew[8] to Lucie A. Davis. SAMUEL A. HEADLEY, farmer, age 27, single, b. and res. Northumberland Co., s/o Lindsey and Elizabeth [Ann Rock] Headley, to LUCIE A. DAVIS, age 22, single, b. Richmond Co., d/o Robert H. and Lucy Davis. Consent by bride, wit. Kenner R. Cralle. Lloyd Moore.[9] 13 MAY 1860. [C2, R:153, R1:8]

Headley, Samuel Andrew to Willie A. Williams. SAMUEL A. HEADLEY, carpenter, age 34, widower, b. Northumberland Co., s/o Lindsey and Elizabeth [Ann Rock] Headley, to WILLIE A. WILLIAMS, age 20, single, b. Richmond Co., d/o Elijah and Julia A. Williams. Consent 6 AUG 1866 by bride and E.L. Williams, wit. L.O. Davenport. Elijah L. Williams. 12 AUG 1866 at *Cedar Lane*. [C4, R:272, R1:18]

Headley, Septimus, to Mildred Ann Jones.[10] SEPTIMUS HEADLEY, farmer, age 21, b. Northumberland Co., s/o Landman [H.] and Elizabeth [Rock] Headley,[11] to MILDRED ANN JONES, age 16, b. Richmond Co., d/o Jesse and Affira [Apphia Lewis] Jones.[12] John Goodwin. 11 JAN 1854 at the residence of Jesse Jones. [C1, R, R1:1]

---

[1] Randall Headley and Elizabeth Jones were married by bond 31 DEC 1799 in Richmond Co., by consent of her parents John and Hanner Jones.

[2] John Littrell and Elizabeth Gordon were married by bond 29 MAR 1813 in Richmond Co.

[3] His name also appears as Lewis L. Headley.

[4] Lindsey Headley, widower, and Jane Newsom, ward of Richard Headley, were married by bond 9 JUL 1838 in Northumberland Co.

[5] Elburton H. Sisson and Hannah Elizabeth Hardwick were married 9 JAN 1850 in Richmond Co. by Rev. George Northam.

[6] Napoleon B. Headley (1861-1927) and his first wife Julia A. Clark (b. 29 OCT 1868, d. 5 JUN 1890) are bur. at Totuskey Baptist Church cemetery.

[7] John H. Headley (1833-1899) and his wife Margaret E. Blackerby (b. 1838, d. 21 JUN 1903) are bur. at Bethany Baptist Church cemetery, Callao, Va.

[8] Samuel Andrew Headley served iin Co. B, 40th Reg., Va. Inf., C.S.A., wounded in action in 1864 in Spotsylvania Co.

[9] Minister return notes "'The knot was tied' May the 13, /60." However, the license notes date 16 MAY 1860.

[10] Septimus Headley (b. 14 JUL 1833 in Heathsville, Va., d. 23 AUG 1908) and wife Mildred A. Jones (b. 19 FEB 1838, d. 24 FEB 1909 in Heathsville, Va.) are bur. in Coan Baptist Church cemetery.

[11] Landham Headley and Elizabeth Rock were married by bond 25 JAN 1832 in Northumberland Co.

[12] Jesse Jones and Apphia Lewis were married by bond 25 APR 1837 in Richmond Co.

Headley, Thomas William to Willie Ann Allison.[1] THOMAS W. HEADLEY, oysterman, age 25y3m, single, b. Richmond Co., s/o Henry W. and Mary C. [Thrift] Headley,[2] to WILLIE ANN ALLISON, age 21y3m, single, b. Richmond Co., d/o Capt. William and Margaret Ann [Jones] Allison.[3] Oath by John R. [his X mark] Luckham as to age of bride, wit. T.W. Headley. A.B. Dunaway. 19 DEC 1875 at the house of Capt. Allison. [C7, R1:39]

Healey, Ellis E. to Mary Florence Hall. ELLIS E. HEALEY, merchant, age 22, single, b. and res. Westmoreland Co., s/o S.L.S. [Samuel] and Elizabeth A. [Redman] Healey,[4] to MARY FLORENCE HALL, age 22, single, b. Richmond Co., d/o Julius Bass Hall and Elizabeth Bagby. Consent 20 NOV 1888 by bride, no wit. F.B. Beale. 21 NOV 1888 at *Farmer's Hall.* [C12, R:317, R1:73]

Henderson, Frederick (Col.) to Rosa Rich (Col.). FREDERICK HENDERSON, oystering, age 26, single, b. Richmond Co., s/o Frederick and Eliza Henderson, to ROSA RICH, age 21, single, b. Richmond Co., d/o Henry and Jane Rich. Consent 26 DEC 1887 by bride, [her X mark], wit. Robt. [his X mark] Sorrell. Rev. W. Carter. 26 DEC 1887 at Ivanhoe, Va. [C11, R:293, R1:71]

Henderson, John (Col.) to Rachel Napper (Col.). JOHN HENDERSON, farming, age 25, single, b. Westmoreland Co., s/o Carter Henderson and Ann Henderson now Washington, to RACHEL NAPPER, age 20, single, b. Richmond Co., d/o William and Agnes Napper. Rev. Robert Lewis. 2 FEB 1882. [C9, R:312, R1:55]

Henry, Anderson (Col.) to Diana Currie (Col.). ANDERSON HENRY, farmer, age 22, single, b. Richmond Co., s/o Peter and Ellen Henry, to DIANA CURRIE, age 21, single, b. Richmond Co., d/o George and Frances Currie. Consent 20 FEB 1878 by bride Dianah [her X mark] Currie, wit. A.P. Wilson. George Laws. 21 FEB 1878 at *Mulberry Island.* [C8, R:310, R1:44]

Henry, Michael (Col.) to Flossie Cole (Col.). MICHAEL HENRY, farming, age 22, single, b. Richmond Co., s/o Peter and Ellen Henry, to FLOSSIE COLE, age 23, single, b. Westmoreland Co., d/o Annie Cole. Consent 15 JAN 1890 by bride, wit. Robt. Dandridge. George Laws. 16 JAN 1890 at *Waterview.* [C12, R:323, R1:76]

Henry, Millard (Col.) to Mary E. "Lizzie" Blue (Col.). MILLARD HENRY, farmer, age 21y4m6d, single, b. Westmoreland Co., s/o Frederick and Hannah Henry, to MARY LIZZIE BLUE, age 19, single, b. Westmoreland Co., d/o George and Fanny Blue. Consent by mother Fanny [her X mark] Blue, wit. T.N. Balderson, Richard [his X mark] Lee. D.M. Wharton. 18 JUL 1878 at res. of the minister in Westmoreland Co. [C8, R:311, R1:45]

Heyward, John (Col.) to Louise Corbin (Col.). JOHN HEYWARD, laborer, age 24, single, b. Charleston, S.C., s/o John and Judy Heyward, to LOUISE CORBIN, age 23, single, b.

---

[1] Thomas W. Headley (b. 8 SEP 1850, d. 21 MAY 1933) and wife Willie Anne Allison (b. 29 SEP 1854, d. 21 APR 1938 in Baltimore, Md.) are bur. in Farnham Baptist Church cemetery.
[2] Henry W. Headley and Catharine M. Thrift were married by bond 25 JAN 1849 in Richmond Co.
[3] William Allison (b. 1 JUN 1824, d. 7 JUL 1901) and wife Margaret Ann Allison (b. 1 NOV 1832, d. 11 OCT 1894), bur. at Farnham Baptist Church cemetery. William Allison and Margaret Ann Jones were married by bond 1 MAY 1850 in Richmond Co.
[4] Samuel L.S. Healy and Elizabeth A. Redman were married by bond 13 NOV 1847 in Westmoreland Co.

Richmond Co., d/o Travers and Virginia Corbin. Chauncey Leonard. 3 JUN 1871 at Suggett's Point.[1] [C5, R:244, R1:30]

Hill, Bartlett (Col.) to Mary Baylor (Col.). BARTLETT HILL, farmer, age 63, single, b. Richmond Co., s/o Talbot and Arabella Hill, to MARY BAYLOR, age 40, single, b. Richmond Co., d/o William and Patty Palmer. Thomas G. Thomas. 26 OCT 1867 at res. of Thos. [Date]. [C4, R:287, R1:21]

Hill, Warren Pollard to Maria Elizabeth Yerby. WARREN POLLARD HILL, farmer, age 22½, single, b. Lancaster Co., res. Westmoreland Co., s/o Warren P. Hill and Mildred Carter,[2] to MARIA ELIZABETH YERBY, age 21¼, b. Lancaster Co., res. Richmond Co., d/o Jas. [T.] Yerby and Cath. Basye.[3] Consent 1 JAN 1858 by bride, wits. H.L. Biscoe, Wm. W. Rains. Robert Williamson, M.G. 14 FEB 1858 at *Edge Hill*. [C1, R:138, R1:6]

Hill, William (Col.) to Caroline Wright (Col.). WILLIAM HILL, laborer, age 26, single, b. Richmond Co., s/o Bartly and Peggy Hill, to CAROLINE WRIGHT, age 21, single, b. Richmond Co., d/o Joseph and Sally Wright. Thomas G. Thomas. 24 DEC 1866 at house of Joseph Wright. [C4, R:273, R1:19]

Hinson, Charles L. to Anna E. Stewart. CHARLES L. HINSON, merchant, age 28, single, b. Westmoreland Co., s/o Reuben and Mary [M. Hinson] Hinson,[4] to ANNA E. STEWART, age 18, single, b. Baltimore, Md., d/o Richard B. and Ann Stewart. Consent 17 OCT 1866 by father R.B. Stewart, wit. Reverdy B. Stewart. J.H. Davis. 17 OCT 1866 at house of R.B. Stewart. [C3, C4, R:272, R1:18]

Hinson, Charles to Etta M. Luckham. CHARLES HINSON, oystering, age 23, single, b. Richmond Co., s/o Philip and Lucy Hinson, to ETTA M. LUCKHAM, age 16, single, b. Richmond Co., d/o Thomas B. and Mary A. [Brooks] Luckham. Consent 1 DEC 1885 by bride, wit. T.B. Luckham, M.A. Luckham, Richard H. Luckham [reverse]. Robert Williamson. 7 DEC 1885 at Farnham Baptist Church. [C11, R:318, R1:65]

Hinson, Clifton to Mrs. Bettie Saunders, widow of Reuben Jenkins. CLIFTON HINSON, laborer, age 20y4m, single, b. Westmoreland Co., s/o George [W.] and Jane E. [Poe] Hinson,[5] to BETTIE JENKINS, age 26, widow, b. Richmond Co., d/o George and Frances [Jennings] Saunders.[6] Consent 12 FEB 1884 by bride, wits. Fairfax Saunders, Jane C. Hinson. R.N. Reamy. 17 FEB 1884. [C10, R:353, R1:61]

Hinson, Frederick to Millie Ann Bowen. FREDERICK HINSON, farmer, age 21, single, b. and res. Westmoreland Co., s/o Thomas and Ann [Riley] Hinson,[7] to MILLIE ANN BOWEN, age 26, single, b. Richmond Co., d/o William and Peggy Bowen. D.M. Wharton, Rector of Montross Parish. 31 DEC 1867 at the house of the minister. [C4, R:287, R1:22]

---

[1] Suggett's Point is located on the Rappahannock River between Richardson and Farnham Creeks near the south end of Route 614. It was named for John Suckett or one of his descendants.
[2] Bond in Lee, p. 32, is for Thomas P. Hill to Milly E. Carter, d/o James Carter, 22 DEC 1842.
[3] James T. [or W.] Yerby and Catherine Basye were married by bond 17 MAR 1835 in Lancaster Co.
[4] Reuben Hinson and Mary M. Hinson were married by bond 21 SEP 1833 in Westmoreland Co.
[5] George W. Hinson and Jane E. Poe were married by bond 2 APR 1857 in Westmoreland Co.
[6] George Saunders and Frances Jennings were married by bond 23 DEC 1847 in Westmoreland Co.
[7] Thomas Hinson and Ann Riley were married by bond 22 SEP 1841 in Westmoreland Co.

Hinson, James Henry,[1] to Elizabeth F. Hinson. JAMES H. HINSON, farmer, age 21, single, b. Richmond Co., s/o Meredith and Nellie [Coates] Hinson,[2] to ELIZABETH F. HINSON, age 24, single, b. Richmond Co., d/o Reuben and Polly [Mary M.] Hinson.[3] Consent 2 JAN 1866 by bride, wit. D.B. Carter, Arthur [his X mark] Carter. Father Reubin [his X mark] Hinson swears his daughter is over age 21 and he has no objection. Robert N. Reamy. 4 JAN 1866 at res. of Reuben Hinson. [C3, R:270, R1:16]

Hinson, Lewis Alexander Washington to Lucy Bladen Hall.[4] LEWIS A.W. HINSON, farmer, age 32, single, b. Richmond Co., s/o Daniel and Sophia [Newman] Hinson,[5] to LUCY B. HALL, age 20, single, b. Richmond Co., d/o Bladen and Frances [Ann Morris] Hall. Consent 2 JAN 1877 by Bladen Hall. Beverley D. Tucker. 3 JAN 1877 at Cobham Park. [C8, R:306a, R1:42]

Hinson, Philemon H.J. to Mrs. Lucy E.R. Luckham. Consent 11 JUN 1857 by bride Lucy E. [her X mark] Luckum [sic], wits. Wm. T. Tebbs, Lawrence Jones. No license or minister return. [C1]

Hinson, Phillip H.J. to Jane E. Self. PHILLIP H.J. HINSON, farmer, age 35, widowed, b. Richmond Co., s/o Thornton and Bethia [Sandford] Hinson,[6] to JANE E. SELF, age 18, single, b. Richmond Co., d/o John and Martha A. Self. Consent 31 DEC 1864 by mother Martha A. [her X mark] Self, wit. John T. Cooke. Robert Williamson, M.G. 9 JAN 1865 at the res. of the bride's mother in Farnham Parish. [C3; R:204, R1:14]

Hinson, Presley L. to Ruth E. Hinson. PRESLEY L. HINSON, farming, age 38, single, b. Richmond Co., s/o Joshua R. and Susan [Hinson] Hinson,[7] to RUTH E. HINSON, age 28, single, b. Richmond Co., d/o John and Elizabeth Hinson. Consent in FEB 1890 by parties, unsigned. R.N. Reamy. 5 FEB 1890. [C12, R:323, R1:76]

Hinson, Reuben to Susan Williams Hall. REUBEN HINSON, farmer, age 50, widower, b. Richmond Co., s/o James and Ann Hinson, to SUSAN WILLIAMS HALL, age 36, single, b. Richmond Co., d/o Newman and Susan [Williams Gutridge] Hall. Consent 23 JUL 1863 by bride Susan W. [her X mark] Hall, wits. Bladen Hall, John Pullen. John Pullen. 23 JUL 1863 at Bladen Hall's. [C3, R:160, R1:12]

Hinson, Robert Walter to Sarah J. Reamy. ROBERT WALTER HINSON, farmer, age 29, single, b. Richmond Co., s/o Daniel and Sophia [Newman] Hinson,[8] to SARAH J. REAMY, age 22, single, b. Richmond Co., d/o Robert N. [Sr.] and Jane Reamy. Consent 25 MAY 1882 from Stonewall Magisterial District. H.H. Fones. 8 JUN 1882. [C9, R:313, R1:56]

Hinson, Taylor F. to Mrs. Mary Jane Jenkins, widow of Robert Bispham. TAYLOR F. HINSON, farmer, age 21, single, b. Westmoreland Co., s/o William F. and Mary A. [Ann Neale] Hinson,[9]

---

[1] James Henry Hinson, Jr. served in Co. D, 40th Reg. Va. Inf., C.S.A., and was sent to Libby Prison.
[2] Meredith Hinson and Nelly Coates were married by bond 7 MAY 1839 in Westmoreland Co.
[3] Reuben Hinson and Mary M. Hinson, d/o William Hinson, were married y bond 25 SEP 1833 in Westmoreland Co.
[4] L.A.W. Hinson [also Hynson] (b. 7 DEC 1842, d. 10 DEC 1921 near Wellford's Wharf) and his wife Lucy Bladen Hall (b. 3 FEB 1856, d. 31 MAY 1927 near Sharps, Va.) is bur. in Cobham Park Baptist Church cemetery. He served in Co. G, 15th Va. Cav., C.S.A.
[5] Daniel Hinson and Sophia Newman were married by bond 20 JAN 1840 in Richmond Co.
[6] Thornton Hinsonn and Bethia Sandford were married by bond 25 JUL 1816 in Westmoreland Co.
[7] Joshua R. Hinson and Susan Hinson were married by bond 6 MAY 1845 in Westmoreland Co.
[8] Daniel Hinson and Sophia Newman were married by bond 20 JAN 1840 in Richmond Co.
[9] William F. Hinson and Mary Ann Neale, d/o Lucinda Miller, were married by bond 23 JAN 1826 in Westmoreland Co.

to MARY J. BISPHAM, age 28, widow, b. Richmond Co., d/o William B. and Felicia Jenkins. D.M. Wharton. 12 DEC 1866 at the res. of the bride. [C4, R:272, R1:18]

Hinson, Warren to Catherine Hynson. WARREN HINSON, farmer, age 23, single, b. Richmond Co., res. Westmoreland Co., s/o Joshua [R.] and Susan [Hinson] Hinson, to CATHERINE HYNSON,[1] age 22, single, b. Richmond Co., d/o Reuben and Polly Hinson. Consent undated by bride Catharine Hynson, no wit. R.N. Reamy. 30 DEC 1875 at R. Hinson's. [C7, R:262, R1:39]

Hinton, William George to Emma Everett Bryant.[2] WILLIAM GEORGE HINTON, carpenter, age 29, single, b. Richmond Co., res. Northumberland Co., s/o George Hinton and Margaret Hinton (née Brown),[3] to EMMA E. BRYANT, age 21, single, b. Richmond Co., d/o Richard P. [Payne] Bryant.[4] Consent by bride, wit. F. Settle. F.W. Claybrook. 30 MAY 1882 at Richard Bryant's. [C9, NN:2 JUN 1882, R:313, R1:56]

Hinson, William Wellford to Jane Bowen. WILLIAM W. HINSON, farmer, age 50, widowed, b. Richmond Co., s/o William [Sr.] and Mary [Ball] Hinson, to JANE BOWEN, age 21, single, b. Richmond Co., d/o Joseph and Ann Bowen. Consent by bride, wit. James Scates. R.N. Reamy. 11 JUN 1878. [C8, R:311, R1:45]

Hinson, William Wellford to Bettie A. Franklin. WILLIAM W. HINSON, farmer, age 49, widowed, b. Richmond Co., s/o William [Sr.] and Mary [Ball] Hinson, to BETTIE A. FRANKLIN, age 37, single, b. Westmoreland Co., d/o Zachariah and Lucy [Hinson] Franklin.[5] Consent 14 FEB 1877 by bride, wit. Mary S. Balderson. Robert N. Reamy. 14 FEB 1877 at res. of James Balderson. [C8, R:306a, R1:42]

Hints, James (Col.) to Ellen Thompson (Col.), alias Croxton. JAMES HINTS, laborer, age 22, single, b. Essex Co., s/o Louis and Phebe Hints, to ELLEN THOMPSON, age 21, single, b. Richmond Co., d/o Thomas and Maria Croxton. Consent 27 DEC 1875 by bride Ellen [her X mark] Thompson, wits. Cyrus Harding, Ned Dunaway, Sr. Allen Brown, minister. 30 DEC 1875 at *Edge Hill*. [C7, R:262, R1:39]

Hoble, Major (Col.) to Lucy Middleton (Col.). MAJOR HOBLE, laborer, age 24, single, b. St. Mary's Co., Md., s/o Clem and Mary L. Dorsey, to LUCY MIDDLETON, age 21, single, b. Richmond Co., d/o William and Rose Middleton. Robert Williamson, M.G. 9 JUN 1866 at *Marleton*. [C4, R:271, R1:17]

Holmes, Straughan (Col.) to Mrs. Lavinia Thornton Harding (Col.). STRAUGHAN HOLMES, farmer, age 30, single, b. Essex Co., s/o Anderson and Alice Holmes, to LAVINIA HARDING, age 30, widow, b. Richmond Co., d/o David and Winney Thornton. Allen Brown, minister. 15 JUL 1872 at the res. of the bride. [C6, R:238, R1:32]

---

[1] Spelling Hyson based on the bride's signature on her consent.
[2] William G. Hinton (b. 23 JUN 1853, d. 24 MAY 1926) and his wife Emma E. Bryant (b. 22 AUG 1860, d. 29 JAN 1931) are bur. in the Hinton Family Cemetery near Farnham, Va.
[3] George Hinton and Margaret Brown were married by bond 19 FEB 1842 in Westmoreland Co.
[4] Capt. Richard P. Bryant (b. 30 AUG 1824, d. 22 APR 1905) is bur. in Farnham Baptist Church cemetery.
[5] Zachariah Franklin and Lucy Hinson were married by bond 2 FEB 1825 in Westmoreland Co.

Holmes, Travers (Col.) to Rose Stewart (Col.). TRAVERS HOLMES, oystering, age 25, single, b. Richmond Co., s/o James and Louisa Holmes, to ROSE STEWART, age 23, single, b. Richmond Co., d/o Henry Stewart (dec'd.) and Hannah Stewart. Consent 22 DEC 1882 by bride Rose [her X mark] Stewart, wit. A.C. Pearson. Charles Sparks. 21 DEC 1882. [C10, R:314, R1:57]

Homes, Edmond (Col.) to L.A. Jackson (Col.). EDMOND HOMES, laborer, age 35, single, b. Essex Co., s/o Willis Homes (dec'd.) and Amey Homes, to L.A. JACKSON, age 35, single, b. Essex Co., d/o James and Winnie Jackson. Oath 30 APR 1880 by Samuel G. Dishman to ages, wit. C.B. Gray. George Laws. 18 MAY 1880. [C9, R:315, R1:50]

Homes, J. to Willie Saunders. Consent 22 JUL 1881 bride, wit. S.W. Brooks. No license or minister return. [C9, R1:54]

Homes, James (Col.) to Cealia Gordon (Col.). JAMES HOMES, farming, age 54, widowed, b. Richmond Co., s/o Phil and Daphne Homes, to CEALIA GORDON, age 28, single, b. Richmond Co., d/o Ellic and Maria Gordon. Oath 7 APR 1879 by Samuel G. Dishman as to age. T.G. Thomas at the res. of James Homes. 10 APR 1879. [C8, C9, R:307, R1:47]

Hoomes, John Marshall (Col.) to Louisa Corbin (Col.). JOHN MARSHALL HOOMES, laborer, age 27, single, b. Essex Co., s/o Anderson and Alcey Hoomes, to LOUISA CORBIN, age 20y11m, single, b. Richmond Co., d/o Samuel and Lucy Corbin. Robert Williamson, M.G. 15 NOV 1871 at Middleton Hall's. [C6, R1:30]

Hornsby, John to Mrs. Ann B. Lewis Sebree. JOHN HORNSBY, age 60, widowed, b. Richmond Co., s/o James and Rachel [Webb] Hornsby, to ANN B. SEBREE, age 43, widow, b. Richmond Co., d/o Charles and Sarah Lewis. Consent 8 JAN 1870 by bride Ann [her X mark], wit. E.M. Rains. Bartholomew Dodson, Parson. 11 JAN 1870. [C5, R:233, R1:27]

Howe, John Milton to Frances E. Scott.[1] JOHN M. HOWE, age 29, single, b. Richmond Co., s/o Thomas and Sally [Tune] Howe,[2] to FRANCES E. SCOTT, age 22, single, b. Westmoreland Co., d/o James and Frances Scott. Consent by bride, wits. John B. Sisson and Samuel E. Sandy. No minister return. 8 FEB 1860 at Henry Scott's. [C2, R:153, R1:8]

Hubbard, James (Col.) to Mary Sophia Jackson (Col.). JAMES HUBBARD, farmer, age 30, single, b. Westmoreland Co., s/o Taliaferro and Mary Hubbard, to MARY SOPHIA JACKSON, age 20, single, b. Richmond Co., d/o Robert and Polly Jackson. George Laws. 19 DEC 1872 at Robert Jackson's. [C6, R:238, R1:33]

Hudland, John Robert (Col.) to Mary Jane Conner (Col.). JOHN ROBERT HUDLAND, mechanic, age 24, single, b. Richmond Co., s/o John and Lucy Hudland, to MARY JANE CONNER, age 20, single, b. Richmond Co., d/o John W. and Susan Jane Conner. Rev. W. Carter. 10 JUN 1880 at the bride's home. [C9, R:315, R1:50]

---

[1] John M. Howe (b. 11 JUL 1830, d. 29 MAY 1920) and wife Frances E. Scott (b. 2 JAN 1837, d. 19 SEP 1913) are bur. at Wicomico United Methodist Church Cemetery, Northumberland Co.
[2] Thomas Howe and Sally Tune were married by bond 22 DEC 1821 in Richmond Co.

Hudson, James S. to Mrs. Maria C. Dobyns Dameron.[1] JAMES S. HUDSON, farmer, age 30, single, b. Richmond Co., s/o Henry O. and Catharine [S.J. Gordon] Hudson,[2] to MARIA C. DAMERON, age 24, widow, b. Richmond, d/o Joseph [A.] and Elizabeth [M. Gordon] Dobyns.[3] Consent 15 JAN 1869 by bride, wit. Richard H. Sisson. Robert Williamson, M.G. 21 JAN 1869 at Union Village. [C5, R, R1:25]

Hudson, Joseph D. to Naomi Virginia Bulger. JOSEPH D. HUDSON, farmer, age 48, widowed, b. and res. Westmoreland Co., s/o William R. and Catharine [Davis] Hudson,[4] to NAOMI VIRGINIA BALGER, age 25, single b. Westmoreland Co., d/o Latham and Margaret Bulger. R.A. Castleman. 23 APR 1890 at the res. of the groom in Westmoreland Co. [C12, R:323a, R1:77]

Hudson, Matthew S.[5] to Eliza A. Hale. MATTHEW S. HUDSON, age 26, single, b. Richmond Co., s/o Samuel and Nancy [Lewis] Hudson,[6] to ELIZA A. HALE, age 22, single, b. Richmond Co., d/o William S. and Bisea [Furdelia Biskey King] Hale.[7] Consent 20 SEP 1861 by bride Eliza A. [her X mark] Hale, wits. B.B. King, Wm. H. Hale. O.M.T. Samuels. 22 SEP 1861 at Union [Cones], Westmoreland Co. [C3, R:123 partial, R1:11]

Hudson, Presley James to Sarah Ann Balderson.[8] PRESLEY J. HUDSON, farmer, age 24, single, b. Richmond Co., s/o Samuel and Nancy [Lewis] Hudson, to SARAH A. BALDERSON, age 26, single, b. Richmond Co., d/o John [Lee] and Lucy [Pearce Tune] Balderson.[9] Consent 28 MAR 1861 by bride, wits. Benj. Tucker, Thos. [his X mark] Vandingham. [C3, R:123, R1:10]

Hutchinson, John T. to Lizzie V. Taylor. JOHN T. HUTCHINSON, farmer, age 21, single, b. New Jersey, s/o Francis and Mary Hutchinson, to LIZZIE V. TAYLOR, age 22, single, b . Richmond Co., d/o Daniel and Lydia Taylor. G.H. Northam. 25 MAR 1873 at *Woodbine* in Westmoreland Co. [C6, R:235, R1:34]

Hutt, Augustus G.L.[10] to Ophelia B. Northen. AUGUSTUS G.L. HUTT, farming, age 22, single, b. Richmond Co., s/o Augustus N. [Neal] and Cornelia [A. Northen] Hutt, *q.v.*, to OPHELIA B. NORTHEN, age 18, single, b. Richmond Co., d/o George D. Northen and Mary C. Northen, *q.v.* Consent 7 JAN 1884 by father George D. Northen, wit. C.J. Bronner. G.H. Northam. 9 JAN 1884 at G.D. Northen's. [C10, R:353, R1:61]

Hutt, Augustus Neal[11] to Cornelia A. Northen. AUGUSTINE N. HUTT, farmer, age 23, single, b. and res. Westmoreland Co., s/o Steptoe D. and Nancy N. [Moxley] Hutt,[12] to CORNELIA A. NORTHEN, age 15, single, b. Richmond Co., d/o George and Elizabeth [H. Bryant] Northen.[13]

---

[1] James S. Hudson (1831-1890) and wife Maria C. Dameron (1843-1917) are bur. in Gibeon Baptist Church cemetery.
[2] Henry O. Hudson and Kitty S.J. Gordon were married by bond 14 JUN 1822 in Richmond Co.
[3] Joseph A. Dobyns and Elizabeth M. Gordonn were married by bond 20 DEC 1839 in Richmond Co.
[4] William R. Hudson and Catharine Davis were married by bond 18 DEC 1828 in Richmond Co., by consent of his mother Martha Hudson, and consent of her mother and guardian Caty Alderson.
[5] Matthew Hudson served in Co. K, 9th Va. Cav., C.S.A.
[6] Samuel Hudson and Nancy Lewis were married by bond 9 AUG 1825 in Richmond Co.
[7] William S. Hale and Furdelia Bisky King were married by bond 29 JAN 1837 in Richmond Co.
[8] Presley J. Hudson (b. 7 OCT 1836, d. 19 NOV 1925) and his wife Sarah A. Balderson (b. 30 OCT 1832, d. 26 SEP 1887) are bur. at Totuskey Baptist Church cemetery. He served in Co. K, 9th Va. Cav., C.S.A.
[9] John Balderson and Lucy Tune were married by bond 1 JAN 1831 in Richmond Co.
[10] Augustus G.L. Hutt (b. 9 JAN 1862, d. 28 OCT 1942) is bur. at Jerusalem Baptist Church cemetery.
[11] Private Augustus Neal Hutt (b. 23 SEP 1837, d. 16 JUN 1862) is bur. in Hollywood Cemetery. He served in Co. C, 9th Va. Cav., C.S.A.
[12] Steptoe D. Hutt, of Alabama, and Nancy N. Moxley were married by bond 20 OCT 1836 in Richmond Co.
[13] George Northen and Elizabeth H. Bryant were married by bond 17 FEB 1835 in Richmond Co.

Consent 8 OCT 1860 by George Northen, wit. A.N. Bramham. Elder O.M.T. Samuels. 10 OCT 1860. [C2, R:154, R1:9]

Hutt, Ernest L. to Mollie Omohundro. ERNEST L. HUTT, merchant, age 26, single, b. Westmoreland Co., s/o Edwin and Susan [J. Brown] Hutt,[1] to MOLLIE OMOHUNDRO, age 24, single, b. Richmond Co., d/o William H. and Eliza [Ann Hutt] Omohundro.[2] Consent 13 JUL 1887 by bride. J.F. Robins. 14 JUL 1887 at the late residence of Wm. Omohundro (dec'd.). [C11, R:292, R1:70]

Hutt, Hiram M.[3] to Sallie Lucia Omohundro.[4] HIRAM M. HUTT, merchant, age 33, single, b. and res. Westmoreland Co., s/o Edwin[5] and Nancy [Ann N. McClanahan] Hutt, to SALLIE LUCIA OMOHUNDRO, age 24, single, b. Richmond Co., d/o William H. and Eliza [Ann Hutt] Omohundro. Oath 26 MAY 1880 by Wm. H. Omohundro as to age of the bride. W.A. Crocker. 27 MAY 1880. [C9, R:315, R1:50]

Hynes, John E. to Sarah A. Self. JOHN E. HYNES, mechanic, age 30, single, b. Ireland, res. Westmoreland Co., s/o Edward and Mary Hynes, to SARAH A. SELF, age 35, single, b. Richmond Co., d/o Moses and Mary S. [Smith] Self.[6] Consent 24 NOV 1880 by bride, wit. William Allison. Beverley D. Tucker. 24 NOV 1880 at St. John's Chapel. [C9, R:316, R1:51]

I

Ingram, Charles H. to Bettie H. Callahan. CHARLES H. INGRAM, farmer, age 24, single, b. and res. Northumberland Co., s/o Griffin and Frances H. Ingram, to BETTIE H. CALLAHAN, age 20, single, b. Westmoreland Co., d/o William C. and Mary R. [Rice] Callahan.[7] G.H. Northam. 19 DEC 1867 at Warsaw, Va. [C4, R:287, R1:22]

J

Jackson, Andrew (Col.) to Mrs. Addie Stevens (Col.). ANDREW JACKSON, oystering, age 35, widowed, b. Lancaster Co., res. Maryland, s/o James and Hagar Jackson, to ADDIE STEVENS, age 30, widow, b. Richmond Co., d/o [blank] and Susan Johnson. Consent from Ivanhoe, Va. 1 OCT 1885 by bride Addie [her X mark] Stevens, wit. T.J. Comodore. Rev. W. Carter. 1 OCT 1885 at the res. of the bride. [C10, R:317, R1:65]

Jackson, Austin (Col.) to Betsey Ann Lucas (Col.). AUSTIN JACKSON, laborer, age 21y7m10d, single, b. Richmond Co., s/o Samuel and Martha Jackson, to BETSEY ANN LUCAS, age 20, single, b. Richmond Co., d/o Niel and Rebecca Lucas. Consent unsigned, wit. ReBecker [her X mark] Cokers, Wm. N. [his X mark] Rich. Rev. [L.] Marshall. 2 JAN[8] 1884 at the Second Baptist Church. [C10, R:353, R1:61]

---

[1] Edwin Hutt and Susan J. Brown were married 28 NOV 1856 in Westmoreland Co.
[2] William H. Omohundro and Eliza Ann Hutt were married 16 DEC 1851 in Richmond Co. by Rev. Alfred Wiles.
[3] Hiram M. Hutt, Sr. (1846-1918 [tombstone gives year 1917]) is bur. at Calvary United Methodist Church cemetery.
[4] NN:11 JUN 1880 announces marriage of Hiram and Sallie; NN:13 JN 1882 announces the death of Hiram M. Hutt's wife.
[5] Edwin Hutt (b. 8 JAN 1819, d. 6 MAY 1889), bur. at St. Paul's Episcopal Church cemetery at Nomini Grove, Va. He served in Co. 4, 111th Va. Mil., C.S.A. Edwin Hutt, s/o Gerard Hutt, and Nancy N. McClannahan, d/o John McClannahan, were married by bond 29 NOV 1837 in Westmoreland Co.
[6] Moses Self and Mary S. Smith were married by bond 5 JAN 1826 in Westmoreland Co.
[7] William C. Callahan and Mary R. Rice were married by bond 25 MAR 1844 in Westmoreland Co.
[8] The license gives date of marriage as 2 FEB 1884, while the return provides 2 JAN 1884.

Jackson, Dennis (Col.) to Charlotte L.V. Adkins (Col.). DENNIS JACKSON, farming, age 35, widowed, b. Richmond Co., [names of parents not completed], to CHARLOTTE L.V. ADKINS, age 17, single, b. Richmond, d/o Nelson and Fanny Adkins. Charles Sparks. 26 DEC 1886 at Nelson's house. [C11, R:317, R1:68]

Jackson, Fleet (Col.) to Betsey Ann Davis (Col.). FLEET JACKSON, laborer, age 22y2m, single, b. Westmoreland Co., s/o David and Eliza Jackson, to BETSEY ANN DAVIS, age 23, single, b. Richmond Co., d/o Edward and Betsey Davis. Thomas G. Thomas. 25 DEC 1872 at house of Charles Lee. [C6, R:238, R1:33]

Jackson, George (Col.) to Winnie Munroe (Col.). GEORGE JACKSON, farming, age 25, single, b. Richmond Co., s/o Robert and Polly Jackson, to WINNIE MUNROE, age 21, single, b. Richmond Co., d/o James and Fanny Munroe. Consent 2 MAY 1879 by James Hubbard. Allen Brown, minister. 4 MAY 1879 at the home of the bride. [C8, R:307, R1:47]

Jackson, Henry (Col.) to Florence Griggs (Col.). HENRY JACKSON, farmer, age 23, single, b. Richmond Co., s/o George and Jane Jackson, to FLORENCE GRIGGS, age 18, single, b. Westmoreland Co., d/o Martha Griggs [father not known]. George [his X mark] Laws. 7 FEB 1884 at *Mulberry Island.* [C10, R:353, R1:61]

Jackson, James (Col.) to Frances Fauntleroy (Col.). JAMES JACKSON, farmer, age 52, single, b. Westmoreland Co., s/o James and Atha Jackson, to FRANCES FAUNTLEROY, age 30, single, b. Westmoreland Co., d/o Simon and Alice Fauntleroy. Jeremia[h] Graham. 13 MAR 1868 at Abraham Proctor's. [C4, R:253, R1:23]

Jackson, Lewis (Col.) to Ophelia Bailor (Col.). LEWIS JACKSON, oystering, age 23, single, b. Essex Co., s/o Lewis and Charlotte Ann Jackson, to OPHELIA BAILOR, age 20, single, b. Richmond Co., d/o John and Louisa Bailor. Rev. L. Marshall. 29 DEC 1885 at *Sabine Hall*.[1] [C10, R:318, R1:65]

Jackson, Meredith (Col.) to Fanny Ellen Jackson (Col.). MEREDITH JACKSON, farming, age 22y7m, single, b. Richmond Co., s/o William and Emily Jackson, to FANNY ELLEN JACKSON, age 28, single, b. Richmond Co., d/o Samuel and Martha Jackson. David Veney. 17 JAN 1880 at Samuel Jackson's house called Wilson's Place. [C9, R:314, R1:49]

Jackson, Nelson (Col.) to Eugenia Thompson (Col.). NELSON JACKSON, oysterman, age 29, single, b. King and Queen Co., s/o Cesar and Hannah Jackson, to EUGENIA THOMPSON, age 22, single, b. Richmond Co., d/o Harvey and Harriet Thompson. Allen Brown, minister. 25 DEC 1873 at the res. of the bride. [C6, R:236, R1:35]

Jackson, Robert (Col.) to Annie Norris (Col.). ROBERT JACKSON, oystering, age 33, widowed, b. Richmond Co., s/o Mary Jackson, to ANNIE NORRIS, age 24, single, b. Richmond Co., d/o Cyrus and Sina Norris. Affidavit to age of bride by J.W. Chinn. Rev. W. Carter. 16 AUG 1885 at the res. of the bride. [C10, R:317, R1:65]

---

[1] *Sabine Hall* was established by Landon Carter and is located on the south side of Route 360 near Warsaw, Va.

Jackson, Thomas to Mary L. Newman. THOMAS JACKSON, farmer, age 26, single, b. Richmond Co., s/o William and Apphia Jackson, to MARY L. NEWMAN, age 21, single, b. Richmond Co., d/o John and Millie Newman. E.L. Williams. 4 JAN 1866 at Corbin Parke's. [C4, R:270, R1:16]

Jackson, William [FB] to Emily Ann Veney [FB]. Consent 18 JUN 1856 by bride Emaly [her X mark] Venie, wits. Humphrey Venie, William [his X cross] Venie. No license or minister return. [C1]

Jackson, William (Col.) to Eliza Rich (Col.). WILLIAM JACKSON, age 38, widower, b. Richmond Co., s/o William and Apphia Jackson, to ELIZA RICH, age 22, single, b. Richmond Co., d/o James and Kitty Rich. Thomas G. Thomas. 24 JUL 1873 at Kate Rich's house. [C6, R:235, R1:34]

Jackson, William H. (Col.) to Elmira E. Newman (Col.). WILLIAM H. JACKSON, farmer, age 22, single, b. Richmond Co., s/o Samuel and Martha Jackson, to ELMIRA E. NEWMAN, age 19, single, b. Richmond Co., d/o John and Millie Newman. Andrew Fisher. 8 FEB 1867 at *Belleville*.[1] [C4, R:285, R1:20]

Jeffries, Isaac S. to Dorathea "Dollie" Belfield.[2] ISAAC S. JEFFRIES, farmer, age 20, single, b. Richmond Co., s/o Ebenezer C. and Ann A. [Jeffries] Jeffries, to DOLLIE BELFIELD, age 22, single, b. Richmond Co., d/o Richard C. and Mary F. [Frances Harwood] Belfield.[3] Consent 31 OCT 1874 by bride. H.H. Fones. 1 NOV 1874. [C7, R:230, R1:37]

Jenkins, Benjamin T., to Mrs. Saluda F. Hudson, widow of Thomas N. Reynolds. BENJAMIN T. JENKINS, oysterman, age 40, widowed, b. Gloucester Co., s/o Miles and Catharine Jenkins, to SALUDA F. REYNOLDS, age 33, widow, b. Charlotte Co., N.C., d/o Ward and Martha Hudson. Robert Williamson, M.G. 10 MAY 1866 at the bride's res. near Durrettsville, Va. [C4, R:271, R1:17]

Jenkins, Carter to Austenia Blanche Richards. CARTER JENKINS, mariner, age 23y9m3d, single, b. Richmond Co., s/o Thomas A. and Martha [Brewer Sanford] Jenkins (dec'd.), to AUSTENIA BLANCHE RICHARDS, age 21y8m12d, single, b. Richmond Co., d/o [Austin] N. and Martha C. [Drake] Richards.[4] Consent 19 JAN 1882 by bride, wit. A.N. Richards. F.B. Beale. 22 JAN 1882. [C9, R:312, R1:55]

Jenkins, Dangerfield to Susan E. Sandy. DANGERFIELD JENKINS, farmer, age 21, single, b. Richmond Co., s/o William [B.] and Felicia J. Jenkins, to SUSAN E. SANDY, age 21, single, b. Richmond Co., d/o Samuel and Elizabeth [Pullen] Sandy.[5] G.H. Northam. 15 FEB 1869. [C5, R, R1:25]

Jenkins, Dangerfield to Belle Thrift. DANGERFIELD JENKINS, farmer, age 28, widowed, b. Richmond Co., s/o William [B.] and Felicia [J.] Jenkins, to BELLE THRIFT, age 26, single, b.

---

[1] Belleville or Belle Ville was in early times the property of George Berrick, and later Moore Fauntleroy Brockenbrough.
[2] Isaac S. Jeffries (b. 1856, d. 17 APR 1928 in Warsaw, Va.) and wife Dorathea Belfield (1852-1891) are bur. in St. John's Episcopal Church cemetery.
[3] Richard C. Belfield and Mary Frances Harwood were married 31 MAR 1847 in Richmond Co. by Rev. John Pullen.
[4] Austin N. Richards and Martha Drake were married 18 DEC 1845 in Richmond Co. by Rev. John Pullen.
[5] Samuel Sandy and Elizabeth Pullen were married by bond 8 JAN 1822 in Richmond Co.

Richmond Co., d/o Samuel B. and Mary A. [Webb] Thrift.[1] G.H. Northam. 7 DEC 1876. [C7, R:306, R1:41]

Jenkins, David (Col.) to Mrs. Matilda Blair (Col.). DAVID JENKINS, farming, age 60, widowed, b. Richmond Co., s/o Peter and Beckey Jenkins, to MATILDA BLAIR, age 37, widow, b. Richmond Co., d/o Osborn Blair. Consent by David Jenkins, wit. George R. Northam; consent 4 DEC 1882 by bride Malinda [her X mark] Blair, wit. M.S. Delano. G.H. Northam. 6 DEC 1882. [C9, R:314, R1:57]

Jenkins, Fleet (Col.) to Rose Fouchee (Col.). FLEET JENKINS, farming, age 24, single, b. Richmond Co., s/o George Jenkins and Jane Ball, to ROSE FOUCHEE, age 18, single, b. Richmond Co., d/o Daniel and Dolly Fouchee. Consent 26 DEC 1884 from Sharps Wharf by Daniel Fouchee, Fleet Jenkins. N. Atkins. 28 DEC 1884 at res. of Daniel Fouchee. [C10, R:356, R1:63]

Jenkins, James to Mrs. Frances France Jenkins. JAMES JENKINS, farmer, age 49, widowed, b. Richmond Co., s/o John and Becky Jenkins, to FRANCES JENKINS, age 35, widow, b. Richmond Co., d/o Reuben Marks and Fanny France.[2] John Pullen. 20 FEB 1862 at James Jenkins'. [C3, R:140, R1:11]

Jenkins, James to Mrs. Susan Oliff, widow of Octavus Hall. JAMES JENKINS, farmer, age 40, widowed, b. Richmond Co., s/o Benjamin and Susan [Pullen] Jenkins,[3] to SUSAN HALL, age 27, widow, b. Richmond Co., d/o James and Lucy Oliff. D.M. Wharton. 22[4] AUG 1867 in the public road near the minister's house. [C4, R:287, R1:21]

Jenkins, James A. to Jenue A. Saunders. JAMES A. JENKINS, carpenter, age 34, single, b. Richmond Co., s/o Thomas A. and Julia A. [Saunders] Jenkins,[5] to JENUE A. SANDERS [sic], age 17, single, b. Richmond Co., d/o A.J. [Allen James] and Alice D.C. [Newman] Saunders. Consent 26 NOV 1872 by mother Alice D.C. Sanders and bride. G.H. Northam. 28 NOV 1872. [C6, R:238, R1:32]

Jenkins, James B. to Mrs. M.V. Oliff. JAMES B. JENKINS, farming, age 23, single, b. Richmond Co., s/o James and Ann Jenkins, to M.V. OLIFF, age 23, widowed, b. Richmond Co., d/o Welford W. and Maria Hinson. Consent 5 JAN 1885 by bride, wit. Charles H. Balderson, J.P. R.N. Reamy. 8 JAN 1885. [C10, R:316, R1:64]

Jenkins, James Henry to Amelia S. Saunders.[6] JAMES H. JENKINS, farmer, age 25, single, b. Richmond Co., s/o George and Mary Jenkins. to AMELIA S. SAUNDERS [sic], age 13y6m, single, b. Richmond Co., d/o William A.H. and Margaret A. [Ann Morris] Saunders. Consent 13 JAN 1866 by father Wm. A.H. Saunders [sic], wit. Robert Hall, clerk. John Pullen. 16 JAN 1866 at William A.H. Saunders'. [C3, C4, R:270, R1:16]

---

[1] Samuel B. Thrift and Mary A.G. Webb were married by bond 4 MAY 1844 in Richmond Co.
[2] Reuben Marks and Fanny France were married by bond 12 JAN 1819 in Richmond Co. She was d/o John France and Catharine Fones.
[3] Benjamin Jenkins and Susan Pullen were married by bond 14 JAN 1817 in Westmoreland Co.
[4] The license gives date of marriage 22 AUG 1867, while the return notes 21 AUG 1867.
[5] Thomas Jenkins and Julia Saunders were married by bond 11 APR 1838 in Richmond Co. by Rev. Thomas M. Washington.
[6] James H. Jenkins (b. 1841, d. 30 JUN 1900 at Foneswood, Va.) and his wife Amelia S. Saunders (b. 13 JUL 1851, d. 13 MAY 1936 at Colonial Beach, Westmoreland Co.) are bur. in the Jenkins Family Graveyard near Foneswood, Va. He served as a private and musician in Co. D, 40th Va. Inf., C.S.A.

Jenkins, John to Caroline Jones. JOHN JENKINS, mechanic, age 23, single, b. Richmond Co., s/o Matthew and Eliza [Richards] Jenkins,[1] to CAROLINE JONES, age 24, single, b. Richmond Co., d/o Samuel and Emily Jones. Robert Williamson, M.G. 24 FEB 1867 at Durrettsville, Va. [C4, R:285, R1:20]

Jenkins, John to Mrs. Ann Habron Saunders. JOHN JENKINS, farmer, age 30, widower, b. Richmond Co., s/o Matthew and Eliza [Richards] Jenkins, to ANN SAUNDERS, age 30, widow, b. Richmond Co., d/o Benjamin and Serena [Sanford] Habron.[2] G.H. Northam. 4 MAR 1873. [C6, R:235, R1:33]

Jenkins, Leroy (Col.) to Mrs. Lear Lewis (Col.). LEROY JENKINS, laborer, age 40, widowed, b. Richmond Co., s/o David and Maria Jenkins, to LEAR LEWIS, age 40, widow, b. Richmond Co., parents unknown. Consent 29 FEB 1888 by Lear [her X mark] Lewis. Rev. Walker Carter. 2 MAR 1888 at the home of the bride. [C11, R:315, R1:72]

Jenkins, Payton to Eliza A. Allison. PAYTON JENKINS, farming, age 28, single, b. Richmond Co., s/o Matthew [Jr.] and [Emmaline] Susan [Harper] Jenkins,[3] to ELIZA A. ALLISON, age 22, single, b. Richmond Co., d/o William Allison. Consent undated by bride, wit. D.E. Douglass. G.H. Northam. 28 AUG 1879 at *Glenmore*. [C8, R:308, R1:47]

Jenkins, Peter (Col.) to Millie Newton (Col.). PETER JENKINS, farming, age 44, widowed, b. Richmond Co., s/o Peter and Rebecca Jenkins, to MILLIE NEWTON, age 38, single, b. Richmond Co., d/o Isaac and Polly Newton. Edmond Rich. 7 MAR 1888 at the res. of the minister. [C11, R:315, R1:72]

Jenkins, Reuben to Bettie Saunders. REUBEN JENKINS, farmer, age 21, single, b. Richmond Co., s/o George and Mary Jenkins, to BETTIE SANDERS [sic], age 21, single, b. Richmond Co., d/o George and Frances Sanders. Consent 26 MAY 1873 by bride, wit. B.B. Smoot. Robert N. Reamy. 29 MAY 1873 at the house of the minister. [C6, R:235, R1:34]

Jenkins, Robert S. to Mary E. Boswell. ROBERT S. JENKINS, farming, age 34y on 9 JAN 1889, widowed, b. Richmond Co., s/o Mathew Jenkins, to MARY E. BOSWELL, age 28, single, b. Richmond Co., d/o J.T. and Sarah H. Boswell. Consent 1 JAN 1888 from Emmerton, Va. by bride. G.H. Northam. 1 JAN 1889 at res. of J.T. Boswell. [C12, R:327, R1:74]

Jenkins, Robert Samuel to Eliza Ann Douglass. ROBERT SAMUEL JENKINS, farmer, age 27, single, b. Richmond Co., s/o Matthew [Jr.] and [Emmaline] Susan [Harper] Jenkins, to ELIZA ANN DOUGLASS, age 25, single, b. Richmond Co., d/o Thomas [H.] and Malinda [Douglass] Douglass.[4] Consent by parties, wit. H.P. Harper. G.H. Northam. 15 DEC 1880. [C9, R:316, R1:51]

Jenkins, Samuel to Willie Ann Clarke. SAMUEL JENKINS, farming, age 30, widowed, b. Richmond Co., s/o Matthew and Susan Jenkins, to WILLIE ANN CLARKE, age 22, single, b. Richmond

---

[1] Matthew Jenkins and Eliza Richards were married 8 DEC 1840 in Richmond Co. by Rev. John M. Waddey.
[2] Benjamin Habron and Rany Sanford were married by bond 14 SEP 1832 in Richmond Co.
[3] Matthew Jenkins, Jr. and Emmaline Susan Harper were married 28 NOV 1849 in Richmond Co. by Rev. William N. Ward.
[4] Thomas H. Douglass and Malindy Douglass were married 4 APR 1845 in Richmond Co. by Rev. E.L. Williams.

Co., d/o Addison and Sarah Clarke. Consent 17 JUL 1884 by bride, wit. C.H. Jones. G.H. Northam. 17 JUL 1884 at res. of James Brand. [C10, R:355, R1:62]

Jenkins, Thomas A. to Mrs. Martha Brewer Sandford. THOMAS A. JENKINS, farming, age about 40, widower, b. upper part of Richmond Co., s/o Thomas Jenkins and wife Mary, to MARTHA SAN[D]FORD, age about 32, widow, b. Westmoreland Co., d/o Thomas Brewer and wife Mary [Hinson].[1] Consent 26 APR 1855 by bride Martha [her X mark] Sandford, wit. Theoderick N. Balderson. John Pullen, M.G. 13 MAY 1855 at Mrs. Sanford's in the upper end of the county. [C1, R:153, R1:2]

Jenkins, Thomas A. to Mrs. Alice D.C. Newman, widow of Allen James Sanders. THOMAS A. JENKINS, farmer, age 57, widowed, b. Richmond Co., names of parents not completed, to ALICE D.C. SANDERS, age 40, widow, b. Richmond Co., d/o Joseph and Sophia [Hinson] Newman.[2] Consent 31 JAN 1874 by bride, wits. G.G. Balderson, J.A. Jenkins. H.H. Fones. 5 FEB 1874. [C7, R:230, R1:36]

Jenkins, Thomas A., Jr. to Lucy Roseley Green. THOMAS A. JENKINS, JR., farmer, age 22, single, b. Richmond Co., s/o Thomas A. Jenkins, Sr. and Martha [Carter] Jenkins,[3] to LUCY ROSELEY GREEN, age 21, single, b. Westmoreland Co., d/o Moses and Amanda Green. Consent 31 DEC 1877 by bride. R.N. Reamy. 3 JAN 1878 at the res. of Thomas Jenkins. [C8, R:310, R1:44]

Jenkins, William to Sarah B. Carpenter. WILLIAM JENKINS, farmer, age 21y4m23d, single, b. Richmond Co., s/o James and Frances Jenkins, to SARAH B. CARPENTER, age 21y15d, single, b. Richmond Co., d/o Eli [C.] and Mary [Carter] Carpenter.[4] Consent 12 DEC 1884 by bride, wit. James A. Yeatman. R.N. Reamy. 14 DEC 1884. [C10, R:356, R1:63]

Jenkins, William Henry to Sarah Olar Lee.[5] WILLIAM HENRY JENKINS, oystering, age 27, single, b. Richmond Co., res. Essex Co., s/o Thomas and Mary Jenkins, to SARAH O. LEE, age 16, single, b. Richmond Co., d/o William H. and Elizabeth Lee. Geo. M. Conley. 25 MAY 1886 at the distillery. [C11, R:316, R1:67]

Jennings, James K. to Mary Jenkins. JAMES K. JENNINGS, farming, age 30 on 11 AUG 1855, single, b. upper district, Richmond Co., s/o Smith Jennings and Elizabeth, to MARY JENKINS, age 20, single, b. upper district, Richmond Co., d/o William Jenkins and Phylitia. Consent 5 JUN 1855 by father William B. Jenkins, wit. Robert Bispham. John Pullen. 10 JUN 1855 at Wm. Jenkins' in upper district of Richmond Co. [C1, R:153, R1:2]

Jeter, William Ryland to Georgianna Garland, b. 5 FEB 1835. WILLIAM RYLAND JETER, age 24, single, b. Dennisville, Amelia Co., res. Petersburg, Va., s/o John A. and Mary C. Jeter, to GEORGIANNA GARLAND, age 23, single, b. Richmond Co., d/o James V. and Juliet F.J. [Lyell]

---

[1] Thomas Brewer and Mary Hinson were married by bond 4 JAN 1821 in Westmoreland Co.
[2] Joseph Newman and Sophia Hinson were married by bond 1 FEB 1830 in Richmond Co.
[3] Thomas A. Jenkins and Martha Carter were married 29 JAN 1852 in Richmond Co. by Rev. William Balderson.
[4] Eli C. Carpenter and Mary Carter were married 30 DEC 1852 in Richmond Co. by Rev. James W. Hunnicutt.
[5] William H. Jenkins (b. 16 OCT 1855, d. 1941) and his second wife Sarah Olar Lee (b. 26 DEC 1867, d. 1956) are bur. in Farnham Baptist Church cemetery.

Garland.[1] Consent 6 MAY 1858 by father J.V. Garland, wit. J.V. Garland, Jr. John G. Rowe, M.G. 25 MAY 1858 at *Plainview* the res. of the bride's father. [C2, R:138, R1:6]

Jett, James H. to Mrs. Elizabeth A., widow of William B. Oliff. JAMES H. JETT, farmer, age 20, single, b. Richmond Co., s/o Mortimer and Cordelia Jett, to ELIZABETH A. OLIFF, age 30, widow, b. Northumberland Co., d/o William and Elizabeth [blank]. Consent 4 JUN 1871 by bride Elizabeth [her X mark] Oliff, wit. T.N. Balderson. H.H. Fones. 11 JUN 1871 at Mrs. Oliff's. [C5, R:244, R1:30]

Johnson, Albert (Col.) to Rose Taliaferro (Col.). ALBERT JOHNSON, laborer, age 21, single, b. Richmond Co., s/o John and Tina Johnson, to ROSE TALIAFERRO, age 21, single, b. Richmond Co., d/o Henry and Nancy Taliaferro. Allen Brown, minister. 16 MAR 1876 at *Shandy Hall*. [C7, R:304, R1:40]

Johnson, Alexander (Col.) to Sarah Jane Veney (Col.). ALEXANDER JOHNSON, oysterman, age 28, single, b. Westmoreland Co., s/o William and Mima Johnson, to SARAH JANE VENEY, age 27, single, b. Richmond Co., d/o Jesse and Charlotte Veney. Consent 16 DEC 1879 by bride Sarah Jane [her X mark] Veney, wit. O.M. Lemoine. David Veney. 16 DEC 1879 at Mulberry Chapel. [C9, R:309]

Johnson, Benjamin to Mrs. Eliza Gaskins. BENJAMIN JOHNSON, farmer, age 26, widowed, b. Richmond Co., s/o Benjamin and Fanny Johnson, to ELIZA GASKINS, age 30, widow, b. Richmond Co., d/o Kellis Johnson. Consent 4 FEB 1869 by bride Eliza [her X mark] Gaskins, no wit. Elder James A. Weaver. 4 FEB 1869 at the res. of M. Self. [C5, R, R1:26]

Johnson, Charles William (Col.) to Tillitha Deleaver (Col.). CHARLES WILLIAM JOHNSON, farming and oystering, age 28, single, b. Richmond Co., s/o Charles and Rachel Johnson, to TILLITHA DELEAVER, age 23, single, b. Baltimore, Md., d/o Elizabeth Deleaver. Consent 27 APR 1887 by bride, her age sworn by Julius C. Johnson. Rev. Jacob Robinson, Pastor of Mt. Zion Church. 28 APR 1887 at the res. of John Deleaver. [C11, R:291, R1:71]

Johnson, Edward (Col.) to Kitty Ward (Col.). EDWARD JOHNSON, farming, age 24, widowed, b. Richmond Co., s/o Ben and Fanny Johnson, to KITTY WARD, age 22, single, b. Richmond Co., d/o Cornelius and Martha Ward. Rev. John Wilkerson. 14 MAY 1882 at *Richmond Hill*.[2] [C9, R:313, R1:56]

Johnson, Elias (Col.) to Mrs. Sarah Laws Gordon (Col.). ELIAS JOHNSON, farmer, age 54, widowed, b. Richmond Co., s/o George Wheeler and Celia Johnson, to SARAH GORDON, age 43, widow, b. Richmond Co., d/o Eppa and Sally Laws. Consent 23 FEB 1875 by bride Sarah [her X mark] Gordon, wits. George W. Saunders, Ellick Johnson. George Laws. 25 FEB 1875 at the house of Elias Johnson. [C7, R:262, R1:38]

---

[1] Library of Virginia, Bible Records, Garland Family Bible Record, 1809-1934, gives births for James V. Garland, son of James V. and Elizabeth Garland, b. 8 JAN 1809, and Juliet F.J. Lyell, daughter of John and Lucy Lyell, b. 28 FEB 1816. James V. and Juliet F.J. were m. 6 FEB 1834 at *Hickory Thicket* by Rev. Richard Brown. James V. Garland departed this life at *Plainview* on 8 MAR 1871 in the 62nd year of his age.
[2] *Richmond Hill* was located on the point where Little Totuskey Creek joins the Big Totuskey Creek, and was first owned by Colonel Barber. A plantation was also named this and was owned by Ann Beale Carter, widow of Charles B. Carter.

Johnson, George (Col.) to Mrs. Anna A. Hill (Col.). GEORGE JOHNSON, farmer, age 26, widowed, b. Richmond Co., s/o Benjamin and Fanny Johnson, to ANNA A. HILL, age 30, widow, b. Dinwiddie Co., d/o Ned and Jennie Jackson. Consent 7 JAN 1871 by bride Anna A. [her X mark] Hill. David Venie, minister. 8 JAN 1871 at res. of Daniel Sydnor. [C5, R:244, R1:50, R1:29]

Johnson, George (Col.) to Mary Cox (Col.). GEORGE JOHNSON, laborer, age 22, single, b. Richmond Co., s/o Ellis and Sarah Johnson, to MARY COX, age 22, single, b. Richmond Co., d/o Neile and Catherine Cox. George [his X mark] Laws, minister, wit. Wm. Y. Chinn. 13 MAY 1880 at *Doctor's Hall*. [C9, R:315]

Johnson, George T. to Emma Myrtle Balderson.[1] GEORGE T. JOHNSON, farming, age 22, single, b. Westmoreland Co., s/o William Johnson, to EMMA MYRTLE BALDERSON, age 16, single, b. Richmond Co., d/o James F. [Franklin] and Mary S. [Susan Carter] Balderson, *q.v.* Consent undated by father Jas. F. Balderson, wit. Hamilton [his X mark] Balderson. R.N. Reamy. 24 DEC 1889 in Westmoreland Co. [C12, R:328, R1:75]

Johnson, Henry (Col.) to Mary S. Palmer. HENRY JOHNSON, farmer, age 22, single, b. Richmond Co., s/o Benjamin and Fanny Johnson, to MARY S. PALMER, age 20, single, b. Richmond Co., d/o Henry and Felicia Palmer. Thomas G. Thomas. 21 JUL 1867 at house of John Wilkenson. [C4, R:287, R1:21]

Johnson, Henry Woodland (Col.) to Hannah Cole (Col.). HENRY WOODLAND JOHNSON, mechanic, age 45y6m, widowed, b. Westmoreland Co., s/o Aaron W. and Ailcie Johnson, to HANNAH COLE, age 24, single, b. Richmond Co., [names of parents not completed]. Consent 5 AUG 1878 by bride Hannah [her X mark] Cole, wit. Lewis McKee. J.B. DeBerry, Pastor Richmond Circuit. 15 AUG 1878 at the parsonage in Farnham. [C8, R:311, R1:45]

Johnson, James A.[2] to Mary S. Clarke. JAMES A. JOHNSON, farmer, age 21, single, b. Richmond Co., s/o James and Mary Johnson, to MARY S. CLARKE, age 17, single, b. Richmond Co., d/o Richard Clarke and Susan N. Clarke.[3] Consent 27 MAR 1866 by mother Susan N. Clarke, Richard Clarke, wit. John R. Davis who also consents. Elijah L. Williams. 29 MAR 1866 at Mrs. Clark's. [C4, R:271, R1:17]

Johnson, John C. (Col.) to Nellie Johnson (Col.). JOHN C. JOHNSON, farming, age 23, single, b. Westmoreland Co., s/o Primus and Sally Johnson, to NELLIE JOHNSON, age 23, single, b. Richmond Co., d/o Elias and Sarah Johnson. Consent undated by bride Nellie [her X mark] Johnson, wit. R.J. Pullen. George Laws. 14 JUN 1888 at *Waterview*. [C11, R:316, R1:72]

Johnson, Julius (Col.) to Eudoria Robinson (Col.). JULIUS JOHNSON, farmer, age 21y3m3d, single, b. Richmond Co., s/o Charles and Rachel Johnson, to EUDORIA ROBINSON, age 19, single, b. Richmond Co., d/o Nelson and Mary Robinson. Consent 4 JAN 1877 by bride's

---

[1] George T. Johnson (b. 22 AUG 1868, d. 28 MAY 1943) and Emma M. Balderson (b. 20 MAY 1874, d. 19 SEP 1947) are bur. at Rappahannock Baptist Church cemetery.
[2] James A. Johnson (b. 17 OCT 1844, d. 13 FEB 1872) is bur. at Jerusalem Baptist Church cemetery.
[3] Richard Clarke, Jr. and Susan N. Clarke were married by bond 17 NOV 1840 in Richmond Co.

parents Nelson [his X mark] Roberson and Mary [her X mark] Roberson,[1] wit. John Lewis. Rev. Peter Blackwell. 7 JAN 1877 at Nelson Robinson's. [C8, R:306a, R1:42]

Johnson, Lieutenant (Col.) to Martha Thompson (Col.). LIEUTENANT JOHNSON, farmer, age about 40, widowed, b. and res. Westmoreland Co., s/o Lewis and Hennah Johnson, to MARTHA THOMPSON, age 19, single, b. Richmond Co., d/o Phillis Johnson [father not known]. Consent 20 NOV 1882 in Westmoreland Co. by Martha [her X mark] Thompson, wit. H.J. Dishman. Consent 21 NOV 1882 by bride's guardian Lucy [her X mark] Henry. Emanuel Watts, Pastor. 23 NOV 1882 at Mount Zion Church. [C9, R:314, R1:57]

Johnson, Ned (Col.) to Bell Lewis (Col.). Ned Johnson, laborer, age 18, single, b. Richmond Co., s/o Ben and Fanny Johnson, to BELL LEWIS, age 24, single, b. Richmond Co., d/o Jane Lewis. Consent by bride, wit. Ben Johnson, Sr. G.H. Northam. 13 APR 1879. [C8, R:307, R1:47]

Johnson, Nelson (Col.) to Amanda C. Maiden (Col.). NELSON JOHNSON, tanner, age 31, single, b. Caroline Co., s/o Felicia Johnson, to AMANDA C. MAIDEN, age 19, single, b. Richmond Co., d/o Hannah Madon [sic]. Consent 24 MAY 1869 by mother Hannah [her X mark] Maiden, wit. Robt. R. Hall, Thomas Maiden. Robert N. Reamy. 27 MAY 1869 at Haner Madon's. [C5, R, R1:26]

Johnson, Orrison (Col.) to Mrs. Martha Ham, widow of Henry Harris (Col.). ORRISON JOHNSON, oysterman and farmer, age 27, single, b. Richmond Co., s/o Natus and Martha Johnson, to MARTHA HARRIS, age 28, widow, b. Richmond Co., d/o Moses and Louisa Ham. Consent 6 FEB 1887 by bride Martha [her X mark] Harris, wit. K.W. [Knowles Wadsworth] Hanks. Rev. Jacob Robinson, Pastor of Mt. Zion Baptist Church, Ivanhoe, Va. 10 FEB 1887 at res. of Orrison Johnson. [C11, R:290, R1:69]

Johnson, Robert (Col.) to Sally Gordon (Col.). ROBERT JOHNSON, farmer, age 21, single, b. Richmond Co., s/o Lawson Johnson and Maria Spurlock, to SALLY GORDON, age 23, single, b. Richmond Co., d/o Samuel and Peggy Gordon. Consent 30 MAR 1875 by bride Sally [her X mark] Gordon, wit. Jane Cox. George Laws. 1 APR 1875 at *Cedar Grove*. [C7, R:262, R1:38]

Johnson, Robert (Col.) to Louisa Jones (Col.). ROBERT JOHNSON, oysterman, age 30, widowed, b. Essex Co., s/o Henry and Betsey Johnson, to LOUISA JONES, age 25, single, b. Richmond Co., [names of parents not inserted]. Consent undated by bride Louisa [her X mark] Jones, wit. Mary Roane. Rev. W. Carter. 14 FEB 1884 at the res. of the bride. [C10, R:353, R1:61]

Johnson, Robert D. (Col.) to Alice Burton (Col.). ROBERT D. JOHNSON, laborer, age 22y1m1d, single, b. Westmoreland Co., s/o Charles and Ann Johnson, to ALICE BURTON, age 20y6m, single, b. Westmoreland Co., d/o James[2] and Lucy Burton. Consent 7 JUN 1879 by mother Lucy [her X mark] Burton, wit. J.T. Sisson, Peter [his X mark] Burton. Edmond Rich. 8 JUN 1879 at the res. of the bride's parents. [C8, R:308, R1:47]

---

[1] The surname of the bride is Robinson in all instances except at the signature block as Roberson for her parents in the consent.
[2] The given name James has been overwritten with another illegible one.

Johnson, Robert S. (Col.) to Julia Ann Stowell (Col.). ROBERT S. JOHNSON, sawyer, age 23, single, b. Essex Co., s/o Henry and Betsey Johnson, to JULIA ANN STOWELL,[1] age 20y6m, single, b. Richmond Co., d/o Margaret Stowells [sic]. Consent 26 MAY 1871 by father-in-law Joseph [his X mark] Newton. Thomas G. Thomas. 27 MAY 1871 at house of Robert Parrot. [C5, R:244, R1:30]

Johnson, Sephus to Malinda Burrell. SEPHUS JOHNSON, farmer, age 35, single, b. Westmoreland Co., s/o Reuben and Fanny Johnson, to MALINDA BURRELL, age 22, single, b. Richmond Co., d/o Spencer and Polly Burrell. James A. Weaver. 18 DEC 1860 at James A. Weaver's in Westmoreland Co. [C2, R:154, R1:9]

Johnson, Thomas Edwin to Mary Ellen Bramham.[2] THOMAS E. JOHNSON, clerk, age 21, single, b. Westmoreland Co., s/o James and Ann Johnson, to MARY E. BRAMHAM, age 21, single, b. Richmond Co., d/o Vincent [Jr.] and M.S. [Mary S. Benneham] Bramham.[3] Consent 17 MAY 1858 by bride, wit. A.N. Bramham. A. Dulaney, minister. 18 MAY 1858. [C2, R1:6]

Johnson, William (Col.) to Julia Smith (Col.). WILLIAM JOHNSON, sailing, age 28, single, b. and res. Philadelphia, Pa., s/o George and Hester Johnson, to JULIA SMITH, age 21, single, b. Richmond Co., d/o Nelson and Mary Smith. George Laws. 5 JAN 1890 at Smoot's Place (Nash's). [C12, R:323, R1:76]

Jones, Charles H. to Georgeanna Bedford Jenkins.[4] CHARLES H. JONES, farming, age 26, single, b. Richmond Co., s/o William and Louisa Jones, to GEORGEANNA JENKINS, age 23, single, b. Richmond Co., d/o Mathew and Susan Jenkins. Consent 19 DEC 1883 from Sharps Wharf by bride, no wit. G.H. Northam. 20 DEC 1883 at Mrs. Jenkins'. [C10, NN:28 DEC 1883, R:357, R1:60]

Jones, Clinton to Dorethea Sanders. CLINTON JONES, farmer, age 21, single, b. Richmond Co., s/o Clinton and Catharine [Brown] Jones,[5] to DORETHEA SANDERS, age 21, single, b. Richmond Co., d/o John and Fanny Sanders. Consent 8 JAN 1872 by bride Dorothea [her X mark] Sanders, wits. Washington [Carter], Henry H. Brown. D.M. Wharton. 10 JAN 1872 at res. of minister in Westmoreland Co. [C6, R:237, R1:31]

Jones, James A. to Edmonia H. Douglass. JAMES A. JONES, oysterman, age 22, single, b. Richmond Co., s/o Samuel and Elizabeth Jones, to EDMONIA H. DOUGLASS, age 21, single, b. Richmond Co., d/o Thomas [H.] and Malinda [Douglass] Douglass.[6] Consent 16 MAY 1881 by bride, wit. D.E. Douglass. G.H. Northam. 17 MAY 1881. [C9, handwritten license; R:336, R1:53]

---

[1] Surname also appears as Stowells.
[2] Thomas Edwin Johnson (b. 13 OCT 1836, d. 4 APR 1901) and wife Mary Ellen Bramham (1836-1906), are bur. in St. John's Episcopal Church Cemetery.
[3] Vincent Bramham, Jr. and Mary S. Benneham were married by bond 8 OCT 1832 in Richmond Co.
[4] Charles H. Jones (b. 18 SEP 1858, d. 20 OCT 1898) and wife Georganna [sic] A. Bedford (b. 16 SEP 1860, d. 29 NOV 1938) are bur. in Calvary United Methodist Church cemetery.
[5] Clinton Jones and Catharine Brown were married 23 JUN 1847 in Richmond Co. by Rev. John Pullen.
[6] Thomas H. Douglass and Malindy Douglass, d/o Ann Douglass, were married 4 APR 1845 in Richmond Co. by Rev. E.L. Williams.

Jones, James Atnine to Esther Rebecca Davis.[1] JAMES A. JONES, oystering, age 29, widowed, b. Richmond Co., s/o Samuel and Emily Jones, to ESTHER R. DAVIS, age 18, single, b. Richmond Co., d/o John Robert and Sarah C. Davis. Consent 23 DEC 1887 by bride's parents, wit. J.P. Brann. Robert Williamson. 25 DEC 1887 at John Robert Davis's. [C11, R:293, R1:71]

Jones, James Henry (Col.) to Sarah Hill (Col.). JAMES HENRY JONES, farmer, age 24, single, b. King and Queen Co., s/o Henry and Fenton Jones, to SARAH HILL, age 24, single, b. Richmond Co., d/o Bartlett and Peggy Hill. Thomas G. Thomas. 28 JUN 1871 at res. of Bartlett Hill. [C5, R:245, R1:30]

Jones, James L. to Eliza Ann Morriss. JAMES L. JONES, [engineer] of steam mill, age about 28, single, b. Spotsylvania Co., s/o Clinton Jones and wife Elizabeth, to ELIZA A. MORRISS, born about 24, single, b. Richmond Co., d/o William H. Morriss and wife Mary. Consent 25 JUN 1856 by William H. Morriss, also signed by bride, wit. John D. Belfield. John Pullen, M.G. 22 JUL 1856 at Wm. H. Morris'. [C1, R]

Jones, James L. to Mary F.E. Saunders. JAMES L. JONES, farming, age 30, single, b. Richmond Co., res. Westmoreland Co., s/o Mary Jones, to MARY F.E. SAUNDERS,[2] age 18, single, b. Richmond Co., d/o William A.H. and Margaret Ann [Morris] Sanders. Consent 5 JAN 1880 by groom and bride Mary F.E. [her X mark] Saunders, wit. Wm. A.H. Saunders. R.N. Reamy. 8 AN 1880. [C9, R:314, R1:49]

Jones, Jesse to Mrs. Margaret N. Booth Self. JESSE JONES, farmer, age 64, widowed, b. Richmond Co., s/o George and Milly Jones, to MARGARET N. SELF, age 37, widow, b. Richmond Co., d/o William Booth. Consent 14 NOV 1874 by bride Margaret N. [her X mark] Self, wit. James P. [his X mark] Brann. G.H. Northam. 17 NOV 1874. [C7, R:230, R1:37]

Jones, Joseph W. (Col.) to Ann Clark (Col.). JOSEPH W. JONES, farming, age 22, single, b. and res. Westmoreland Co., s/o Henry Jones and Mary Lewis, to ANN CLARK, age 21y10m, single, b. Westmoreland Co., d/o Frederick and Anna Clark. Rev. Robert Lewis. 3 FEB 1887 at the res. of Frederick Clark. [C11, R:290, R1:69]

Jones, Lawson C.[3] to Virginia H. Payton. LAWSON C. JONES, farming, age about 24, single, b. and res. King George Co., s/o Standfield and Frances P. Jones, to VIRGINIA H. PAYTON, age about 17, single, b. Richmond Co., d/o John and Elizabeth Payton. Consent 29 MAR 1858 by bride, wits. T.N. Balderson, H.J. Jett. John Pullen, M.G. 1 APR 1858 at Mrs. Elizabeth Morris'. [C1, C2, R:138, R1:6]

Jones, Robert W. to Mary Jane Jones. ROBERT W. JONES, farmer, age 23, single, b. Richmond Co., s/o Mary Jones, to MARY JANE JONES, age 18, single, b. Richmond Co., d/o Robert William and Lucy Jones. Consent 11 JAN 1876 by father Robert W. [his X mark] Jones, wit. Thornton Saunders. Robert N. Reamy. 13 JAN 1876 at Robert Jones'. [C7, R:304, R1:39]

---

[1] James Atnine Jones (b. 1857, d. 12 JUL 1914) and his second wife Esther Rebecca Davis (b. 1870, d. 26 JAN 1933) are bur. in Farnham Baptist Church cemetery.
[2] The surname also appears as Sanders.
[3] A Lawson C. Jones served in Co. D, 40th Reg., Va. Inf., C.S.A., and was sent to Point Lookout, and bur. there.

Jones, Robert W. to Mrs. Maria Elizabeth Settle Atkins. ROBERT W. JONES, farming, age 50, widowed, b. Richmond Co., [names of parents not completed], to MARIA ELIZABETH ATKINS, age 45, widow, b. King George Co., Mr. and Mrs. Settle. Consent 21 APR 1880 by Maria E. Atkins, wit. Charles H. Balderson. R.N. Reamy. 25 APR 1880. [C9, R:315, R1:50]

Jones, Samuel to Susan F. Fones. SAMUEL JONES, carpenter, age 50, widowed, b. King George Co., s/o Peter and Susan [Strother] Jones,[1] to SUSAN F. FONES, age 20, single, b. Richmond Co., d/o Thomas B. and Nancy [Richards] Fones. Consent 31 DEC 1861 by father Thomas B. Fones, wit. Benj. P. Atwill. E.L. Williams. 2 JAN 1862 at Thos. Fones'. [C3, R:140, R1:11]

Jones, Thomas D. to Sally Martin. THOMAS D. JONES, farmer, age 34, widowed, b. Richmond Co., s/o Thomas D. and Violet [Broocke] Jones,[2] to SALLY MARTIN, age 23, single, b. and res. King and Queen Co., parents unknown. No minister return. 13 DEC 1860. [C2, R:154, R1:9]

Jones, Thomas Edwin to Florence L. France.[3] THOMAS EDWIN JONES, fishing, age 22y10m, single, b. Richmond Co., s/o Thomas and Margaret Jones, to FLORENCE L. FRANCE, age 21, single, b. Richmond Co., s/o Rodney and Luvinia France. Consent 6 APR 1883 from *Cobham Park* by bride, wit. John A. France. G.H. Northam. 8 APR 1883 at *Cobham Park*. [C10, R:356, R1:58]

Jones, William H. to Fanny Sanders. WILLIAM H. JONES, farming, age 23, single, b. Westmoreland Co., s/o Robert and Lucy Jones, to FANNY SANDERS, age 23, single, b. Richmond Co., d/o George and Frances Sanders. Consent 17 MAR 1879 by bride, wit. J.T. Carpenter. R.N. Reamy. 20 MAR 1879 at B. Smoot's. [C8, R:307, R1:47]

Jones, William S. to Mary A. Brown. WILLIAM S. JONES, farming, age 21y7m, single, b. Richmond Co., s/o Samuel and Susan F. [Fones] Jones, *q.v.*, to MARY A. BROWN, age 18, single, b. Richmond Co., d/o John C. and Martha [France] Brown, *q.v.* Consent undated by mother Marthey Brown, wit. Geo. M. Conley. Geo. M. Conley. 7 MAR 1886 at *Cherry Hill*. [C11, R:315, R1:67]

Jordan, Thomas A. (Col.) to Louisa Corsett (Col.). THOMAS A. JORDAN,[4] ditcher, age 37, single, b. Chowan Co., N.C., s/o John and Mary Jordan, to LOUISA CORSETT, age 32, single, b. Lancaster Co., parents unknown. Allen Brown, minister. 22 MAY 1872 at house of Edgar T. Lemoine. [C6, R:237, R1:31]

K

Kelley, Eppy (Col.) to Mariah Veney (Col.). EPPY KELLEY, farmer, age 23, single, b. Richmond Co., s/o Isaac and Fanny Kelly [sic], to MARIAH VENEY, age 22, single, b. Richmond Co., d/o Jerry and Charlotte Veney. Consent 25 MAR 1870 by parties Eppy [his X mark] and Mariah [her X mark] Veney. Robert N. Reamy. 27 MAR 1870. [C5, R:233, R1:27]

Kelly, Aaron A. [FB] to Margaret Rich [FB]. AARON A. KELLY, farmer, age 22, single, b. and res. Westmoreland Co., s/o Vincent and Attaway Kelly, to MARGARET RICH, age 23, single, b.

---

[1] Peter Jones and Susannah Strother were married by bond 26 MAY 1800 in King George Co.
[2] Thomas Jones and Violett Broocke, widow, were married by bond 20 FEB 1821 in Richmond Co.
[3] Florence F. Jones (1863-1949) is bur. in Cobham Park Baptist Church cemetery.
[4] The Register records the groom's name as Thomas A. Gordon, but his parents' surname as Jordan.

Richmond Co., d/o Lindsay and Felicia Rich. Consent 28 JAN 1862 by bride Margaret [her X mark] Rich, wit. Wm. H. Newman. James A. Weaver. 30 JAN 1862 at home of Lindsay Rich [FB]. [C3, R:140, R1:11]

Kelsick, Harry (Col.) to Nuttie Yeatman (Col.). HARRY KELSICK, laborer, age 26y6m, single, b. Richmond Co., s/o Samuel and Hannah Kelsick, to NUTTIE YEATMAN, age 21, single, b. Richmond Co., d/o Joseph and Letta Yeatman. Rev. T.G. Thomas. 6 JAN 1881. [C9, R:335, R1:52]

Kennan, Thomas L.[1] to Catharine L. Miskill. THOMAS L. KENNAN, age 24, single, b. Richmond Co., res. Bowlers Rock Light Vessel, s/o William Kennan and Mahala Davis,[2] to CATHARINE L. MISKILL, age 18, single, b. Richmond Co., res. Downmanville,Va., d/o William D. and Lucy [English] Miskill. Consent 21 FEB 1858 by father William D. [his X mark] Miskill, wit. Thomas W. English. E.L. Williams, minister. 23 FEB 1858 at Downmanville, Va. [C1, R:138, R1:6]

Kennan, William J. to Mrs. Arrabella M. Lyell Cox. WILLIAM J. KENNAN, school teacher, age 27, single, b. Richmond Co., s/o Lefever and Elizabeth [Miskell] Kennan,[3] to ARRABELLA M. COX, age 27, widow, b. Northumberland Co., d/o Thomas [S.] and Mary [E. Graham] Lyell.[4] Consent 27 AUG 1863 by bride, wit. H. Oldham. Robert Williamson. 27 AUG 1863 at Farnham Church. [C3, R:160, R1:13]

Keyser, Ander D. to Mrs. Georgeanna E.C. Hale. ANDER D. KEYSER, laborer, age 25, widowed, b. and res. Northumberland Co., s/o Braxton and Eliza Keyser, to GEORGEANNA E.C. HALE, age 27, widow, b. Richmond Co., d/o William C. and M.A.G. [Martha Ann Garland Lewis] Bryant.[5] Consent 24 NOV 1879 by bride and groom Ander D. [his X mark] Keyser, wit. Martha A. [her X mark] Bryant. G.H. Northam. 24 NOV 1879. [C8, R:309, R1:48]

King, Benjamin L. to Catharine Sydnor. BENJAMIN L. KING, farmer, age 35, widowed, b. Westmoreland Co., s/o John W. and Harriet A. King, to CATHARINE SYDNOR, age 19, single, b. Richmond Co., d/o William B. and Ann [Hale] Sydnor.[6] Consent 13 AUG 187[7] by bride, wit. William B. Sydnor. G.H. Northam. 14 AUG 1878. [C8[7]; R:307, 311, R1:43 and 45]

King, Benjamin L. to Edmonia Hudson. B.L. KING, farming, age 47, widowed, b. Westmoreland Co., s/o J.W. [John] and Harriet [A.] King, to EDMONIA HUDSON, age 22, single, b. Richmond Co., d/o Matthew [S.] and Eliza Ann [Hale] Hudson, *q.v.* Consent 17 MAY 1887 by parties and their marks, wit. Judson [his X mark] Sydnor. G.H. Northam. 18 MAY 1887 at Mr. King's. [C11, R:291, R1:70]

King, George W. to Anna Clark. GEORGE W. KING, farming, age 28, widowed, b. Richmond Co., s/o William and Martha M. King, to ANNA CLARK, age 21, single, b. Richmond, d/o Spilman B. and Margaret [Hale] Clark, *q.v.* Consent 10 DEC 1888 by bride's parents, wit. by bride and Floid Davis. W.A. Crocker. 12 DEC 1888 at the res. of the bride. [C12, R:317, R1:73]

---

[1] Thomas Kennan served in Co. D, 47th Va. Inf., C.S.A.
[2] The marriage bond 3 DEC 1832 in Richmond Co. is for William Kennan and Mahalah B. Hazard, d/o William Hazard.
[3] Lefevre Kennon and Elizabeth Miskell were married by bond 25 JUN 1828 in Richmond Co.
[4] Thomas S. Lyell and Mary E. Graham were married by bond 13 JAN 1825 in Westmoreland Co.
[5] William C. Bryant and Martha Ann Garland Lewis were married 20 OCT 1845 in Richmond Co. by Rev. E.L. Williams.
[6] William B. Sydnor and Ann Hale were married by bond 13 DEC 1836 in Northumberland Co.
[7] The license is filmed with 1878 records.

King, George Washington to Dorathia Blanche Clark.[1] GEORGE W. KING, farmer, age 17, single, b. Richmond Co., s/o William and Martha [Ann Kent] King, to DORATHIA CLARK, age 23, single, b. Richmond Co., d/o Joseph and Nancy Clarke [sic]. Consent 24 FEB 1875 by bride, wit. Marthy [her X mark] W. King. G.H. Northam. 25 FEB 1875. [C7, R:262, R1:38]

King, Louis Andrew to Cornelia Sydnor. LOUIS A. KING, farming, age 20y8m, single, b. Westmoreland Co., s/o Benjamin King and Susan King née Wilkins, to CORNELIA SYDNOR, age 20, single, b. Richmond Co., d/o Addison and Caroline [Hudson] Sydnor, *q.v.* Consent undated by bride Cornelia [her X mark] Sydnor, Ben [his X mark] King, Addison [his X mark] Sydnor, wit. Judson [his X mark] Sydnor. Charles N. Betts. 29 APR 1888 at the res. of Susan King. [C11, R:315, R1:72]

King, Octavius T. to Harriet S. Franklin. OCTAVIUS T. KING, carpenter, age 25 on 14 MAR 1869, single, b. and res. Westmoreland Co., s/o Griffin and [Ann] H. [English] King,[2] to HARRIET S. FRANKLIN, age 20 on 8 APR 1869, single, b. Richmond Co., d/o Samuel R. and Susan S. [Sisson] Franklin. G.H. Northam. 16 MAR 1869. [C5, R, R1:25]

King, Richard Henry to Elsiebeth J. Self.[3] RICHARD KING, farming, age nearly 23, single, b. Richmond Co., s/o William and Martha King, to ELIZABETH SELF [sic], age 22, single, b. Richmond Co., d/o Moses A. [Andrew] and Lucy [Ann Sydnor] Self. Consent 1 MAR 1883 by bride, wit. Henry W[ad]kins. G.H. Northam. 4 MAR 1883. [C10, R:355, R1:58]

King, Thomas William to Josephine Marian Bell.[4] THOMAS W. KING, merchant, age 22, single, b. Richmond Co., s/o Albert S. [Sydnor] and Jane [Sydnor] King,[5] to JOSIE M. BELL, age 22, single, b. Richmond Co., d/o R.L. [Robert Lewis] and [Mary] Susan [Self] Bell. Consent undated by parties, wit. Wm. E. Woolard. J. Manning Dunaway. 9 APR 1890 at the bride's residence. [C12, R:323a, R1:77]

King, William to Tamina Lambert. WILLIAM KING, farmer, age 20y6m, single, b. Richmond Co., s/o William and Martha [Ann Kent] King,[6] to TAMINA LAMBERT, age 18, single, b. Richmond Co., d/o William and Frances [Clarke] Lambert.[7] Consent by father William Lambert and Martha King, wit. H. Clarke. G.H. Northam. 26 MAY 1872. [C6, R:237, R1:31]

Knox, Douglas Hamilton to Loula Sclater Brockenbrough.[8] DOUGLAS HAMILTON KNOX, merchant, age 39, single, b. and res. Fredericksburg, Va., s/o Thomas F. and Virginia A. [Soulter] Knox,[9] to LOULA SCLATER BROCKENBROUGH, age 20, single, b. Richmond Co.,

---

[1] George W. King (b. 7 JUN 1858, d. 21 JUN 1912) and his first wife Dorathia B. Clark (b. 1852, d. 30 JAN 1888 in childbirth) are bur. at Totuskey Baptist Church cemetery.
[2] Griffin King and Ann H. English were married by bond 13 APR 1824 in Westmoreland Co.
[3] Richard H. King (b. 30 NOV 1860, d. 14 AUG 1925) and his wife Elsiebeth J. Self (b. 9 NOV 1859, d. 29 SEP 1949) are bur. at Totuskey Baptist Church cemetery.
[4] Thomas W. King (b. 3 AUG 1867, d. 20 FEB 1926) and his wife Josephine M. Bell (b. 18 MAY 1865, d. 13 FEB 1949) are bur. at Totuskey Baptist Church cemetery.
[5] Albert S. King (b. 1843, d. 10 MAR 1928) and his first wife Jane Sydnor (b. 15 JUN 1845, d. 4 DEC 1907) are bur. at Totuskey Baptist Church cemetery.
[6] William King and Martha Ann Kent, d/o Lucy Sydnor, were married by bond 6 AUG 1842 in Richmond Co.
[7] William Lambert and Frances Clarke were married by bond 16 FEB 1846 in Richmond Co.
[8] Douglas Hamilton Knox (b. JUL 1847, d. 14 FEB 1914) and wife Loula S. Brockenbrough (b. JUL 1866, d. AUG 1946) are bur. in the Confederate Cemetery at Fredericksburg, Va.
[9] Thomas F. Knox and Virginia A. Soulter were married 24 MAY 1832 in Norfolk, Va.

d/o William A. and Lutie B. [Beadles] Brockenbrough.[1] A.B. Kinsolving. 27 APR 1887 at the house of Wm. A. Brockenbrough. [C11, R:291, R1:71]

Knox, Robert Taylor[2] to Mary G. Brockenbrough. ROBERT T. KNOX, merchant, age 31, single, b. and res. Fredericksburg, Va., s/o Thomas F. and Virginia A. [Soulter] Knox, to MARY G. BROCKENBROUGH, age 27, single, b. Richmond Co., d/o Moore F. [Fauntleroy] and Sarah [Smith] Brockenbrough. Andrew Fisher. 10 NOV 1868 at Warsaw, Va. [C5, R:254, R1:24]

L

Lamb, James Christian to Sarah "Saide" Smith Brockenbrough.[3] JAMES C. LAMB, lawyer, age 32, widowed, b. Charles City Co., res. Richmond, Va., s/o L.A. [Lycurgus Anthony] and Anne E. [Ann Elizabeth Christian] Lamb, to SAIDE BROCKENBROUGH, age 23, single, b. Richmond Co., d/o William F. [Fauntleroy] and E.B. [Eliza Bland Smith] Brockenbrough.[4] Rev. Martin Johnson. 1 DEC 1885 at St. John's Church in Warsaw, Va. [C10, R:318, R1:65]

Lamkin, Austin to Frances M. Elmore. AUSTIN LAMPKIN [sic],[5] farmer, age 4[0], widowed, single, b. Northumberland Co., s/o Charles Lampkin and Elizabeth [Kenner],[6] to FRANCES M. ELMORE, age 22, single, b. Richmond Co., d/o Rawleigh Elmore and Catharine Bryant.[7] Consent 28 DEC 1859 by bride Frances M. [her X mark] Elmore, wits. Cathrine [her X mark] Elmore, Charles R. Keyser. Barth. Dodson, Baptist parson. 2 JAN 1860. [C2, R:153, R1:8]

Lamkin, James L. and Olivia C. Dulaney. Consent 11 OCT 1855 by bride, wit. Jas. H. Dulaney. No license or minister return. [C1]

Lamkin, Robert James, Corp. to Annie Maria George.[8] ROBERT J. LAMKIN, soldier, age 22, single, b. Northumberland Co., s/o James L. and Judy [Judith Sampson] Lamkin,[9] to ANNIE M. GEORGE, age 18, single, b. Cecil Co., Md., d/o [Nicholas] and Araminta George. Consent 8 FEB 1862 by bride, signed by Arriminta Dulany, wit. T.E. Johnson. Andrew Fisher. 9 FEB 1862 at the res. of Araminta Dulany. [C3, R:140, R1:11]

Landman, George L. to Dorothea Ida Lee.[10] GEORGE LANDMAN, oystering, age 28, single, b. Richmond Co., s/o Betty Landman, to DOROTHEA IDA LEE, age 18, single, b. Richmond Co., d/o William H. and Elizabeth Jane Lee. Geo. M. Conley. 12 JUN 1887 in Warsaw, Va. [C11, R:292, R1:70]

---

[1] Dr. William A. Brockenbrough (11 DEC 1836-2 AUG 1896) and his two wives: Lutie Beadles (15 JAN 1844-2 MAR 1878), and Sallie Maxwell (11 SEP 1844-12 MAR 1901) are bur. at Emmanuel Episcopal Church cemetery, near Emmerton, Va.
[2] Lieut. Robert Taylor Knox, C.S.A. (b. 24 JUL 1837 in Fredericksburg, Va., d. 10 MAR 1915), is bur. in the Confederate Cemetery at Fredericksburg, Va. Also there is his wife, and her tombstone inscription is for Etta Brockenbrough (1840-1898).
[3] Judge James Christian Lamb (b. 18 NOV 1853, d. 1 JAN 1903 in Richmond, Va.) and his second wife Sarah Smith Brockenbrough (b. 1 JUL 1862, d. 8 MAY 1949 in Warsaw, Va.) are bur. in Hollywood Cemetery, Richmond, Va.
[4] William Fauntleroy Brockenbrough (b. 1826, d. 10 JUN 1890) and wife Eliza Bland Smith (b. 13 MAR 1838, d. 19 JUL 1905) are bur. in St. John's Episcopal Church Cemetery.
[5] Spelling also as Lamkin.
[6] Charles Lamkin and Elizabeth Kenner were married by bond 8 APR 1815 in Northumberland Co.
[7] Rawleigh Elmore and Catharine Bryant were married by bond 24 FEB 1835 in Richmond Co.
[8] Robert J. Lamkin (b. 28 SEP 1839 in Northumberland Co., d. 30 MAR 1879) and wife Annie M. George (b. 7 NOV 1843 in Cecil Co., Md., d. 21 AUG 1916), d/o Nicholas and Araminta George, are bur. at Calvary United Methodist Church cemetery. Also see Library of Virginia, Bible Records, Lamkin Family Bible Record. He served in Co. B, 40th Reg., Va. Inf., C.S.A.
[9] James L. Lamkin and Judith Sampson were married by bond 19 SEP 1838 in Northumberland Co.
[10] George L. Landman (1856-1940) and wife Dorothy Ida Lee (b. SEP 1869, d. 26 JAN 1925 in D.C.) are bur. at Cedar Hill Cemetery, Suitland, Md.

Landman, Henry Wise to Ann Jackson. HENRY WISE LANDMAN, laborer, age 23, single, b. Richmond Co., s/o Travers and Sally Landman, to ANN JACKSON, age 24, single, b. Richmond Co., d/o George and Maria Hale Jackson. Consent 22 MAY 1878 by bride Ann [her X mark] Jackson, wit. D.L. Lankford. G.H. Northam. 22 MAY 1878. [C8, R:311, R1:45]

Landman, James M. to Alice Reynolds. JAMES M. LANDMAN, farmer, age 25, single, b. Richmond Co., s/o Travers and Sally Landman, to ALICE REYNOLDS, age 31, single, b. Richmond Co., d/o Edwin [J.] and Mary [Mozingo] Reynolds.[1] G.H. Northam. 23 DEC 1878. [C8, R:312, R1:46]

Landon, Newman (Col.) to Eliza Laws (Col.). NEWMAN LANDON, farming, age 23y10m19d, single, b. Richmond Co., s/o William and Louisa Landon, to ELIZA LAWS, age 27, single, b. Richmond Co., d/o George and Judy Laws. Consent 11 SEP 1883 by bride. Rev. T.G. Thomas. 12 NOV[2] 1883 at the minister's house. [C10, R:357, R1:59]

Lane, Sidney to Mrs. Jane Ann McCarty. SIDNEY LANE, merchant, age 36, widowed, b. Mathews Co., s/o Wm. and Dorathy Lane, to JANE ANN McCARTY, age 31, widow, b. Richmond Co., d/o Chas. W. and Maria S.J. Smith. Andrew Fisher. 1 SEP 1859 at *Laurel Grove*. [C2, R:165, R1:7]

Lawrence, Mac (Col.) to Nancy Phillips (Col.). MAC LAWRENCE, oystering, age 21, single, b. Richmond Co., s/o Jos. Lawrence and Julia Veney, to NANCY PHILLIPS, age 18, single, b. Richmond Co., d/o Charles and Adlena Phillips. Rev. W. Carter. 17 DEC 1890 at the bride's home. [C12, R:324, R1:78]

Lawrence, Richard (Col.) to Hannah Palmer (Col.). RICHARD LAWRENCE, farmer, age 21y6m, single, b. Richmond Co., s/o Jack and Rose Lawrence, to HANNAH PALMER, age 21, single, b. Richmond Co., d/o Harry and Philis Palmer. Consent 29 DEC 1869 unsigned. Davy Veney. 30 DEC 1869 at Goddy's Mill. [C5, R, R1:27]

Laws, Baldwin (Col.) to Hannah Veney (Col.). BALDWIN LAWS, farmer, age 45, single, b. Northumberland Co., s/o Maria Laws, to HANNAH VENEY, age 40, single, b. Richmond Co., d/o Travis and Anna Veney. Consent 1 FEB 1864 by bride Hannah [her X mark] Veney, wit. Saml. Gresham. Robert Williamson, M.G. 3 FEB 1864 at Farnham. [C3, R:139, R1:13]

Laws, Daniel (Col.) to Lucy Saunders (Col.). DANIEL LAWS, farmer, age 23, single, b. Richmond Co., s/o George and Judy Laws, to LUCY SAUNDERS, age 22, single, b. Richmond Co., d/o James and Ann Saunders. Consent 12 NOV 1874 by bride Lucy [her X mark] Saunders, wit. Samuel Cox. Thomas G. Thomas. 15 NOV 1874 at the church at [*Nomini*] Grove. [C7, R:230, R1:37]

Laws, George, Rev. (Col.) to Mrs. Nancy Willis Parker (Col.). GEORGE LAWS, preacher, age 49, widowed, b. Richmond Co., s/o Eppa and Sally Laws, to NANCY PARKER, age 45, widow, b. Richmond Co., d/o Franklin Willis. Thomas G. Thomas. 18 DEC 1879 at the house of the minister. [C9, R:309, R1:48]

---

[1] Edwin J. Reynolds and Mary Mozingo were married 29 DEC 1842 in Richmond Co. by Rev. William N. Ward.
[2] The license gives marriage date as 12 SEP 1883, while the minister return shows 12 NOV 1883.

Lawson, Thomas (Col.) to Maria L. McIlroy (Col.). THOMAS LAWSON, laborer, age 50, single, b. Richmond Co., s/o Goen and Ibby Lawson, to MARIA L. McILROY, age 21, single, b. King and Queen Co., [name of parents blank]. Thomas G. Thomas. 10 APR 1869 at Austin Richards'. [C5, R, R1:25]

Learch, William C. to Lucy Ann Elmore. WILLIAM C. LEARCH, mechanic, age 29, single, b. Hanneberg Co., Prussia, res. Montross, Westmoreland Co., s/o Dorthea Learch, to LUCY ANN ELMORE, age 23, single, b. Richmond Co., d/o J.W. [John William] Elmore and Winnie [Winnefred] Jackson.[1] Consent undated by John W. Elmore, wits. John Littrell, J.B. Northam. B.W. Nash, of Union Baptist Church. 5 APR 1858. [C2, R:138, R1:6]

Lee, Andrew (Col.) to Sophia Corbin (Col.). ANDREW LEE, oystering and farming, age 23, single, b. Richmond Co., s/o Henry and Sally Lee, to SOPHIA CORBIN, age 19, single, b. Richmond Co., d/o Cornelius and Nancy Corbin. Consent 25 MAR 1889 by Sophia Corbin, wit. Nancie Corbin. Rev. L. Harrod, Pastor, Ebenezer, at Ebenezer Baptist Church. [C12, R:327, R1:74]

Lee, Charles (Col.) to Fanny Rich (Col.). CHARLES LEE, farmer, age 21, single, b. Richmond Co., s/o Peter and Lydia Ann Lee, to FANNY RICH, age 22, single, b. Richmond Co., d/o Jack Taylor and Mary Rich. Consent 9 AUG 1869 by mother Mary Rich and by Junius [his X mark] Bowser. Thomas G. Thomas. 9 AUG 1869 at res. of Mary Rich. [C5, skipped on film, R, R1:26]

Lee, Charles (Col.) to Ellen Johnson (Col.). CHARLES LEE, laborer, age 25, single, b. Westmoreland Co., s/o Richard and Lydia Lee, to ELLEN JOHNSON, age 23, single, b. Richmond Co., d/o Abby Johnson. Consent 2 JUL 1880 by bride Ellen [her X mark] Johnson, wit. Simon Sydnor. D.M. Wharton. 4 JUL 1880 at the res. of the minister in Westmoreland Co. [C9, R:315, R1:51]

Lee, George (Col.) to Alice Fossett (Col.). GEORGE LEE, farming, age 24y4m, single, b. and res. Westmoreland Co., s/o Humphrey and Lucy Lee, to ALICE FOSSETT, age 18, single, b. Richmond Co., d/o Henry and Sally Fossett. Consent 17 DEC 1884 by bride, wit. William [his X mark] [Newland]. Charles C. Washington. 18 DEC 1884 at the res. of the girl's parents. [C10, R:355, R1:63]

Lee, Henry Thomas (Col.) to Emma E. Gordon (Col.). HENRY THOMAS LEE, farming, age 26y4m8d, single, b. and res. Westmoreland Co., s/o Humphrey and Lucy Lee, to EMMA E. GORDON, age 25, single, b. Richmond Co., d/o Stafford and Amanda Gordon. Consent 1 JAN 1884 by bride Emma E. [her X mark] Gordon, wit. E.C. Edwards. Rev. Robert Lewis. 3 JAN 1884 at *Belle Mount*.[2] [C10, R:353, R1:61]

Lee, Richard Henry to Mary Ellen Yeatman. RICHARD HENRY LEE, farmer, age 23, single, b. Richmond Co., s/o William H. and Elizabeth J. Lee, to MARY ELLEN YEATMAN, age 22, single, b. Westmoreland Co., d/o Sopha Yeatman [name of father not given]. Consent undated by Sopha [her X mark] Yeatman, wit. Lewis H. Sisson, also signed by bride. Beverley D. Tucker. 11 DEC 1881 at St. John's Rectory in Warsaw, Va. [C9, R:338, R1:54]

---

[1] John William Elmore and Winnefred Jackson were married by bond 22 MAY 1833 in Richmond Co. by consent of his father Thomas Elmore.
[2] *Belle Mount* was located on a bluff overlooking the Rappahannock River and was northeast of *Mount Airy* and beyond Cat Point Creek.

Lee, Squire (Col.) to Lizzie Lewis (Col.). SQUIRE LEE, oysterman, age 24, single, b. Richmond Co., s/o Solomon and Harriet Lee, to LIZZIE LEWIS, age 20, single, b. Richmond Co., d/o John and Mary Lewis. [Note that Lizzie Lewis is the granddaughter of Alfred Churchwill.] Rev. W. Carter. 13 DEC 1882 at the church. [C9, R:314, R1:57]

Lemoine, John Harding[1] to Esther Stuart Hill. JOHN H. LEMOINE, merchant, age 37, single, b. Richmond Co., s/o Feriol [Jr.] and Ann M. [Maria Saunders] Lemoine, to ESTHER STUART HILL, age 21, single, b. Richmond Co., d/o William E. and Virginia A. [Benneham] Hill. Everard Meade. 2 JUN 1884 at St. John's Church, Warsaw. [C10, NN:6 JUN 1884, R:354, R1:62]

Levier, Joseph (Col.) to Alice Conner (Col.). JOSEPH LEVIER, hauling, age 25, single, b. Richmond Co., s/o Joseph Levier (dec'd.) and Jennie Rich, to ALICE CONNER, age 22, single, b. Richmond Co., d/o John and Susan Conner. Consent 26 JUL 1886 by bride Alice [her X mark] Conner, wit. Winnie Washington. Daniel Payne. 28 JUL 1886. [C11, R:316, R1:68]

Levier, William (Col.) to Mary E. Banks (Col.). WILLIAM LEWIS, farmer, age 25, single, b. Richmond Co., s/o Joseph Levier and Jane Rich, to MARY E. BANKS, age 21, single, b. Richmond Co., d/o Emanuel and Aphia Banks. Consent 23 MAY 1876 by bride, wit. Richd. Lewis. A.B. Dunaway. 25 MAY 1876. [C7, R:304, R1:40]

Lewis, Andrew Jackson[2] to Frances Mozingo. ANDREW J. LEWIS, farmer, age 21, single, b. Richmond Co., s/o John [Ball] and Alice [Virginia Roeick] Lewis,[3] to FRANCES MOZINGO, age 19, single, b. Baltimore, Md., d/o Jonathan B. and Matilda [Efford] Mozingo.[4] Robert Williamson, M.G. 16 JAN 1868 at *Marleton*. [C4, R:253, R1:23]

Lewis, Calvin G. to Mary J. Bryant. CALVIN G. LEWIS, farmer, age 22, single, b. Richmond Co., s/o Charles Lewis and wife Sarah, to MARY J. BRYANT, age 16, single, b. Northumberland Co., d/o Samuel Bryant and wife Olivia. Consent proved 15 JUL 1856 by mother Olivia N. Bryant, wits. [S.R.] Forester, R.D. Bryant. E.L. Williams, minister. 28 JUL 1856. [C1, R, R1:3]

Lewis, Cephas Moon to Sarah J. Straughan.[5] CEPHAS M. LEWIS, farmer, age 22, single, b. and res. Northumberland Co., s/o John W. and Elizabeth J. [Jones] Lewis, to SARAH J. STRAUGHAN, age 19, single, b. Westmoreland Co., d/o Thomas N. and Sarah E. [Oldham] Straughan.[6] Consent 16 JAN 1876 by bride and her mother Sarah E. Straughan, wit. John A. Thrift. G.H. Northam. 19 JAN 1876. [C7, R:304, R1:39]

Lewis, Charles, to Zerline Newgent. CHARLES LEWIS, tailor, age 23, single, b. Northumberland Co., s/o Charles Lewis and Sarah [B.] Cockerill [sic Clockrell],[7] to ZERLINE NEWGENT, age

---

[1] John Harding Lemoine served in Co. B, 40th Reg., Va. Inf., C.S.A. and was a prisoner at Point Lookout, Md. He died 25 JAN 1905 in Ivondale, Va.
[2] Andrew J. Lewis (b. 11 OCT 1846, d. 7 SEP 1913) and wife Frances A. Mozingo (b. 7 JUL 1848, d. 31 JUL 1930) are bur. in Oakland United Methodist Church cemetery.
[3] John B. Lewis (b. 19 MAY 1821, d. 5 MAY 1893) and wife Alice V. Roeick (b. 22 DEC 1824, d. 9 SEP 1892) are bur. in Oakland United Methodist Church cemetery.
[4] Jonathan B. Mozingo and Matildy Efford were married by bond 8 MAY 1847 in Richmond Co.
[5] Cephas Moon Lewis (1856-1915) and wife Sarah J. Straughan (1857-1924) are bur. at Bethany Baptist Church cemetery.
[6] Thomas N. Straughan and Sarah E. Oldham, d/o John F. Oldham, were married by bond 18 JAN 1847 in Westmoreland Co.
[7] Charles Lewis, widower, and Sally B. Cockerill were married by bond 11 JAN 1816 in Richmond Co.

19, single, b. Richmond Co., d/o George Newgent and Sarah Nash.[1] William H. Kirk, M.G. 10 JAN 1855 at Charles Barrock's. [C1, R:153, R1:2]

Lewis, Charles H. (Col.) to Mary E. Stevens (Col.). CHARLES H. LEWIS, oystering and farming, age 21, single, b. Richmond Co., res. Maryland, s/o Lucius and Frances Lewis, to MARY E. STEVENS, age 18, single, b. Richmond Co., d/o Samuel Stevens and wife now Addie Jackson. Consent 2 OCT 1885 from Ivanhoe, Va. by bride Mary E. [her X mark] Stevens, wit. mother Addie [her X mark] Jackson. Rev. W. Carter. [C10, R:317, R1:65]

Lewis, Charles Henry to Dorathy Jane Mozingo.[2] CHARLES H. LEWIS, oysterman, age 25, widowed, b. Richmond Co., s/o John B. [Ball] and Ailcey [Alice Virginia Roeick] Lewis, to DORATHY J. MOZINGO, age 17, single, b. Richmond Co., d/o Jonathan B. and Matilda [Efford] Mozingo. Oath to ages of parties by Matilda Mozingo, wit. by parties. G.H. Northam. 6 APR 1876. [C7, R:304, R1:40]

Lewis, Daniel (Col.) to Nellie Fushee (Col.). DANIEL LEWIS, oysterman, age 21, single, b. Richmond Co., s/o Henry and Delia Lewis, to NELLIE FUSHEE, age 21, single, b. Richmond Co., d/o John and Crisse Fushee. Allen Brown, minister. 28 MAR 1878 at the home of the bride. [C8, R:311, R1:44]

Lewis, Fairfax to Zepporrah E. Hale.[3] FAIRFAX LEWIS, farming, age 20, single, b. Richmond Co., s/o Middleton C. and Sarah [Ann Clark] Lewis, to ZEPPORRAH E. HALE, age 22, single, b. Richmond Co., d/o Moses and Nancy E. [Sydnor] Hale. Consent by bride. Consent by groom's mother Sarah [her X mark] Lewis, wits. George W. Wilkins, Thos. F. Hammack. G.H. Northam. 17 DEC 1882. [C9, R:314, R1:57]

Lewis, Henry C. to Mrs. Elizabeth F. Haydon. HENRY C. LEWIS, mechanic, age 32, single, b. Richmond Co., s/o Henry C. and Fanny Lewis, to ELIZABETH F. HAYDON, age 26, widow, b. Richmond Co., names of parents "omitted for good cause." Consent 30 MAR 1866 by bride Elizabeth F. [her X mark] Haydon, wit. Mary A. Douglas. Barth. Dodson, Parson. 3 APR 1866 at Elizabeth Haydon's house. [C4, R:271, R1:17]

Lewis, Hiram Frederick to Mary Elizabeth "Lizzie" Wagner.[4] HIRAM F. LEWIS, farming, age 28y11m27d, single, b. and res. Northumberland Co., s/o James C. and Mary S. [Harrison] Lewis,[5] to MARY ELIZABETH WAGNER, age 21y11m17d, single, b. Richmond Co., d/o John and Maggie Wagner. Consent by bride, wit. Maggie Wagner. W.H. Edwards. 23 DEC 1884 at Oakland Church. [C10, R:356, R1:63]

Lewis, James (Col.) to Henrietta Gaines (Col.). JAMES LEWIS, farmer, age 21y10m, single, b. Richmond Co., s/o Henry and Diley Lewis, to HENRIETTA GAINES, age 21y3m, single, b.

---

[1] George Newgent and Sarah Nash were married by bond 21 DEC 1824 in Richmond Co.
[2] Charles H. Lewis (b. 6 FEB 1849, d. 13 OCT 1932 at Sharps, Va.) and wife Dorathy Jane Mozingo (b. 15 SEP 1858, d. 8 JUL 1945 at Sharps, Va.) are bur. at Milden Cemetery.
[3] Fairfax Lewis (b. 10 MAY 1863, d. 9 OCT 1921) and wife Ella Sipporah Hale (b. 26 JAN 1859, d. 14 AUG 1929) are bur. in White Stone Baptist Church cemetery.
[4] Hiram F. Lewis (b. 26 DEC 1855, d. 18 SEP 1918) and wife Mary L. Wagner (b. 6 JAN 1869 in N.Y., d. 19 MAY 1953) are bur. at Calvary United Methodist Church cemetery.
[5] James C. Lewis and Mary S. Harrison, d/o Ann T. Harrison, were married by bond 19 DEC 1848 in Northumberland Co.

Richmond Co., d/o John F. and Ann Gaines. Thomas G. Thomas. 27 MAR 1869 at Henry Yeatman's. [C5, R, R1:25]

Lewis, James Edwin to Malvania Virginia Douglass.[1] JAMES E. LEWIS, farming, age 21y6m, single, b. and res. Northumberland Co., s/o James C. and Mary S. [Harrison] Lewis, to MALVANIA VIRGINIA DOUGLASS, age 17, single, b. Richmond Co., d/o William G. and Mary Ann [Hayden] Douglass. Consent 28 APR 1883 by bride Malvanie [her X mark] Douglass, and W.J. Douglass, wit. Charley Dodson. W.E. Allen. 2 MAY 1883. [C10, R:356, R1:59]

Lewis, James M. to Georgie A. Douglass. JAMES M. LEWIS, farming, age 21y6m, single, b. Richmond Co., s/o Richard C. Lewis and Elizabeth [Douglas], *q.v.*, to GEORGIA A. DOUGLAS, age 21y6m, single, b. Richmond Co., d/o Samuel and Ann E. Douglass. Consent 10 NOV 1879 by bride, sworn S. Bryant. W.A. Crocker. 12 NOV 1879 at the res. of the bride's father. [C8, R:308, R1:48]

Lewis, John (Col.) to Martha Ellen Shelton (Col.). JOHN LEWIS, oystering, age 24, widowed, b. Richmond Co., s/o Henry Lewis (dec'd.) and Lucy Lewis, to MARTHA ELLEN SHELTON, age 20, single, b. Richmond Co., d/o Major and Sarah Shelton. Peter Blackwell. 20 APR 1882 at res. of Major Shelton. [C9, R:312, R1:56]

Lewis, John (Col.) to Ann Conevey (Col.). JOHN LEWIS, oysterman, age 24, single, b. Richmond Co., s/o Henry and Delee Lewis, to ANN CONEVEY, age 21, single, b. Northumberland Co., d/o Oliver and Jane Conevey. Peter Blackwell. 9 JAN 1879 at Mr. Downing's. [C8, R:307, R1:46]

Lewis, John to Sophia Carter. JOHN LEWIS, oysterman, age 29, widowed, b. Northumberland Co., s/o James and Betsy Lewis, to SOPHIA CARTER, age 21, single, b. Lancaster Co., d/o Isaac and Mary Carter. Consent 15 DEC 1869 by bride Sophia [her X mark] Carter, wit. Washington Veney. Robert Williamson, M.G. 16 DEC 1869 at *Waverly*, Farnham Parish. [C5, R, R1:27]

Lewis, John B. to Mary Rice. JOHN B. LEWIS, farming, age 62, widowed, b. Northumberland Co., s/o Charles H. and Sally Lewis, to MARY RICE, age 43, single, b. Richmond Co., d/o Thomas and Nancy Rice. Consent 21 APR 1883 by bride, wit. M.C. Lewis. F.W. Claybrook. 23 APR 1883 at the res. of Sally Rice. [C10, NN:4 MAY 1883, R:356, R1:58]

Lewis, Meredith Columbus to Mary Samuel Douglass.[2] MEREDITH C. LEWIS, farmer, age 21, single, b. Richmond Co., s/o John B. [Ball] and Alice [Virginia Roeick] Lewis, to MARY S. DOUGLASS, age 17, single, b. Richmond, s/o William G. and Mary [Ann Hayden] Douglass. Consent 18 APR 1881 by bride. A. Wiles. 21 APR 1881 at the res. of the bride's father. [C9, R:335, R1:53]

Lewis, Middleton C. to Sarah Ann Clark. Consent 20 MAR 1854 by mother Elizabeth Clark, wit. John Harrison. No license or minister return. [C]

---

[1] James E. Lewis (b. 31 OCT 1866 [tombstone], d. 2 AUG 1936) and wife Malvania V. Douglas (b. 10 JAN 1865, d. 8 JUN 1937) are bur. in Oakland United Methodist Church cemetery.
[2] Meredith C. Lewis (b. 29 AUG 1859, d. 23 AUG 1941) and wife Mary S. Douglass (b. 27 MAR 1864, d. 31 JAN 1946) are bur. in Oakland United Methodist Church cemetery.

Lewis, Peter (Col.) to Trinity Ann Bryant (Col.). PETER LEWIS, oysterman, age 28, single, b. Richmond Co., s/o Harrison and Fanny Lewis, to TRINITY ANN BRYANT, age 19, single, b. Richmond Co., d/o Joseph Bryant and Charlott[e] Veney. Consent by mother of the bride Sharlott [her X mark] Veney, Trinity A. [her X mark] Bryant, wit. James Veney. David Veney. 20 JUN 1868 at Washington Veney's. [C4, C5, R:254, R1:24]

Lewis, Richard C. to Elizabeth Douglas. RICHARD C. LEWIS, farmer, age 25, single, b. Richmond Co., s/o Richard and Elizabeth Lewis, to ELIZABETH DOUGLAS, age 22, single, b. Richmond Co., d/o Jerry and Winnie Douglas. Consent 24 OCT 1877 by bride Elsbeth [her X mark] Douglas, sworn John T. Waterfield. J.B. DeBerry, P.C. 28 OCT 1877 at the res. of the bride's father. [C8, R:307, R1:43]

Lewis, Thomas Daniel, b. 14 AUG 1859, to Mrs. Virginia A. Lewis, widow of John W. Walker.[1] THOMAS D. LEWIS, farming, age 23y7m, single, b. Richmond Co., res. Lancaster Co., s/o Jeremiah and Mariah Lewis, to VIRGINIA A. WALKER, age 22, widow, b. Richmond Co., d/o John B. and Elsie Lewis. Consent 21 JAN 1884 by bride, wit. R. Dodson. W.E. Allen. 23 JAN 1884 at John B. Lewis'. [C10, R:353, R1:61]

Lewis, Thomas P., Jr. to Dorathy A. Bartlett.[2] THOMAS P. LEWIS, JR., farmer, age 39, widowed, b. Richmond Co., res. Northumberland Co., s/o Thomas P. [Sr.] and Elizabeth [Dameron] Lewis, to DORATHY A. BARTLETT, age 26, single, b. Richmond Co., [names of parents not completed]. Consent 7 JAN 1876 by bride Dorathy A. [her X mark] Bartlett. G.H. Northam. 9 JAN 1876. [C7, R:304, R1:39]

Lewis, William Addison to Virginia Ann Douglass.[3] WILLIAM A. LEWIS, farmer, age 23, single, b. Richmond Co., s/o John B. [Bell] and Alice [Virginia Roeick] Lewis, to VIRGINIA A. DOUGLASS, age 22, single, b. Richmond Co., d/o John and Elizabeth Douglass. Consent 22 OCT 1866 by bride Virginia A. [her X mark] Douglas, wits. Lindsey Headley, John Douglas. Robert Williamson, M.G. 24 OCT 1866 at John Douglass' near Union Village. [C3, C4, R:272, R1:18]

Lewis, William M. to Evalinor McGuire. WILLIAM M. LEWIS, farmer, age 54, widowed, b. and res. Northumberland Co., s/o William Lewis, Jr. and Frances Lewis, to EVALINOR McGUIRE, age 33, single, b. Northumberland Co., d/o John and Malinda [T. Hudson] McGuire.[4] Consent 27 AUG 1879 by bride Evalinor [her X mark] McGuire, wit. James W. Beacham. R.N. Reamy. 28 AUG 1879 at W. McGuire's. [C8, R:308, R1:47]

Lewis, Zebedee M. to Luemma Brann. ZEBEDEE LEWIS, farmer, age 21, single, b. Richmond Co., s/o Austin D. and Nancy Lewis, to LUEMMA BRANN, age 18, single, b. Richmond Co., d/o William and Frances Brann. Robert Williamson, M.G. 7 MAY 1867 at Thomas [Bragg's]. [C4, R:286, R1:21]

---

[1] Thomas D. Lewis (1860-1932) and wife Virginia L. (1864-1951) are bur. in Oakland United Methodist Church cemetery. Note difference in birth year for Thomas between Bible record and tombstone.
[2] Dorothey A. Lewis (1849-1918) is bur. in Gibeon Baptist Church cemetery on the same marker with her son Warren J. Lewis.
[3] William A. Lewis (b. 20 AUG 1843, d. 10 SEP 1916 in Arlington Co.) and wife Virginia A. Douglass (b. 16 JAN 1845, d. 19 JAN 1929 in Arlington Co.) are bur. in Oakwood Cemetery, Falls Church, Va.
[4] John McGuire and Malinda T. Hudson were married by bond 15 FEB 1838 in Northumberland Co.

Lewis, Zebedee M. to Mary F. Jones. ZEBEDEE M. LEWIS, miller, age 40, widowed,[1] b. Richmond Co., s/o Austin D. and Nancy Lewis, to MARY F. JONES, age 24, single, b. Richmond Co., [names of parents not completed]. Consent 28 FEB 1890 unsigned. G.H. Northam. 12 FEB 1890 at Mr. Lowery's, Farnham, Va. [C12, R:323, R1:76]

Lindon, C.C. to Carrie Davis. C.C. LINDON, merchant, age 25, single, b. Baltimore, Md., s/o Clarence C. and Elizabeth Lindon, to CARRIE DAVIS, age 24, single, b. Richmond Co., d/o Joseph and Martha Davis. G.H. Northam. 29 DEC 1885 at *Glenmore*. [C11, NN:15 JAN 1886, R:318, R1:66]

Littrell, James W. to Fanny C. Sisson. JAMES W. LITTRELL, carpenter, age 25, single, b. Richmond Co., s/o Alfred Littrell and Jane [Thrift] Littrell[2] now Wilson, to FANNY C. SISSON, age 25, single, b. Richmond Co., d/o Hiram and Sarah [Littrell] Sisson.[3] G.H. Northam. 8 JUL 1879. [C8, R:308, R1:47]

Littrell, John to Sarah C. Northen. JOHN LITTRELL, shoemaker, age 37y3m20d, single, b. Richmond Co., s/o John and Elizabeth Littrell, to SARAH C. NORTHEN, age 27y5m, single, b. Richmond Co., d/o George and Elizabeth [H. Bryant] Northen.[4] Andrew Fisher. 30 JUL 1863 at res. of George Northen. [C3, R:160, R1:13]

Littrell, John Edmund[5] to Etta Blanch Jett. JOHN EDMUND LITTRELL, clerking in store, age 24, single, b. Richmond Co., s/o Alfred and Jane G. [Thrift] Littrell, to ETTA BLANCH JETT, age 24, single, b. King George Co., d/o Henry S. and Martha A. [Ann Jones] Jett.[6] F.W. Claybrook. 6 FEB 1883 at *Indian Banks*. [C10, R:355, R1:58]

Littrell, John Mitchell to Mrs. Zaeline Elizabeth Lewis. JOHN M. LITTRELL, farmer, age 35, single, b. Northumberland Co., s/o John and Lucy [Rice] Littrell,[7] to ZAELINE E. LEWIS, age 22, widow, b. Richmond Co., d/o George and Sarah [Nash] Newgent. Consent 31 DEC 1858 by bride, Zaeline [her X mark] Lewis. Robert Williamson, M.G. 6 JAN 1859 at *California*.[8] [C2, R:165, R1:7]

Liverpool, Jesse (Col.) to Elizabeth Yerby (Col.). JESSE LIVERPOOL, ferry man, age 21, single, b. Richmond Co., s/o Peter and Mary Liverpool, to ELIZABETH YERBY, age 19, single, b. Richmond Co., d/o Isaac and Betsy Yerby. Thomas G. Thomas. 25 JAN 1867 the house of Sister Yerby. [C4, R:285, R1:19]

Liverpool, Stewart (Col.) to Lucy Ann Beale (Col.). STEWART LIVERPOOL, laborer, age 22, single, b. Essex Co., s/o John and Elizabeth Liverpool, to LUCY ANN BEALE, age 22, single, b. Westmoreland Co., [names of parents left blank]. George Laws. 3 MAY 1873. [C6, R:235, R1:34]

---

[1] Zebedee M. Lewis was previously married 7 MAY 1867 in Richmond Co. to Luemma Brann.
[2] Alfred Littrell and Jane Thrift were married 9 JAN 1852 in Richmond Co. by Rev. Elijah L. Williams.
[3] Hiram Sisson [Hierome] and Sally Littrell were married by bond 24 FEB 1840 in Richmond Co.
[4] George Northen and Elizabeth H. Bryant were married by bond 17 FEB 1835 in Richmond Co.
[5] The marriage license gives name John Edwin Littrell.
[6] Henry S. Jett and Martha Ann Jones were married 5 APR 1848 in King George Co. by Rev. Philip Montague. He served in the 15th Va. Cav., C.S.A., and he (d. 22 FEB 1896) is bur. in Farnham Baptist Church cemetery.
[7] John Littrell and Lucy Rice were married by bond 21 DEC 1810 in Northumberland Co.
[8] *California* was a tract purchased by Addison L. Carter in 1850 at the height of the California gold rush. It is about 2 miles from the line with Northumberland Co. at Moon, Va.

Lloyd, Bernard to Ora B. Franklin. BERNARD LLOYD, dairyman, age 25, single, b. Charles Co., Md., res. Anne Arundel Co., Md., s/o Thomas and Mary E. Lloyd, to ORA B. FRANKLIN, age 20, single, b. Richmond Co., d/o Philip M. and Mary S. Franklin. Everard Meade. 23 JUN 1890 at St. John's Church. [C12, R:323a, R1:77]

Lomax, Lawrence (Col.) to Susan Ball (Col.). LAWRENCE LOMAX, oysterman, age 23, single, b. Essex Co., s/o Ben and Clara Lomax, to SUSAN BALL, age 22, single, b. Richmond Co., d/o Butler and Easter Ball. Consent 29 DEC 1880 from *Ivanside* by bride Susan [her X mark] Ball, wit. Ben Young. Rev. Peter Blackwell. 30 DEC 1880. [C9, R:317, R1:51]

Loper, Edmond (Col.) to Julia Newton (Col.). EDMOND LOPER, laborer, age 24, widowed, b. Delaware, s/o Peter and Harriet Loper, to JULIA NEWTON, age 22, single, b. Richmond Co., d/o Isaac and Polly Newton. Consent 6 MAY 1878 by bride Julia [her X mark] Newton. Edmond Rich. 9 MAY 1878 at the house of Samuel Pursell. [C8, R:311, R1:45]

Lowery, Cornelius Franklin to Henrietta Balderson.[1] CORNELIUS F. LOWRY [sic], farming, age 35, widowed, b. and res. Northumberland Co., s/o Warren [and Rebecca Beacham] Lowry, to HENRIETTA BALDERSON, age 22, single, b. Westmoreland Co., d/o Ransdal and Jemima Balderson. Consent 31 JAN 1888 by parties Henretter S. Baldson [sic] and Cornelious F. Lowry [sic]. Rev. A. Judson Reamy. 8 FEB 1888. [C11, R:315, R1:72]

Lowery, James to Julia A. French.[2] JAMES LOWERY, carpenter, age 23, single, b. Richmond Co., s/o Gowen T. and Mary J. [Pearce] Lowery,[3] to JULIA A. FRENCH, age 25, single, b. Va., d/o Rhodam and Hannah [Haydon] French. Consent 10 DEC 1872 by bride, wit. Harvey T. French. William H. Kirk. 12 DEC 1872 at Mrs. French's. [C6, R:238, R1:32]

Lowery, James Oliver to Martha E. Connellee.[4] JAMES O. LOWRY [sic],[5] farmer, age 30y8m, single, b. Caroline Co., s/o Jordan B. and Fanny E. Lowry, to MARTHA E. CONNELLEE, age 26, single, b. Richmond Co., d/o James D. and Mary W. Connellee. G.H. Northam. 15 DEC 1874. [C7, R:230, R1:37]

Lowery, Jordan B. to Mrs. Elizabeth Grant Marshall. JORDAN B. LOWERY, farmer, age 37, widowed, b. Hanover Co., s/o Overton Lowery and wife Ela [sic], to ELIZABETH MARSHALL, age 25, widow, b. King George Co., d/o Wm. Grant. G.H. Northam, minister of the Baptist persuasion. 8 APR 1857 at *Mount Airy*. [C1, R:159, R1:4]

Lowery, Joseph W.[6] to Almeda F. Lewis. JOSEPH W. LOWRY [sic], oystering, age 28, single, b. and res. Northumberland Co., s/o [Orange] and Rebecca [Beacham] Lowery,[7] to ALMEDA F. LEWIS, age 18, single, b. Richmond Co., d/o Thomas P. and Virginia Lewis. Consent undated

---

[1] Cornelius F. Lowery (b. 1 MAY 1849, d. 22 NOV 1913 in Baltimore, Md.) and wife Henrietta Balderson are bur. in Roseland Cemetery, Reedville, Va.
[2] Perhaps Julia A. Lowery (1851-1935) is bur. in Hopewell Methodist Church cemetery, with other members of the French Family.
[3] Goin D. Lowry, ward of H. Stott, and Mary J. Pearce, d/o Margaret Winstead, were married by bond 16 DEC 1844 in Northumberland Co.
[4] James Oliver Lowery (b. 7 MAY 1840 in Caroline Co., d. 20 APR 1920 at *Distillery Farm*) and wife Martha E. Connellee (b. 23 JUN 1840, d. 1 MAY 1919) are bur. at Warsaw United Methodist Church cemetery. He served in C.S.A.
[5] The surname also appears as Lowery.
[6] Joseph W. Lowry (1860-1896) is bur. in Gibeon Baptist Church cemetery.
[7] Orange Lowery and Rebecca Beacham were married by bond 28 DEC 1841 in Northumberland Co.

by parties, wits. Thomas J. [his X mark] Lewis, L.W. Thrift. R.N. Reamy. 9 MAY 1888. [C11, R:316, R1:72]

Lowery, William B. to Annie Richards.[1] WILLIAM B. LOWERY, farmer, age 22y9m, single, b. Hanover Co., s/o Jordan B. and Fanny Lowery, to ANNIE RICHARDS, age 18, single, b. Richmond Co., d/o John and Mary [Webb] Richards.[2] Consent 24 MAR 1871 by mother Mrs. Mary Richards. Andrew Fisher. 24 JAN 1871 at Laurel Brook Church. [C5, R:244, R1:29]

Luckham, Edward to Mrs. Martha Clarke, widow of Robert Morris. EDWARD LUCKHAM, farming, age 38, single, b. Richmond Co., res. Lancaster Co., s/o William and Jane Luckham, to MARTHA MORRIS, age 28, widow, b. Richmond Co., d/o Joseph and Nancy Clarke. G.H. Northam. 4 JAN 1879. [C8, R:307, R1:46]

Luckham, John R. to Naomi Thompson. JOHN R. LUCKHAM, oystering, age 29y5m, single, b. Richmond Co., s/o John and Lucy [E. Jones] Luckham, to NAOMI THOMPSON, age 24y10m28d, single, b. King George Co., d/o William D. Thompson and Ellen [Moxley] Thompson now Jett. F.W. Claybrook. 17 MAY 1883. [C10, R:356, R1:59]

Luckham, Thomas B. to Mary Ann Brooks. THOMAS B. LUCKHAM, farmer, age 26, single, b. Richmond Co., s/o William and Mahala [Hazard] Luckham,[3] to MARY A. BROOKS, age 23, single, b. Richmond Co., d/o Richard H. and Jane Brooks. Consent 5 DEC 1859 by bride, wit. Jas. McCarty. Robert Williamson, M.G. 8 DEC 1859. [C2, R:165, R1:8]

Lumpkin, James T.B. to Emma L. Hutchinson. JAMES T.B. LUMPKIN, merchant, age 26, single, b. King and Queen Co., res. Essex Co., s/o Robert and Mary E. Lumpkin, to EMMA L. HUTCHINSON, age 20, single, b. Fauquier Co., d/o F.M. and Rosa L. Hutchinson. H.H. Fones. 14 MAR 1881. [C9, R:335, R1:52]

Lusby, Thomas Washington[4] to Mrs. Martha A. Dunnaway. THOMAS W. LUSBY, farmer, age 22, single, b. Westmoreland Co., s/o John T. Lusby and Margaret B. Self,[5] to MARTHA A. DUNNAWAY, age 26, widow, b. Northumberland Co., d/o Edward Sebree and Nancy Crowder. Consent 15 JAN 1857 by bride Marthia A. [her X mark] Dunaway [sic], wit. J.W. Bryant. Barth. Dodson, M.G., Baptist. 22 JAN 1857. [C1, R:159, R1:4]

Lusby, Thomas Washington to Frances Jane "Fannie" Dameron.[6] THOMAS W. LUSBY, farmer, age 35, widower, b. Richmond Co., s/o John T. and Margaret B. [Self] Lusby, to FANNIE J. DAMERON, age 21, single, b. Richmond Co., d/o Charles and Lucy [Douglas] Dameron.[7] Consent 21 MAY 1870 by bride, wits. Jno. F. Thrift and James Lowery, proved by the oath of James Lowery. Wm. H. Kirk. 25 MAY 1870 at the res. of Charles Dameron. [C5, R:233, R1:28]

---

[1] William B. Lowery (1847-1906) and wife Annie Richards (1853-1926) are bur. at Warsaw United Methodist Church cemetery. These are the parents of William Wesley Lowery (1883-1964) who founded Lowery's Restaurant in Tappahannock, Va.
[2] John Richards and Mary Webb were married by bond 5 MAR 1841 in Richmond Co. by Rev. William N. Ward.
[3] William Luckham and Mahala Hazard were married by bond 6 FEB 1816 in Richmond Co.
[4] Thomas W. Lusby served in Co. E, 40th Reg., Va. Inf., C.S.A.
[5] John Lusby and Margaret Self were married by bond in DEC 1833 in Westmoreland Co.
[6] Thomas W. Lusby (b. 31 OCT 1835, d. 2 FEB 1906 in Robley, Va.) and wife Frances J. Dameron (b. 14 AUG 1849, d. FEB 1927 in Alexandria, Va.) are bur. in Farnham Baptist Church cemetery. He served in Co. E, 40th Reg., Va. Inf., C.S.A.
[7] Charles Y. Dameron and Lucy Douglas were married by bond 1 OCT 1833 in Northumberland Co.

Luttrell, James Leroy to Julia A. Rock. JAMES LEROY LUTTRELL, age 36, widowed, b. Richmond Co., s/o John P. and Nancy H. [Davenport] Luttrell,[1] to JULIA A. ROCK, age 21, single, b. Richmond Co., d/o James and Sarah [Ann Hardwick] Rock.[2] Consent 24 JAN 1865 by bride, wit. W.M. Rock. William F. Bain. 26 JAN 1865 at James Rock's. [C3, R:204, R1:14, R1:56]

Luttrell, James L. to Nancy Jane Elmore.[3] JAMES L. LUTTRELL, farmer, age 52, widower, b. Richmond Co., s/o John [P.] and Nancy [H. Davenport] Luttrell, to NANCY JANE ELMORE, age 26, single, b. Richmond Co., d/o Henry and Mary [Ann Headley] Elmore.[4] Robert Williamson. 7 SEP 1882 at *Laurel Hill.* [C9, R:313]

Luttrell, Leroy M. to Mrs. Virginia A. Haynie, widow of William J. Davenport.[5] LEROY M. LUTTRELL, farmer, age 27, single, b. and res. Northumberland Co., s/o James M. and Maria A. Luttrell, to VIRGINIA A. DAVENPORT,[6] age 25, widow, b. Richmond Co., d/o Joseph Haynie and Elizabeth Haynie née Norris.[7] Consent 16 APR 1889 by bride. E.P. Parham, minister M.E. Church. 17 APR 1889 at the bride's residence. [C12, R:327, R1:74]

Luttrell, William Filmore to Willie M. Hanks.[8] WILLIAM F. LUTTRELL, farmer, age 2[2]y5m, single, b. Richmond Co., s/o Joseph [R.] and Rebecca [A. Lewis] Luttrell,[9] to WILLIE M. HANKS, age 19, single, b. Richmond Co., d/o William E. and Virginia [Dunaway] Hanks, *q.v.* Consent 26 NOV 1877 by bride and William E. Hanks. J.B. DeBerry, P.C. 28 NOV 1877 at the res. of the bride's father. [C8, R:307, R1:43]

Lyell, Charles B. to Indiana M. Middleton. CHARLES B. LYELL, farming, age 21, single, b. Northumberland Co., s/o Thomas S. and Mary E. [Graham] Lyell,[10] to INDIANA M. MIDDLETON, age 15, single, b. Northumberland Co., d/o William and Mary E. [DeShields] Middleton.[11] Consent 31 MAY 1861 by B.S. [Benjamin Smith] Middleton,[12] uncle and ward of Indiana, also signed by parties, wits. [Wm.] L. Middleton. Robert Williamson, M.G. 6 JUN 1861 at *Edge Hill.* [C3, R:123, R1:10]

Lyell, Dennis (Col.) to Frances Lomax (Col.). DENNIS LYELL, laborer, age 22, single, b. Northumberland Co., s/o Dennis and Ellen Lyell, to FRANCES LOMAX, age 28, single, b. Richmond Co., d/o Mary Barber. Thomas G. Thomas. 19 DEC 1878. [C8, R:312, R1:46]

---

[1] Johhn P. Luttrell and Ann H. Davenport were married by bond 7 AUG 1826 in Richmond Co.

[2] James Rock and Sarah Ann Hardwick were married by bond 5 JAN 1837 in Richmond Co.

[3] James L. Luttrell (b. 18 DEC 1827, d. 16 NOV 1910) and his second wife Nancy Jane Elmore (b. 3 JUN 1854, d. 6 MAR 1924) are bur. in the Richardson Family Graveyard near Luttrellville, Va.

[4] Henry Elmore and Mary Ann Headley were married 8 JUL 1852 in Northumberland Co.

[5] Leroy W. Luttrell (b. 21 NOV 1861, d. 14 AUG 1952) and his wife Virginia A. Davenport (b. 28 NOV 1863, d. 20 JAN 1939) are bur. in Hopewell Methodist Church cemetery.

[6] The surname also appears as Devenport and Deavenport.

[7] Joseph Haynie and Elizabeth Morris were married by bond 1 JAN 1850 in Lancaster Co.

[8] William F. Luttrell (b. 2 APR 1856, d. 17 JAN 1929 in Downings, Va.) and wife Willie M. Hanks (1858-1934) are bur. in Farnham Baptist Church cemetery.

[9] Joseph R. Luttrell and Rebecca A. Lewis were married 20 MAR 1853 in Northumberland Co.

[10] Thomas S. Lyell and Mary E. Graham were married by bond 13 JAN 1825 in Westmoreland Co.

[11] William Middleton and Mary E. DeShields were married by bond 29 JUN 1836 in Northumberland Co.

[12] Dr. B.S. Middleton (b. 20 MAY 1816 in Westmoreland Co., d. 3 JUL 1892 at his home in Richmond Co.), s/o William Middleton, Jr. and Maria Smith Redman. In 1847 he was married to Sarah Ann Cox who d. 11 DEC 1848. Married second on 27 MAR 1855 to Caroline Virginia Coffin. He practiced medicine near Emmerton, Va.

Lyell, Edwin to Martha E. Jeffries.[1] EDWIN LYELL, farmer, age 27, single, b. and res. Westmoreland Co., s/o Thomas S. and Mary E. [Graham] Lyell,[2] to MARTHA E. JEFFRIES, age 20, single, b. Richmond Co., d/o Richard O. [Orlando] and Emily [Rockwell] Jeffries.[3] Consent 4 FEB 1860 by bride and Emily Jeffries, wit. Seth Rockwell. Lloyd Moore. 15 FEB 1860. [C2, R:153, R1:8]

Lyell, Henry to Lucy E. Lyell. HENRY LYELL, farmer, in his 31st year, widower, b. Richmond Co., s/o Thomas J. Lyell and wife Mary E., to LUCY E. LYELL, in her 22nd year, single, b. Richmond Co., d/o Samuel M. Lyell and wife Felicia A. [Ann Garland].[4] William N. Ward, M.G. 26 FEB 1856 in Warsaw, Va. [C1, R, R1:3]

Lyell, John Middleton to Anna Doswell Booker.[5] JOHN M. LYELL, merchant, age 26, single, b. Northumberland Co., s/o Thomas S. and Mary E. [Graham] Lyell, to ANNA D. BOOKER, age 22, single, b. Richmond Co., d/o E.D. [Erasmus Derwin][6] and Olivia C. [Carrington Anderson] Booker. Consent 30 OCT 1871 at Farnham by bride, wits. E.C. Booker and R.H. Lyell. Robert Williamson. 31 OCT 1871 at *Cedar Grove*. [C6, R:245, R1:30]

Lyell, Robert Hudson to Ada Maria Terrell Booker.[7] ROBERT H. LYELL, merchant, age 33y4m, single, b. Northumberland Co., res. Baltimore, Md., s/o Thomas S. and Mary E. [Graham] Lyell, to ADA MARIA TERRELL BOOKER, age 21, single, b. Richmond Co., d/o Erasmus D. [Derwin] and Olivia [Carrington Anderson] Booker. Consent 21 NOV 1881 from *Cedar Grove* by bride. F.W. Claybrook. 22 NOV 1881 at Farnham Baptist Church. [C9, NN:2 DEC 1881, R:338, R1:54]

M

Maden, Alexander (Col.) to Maria Diggs (Col.). ALEXANDER MADEN, oysterman, age 36, single, b. Richmond Co., s/o John and Jennie Maden, to MARIA DIGGS, age 23, single, b. Northumberland Co., d/o Nelson and Maria Diggs. Thomas G. Thomas. 1 FEB 1871 at house of Nelson Diggs. [C5, R:244, R1:29]

Maden, Spencer (Col.) to Mrs. Mary Johnson (Col.). SPENCER MADEN,[8] farmer, age 50, widowed, b. Richmond Co., s/o William and Elsie Maden, to MARY JOHNSON, age 50, widow, b. Richmond Co., d/o Rachel Carter. Thomas G. Thomas. 6 NOV 1869 at res. of the minister. [C5, R, R1:26]

---

[1] Edwin Lyell (b. 29 MAR 1832, d. 12 DEC 1907) and wife Martha E. Jeffries (b. 3 AUG 1843, d. 9 MAY 1908) are bur. at Calvary United Methodist Church cemetery. He served in Co. C, 41st Va. Inf., C.S.A.
[2] Thomas S. Lyell and Mary E. Graham were married by bond 13 JAN 1825 in Westmoreland Co.
[3] Richard O. Jeffries and Emily Rockwell were married by bond 16 OCT 1838 in Richmond Co. by consent of her father Seth Rockwell.
[4] Samuel M. Lyell and Felicia Ann Garland were married by bond 9 JUL 1833 in Richmond Co. The bond states the bride is an orphan of Vincent Garland, Jr., dec.
[5] John Middleton Lyell (b. 22 AUG 1845, d. 10 SEP 1916 at *Walnut Lawn*) and wife Anna Doswell Booker (b. 11 APR 1849, d. 10 DEC 1891) are bur. at Farnham Baptist Church cemetery. He served in Co. D, the 9th Va. Cav., C.S.A., and lived post war at *Linden Farm*.
[6] Dr. Erasmus Derwin Booker, s/o James Booker and Ann Throckmorton, and grandson of Revolutionary War soldier Capt. Lewis Booker of *Laurel Grove*, near Millers Tavern, Essex. Co. On 6 APR 1848 he was married to Olivia Carrington Anderson, d/o John Trevillian Anderson and Ann Rebecca Doswell of *Verdun*, King William Co. Olivia d. 28 JUN 1863 and Dr. Booker married second 2 AUG 1866 to Elizabeth E. Eubank, d/o Col. Thomas Dunaway Eubank and Elizabeth Downing. Dr. Erasmus D. Booker (b. 10 SEP 1825 near New Market, Shenandoah Co., d. 20 JAN 1898), and wife Bettie E. (d. 17 JUN 1900 age 53y9m14d) are bur. in Farnham Baptist Church cemetery.
[7] Robert Hudson Lyell (b. 27 JUL 1848, d. DEC 1925 in Baltimore, Md.) and wife Ada Booker (b. 6 DEC 1859, d. 30 DEC 1937 in Lynchburg, Va.) are bur. in Farnham Baptist Church cemetery.
[8] The surname also appears as Maiden.

Maiden, Elijah (Col.) to Emily Jones (Col.). ELIJAH MAIDEN, laborer, age 27, single, b. Richmond Co., s/o Powell Maiden and Lilla Maden (dec'd.), to EMILY JONES, age 26, single, b. Richmond Co., d/o Lewis and Ellen Jones. Consent 18 DEC 1882 by bride Emily [her X mark] Jones, wit. O.M. Lemoine. Charles Sparks. 24 DEC 1882. [C10, R:314, R1:57]

Maiden, Powell (Col.) to Harriet Rankings (Col.). POWELL MAIDEN, oysterman, age 40, widowed, b. Richmond Co., s/o John and Virginia Maiden, to HARRIET RANKINGS, age 26, single, b. Richmond Co., d/o Robert and Julia Ann Rankings. Allen Brown, minister. 21 DEC 1877 at the bride's home. [C8, R:308, R1:43]

Maiden, Powell (Col.) to Rachel Bailey (Col.). POWELL MAIDEN, oysterman and farmer, age 50, widowed, b. Richmond Co., s/o John and Jennie Maiden, to RACHEL BAILEY, age 32, single, b. Richmond Co., d/o Simon Bailey and Lucy Castor. N. Atkins. 22 MAY 1884 at *Shandy Hall*. [C10, R:354, R1:62]

Maiden, Thomas [FB] to Virginia Cox [FB]. THOMAS MAIDEN, farmer, age 22, single, b. Baltimore, Md., s/o Hannah Maiden [FB], to VIRGINIA COX, age 21, single, b. Richmond Co., d/o Del[l] and Charlotte Cox [FB]. Consent 6 JAN 1863 by R.F. Mitchell.[1] John Pullen. 15 JAN 1863 at Dell Cox's. [C3, R:160, R1:12]

Malone, James to Mrs. Mary J. Lewis. JAMES MALONE, farmer, age 29, single, b. Cross Maglenn, Ire., s/o Cornelius and Mary Malone, to MARY J. LEWIS, age 26, widow, b. Northumberland Co., [names of parents blank]. Barth. Dodson, Parson. 13 MAR 1866 at the house of Mary J. Lewis. [C4, R:270, R1:16]

Marks, Christopher Columbus to Lavinia Elgier Hinson. CHRISTOPHER C. MARKS, farmer, age 21, single, b. Richmond Co., s/o Vincent and Mary [France] Marks, to LAVINIA E. HINSON, age 20, single, b. Richmond Co., d/o W.W. [William] and Maria [Scates] Hinson.[2] H.H. Fones. 6 DEC 1876. [C7, R:306, R1:41 and 43]

Marks, Daingerfield to Elizabeth Sanders. DAINGERFIELD MARKS, farmer, age 21, single, b. Richmond Co., s/o Samuel and Frances [Hinson] Marks,[3] to ELIZABETH SANDERS, age 19, single, b. Richmond Co., d/o James C. and Sally Sanders. Consent 7 MAR 1861 by father James C. Sanders, wit. Robert H. Brown. John Pullen. 7 MAR 1861 at father's. [C3, R:123, R1:10]

Marks, Henry T. to Eliza A. France.[4] HENRY T. MARKS, farming, age 22, single, b. Richmond Co., s/o Thomas R. and Ann [Hall] Marks, *q.v.*, to ELIZA A. FRANCE, age 18y8m, single, b. Richmond Co., d/o William and Mary Jane [Weeden] France, *q.v.* Consent 16 JAN 1884 by William France, wit. William H. Marks. H.H. Fones. 17 JAN 1884. [C10, R:353, R1:61]

Marks, John to Nancy Strawn. JOHN MARKS, wagoner, age 37, widowed, b. Richmond Co., s/o Marshal Anthony Malone and Nancy Marks, to NANCY STRAWN,[5] age 23, single, b. Richmond

---

[1] "Thomas Maiden & Virginia Cox are free negroes of this county, and wish to get married after the fashion of white folks, I presume you can fix them off." R.F. Mitchell.
[2] William W. Hinson and Maria Scates were married 13 MAR 1850 in Richmond Co. by Rev. William Balderson.
[3] Samuel Marks and Frances Hinson were married by bond 6 MAR 1838 in Richmond Co. by Rev. Thomas M. Washington.
[4] Henry T. Marks (1861-1941) and wife Eliza A. France (1865-1921) are bur. in Rappahannock Baptist Church cemetery.
[5] Spelling may be a form of the surname Straughan.

Co., d/o John and Jenny Strawn. Consent 5 NOV 1868. David Veney, minister. 8 NOV 1868 at Mulberry Chapel Church. [C5, R:254, R1:24]

Marks, John R.[1] to Ada Jane Brown. JOHN K. MARKS, farmer, age 23, single, b. Richmond Co., s/o Vincent and Mary [V. France] Marks,[2] to ADA J. BROWN, age 19, single, b. Richmond Co., d/o Robert H. and Sally Ann Brown. Consent by Robert H. Brown, wit. James H. Anthony. G.H. Northam. 18 JUN 1876 at [Cobham] Park. [C7, R:305, R1:40]

Marks, Lemuel to Mary Ann Sanders. LEMUEL MARKS, farming, age 22, single, b. Lunenburg Parish, s/o John Marks and Catharine [Marks],[3] to MARY A. SANDERS, age 22, single, b. Lunenburg Parish, d/o James C. Sanders and Sally [Hinson]. Consent 17 JAN 1854 by bride, wit. Samson Markes, Jas. C. Sanders, Joseph F. Sanders, James M. Morris. Return by Rev. John Pullen, at James C. Sanders in Richmond Co., Lunenburg Parish. 19 JAN[4] 1854. [C, R, R1:1]

Marks, Lemuel to Berthia E. Robinson. LEMUEL MARKS, farmer, age 18, single, b. Richmond Co., s/o Lemuel Marks and Mary A. Nevitt, to BERTHIA E. ROBINSON, age 22, single, b. Westmoreland Co., d/o John and Charlotte [T. Hall] Robinson.[5] Consent 5 MAR 1877 by bride, wit. John A. France; consent 5 MAR 1877 by Mary A. Nevitt, wit. John A. France. G.H. Northam. 8 MAR 1877. [C8, R:306a, R1:42]

Marks, Lemuel to Florence B. Balderson. LEMUEL MARKS, fishing and oystering, age 23, widowed, b. Richmond Co., s/o Lemuel Marks and Mary Marks née Saunders, *q.v.*, to FLORENCE B. BALDERSON, age 21, single, b. Richmond Co., d/o Thomas G. [Gilbert] and Mary F. [Frances Davis] Balderson, *q.v.* Oath by T.C. [Tasker Carter] Crabb as to the age of bride. G.M. Conley. 24 DEC 1885 at *River Dale*. [C11, R:318, R1:65]

Marks, Miskell L. to Julia Ann Bowen. MISKELL L. MARKS, white, farmer, age 23, single, b. Richmond Co., s/o Samuel and Lucy Marks, to JULIA ANN BOWEN, age 23, single, b. Richmond Co., d/o Martin and Patty [Sanders] Bowen.[6] Consent 31 MAR 1871 by bride, wit. Robert H. Brown. H.H. Fones. 2 APR 1871 at Mrs. Patty Bowen's. [C5, R:244, R1:29]

Marks, Paltine C.[7] to Sally F. Nash. PALTINE C. MARKS, carpenter, age 23, single, b. Richmond Co., s/o Thornton and Jennie [Jane Hinson] Marks,[8] to SALLY F. NASH, age 21, single, b. Richmond Co., d/o Zachariah and Polly [Mary Marks] Nash.[9] Consent 22 DEC 1865 by father Zachariah Nash, wits. Thos. E. Pullen, William D. Olliff who proves age of parties. John Pullen. 28 DEC 1865 at Zachariah Nash's. [C3, R:205, R1:15]

Marks, Samuel Daingerfield to Myrtle Sedonia Marks. SAMUEL D. MARKS, farmer, age 25, single, b. Richmond Co., s/o Daingerfield and Elizabeth [Sanders] Marks, *q.v.*, to MYRTLE S. MARKS,

---

[1] John R. Marks (b. 1853, d. 16 OCT 1916) is bur. in Cobham Park Baptist Church cemetery.
[2] Vincent Marks and Mary France were married by bond 9 MAY 1850 in Richmond Co.
[3] John Marks and Catharine Marks were married by bond 15 JAN 1821 in Westmoreland Co.
[4] The Register gives date of marriage 19 MAR 1854.
[5] John Robinson and Charlotte T. Hall were married by bond 15 OCT 1846 in Richmond Co. by consent of her father Robert Hall.
[6] Martin V. Bowen and Martha Sanders were married 3 OCT 1845 in Richmond Co. by Rev. John Pullen.
[7] Paltine C. Marks served in Co. D, 40th Reg., Va. Inf., C.S.A.
[8] Thornton Marks and Jane Hinson were married by bond 30 APR 1836 in Richmond Co.
[9] Zachariah Nash and Mary Marks were married by bond 12 MAR 1833 in Richmond Co.

age 18, single, b. Richmond Co., d/o M.L. [Miskell] and Julia A. [Ann Bowen] Marks, *q.v.* G.M. Conley. 7 JAN 1890 at *The Hermitage.* [C12, R:323, R1:76]

Marks, Thomas Dennard[1] to Jeannette J. Peed. THOMAS D. MARKS, farmer, age 27, single, b. Richmond Co., s/o William B. and Mary [Weadon] Marks,[2] to JEANNETTE J. PEED, age 18, single, b. Richmond Co., d/o John R. and Almira Peed. Consent 6 JUN 1879 by father J.R. Peed, wit. T.W. Bowen. Z. Parker Richardson. 4 JUN 1879 at *Foneswood,*[3] the res. of the bride's father. [C8, R:308, R1:9, R1:47]

Marks, Thomas to Ann Hall.[4] THOMAS MARKS,[5] farmer, age 32, single, b. Richmond Co., s/o Reuben and Fanny [France] Marks,[6] to ANN HALL, age 18, single, b. Richmond Co., d/o Stephen and Mary A. [Ann Hall] Hall.[7] Consent 11 DEC 1860 by mother Mary A. Jones, wit. Samuel [his X mark] Markes. John Pullen. 13 DEC 1860. [C2, R:154]

Marks, Vincent, Jr. to Mary A. Cash. VINCENT MARKS, JR., farmer, age 22, single, b. Richmond Co., s/o Vincent [Sr.] and Mary [France] Marks,[8] to MARY A. CASH, age 22, single, b. Richmond Co., d/o [William and] Felicia [France] Cash. Consent 27 AUG 1872 by bride, also signed by her mother Felicia Cash, no wit. D.M. Wharton. 29 AUG 1872 at res. of minister in Westmoreland Co. [C6, R:238, R1:32]

Marks, Washington L. to Persiler A. Scates. WASHINGTON L. MARKS, farming, age 23, single, b. Richmond Co., s/o Thomas and Ann [Hall] Marks, *q.v.*, to PERSILER A. SCATES, age 18, single, b. Richmond Co., d/o Joseph and Sarah [A. Hinson] Scates, *q.v.* Consent 7 MAY 1888 by bride, wit. Sarah A. Scates, R.A. Conley. Geo. M. Conley. 9 MAY 1888 at the res. of Mrs. Sarah Scates. [C11, R:316, R1:72]

Martin, Henry (Col.) to Nancy Branch (Col.). HENRY MARTIN, coach maker, age supposed to be about 40, single, b. Richmond Co., s/o Norsaw and Lucy Martin, to NANCY BRANCH, age 34, single, b. Petersburg, Va., d/o Vollin and Kitty Branch. G.H. Northam. 10 MAR 1866 at Warsaw, Va. [C4, R:270, R1:16]

Mason, Edward (Col.) to Ella Lee (Col.). EDWARD MASON, sailing, age 26, single, b. Richmond Co., s/o LeRoy and Tabitha Mason, to ELLA LEE, age 21, single, b. Lancaster Co., d/o Alice Conway. Consent 5 FEB 1887 by bride Ella [her X mark] Lee, wit. G.F. Green. Charles Sparks. 6 FEB 1887 at Henry Green's house at 7 o'clock. [C11, R:290, R1:69]

Mason, Leroy (Col.) to Emma Tolliver (Col.). LEROY MASON, sailing, age 24, single, b. Richmond Co., s/o Leroy and Tabitha Mason, to EMMA TOLLIVER, age 19, single, b. Richmond Co., d/o Rose Johnson. Consent 24 FEB 1890 from Ivanhoe, Va. by bride, wit. Sydnor Veeney. Rev. Jacob Robinson. 26 FEB 1890 at Mt. Zion Church, Ivanhoe. [C12, R:323a, R1:76]

---

[1] Thomas D. Marks (b. 1852, d. 21 JUL 1921), farmer, is bur. Rappahannock Baptist Church cemetery.
[2] William B. Marks and Mary Weadon were married 6 FEB 1850 in Richmond Co. by Rev. John Pullen.
[3] Foneswood, Va. is a locality on Route 624 close to the county's north boundary. An early owner of property here was Thomas Fones.
[4] Thomas Marks (b. 9 DEC 1828, d. 9 APR 1908 of Bright's disease) and wife Ann Hall (b. 10 NOV 1841, d. 8 FEB 1925) are bur. Rappahannock Baptist Church cemetery.
[5] Spelling also appears as Markes.
[6] Reuben Marks and Fanny France were married by bond 12 JAN 1819 in Richmond Co.
[7] Stephen Hall and Mary Ann Hall were married by bond 5 OCT 1829 in Richmond Co.
[8] Vincent Marks and Mary France were married by bond 9 MAY 1850 in Richmond Co.

Mason, Oskar (Col.) to Mrs. Susan Tucker Gaskins (Col.). OSKAR MASON, farmer, age 24, single, b. Richmond Co., s/o Leroy and Tabitha Mason, to SUSAN GASKINS, age 23, widow, b. Richmond Co., d/o John and Winefred Tucker. Consent 22 DEC 1868 by bride Susan [her X mark] Gaskins, wit. Jerry [his X mark] Middleton. Robert Williamson, M.G. 24 DEC 1868 at *Locust Hill*. [C5, R:254, R1:25]

Mason, Willis (Col.) to Mrs. Mary Ann Diggs (Col.). WILLIS MASON, age 29, widowed, b. Richmond Co., s/o Leroy and Tabb[y] Mason, to MARY ANN DIGGS, age 35, widow, b. Richmond Co., d/o Addison and Nellie Drake. Consent 26 JUL 1876 by bride Mary Ann [her X mark] Diggs, wit. R.H. Lyell. Rev. Daniel R. Payne. 27 JUL 1876 at the res. of Mrs. Diggs. [C7, R:305, R1:40]

Mason, Willis (Col.) to Fanny Jackson (Col.). WILLS MASON, farmer, age 22, single, b. Richmond Co., s/o Leroy and Tabby Mason, to FANNY JACKSON, age 22, single, b. Richmond Co., d/o James and Hagar Jackson. Consent undated by bride, wit. Cyrus Harding, Jr. Robert Williamson, M.G. 24 DEC 1869 at *Beaver Hill*, Farnham. [C5, R, R1:27]

Mathews, Lee Roy (Col.) to Gertrude Basye (Col.). LEE ROY[1] MATHEWS, farming, age 23, single, b. Richmond Co., s/o Lee Roy and Adeline Mathews, to GERTRUDE BASYE, age 22, single, b. Westmoreland Co., d/o Aldsman Basye and Sally Johnson. Consent 17 DEC 1884 by bride, wit. Richard France. George Laws. 18 DEC 1884. [C10, R:355, R1:63]

Matthews, Alexander (Col.) to Susan Ann Parker (Col.). ALEXANDER MATTHEWS, farming, age 27, single, b. Richmond Co., s/o Leroy and Adaline Matthews, to SUSAN ANN PARKER, age 21, single, b. Richmond Co., d/o James and Lucy Parker. Consent 28 DEC 1880 by bride, wit. John Saunders. George Laws. 30 DEC 1880 at *Grove Mount*. [C9, R:317, R1:51]

McCarty, Ovid Downman to Martha Lucinda Carter Hill.[2] OVID D. McCARTY, age not given, single, b. Richmond Co., s/o [Capt.] William D. [Downman] and Frances R. [Ravenscroft Ball] McCarty, to MARTHA L. HILL, age not given [d/o Col. William Hill and Harriet A. Moss],[3] single, b. Richmond Co., d/o Wm. Hill. W.H. Coffin. 27 NOV 1854. [C1, R, R1:1]

McCarty, Robert M.[4] to Sydney B. Sisson. ROBERT M. McCARTY, teacher, age 32, widowed, b. Richmond Co., s/o Madison P. (age 66) and Olivia A. [Ann Mitchell] McCarty (age 53),[5] to SYDNEY B. SISSON, age 19, single, b. Richmond Co., d/o William H. (age 69) and Elizabeth Sisson (age 56). Consent 8 DEC 1874 by parties. H.H. Fones. 8 DEC 1874. [C7, R:230, R1:37]

McGinnis, Alexander Washington to Jenetta Balderson.[6] ALEXANDER W. McGINNIS, age 27, single, b. Richmond Co., s/o Richard and Phelista [Colista E. Reamy] McGinnis,[7] to JENETTA BALDERSON, age 19, single, b. Richmond Co., d/o Hazzard and Betsy Balderson. Consent

---

[1] Name also appears as Lee Roy Mathews.
[2] Ovid D. McCarty (b. 16 JUL 1830, d. 17 MAY 1881) and wife Martha L.C. Hill (b. 22 FEB 1829, d. 28 FEB 1879) are bur. at Loudon Park Cemetery, Baltimore, Md.
[3] William H. Hill and Harriet A. Moss were married by bond 8 MAR 1828 in Richmond Co.
[4] Robert M. McCarty, "a true soldier" of Co. B, 40th Va., 1840-1928, is bur. at Menokin Baptist Church cemetery.
[5] Madison P. McCarty and Olivia Ann Mitchell were married by bond 10 JAN 1838 in Richmond Co.
[6] Alexander W. McGinniss [or McGuiness] (b. 5 AUG 1835, d. 2 OCT 1922) and wife Jeanette Balderson (b. 2 OCT 1848, d. 2 MAR 1917) are bur. in the McGuinness Family Cemetery off of Route 645. He served in Co. G, 15th Va. Cav., C.S.A.
[7] Richard McGinnis and Calista E. Bartlett were married by bond 14 DEC 1835 in Westmoreland Co.

15 DEC 1866 by T.N. Balderson, guardian, and Presley A. Carter, wit. Presley A. Carter. John Pullen. 18 DEC 1866 at Betsy Balderson's. [C4, R:272, R1:18]

McGuinness, Richard W. to Banton A. Reamey. Note from Edgar A. Hamilton, Major 1st N.Y. M.C. Rifles in charge of the Northern Neck of Virginia regarding oath of allegiance and marriage of the parties. John Pullen. 8 JUN 1865 at *Stony Hill.* No license or minister return. [C3]

McGuire, William H. to Sarah F. Howe. WILLIAM H. McGUIRE, carpenter, age 30, widowed, b. and res. Westmoreland Co., s/o William A. and Lucy A. [Thomas] McGuire,[1] to SARAH F. HOWE, age 30, single, b. Richmond Co., d/o Thomas Howe. Consent 2 APR 1872 by bride, wit. G. Sydnor. Elder James A. Weaver. 2 APR 1872 at the res. of John Davis. [C6, R:237, R1:31]

McGuire, William M. to Elizabeth Sydnor. Consent 26 NOV 1856 by father William B. [his X mark] Sydnor, wit. Ro. R. Middleton. No license or minister return. [C1]

McKee, James Williams (Col.) to Emma Garrison Corbin (Col.). JAMES WILLIAMS McKEE, oystering, age 26, single, b. Richmond Co., s/o Thomas and Mary McKee, to EMMA GARRISON CORBIN, age 18, single, b. Richmond Co., d/o Gawen and Catharine Corbin. N.A. Atkins. 5 MAR 1885.[2] [C10, R:316, R1:64]

McKenney, Charles W. to Susan E. Haynes. CHARLES W. McKENNEY, farmer, age 28, single, b. Richmond Co., s/o William R. and Elizabeth K. [Webb] McKenney,[3] to SUSAN E. HAYNES, age 27, single, b. Richmond Co., d/o William C. and L.R. [Louisa R. Harwood] Haynes.[4] Consent 25 JUN 1879 by bride, wit. R.R. Haynes. F.B. Beale. 26 JUN 1879 at Menokin Church. [C8, R:308, R1:47]

McKenney, Vincent H. to Mary L. Barbour. VINCENT H. McKENNEY, farmer, age 26, single, b. and res. Westmoreland Co., s/o Samuel H. and Priscilla R. [Sutton] McKenney,[5] to MARY L. BARBOUR, age 16, single, b. Westmoreland Co., d/o James and Mary A. [Barbour or Barber]. Consent 17 DEC 1874 by father Mary A. Barber [sic], wit. R.H. Mothershead. G.H. Northam. 22 DEC 1874. [C7, R:230, R1:37]

McTyre, Adolphus to Mary Elizabeth Anton.[6] ADOLPHUS McTYRE, house carpenter, age 28, single, b. Middlesex Co., res. Essex Co., s/o William G. and Elizabeth P. McTyre, to MARY E. ANTON, age 26, single, b. Essex Co., d/o Thomas and Polly Anton.[7] John Pullen. 2 NOV 1865 at Thomas Anton's. [C3, R:204, R1:15]

Mealy, Edward W., b. 28 DEC 1857, to Laura V. Newsome.[8] EDWARD MEALY, oysterman, age 23, single, b. Richmond Co., s/o Jesse and [Sarah] Mealy, to LAURA V. NEWSOME, age 23, single, b. Richmond Co., d/o Sarah Newsome. Consent 28 NOV 1881 by bride. G.H. Northam. 29 NOV 1881 at Jerusalem Church. [C9, R:338, R1:54]

---

[1] William McGuire and Lucy Thomas were married by bond 7 FEB 1827 in Westmoreland Co.
[2] Place of marriage is illegible on the minister return, but may be *Totuskey Farm.*
[3] William R. McKenny and Elizabeth K. Webb were married by bond 24 JAN 1838 in Richmond Co. by Rev. Thomas M. Washington.
[4] William C. Haynes and Louisa R. Harwood were married 30 MAR 1848 in Richmond Co. by Rev. George Northam.
[5] Samuel McKenney and Priscilla R. Sutton were married by bond 5 JAN 1847 in Westmoreland Co.
[6] Adolphus McTyre (1827-1916) and wife Mary E. Anton (d. 30 AUG 1883 of paralysis) are bur. at *Marl's Old Field* (*Mount Venus*) in Essex Co. He served in the C.S.A.
[7] A Thomas Anton and Patsy Vawter were married by bond 21 DEC 1835 in Essex Co.
[8] Laura Newsome Mealey (1858-1928) is bur. at Jerusalem Baptist Church cemetery.

Mealy, William, to Mary E. Harriss. WILLIAM MEALY, farmer, age 26, single, b. Lancaster Co., s/o John and Fanny Mealy, to MARY E. HARRISS, age 27, single, b. Richmond Co., d/o Henry M. and Frances A. Harriss. Robert Williamson, M.G. 23 DEC 1866 at John Thrift's. [C4, R:273, R1:19]

Meekins, Thomas G. to Matta E. Reynolds. THOMAS G. MEEKINS, oysterman, age 38, single, b. Maryland, res. Lancaster Co., s/o Thomas [D.] and Eliza [Jackson] Meekins,[1] to MATTA E. REYNOLDS, age 20, single, b. Richmond Co., d/o Thomas and Saluda F. Reynolds. Consent 1 JUN 1878 by bride and Saluda Jenkins, wit. J.B. Roe. G.H. Northam. 2 JUN 1878 at Jerusalem Church. [C8, R:311, R1:45]

Meekins, William Z.[2] to Mary S. Luttrell. WILLIAM Z. MEEKINS, oysterman, age 29, single, b. and res. Lancaster Co., s/o Calvinbos[tra] and Emily Meekins, to MARY S. LUTTRELL,[3] age 18, single, b. Richmond Co., d/o Alfred Littrell and Jane [Thrift] Littrell now Wilson. Consent 25 NOV 1878 by mother Jane Wilson, wit. James W. Luttrell. G.H. Northam. 26 NOV 1878. [C8, R:312, R1:46]

Middleton, Jerry (Col.) to Mrs. Winny Foshee (Col.). JERRY MIDDLETON, carpenter, age 55, widow, b. Richmond Co., s/o James and Winny Haynie, to WINNY FOSHEE, age 40, widow, b. Essex Co., d/o Ceasar and Elmira Smith. Robert Williamson, M.G. 19 DEC 1867 at [S]ion House. [C4, R:287, R1:22]

Middleton, William J. to Catharine Ann Webb. WILLIAM J. MIDDLETON, age 23, single, b. Northumberland Co., s/o William and Mary E. [DeShields] Middleton,[4] to CATHARINE ANN WEBB, age 23, single, b. Richmond Co., d/o William and Margaret [M.C. Shepherd] Webb.[5] Consent 14 AUG 1861 by bride, wit. Charles B. Lyell. H.F. Cundiff. 15 AUG 1861 at *Millwood*. [C3, R:123, R1:10]

Midwig, Casper to Bettie P. Garner. CASPER MIDWIG, engineer, age 23y4m, single, unknown place of birth, res. York Co., Pa., s/o Francis and Catherine Midwig, to BETTIE P. GARNER, age 22, single, b. Lancaster Co., d/o William and Sarah [Davenport Berrick] Garner.[6] Consent 4 DEC 1872 by bride, wit. Joseph Barrack. William H. Kirk. 6 DEC 1872 at the res. of Charles Barrack. [C6, R:238, R1:32]

Miller, Edward M., Jr. to Lulia L. Lowery. EDWARD M. MILLER, laborer, age 26, single, b. and res. York Co., Pa., s/o Edward M. Miller, Sr. and Rebecca Miller, to LULIA L. LOWERY, age 22, single, b. Richmond Co., d/o G.T. and Mary Lowery. Consent 25 NOV 1879 by bride, wits. Alfonso Barrack, G.T. Lowery. G.H. Northam. 27 NOV 1879. [C8, R:309, R1:48]

Miller, Thomas F. to Mary V. Waltz. THOMAS F. MILLER, blacksmith, age 42, widowed, b. Caroline Co., res. Lancaster Co., s/o C.P. and Eliza Miller, to MARY V. WALTZ, age 23, single, b. Delaware, d/o Jacob and Barbara Waltz. Consent 17 SEP 1886 by bride, wit. W.H. Bromley. Rev. R.H. Potts. 19 SEP 1886. [C11, R:316, R1:68]

---

[1] Thomas D. Meekins and Elizabeth Jackson were married by bond 9 NOV 1826 in Richmond Co.
[2] W.Z. Meekins (1850-1913) is bur. at Jerusalem Baptist Church cemetery.
[3] Surname is also spelled Littrell.
[4] William Middleton, Jr. and Mary E. DeShields, d/o Joseph DeShields, were married by bond 29 JUN 1835 in Northumberland Co.
[5] William Webb and Margaret M.C. Shepherd were married by bond 17 NOV 1825 in Richmond Co.
[6] William Garner and Sarah Davenport Berrick were married by bond 17 JUN 1846 in Lancaster Co.

Mills, Henry J. to Lucy R. Saunders. HENRY J. MILLS, clerking in store, age 21y13d, single, b. Manchester, Va., s/o James H. and Sarah Mills, to LUCY R. SAUNDERS, age 17y10m13d, single, b. Richmond Co., d/o A.N. [Augustine] Saunders, M.D. and Mary C. [Catharine Sands] Saunders.[1] Martin Johnson. 14 MAY 1884 at St. John's Church, Warsaw. [C10, NN:16 MAY 1884, R:354, R1:62]

Minor, Bushrod Beverly to Althea Ann Mothershead.[2] BUSHARD B. MINOR [sic], farming, age 23, single, b. Richmond Co., res. Northumberland Co., s/o James [E.] and Margaret [A. Sanders] Minor, to ALTHEA A. MOTHERSHEAD, age 20, single, b. Richmond Co., d/o William H. [Hudson] and Rebecca [Pullen] Mothershead. Consent 19 AUG 1884 by bride, wit. George M. Conley. R.N. Reamy. 21 AUG 1884. [C10, R:355, R1:62]

Minor, Charles H. to Sarah F. Sisson. CHARLES H. MINOR, farmer, age 24y4m, single, b. King William Co., s/o Reuben and Malissa J. Minor, to SARAH F. SISSON, age 20, single, b. Richmond Co., d/o Robert and Amanda [Ann Sanders] Sisson.[3] Consent 30 JAN 1876 by father Robert Sisson, also signed by bride, no wit. H.H. Fones. 2 FEB 1876. [C7, R:304, R1:40]

Minor, Elliott S. to Sybella "Sibbie" Sisson.[4] ELLIOTT S. MINOR, age 26, single, b. and res. Westmoreland Co., s/o Beverly and Lucy [Lucinda B. McKenney] Minor,[5] to SIBBIE SISSON, age 20, single, b. Richmond Co., d/o Wm. H. and Betsy Sisson. Consent 26 JAN 1865/6 by father Wm. H. Sisson, wit. J.M. Scates. G.H. Northam. 27 DEC 1865 at *Piney Grove*. [C3, R:205, R1:15]

Minor, James (Col.) to Alice Corbin (Col.). JAMES MINOR, oystering, age 24, single, b. Richmond Co., s/o William and Jane Minor, to ALICE CORBIN, age 22, single, b. Richmond Co., d/o Travers and Virginia Corbin. Charles Sparks. 5 MAY 1887 at Dr. Motley's. [C11, R:291, R1:71]

Minor, James E. to Margaret A. Sanders. JAMES E. MINOR, carpenter, age 21, single, b. Westmoreland Co., s/o Beverley and Lucy [Lucinda B. McKenney] Minor, to MARGARET A. SANDERS, age 19, single, b. Richmond Co., d/o James L. and Peggy Sanders. Consent 21 MAY 1860 by Mrs. Peggy Sanders, also signed by bride, wit. James M. Scates. John Pullen. 31 MAY 1860. [C2, R:153, R1:8]

Mitchell, Charles W. to Elizabeth Ann Lemoine. CHARLES W. MITCHELL, farmer, age 25, single, b. Richmond Co., s/o John C. and Sarah E. [Chinn] Mitchell,[6] to ELIZABETH ANN LEMOINE, age 24, single, b. Richmond Co., d/o Feriol [Jr.] and Maria Ann [Saunders] Lemoine.[7] Consent 4 NOV 1876 by bride, wit. M.L. Pitts. Beverley D. Tucker. 8 DEC 1876 at Farnham Church. [C7, R:305, R1:41]

---

[1] Augustine N. Saunders, Dr., and Mary Catharine Sands, d/o O.H. and Maria Sands, were married by bond 5 DEC 1845 in Richmond Co.

[2] Bushrod B. Minor (b. 14 APR 1861, d. 21 NOV 1938) and wife Althea A. Mothershead (b. 16 APR 1853, d. 18 MAY 1940) are bur. in Rappahannock Baptist Church cemetery.

[3] Robert Sisson and Amanda Ann Sanders were married by bond 5 AUG 1847 in Richmond Co.

[4] Elliott S. Minor (d. 30 AUG 1911 of heart trouble, age 75) and wife Sibbie Sisson (d. 12 SEP 1922 age 79) are bur. in the Minor Family Cemetery off Route 621. He served in Co. G, 15th Va. Cav., C.S.A.

[5] Beverly Minor and Lucinda B. McKenney were married by bond 27 APR 1835 in Westmoreland Co.

[6] John C. Mitchell and Sally E. Chinn were married 4 MAY 1841 in Richmond Co. by Rev. William N. Ward.

[7] Feriol Lemoine, Jr. and Ann Maria Saunders were married by bond 5 FEB 1833 in Richmond Co.

Mitchell, Frederick, to Mrs. Lucy Carter. FREDERICK MITCHELL, saw mill hand, age 25, widowed, b. Westmoreland Co., s/o Peter and Soph[i]a Mitchell, to LUCY CARTER, age 23, widow, b. Richmond Co., d/o John and Julia Parker. Jerry Graham, Sr. 25 MAR 1869. [C5, R, R1:25]

Mitchell, Robert (Col.) to Emma Johnson (Col.). ROBERT MITCHELL, laborer, age 37, single, b. Lancaster Co., s/o Robert Mitchell and Eliza Rich, to EMMA JOHNSON, age 21, single, b. Richmond Co., d/o Elic Lane and Delia Johnson. Consent 23 JUN 1883 by bride Emma [her X mark] Johnson, wit. [J.]W. Hanks. Rev. W. Carter. 24 JUN 1883 at the bride's home. [C10, R:357, R1:59]

Mitchell, Robert Carter to Genevieve S. Shackleford. ROBERT CARTER MITCHELL, farming, age 41, single, b. Richmond Co., s/o John C. and Sally [E. Chinn] Mitchell,[1] to GENEVIEVE S. SHACKLEFORD, age 39, single, b. Richmond Co., d/o Lyne and Juliet A. [Ann Saunders] Shackleford.[2] R.A. Castleman. 23 OCT 1890 at St. John's Church, Warsaw, Va. [C12, R:324, R1:77]

Mitchell, William Bladen[3] to Mary Julia Lemoine. WILLIAM BLADEN MITCHELL, farmer, age 50, widowed, b. Richmond Co., s/o Robert Bladen Mitchell and Julia Maria Mitchell, to MARY JULIA LEMOINE, age 32, single, b. Richmond Co., d/o [Feriol, Jr.] and Ann [Maria Saunders] Lemoine. Consent 10 OCT 1875 by bride, wit. Maria L. Pitts. Beverley D. Tucker. 13 OCT 1875 at res. of F. Lemoine in Farnham Township. [C7, R:262, R1:38]

Mitchell, William Bladen to Willie T. Crabb. WILLIAM B. MITCHELL, farmer, age 38, widowed, b. Richmond Co., s/o Robert B. [Bladen] and Julia Ann Mitchell, to WILLIE T. CRABB,[4] age 21, single, b. Richmond Co., d/o William M.M. and Ann T.C. [Peck] Crabb.[5] Peter Ainslie. 30 SEP 1863 at [*Laurel*] *Brook*. [C3, R:160, R1:13]

Monroe, Howard (Col.) to Louisa Young (Col.). HOWARD MONROE, oysterman, age 24, single, b. Richmond Co., s/o James and Fanny Monroe, to LOUISA YOUNG, age 22, single, b. Richmond Co., d/o Alice Fauntleroy. Allen Brown, minister. 14 JAN 1873 at the bride's house. [C6, R:235, R1:33]

Monroe, Thornton (Col.) to Lucy Anna Bowler (Col.). THORNTON MONROE, oystering, age 23y2m, single, b. Richmond Co., s/o James and Fanny Monroe, to LUCY ANNA BOWLER, age 21, single, b. Richmond Co., d/o Mary Campbell [name of father not given]. Consent 19 DEC 1881 by mother Mary [her X mark] Cambell [sic], and by bride Lucy Anna [her X mark] Bowler. Allen Brown, minister. 22 DEC 1881 at the bride's home. [C9, R:337, R1:54]

Montgomery, Adorinam Judson[6] to Luemma F. Garland. A. JUDSON MONTGOMERY, mechanic, age 23, single, b. Richmond Co., res. Baltimore, Md., s/o Robert L. and Elizabeth T. [Reynolds]

---

[1] John C. Mitchell and Sally E. Chinn were married 4 MAY 1841 in Richmond Co. by Rev. William N. Ward.

[2] Lyne Shackleford (b. 16 FEB 1809, d. 15 MAR 1859) and his wife Juliet A. Saunders (b. 29 JAN 1824, d. 12 OCT 1895) are bur. in the Shackleford Family Cemetery near Warsaw, Va. Also see Richmond Co. Deeds, Bk. 262, p. 237. Lyne Shackleford and Juliet Ann Saunders were married by bond 5 JAN 1847 in Richmond Co.

[3] William Bladen Mitchell (b. 2 MAY 1824 at *Grove Mount*, d. 25 NOV 1895 at *Belle Mount*), served in Co. B and D, 40th Reg., Va. Inf., C.S.A. He also served in the 55th Reg. for a while.

[4] Surname appears as Crabb and Crabbe.

[5] William M.M. Crabb and Ann T. Peck were married 22 FEB 1838 in Richmond Co. by Rev. Lovell Marders.

[6] Adorinam Judson Montgomery served in Co. B, 40th Reg., Va. Inf., C.S.A., imprisoned at Point Lookout, d. 15 MAR 1896 of consumption in Warsaw, Va.

Montgomery,[1] to LUEMMMA F. GARLAND, age 21, single, b. Richmond Co., d/o Moore F. [Fauntleroy] and Elizabeth P. [Cooke] Garland.[2] Andrew Fisher. 8 AUG 1866 at Warsaw, Va. [C4, R:272, R1:18]

Montgomery, Henry I.[3] to Sarah J. Yeatman. HENRY I. MONTGOMERY, soldier, age 21, single, b. Richmond Co., s/o Robert L. and Elizabeth T. [Reynolds] Montgomery,[4] to SARAH J. YEATMAN, age 17, single, b. Westmoreland Co., d/o Thomas [J.] and Susan [P. Hunter] Yeatman. James F. Brannin. 8 OCT 1861 at the parsonage, Warsaw. [C3, R:124, R1:11]

Montgomery, Robert Hill[5] to Branche Brockenbrough. ROBERT H. MONTGOMERY, farmer, age 26, single, b. and res. King George Co., s/o Robert H. [Hill] and Sarah [B. Arnold] Montgomery,[6] to BRANCHE BROCKENBROUGH, age 25, single, b. Richmond Co., d/o William A. [Austin] and Mary C. [Carter Gray] Brockenbrough.[7] Beverley D. Tucker. 20 DEC 1877 at *Waveland*, Farnham. [C8, R:308, R1:43]

Moore, Peter (Col.) to Ella Eatman (Col.). PETER MOORE, farmer, age 20y8m, single, b. Richmond Co., s/o Agnes Moore, father unknown, to ELLA EATMAN, age 20, single, b. Richmond Co., d/o Richard and Sally Eatman. Consent 2 OCT 1873 by father Richard [his X mark] Eatman, wit. Wm. H. Omohundro. Thomas G. Thomas. 4 OCT 1873. [C6, R:235, R1:34]

Moore, Thomas Jefferson to Ellen Mothershead. THOMAS JEFFERSON MOORE, farming, age 24y2d, single, b. Caroline Co., s/o Charles W. Moore and Mary Ann White, to ELLEN [or Ella] MOTHERSHEAD, age 23y1d, single, b. Richmond Co., d/o Washington and Amanda [Edmonds] Mothershead, *q.v.* Consent 2 MAY 1883 by father Washington Mothershead. R.N. Reamy. 11 APR 1883. [C10, R:356, R1:58]

Moore, William to Arbella Lewis. WILLIAM MOORE, laborer, age 30, single, b. Germany, res. Baltimore, Md., s/o Christopher Moore, to ARBELLA LEWIS, age 25, single, b. Richmond Co., d/o Valentine and Mildred [Stott] Lewis.[8] Consent 24 SEP 1872 by father Valtine [sic] Lewis. G.H. Northam. 25 SEP 1872. [C6, R:238, R1:32]

Morgan, James Madison[9] to Mary A. Montgomery. JAMES M. MORGAN, coach maker, age 25, single, b. Richmond Co., s/o Josiah Morgan and Mel [Malvina] Weathers,[10] to MARY A. MONTGOMERY, age 21, single, b. Richmond Co., d/o L. and R.S. Montgomery. Consent 19 JAN 1857 by bride, wit. H.P.A. Montgomery. G.H. Northam, minister of the Baptist denomination. 22 JAN 1857 at *Bunkers Hill*. [C1, R:159, R1:4]

---

[1] Robert L. Montgomery and Elizabeth T. Reynolds were married by bond 28 NOV 1835 in Richmond Co.

[2] Moore Fauntleroy Garland (1821-1856) and wife Elizabeth P. Cook (b. 27 JUL 1823, d. 26 APR 1888) are buried at *Walnut Lawn*, just south of Warsaw, Va. Moore F. Garland and Elizabeth P. Cooke were married by bond 15 NOV 1841 in Richmond Co.

[3] Henry I. Montgomery served in Co. B, 40th Reg., Va. Inf., C.S.A.

[4] Robert L. Montgomery (b. 2 JUN 1802, d. 6 NOV 184[5]) and his wife Elizabeth T. (b. 19 JUN 1805, d. 24 MAY 1858) are bur. at *Cloverdale Farm* off of Route 3.

[5] Robert Hill Montgomery (1850 [0 over 4]-1889 [9 over 8]) is bur. at Emmanuel Episcopal Church cemetery at Emmerton, Va.

[6] Robert H. Montgomery and Sarah B. Arnold were married 8 DEC 1840 in King George Co. by Rev. Philip Montague. Robert Hill Montgomery (b. 18 AUG 1815, d. 21 APR 1850) and Sarah B. Arnold (b. 4 FEB 1821, d. 9 FEB 1851), d/o John and Frances B. Arnold, are bur. in the Arnold Family Cemetery at *Willow Hill*, King George Co.

[7] William Austin Brockenbrough (b. 1809, d. 13 NOV 1858 in Tappahannock, Essex Co.), s/o Austin Brockenbrough, and his wife Mary C. Gray (c.1811-c.1860) were married 12 AUG 1832 in Essex Co.

[8] Valentine Lewis and Milly Stott were married by bond 5 FEB 1824 in Northumberland Co.

[9] James M. Morgan (b. 10 DEC 1831 in Gloucester Co., d. 17 NOV 1912 of cancer in Warsaw, Va.) is bur. at Warsaw United Methodist Church cemetery. He served in Co. B, 40th Reg., Va. Inf., C.S.A.

[10] Josiah Morgan, of Gloucester Co., and Malvina Weathers, were married by bond 28 JUL 1828 in Richmond Co.

Morris, Hamilton H. to Fanny E. Gouldman. HAMILTON H. MORRISS [sic], farmer, age 25, single, b. Richmond Co., res. Lancaster Co., s/o James [M.] and Amelia [D. Newman] Morriss, to FANNY E. GOULDMAN, age 22, single, b. Essex Co., d/o Hiram and Sarah A. [Ann Gray] Gouldman.[1] H.H. Fones. 19 MAY 1871 at res. of Jno. Dishman. [C5, R:244, R1:29]

Morris, Hamilton H. to Lou D. Scott. H.H. MORRIS, farming, age 4[2]y8m, widowed, b. Richmond Co., s/o James [M.] and Amelia D. [Newman] Morris,[2] to LOU D. SCOTT, age 22, single, b. Richmond Co., d/o James Scott. Consent 5 OCT 1887 by parties. Geo. M. Conley. 9 OCT 1887 near Newland, Va. [C11, R:292, R1:70]

Morriss, John to George Etta Saunders. JOHN MORRISS, fisherman, age 36, single, b. Richmond Co., s/o John and Betsey Morriss, to GEORGE ETTA SAUNDERS, age 20y, single, b. Richmond Co., d/o James C. and Nancy Saunders. Consent 1 NOV 1875 by bride Georgie E. [her X mark] Saunders, and James C. Saunders, wit. A.L. Saunders. Robert N. Reamy. 11 NOV 1875 at J.C. Saunders'. [C7[3], R:262, R1:39]

Morris, Leason Fairfax to Mary Virginia Reamy.[4] LEASON F. MORRIS, farmer, age 26, single, b. Richmond Co., s/o James M. and Amelia[5] D. [Newman] Morriss [sic], to MARY V. REAMY, age 20, single, b. Richmond Co., d/o Saml. H. and Susan C. [Caroline E. Fones] Reamy. Robert N. Reamy. 20 AUG 1868 at S.T. Reamy's. [C5, R:254, R1:24]

Morris, Oscar P., Jr., to Annie Maria Saunders. OSCAR P. MORRIS, JR., farmer, age 24, single, b. Richmond Co., s/o Wm. H. and Maria Morris[s], to ANNIE MARIA[6] SAUNDERS, age 20, single, b. Richmond Co., d/o Aug. N. [Augustine] and Mary C. [Catharine Sands] Saunders.[7] Consent 4 FEB 1870 by parties, wit. N. Saunders. G.H. Northam. 6 FEB 1870. [C5, R:233, R1:27]

Morris, Robert to Martha Clarke. ROBERT MORRIS, carpenter, age 29, single, b. Spotsylvania Co., s/o James and Sarah Morris, to MARTHA CLARKE, age 19, single, b. Richmond Co., d/o Joseph and Sarah [Haydon] Clarke.[8] Consent 14 MAY 1869 by mother Sophia [her X mark] Clarke, wit. Jos. Clarke. J.H. Davis. 16 MAY 1869 at the home of Jos. Clarke. [C5, R, R1:26]

Morriss, William H., Jr. to Doretha L. Scates. WILLIAM H. MORRISS, JR., merchant, age 25, single, b. Richmond Co., s/o William H. [Sr.] and Mary Morriss, to DORETHA L. SCATES, age 19, single, b. Richmond Co., names of parents "omitted for good cause." Consent 15 JUN 1868 by parties, wit. Elizabeth [her X mark] Scates, wit. L.J. Morriss. Robert N. Reamy. 18 JUN 1868 at Mrs. B. Scates'. [C4, C5, R:254, R1:24]

Morriss, William K. to Mrs. Lucy A. Hart, widow of James Reamy. WILLIAM K. MORRISS, farmer, age 45, widower, b. Richmond Co., s/o William K. and Frances Morriss, to LUCY A. REAMY,

---

[1] Hiram Gouldman and Sarah Ann Gray were married 8 MAY 1840 in Essex Co.
[2] James M. Morris and Parmela Newman were married by bond 11 OCT 1834 in Richmond Co.
[3] Consent and license are not filmed together.
[4] Leason F. Morris (1842-1907) and wife Mary V. Reamy (b. 20 JUL 1848, d. 4 OCT 1937) are bur. in Rappahannock Baptist Church cemetery. He served in Co. D, 40th Va. Inf., C.S.A.
[5] Her name may be Parmela as found on the 1834 marriage bond to James M. Morris in Richmond Co.
[6] Her middle name appears as Marie and Maria, but the latter is taken from her signature on the consent.
[7] Augustine N. Saunders and Mary Catharine Sands were married by bond 5 DEC 1845 in Richmond Co.
[8] Joseph Clarke and Sarah Haydon were married by bond 20 OCT 1838 in Northumberland Co.

age 26, widow, b. Caroline Co., d/o Philine [Fielding] and Ann [E. Pittman] Hart.[1] John Pullen. 2 OCT 1866 at William K. Morriss'. [C4, R:272, R1:18]

Moss, Arthur to Susan Sanders. ARTHUR MOSS, farmer, age 21y10m, single, b. Richmond Co., s/o Thomas and Cordelia Moss, to SUSAN SANDERS, age 24, single, b. Richmond Co., d/o George and Frances Sanders. Consent 19 JUN 1871 by bride, wit. Eliza Ambers. Robert N. Reamy. 22 JUN 1871 at res. of the minister. [C5, R:245, R1:30]

Moss, George to Emily J. Balderson. GEORGE MOSS, farming, age about 23, single, b. upper district of Richmond Co., s/o Thomas Moss and wife Mary, to EMILY J. BALDERSON, age about 23, single, b. upper district of Richmond Co., d/o William R. Balderson and wife Amelia [Ambrose].[2] Consent 29 JAN 1856 by William R. Balderson, wits. William Carter, George W. Quisenberry. John Pullen, M.G. 30 JAN 1856 at *Wave Hill* res. of John Pullen. [C1, R1:3]

Moss, Stephen[3] to Elizabeth Ann Yardly. STEPHEN MOSS, farmer, age 25, single, b. Richmond Co., s/o Thomas and Mary Moss, to ELIZABETH A. YARDLY, age 24, single, b. Westmoreland Co., d/o James and Matilda Yardly. Consent 27 DEC 1865 by bride Elizabeth Ann [her X mark] Yardly, wit. Geo. W. Balderson who proved certificate. John Pullen. 28 DEC 1865 at John Pullen's. [C3, R:205, R1:15]

Mothershead, George Henry to Luticia Ellen Reamy.[4] GEORGE H. MOTHERSHEAD, farmer, age 24, single, b. Richmond Co., s/o [James] Henry and Eliza [Peed] Mothershead,[5] to LUTICIA E. REAMY, age 25, single, b. Richmond Co., d/o Robert N. [Neale] and [Virginia] Jane [Owens] Reamy. John Pullen. 25 AUG 1864 at Robert N. Reamy's. [C3, R:139, R1:14]

Mothershead, George M. to Eliza Jane Straughan. GEORGE M. MOTHERSHEAD, post rider, age 25, widowed, b. Richmond Co., s/o George and Pollie Mothershead, to ELIZA JANE STRAUGHAN, age 30, single, b. Westmoreland Co., d/o Richard and Pollie Straughan. Consent 6 FEB 1856 by bride, wit. John Sutton. Elijah L. Williams, minister. 7 FEB 1856. [C1, R, R1:3]

Mothershead, George M. to Mrs. Mary C. Middleton, widow of James W. Bailey. GEORGE M. MOTHERSHEAD, farmer, age 35, widower, b. Richmond Co., res. Westmoreland Co., s/o George and Mary Mothershead, to MARY C. BAILEY, age 33, widow, b. Westmoreland Co., d/o Jeremiah and Nancy [S. Harrison] Middleton.[6] Robert Williamson, M.G. 30 AUG 1865 at James W. Brown's. [C3, R:204, R1:15]

Mothershead, John O. to Alice C. Cralle. Consent 7 AUG 1867 by T.N. Balderson, guardian. No license or minister return. [C5]

---

[1] Fielding Hart and Ann E. Pittman were married by bond 8 AUG 1836 in Caroline Co.
[2] William Balderson, Jr. and Amelia Ambrose were married by bond 5 FEB 1833 in Richmond Co.
[3] Stephen Moss served in Co. D, 40th Reg., Va. Inf., C.S.A., deserted and sentenced to 12 months hard labor.
[4] George H. Mothershead (b. 29 NOV 1839, d. 5 DEC 1887) and his wife Luticia E. Reamy (b. 11 APR 1838, d. 28 MAY 1916) are bur. in the Reamy Family cemetery at Foneswood, Va. He served in Co. G, 15th Va. Cav., C.S.A.
[5] James H. Mothershead and Eliza Peed were married by bond 21 DEC 1829 in Westmoreland Co.
[6] Jeremiah Middleton, of Westmoreland Co., and Nancy S. Harrison, were married by bond 28 MAY 1808 in Richmond Co.

Mothershead, M. Fairfax. to Lucinda A. Scates. M. FAIRFAX MOTHERSHEAD, farmer, age 23, single, b. Richmond Co., s/o William H. and Rebecca [Pullen] Mothershead,[1] to LUCINDA A. SCATES, age 18, single, b. Richmond Co., d/o James A. and Virginia [A. Hinson] Scates, *q.v.* Consent 7 MAY 1883 by father James A. Scates, wit. J.M. Scates. H.H. Fones. 9 MAY 1883. [C10, R:356, R1:59]

Mothershead, Walker to Martha Bowen. WALKER MOTHERSHEAD, farmer, age 24, single, b. Richmond Co., s/o Henry and Rose Mothershead, to MARTHA BOWEN, age 24, single, b. Richmond Co., d/o John and Maria Bowen. Consent 14 NOV 1868 by bride Marthy [her X mark] Bowing, wit. Thomas Talbert. G.H. Northam. 19 NOV 1868. [C4, C5, R:254, R1:24]

Mothershead, Washington to Amanda Edmonds. WASHINGTON MOTHERSHEAD, farming, age about 24, single, b. Richmond Co., s/o William Mothershead and Sarah, to AMANDA EDMONDS, age about 24, single, b. Westmoreland Co., d/o Rictchard [sic] Edmonds and Peanelopy [Marks].[2] Consent 2 SEP 1856 by father Richard [his X mark] Edmons [sic], wits. George Edmonds, Joseph Bowen. John Pullen, M.G. 3 SEP 1856 at Richard Edmonds'. [C1, R:148, R1:4]

Mothershead, William H. to Priscilla A. Settle. WILLIAM H. MOTHERSHEAD, merchant, age 23, single, b. Richmond Co., res. Westmoreland Co., s/o Richard H. and Frances S. [McKenney] Mothershead,[3] to PRISCILLA A. SETTLE, age 21, single, b. Richmond Co., d/o Frederick and Diana [T. Claughton] Settle. Consent 30 JUL 1872 by bride, no wit. G.H. Northam. 30 JUL 1872 at *Woodbine*. [C6, R:238, R1:32]

Motley, James Lewis, Jr. to Emma Jane "Nana" Leonard.[4] JAMES L. MOTLEY, JR., farmer, age 36, single, b. Richmond Co., s/o [Dr.] James L. Motley, Sr. and Louisa [Tod] Motley,[5] to EMMA J. LEONARD, age 20, single, b. Reedsburg, Wis., d/o A.F. [Alfred Frederick] and Jerusha [Dewey] Leonard.[6] Consent 30 MAY 1881 from Farnham by A.F. Leonard, wit. R.L. Reynolds. F.W. Claybrook. 1 JUN 1881 at Farnham Baptist Church. [C9, NN:3 JUN 1881, R:336, R1:53]

Mozingo, Alexander to Mary Scates. ALEXANDER MOZINGO, farmer, age 20y6m, single, b. Richmond Co., s/o Pierce and Sally [Sarah P. Barrett] Mozingo, *q.v.*, to MARY SCATES, age 25, single, b. Richmond Co., d/o Joseph and Roberta [W. Butler] Scates.[7] Consent 10 NOV 1875 by bride Mary [her X mark] Scates, wits. Richard H. Mozingo, Fauntleroy Mozingo. D.M. Wharton. 11 NOV 1875 at the res. of the minister in Westmoreland Co. [C7, R:262, R1:38]

---

[1] William H. Mothershead and Rebecca Pullen, d/o John and Henrietta Pullen, were married 10 MAR 1852 by Rev. John Pullen.

[2] Richard Edmonds and Penelope Marks were married by bond 3 JAN 1820 in Westmoreland Co.

[3] Richard H. Mothershead and Frances S. McKenney were married 1 JAN 1846 in Richmond Co. by Rev. John Pullen.

[4] James L. Motley, Jr. (b. 5 MAR 1845 at *Woodberry*, d. 6 JAN 1914) and wife Emma J. Leonard (b. 1860, d. 12 SEP 1940) are bur. in Farnham Baptist Church cemetery. He served in Co. K, 9th Va. Cav., C.S.A.

[5] Dr. James L. Motley, Sr. (b. 14 DEC 1816 in King & Queen Co., d. 11 SEP 1893 at his home *Woodberry*) and wife Louisa (b. 22 JAN 1818, d. 21 AUG 1895) are bur. in Farnham Baptist Church cemetery. James L. Motley and Louisa Tod, d/o George Thompson Tod (c.1771-1859) and Mary Hart Smith, d/o William (1746-1802) and Mary Smith (1750-1822) of Fredericksburg, Va., were married 24 JUN 1841 in Caroline Co. James was s/o John Motley and his first wife Frances Lewis Watts.

[6] Alfred Frederick Leonard (1821-1894) lived at *Locust Grove* at Farnham, Va., and is bur. with his wife in Farnham Baptist Church cemetery. Jerusha (b. 7 JUL 1837, d. 29 JAN 1915) was born at Franklin, Portage Co., Ohio, and moved to Wisconsin where she was a school teacher in Reedsville when she met and married Mr. Leonard in 1856.

[7] Joseph Scates and Roberta W. Butler were married by bond 3 MAR 1845 in Richmond Co.

Mozingo, Charles B. to Lillie A. Hale.[1] CHARLES B. MOZINGO, farming, age 25, single, b. Richmond Co., s/o John [Jonathan] B. and Matilda [Efford] Mozingo,[2] to LILLIE A. HALE, age 21y8m, single, b. Richmond Co., d/o Moses and Georgeanna [Bryant] Hale.[3] Consent by parties. G.H. Northam. 16 DEC 1883 at S. Clark's. [C10, R:357, R1:60]

Mozingo, Edward to Sarah Mozingo. EDWARD MOZINGO, mill hand, age 21y4m, single, b. Richmond Co., s/o John and Catharine [A. Jones] Mozingo, *q.v.*, to SARAH MOZINGO, age 20y4m, single, b. Richmond Co., d/o Pierce and Sally [Sarah P. Barrett] Mozingo, *q.v.* Consent by bride Sarah [her X mark] Mozingo, and father Pierce [his X mark] Mozingo, wit. Wm. R. [his X mark] Mozingo. G.M. Conley. 26 DEC 1889 at *Millview*. [C12, R:328, R1:75]

Mozingo, Fauntleroy to Isabella Weaver. FAUNTLEROY MOZINGO, farmer, age 20y9m, single, b. Richmond Co., s/o Pierce and Sally [Sarah P. Barrett] Mozingo (dec'd.), to ISABELLA WEAVER, age 33y10m11d, single, b. Richmond Co., d/o Henry and Nancy Weaver. Consent 5 JAN 1878 by bride and Nancy Weaver, wit. Pierce Mozingo. D.M. Wharton. 8 JAN 1878 at the res. of the minister in Westmoreland Co. [C8, R:310, R1:44]

Mozingo, Fauntleroy W.[4] to Mildred A. Reynolds. Consent 19 JUN 1854 by bride Mildred A. Reynolds, wit. Thomas H. Reynolds. No license or minister return. [C1]

Mozingo, Fauntleroy W. to Sarah Ella Latham.[5] FAUNTLEROY W. MOZINGO, mechanic, age 40, widower, b. Richmond Co., s/o Christopher [B.] and Frances [Barnes] Mozingo,[6] to SARAH E. LATHAM, age 23, single, b. and res. Essex Co., d/o Jonathan and Elizabeth [Fowler] Latham.[7] Robert Williamson, M.G. 4 OCT 1870 at Calvary Church. [C5, R:233, R1:28]

Mozingo, John to Mrs. Catharine A. Jones. JOHN MOZINGO, farmer, age 46, widowed, b. Richmond Co., s/o Thomas [C.] and Rebecca [Jones] Mozingo,[8] to CATHARINE A. JONES, age 35, widow, b. Richmond Co., d/o Thomas and Sally Brown. Consent 17 AUG 1863 by bride. G.H. Northam. 24 SEP 1863. [C3, R:160, R1:13]

Mozingo, John B. to Mrs. Mary J. Fidler Brizendine. JOHN B. MOZINGO, farming, age 27, single, b. Richmond Co., s/o J.B. [Jonathan] and Matilda [Efford] Mozingo, to MARY J. BRIZENDINE, age 32, widow, b. Richmond Co., d/o Joseph and Susan Fidler. Consent undated by bride. G.H. Northam. 25 FEB 1880. [C9, R:314, R1:50]

Mozingo, John B. to Willie A. Woollard. JOHN B. MOZINGO, farming, age 35, widowed, b. Richmond Co., s/o J.B. [Jonathan] and Matilda [Efford] Mozingo, to WILLIE A. WOOLLARD, age 21, single, b. Richmond Co., d/o James G. and Sophia Woollard. Consent 23 JUN 1888 from Emmerton, Va. by bride, wit. John W. Rowe. G.H. Northam. 24 JUN 1888 at res. of John Rowe. [C11, R:316, R1:73]

---

[1] Charles B. Mozingo (1860-1931) and his wife Lillie A. Hale (1865-1944) are bur. in Jerusalem Baptist Church cemetery.

[2] Jonathan B. Mozingo and Matildy Efford were married by bond 8 MAY 1847 in Richmond Co.

[3] Moses Hale and Georgiana Bryant were married 17 NOV 1864 in Northumberland Co.

[4] A Fauntleroy Washington Mozingo served in Co. B, 40th Reg., Va. Inf., C.S.A., then Co. B, 15th Va., d. 28 MAR 1891 in Lancaster Co., bur. Farnham Baptist Church cemetery.

[5] Sarah Ella Latham (b. 16 DEC 1847, d. 8 JAN 1939), w/o Fauntleroy W. Mozingo, is bur. in Farnham Baptist Church cemetery.

[6] Christopher B. Mozingo and Fanny Barnes were married by bond 2 JAN 1821 in Richmond Co.

[7] Jonathan Lathom and Elizabeth B. Fowler were married 18 AUG 1832 in Essex Co.

[8] Thomas C. Mozingo and Rebecca Jones were married by bond 1 FEB 1813 in Richmond Co.

Mozingo, Meredith M.[1] to Sarah J. Jackson. MEREDITH M. MOZINGO, farmer, age 22, single, b. Richmond Co., s/o Christopher [B.] and Frances [Barnes] Mozingo,[2] to SARAH J. JACKSON, age 17,[3] single, b. Richmond Co., d/o George and Mariah [Hale] Jackson.[4] Consent 5 AUG 1859 by bride Sarah J. [her X mark] Jackson, wits. Geo. A. Carter, H.P. Harper. James A. Weaver. 8 AUG 1859 at Daniel Jackson's. [C2, R:165, R1:7]

Mozingo, Pierce,[5] to Sarah P. Barrett. PIERCE MOZINGO, farmer, age 27, single, b. Westmoreland Co., s/o Thomas [C.] Mozingo and Rebecca [Jones], to SARAH P. BARRETT, age 18, single, b. Richmond Co., d/o John Barrett and Mary. Consent by father John [his X mark] Barrett, wit. Robert Bispham. John Pullen, M.G. 11 JAN 1855 at John Barrett's. [C1, R:153, R1:2]

Mozingo, Richard[6] to Mrs. Martha J. Sutton Brown. RICHARD MOZINGO, farmer, age 49, single, b. Westmoreland Co., s/o Pierce and Nancy [Sutton] Mozingo, to MARTHA J. BROWN, age 35, widow, b. Westmoreland Co., d/o William and Catherine [Nash] Sutton.[7] Consent 11 JAN 1871 by bride Martha J. [her X mark] Brown, wit. Thos. M. Omohundro. D.M. Wharton, Rector, Montross Parish. 12 JAN 1871 at res. of minister. [C5, R:244, R1:29]

Mozingo, Richard C. to Kaziah "Kissie" Bowen. RICHARD C. MOZINGO, farmer, age 24, single, b. Westmoreland Co., s/o William C. and Elizabeth [Barrett] Mozingo,[8] to KAZIAH BOWEN, age 23, single, b. Richmond Co., d/o John Bowen, Sr. and Maria Bowen. Consent 20 DEC 1878 by John Bowen. F.B. Beale. 25 DEC 1878. [C8, R:312, R1:46]

Mozingo, Thomas to Emma J. Davis. THOMAS MOZINGO, farmer, age 24, single, b. Richmond Co., s/o John and Rutha Mozingo, to EMMA J. DAVIS, age 25, single, b. Richmond Co., d/o Henry and Elizabeth Davis. Consent 15 JUN 1875 by bride Emer [sic] J. [her X mark] Davis, wit. Pierce [his X mark] Mozingo. D.M. Wharton. 15 JUN 1875 at the res. of the minister. [C7, R:262, R1:38]

Mozingo, William R. to Maria J. Barrett. WILLIAM R. MOZINGO, farming, age 26y11m, single, b. Richmond Co., s/o Pierce Mozingo and Sally [Sarah P.] Barrett, to MARIA J. BARRETT, age 33, single, b. Richmond Co., d/o James and Amelia Barrett. Consent 28 JUL 1887 by bride. Geo. M. Conley. 28 JUL 1887 . [C11, R:292, R1:70]

Muir, William M. "Squire", Jr. to Morgie L. McClannahan.[9] WILLIAM M. MUIR, JR., farming, age 32, widowed, b. Scotland, s/o William M. Muir, Sr. and Grace Muir, to MORGIE L. McCLANNAHAN, age 29, single, b. Richmond Co., d/o Meredith M. and Jane McClannahan. Rev. W.W. Walker, minister M.E. Church South. 12 SEP 1888 at the home of Mrs. Jane McClannahan. [C11, R:316, R1:73]

---

[1] Meridith Mozingo served in Co. K, 9th Va. Cav., and d. at Fort Delaware, bur. in New Jersey.
[2] Christopher B. Mozingo and Fanny Barnes were married by bond 2 JAN 1821 in Richmond Co.
[3] The application gives the age of the bride as 17 years.
[4] George Jackson and Maria Hale were married by bond 9 OCT 1834 in Northumberland Co.
[5] Pierce Mozingo served in Co. G, 15th Va. Cav., C.S.A.
[6] Richard Mozingo served in Co. G, 15th Va. Cav., C.S.A.
[7] William Susson and Kitty Nash were married by bond 6 DEC 1835 in Westmoreland Co.
[8] William Mozingo and Elizabeth Barrett were married 24 APR 1851 in Richmond Co. by Rev. George Northam.
[9] William M. Muire (b. 30 OCT 1856, d. 26 JUN 1943) and wife Morgie L. McClannahan (b. 17 NOV 1859, d. 2 APR 1919) are bur. in St. John's Episcopal Church cemetery.

Mullen, Francis William to Mary Jane Miskill.[1] FRANCIS W. MULLIN, waterman, age 25, single, b. Staten Island, N.Y., s/o Barnard and Charlotte Mullin, to MARY J. MISKILL, age 16, single, b. Richmond Co., d/o William D. and Lucy [English] Miskill.[2] Consent 20 DEC 1860 by father Wm. D. Miskill, wit. William English. E.L. Williams. 25 DEC 1860. [C2, R:154, R1:9]

Murren, James to Lavinia Elmore. JAMES MURREN, age 27, single, b. Richmond Co., s/o William T. [Thompson] and Mary J. [McPherson] Murren,[3] to LAVINIA ELMORE, age 26, single, b. Richmond Co., d/o Frances Elmore. Beverley D. Tucker. 5 DEC 1878 at the res. of Mr. Sanford near Warsaw, Va. [C8, R:312, R1:46]

Murren, James to Mrs. Mary Ann Gregory. G.H. Northam. JAMES MURREN, farming, age 32y4m5d, widowed, b. Richmond Co., s/o William Thompson Murren and Mary A. [McPherson] Murren, to MARY ANN GREGORY, age 33, widow, b. Richmond Co., d/o John and Martha Shackleford. 29 MAR 1883. [C10, R:356, R1:58]

N

Napper, William (Col.) to Lucy Atwell (Col.). WILLIAM NAPPER, farmer, age 26y10m, widowed, b. Richmond Co., s/o Spencer and Mary Napper, to LUCY ATWELL, age 28, widow, b. Northumberland Co., d/o James Atwell. Thomas G. Thomas. 8 JAN 1870 at James Garland's. [C5, R:233, R1:27]

Napper, William (Col.) to Matilda Ann Newton (Col.). WILLIAM NAPPER, farmer, age 27, widowed, b. Richmond Co., s/o Spencer and Mary Napper, to MATILDA ANN NEWTON, age 22, single, b. Richmond Co., d/o Glasco and Ellen Newton. Thomas G. Thomas. 7 MAR 1872 at the house of James Evans. [C6, R:237, R1:31]

Nash, Alexander Maxwell to Ella P. Balderson. ALEXANDER MAXWELL NASH, farmer, age 22, single, b. Richmond Co., s/o Curtis M. and Susan A. [Ann Bowen] Nash, *q.v.*, to ELLA P. REAMY, abe 16, single, b. Spotsylvania Co., d/o William O. and Julia A. [Ann Sanders] Balderson.[4] R.N. Reamy. 12 JAN 1881 at *Morris Hill*. [C9, R:335, R1:52]

Nash, Curtis M. to Susan Ann Bowen.[5] CURTIS M. NASH, farming, age about 21, single, b. upper district of Richmond Co., s/o Zacariah [sic] Nash and wife Mary [Marks],[6] to SUSAN ANN BOWEN, age about 18, single, b. upper district of Richmond Co., d/o William S. Bowen and wife Nancy. Consent 25 JUL 1857 by John Pullen, guardian of bride, wits. John A. Coates, Geo. W. Sanders. John Pullen, M.G. 2 AUG 1857 at Mrs. Nancy Bowen's. [C1, R:159, R1:5]

Nash, Hamilton to Willia Ann Emdora Hinson. HAMILTON NASH, farming, age 21, single, b. Richmond Co., s/o Curtis M. and Susan Ann [Bowen] Nash, *q.v.*, to WILLIA ANN EMDORA HINSON, age 2[2], single, b. Richmond Co., d/o W.W. [Welford] and Maria Hinson. Consent 23 FEB 1886 by bride. R.N. Reamy. 24 FEB 1886 at res. of A. Nash. [C11, R:315, R1:67]

---

[1] Francis W. Mullen (d. 10 JAN 1917) and wife Mary J. Miskell (b. 15 AUG 1846, d. 12 JUL 1928) are bur. at Jerusalem Baptist Church cemetery. Her served in Co. B, 41st Va. Mil., C.S.A.
[2] William D. Miskell and Lucy English were married by bond 31 MAR 1836 in Richmond Co.
[3] William Thompson Murren and Mary McPherson, ward of Benjamin Clark, were married 19 JAN 1826 in Fredericksburg.
[4] William O. Balderson and Julia Ann Sanders were married 11 SEP 1849 in Richmond Co. by Rev. William N. Ward.
[5] Curtis M. Nash (b. 8 MAY 1835, d. 27 AUG 1913) and wife Susan A. Bowen (b. 16 MAY 1839, d. 4 JAN 1903) are bur. in Rappahannock Baptist Church cemetery. He served in Co. D, 40th Va. Inf., C.S.A., prisoner of war at Falling Waters.
[6] Zachariah Nash and Mary Marks were married by bond 12 MAR 1833 in Richmond Co.

Nash, Nathaniel Brook to Frances A. Scates. NATHANIEL B. NASH, farmer, age 25, single, b. Richmond Co., s/o Zachariah and Mary [Marks] Nash,[1] to FRANCES A. SCATES, age 21, single, b. Richmond Co., d/o John B. and Elizabeth [Marks] Scates.[2] Consent 14 SEP 1866 by Elizabeth Scates and bride Frances A. Scates, wit. R.H. Brown. John Pullen. 16 SEP 1866 at Elizabeth Scates'. [C4, R:272, R1:64, R1:18]

Nash, Nathaniel Brook to Mrs. Virginia Ansophia "Jennie" Sanders Jenkins.[3] NATHANIEL BROOK NASH, mechanic, age 43, widowed, b. Richmond Co., s/o Zachariah and Mary [Marks] Nash, to JENNIE A.S. JENKINS, age 29, widow, b. Richmond Co., d/o Allen J. and Alice D.C. [Newman] Sanders, *q.v.* Consent 23 JUN 1885 by bride to marry "Bruks" Nash. R.N. Reamy. 24 JUN 1885. [C10, R:317]

Nash, William A. to Virginia E. Coates. WILLIAM A. NASH, farming, age 23, single, b. Richmond Co., s/o C.M. [Curtis] and Susan Ann [Bowen] Nash, *q.v.*, to VIRGINIA E. COATES, age 18, single, b. Essex Co., d/o Edward Coates and Sarah A. [Ann] Jenkins née Morriss, *q.v.* Consent 25 DEC 1882 by bride, wits. [A.]A. Jenkins, R.A. Jenkins, Lucy A. Jenkins, W. [his X mark] Oliff. R.N. Reamy. 27 DEC 1882. [C10, R1:57]

Nash, William H. to Amanda Morriss. WILLIAM H. NASH, farmer, age 22, single, b. Westmoreland Co., s/o Samuel and Sarah [Green] Nash,[4] to AMANDA MORRISS, age 23, single, b. Richmond Co., d/o William H. and Mary Morriss. Consent 20 DEC 1870 by bride, her age sworn by E.H. Coates. H.H. Fones. 21 DEC 1870 at res. of Saml. Fones.[5] [C5, R:234, R1:28]

Nash, Zachariah to Mrs. Rose A. Cash Moss. ZACHARIAH NASH, farmer, age 59, widowed, b. Richmond Co., s/o James and Betsy Nash, to ROSE A. MOSS, age 33, widow, b. Richmond Co., d/o William and Felicia [France] Cash.[6] D.M. Wharton. 11 APR 1867[7] at res. of the minister. [C4, R:286, R1:21]

Neasom,[8] James R. to Lucy Efford. Consent 21 MAR 1854 by mother Nancy Efford, wit. William English. No license or minister return. [C]

Nevitt, Edwin Belley to Mrs. Mary Ann Sanders, widow of Lemuel Marks. EDWIN BELLEY NEVITT, farmer, age 23, single, b. District of Columbia, s/o Robert [K.] & L.C. [Lettice C. Moore] Nevitt,[9] to MARY ANN MARKS, age 2[5], widow, b. Richmond Co., d/o J.C. [James C.] and Sarah [Hinson] Saunders [sic]. Consent 30 MAY 1870 by bride, signed Mrs. Mary A. Marks, M.A. Saunders. H.H. Fones. 1 JUN 1870 at res. of J.C. Saunders. [C5, R:233, R1:28]

Newman, Frederick (Col.) to Sarah Johnson (Col.). FREDERICK NEWMAN, farmer, age 29, single, b. and res. Westmoreland Co., s/o Thomas and Fanny Carey, to SARAH JOHNSON, age 21, single, b. Westmoreland Co., d/o Sally Johnson. Consent 7 MAR 1878 by bride, wit. Thomas Johnson. George Laws. 7 MAR 1878 at *Kinderhook*. [C8, R:310, R1:44]

---

[1] Zachariah Nash and Mary Marks were married by bond 12 MAR 1833 in Richmond Co.
[2] Johnn B. Scates and Betsy Marks were married by bond 10 MAR 1830 in Richmond Co.
[3] Virginia Rock (b. 1855, d. 8 DEC 1940) is buried at Welcome Grove Baptist Church cemetery.
[4] Samuel Nash and Sarah Green, d/o George Green, were married by bond 6 NOV 1843 in Westmoreland Co.
[5] Place of marriage on license; however, minister return notes place of marriage as the residence of Griffin Sanders.
[6] Willliam Cash and Fillishsha France, d/o John France and Catharine Fones, were married by bond 7 JAN 1828 in Richmond Co.
[7] Minister return gives date of marriage as 3 OCT 1867.
[8] This may be James Newsome.
[9] Robert K. Nevitt and Lettice C. Moore were married by license 20 DEC 1836 in D.C.

Newman, George (Col.) to Mima Johnson (Col.). GEORGE NEWMAN, laborer, age 20y10m, single, b. Richmond Co., s/o Richard and Milly Newman, to MIMA JOHNSON, age 24, single, b. Richmond Co., d/o Ben and Fanny Johnson. Consent by parties and Milly [her X mark] Newman, wit. Oliver Henry. Edmond Rich. 16 APR 1878 at the house of J.P. Delano. [C8, R:311, R1:44]

Newman, George H. to Myra N. Balderson. GEORGE H. NEWMAN, farming, age 23, single, b. Richmond Co., Upper Parish, s/o Joseph Newman and Sophia [Hinson],[1] to MYRA N. BALDERSON, age 19, single, b. Richmond Co., Upper Parish, d/o Gilbert H. [Hardwick] Balderson and Elizabeth [Pope].[2] John Pullen, M.G. 25 MAY 1854 at T.N. Balderson's. [C1, R, R1:1]

Newman, George H. to Lucy Jenkins. GEORGE H. NEWMAN, farming, age 52, widowed, b. Richmond Co., s/o Joseph Newman and Sophia Newman née [Hinson], to LUCY JENKINS, age 21, single, b. Richmond Co., d/o Thomas A. and Martha [Brewer Sandford] Jenkins, *q.v.* Consent 27 JUL 1885 by bride Lucy [her X mark] Jenkins, wit. R.W. Hinson. R.N. Reamy. 30 JUL 1885. [C10, R:317, R1:64]

Newman, Henry (Col.) to Sophia Wright (Col.). HENRY NEWMAN, farming, age 39, widowed, b. Westmoreland Co., s/o George and Mary Newman, to SOPHIA WRIGHT, age 22y10m, single, b. Richmond Co., d/o Jacob and Gracy Wright. Thomas G. Thomas. 23 NOV 1879 at the res. of the minister. [C8, R:309, R1:48]

Newman, Henry to Elizabeth Pugh. Consent 18 SEP 1857 by bride Elizabeth [her X mark] Pugh, wit. James Pare. No license or minister return. [C1]

Newman, James W. (Col.) to Ellen Fosset (Col.). JAMES W. NEWMAN, laborer, age 19y10m, single, b. and res. Westmoreland Co., s/o Jane Newman [name of father not given], to ELLEN FOSSET, age 22, single, b. Richmond Co., d/o Henry and Sally Fosset. Consent 14 DEC 1882 from Montross, Va. by Jane [her X mark] Newman, wit. Wm. Reed. M.F. Sanford. 14 DEC 1882 at the home of the bride. [C10, R1:57]

Newman, Jessie (Col.) to Mrs. Margaret Dandridge, widow of Alexander Gray (Col.), widow of Alexander Gray. JESSIE NEWMAN, laborer, age 27, single, b. Richmond Co., s/o Abram and Sarah Newman, to MARGARET GRAY, age 35, widow, b. Richmond Co., d/o [George and] Bekky Dandridge. Consent 4 APR 1885 by bride who is age 35. George Laws. 5 APR 1885 at New Zion Church. [C10, R:316, R1:64]

Newman, John H. (Col.) to Frances A. Thompson (Col.). JOHN H. NEWMAN, farming, age 3[0], widowed, b. Richmond Co., s/o Cephas and Dorcas Newman, to FRANCES A. THOMPSON, age 21y2m8d, single, b. Richmond Co., d/o John Thompson and Betsey Thompson now Veney. Allen Brown, minister. 19 FEB 1882 at the bride's home. [C9, R:312, R1:55]

Newman, John H. (Col.) to Lucy Croxton (Col.). JOHN H. NEWMAN, farmer, age 27y10m, single, b. Richmond Co., s/o Cephas and Dorcas Newman, to LUCY CROXTON, age 21, single, b.

---

[1] Joseph Newman and Sophia Hinson were married by bond 1 FEB 1830 in Richmond Co.
[2] Gilbert H. Balderson was married by bond 12 APR 1834 in Richmond Co. to Elizabeth Pope.

Richmond Co., d/o Jerry and Mary Croxton. Allen Brown, minister. 23 MAY 1878 at the bride's home. [C8, R:311]

Newsom, Joseph E. to Melissa E. Forester.[1] JOSEPH E. NEWSOM, farming, age 47 single, b. Richmond Co., s/o Samuel and Ann Newsom, to MELISSA E. FORESTER, age 16, single, b. Richmond Co., d/o Richard P. and Sally E. [Hynson] Forester, *q.v.* Consent 21 SEP 1881 by Richard P. Forester. W.A. Crocker. 25 SEP 1881 at Calvary Church. [C9, R:338, R1:54]

Newton, Frederick (Col.) to Mary Jane Newman (Col.). FREDERICK NEWTON, sailing and oystering, age 21y9m, single, b. Richmond Co., s/o Peter and Eliza Newton, to MARY JANE NEWMAN, age 25, single, b. Richmond Co., d/o Ths. H. and Willie A. Newman. Consent 15 FEB 1890 by T.H. Newman, wit. Winnie A. Newman. Rev. L. Marshall. 16 FEB 1890 at Second Baptist [Church]. [C12, R:323, R1:76]

Newton, Henry (Col.) to Felicia Coats (Col.). HENRY NEWTON, laborer, age 24, single, b. Richmond Co., s/o Glasco and Ellen Newton, to FELICIA COATS, age 16y11m, single, b. Richmond Co., s/o Sandy and Lucinda Coats. Consent 2 FEB 1881 by bride Lucind [her X mark] Costs, wit. John [his X mark] Tate. Rev. Robert Lewis. 3 FEB 1881. [C9, R:335, R1:52]

Newton, Isaac (Col.) to Lucy Ellen Fitzhugh (Col.). ISAAC NEWTON, oystering, age 23, single, b. Richmond Co., s/o Charles and Emily Newton, to LUCY ELLEN FITZHUGH, age 21, single, b. Richmond Co., d/o Daniel and Lucy Fitzhugh. Consent 20 DEC 1887 by Isaac [his X mark] Newton and Jonas [his X mark] Minor, wit. L.D. Warner, clerk. Rev. Jacob Robinson. 21 DEC 1887 at Mr. [Jackins] at *Ivandale* [sic].[2] [C11, R:293, R1:71]

Newton, John (Col.) to Maria Johnson (Col.). JOHN NEWTON, oystering, age 28, single, b. Richmond Co., s/o Henry and Kitty Newton, to MARIA JOHNSON, age 26, single, b. Richmond Co., d/o Orrison and Ann Johnson. Consent 24 DEC 1885 by bride. Rev. Jacob Robinson. 24 DEC 1885 at Mt. Zion Church, Ivanhoe. [C11, R:318, R1:65]

Newton, William (Col.) to Mary Glasco (Col.). WILLIAM NEWTON, oysterman, age 24, single, b. Richmond Co., s/o Isaac and Fanny Newton, to MARY GLASCO, age 20, single, b. Richmond Co., d/o Thomas and Emma Glasco. Allen Brown, minister. 20 DEC 1877 at the bride's home. [C8, R:307, R1:43]

Newton, William (Col.) to Emma Carter (Col.). WILLIAM NEWTON, farming, age 3[7], widowed, b. Richmond Co., s/o Isaac and Fanny Newton, to EMMA CARTER, age 23, single, b. Richmond Co., d/o John and Ellen Carter. Consent 28 JAN 1889 by Joseph Heintze by Rev. L. Harrod, wit. James Darby. Rev. Lucius Harrod, Pastor Ebenezer Baptist Church. 29 JAN 1889, at the res. of Emily Heintze. [C12, R:327, R1:74]

Newton, William H. (Col.) to Sophy Ann Martin (Col.). WILLIAM H. NEWTON, farmer, age 20, single, b. Richmond Co., s/o Milly Newton (father not known), to SOPHY ANN MARTIN, age 20, single, b. Richmond Co., d/o Ann Martin (father not known). Edmond Rich. 5 JUN 1884 at the res. of Milly Newton. [C10, R:354, R1:62]

---

[1] Joseph E. Newsom (b. 16 MAR 1834, d. 11 JUN 1902) and his wife Melissa E. Forrester (b. 1864, d. 27 APR 1927) are bur. at Farnham Baptist Church cemetery.
[2] Ivondale is a locality at the junction of Routes 608, 610 and 613, and was known as Central, Va. before the Civil War.

Norris, Andrew J. to Emma E. Hanks.[1] ANDREW J. NORRIS, farming, age 27, single, b. and res. Lancaster Co., s/o Henry C. and Elizabeth [D. Hazzard],[2] to EMMA E. HANKS, age 25, single, b. Richmond Co., d/o William and Virginia [Dunaway] Hanks. Consent 30 APR 1889 by bride. Robert Williamson. 2 MAY 1889 at res. of William Hanks near Farnham, Va. [C12, R:327, R1:74]

Norris, Henry C. to Maria A. Barnes. HENRY C. NORRIS, bricklayer, age 27, widowed, b. and res. Lancaster Co., s/o Richard and Sarah [Stott] Norris,[3] to MARIA A. BARNES, age 21, single, b. Richmond Co., d/o [Kan.] C. and Fanye Barnes. William F. Bain. 6 MAR 1867 at William E. Deane. [C4, R:286, R1:20]

Norris, Julius (Col.) to Maria Williams (Col.). JULIUS NORRIS, oystering, age 23, single, b. Richmond Co., s/o Cyrus and [L]ina Norris, to MARIA WILLIAMS, age 26, single, b. Richmond Co., d/o Patty Williams [name of father not given]. Rev. W. Carter. 23 DEC 1883 at the church. [C10, R:357, R1:60]

Northam, Rev. George Henry to Catharine A. Saunders.[4] GEORGE H. NORTHAM, Baptist minister, age 29, widowed, b. Middlesex Co., res. Westmoreland Co., s/o George and Nancy Northam, to CATHARINE A. SAUNDERS, age 22, single, b. Richmond Co., d/o Richard and Alice Saunders. Consent 7 NOV 1857 by bride, wit. Melville Biscoe. Robert Williamson, M.G. 10 NOV 1857 at Farnham house. [C1, R:160, R1:5]

Northen, Alfred G.[5] to Mrs. Lillie A. Efford Scrimger. ALFRED G. NORTHEN, farming, age 63, widowed, b. Richmond Co., s/o Samuel and Sarah [Ann Baker] Northen,[6] to LILLIE A. SCRIMGER, age 40, widow, b. Richmond Co., d/o Williamson Efford.[7] Consent in OCT 1879 by bride Lillie A. [her X mark] Scrimger. G.H. Northam. 8 OCT 1879 at Mrs. Scrimger's. [C8, R:308, R1:48]

Northen, Alonzo to Octavia C. Clark. ALONZO NORTHEN, farmer, age 20y10m10d, single, b. Richmond Co., s/o George and Elizabeth H. [Bryant] Northen,[8] to OCTAVIA C. CLARK, age 16y3m, single, b. Richmond Co., d/o John H. and Lucinda [Bryant] Clark. Consent 26 FEB 1877 by bride Octavia C. Clarke [sic], wit. Lucinda [her X mark] Clark, B.E. Bell; consent by George Northen. W.A. Crocker. 27 FEB 1877 at res. of George Northen. [C8, R:306a, R1:42]

Northen, Alonzo C.[9] to Catharine S. Northen. ALONZO C. NORTHEN, farming, age 27, widowed, b. Richmond Co., s/o George and Elizabeth [H. Bryant] Northen, to CATHARINE S. NORTHEN, age 19, single, b. Richmond Co., d/o Thomas W. and Lucy Jane [Northen] Northen, *q.v.* Consent 6 NOV 1885 by bride, wit. Alonzo C. Northen. G.H. Northam. 10 NOV 1885 at the res. of Thomas W. Northen. [C10, NN:27 NOV 1885, R:318, R1:65]

---

[1] Andrew J. Norris (1859-1923) and wife Emma Hanks (1860-1943) are bur. in Farnham Baptist Church cemetery.
[2] Henry C. Norris and Elizabeth D. Hazzard were married 25 DEC 1854 in Lancaster Co.
[3] Richard Norris and Sarah Stott were married by bond 19 DEC 1820 in Lancaster Co.
[4] Rev. George Henry Northam (b. 1828, d. 5 JUN 1896) and his wife Catharine A. Saunders (b. 1836, d. 25 MAR 1911 in Baltimonre Co., Md.) are bur. at Jerusalem Baptist Church cemetery.
[5] As Albert G. Northern, served in Co. E, 40th Reg., Va. Inf., C.S.A., as carpenter.
[6] Samuel Northen and Sarah Ann Baker were married by bond 13 NOV 1815 in Richmond Co.
[7] Williamson Efford and Ann Jesper were married by bond 2 SEP 1824 in Richmond Co.
[8] George Northen and Elizabeth H. Bryant were married by bond 17 FEB 1835 in Richmond Co.
[9] Alonzo C. Northen (1856-1925) is bur. in Jerusalem Baptist Church cemetery.

Northen, Charles Alexander to Sarah Rebecca Bell. CHARLES A. NORTHEN, farmer, age 28, single, b. Richmond Co., s/o George and Elizabeth H. [Bryant] Northen, to SARAH R. BELL, age 29, single, b. Richmond Co., d/o Lemuel G. and Ann [Morris] Bell.[1] Consent 8 FEB 1864 by bride. William F. Bain. 11 FEB 1864 at Lemuel G. Bell's. [C3, R:139, R1:13]

Northen, George D. to Mary C. Northen.[2] GEORGE D. NORTHEN, farmer, age 23, single, b. Richmond Co., s/o George and Elizabeth H. [Bryant] Northen, to MARY C. NORTHEN, age 24, single, b. Richmond Co., d/o Edward J. and Catharine J. [Northen] Northen.[3] Consent 25 APR 1865 by bride, wit. E.J. Northen. Robert Williamson, M.G. 26 APR 1865 at Edward J. Northen's. [C3, R:204, R1:15]

Northen, James Edward[4] to Mrs. Sarah Connelly Brown. JAMES E. NORTHEN, farmer, nearly 21, single, b. Richmond Co., s/o Edward J. and Catherine M. [Northen] Northen,[5] to SARAH C. BROWN, age 25, widow, b. Westmoreland Co., d/o O. and Julia Connelly. Consent 13 SEP 1869 by bride, no wit. G.H. Northam. 15 SEP 1869. [C5, R, R1:26]

Northen, James Edward to Henrietta E. Northen.[6] JAMES EDWARD NORTHEN, farmer, age 28, widowed, b. Richmond Co., s/o Edward [J., Jr.] and Catherine [M. Northen] Northen, to HENRIETTA E. NORTHEN, age 20, single, b. Richmond Co., d/o George and Elizabeth [H. Bryant] Northen. Consent 9 JAN 1878 by father George Northen. J.B. DeBerry, P.C. 10 JAN 1878 at the res. of the bride's father. [C8, R:310, R1:44]

Northen, Peter S. to Adethia A. Hanks. PETER S. NORTHEN, farmer, age 58, widowed, b. Richmond Co., s/o James and Catharine [Gwinn Smith] Northen,[7] to ADETHIA A. HANKS, age 25, single, b. Richmond Co., d/o Joseph [T.] and Judy [Judith P. Hanks] Hanks.[8] Consent 9 JUL 1864 by bride Adithia A. Hanks, wit. J.H. Bryant. Robert Williamson, M.G. 12 JUL 1864 at Beard's Store. [C3, R:139, R1:13]

Northen, Thomas S. to Mary A.K. Robertson. THOMAS S. NORTHEN, carpenter, age 26, single, b. Richmond Co., s/o Edward J. and Catharine M. [Northen] Northen, to MARY E.K. ROBERTSON, age 21, single, b. Lancaster Co., d/o Sidney T. Robertson (father's name unknown[9]). Consent 9 FEB 1861 by bride, wit. Joseph Davis. E.L. Williams. 14 FEB 1861. [C3, R:123, R1:10]

Northen, Thomas W. to Lucy Jane Northen. THOMAS W. NORTHEN, farmer, age 31, single, b. Richmond Co., s/o Peter S. and Harriet S. [Montague] Northen,[10] to LUCIE J. NORTHEN, age 24, single, b. Richmond Co., d/o Edward J. and Catharine [M. Northen] Northen. Consent 20 FEB 1866 by bride, wit. G.A. Carter. Robert Williamson, M.G. 1 MAR 1866 at Mrs. Edward Northen's. [C4, R1:16]

---

[1] Lemuel G. Bell and Ann Morris were married by bond 27 JAN 1829 in Richmond Co.
[2] George D. Northen (b. 4 JAN 1842, d. 8 JUN 1902) and his wife Mary C. Northen (b. 24 MAY 1839, d. 16 APR 1923) are bur. in Jerusalem Baptist Church cemetery. He served as a private in Co. D, 9th Va. Cav., C.S.A. under the name George D. Northern.
[3] Edward J. Northen, Jr. and Catharine M. [sic] Northen were married by bond 7 DEC 1832 in Richmond Co.
[4] James E. Northen (b. 1848, d. 1900) is bur. at Calvary United Methodist Church cemetery.
[5] Edward J. Northen, Jr. and Catharine M. [sic] Northen were married by bond 7 DEC 1832 in Richmond Co.
[6] James E. Northen (1848-1900) and wife Henrietta E. Northen (1848-1933) are bur. at Calvary United Methodist Church cemetery.
[7] James Northen and Catharine Gwinn Smith were married by bond 22 DEC 1800 in Richmond Co.
[8] Joseph T. Hanks and Judith P. Hanks, widow, were married by bond 12 SEP 1837 in Richmond Co.
[9] Andrew Robertson and Sidney T. Hathaway were married by bond 20 APR 1835 in Lancaster Co.
[10] Peter S. Northen and Harriet S. Montague, d/o Thomas Tarpley Montague and Elizabeth Montague, were married by bond 14 MAR 1833 in Richmond Co.

Northen, Thomas W. to Catharine J. Davis. THOMAS W. NORTHEN, farming, age 47, widowed, b. Richmond Co., s/o Peter S. and Harriet S. [Montague] Northen, to CATHARINE J. DAVIS, age 25, single, b. Richmond Co., d/o John R. [Robeson] and Isabella [L. Hammack] Davis, *q.v.* G.H. Northam. 12 OCT 1884 at res. of Robinson Davis. [C10, R:355, R1:62]

Northen, William A. to Julia J. Williams. WILLIAM A. NORTHEN, farming, age 33, single, b. Richmond Co., s/o William [S.] and Sarah A. [Davis] Northen,[1] to JULIA J. WILLIAMS, age 18, single, b. Richmond Co., d/o Elijah and Julia A. Williams. Consent 13 SEP 1868 by mother. G.H. Northam. 16 SEP 1868 at Farnham Church. [C5, R:254, R1:24]

Northen, William Dandridge[2] to Fanny Lowery. WILLIAM DANDRIDGE NORTHEN, farmer, age 28, single, b. Richmond Co., s/o Alfred G. Northen and Harriet Jesper,[3] to FANNY LOWERY, age 21y8m, single, b. Richmond Co., d/o J.B. and F.W. Lowery. Consent in NOV 1875 by parties. W.A. Crocker. 8 DEC 1875. [C7, R:262, R1:39]

Northen, William Fitzhugh Lee to Mary E. Cook.[4] WILLIAM F.L. NORTHEN, farming, age 25, single, b. Richmond Co., s/o George and Elizabeth [Henrietta Bryant] Northen,[5] to MARY E. COOK, age 17, single, b. Richmond Co., d/o Alexander B. and Sarah A. [Ann Johnson] Cook, *q.v.* Consent 20 DEC 1888 by Sarah A. Cook, wit. W.F.L. Northen. W.A. Crocker. 27 DEC 1888 at the res. of the bride's mother. [C12, R:317, R1:73]

Northup, Frederick Updike[6] to Leafie Lowry. FREDERICK UPDIKE NORTHUP, clerk, age 35, single, b. New York City, s/o Fred B. and Sophia U. Northup, to LEAFIE LOWRY, age 19, single, b. Richmond Co., d/o J.B. and Elizabeth Lowry. G.H. Northam. 9 JUN 1884. [C10, NN:13 JUN 1884, R:354, R1:62]

O

Oakley, Israel to Ida B. Jett. ISRAEL OAKLEY, mechanic, age 28, single, b. Richmond Co., s/o George K. and Emily A. Oakley, to IDA B. JETT, age 20, single, b. King George Co., d/o H.S. [Henry] and Martha [Ann Jones] Jett.[7] Consent 13 MAR 1884 from *Indian Banks* by H.S. Jett and Cary J. Jett, no wit. F.W. Claybrook. 18 MAR 1884 at *Indian Bank*. [C10, R:354, R1:61]

Oakley, Newton Zeluff to Maria Collins Allison.[8] NEWTON Z. OAKLEY, oysterman, age 25y5m, single, b. New York City, s/o George T. and Emily A. Oakley,[9] to MARIA C. ALLISON, age 20y8m, single, b. Richmond Co., d/o William and Margaret A. [Ann Jones] Allison. Consent 13 DEC 1883 by William Allison., wit. Geo. W. Allison. F.W. Claybrook. 18 DEC 1883 at the res. of Capt. Allison. [C10[10], R:357, R1:60]

---

[1] William S. Northen and Sarah A. Davis were married by bond 20 DEC 1832 in Richmond Co. He was sheriff of Richmond Co. from 1 JAN 1856 to 2 AUG 1869.
[2] William D. Northen is bur. at Warsaw United Methodist Church cemetery. He served in Co. C, 40th Va. Inf., C.S.A.
[3] Albert G. Northen and Harriet Jesper were married 24 OCT 1844 in Richmond Co. by Rev. William N. Ward.
[4] W.F.L. Northen (b. 16 JUN 1863, d. 17 JAN 1938) and wife Mary E. Cook (b. 27 DEC 1872, d. 9 DEC 1930) are bur. in Calvary United Methodist Church cemetery.
[5] George Northen and Elizabeth H. Bryant were married by bond 17 FEB 1835 in Richmond Co.
[6] Frederick U. Northup (b. 16 NOV 1842, d. 1 JUN 1916), is memorialized on a tablet in St. John's Episcopal Church.
[7] Henry S. Jett and Martha Ann Jones were married 5 APR 1848 in King George Co. by Rev. Philip Montague.
[8] Newton Z. Oakley (b. 16 MAY 1858, d. 14 JUN 1925 in Simonson, Va.) and wife Maria C. Allison (b. 22 APR 1863, d. 16 MAY 1943) are bur. in Farnham Baptist Church cemetery. Simonson is a locality at the southwest corner of the County on the narrow peninsula between the mouths of Morattico and Lancaster Creeks.
[9] Emily A. Oakley (b. 17 APR 1835, d. 23 JAN 1916) is bur. in Farnham Baptist Church cemetery.
[10] The consent and license are not together on microfilm, see after record No. 58 for consent.

Oldham, Thomas Newton to Mary Curtis Davenport.[1] THOMAS N. OLDHAM, farmer, age 29, single, b. Richmond Co., s/o William C. and Virginia [Ficklin] Oldham,[2] to MARY C. DAVENPORT, age 20, single, b. Richmond Co., d/o L.O. [Linsey] and Maria S. [Davis] Davenport.[3] Consent 20 DEC 1875 by bride's parents L.O. Davenport and Maria S. Davenport, wit. L.A. Weaver. G.H. Northam. 22 DEC 1875. [C7, NN:22 APR 1881, R:262, R1:39]

Oliff, Benjamin Walt to Olivia R. Marks.[4] BENJAMIN W. OLIFF, merchant, age 25, single, b. Richmond Co., res. King George Co., s/o Bailey and Elizabeth Oliff, to OLIVIA R. MARKS,[5] age 24, single, b. Richmond Co., d/o Vincent and Mary [France] Marks. Consent 13 APR 1889 by bride Livie R. Marks, no wit. Geo. M. Connelley. 14 APR 1889 at Oak Row. [C12, R:327v]

Oliff, Charles W. to Mary J. Hinson. CHARLES W. OLIFF, farmer, age 24y2d, single, b. Richmond Co., s/o Henry V. [Vincent] and Elizabeth [Bowen] Oliff, *q.v.*, to MARY J. HINSON, age 23, single, b. Richmond Co., d/o John and Elizabeth Hinson. Consent by bride, wit. T.M.L. Reamy. R.N. Reamy. 18 MAR 1880 at John Hinson's. [C9, R:314, R1:50]

Oliff, George Washington to Martha Ellen Jenkins.[6] GEORGE WASHINGTON OLIFF, farming, age 22, single, b. Richmond Co., s/o James P. and Elizabeth [A. Oliff] Oliff, *q.v.*, to MARTHA E. JENKINS, age 21, single, b. Richmond Co., d/o Thomas [A.] and Martha [Brewer Sandford] Jenkins, *q.v.* Consent undated by bride and Alice D.C. Jenkins, wit. Wm. Nash. G.M. Conley. 5 NOV 1889 at *Millview*. [C12, R:328, R1:75]

Oliff, Hannibal Wesley to Mrs. Augusta A. Balderson,[7] widow of Robert L. Sanders. HANNIBAL W. OLIFF, farming, age 26, single, b. Richmond Co., s/o W.D. [William] and Elizabeth [Nash] Oliff, *q.v.*, to AUGUSTA A. SANDERS, age 25, widow, b. Richmond Co., d/o G.G. [George Graham] and Elizabeth Ann [Newman] Balderson, *q.v.* Consent 7 OCT 1889 by bride, no wit. G.M. Connelly. 9 OCT 1889 near Newland, Va. [C12, R:328, R1:74]

Oliff, Henry Carter to Mary A. Hill. HENRY C. OLIFF, farmer, age 3[0], single, b. Richmond Co., s/o William [Jr.] and Sophia [Carter] Oliff, to MARY A. HILL, age 33, single, b. Richmond Co., d/o William Hill. G.H. Northam. 25 APR 1869. [C5, R, R1:25]

Oliff, Henry Carter to Martha Virginia Hall.[8] HENRY CARTER OLIFF, miller and carpenter, age 37, widowed, b. Richmond Co., s/o William [Jr.] and Sophia [Carter] Oliff, to MARTHA[9] VIRGINIA

---

[1] Thomas Newton Oldham (1846-1925) and wife Mary Curtis Davenport (b. 4 AUG 1856, d. 26 NOV 1930) are bur. in Jerusalem Baptist Church cemetery.

[2] William C. Oldham (b. 1820, d. 5 JUN 1869) and wife Virginia Ficklin (b. 27 NOV 1826, d. 9 AUG 1879) are bur. in Jerusalem Baptist Church cemetery. William C. Oldham and Virginia Ficklin were married by bond 8 AUG 1843 in Richmond Co., with consent of her father C.D. Ficklin. He was sheriff of Richmond Co. from 1 JAN 1861 to 1 JAN 1865.

[3] Linsey O. Davenport and Maria S. Davis were married 20 AUG 1851 in Richmond Co. by Rev. John Godwin, with consent of her father Robert H. Davis.

[4] Benjamin W. Oliff (b. 13 DEC 1861, d. 23 APR 1908) and wife Olivia R. Marks [Jones] (b. 12 MAR 1864, d. 14 JUL 1948) are bur. in Rappahannock Baptist Church cemetery.

[5] The license notes that the bride Olivia alias Livie R. Marks.

[6] George W. Oliff (b. 2 FEB 1867, d. 3 AUG 1941) and his first wife Martha E. Jenkins (b. 1868, d. 22 MAY 1919) are bur. in Rappahannock Baptist Church cemetery.

[7] Hannibal W. Oliff (b. 24 AUG 1863, d. OCT 1894) and his wife Augusta A. Balderson (b. 17 SEP 1863, d. 23 FEB 1935) are bur. in Rappahannock Baptist Church cemetery.

[8] Henry Carter Oliff (1838-1892) and his second wife Martha Virginia Hall (1840-1928) are bur. in Menokin Baptist Church cemetery. He served in Co. D, 40th Reg., Va. Inf., C.S.A.

[9] Each instance of Martha appears to have been altered and may be Mary.

HALL, age 35, single, b. Richmond Co., d/o Robert and [Sibie] Hall. H.H. Fones. 26 DEC 1875. [C7, R:262, R1:39]

Oliffe, Henry Vincent, to Elizabeth Bowen. HENRY VINCENT OLIFFE, farmer, age 33 on 16 MAR 1855, single, b. Richmond Co., upper end, s/o James Oliffe and Susan, to ELIZABETH BOWEN, age 22, single, b. Richmond Co., upper end, d/o Kelley H. Bowen and Mariah [Fegget].[1] Consent by bride Elizebeth [her X mark] Bowen, wits. James Morris, Wm. A.H. Saunders. John Pullen, M.G. 26 APR 1855 at *Wave Hill*, res. of John Pullen. [C1, R:153, R1:2]

Oliff, Hudson to Mary Jane Balderson. HUDSON OLIFF, farmer, age 21, single, b. Richmond Co., s/o William [Jr.] and Sophia [Carter] Oliff, to MARY JANE BALDERSON, age 27y7m, single, b. Richmond Co., d/o Leonard and Mahala [Ambrose] Balderson.[2] Consent 9 MAR 1874 by bride, wit. Joseph Ambers. Robert N. Reamy. 15 MAR 1874 at James Jenkins'. [C7[3], R:230, R1:36]

Oliff, James Henry to Mary Altha Jenkins. JAMES HENRY OLIFF, farmer, age 26, single, b. Richmond Co., s/o Henry Vincent and Elizabeth Oliff, to MARY ALTHA JENKINS, age 20, single, b. Richmond Co., d/o James Henry and Martha Eltha Jenkins. Consent 2 APR 1887 from Foneswood, Va. by parents of the bride, wit. Willie B. Reamey. R.N. Reamy. 6 APR 1887. [C11, R:291, R1:69]

Oliff, James P. to Elizabeth A. Oliff. JAMES P. OLIFF, farmer, age 21, single, b. Richmond Co., s/o William [Jr.] and Sophia [Carter] Oliff,[4] to ELIZABETH A. OLIFF, age 30, single, b. Richmond Co., d/o James and Lucy Oliff. Consent 23 APR 1866 by parties, wit. Jos. A. Pullin. John Pullen. 25 APR 1866 at Lucy Oliff's. [C4, R:271, R1:17]

Oliff, John A. to Martha Melveine Hinson. JOHN A. OLIFF, farmer, age 22, single, b. Richmond Co., s/o William D. [Davis][5] and Mary [Ann Bowen] Oliff,[6] to MARTHA MELVEINE HINSON, age 20, single, b. Richmond Co., d/o W.W. [William] and Maria [Scates] Hinson.[7] Consent 9 SEP 1880 by bride, signed Martha Mell Viene Hinson. R.N. Reamy. 12 SEP 1880. [C9, R:316, R1:51]

Oliffe, Octavus to Mrs. Susan Carter. OCTAVOUS [sic] OLIFFE, farming, age about 24, single, b. Westmoreland Co., s/o Lofty Oliffe and wife Susan [Jones],[8] to SUSAN CARTER, age about 40, widow, b. Richmond Co., d/o James Coates and wife Elizabeth. Consent 6 OCT 1856 by bride Susan [her X mark] Carter, wits. John Morriss, James Reamy. John Pullen, M.G. 29 OCT 1856 at Susan Carter's. [C1, R:148, R1:4]

---

[1] Kelly H. Bowen and Mariah Fegget were married by bond 17 DEC 1827 in Westmoreland Co.
[2] Leonard Balderson and Mahala Ambrose were married by bond 22 MAR 1842 in Richmond Co. by Rev. William Balderson.
[3] Two copies of this license appears, one that is crossed through gives date of marriage 13 MAR 1874.
[4] William Oliff, Jr. and Sophia Carter were married by bond 23 DEC 1835 in Richmond Co.
[5] William Davis Oliff (d. 15 MAY 1873 age 45) is listed among the deaths at the Poor House for Westmoreland County.
[6] William D. Olliff and Mary Ann Bowen were married 15 MAY 1850 in Richmond Co. by Rev. John Pullen, with consent of the bride's parents William S. and Nancy Bowen.
[7] William W. Hinson and Maria Scates were married 13 MAR 1850 in Richmond Co. by Rev. William Balderson.
[8] Lofty Oliffe and Susannah Jones were married by bond 23 AUG 1819 in Westmoreland Co.

Oliff, Robert H. to Shady Jett. ROBERT H. OLIFF, farmer, age 23, single, b. Richmond Co., s/o Jesse and Bethuel [Jenkins] Oliff, to SHADY JETT, age 21, single, b. Richmond Co., d/o Mortimer and Cordelia Jett. R.N. Reamy. 7 or 12[1] FEB 1867 at Mrs. Jetts'. [C4, R:285, R1:20]

Oliff, Samuel to Mary F. Hall. SAMUEL OLILFF, farming, age 21y10m, single, b. Richmond Co., s/o Henry Vincent and Blazie Oliff, to MARY F. HALL, age 19, single, b. Richmond Co., d/o William Hall and Susan Hall (dec'd.). H.H. Fones. 15 MAR 1882. [C9, R:312, R1:56]

Oliff, Thomas to Mahaly Hinson. THOMAS OLIFF, farmer, age 19, single, b. Richmond Co., s/o Jesse and [Bethuel] Oliff, to MAHALY HINSON, age 22, single, b. Richmond Co., d/o George Hinson. Consent 5 DEC 1873 by bride, also Jesse Oliff, wit. W.H. Balderson. B.R. Battaile. 11 DEC 1873 in Westmoreland Co. [C6, R:236, R1:35]

Oliff, William D. to Elizabeth Nash. WILLIAM D. OLIFF, miller, age 32, widowed, b. Westmoreland Co., s/o William S. and Ann [Drake] Oliff,[2] to ELIZABETH NASH, age 19, single, b. Richmond Co., d/o Zachariah and Mary [Marks] Nash.[3] Consent 3 JAN 1861 by father Zachariah Nash, wits. Jos. A. Pullen, Jackson Marks. John Pullen. 17 JAN 1861. [C3, R:123, R1:10]

Oliff, William J. to Adella F. Nash. WILLIAM J. OLIFF, farming, age 24, single, b. Richmond Co., s/o W.D. [William] and Elizabeth J. Oliff, to ADELLA F. NASH, age 19, single, b. Richmond Co., d/o Curtis M. and Susan [Ann Bowen] Nash, *q.v.* Consent 30 NOV 1885 by parents of the bride, wit. Robert France. R.N. Reamy. 2 DEC 1885. [C11, R:319, R1:66]

Omohundro, Benjamin P. to Frances A. Cralle. BENJAMIN P. OMOHUNDRO, farmer, age 22, single, b. Richmond Co., s/o Thomas and Sally Omohundro, to FRANCES A. CRALLE, age 21, single, b. Richmond Co., d/o Samuel [Jr.] and Frances M. [Belfield] Cralle.[4] Consent 16 APR 1862 by bride, wit. Wm. H. Omohundro. G.H. Northam. 16 APR 1862 at the res. of the bride's mother. [C3, R:140, R1:11]

Omohundro, George Edward to Mary Daingerfield Saunders. GEORGE EDWARD OMOHUNDRO, farmer, age 29, single, b. Westmoreland Co., s/o E.B. [Edward] and Sarah [Ann] F. [Reamy] Omohundro, to MARY DANGERFIELD SAUNDERS [sic], age 23, single, b. Richmond Co., d/o E.S. [Edward S.] and Maria [Belfield] Saunders. G.H. Northam. 15 DEC 1870 at *Spring Hill.* [C5, R:234, R1:28]

Omohundro, George Edward to Edwina S. Saunders. GEORGE E. OMOHUNDRO, farmer, age 33, widowed, b. Westmoreland Co., s/o Edward B. and Sarah Ann [F. Reamy] Omohundro,[5] to EDWINA S. SAUNDERS, age 26, single, b. Richmond Co., d/o Edward S. and Maria [Belfield] Saunders.[6] H.H. Fones. 5 JAN 1876 at *Spring Hill.* [C7, R:304, R1:39]

---

[1] Certificate gives date of marriage 7 FEB 1867, but return notes 12 FEB 1867.
[2] William Olliffe and Ann Drake were married by bond 1 JUN 1819 in Westmoreland Co.
[3] Zachariah Nash and Mary Marks were married by bond 12 MAR 1833 in Richmond Co.
[4] Samuel Cralle, Jr. and Frances M. Belfield, d/o Joseph Belfield, were married by bond 10 SEP 1832 in Richmond Co.
[5] Edward B. Omohundro and Sarah A. Reamy were married by bond 1 JUL 1839 in Westmoreland Co.
[6] Edward S. Saunders and Maria Belfield were married by bond 8 MAY 1833 in Richmond Co.

Omohundro, John Orson to Alice C. Cralle.[1] JOHN C. OMOHUNDRO, farmer, age 22, single, b. Westmoreland Co., s/o Edward B. and Sarah A.F. [Reamy] Omohundro, to ALICE C. CRALLE, age 20, single, b. Richmond Co., d/o Samuel [Jr.] and Fanny [M. Belfield] Cralle. D.M. Wharton. 10 AUG 1871 at the res. of the bride's mother. [C6, R:245, R1:30]

Owens, John Benjamin to Frances E. Carter.[2] JAMES B. OWENS, farmer, age 23, single, b. Westmoreland Co., res. Richmond Co., s/o William [W.] and Betsy [Elizabeth Simmes] Owens,[3] to FRANCES E. CARTER, age 21, single, b. Richmond Co., d/o William and Mary [Ann Scrimger] Carter.[4] Consent 16 SEP 1859 by bride, wit. M.A. Carter who also certifies bride if of age 21 years. John Pullen. 20 SEP 1859 at Mrs. W. Carter's. [C2, R:165, R1:7]

Owens, William Minor[5] to Emma J. Balderson. WILLIAM M. OWENS, farming, age 24, single, b. Richmond Co., s/o John B. [Benjamin] and Frances E. [Carter] Owens, *q.v.*, to EMMA J. BALDERSON, age 22, single, b. Fredericksburg, Va., d/o Octavius and Julia Balderson. Consent 30 AUG 1884 by bride. R.N. Reamy. 3 SEP 1884. [C10, R:355, R1:62]

P

Packett, Eli Patterson[6] to Ella Susan Sisson.[7] ELI PACKETT, farmer, age 18, single, b. Richmond Co., s/o John [Scrimger] and Maria [Courtney] Packett,[8] to ELLA SISSON, age 17, single, b. Richmond Co., d/o James and Susan [Crowder] Sisson.[9] Consent 20 OCT 1859 by James L. Packett, guardian of bride, wit. Wm. H. Packett. Lloyd Moore. 20 OCT 1859. [C2, R:165, R1:7]

Packett, Henry to Mary Jane Lewis. Return by Rev. William N. Ward. 3 JAN 1854. No license. [C]

Packett, Henry to Emily Reynolds. HENRY PACKETT, farmer, age 35, widowed, b. Richmond Co., s/o Henry and Ann Packett, to EMILY REYNOLDS, age 20, single, b. Richmond Co., d/o Richard and Maria [Webb] Reynolds.[10] Lloyd Moore. 4 AUG 1859. [C2, R:165, R1:7]

Packett, Henry to Susan H. Drake. HENRY PACKETT, farmer, age 31, widowed, b. Richmond Co., s/o Henry and Ann Packett, to SUSAN H. DRAKE, age 18, single, b. Richmond Co., d/o Richard and Ann Drake. E.L. Williams, M.G. 28 DEC 1854 at Totuskey Mill. [C1, R, R1:3]

Packett, James William to Willie Ann Sisson.[11] JAMES W. PACKETT, carpenter, age 24, single, b. Richmond Co., s/o James L. [Lewis] and Virginia [Parr] Packett,[12] to WILLIE A. SISSON, age 25, single, b. Richmond Co., d/o William H. and Lucy Ann [Latham] Sisson.[13] Consent 2 AUG

---

[1] John Orson Omohundro (b. 23 APR 1848, d. 2 MAY 1885) and wife Alice C. Cralle (b. 22 OCT 1850, d. 22 OCT 1911) were bur. at Belfield Family cemetery.

[2] Frances E. Owens (b. 12 JUL 1838, d. 30 NOV 1915) is bur. in Rappahannock Baptist Church cemetery.

[3] William W. Owens and Elizabeth Simmes were married by bond 24 SEP 1832 in Westmoreland Co.

[4] William Carter and Mary Ann Scrimger were married by bond 24 APR 1834 in Richmond Co.

[5] William M. Owens (b. 23 AUG 1860, d. 10 SEP 1906) is bur. at Currioman Baptist Church cemetery, Chiltons, Va.

[6] Eli Patterson Packett (b. 19 DEC 1841, d. SEP 1871, served in 15th Reg. Va. Cav., C.S.A.) is bur. in the Packett Family Burial Ground at *Sabine Hall* near Warsaw, Va.

[7] Ella Susan Sisson Packett (1840-1911), first wife of Eli Patterson Packett, is bur. in the Packett-Delano Family Burial Ground near Warsaw, Va.

[8] John Packett and Maria Courtney were married 4 FEB 1841 in Richmond Co. by Rev. William N. Ward.

[9] James Sisson andd Susan Crowder were married by bond 16 DEC 1828 in Richmond Co.

[10] Richard Reynolds and Maria Webb were married by bond 11 JUN 1835 in Richmond Co.

[11] James William Packett (b. 11 DEC 1857, d. 3 JUL 1887) is bur. at the Packett-Delano Family Burial Ground, near Warsaw, Va.

[12] James L. Packett and Virginia Parr were married 28 OCT 1852 in Richmond Co. by Rev. Elijah L. Williams.

[13] William H. Sisson and Lucy A. Latham were married 7 APR 1853 in Richmond Co. by Rev. William N. Ward.

1882 by parties, wit. J.E. Gallagher. G.H. Northam. 3 AUG 1882 at *Mt. Airy Mill*. [C9, R:313, R1:56]

Packett, John Henry to Ida Augusta Fones.[1] JOHN H. PACKETT, laboring and farming, age 24, single, b. Richmond Co., s/o James L. [Lewis] and Virginia [Parr] Packett,[2] to IDA A. FONES, age 22, single, b. Richmond Co., d/o William H. [Henry] and Mary E. [Elizabeth Wilson] Fones. G.M. Conley. 3 FEB 1889 near Warsaw, Va. [C12, R:327, R1:74]

Packett, John Scrimger to Virginia A. Parr.[3] JOHN S. PACKETT, farmer, age 23, single, b. Richmond Co., s/o John [Scrimger] and Maria [Courtney] Packett,[4] to VIRGINIA A. PARR, age 18, single, b. Richmond Co., d/o James and Ann [Packett] Parr.[5] G.H. Northam. 25 SEP 1873. [C6, R:235, R1:34]

Packett, Richard Hugh to Joanna "Josey" Hall.[6] RICHARD H. PACKETT, fishing and farming, age 23, single, b. Richmond Co., s/o James L. [Lewis] Packett (dec'd.) and Virginia [Parr] Packett, to JOANNA HALL, age 19, single, b. Richmond Co., d/o Bladen and Frances [Ann Morris] Hall.[7] Consent undated by R.H. Packett, wit. B. Hall. G.H. Northam. 15 MAY 1884 at Jerusalem Baptist Church. [C10, R:354, R1:62]

Packett, William Harford, Jr., to Louemma Clarke.[8] WILLIAM H. PACKETT, JR.,[9] farmer, age 24, single, b. Richmond Co., s/o John and Maria [Courtney] Packett, to LOUEMMA CLARKE, age 18, single, b. Richmond Co., d/o John [Henry] and Lucy [Lucinda Jane Bryant] Clarke.[10] G.H. Northam. 11 MAR 1873. [C6, R:235, R1:33]

Page, Chapman (Col.) to Virginia Thompson (Col.). CHAPMAN PAGE, farmer, age 39, single, b. Richmond Co., s/o Thomas and Winny Page, to VIRGINIA THOMPSON, age 21, single, b. Richmond Co., d/o Daniel and Hannah Thompson. Thomas G. Thomas. 6 JAN 1870 at Daniel Thompson's. [C5, R:233, R1:27]

Page, Chapman (Col.) to Sally Jane Scott (Col.). CHAPMAN PAGE, mechanic, age 49, widowed, b. Richmond Co., s/o Thomas and Winnie Page, to SALLY JANE SCOTT, age 40, single, b. Richmond Co., [names of parents blank]. Thomas G. Thomas. 9 JAN 1876 at the house of Edward Parker. [C7, R:304, R1:39]

Page, William Emerson (Col.) to Lucy Ellen Roy (Col.). WILLIAM EMERSON PAGE, oystering, age 22y2m3d, single, b. Richmond Co., s/o Thomas B. and Sally F. Page, to LUCY ELLEN ROY, age 22y1m11d, single, b. Richmond Co., d/o Lee Roy and Mary Ann Roy (dec'd.). Consent 21

---

[1] John Henry Packett (b. 7 OCT 1863, d. 7 APR 1924) and Ida Augusta Fones (1866-1925) are bur. in the Packett-Delano Family Burial Ground, near Warsaw, Va.
[2] James L. Packett and Virginia Parr were married 28 OCT 1852 in Richmond Co. by Rev. Elijah L. Williams.
[3] John Scrimger Packett (b. 1 JUN 1849, d. 3 APR 1927) and his wife Virginia A. Parr (b. 16 AUG 1855, d. 7 MAR 1929 in Warsaw, Va.) are bur. in Warsaw Baptist Church cemetery.
[4] John Packett and Maria Courtney were married 4 FEB 1841 in Richmond Co. by Rev. William N. Ward.
[5] James Parr and Ann Packett, d/o Henry and Anne Packett, were married by license 1 JUN 1853 in Richmond Co.
[6] Richard Hugh Packett (b. 15 AUG 1860, d. 29 APR 1947) and his wife Joanna Hall (b. 28 JUL 1864, d. 9 SEP 1933) are bur. in the Packett-Delano Family Burial Ground, near Warsaw, Va.
[7] Bladen Hall and Frances Morris were married 8 FEB 1849 in Richmond Co. by Rev. John Pullen.
[8] Louemma Clarke Packett (b. 11 OCT 1855, d. 14 JUN 1885) is bur. in the Packett-Delano Family Burial Ground near Warsaw, Va.
[9] Surname also appears as Packet.
[10] John H. Clarke and Lucy Bryant were married by bond 24 FEB 1835 in Richmond Co.

MAR 1883 from Ivanhoe, Va. by bride Lucy E. [her X mark] Roy, and father Lee Roy, wit. J.A. [his X mark] Page. Rev. W. Carter. 22 MAR 1883 at the church. [C10, R:355, R1:58]

Palmer, Atwell (Col.) to Willie Ann Newton (Col.). ATWELL PALMER, farming, age 50, widowed, b. Richmond Co., s/o Samuel and Hannah Palmer, to WILLIE ANN NEWTON, age 26, single, b. Richmond Co., d/o Isaac and Polly Newton. Edmond Rich. 21 DEC 1881 at the res. of the minster. [C9, R:337, R1:54]

Palmer, Edward (Col.) to Rebecca Woody (Col.). EDWARD PALMER, oystering, age 23, single, b. Essex Co., s/o William and Nellie Palmer, to REBECCA WOODY, age 20, single, b. Essex Co., d/o Robert and Winnie Woody. Rev. John Wilkerson. 18 MAR 1886 at *River Dail.* [C11, R:315, R1:67]

Palmer, Henry (Col.) to Catherine Martin (Col.). HENRY PALMER, farmer, age 24, single, b. Richmond Co., s/o Peter and Lila Palmer, to CATHERINE MARTIN, age 19, single, b. Richmond Co., d/o Henry and Nancy Martin. George Laws. 26 NOV 1868 at Henry Martin's. [C5, R:254, R1:24]

Palmer, Henry (Col.) to Matilda Ann Dunaway (Col.). HENRY PALMER, farming, age 39, widowed, b. Richmond Co., s/o Henry and Felicia Palmer, to MATILDA ANN DUNAWAY, age 15, single, b. Richmond Co., d/o William H. and Eliza Ann Dunaway. Consent 10 DEC 1888 from Farnham, Va. by bride. Rev. Jacob Robinson. 13 DEC 1888 at William Dunaway's house. [C12, R:317, R1:73]

Parker, Peyton, of Greenlaw's Wharf, King George Co., to Bettie H. Snyder. PEYTON[1] PARKER, merchant, age 33, widowed, b. Essex Co., res. King George Co., s/o William H. and Frances [F. Parker] Parker,[2] to BETTIE H. SNYDER, age 19, single, b. Richmond City, Va., d/o Henry J. and A.G. Snyder. Consent 30 APR 1884 by father H.J. Snyder; consent by bride. R.N. Reamy. 18 MAY 1884. [C10, R:354, R1:62]

Parker, Thomas (Col.) to Polly Henry (Col.). THOMAS PARKER, oystering, age 29, single, b. Richmond Co., s/o Scott Parker and Maria Clayton, to POLLY HENRY, age 30, single, b. Caroline Co., d/o Edmond and Millie Henry. Charles Sparks. 23 JAN 1884 at Ebenezer Baptist Church. [C10, R:353, R1:61]

Parr, James P. to Mrs. Frances A. Pew Smither. JAMES P. PARR, farmer, age 32, widowed, b. Spotsylvania Co., s/o Henry and Harriet Parr, to FRANCES A. SMITHER, age 30, widow, b. Richmond Co., d/o Martin [Lewis] and Nancy [Habron] Pew.[3] Consent 21 SEP 1861 by bride Frances A. [her X mark] Smither, wit. Henry Newman. E.L. Williams. 22 SEP 1861 at the brick house. [C3, R:123, R1:11]

Parsons, Lewis N. to Alva C. Efford. LEWIS N. PARSONS, carpenter, age 26, single, b. Baltimore Co., Md., s/o Stephen P. and Annie E. Parsons,[4] to ALVA E. EFFORD, age 25, single, b. Richmond Co., d/o George W. [Jr.] and Julia Ann [Harrison] Efford, *q.v.* Consent 16 APR 1888

---

[1] Given name also found as Payton.
[2] William H. Parker and Frances F. Parker were married 14 OCT 1853 in Essex Co. by Rev. John Bird.
[3] Martin Pew and Nancy Habron were married by bond 26 FEB 1824 in Richmond Co. by Rev. Charles Bell.
[4] Stephen P. Parsons (1832-1898) and wife Annie E. (1836-1911) are bur. in Farnham Baptist Church cemetery.

from Ivanhoe, Va. by bride, wit. Julie A. [her X mark] Efford. Robert Williamson. 17 APR 1888 near Ivanhoe, Va. [C11, R:315, R1:72]

Patterson, Joseph Warner to Mary S. Davis. JOSEPH W. PATTERSON, farmer, age 24, single, b. Richmond Co., s/o Richard and Sarah Clark [sic], to MARY S. DAVIS, age 25, single, b. Richmond Co., d/o Richard and Sarah Davis. Robert Williamson, M.G. 2 JAN 1868 at *Wakefield*. [C4, R:253, R1:23]

Patterson, Joseph Warner[1] to Clementine F. Hale. JOSEPH W. PATTERSON, farming, age 37, widowed, b. Richmond Co., s/o Richard and Sarah Patterson, to CLEMENTINE F. HALE, age 25, single, b. Richmond Co., d/o James S. and Elizabeth Hale. Consent 31 OCT 1878 by bride Clementine [her X mark] F. Hale, wit. Robert J. Lumkin. G.H. Northam. 3 NOV 1878. [C8, R:312, R1:45]

Paul, William James to Miranda Dameron. WILLIAM JAMES PAUL, farmer, age 28, single, b. Dorchester Co., Md., s/o Robert and Elizabeth Paul, to MIRANDA DAMERON, age 22, single, b. Richmond Co., d/o Charles [Y.] and Lucy [Douglas] Dameron. Consent 2 JUL 1866 by bride, daughter of Charles Dameron, wit. E.D. Booker. Barth. Dodson, Parson. 3 JUL 1866 at res. of Charles Dameron. [C4]

Payton, William H. to Frances R. Saunders. WILLIAM H. SAUNDERS, farmer, age 22, single, b. Richmond Co., s/o John A. and Elizabeth [Morris] Payton,[2] to FRANCES R. SAUNDERS, age 21, single, b. Richmond Co., d/o Edward S. and Maria [Belfield] Saunders. G.H. Northam. 7 FEB 1867. [C4, R:285, R1:20]

Pearse, Thornton W., to Martha C. Wan. Consent 19 DEC 1854 by parties, wit. Wm. P. Middleton, Eliza C. Wan. No license or minister return. [C1]

Pearson, Arthur C. to Fannie G. Lyell. ARTHUR C. PEARSON, merchant, age 33, single, b. Richmond Co., s/o Lawson T. [Sr.] and Alice M. [Saunders] Pearson,[3] to FANNIE G. LYELL, age 23, single, b. Richmond Co., d/o Edwin and Martha [E. Jeffries] Lyell, *q.v.* Consent 11 OCT 1886 by bride, wit. Edwin Lyell. M.S. Colonna. 12 OCT 1886 at Calvary Church. [C11, R:316, R1:68]

Pearson, John T. to Georgeanna Boswell. JOHN T. PEARSON, millwright, age 44, widowed, b. Maryland, s/o Allen and Phoebe Pearson, to GEORGEANNA BOSWELL, age 25, single, b. Richmond Co., d/o John T. and Sarah N. [Northen] Boswell.[4] G.H. Northam. 17 JAN 1882 at Mr. Boswell's. [C9, R:312, R1:55]

Pearson, Lawson T., Jr., to Louisa J. Oldham.[5] LAWSON T. PEARSON, JR., farmer, age 29, single, b. Richmond Co., s/o [Capt.] Lawson T. [Sr.] and Alice M. [Saunders] Pearson, to LOUISA J. OLDHAM, age 29, single, b. Richmond Co., d/o William C. and Virginia [Ficklin]

---

[1] Joseph W. Patterson, merchant, served in Co. E, 40th Reg., Va. Inf., C.S.A. and d. 1919 in Lancaster Co., age 77.
[2] John A. Payton and Elizabeth Morris were married by bond 11 NOV 1828 in Richmond Co.
[3] Capt. Lawson T. Pearson and Alice M. Saunders were married by bond 26 NOV 1842 in Richmond Co.
[4] John H. Boswell (b. 22 OCT 1832, d. 14 JAN 1898, 9th Va. Cav., C.S.A.) and his wife Sarah Northen (b. 8 OCT 1836, d. 19 MAY 1913) are bur. in the Boswell Family Cemetery on Route 614.
[5] Lawson T. Pearson and wife Lou Oldham (1845-1923) are bur. at Jerusalem Baptist Church cemetery.

Oldham.[1] Consent 24 MAY 1875 by bride, wit. L.A. Weaver. G.H. Northam. 26 MAY 1875. [C7, R:262, R1:38]

Pearson, William L. to Bettie Oldham.[2] WILLIAM L. PEARSON, farmer, age 26, single, b. Richmond Co., s/o Lawson T. [Sr.] and Alice M. [Saunders] Pearson, to BETTIE OLDHAM, age 24, single, b. Richmond Co., d/o William C. and Virginia [Ficklin] Oldham.[3] Consent 5 OCT 1878 by bride, wit. Thomas N. Oldham. G.H. Northam. 8 OCT 1878. [C8, R:311, R1:45]

Peed, Miskel S. [b. 23 MAY 1857] to Martha E. Bispham. MISKEL S. PEED, age 20y7m, single, b. and res. Westmoreland Co., s/o John [P.] and Catharine R. [Saunders] Peed,[4] to MARTHA E. BISPHAM, age 17, single, b. Richmond Co., d/o Robert Bispham and Jane Bispham now Hinson. Consent by mother Catharine R. Peed, wit. James E. Thomas. R.N. Reamy. 27 DEC 1877 at M. Hinson's. [C8, R:308, R1:43]

Peed, Richard Carter[5] to Cornelia Arabelle J. Sanders. RICHARD C. PEED, farmer, age 24, single, b. and res. Westmoreland Co., s/o John P. and Catharine [R. Saunders] Peed, to CORNELIA A.J. SANDERS, age 15, single, b. Richmond Co., d/o James A.B. and Susan [Sanders] Sanders. Consent 18 SEP 1876 by James A.B. Sanders, wit. G.H. Mothershead. H.H. Fones. 20 SEP 1876. [C7, R:305, R1:41]

Peed, Richard Carter to Anne Mae Jett.[6] RICHARD C. PEED, farming, age 35, widowed, b. Westmoreland Co., s/o Richard C. Peed, to ANNIE M. JETT [sic], age 17, single, b. Richmond Co., d/o James H. and Elizabeth [A. Oliff] Jett, *q.v.* Consent 29 JAN 1890 by father James H. Jett, wit. Hamilton E. Balderson. H.H. Fones. 26 JAN 1890. [C12, R:323, R1:76]

Peterson, Emanuel (Col.) to Fanny Johnson (Col.). EMANUEL PETERSON, laborer, age 22, single, b. Richmond Co., s/o Armistead and Lucy Peterson, to FANNY JOHNSON, age 21, single, b. Richmond Co., d/o Peter and Peggy Johnson. Thomas G. Thomas. 29 SEP 1866 at the res. of J.B. Lowry. [C4, R:272, R1:18]

Peterson, John (Col.) to Louisa Sorrell (Col.). JOHN PETERSON, farmer, age 23, single, b. Lancaster Co., s/o Henry and Jane Peterson, to LOUISA SORRELL, age 22, single, b. Richmond Co., d/o Davy and Ellen Sorrell. Travis Corbin, M.G. 11 APR 1868. [C4, R:253, R1:23]

Pew, James to Mary Frances Marshall. JAMES PEW, farmer, age 25, single, b. Richmond Co., s/o Martin [Lewis] and Nancy [Habron] Pew, to MARY FRANCES MARSHALL, age 19, single, b. Albemarle Co., d/o George Marshall and Jane T. Seymore. Consent 11 MAR 1869 by mother Jane T. Seymore. Robert Williamson, M.G. 24 MAR 1869 at Mr. R. Hammack's. [C5, R, R1:25]

---

[1] William C. Oldham and Virginia Ficklin were married by bonnd 8 AUG 1843 in Richmond Co. by Rev. Nathan Healy.
[2] William L. Pearson (b. 18 JAN 1852, d. 8 DEC 1883) and his wife Elcybeth Oldham (b. 20 NOV 1852, d. 10 DEC 1881) are bur. in Jerusalem Baptist Church cemetery.
[3] William C. Oldham and Virginia Ficklin were married by bonnd 8 AUG 1843 in Richmond Co. by Rev. Nathan Healy.
[4] John Peed and Catharine R. Saunders were married by bond 6 MAR 1848 in Richmond Co.
[5] Richard C. Peed (b. 5 FEB 1852, d. 7 JAN 1921 in Foneswood, Va.) is bur. Rappahannock Baptist Church cemetery.
[6] Richard C. Peed (b. 5 FEB 1852, d. 7 JAN 1921) and his second wife Anne Mae Jett (b. 1872, d. 24 SEP 1952) are bur. at Foneswood, Va.

Pew, Martin Lewis[1] to Maria E. Hammack. MARTIN L. PEW, farmer, age 22, single, b. Richmond Co., s/o Martin [Lewis] and Nancy [Habron] Pew, to MARIA E. HAMMACK, age 18, single, b. Richmond Co., d/o Benedict and Ellen [B. Polk] Hammack.[2] Consent 26 DEC 1860 by father Benedict Hammack, wit. Barnes B. Mozingo. E.L. Williams. 27 DEC 1860. [C2, R:154, R1:9]

Pew, William Samuel to Elizabeth Alice Wright.[3] WILLIAM S. PEW,[4] farmer, age 30, single, b. Richmond Co., s/o Martin [Lewis] and Nancy [Habron] Pew, to ELIZABETH A. WRIGHT, age 16, single, b. Richmond Co., d/o John M. and Elizabeth [T. Dudley] Wright. Consent 20 DEC 1872 by Andrew Wright, guardian, no wit. G.H. Northam. 24 DEC 1872. [C6, R:238, R1:33]

Phillips, Baylor (Col.) to Matilda Ann Johnson (Col.). BAYLOR PHILLIPS, oystering, age 44, widowed, b. Richmond Co., s/o Hannah Phillips, to MATILDA ANN JOHNSON, age 28, single, b. Richmond Co., d/o William and Delia Johnson. Rev. W. Carter. 19 MAR 1885 at the res. of the bride. [C11, R:316, R1:64]

Phillips, Charles (Col.) to Adelaide Yerby (Col.). CHARLES PHILLIPS, farmer, age 24, single, b. Richmond Co., s/o John and Sallie Phillips, to ADELAIDE YERBY, age 18, single, b. Richmond Co., d/o Shedrick and Nancy Yerby. Travis Corbin. 7 JAN 1868 at *Moratico Hall*. [C4, R:253, R1:23]

Phillips, Charles (Col.) to Mrs. Virginia Veney (Col.). CHARLES PHILLIPS, oystering, age 43, widowed, b. Richmond Co., s/o Jack and Sallie Phillips, to VIRGINIA VENEY, age 23, widow, b. Richmond Co., d/o George and Martha Ann Veney. Rev. W. Carter. 13 MAY 1888 at the bride's home. [C11, R:316, R1:72]

Phillips, Edward W. to Mary J. Northen. EDWARD W. PHILLIPS, teacher, age 28, single, b. Smith Co., Tenn., res. Goochland Co., s/o Bernard and Sarah Phillips, to MARY J. NORTHEN, age 21, single, b. Richmond Co., d/o William S. and Sarah [A. Davis] Northen.[5] Andrew Fisher, of Episcopal Church. 20 DEC 1860. [C2, R:154, R1:9]

Phillips, Eugene S. to Mary Elizabeth Grey. EUGENE S. PHILLIPS, merchant, age 33, single, b. Richmond Co., s/o John W. and [Mrs.] Maria L. [Louisa Headley Fogg] Phillips,[6] to MARY ELIZABETH GREY, age 18, single, b. King George Co., d/o P.P. and Caroline Virginia Gray [sic]. Beverley D. Tucker. 28 JUL 1880 at the house of the bride's father. [C9, R:316, R1:51]

Phillips, James Wilton to Maria Susan Jeffries.[7] JAMES WILTON PHILLIPS, farmer, age 23, single, b. and res. Essex Co., s/o George W. and Susan E. [Clarkson] Phillips,[8] to MARIA SUSAN

---

[1] Martin L. Pew (d. 5 MAY 1862 in Ashland, Va.) is bur. in an unmarked grave at Woodland Cemetery. He served in Co. K, 9th Va. Cav., C.S.A.
[2] Benedict Hammack and Ellen B. Polk were married by bond 23 DEC 1834 in Richmond Co.
[3] William S. Pugh (b. 1836, d. 15 MAR 1884) and wife Elizabeth Alice Wright (b. 7 APR 185[8], d. 14 FEB 1930) are bur. in Farnham Baptist Church cemetery.
[4] The surname also appears as Pugh.
[5] William S. Northen and Sarah A. Davis were married by bond 20 DEC 1832 in Richmond Co.
[6] John W. Phillips and Mrs. Maria L. Fogg were married 7 JUN 1842 in Richmond Co. by Rev. William N. Ward.
[7] James W. Phillips (b. 26 DEC 1844, d. 3 NOV 1916) and his wife Maria S. Jeffries (b. 6 JUN 1844, d. 4 JAN 1924) are bur. in Ephesus Baptist Church cemetery at Dunnsville, Essex Co., Va. He served in Co. F, 9th Va. Cav., C.S.A.
[8] George W. Phillips and Susan E. Clarkson were married 17 JAN 1842 in Essex Co.

JEFFRIES, age 24, single, b. Richmond Co., d/o John F.B.[1] and Matilda A.E. [Jeffries] Jeffries.[2] Andrew Fisher. 16 DEC 1868 at Warsaw, Va. [C5, R:254, R1:24]

Phillips, John (Col.) to Addie L. Lemoine (Col.). JOHN PHILLIPS, oysterman, age 28, single, b. Richmond Co., s/o John and Mary Phillips, to ADDIE L. LEMOINE, age 22, single, b. Richmond Co., d/o Edgar Lemoine and Hannah Jessup. Consent 5 FEB 1883 by bride, wit. J.F. Clayton; consent 5 FEB 1883 by John Phillips for his niece Addie. Charles Sparks. 7 FEB 1883. [C10, R:355, R1:58]

Phillips, Kirwan Plummer to Rosine Linwood Northam.[3] KIRWAN PLUMMER PHILLIPS, sailing, age 23, single, b. Richmond Co., s/o John W. and Maria L. [Louisa Headley Fogg] Phillips, to ROSINE LINWOOD NORTHAM, age 18, single, b. Westmoreland Co., d/o George H. [Henry] and Catherine A. [Saunders] Northam. Consent 22 MAY 1882 from *Glenmore* by G.H. Northam, wit. George R. Northam. Robert Williamson. 23 MAY 1882 at Jerusalem Baptist Church. [C9, R:313, R1:56]

Pierson, John W. to Themedore P. Phillips.[4] JOHN W. PIERSON, oyster planting, age 34, single, b. Newport, N.J., s/o Jonathan L. and Rhoda Pierson, to THEMEDORE PHILLIPS, age 28, single, b. Richmond Co., d/o John W. and Maria L. [Louisa Headley Fogg] Phillips. Robert Williamson. 22 AUG 1888 at Farnham Village. [C11, R:316, R1:73]

Pitts, William Dandridge, Capt., to Julia Kate Lyell.[5] WILLIAM D. PITTS, merchant, age 42, single, b. Essex Co., s/o [R.]L. [Reuben Lindsay] and Maria L. [Dobyns] Pitts,[6] to JULIA KATE LYELL, age 25, single, b. Richmond Co., d/o R.H. [Richard] and Elizabeth [T. Tapscott] Lyell.[7] Consent 22 NOV 1880 from Farnham Church by R.H. Lyell, wits. Willie R. Jeter, R.L. Reynolds. W.A. Crocker. 23 NOV 1880 at Calvary Church. [C9, NN:26 NOV 1880, R:316, R1:51]

Pitts, William H. to Emeline Carter. WILLIAM H. PITTS, farmer, age 27, single, b. Westmoreland Co., s/o William and Martha [Pitts] Pitts,[8] to EMELINE CARTER, age 28, single, b. Richmond Co., d/o Daniel and Sally Carter. Consent 18 OCT 1864 by bride, wits. E.A. Brewer, George A. Edmonds. John Pullen. 20 OCT 1864 at Daniel Carter's. [C3, R:139, R1:14]

Pitts, William Madison to Virginia Elizabeth Jackson.[9] WILLIAM M. PITTS, mechanic, age 24, single, b. and res. Lancaster Co., s/o Washington Pitts and Dorathea Ann Pitts now Miller, to VIRGINIA ELIZABETH JACKSON, age 23y4m21d, single, b. Richmond Co., d/o Daniel S. and Mildred Elizabeth [Sydnor] Jackson. G.H. Northam. 17 DEC 1885 at *Edge Hill*. [C11, NN:25 DEC 1885, R:318, R1:66]

---

[1] The Richmond Enquirer, 16 JUN 1848, noted "At a Court of Monthly Session, held for Richmond Co., at the Court House, on Mon., the 5th of June, 1848: ... Clerk, John F.B. Jeffries, Esq., who has for more than ten years discharged the duties of said office ..."
[2] John F.B. Jeffries and Matilda Jeffries were married by bond 17 DEC 1818 in Essex Co.
[3] Kirwan P. Phillips (b. 20 NOV 1858, d. 6 JAN 1914) and his wife Rosa Linwood Northam (b. 7 NOV 1865, d. 31 OCT 1905) are bur. in Jerusalem Baptist Church cemetery.
[4] John W. Pierson (1852-1923) and wife Themedore P. Phillips (1857-1910) are bur. in Jerusalem Baptist Church cemetery.
[5] William D. Pitts (b. 12 AUG 1837, d. 25 JUL 1894) and Julia Kate Lyell (b. 11 SEP 1853, d. 13 OCT 1889) are bur. in Calvary United Methodist Church cemetery. He served as second lieutenant and Captain in Co. B, 40th Va. Inf., C.S.A.
[6] Reuben L. Pitts, of Essex Co., and Maria L. Dobyns, were married by bond 7 DEC 1830 in Richmond Co.
[7] Richard H. Lyell and Elizabeth T. Tapscott were married by bond 5 OCT 1840 in Richmond Co.
[8] William Pitts and Martha Pitts were married by bond 14 DEC 1821 in Essex Co.
[9] William M. Pitts (b. 24 DEC 1860, d. 8 NOV 1908) and wife Virginia E. Jackson (b. 26 JUL 1860, d. 5 JUN 1928) are bur. at Totuskey Baptist Church cemetery.

Pollard, Edward Spotswood to Mary Beverley Douglas.[1] EDWARD S. POLLARD, farmer, age 32, single, b. and res. King William Co., s/o Robert and Evelyn B. [Byrd Chamberlayne] Pollard, to MARY DOUGLAS, age 20, single, b. New Kent Co., d/o Wm. R.C. and Lucy [Hankins] Douglas. Consent 30 NOV 1864 by father Wm. R.C. Douglas, notary J.J. White. Andrew Fisher. 15 DEC 1864 at *Edge Hill*. [C3, R:139, R1:14]

Pope, Joseph to Frances E. Miskill. JOSEPH POPE, taylor, age 26, single, b. Richmond Co., s/o Leroy and Hannah [Nash] Pope,[2] to FRANCES E. MISKILL, age 15, single, b. Richmond Co., d/o William H. and Frances [E. Downman] Miskill.[3] Consent 15 NOV 1854 by father [Wm.] Miskill, wit. Charles B[ar]rock. William H. Kirk. 23 NOV 1854 at Wm. H. Miskill's. [C1, R, R1:1]

Pope, Nathan M. to Josephine J. Belfield. NATHAN M. POPE, farmer, age 30, single, b. and res. Westmoreland Co., s/o Elliott and Elizabeth Pope,[4] to JOSEPHINE J. BELFIELD, age 20, single, b. Richmond Co., d/o John W. Belfield, Jr. and Mary E. [Payton] Belfield.[5] D.M. Wharton. 9 MAR 1876 at *Kelvin Grove*, the res. of her father. [C7, R:304, R1:40]

Pope, Samuel to Myrtle Morriss. SAMUEL POPE, sailing, age 23, single, place of birth and residence not given, [names of parents not given], to MYRTLE MORRISS, age 21, single, b. Richmond Co., d/o Fairfax and Virginia Morriss. G.M. Conley. 14 NOV 1889 near Reamy's. [C12, R:328, R1:75]

Porter, William Horace to Mary Ann Omohundro.[6] WILLIAM H. PORTER, soldier, age 35, single, b. and res. Westmoreland Co., s/o Samson and Catharine [Neasom] Porter,[7] to MARY A. OMOHUNDRO, age 23, single, b. Richmond Co., s/o Thomas [M.] and Sally Omohundro. Consent 27 AUG 1862 by bride. James S. Porter, M.G. 28 AUG 1862 at the res. of Thos. Omohundro. [C3, R:140, R1:12]

Potter, Charles Edward to Frances A. Sacra. CHARLES EDWARD POTTER, farmer, age 25, single, b. Richmond Co., s/o James and Catherine [S. Courtney] Potter,[8] to FRANCES A. SACRA, age 22, single, b. Richmond Co., d/o Charles C. and Mary [Harford] Sacra.[9] Consent by bride, no wit. James A. Weaver. 10 JAN 1870 at the res. of Jeremiah Courtney. [C5, R:233, R1:27]

Potter, Charles Edward to Mary Isabella Murren. CHARLES E. POTTER, farming, age 39, widowed, b. Richmond Co., s/o James and Catharine [S. Courtney] Potter,[10] to MARY ISABELLA MURREN, age 35, single, b. Richmond Co., d/o [William] Thompson and Mary

---

[1] Edward S. Pollard (b. 7 JUL 1832, d. 15 MAR 1909) and wife Mary B. Douglas (b. 11 OCT 1843, d. 30 MAY 1902) are bur. at *Mt. Zoar*, King William Co.
[2] Leroy Pope and Hannah Nash were married by bond 21 DEC 1824 in Richmond Co.
[3] William H. Miskell and Frances E. Downman were married by bond 23 MAR 1832 in Richmond Co.
[4] An Elliott Pope and Eliza Healy were married by bond 21 OCT 1834 in Middlesex Co.
[5] John W. Belfield, Jr. and Mary E. Payton were married by bond 13 AUG 1849 in Richmond Co.
[6] William H. Porter (1828-1901) and wife Mary A. Omohundro (b. 30 SEP 1836, d. 16 JAN 1872) are likely bur. in the Porter Family Cemetery near Lyells, Va. He served in Co. C, 9th Va. Cav., C.S.A.
[7] Samson Porter, of Westmoreland Co., and Catharine Neasom, were married by bond 23 MAR 1827 in Richmond Co.
[8] James Potter and Catharine S. Courtney were married 28 OCT 1841 in Richmond Co. by Rev. William N. Ward.
[9] Charles C. Sacra and Mary Harford were married by bond 1 SEP 1834 in Richmond Co.
[10] James Potter and Catharine S. Courtney were married 28 OCT 1841 in Richmond Co. by Rev. William N. Ward.

[McPherson] Murren.[1] Rev. Martin Johnson. 5 FEB 1884 at St. John's Chapel at 8 p.m. [C10, NN:8 FEB 1884, R:353, R1:61]

Potter, James to Mrs. Catharine Sanford. JAMES POTTER, boat and shoe maker, age 41, widower, b. Westmoreland Co., s/o James Potter and Mary, to CATHARINE SANFORD, age 31, widow, b. Richmond City, d/o William Thrif[t] and Sarah. Consent 11 OCT 1854 by bride, wits. William H. Sisson, James Gallagher. William N. Ward, M.G. 11 OCT 1854. [C1, R, R1:1]

Potter, James Meredith to Mary Catherine Pritchet. JAMES MEREDIDTH POTTER, farmer, age 40, single, b. Westmoreland Co., s/o William and Maria Potter, to MARY CATHERINE PRITCHET, age 27, single, b. Richmond Co., d/o Harry and Alsie Pritchet. Consent c.1 DEC 1873 by bride. Elder James A. Weaver. 3 DEC 1873 at the res. of William Lee. [C6, R:236, R1:35]

Potter, Richard Lewis to Sarah Louisa Courtney. RICHARD LEWIS POTTER, farming, age 35, single, b. Richmond Co., s/o James and Catharine [S. Courtney] Potter, to SARAH LOUIS COURTNEY, age 21y1m5d, single, b. Richmond Co., d/o Jeremiah and Mary Elizabeth [Pritchard] Courtney, *q.v.* Consent undated by bride S.L. [her X mark] Courtney, wit. Wm. H. [his X mark] Lee. Geo. M. Conley. 11 DEC 1888 at *Coal Hill*. [C12, R:317, R1:73]

Pound, Robert C. to Lenora Jackson Hinson.[2] ROBERT C. POUND, farming, age 27, single, b. and res. Westmoreland Co., s/o William [H.] and Martha [Green] Pound,[3] to LENORA J. HYNSON [sic], age 22, single, b. Richmond Co., d/o Reuben and Susan [Williams Hall] Hynson [Hinson], *q.v.* Consent by bride, wit. Thos. L. Callis. R.N. Reamy. 21 DEC 1887. [C11, R:293, R1:71]

Prescott, William to Delila Brown. WILLIAM PRESCOTT, farmer (at present soldier in the U.S. service), age 26, single, b. and res. Belknap Co., N.H., s/o William and Hannah Prescott, to DELILA BROWN, age 18, single, b. Richmond Co., d/o William and Mary Brown. William F. Bain. 14 SEP 1865 at Wm. Brown's. [C3, R:204, R1:15]

Price, Albert to Sophronia Isabella Rice.[4] ALBERT PRICE, farmer, age 23, single, b. Maryland, res. Lancaster Co., s/o George W. to Mary F. Price, to SOPHRONIA I. RICE, age 23, single, b. Richmond Co., d/o Peter W. and Judith [C. Pursell] Rice. Consent by bride 21 FEB 1876, wit. K.R. Cralle. A.B. Dunaway. 23 FEB 1876 at the house of Peter Rice. [C7, R:304, R1:40]

Pridham, John C.[5] to Martha A.E. George. JOHN C. PRIDHAM, farmer, age 21, single, b. Richmond Co., s/o William R. Pridham and wife Sarah [Morris],[6] to MARTHA A.E. GEORGE, age 15, single, b. Lancaster Co., Va., d/o William P. George and wife Lucy Ann [West].[7] Consent 6 JUN 1855 by father William P. George, wit. L.G. Bell. William N. Ward, M.G. 20 JUN 1855. [C1, R:153, R1:2]

---

[1] William T. Murren and Mary McPherson, ward of Benjamin Clark, of Fredericksburg, Va., were married 19 JAN 1826 by Rev. Henry Slicer.
[2] Robert C. Pound (b. 17 SEP 1859, d. 7 AUG 1938) and wife Lenora J. Hinson are bur. at Pope's Creek Baptist Church cemetery, as is his mother Martha Pound (b. 29 OCT 1833, d. MAY 1919).
[3] William H. Pound and Martha Green, d/o George Green, were married by bond 17 AUG 1849 in Richmond Co.
[4] Albert Price (b. 25 APR 1852, d. 28 JUN 1931) and his wife Sophronia Isabella Rice (b. 14 FEB 1853, d. 11 MAY 1878) are bur. at Farnham Baptist Church cemetery.
[5] John C. Pridham served in Co. D, 47th Reg., Va. Inf., C.S.A.
[6] William R. Pridham and Sally Morris were married by bond 11 FEB 1833 in Westmoreland Co.
[7] William P. George and Lucy A. West were married by bond 2 MAR 1837 in Lancaster Co.

Pritchett, George F. to Matilda A. Jeffries. GEORGE F. PRITCHETT, store clerk, age 29, widowed, b. Norfolk, Va., res. Baltimore, Md., s/o John and Helen Pritchett, to MATILDA A. JEFFRIES, age 28, single, b. Richmond Co., d/o John F.B. and Matilda A.E. [Jeffries] Jeffries. Anthony Fisher. 28 SEP 1858 at *The Glebe.* [C2, R:138, R1:6]

Pritchett, Thomas R. to Mary E. Sacra. THOMAS R. PRITCHETT, farmer, age 25, single, b. Westmoreland Co., s/o Henry and Alice [R. Sanford] Pritchett,[1] to MARY E. SACRA, age 23, single, b. Richmond Co., d/o Charles C. and Polly [Mary Harford] Sacra.[2] Consent 11 JAN 1859 by bride, wit. Austin N. Richards. No minister return. 12 JAN 1859 at Austin N. Richards'. [C2, R:165, R1:7]

Purcell, John Henry to Sarah Ann Lewis.[3] JOHN HENRY PURCELL, farmer, age 23, single, b. Richmond Co., s/o Samuel and Mary [E. McKenney] Purcell, to SARAH ANN LEWIS, age 17, single, b. Richmond Co., d/o John B. and Alice Lewis. Consent 1 MAR 1871 by father John B. [his X mark] Lewis, wit. Sarah A. Lewis. Barth. Dodson, parson. 3 MAR 1872. [C6, R:237, R1:31]

Purcell, William Northen to Lucy Lee Johnson.[4] WILLIAM N. PURCELL, farming, age 20y8m, single, b. and res. Westmoreland Co., s/o Stephen[5] and Julia [F.] Purcell, to LUCY L. JOHNSON, age 19, single, b. Westmoreland Co., d/o James W. [William] and Augusta L. [Barker] Johnson.[6] Consent 2 MAY 1884 by Stephen [his X mark] Purcell, wit. John F. Miller. R.N. Reamy. 4 MAY 1884. [C10, R:354, R1:62]

Pursell, William Henry to Mary C. Hudson. WILLIAM HENRY PURSELL, farmer, age 30, widowed, b. Westmoreland Co., res. Northumberland Co., s/o William P. and Polly Pursell, to MARY C. HUDSON, age 25, single, b. Westmoreland Co., d/o William R. Hudson. Consent 6 AUG 1862 by bride, wit. R. Dawson. James A. Weaver. 6 AUG 1862. [C3, R:140, R1:12]

R

Rains, William W.[7] to Sarah Jeter Biscoe. WILLIAM W. RAINS, farmer, age 19, single, b. Richmond Co., s/o Alfred J. and Elizabeth [Webb] Rains,[8] to SARAH J. BISCOE, age 15, single, b. Lancaster Co., d/o Henry L. and Sarah C. [Blakemore] Biscoe.[9] Consent 11 FEB 1859 by Th. Oldham, guardian of William, wits. R.H. Lyell, James M. Stiff. Robert Williamson, M.G. 13 FEB 1859. [C2, R:165, R1:7]

Randall, Philip (Col.) to Judy Ann Blackwell (Col.). PHILIP RANDALL, oysterman, age 23, single, b. Gloucester Co., s/o John and Fanny Randall, to JUDY ANN BLACKWELL, age 17, single,

---

[1] Henry Pritchet and Alice R. Sanford were married by bond 7 JAN 1825 in Westmoreland Co.
[2] Charles C. Sacra and Mary Harford were married by bond 1 SEP 1834 in Richmond Co. with consent by Martha Harford.
[3] John Henry Purcell (b. 21 JUN 1849, d. 24 FEB 1904 in Robley, Va.) and wife Sarah Ann Lewis (b. 17 SEP 1855, d. 9 NOV 1898 in Robley, Va.) are bur. in Farnham Baptist Church cemetery.
[4] William N. Purcell (b. 11 SEP 1863, d. 6 AUG 1941) and wife Lucy L. Johnson (b. 28 APR 1863, d. 8 APR 1935) are bur. at Oak Grove Cemetery.
[5] Stephen Purcell (1834-1908) is bur. in the Purcell Family Cemetery at *Chesterfield Farm* off of Route 640. He served in Co. C, 47th Va. Inf., C.S.A.
[6] The couple are thought to be bur. in the Johnson Family Cemetery near the intersection of Routes 3 and 204.
[7] Private William W. Rains, b. 1840, d. 1914 in Bowling Green, Caroline Co., Va., bur. Lakewood Cemetery there, served in Co. K, 9th Va. Cav., C.S.A.
[8] Alfred J. Rains and Elizabeth Webb were married by bond 12 JAN 1830 in Richmond Co.
[9] Henry L. Biscoe and Sarah C. Blakemore were married by bond 15 DEC 1834 in Westmoreland Co. Also, Harry L. Biscoe and Sarah C. Blakemore had a bond 16 DEC 1834 in Lancaster Co.

b. Richmond Co., d/o John Blackwell and Mary Sorril formerly Mary Blackwell. Consent by mother Mary [her X mark] Sorril, wit. Lucius Lewis. Peter Blackwell. 21 FEB 1878 at res. of Mary Sorril. [C8, R:310, R1:44]

Reamy, Alexander to Margaret "Maggie" P. Reamy.[1] ALEXANDER REAMY, farming, age 33, single, b. Westmoreland Co., res. King George Co., s/o Joseph J. [Jett] and Jane A. [Anmon] Reamy, to MAGGIE P. REAMY, age 22, single, b. Richmond Co., d/o Robert N. [Sr.] and Jane [Owens] Reamy. Consent 29 DEC 1884 by bride, wit. B.W. Oliff. H.H. Fones. 30 DEC 1884. [C10, R:356, R1:63]

Reamy, J.B. to Mary E. Dobyns. J.B. REAMY, sawyer, age 30, widowed, b. Richmond Co., s/o Robert N. Reamy [name of mother not given], to MARY E. DOBINS sic], age 22, single, b . Richmond Co., d/o Augustus [Dobyns] [name of mother not given]. Consent 28 JUL 1884 by bride Mary E. [her X mark] Dobins, wit. Robert H. Thrift. G.H. Northam. 29 JUL 1884. [C10, NN:8 AUG 1884, R:355, R1:62]

Reamy, James to Lucy A. Hart. JAMES REAMY, merchant's clerk, single, b. Richmond Co., s/o Samuel T. and Susan [C. Fones] Reamy, to LUCY A. HART, single, birthplace unknown, d/o (unknown) Fielding and Ann Eliza Hart. Consent 3 AUG 1855 by father Samuel T. Reamy and ward for Lucy A. Hart, wits. Theoderick N. Balderson, William J. Reamy. William A. Baynham, M.G. 14 AUG 1855. [C1, R:153, R1:2]

Reamy, John Brooks[2] to Martha Jane Bryant. J.B. REAMEY [sic], farmer, age 24, single, b. Richmond Co., s/o Robert G. and Maria [L. Carter] Reamy,[3] to MARTHA JANE BRYANT, age 23, single, b. Richmond Co., d/o Richard [D.] and Lucy [C. Elmore] Bryant. Consent 2 MAR 1874 by bride Martha [her X mark] Jane Bryant, wit. R.[G.] Scates. Elder James A. Weaver. 4 MAR 1874 at the res. of Richard Scates. [C7, R:230, R1:36]

Reamy, John Taliaferro[4] to Julia Purssell. JOHN T. REAMY, farmer, age 28, single, b. Richmond Co., res. Westmoreland Co., s/o Robert N. [Neale] and [Mary] Jane [Owens] Reamy, to JULIA PURSSELL, age 23, single, b. Richmond Co., d/o V.R. and Ann Purssell. Consent 20 JAN 1876 by bride, no wit. Robert N. Reamy. 20 JAN 1876 at V.R. Purssell's. [C7, R:304, R1:40]

Reamy, Richard Randell to Agnes Baynham Balderson.[5] RICHARD R. REAMY, farming, age 22, single, b. and res. Westmoreland Co., s/o Richard T. [Temple] and Frances A. [Ann Fones] Reamy, to AGNES B. BALDERSON, age 18, single, b. Richmond Co., d/o Charles H. [Hiram] and Virginia [J. Coates] Balderson, *q.v.* Consent 24 FEB 1885 by father Charles H. Balderson, wit. C.C. Balderson. H.H. Fones. 26 FEB 1885. [C10, R:316, R1:64]

Reamy, Robert N., Jr. to Alcinda Reamy. ROBERT N. REAMEY [sic], farmer, age 24, single, b. Richmond Co., res. King George Co., s/o Robert N. [Sr.] and Jane [Owens] Reamey,[6] to

---

[1] Alexander Reamy (1851-1918) and wife his first wife Margaret Reamy are bur. in Oakland Baptist Church cemetery, King George Co., Owens, Va.
[2] John B. Reamy, b. 8 OCT 1849, d. 1898 in Callao, Va., and his wife Martha was b. 1851, d. 1877.
[3] Robert G. Reamy and Maria L. Carter were married 27 DEC 1849 in Richmond Co. by Rev. John Pullen.
[4] John T. Reamy (b. 7 AUG 1847, d. 31 JAN 1923 in Richmond, Va.) is bur. in Hollywood Cemetery, Richmond, Va. He served in Co. C, 47th Va. Inf., C.S.A.
[5] Richard R. Reamy (b. 7 OCT 1862, d. 26 APR 1927) and wife Agnes B. Balderson (b. 15 AUG 1866, d. 27 DEC 1898) bur. in Rappahannock Baptist Church cemetery.
[6] Robert Reamy and Jane Owens were married in JUL 1837 in King George Co.

ALCINDA REAMEY, age 22, single, b. Richmond Co., d/o James O. and [Mary] Jane [Morris] Reamey.[1] Consent 1 DEC 1873 by bride, no wit. G.W. Beale, minister. 4 [DEC[2]] 1873 at Mrs. Jane Reamey's. [C6, R:236, R1:34]

Reamy, William J.[3] to Jane E. Morriss. WILLIAM J. REAMEY [sic], mechanic, age about 23, single, b. Westmoreland Co., s/o Samuel T. Reamey and wife Susan [C. Fones],[4] to JANE E. MORRISS, age about 18, single, b. Richmond Co., d/o James M. Morriss and wife Amelia A.D. [Newman].[5] John Pullen, M.G. 3 MAR 1856 at *Cherry Hill*. [C1, R, R1:3]

Reamy, William Taylor[6] to Catharine N. Morris. WILLIAM T. REAMY, farming, age 31, single, b. Richmond Co., s/o William J. and Jane E. [Morriss] Reamy, *q.v.*, to CATHARINE N. MORRISS [sic], age 17, single, b. Richmond Co., d/o Oscar P. and Annie Maria [Saunders] Morris, *q.v.* H.H. Fones. 21 MAR 1888. [C11, R:315, R1:72]

Reed, Edwin to Virginia Sanders. EDWIN REED, mechanic, age 23y4m22d, single, b. and res. Westmoreland Co., s/o Lewis and Betsey Reed, to VIRGINIA SANDERS, age 22, single, b. Richmond Co., d/o Vincent and Mary Sanders. Consent 22 SEP 1874 by bride, wit. E.H. Coats. Robert N. Reamy. 24 SEP 1874 at M. Coats'. [C7, R:230, R1:37]

Reed, James (Col.) to Alice Taylor (Col.). JAMES REED, oystering, age 28, single, b. Richmond Co., s/o Nelson Reed and Charlotte Reed now Veney, to ALICE TAYLOR, age 18, single, b. Richmond Co., d/o Shadrack Taylor and Lettie Taylor now Conley. Consent 14 MAR 1884 by mother Lettie Connley, wit. George Veney. Rev. W. Carter. 16 MAR 1884 at the home of the bride. [C10, R:354, R1:61]

Reed, James A. (Col.) to Lou Emma Blackwell (Col.). JAMES A. REED, farmer, age 34, widowed, b. Richmond Co., s/o Nelson and Charlotte Reed, to LOU EMMA BLACKWELL, age 23, single, b. Richmond Co., d/o Jerry and Margaret Blackwell. Handwritten license. Rev. W. Carter. 7 APR 1890 at the bride's home. [C12, R:323a, R1:76]

Reed, James B.[7] to Lucy J. Mothershead. JAMES B. REED, farmer, age 25, single, b. and res. Westmoreland Co., s/o Joseph B. and Elizabeth Reed, to LUCY J. MOTHERSHEAD, age 17, single, b. Richmond Co., d/o Richard H. and Frances S. [McKenney] Mothershead.[8] G.H. Northam. 29 MAR 1866. [C4, R:271, R1:17]

Reynolds, Charles Edward to Mrs. Alice Finnick. CHARLES EDWARD REYNOLDS, farming, age 34, widowed, b. Richmond Co., s/o Edward J. [sic] and Mary [Mozingo] Reynolds,[9] to ALICE FINNICK, age 25, widow, b. Richmond Co., d/o John [Thomas] and Rachel [Clark] Waterfield, *q.v.* Consent by parties Charles [his X mark] Reynolds, and Mrs. Alice [her X mark] Fenwick [sic], wit. Frederick R. Austin. W.H. Gregory. 21 JUL 1884. [C10, R:355, R1:62]

---

[1] James O. Reamy and Mary Jane Morris were married by bond 14 SEP 1843 in Richmond Co.
[2] The minister return gives 4 NOV 1873, but this is an apparent error since the license was issued 1 DEC 1873.
[3] William J. Reamy served in Co. K, 9th Va. Cav., C.S.A., was wounded at Chancellorsville.
[4] Samuel T. Reamy, s/o Beriman Reamy, and Susan C. Fones, were married by bond 25 APR 1832 in Westmoreland Co.
[5] James M. Morris and Parmela Newman were married by bond 11 OCT 1834 in Richmond Co.
[6] William T. Reamy (b. 29 JAN 1857, d. 26 JAN 1935) is bur. at Rappahannock Baptist Church cemetery.
[7] James B. Reed (1841-1910) is bur. at Nomini Baptist Church, Templeman's, Va. He served in Co. A, 15th Va. Cav., C.S.A., occupation as carpenter, resided in 1906 in Templeman's, Va.
[8] Richard H. Mothershead and Frances S. McKenney were married 1 JAN 1846 in Richmond Co. by Rev. John Pullen.
[9] Edwin J. Reynolds and Mary Mozingo were married 29 DEC 1842 in Richmond Co. by Rev. William N. Ward.

Reynolds, John B. to Mary S. Scates. JOHN B. REYNOLDS, farmer, age 22, single, b. Richmond Co., s/o John J. and Jane P. [Reynolds] Reynolds,[1] to MARY S. SCATES, age 21, single, b. Richmond Co., d/o Thos. and Susan [Sanders] Scates. Consent 24 AUG 1869 by bride Mary S. [her X mark] Scates, wit. T.N. Balderson. H.H. Fones. 26 AUG 1869 at Mrs. Susan Scates'. [C5, R, R1:26]

Reynolds, John James to Rebecca Bell Hall. JOHN JAMES REYNOLDS, mechanic, age 26, single, b. and res. Westmoreland Co., s/o Edward and Mary Ann Reynolds, to REBECCA BELL HALL, age 17, single, b. Richmond Co., d/o William J. and Mary Jane [Conley] Hall, *q.v.* G.M. Conley. 6 NOV 1889 near Lyells, Va. [C12, R:328, R1:75]

Reynolds, John W. to Louisa W. Reynolds. JOHN W. REYNOLDS, farmer, age 23y5m, single, b. Richmond Co., s/o William and Hannah [Wilcox] Reynolds,[2] to LOUISA W. REYNOLDS, age 23y10m, single, b. Richmond Co., d/o William and [Lucetta W. McKenney] Reynolds. Consent 14 JUN 1872 by bride Liouzer [her X mark] Reynolds, wit. G. Talbert. Elder James A. Weaver. 15 JUN 1872 at the res. of the bridegroom. [C6, R:237, R1:32]

Reynolds, Richard T. to Hannah Elizabeth Reynolds. RICHARD T. REYNOLDS, farmer, age 29, single, b. Richmond Co., s/o William H. and Laura Ann Reynolds, to HANNAH ELIZABETH REYNOLDS, age 29, single, b. Richmond Co., d/o William and Hannah [Wilcox] Reynolds. G.H. Northam. 15 APR 1880. [C9, R:315, R1:52]

Reynolds, Robert L. to Mary Saunders. ROBERT L. REYNOLDS, farmer, age 24, single, b. Richmond Co., s/o William [H.] and Laura [Ann] Reynolds, to MARY SAUNDERS, age 21, single, b. Richmond Co., d/o James and Elizabeth Saunders. Consent by bride, wit. A.N. [his X mark] Richards. G.H. Northam. 1 DEC 1870. [C5, R:234, R1:28]

Reynolds, Robert L. and Thebedo Packett. ROBERT REYNOLDS, farmer, age 33, widowed, b. Westmoreland Co., s/o William [H.] and Laura [Ann] Reynolds, to THEBEDO PACKETT, age 21, single, b. Richmond Co., d/o Henry and Susan [F. Drake] Packett. G.H. Northam. 20 FEB 1879. [C8, R:307, R1:46]

Reynolds, Robert Lunsford[3] to Narcissa Elizabeth Taylor, b. 11 OCT 1850. ROBERT L. REYNOLDS, trader, age 33, single, b. Caroline Co., d/o McKenzie and Martha Reynolds, to NARCISSA E. TAYLOR, age 28, single, b. Northumberland Co., d/o Joseph H. and Frances [H. Street] Taylor.[4] Consent 14 DEC 1874 by bride, wit. Willie B. Scott. A.B. Dunaway. 22 DEC 1874 at the house of K.R. Cralle. [C7, R:231, R1:38]

Reynolds, Thomas N.[5] to Saluda F. Hudson. Consent 31 OCT 1854 by bride, wit. S.E. Tune. No license or minister return. [C1]

---

[1] John J. Reynolds and Jane P. Reynolds were married by bond 2 FEB 1843 in Richmond Co. by Rev. Nathan Healy.
[2] William Reynolds and Hannah Wilcox were married by bond 20 MAY 1841 in Richmond Co.
[3] Library of Virginia, Bible Records, Reynolds Family Bible Record, 1813-1927, "Robert Lunsford Reynolds died at 1407 West Lexington St., Baltimore, Md., of pneumonia, April 15, 1901 in his 57th year, was taken to Va. for interment." He and his wife Narcissa E. Taylor (b. 11 OCT 1850, d. 30 NOV 1929) are bur. in Farnham Baptist Church cemetery.
[4] Joseph H. Taylor and Frances H. Street, d/o Elizabeth Street, were married by bond 17 JUL 1841 in Richmond Co.
[5] Son of Vincent Reynolds and Elizabeth Alloway who were married by bond 28 DEC 1803 in Richmond Co.

Reynolds, William A. to Eley Pritchett. WILLIAM A. REYNOLDS, farming, age 29, single, b. Richmond Co., s/o William [H.] and Laura [Ann] Reynolds, to ELEY PRITCHETT, age 19, single, b. Richmond Co., d/o Thomas Pritchett and Mary Sacre his wife now Courtney. Consent by mother Mary Courtney. G.H. Northam. 25 SEP 1879. [C8, R:308, R1:47]

Rhoda, George to Frances Sydnor. GEORGE RHODA, farmer, age 28, single, b. Indiana, s/o George and Catharine Rhoda, to FRANCES SYDNOR, age 20, single, b. Richmond Co., d/o William B. and Ann [Hale] Sydnor. Elder James A. Weaver. 7 FEB 1867. [C4, R:285, R1:20]

Rice, John W. to Frances S. Winstead.[1] JOHN W. RICE, farmer, age 23, single, b. and res. Northumberland Co., s/o Isaac and Nancy W. [Dodson] Rice, to FRANCES WINSTEAD, age 15, single, b. Northumberland Co., d/o [Mottrom] and Polly [H. Dawson] Winstead.[2] Consent 8 APR 1868 by Polly H. Dodson and Frances Winstead, wit. Dandridge C. Winstead. Wm. H. Kirk. 14 APR 1868 at Bartholomew Dodson's. [C4, C5, R:253, R1:23]

Rice, John W. to Alphonesy Barrack.[3] JOHN W. RICE, farmer, age 28, single, b. Richmond Co., s/o Peter W. and Judith [C. Pursell] Rice, to ALPHONESY BARRACK, age 17, single, b. Richmond Co., d/o Charles and Margaret Barrack. Consent 10 FEB 1875 by bride, wit. K.R. Cralle; consent 13 FEB 1875 by father Charles [his X mark] Barrack, wit. Alfonso Barrack. A.B. Dunaway. 17 FEB 1875 at the house of Charles Barrack. [C7, R:262, R1:38]

Rice, Thomas J. to Annie M. Barrack.[4] THOMAS J. RICE, farmer, age 24, single, b. Lancaster Co., s/o Thomas and Nancy H. [Hazzard] Rice,[5] to ANNIE M. BARRACK, age 22, single, b. Lancaster Co., d/o Nuby and Elizabeth Barrack. William F. Bain. 6 FEB 1867 at house of Charles Barrack. [C4, R:285, R1:19]

Rice, William Hugh, Rev. to Hester Emma Douglas.[6] WILLIAM H. RICE, farming, age 21y1m, single, b. and res. Lancaster Co., s/o Thomas and Ann [Nancy C. Hazzard] Rice, to HESTER EMMA DOUGLAS, age 17, single, b. Lancaster Co., d/o Pharaoh and [Jerusha] Ann [Elmore] Douglas. Consent 18 DEC 1888 by bride and Mrs. Ann Douglas, wit. John A. [his X mark] Hazzard. Jas. T. Eubank. 23 DEC 1888 at Mrs. Pharoah Duglas [sic]. [C12, R:317, R1:73]

Rich, Daniel (Col.) to Mary Frances Johnson (Col.). DANIEL RICH, oysterman, age 26, single, b. Richmond Co., s/o William and Lucinda Rich, to MARY FRANCES JOHNSON, age 19, single, b. Richmond Co., d/o John and Teaney Johnson. Consent 3 AUG 1871 by Teaney [her X mark], wits. Dennis [his X mark] Jackson, and Wm. W. Ficklin. Rev. Chauncey Leonard. 5 AUG 1871 at *Westview*. [C6, R:245, R1:30]

Rich, David (Col.) to Julia Ann Veney (Col.). DAVID RICH, farming, age 31, single, b. Richmond Co., s/o [Beverly] and Mary [Luin] Rich, to JULIA ANN VENEY, age 22, single, b. Richmond

---

[1] John W. Rice (1844-1916) and his wife Frances S. Winstead (1853-1925) are bur. at Lebanon Baptist Church cemetery, Lancaster Co.

[2] Mottrom Winstead, widower, and Polly H. Dawson, were married by bond 30 DEC 1833 in Northumberland Co.

[3] John W. Rice (1846-1924) and wife Alphronesy Barrack (1857-1946) are bur. in Farnham Baptist Church cemetery.

[4] Thomas J. Rice (b. 3 NOV 1843, d. 7 APR 1911) and wife Annie M. Barrack (b. 22 APR 1844, d. 1 FEB 1926) are bur. in Lebanon Baptist Church cemetery, Lancaster Co.

[5] Thomas Rice and Nancy C. Hazzard were married by bond 6 MAR 1838 in Lancaster Co.

[6] Rev. William Hugh Rice (b. 17 NOV 1867, d. 7 DEC 1943) and his wife Hester Emma Douglas (b. 29 APR 1871, d. 4 FEB 1933 in Charlottesville, Va., d/o Pharaoh Douglas and Jerusha Ann Elmore) are bur. in Warsaw Baptist Church cemetery.

Co., d/o Lewis and Adeline Veney. Rev. John Wilkerson. 15 MAR 1888 at res. of Jefferson Veney, Farnham, Va. [C11, R:315, R1:72]

Rich, Edmond [FB] to Ann B. Newman [FB]. Consent 4 JAN 1854 by mother Jane Newman, wit. by Wm. H. Newman. No license or minister return. [C]

Rich, George (Col.) to Catharine Ann Griffin (Col.). GEORGE RICH, laborer, age 24, single, b. Richmond Co., s/o Henry and Sally Rich (dec'd.), to CATHARINE ANN GRIFFIN, age 25, single, b. Richmond Co., d/o John (dec'd.) and Sarah Griffin (dec'd.). Consent 20 DEC 1877 by bride. David Veney, pastor. 20 DEC 1877 at *Millwood.* [C8, R:308, R1:43]

Rich, George (Co.) to Sarah Bundy (Col.). GEORGE RICH, farmer, age 24, single, b. Richmond Co., s/o Lindsay and Eliza [Tate] Rich,[1] to SARAH BUNDY, age 18, single, b. Richmond Co., d/o Polly Bundy. Andrew Fisher states that parties are free persons of color. Consent 18 JAN 1859 by mother Polly Bundy, wits. Edmond [his X mark] Rich, E.R. Pullin. Andrew Fisher. 26 JAN 1859. [C2, R:165, R1:7]

Rich, James (Col.) to Maria Newton (Col.). JAMES RICH, oystering, age 31, single, b. Richmond Co., s/o Julia Ann Rich now Veney, to MARIA NEWTON, age 27, single, b. Richmond Co., d/o Charles and Emily Newton. N.A. Atkins. 7 NOV 1884 at *C[hest]nut Hall.*[2] [C10, R:355, R1:63]

Rich, John (Col.) to Mrs. Jane Rich (Col.). JOHN RICH, oystering and farming, age 54, widowed, b. Richmond Co., s/o Daniel Rich and Patsy Rich née Laws, to JANE RICH, age 45, widow, b. Northumberland Co., d/o Joseph and Sarah Bee. Consent 31 MAY 1886 by bride Jane [her X mark] Rich, wit. George [his X mark] Rich. Rev. W. Carter. [C11, R:316, R1:68]

Rich, John Melvin (Col.) to Eulis Bailey (Col.). JOHN MELVIN RICH, oysterman, abe 23, single, b. Richmond Co., s/o Beverly and Mary [Luin] Rich, to EULIS BAILEY, age 19, single, b. Richmond Co., d/o Eliza Bailey (father's name unknown). Consent 18 OCT 1882 by Leroy [his X mark] Bailey, wit. Charles L. Bell. G.H. Northam. 19 OCT 1882. [C9, R:313, R1:56]

Rich, Julius (Col.) to Alice Rich (Col.). JULIUS RICH, laborer, age 25, single, b. Richmond Co., s/o Henry and Catherine Rich, to ALICE RICH, age 18, single, b. Richmond Co., d/o Henry Rich, Sr. and Jane Rich. Consent 24 FEB 1880 by the groom's parents Henry [his X mark] Rich, and Jane [her X mark] Rich, wit. Warren [his X mark] Thompson. Walker Carter, minister. 26 FEB 1880 at the res. of the bride. [C9, R:314, R1:50]

Rich, Moses (Col.) to Mrs. Henrietta Corbin Clayton (Col.). MOSES RICH, laborer, age 24, single, b. Richmond Co., s/o Robert and Nancy Rich,[3] to HENRIETTA CLAYTON, age 25, widow, b. Richmond Co., d/o Samuel and Lucy Corbin. Allen Brown, minister. 2 JUN 1877 at the res. of the bride's mother. [C8 R:307, R1:43]

Rich, Philip (Col.) to Prissey A. Thompson (Col.). PHILIP RICH, farming, age 37, single, b. Richmond Co., s/o Lindsey and Phirlisbia Rich, to PRISSEY A. THOMPSON, age 18, single, b. Richmond Co., d/o Daniel and Hannah Thompson. Consent 10 DEC 1879 by bride's parents

---

[1] Linsey Rich and Eliza Tate were married by bond 1 MAY 1823 in Richmond Co.
[2] The original appears to read Calanut Hall.
[3] Robert Rich, Jr. and Nancy Rich were married by bond 23 DEC 1839 in Richmond Co.

Daniel [his X mark] Thompson, and wife Hannah [her X mark] Thompson. G.H. Northam. [C8, R:309, R1:48]

Rich, Robert (Col.) to Georgeanna Jackson (Col.). ROBERT RICH, mechanic, age 50, widowed, b. Richmond Co., s/o Winnie Rich, to GEORGEANNA JACKSON, age 30, widow, b. Westmoreland Co., d/o Armistead and Ellen Jackson. Thomas G. Thomas. 25 JUN 1876 at the house of Armistead Jackson. [C7, R:305, R1:40]

Rich, Samuel E. (Col.) to Edmonia Jackson (Col.). SAMUEL E. RICH, farmer, age 23, single, b. Richmond Co., s/o James and Catherine Rich, to EDMONIA JACKSON, age 21, single, b. Richmond Co., d/o Samuel and Martha Jackson. Davy Veney. 2 MAR 1878 at their residence. [C8, R1:44]

Rich, Simon P. (Col.) to Mary Jane Churchwell (Col.). SIMON P. RICH, age 35, single, b. Richmond Co., s/o Lindsey and Felicie Rich, to MARY AND CHURCHWELL, age 18, single, b. Richmond Co., d/o Samuel and Jane Churchwell. Consent in MAR 1881 by bride, wit. Samuel Churchwell. G.H. Northam. 31 MAR 1881. [C9, R:335, R1:52]

Rich, Thomas (Col.) to Martha Veney (Col.). THOMAS RICH, oysterman, age 25, single, b. Richmond Co., s/o Henry and Sally Rich, to MARTHA VENEY, age 20, single, b. Richmond Co., d/o Joseph and Fanny Veney. Consent 4 JAN 1872 by bride Martha [her X mark] Veney, wit. Jas. C. Bryant, oath by Henry Veney as to age of bride. Robert Williamson, M.G. 4 JAN 1872 at *Laurel Grove*. [C6, R:237, R1:31]

Rich, Warren (Col.) to Anna Christopher (Col.). WARREN RICH, laborer, age 26, single, b. Richmond Co., s/o Lee and Margaret Rich, to ANNA CHRISTOPHER, age 17, single, b. Lancaster Co., d/o Julia Christopher. Rev. W. Carter. 2 JAN 1890. Consent 1 JAN 1890 by bride Anna [her X mark] Christopher, wit. F. Little. [C12, R:323, R1:76]

Rich, William (Col.) to Sally Thompson (Col.). WILLIAM RICH, farmer, age 27, single, b. Richmond Co., s/o James and Kitty Rich, to SALLY THOMPSON, age 25, single, b. Richmond Co., d/o John and Betsey Thompson. David Veney. 10 SEP 1869 at Jordans. [C5, R, R1:26]

Rich, William E. (Col.) to Elenora Mayo (Col.). WILLIAM E. RICH, laborer, age 56, single, b. Richmond Co., s/o Lindsey and Eliza [Tate] Rich, to ELENORA MAYO, age 22, single, b. Richmond Co., d/o Charles Mayo and Pinkey Mayo now Braxton. Rev. T.G. Thomas. 4 MAY 1882 at the house of the minister. [C9, R:313, R1:56]

Rich, William Henry (Col.) to Hannah Landon (Col.). WILLIAM HENRY RICH, laborer, age 25, single, b. Richmond Co., s/o Henry and Peggy Rich, to HANNAH LANDON, age 21, single, b. Richmond Co., d/o Richard and Peggy Landon (dec'd). Thomas G. Thomas. 25 DEC 1877 at Clarksville [Baptist] Church. [C8, R:308, R1:43]

Rich, William Lawson (Col.) to Sylvia Williams (Col.). WILLIAM LAWSON RICH, farming, age 28, single, b. Richmond Co., s/o Beverley and Mary [Luin] Rich,[1] to SYLVIA WILLIAMS, age 22, single, b. Richmond Co., d/o Martin and Hannah Williams. Consent 23 JAN 1884 from

---

[1] Beverly Rich and Mary Luin were married by bond 29 JUN 1850 in Richmond Co.

Emmerton, Va. by bride, wit. William H. Veney. G.H. Northam. 24 JAN 1884 at the colored church. [C10, R:353, R1:61]

Richards, John P. to Eliza J. Peake. JOHN P. RICHARDS, farmer, age 30 on 21 JAN 1855, widower, b. Richmond Co., s/o Joab and Sally S. Richards, to ELIZA J. PEAKE, age 22, single, b. Westmoreland Co., d/o John H. and Lucy E. Peake. Consent 18 DEC 1854 by bride, wit. Wm. B. Mitchell. W.H. Coffin, M.G. 21 DEC 1854. [C1, R, R1:1]

Richardson, Elick [FB] to Gracy H. Weldon [FB]. ELICK RICHARDSON, wood cutter, age 22, single, b. Westmoreland Co., s/o Judy Richardson, [father not known], to GRACY H. WELDON, age 23, single, b. Richmond Co., d/o Sampson Weldon and wife Sally. Consent 21 MAR 1855 by Gracy H. [her X mark] Weldon, wit. George [his X mark] Thompson. License notes parties are people of color. William N. Ward, M.G. 21 MAR 1855 at Sampson Weldon's. [C1, R:153, R1:2]

Richardson, Hannibal (Col.) to Willie Ann Henderson (Col.). HANNIBAL RICHARDSON, farming, age 22, single, b. and res. Westmoreland Co., s/o Henry and Mary Richardson, to WILLIE ANN HENDERSON, age 20, single, b. Richmond Co., d/o Samuel and Amanda Henderson. Rev. [Robt.] Lewis. 26 JUL 1883 at the house of Samuel Henderson. [C10, R:357, R1:59]

Richardson, John Henry (Col.) to Melinda Lawrence (Col.). JOHN HENRY RICHARDSON, farming, age 21, single, b. Westmoreland Co., s/o John and Letta Richardson, to MELINDA LAWRENCE, age 21, single, b. Westmoreland Co., d/o Jack and Rose Lawrence. Consent 4 AUG 1886 by bride Melinda [her X mark] Lawrence, wit. Jno. Campbell. D.M. Wharton. 4 AUG 1886 at the res. of the minister in Westmoreland Co. [C11, R:316, R1:68]

Richardson, William (Col.) to Betty Street (Col.). WILLIAM RICHARDSON, laborer, age 26, single, b. Richmond Co., s/o John and Ara Richardson, to BETTY STREET, age 21, single, b. Essex Co., d/o William and Maria Street. George Laws. 17 FEB 1871 at Warsaw, Va. [C5, R:244, R1:29]

Roane, Alfred (Col.) to Anna Newton (Col.). ALFRED ROANE, farming, age 24, single, b. Lancaster Co., s/o Carter and Mary Ann Roane, to ANNA NEWTON, age 15y6m, single, b. Richmond Co., d/o Henry and Kitty Newton. Consent 20 APR 1881 by father Henry [his X mark] Newton, wit. Albert [his X mark] Smith. Peter Blackwell. 24 APR 1881 at Mount Zion Church. [C9, R:336, R1:53]

Roane, Henry (Col.) to Harriet Ann Lewis (Col.). HENRY ROANE, farming, age 27, single, b. Richmond Co., s/o Thomas and Lucy Roane, to HARRIET ANN LEWIS, age 18y3m26d, single, b. Richmond Co., d/o Benjamin Robert Lewis and Louisa Lewis now Glasgo. Nelson Atkins. 26 OCT 1881 at Ebenezer Baptist Church. [C9, license signed by parties; R:338, R1:54]

Roane, Nicholas (Col.) to Bettie Lee (Col.). NICHOLAS ROANE, laborer, age 29, divorced, b. Westmoreland Co., s/o John and Lucy Roane, to BETTIE LEE, age 28, single, b. Richmond Co., d/o Major Lee and Harriet Lee now Fitzhugh. Rev. Robert Lewis. 23 DEC 1880 at *Bryer's Hill*. [C9, R:317, R1:52]

Roane, Thomas Henry (Col.) to Mary Bettie Smith (Col.). THOMAS HENRY ROANE, oysterman and farmer, age 23, single, b. Richmond Co., s/o Henry Roane and Rosetta Carter, to MARY BETTIE SMITH, age 19, single, b. Richmond Co., d/o Albert and Eliza Ann Smith. Rev. W. Carter. 22 NOV 1882 at the church. [C9, R:313, R1:57]

Roane, Thomas Wesley (Col.) to Fanny Rich (Col.). THOMAS WESLEY ROANE, farming, age 25, single, b. and res. Westmoreland Co., s/o John and Lucy Roane, to FANNY RICH, age 30, single, b. Richmond Co., [names of parents not completed]. E.P. Parham, M.E. Church. 15 APR 1886 at the res. of the groom's mother in Westmoreland Co. [C11, R:315, R1:67]

Robb, Thomas (Col.) to Teaner Johnson (Col.). THOMAS ROBB, farmer, age 26, single, b. Richmond Co., s/o Spencer and Elizabeth Robb, to TEANER JOHNSON, age 25, single, b. Richmond Co., d/o Nancy Johnson. Consent 18 MAY 1872 by bride Teaner [her X mark] Johnson, wit. Fredrick [his X mark] Gray. George Laws. 18 MAY 1872 at *Grove Mount.* [C6, R:237, R1:31]

Robinson, Jacob, Rev. (Col.) to Bertha Weinberg (Col.). JACOB ROBINSON, preaching, age 39, widowed, b. Hanover Co., s/o John and Lucy Robinson, to BERTHA WEINBERG, age 20y6m, single, b. Richmond Co., d/o Adolphus Weinberg and Cornelia Veney. Rev. L. Harrod, Pastor, Ebenezer and Mulberry. 24 DEC 1890 at Mt. Zion Baptist Church. [C12, R:324, R1:78]

Robinson, John to Mildred Augusta Hall. JOHN ROBINSON, farmer, age 42, b. Maryland, res. Westmoreland Co., widower, s/o William and Sophiah Robinson, to MILDRED AUGUSTA HALL, age 20, b. Richmond Co., single, d/o Robert and Libby Hall. Consent 8 APR 1859 by father Robt. Hall, wit. J.W. Porter. H.P.F. King, M.G. 10 AUG 1859 at Robt. Hall's. [C2, R:165, R1:7]

Robinson, Richard (Col.) to Nettie Rockwell (Col.). RICHARD ROBINSON, farming, age 35, single, b. Richmond Co., s/o James Veney and Millie Robinson, to NETTIE ROCKWELL, age 19, single, b. Richmond Co., d/o Judy McKan. Consent 22 APR 1885 by Judy Mackan, wit. Jno. C. Taylor. Charles Sparks. 22 APR 1885 at the res. of Mr. Robinson. [C10, R:317, R1:64]

Rock, Fleet C. to Frances C. Hudson.[1] FLEET C. ROCK, farming, age 31, single, b. Richmond Co., s/o James [and Sarah] Rock, to FANNIE C. HUDSON,, age 20, single, b. Richmond Co., d/o James [S.] and Maria [C. Dobyns Dameron] Hudson, *q.v.* Consent 18 NOV 1890 by bride, wit. Maria Hudson. J. Manning Dunaway. 19 NOV 1890 at the res. of the bride. [C12, R:324, R1:77]

Rock, John F. to Loulie M. Dameron. JOHN F. ROCK, mariner, age 35, single, b. Richmond Co., s/o Wesley Rock and Ann [D.] Thrift,[2] to LOULIE M. DAMERON, age 20, single, b. Richmond Co., d/o Joseph Dameron and Maria C. his wife now Hudson. Consent 1 OCT 1883 by parties, and Maria C. Hudson. G.H. Northam. 6 OCT 1883. [C10, R:357, R1:59]

---

[1] Fleet C. Rock (b. 12 FEB 1852, d. 19 OCT 1927) and wife Frances C. Hudson (b. 7 JAN 1870, d. 11 JUL 1956) are bur. at Totuskey Baptist Church cemetery.
[2] Wesley Rock and Ann D. Thrift were married by bond 29 NOV 1841 in Richmond Co.

Rock, John Franklin to Josephine M. Rock.[1] JOHN FRANKLIN ROCK, farming, age 27, single, b. Richmond Co., s/o Griffin and Julia [Juliet A. Davis] Rock,[2] to JOSEPHINE ROCK, age 25, single, b. Richmond Co., d/o Thomas C. and Ann [Fulks] Rock.[3] Consent 7 DEC 1885 by bride, wit. James L. Davis. G.H. Northam. 10 DEC 1886. [C11, NN:18 DEC 1885, R:319, R1:66]

Rock, Thomas Javan[4] to Arinthea Ann Webb. THOMAS JAVAN ROCK, farming, age 28, single, b. Richmond Co., s/o Griffin and Julia [Juliet A. Davis] Rock, to ARINTHEA ANN WEBB, age 23, single, b. Richmond Co., d/o Beverly and Mary Webb. G.H. Northam. 7 JAN 1885 at Jerusalem Baptist Church. [C10, R:316, R1:64]

Rockwell, Seth, Jr.[5] to Mary Emma Pearson. SETH ROCKWELL, JR., merchant, age 32, single, b. Richmond Co., s/o Seth, Sr. and A.C. Rockwell, to MARY EMMA PEARSON, age 23, single, b. Richmond Co., d/o [Capt. Lawson T.] and Alice [M. Saunders] Pearson.[6] Consent 15 MAR 1870 by bride, no wit. G.H. Northam. 15 MAR 1870 at Farnham house. [C5, R:233, R1:27]

Roe, John, to Mary Coats. Consent 27 FEB 1857 by bride Mary [her X cross] Coats, wit. Thomas English. No license or minister return. [C1]

Roe, John to Georgeanna W. Beverton. JOHN ROE, farmer, age 72, widowed, b. Richmond Co., parents unknown, to GEORGEANNA W. BEVERTON, age 26, single, b. Richmond Co., d/o Henry and [Fi]delia [Ann Drake] Beverton. Consent 11 OCT 1872 by bride, wit. Alfred Scates. G.H. Northam. 13 OCT 1872. [C6, R:238, R1:32]

Rollins, Bailor (Col.) to Maria Banks (Col.). BAILOR ROLLINS, laborer, age 28y9m, single, b. Caroline Co., s/o Michael and Daphne Rollins, to MARIA BANKS, age 23, single, b. Richmond Co., d/o Emmanuel and Apphia Banks. Allen Brown, minister. 11 MAR 1876 at Farnham Church. [C7, R:304, R1:40]

Rowe, John Richard to Louemma Mealy.[7] JOHN R. ROWE, oystering, age 23, single, b. Richmond Co., s/o John and Mary Rowe, to LOU E. MEALEY [sic], age 18, single, b. Richmond Co., d/o William and Mary E. [Harriss] Mealy. Consent 17 MAR 1887 by Mrs. Mary Elizabeth Healey, wit. Joseph A. Schools. G.H. Northam. 20 MAR 1887 at res. of Mrs. Everett. [C11, R:291, R1:69]

Rowe, John W. to Dollie A. Woollard.[8] JOHN W. ROE [sic], farming, age 27, single, b. Richmond Co., s/o Samuel B. and Winnie [Winnefred Woollard] Roe,[9] to DOLLY A. WOOLLARD, age 17, single, b. Richmond Co., d/o John and Elizabeth C. Woollard. Consent 22 DEC 1884 by bride and Elizabeth C. Woollard. G.H. Northam. 24 DEC 1884 at Mrs. B. Woollard's. [C10, R:356, R1:63]

---

[1] James F. Rock and wife Joseph M. Rock are bur. in Calvary United Methodist Church cemetery.
[2] Griffin Rock and Juliet A. Davis were married 28 OCT 1852 in Richmond Co. by Rev. E.L. Williams.
[3] Thomas C. Rock, s/o Alexander Rock, and Ann Fulks were married by bond 30 JUL 1838 in Richmond Co.
[4] Thomas Javan Rock (1855-1892) is bur. in Calvary United Methodist Church cemetery. The death date for wife is blank.
[5] Seth Rockwell enlisted in 1862 in Co. B, 40th Reg., Va. Inf., C.S.A., and was wounded at Gaines Mill.
[6] Lawson T. Pearson and Alice M. Saunders were married by bond 14 JAN 1851 in Richmond Co.
[7] John Richard Rowe (b. 28 JAN 1864, d. 11 FEB 1930 at Emmerton, Va.) and wife Louemma Mealey (b. 14 MAR 1869, d. 4 NOV 1936) are bur. in Jerusalem Baptist Church cemetery.
[8] John W. Rowe (b. 31 DEC 1859, d. 1 MAY 1935) and his wife Dollie A. Woollard (b. 17 CT 1867, d. 21 SEP 1949) is bur. at Jerusalem Baptist Church cemetery.
[9] Samuel B. Roe and Winnefred Woollard were married by bond 29 MAR 1848 in Richmond Co.

Ruby, Edgar H. to Julia O. Lowery. EDGAR H. RUBY, distiller, age 22, single, b. and res. York Co., Pa., s/o George H. and Lydia A. Ruby, to JULIA O. LOWERY, age 21y3m, single, b. Northumberland Co., d/o Gowen T. and Mary Jane [Pearce] Lowery.[1] Consent 24 JUL 1875 by bride Julia O. Lowery, no wit. A.B. Dunaway. 27 JUL 1875 at the house of Mr. Lowery. [C7, R:262, R1:38]

Rucker, Henry (Col.) to Eliza Ward (Col.). HENRY RUCKER, farmer, age 33, bachelor, b. King William Co., s/o Lewis and Maria Rucker, to ELIZA WARD, age 28, single, b. Richmond Co., d/o Ralph and Eliza Ward. Thomas G. Thomas. 5 NOV 1870 at the res. of the minister. [C5, R:234, R1:28]

Rucker, Henry (Col.) to Mrs. Annie Wright (Col.). HENRY RUCKER, ditcher, age 52, widowed, b. King William Co., s/o Lewis and Nannie Rucker, to ANNIE WRIGHT, age 46, widow, b. Richmond Co., [names of parents unknown]. Rev. T.G. Thomas. c.14 JUL 1887 at the house of D. Northen. [C11, R:292, R1:70]

Rude, Lawrence to Corinthia H. Reynolds.[2] LAWRENCE RUDE, mechanic, age 28, single, b. in Massachusetts, s/o Gilbert and Ann Rude, to CORINTHA H. REYNOLDS [sic], age 19y8m, single, b. Richmond Co., d/o Thomas Reynolds and Saluda F. Reynolds now Jenkins. Consent 30 NOV 1875 by mother Saluda F. Jenkins. G.H. Northam. 2 DEC 1875 at Jerusalem Baptist Church. [C7, R:262, R1:39]

Rust, George H.[3] to Malissa S. Lewis. GEORGE RUST, farmer, age 27, single, b. Richmond Co., s/o Elizabeth Rust, to MALISSA S. LEWIS, age 18, single, b. Richmond Co., d/o Robert G. and Matilda [Woollard] Lewis.[4] Consent 4 JAN 1861 by father George Rust and signed by Malissa [her X mark] Lewis, wit. Cyrus Clarke. Robert Williamson, M.G. 10 JAN 1861. [C3, R:123, R1:10]

S

Samuel, Alexander to Milicie Clark. ALEXANDER SAMUEL, farmer, age 21, single, b. Caroline Co., s/o George and Jane [Saunders] Samuel, to MILICIE CLARK, age 21, single, b. Richmond Co., d/o Joseph and Sarah Clark. Consent 25 FEB 1868 by father Joseph [his X mark] Clark and bride, wit. Robert Morriss. Elder James A. Weaver. 27 FEB 1868 at res. of Joseph Clark. [C4, C5, R:253, R1:23]

Samuel, Garland J. to Hester A. Oliff. GARLAND J. SAMUEL, farmer, age 21y9m, single, b. Caroline Co., s/o George and Jane [Saunders] Samuel, to HESTER A. OLIFF, age 21, single, b. Richmond Co., d/o William D. and Mary [Ann Bowen] Oliff.[5] Consent 18 NOV 1876 by bride Hester A. [her X mark] Oliff, wit. R.W. Hinson, father William D. Oliff. H.H. Fones. 21 NOV 1876. [C7, R:306, R1:41]

---

[1] Goin D. Lowry, ward of H. Stott, and Mary J. Pearce, d/o Margaret Winstead, were married by bond 16 DEC 1844 in Northumberland Co.
[2] Lawrence Rude (1847-1939) and his wife Corinthia H. Reynolds (b. 14 APR 1856, d. 8 AUG 1902) are bur. in Jerusalem Baptist Church cemetery.
[3] George Rust served in Co. G, 15th Va. Cav., C.S.A.
[4] Robert Lewis and Matilda Woollard were married by bond 27 APR 1835 in Richmond Co.
[5] William D. Olliff and Mary Ann Bowen were married 15 MAY 1850 in Richmond Co. by Rev. John Pullen.

Sanders, Allen James[1] to Alice D.C. Newman. ALLEN J. SAUNDERS, farming, age 23, single, b. Richmond Co., upper district, s/o James L. Sanders and Peggy [Margaret Marks], to ALICE D.C. NEWMAN, age 21, single, b. Richmond Co., upper district, d/o Joseph Newman and Sophiah [Sophia Hinson].[2] Consent 20 FEB 1855 by bride, wits. James M. Morris, John B. Scates, Samuel [his X mark] Marks. John Pullen, M.G. 21 FEB 1855 at John Pullen's, *Wave Hill*. [C1, R:153, R1:2]

Sanders, Frank Welton to Elizabeth Virginia Brewer.[3] FRANK WELTON SANDERS, farming, age 23, single, b. Maryland, s/o George [Henry] and Frances [Maria Jennings] Sanders, to VIRGINIA BREWER, age 22, single, b. Richmond Co., d/o Richard [Ellett] and Frances [Jane Hinson] Brewer, *q.v.* Consent 11 JAN 1887 by bride, wit. A.W. Sanders. Geo. M. Conley. 13 JAN 1887 at *Locust Grove*. [C11, R:290, R1:69]

Sanders, Hiram to Sophronia E. Saunders. HIRAM SANDERS, farming, age 33, widowed, b. Richmond Co., s/o George [Henry] and Frances [Maria Jennings] Sanders, to SOPHRONIA E. SAUNDERS, age 16, single, b. Richmond Co., d/o William A.H. and Margaret [Morris] Sanders [Saunders]. Consent 3 AUG 1883 by bride and Wm. A.H. Saunders, wit. A.W. Sanders [sic]. R.N. Reamy. 5 AUG 1883. [C10, R:357, R1:59]

Sanders, James to Ann R. Habron. JAMES SANDERS, farmer, age 47y9m, widowed, b. Richmond Co., s/o Thomas and Barsheba Sanders, to ANN R. HABRON, age 25, single, b. Richmond Co., d/o Benjamin and Ranie [Sanford] Habron.[4] Consent 20 AUG 1864 by bride, wit. Martin [his X mark] Lee. E.L. Williams. 25 AUG 1864 at res. of Martin Pugh. [C3, R:139, R1:14]

Sanders, James H. to Frances Marks. JAMES H. SANDERS, farmer, age 24, single, b. Richmond Co., s/o James C. and Sarah Sanders, to FRANCES MARKS, age 23, single, b. Richmond Co., d/o Thornton and Jane [Hinson] Marks.[5] Consent 28 FEB 1865 by bride Frances [her X mark] Marks, wit. Abr. Wilson. John Pullen. 3 or 4[6] MAR 1865 at Zachariah Nash's. [C3, R:204, R1:14]

Sanders, James H. to Anna E. Hinson. JAMES H. SANDERS, farming, age 31, single, b. Richmond Co., s/o Lawson and Peggy Sanders, to ANNA E. HINSON, age 25, single, b. Richmond Co., d/o W.W. [William] and Maria [Scates] Hinson.[7] Consent by bride, wit. R.B. Bartlett. R.N. Reamy. 18 DEC 1878 at Jos. France's. [C8, R:310 and 312, R1:46]

Sanders, John L. to Alice A. Coates. JOHN L. SANDERS, farmer, age 22, single, b. Richmond Co., s/o George W. and Charlotte [Scates] Sanders,[8] to ALICE A. COATES, age 18, single, b. Richmond Co., d/o Edward Coates and Sallie A. who is now Sallie A. Jenkins. Consent 1 JAN 1878 by mother Sallie A. Jenkins, wit. A.L. Saunders. H.H. Fones. 2 JAN 1878. [C8, R:310, R1:44]

---

[1] Allen J. Sanders, b. 1832, d. 1 SEP 1864 at Point Lookout, Md., served in Co. D, 40th Inf., Va. Reg., C.S.A.
[2] Joseph Newman and Sophia Hinson were married by bond 1 FEB 1830 in Richmond Co.
[3] Frank W. Sanders (b. 15 MAR 1863, d. 2 MAR 1942) and wife Elizabeth V. Brewer (b. 1867, d. 10 APR 1916) are bur. at Norwood Baptist Church cemetery.
[4] Benjaminn Habron and Rany Sanford were married by bonnd 14 SEP 1832 in Richmond Co.
[5] Thornton Marks and Jane Hinson were married by bond 30 APR 1836 in Richmond Co.
[6] The certificate has marriage date 3 MAR 1865, while the return states 4 MAR 1865.
[7] William W. Hinson and Maria Scates were married 13 MAR 1850 in Richmond Co. by Rev. William Balderson.
[8] George W. Sanders and Charlotte Scates were married 27 MAR 1851 in Richmond Co. by Rev. John Pullen.

Sanders, Lemuel to Elizabeth Scates. LEMUEL SANDERS, farming, age about 22, single, b. upper district of Richmond Co., s/o James C. Sanders and wife Sally, to ELIZABETH SCATES, age about 22, single, b. upper district of Richmond Co., d/o John B. Scates and wife Elizabeth [Marks].[1] Consent 5 APR 1856 by bride, signed by John B. Scates, Elizabeth Scates, and a second Elizabeth Scates, wit. Samuel [his X mark] Marks. John Pullen, M.G. 11 APR 1856 at Capt. John B. Scates'. [C1, R, R1:3]

Sanders, Lovel to Delila Oliff. LOVELL SANDERS, farmer, going on 26, widower, b. upper district of Richmond Co., s/o Thomas Sanders and wife Susanna [Jones],[2] to DELILA OLIFF, age about 26, single, b. Richmond Co., d/o James S. Oliff and wife Lucinda. Consent 17 JAN 1858 by bride Delila [her X mark] Oliff, wits. S.T. Reamy, James Reamy. John Pullen, M.G. 13 JAN 1858 at Vincent Oliff's. [C1, R:138, R1:6]

Sanders, Stephen Horace to Sophronia Ann Hall.[3] STEPHEN H. SANDERS,[4] farmer, age 21½, single, b. Richmond Co., s/o Robert [Christian, Sr.] [1798-1851] and Mary Sanders, to SOPHRONIA ANN HALL, age 18, single, b. Richmond Co., d/o Bladen and Frances [Ann Morris] Hall. Consent 17 MAY 1871 by father Bladen Hall, wit. B.W. Brockenbrough. Robert N. Reamy. 18 MAY 1871 at *Level Green*. [C5, R:244, R1:29]

Sanders, Thornton to Henrietta Edmonds. THORNTON SANDERS, farming, age about 24, single, b. upper district of Richmond Co., s/o Henry V. Sanders and wife Lucy [Marks],[5] to HENRIETTA EDMONDS, age about 25, single, b. Westmoreland Co., d/o Ritchard Edmons [sic] and wife Penolopy [Marks].[6] Consent 28 SEP 1857 by bride, also signed by Thornton Sanders, wits. C.H. Balderson, George Edmonds. John Pullen, M.G. 30 SEP 1857 at John Pullen's. [C1, R:159, R1:5]

Sanders, William A. to Sarah Saunders. WILLIAM A. SANDERS,[7] fisherman, age 25, single, b. Richmond Co., s/o William A.[H.] and Margaret A. [Morris] Sanders,[8] to SARAH SAUNDERS, age 19, single, b. Richmond Co., d/o George and Frances Saunders. Consent 20 DEC 1872 by bride, wits. George Saunders, Frances Saunders, Hiram Saunders. Robert N. Reamy. 26 DEC 1872 at res. of George Saunders. [C6, R:238, R1:33]

Sanders, William Henry[9] to Mrs. Lavina Elgier Hinson, widow of Christopher Columbus Marks. WILLIAM H. SANDERS, farming, age 38, widowed, b. Richmond Co., s/o Reuben K. and Patsy Sanders, to LAVINA E. MARKS, age 27, widow, b. Richmond Co., d/o W.W. [William] and Maria [Scates] Hinson. Consent 17 OCT 1885 by bride. R.N. Reamy. 21 OCT 1885. [C10, R:318, R1:65]

---

[1] John B. Scates and Betsy Marks were married by bond 10 MAR 1830 in Richmond Co.
[2] Thomas Sanders and Susannah Jones were married by bond 22 SEP 1819 in Richmond Co.
[3] Stephen Horace Sanders (b. 29 OCT 1849, d. 26 APR 1941) is bur. in the Sanders Family Cemetery near Warsaw, Va., and his wife Sophronia Ann Hall (b. 25 APR 1859, d. 22 MAR 1893) is bur. in Cobham Park Baptist Church cemetery.
[4] The marriage record can be found spelled Saunders; but his tombstone is Sanders.
[5] Henry V. Sanders and Lucy Marks were married by bond 21 NOV 1821 in Richmond Co.
[6] Richard Edmonds and Penelope Marks were married by bond 3 JAN 1820 in Westmoreland Co.
[7] The surname also appears as Saunders.
[8] William A.H. Sanders and Margaret Morris were married 29 DEC 1842 in Richmond Co. by Rev. R.N. Herndon.
[9] William H. Sanders (1840-1912) is bur. at Welcome Grove Baptist Church cemetery.

Sanders, Willie X. to Ida S. Sanders. WILLIE X. SANDERS,[1] farming, age 21y2m, single, b. Richmond Co., s/o L.M. and Elizabeth Sanders, to IDA S. SANDERS, age 18, single, b. Richmond Co., d/o Thornton and Henrietta [Edmonds] Sanders, *q.v.* Consent 23 FEB 1880 by father [Thornton] Sanders, wit. M.D. Sanders. R.N. Reamy. 26 FEB 1880. [C9, R:314, R1:50]

Sandford, Lucius E. to Ellen D. Fauntleroy. LUCIUS E. SANDFORD, soldier, age 31, widowed, b. and res. Westmoreland Co., s/o Ethelwald and Sarah M. Sandford, to ETTA D. FAUNTLEROY, age 22, single, b. Richmond Co., d/o Henry and Annette L. Fauntleroy. Consent 11 JAN 186[4] by mother A. Fauntleroy, wit. B.J. Faunt LeRoy. William F. Bain. 18 JAN 1864 at *Naylors Hold* [sic], the res. of Mrs. Fauntleroy. [C3, R:139, R1:13]

Sandford, Richard H. to Catharine M. Lewis. RICHARD H. SANDFORD, miller, age 29, single, b. Westmoreland Co., s/o William and Nancy Sandford, to CATHARINE M. LEWIS, age 22, single, b. Richmond Co., d/o Robert G. and Matilda Lewis. Consent 27 DEC 1862 signed by parties, wits. Richard W. Lewis, R.G. Lewis. E.L. Williams. 28 DEC 1862 at Cyrus Clarke's. [C3, R:140, R1:12]

Sandy, Ellison P.[2] to Catharine A. Reamy. ELLISON P. SANDY, farmer, age 23, single, b. Richmond Co., s/o Samuel and Elizabeth [Pullen] Sandy,[3] to CATHARINE A. REAMY, age 23, single, b. Richmond Co., d/o Samuel T. and Susan [Fones] Reamy.[4] Age of parties proved by oath of H.M. Sandy. John Pullen. 5 JUL 1866 at the res. of S.T. Reamy. [C4, R:271, R1:17]

Sandy, Frank to Maggie J. Harrison. FRANK SANDY, farming, age 23, single, b. Richmond Co., s/o Samuel and Elizabeth [Pullen] Sandy, to MAGGIE J. HARRISON, age 23, single, b. Richmond Co., d/o John and Maggie Harrison. Consent 12 DEC 1881 by bride, wit. C.H. Jones. G.H. Northam. 14 DEC 1881 at John Harrison's. [C9, R:337, R1:54]

Sandy, Hiram N.[5] to Mary A. Jennings. HIRAM N. SANDY, farmer, age 28, single, b. Richmond Co., s/o Samuel and Elizabeth [Pullen] Sandy, to MARY A. JENNINGS, age 29, widow, b. Richmond Co., d/o William B. and Elisha Jennings. John Pullen. 14 FEB 1866 at William Jenkins'. [C4, R:270, R1:16]

Sandy, Hiram N. to Rosella F. Winstead. HIRAM N. SANDY, farmer, age 36, widowed, b. Richmond Co., res. Northumberland Co., s/o Samuel and Elizabeth [Pullen] Sandy, to ROSELLA F. WINSTEAD, age 31, single, b. Richmond Co., s/o George L. and Martha H.B. [Headley] Winstead. A.B. Dunaway. 4 FEB 1877 at the house of George Winstead. [C8, R:306a, R1:42]

Sandy, Samuel E. to Mary J. Reamy. SAMUEL E. SANDY, shoemaker, age 30, single, b. Richmond Co., s/o Samuel and Elizabeth [Pullen] Sandy, to MARY J. REAMY, age 24, single, b. Richmond Co., d/o John and Catharine Reamy. John Pullen. 13 OCT 1867 at S.T. Reamy's. [C4, R:287, R1:21]

---

[1] The surname is interchanged between Saunders and Sanders within the same record.
[2] Ellison Sandy served in Co. G, 15th Va. Cav., C.S.A.
[3] Samuel Sandy and Elizabeth Pullen were married by bond 8 JAN 1822 inn Richmond Co.
[4] Samuel T. Reamy and Susan Fones were married by bond 26 APR 1832 in Westmoreland Co.
[5] Listed as Hiram M. Sandy, enlisted in Co. D, 40th Reg., Va. Inf., C.S.A., wounded in knee at Chancellorsville.

Sandy, Thomas E.[1] to Maria H. Dunaway. THOMAS E. SANDY, farmer, age 25, single, b. Richmond Co., s/o William and Harriet [Sanford] Sandy,[2] to MARIA H. DUNAWAY, age 22, single, b. Richmond Co., d/o John [G.] and Martha A. [Sebra] Dunaway.[3] Consent 5 MAR 1880 by bride, wit. John A. Thrift. G.H. Northam. 7 MAR 1880. [C9, R:314, R1:50]

Sandy, Vincent S. to Mrs. Ann Mothershead Barber. VINCENT S. SANDY, farmer, age 61, widowed, b. Richmond Co., res. Northumberland Co., s/o John and Sally Sandy, to ANN BARBER, age 42, widow, b. Westmoreland Co., d/o George and Polly [Howe] Mothershead.[4] W.A. Crocker. 31 MAY 1875. [C7, R:305, R1:40]

Sanford, James to Sarah Weathers. JAMES SANFORD, farmer, age 41, widowed, b. Richmond or Westmoreland Co., s/o Sarah Sanford ("he don't know his father"), to SARAH WEATHERS, age 35, single, b. Richmond Co., d/o William and Fanny [Frances A. Hardwick] Weathers.[5] Consent 27 DEC 1858 by Sarah [her X mark] Weathers, wit. J.G. [his X mark] Moore. No minister return. 30 DEC 1858. [C2, two versions; R:138, R1:6]

Sanford, James H. to Mary Frances Jenkins. JAMES H. SANFORD, farmer, age 21, single, b. Richmond Co., s/o Albert and Martha [Brewer] Sanford, to MARY FRANCES JENKINS, age 21, single, b. Richmond Co., d/o John and Martha [Jenkins] Jenkins.[6] Consent 24 JAN 1871 by Mary Frances Jenkins, wit. Hiram Sanders. Robert N. Reamy. 26 JAN 1871 at res. of T.N. Balderson. [C5, R:244, R1:29]

Sanford, James H. to Martha Marks. JAMES H. SANFORD, farmer, age 23, widowed, b. Richmond Co., s/o Albert and Martha [Brewer] Sanford, to MARTHA MARKS, age 16, single, b. Richmond Co., d/o James and Ann [Bowen] Marks.[7] Consent 18 DEC 1873 by mother Ann [her X mark] Marks, wit. Thomas Jenkins, J.L. Waffull. Robert N. Reamy. 23 DEC 1873 at the res. of the bride. [C6, R:236, R1:35]

Sanford, John B.[8] to Emeline Thrift. Consent undated by bride Emeline [her X mark] Thrift, wit. Hiram Sisson. No license or minister return. [C1]

Sanford, Lewis to Mrs. Elizabeth Coates Fidler. LEWIS SANFORD, farmer, age 23, single, b. Richmond Co., s/o George H. and Elizabeth J. [Jones] Sanford, to ELIZABETH C. FIDLER, age 22, widow, b. Richmond Co., d/o Henry H. and Elizabeth Coates. Consent 3 JAN 1870 by parties. Robert Williamson, M.G. 4 JAN 1870 at the Brookhouse, Farnham. [C5, R:233, R1:27]

Sanford, Richard A. to Mrs. Nancy Sydnor. RICHARD A. SANFORD, miller, age 36, widowed, b. Westmoreland Co., s/o William and Nancy [Sydnor] Sanford,[9] to NANCY SYDNOR, age 30,

---

[1] A Thomas E. Sandy (b. 18 AUG 1851, d. 13 NOV 1901) is bur. in Farnham Baptist Church cemetery.
[2] William Sandy and Harriet Sanford were married 27 NOV 1851 in Richmond Co. by Rev. G.M. Northam.
[3] John G. Dunaway and Martha A. Sebra were married 9 OCT 1850 in Richmond Co. by Rev. Bartholomew Dodson.
[4] George Mothershead and Polly Howe, d/o Ann Howe, were married by bond 7 FEB 1815 in Westmoreland Co.
[5] William Weathers and Frances A. Hardwick, d/o Aaron Hardwick, were married by bond 9 FEB 1809 in Richmond Co.
[6] John Jenkins and Martha Jenkins were married by bond 4 DEC 1848 in Richmond Co.
[7] James Marks and Ann Bowen were married 24 FEB 1853 in Richmond Co. by Rev. John Pullen.
[8] John B. Sanford served in Co. D, 47th Reg., Va. Inf., C.S.A., and was wounded at Seven Pines, Va.
[9] William Sanders and Nancy Sydnor were married by bond 1 NOV 1813 in Richmond Co.

widow, b. Northumberland Co., d/o Austin B. and Nancy [Hale] Lewis.[1] G.H. Northam. 26 MAY 1871 at *Morattico*. [C5, R:244, R1:29]

Sanford, Richard Edward, Jr. to Louisa Jeter Sisson.[2] RICHARD E. SANFORD, farming, age 24y9m19d, single, b. Westmoreland Co., s/o Richard [Edward, Sr.] and Frances [Ann Sydnor] Sanford, to LOUISA J. SISSON, age 17, single, b. Richmond Co., d/o John T. [Taliaferro] and Anna E. [Elizabeth Clarke] Sisson.[3] Consent 26 OCT 1878 by parents J.T. Sisson and Anna E. Sisson. G.H. Northam. 31 OCT 1878. [C8, R:312, R1:45]

Sanford, Richard H. to Emma J. Booker. RICHARD H. SANFORD, miller, age 34, widowed, b. Westmoreland Co., s/o William and Nancy Sanford, to EMMA J. BOOKER, age 23, single, b. Richmond Co., d/o George and Nancy Booker. G.H. Northam. 5 NOV 1867 at Taylor's Mill. [C4, R:287, R1:21]

Sanford, William Henry to Susanna Leftwich Murren.[4] WILLIAM SANFORD, farmer, age 23, single, b. Richmond Co., s/o James and Olivia Sanford, to SUSAN MURRAIN [sic], age 22, single, b. Richmond Co., d/o [William] Thompson and Mary [McPherson] Murren [sic Murrain].[5] Elder James A. Weaver. 14 NOV 1869 at the res. of the bride's father. [C5, R, R1:26]

Sanford, William S., d. 15 JAN 1890, to Louisa Fanny Franklin. WILLIAM S. SANFORD, age 23, single, b. Richhmond Co., s/o George and Elizabeth Sanford, to LOUISA FANNY FRANKLIN, age 21, single, b. Richmond Co., d/o Samuel R. and Susan S. [Sisson] Franklin.[6] G.H. Northam. 19 JAN 1882 at William Richard Webb's. [C9; R:312, R1:55]

Sargent, Charlie H. to Mary A. Barrott. CHARLIE H. SARGENT, laborer, age 33, widowed, b. Kennebec Co., Me., res. Westmoreland Co., s/o Charles and Mariam Sargent, to MARY A. BARROTT, age 34, single, b. Richmond Co., s/o John and Mary Barrott. D.M. Wharton. 5 DEC 1877 at the res. of the minister in Westmoreland Co. [C8, R:307, R1:43]

Saunders, Alexander W. to Elizabeth Scates. ALEXANDER W. SAUNDERS, farmer, age 23, single, b. Richmond Co., s/o William A. and Margaret [Morris] Saunders, to ELIZABETH SCATES, age 17, single, b. Richmond Co., d/o Richard and Mary F. [Brown] Scates.[7] Consent 6 DEC 1879 by bride's guardian J.[M.] Scates. R.N. Reamy. 11 DEC 1879. [C8, R:309, R1:48]

Saunders, Arthur L. to Sophia E. Bowen. ARTHUR L. SAUNDERS, fisherman, age 35, single, b. Richmond Co., s/o John L. and Margaret Saunders, to SOPHIA E. BOWEN, age 24, single, b. Richmond Co., d/o Joseph H. and Sarah A. Bowen. Consent 2 JUN 1878 by bride, wit. T.M. Bowen. H.H. Fones. 5 JUN 1878. [C8, R:311, R1:45]

---

[1] Austin Lewis and Nancy Hale were married by bond 28 DEC 1836 in Northumberland Co.

[2] Richard E. Sanford, Jr. (b. 11 DEC 1853 in Westmoreland Co., d. 13 NOV 1938) and wife Louisa J. Sisson (b. 4 FEB 1863, d. 1948) are bur. at Totuskey Baptist Church cemtery.

[3] John T. Sisson (b. 14 SEP 1829, d. 15 JUL 1899) and wife Anna E. Clarke (b. 14 NOV 1839, d. 25 FEB 1905) are bur. at Totuskey Baptist Church cemetery, along with her father Hempsel Clarke (1810-1886).

[4] William Henry Sanford (b. 1846, d. 24 DEC 1916) and his wife Susanna Leftwich Murren (b. 1849, d. in OCT 1924) are bur. in St. John's Episcopal Church cemetery.

[5] William T. Murren and Mary McPherson, ward of Benjamin Clark, of Fredericksburg, Va., were married 19 JAN 1826 by Rev. Henry Slicer.

[6] Samuel R. Franklin and Susan S. Sisson were married by bond 24 FEB 1841 in Richmond Co.

[7] Richard Scates and Mary F. Brown were married 10 APR 1850 in Richmond Co. by Rev. John Pullen.

Saunders, Augustine N., Jr. to Mrs. Sarah Jackson Mozingo, widow of Robert M. Harris and Meredith M. Mozingo. AUSTIN N. SAUNDERS, JR. [sic], farmer, age 23, single, b. Richmond Co., s/o Austin N. [Sr.] [sic] and Mary C. [Catharine Sands] Saunders,[1] to SARAH HARRIS, age 28, widow, b. Richmond Co., d/o George and Maria [Hale] Jackson. Consent 15 JUN 1874 by bride Sarah [her X mark] Harris, wits. W.G. Wallace, Wm. [his X mark] H. Fones. Elder James A. Weaver. 17 JUN 1874 at the res. of the bride. [C7, R:230, R1:36]

Saunders, Austin N.,[2] Jr. to Sarah A. Self. AUSTIN N. SAUNDERS, JR., age 23, single, b. Richmond Co., s/o A.N. Saunders, Sr. and Mary C. [Catharine Sands], to SARAH A. SELF, no age given, single, b. Richmond Co., d/o Moses and Mary S. [Smith] Self. Consent in APR 1873 by bride, wit. Mary J. Weaver. No license or minister return. [C6, R:235, R1:34]

Saunders, Augustus Washington[3] to Etta B. Balderson. AUGUSTUS W. SAUNDERS [sic], farmer, age 27, single, b. Richmond Co., s/o Griffin and Maria [A. Sanders] Sanders,[4] to ETTA B. BALDERSON, age 18, single, b. Richmond Co., d/o James F. [Franklin] and Mary S. [Susan Carter] Balderson, *q.v.* Consent 14 FEB 1881 by father James F. Balderson, wit. C.R. Balderson. R.N. Reamy. 16 FEB 1881. [C9, R:335, R1:52]

Saunders, Augustus Washington to Anna Wade Balderson. AUGUSTUS W. SANDERS [sic], farming, age 30, widowed, b. Richmond Co., s/o Griffin [d. 1884] and Maria [A. Sanders] Sanders,[5] to ANNA WADE BALDERSON, age 18, single, b. Richmond Co., d/o George W. [Washington] and Sarah Jane [Hart] Balderson.[6] Consent 13 JAN 1885 by father George W. Balderson, wit. Cary M. Scates. R.N. Reamy. 14 JAN 1885. [C10, NN:23 JAN 1885, R:316, R1:64]

Saunders, Charles H. to Susan Gutridge. CHARLES H. SAUNDERS, farmer, age 24, single, b. Richmond Co., s/o John Saunders (dec'd.) and Fanny Saunders, to SUSAN GUTRIDGE, age 18, single, b. Richmond Co., d/o Lucy Coates. Consent 30 AUG 1880 by mother Lucy [her X mark] Coates, wit. Washington [his X mark] Saunders. R.N. Reamy. 1 SEP 1880. [C9, R:316, R1:51]

Sanders, Charles M.G. to Annie E. Balderson. CHARLES M.G. SAUNDERS [sic], farming, age 25, single, b. Richmond Co., s/o Griffin and Maria [A. Sanders] Sanders, to ANNIE E. BALDERSON, age 18, single, b. Richmond Co., d/o G.G. [George Graham] and Elizabeth Ann [Newman] Balderson, *q.v.* Consent 29 MAR 1886 by father G.G. Balderson. R.N. Reamy. 1 APR 1886 at res. of Mr. G. Balderson. [C11, R:315, R1:67]

Saunders, David to Isabella Lewis. DAVID SAUNDERS, farmer, age 21, single, b. Richmond Co., s/o James and Elizabeth Saunders, to ISABELLA LEWIS, age 16, single, b. Richmond Co., d/o Robert Lewis. Robert Williamson, M.G. 4 MAR 1868 at *Moodwood*. [C4, R:253, R1:23]

---

[1] Augustine N. Saunders and Mary Catharine Sands, d/o O.H. and Maria Sands, were married by bond 5 DEC 1845 in Richmond Co.
[2] Probably Augustine N. Saunders, Jr., as above.
[3] Augustus W. Saunders (b. 2 JUL 1852, d. 31 JAN 1944) and his second wife Anna Wade Balderson (b. 23 MAR 1867, d. 20 JUL 1955) are bur. in Rappahannock Baptist Church cemetery.
[4] Griffin Sanders and Maria A. Sanders were married 12 JAN 1843 in Richmond Co. by Rev. R.N. Herndon.
[5] Griffin Sanders and Maria A. Sanders were married 12 JAN 1843 in Richmond Co. by Rev. R.N. Herndon.
[6] George W. Balderson (b. 4 JUL 1844, d. 24 JAN 1926) and wife Sarah J. Hart (b. 12 SEP 1841, d. 27 FEB 1891) are bur. in Rappahannock Baptist Church cemetery.

Saunders, David A. to Eugenia B. Clarke. DAVID A. SAUNDERS, miller, age 28, widowed, b. Richmond Co., s/o James Saunders, to EUGENIA B. CLARKE, age 21, single, b. Richmond Co., d/o John L. and Lucy Clarke. Consent in MAR 1880 by bride, wit. John T. Waterfield. G.H. Northam. 24 MAR 1880. [C9, R:314, R1:50]

Saunders, Fairfax to Dosey Hinson. FAIRFAX SAUNDERS, laborer, age 29, single, b. Richmond Co., s/o Lovel and Malisia Saunders, to DOSEY HINSON, age 16, single, b. Westmoreland Co., d/o George and Jane Hinson. R.N. Reamy. 19 AUG 1883. [C10, R:357, R1:59]

Saunders, Hiram T. to Louisa Marks. HIRAM T. SAUNDERS, white, farmer, age 21, single, b. Richmond Co., s/o George and Frances Saunders, to LOUISA MARKS, age 22, single, b. Richmond Co., d/o Thornton and Virginia Marks. Consent 7 FEB 1871 by parties, wit. A.H. Saunders. Robert N. Reamy. 9 FEB 1871. [C5, R:244, R1:29]

Saunders, Hyram to Felista J. Marks. HYRAM SAUNDERS, farmer, age 27, widowed, b. Richmond Co., s/o George and Frances Saunders, to FELISTA J. MARKS, age 24, single, b. Richmond Co., d/o Thornton and T.J. [Hinson] Marks. R.N. Reamy. 13 JUL 1876. [C7, R1:40]

Saunders, James (Col.) to Frances Cupit (Col.). JAMES SAUNDERS, farming, age 28, widowed, b. Westmoreland Co., s/o Moore and Catherine Saunders, to FRANCES CUPIT, age 30, single, b. Richmond Co., d/o Lewis and Nancy Cupit. George [his X mark] Laws. 17 JAN 1886. [C11, R:315, R1:67]

Saunders, James (Col.) to Mrs. Margaret Washington Smith (Col.). JAMES SAUNDERS, farmer, age 48, widowed, b. Richmond Co., s/o James and Lucinda Saunders, to MARGARET SMITH, age 30, widow, b. Richmond Co., d/o Cyrus and Peggy Washington. Consent 18 DEC 1874 by bride Margaret [her X mark] Smith, wit. Samuel Cox. George Laws. 26 DEC 1874 at the res. of the bride's mother. [C7, R:231, R1:38]

Saunders, James P. to Almonia E. Saunders.[1] JAMES P. SAUNDERS, farmer, age 31, single, b. Lancaster Co., s/o William Saunders and Harriett Kirk,[2] to ALMONIA E. SAUNDERS, age 17, single, b. Richmond Co., d/o Richard Saunders and Alice Chilton. William H. Kirk, M.G. 21 JUN 1855 at Farnham house. [C1, R:153, R1:2]

Saunders, John Henry to Martha R. Bowen.[3] JOHN H. SANDERS [sic],[4] fisherman, age 24, single, b. Richmond Co., s/o James C. and Nancy [Hinson] Sanders,[5] to MARTHA BOWEN, age 25, single, b. Richmond Co., d/o Martin [V.] and "Patty" [Martha Sanders] Bowen. Consent 31 DEC 1875 by bride Marthia [sic] [her X mark] Bowen, wit. A.L. Saunders [sic]. R.N. Reamy. 2 JAN 1876 at L. Marks'. [C7, R:304, R1:39]

Saunders, John Thomas to Mary Ella Dunaway. JOHN THOMAS SAUNDERS, farming and oystering, age 22, single, b. Richmond Co., s/o James Saunders and Ann his wife now Ann

---

[1] James P. Saunders (b. 14 DEC 1823, d. 22 APR 1908) and wife Almonia E. Saunders (b. 12 JUL 1839, d. 2 JAN 1908) are bur. in Farnham Baptist Church cemetery.
[2] William Saunders and Harriett Kirk were married by bond 23 NOV 1820 in Lancaster Co.
[3] John H. Saunders (b. 18 OCT 1851, d. 9 SEP 1915) and wife Martha R. Bowen (1850-1923) are bur. at Welcome Grove Baptist Church cemetery.
[4] Surname also appears as Saunders.
[5] James C. Sanders and Nancy Hinson were married 23 JAN 1851 in Richmond Co. by Rev. William Balderson.

Jenkins, to MARY ELLA DUNAWAY, age 22y6m, single, b. Lancaster Co., d/o R.R. Dunaway and Mary Jane Dunaway (dec'd.). G.H. Northam. 29 APR 1888 at *Oak Farm*. [C11, R:315, R1:72]

Saunders, Julius C. to Sophia A. Balderson. JULIUS C. SAUNDERS, farming, age 24, single, b. Richmond Co., s/o Griffin and Maria [A. Sanders] Saunders, to SOPHIA A. BALDERSON, age 16, single, b. Richmond Co., d/o G.G. [George Graham] and Elizabeth [Ann Newman] Balderson. Consent 4 MAY 1879 by father G.G. Balderson, wit. J.M. Scates. H.H. Fones. 11 MAY 1879. [C8, R:307, R1:47]

Saunders, Lucius C. to Bettie Virginia Sisson. LUCIUS C. SAUNDERS, farming, age 23, single, b. Westmoreland Co., s/o Ovalton and Catharine Saunders, to BETTIE VIRGINIA SISSON, age 18, single, b. Richmond Co., d/o Robert and Amanda Sisson. Consent 14 FEB 1887 by parents of the bride, no wit. Geo. M. Conley. 17 FEB 1887 at *Stony Hill*. [C11, R:290, R1:69]

Saunders, Presley M. to Lucinda Nash. PRESLEY M. SAUNDERS [sic], farmer, age 21, single, b. Richmond Co., s/o Joseph F. and Mary M. [Bowing] Saunders,[1] to LUCINDA NASH, age 21, single, b. Richmond Co., d/o Zachariah and Mary [Marks] Nash. Consent 12 JAN 1871 by bride, wits. L.D. Warner. H.H. Fones. 19 JAN 1871 at Mrs. Mary Saunders'. [C5, R:244, R1:29]

Saunders, Robert C. to Charlotte Hinson. ROBERT C. SAUNDERS, farmer, age 22, single, b. Richmond Co., res. Westmoreland Co., s/o Robert and Mary A. Saunders, to CHARLOTTE HINSON, age 18, single, b. Richmond Co., d/o Reuben and Polly Hinson. Consent 18 JAN 1870 by father Reuben Hinson, no wit. Robert N. Reamy. 20 JAN 1870. [C5, R:233, R1:27]

Saunders, Robert L. to Augusta A. Balderson. ROBERT L. SAUNDERS, farming, age 22, single, b. Richmond Co., s/o Thornton and Henrietta [Edmonds] Saunders, to AUGUSTA A. BALDERSON, age 21y1m, single, b. Richmond Co., d/o Graham G. [George Graham] and Elizabeth A. [Ann Newman] Balderson, *q.v.* Consent 6 OCT 1884 from *Newland* by bride, G.G. Balderson. R.N. Reamy. 16 OCT 1884. [C10, R:355, R1:62]

Sanders, Robert W. to Etta Edmonds. ROBERT W. SAUNDERS [sic], farming, age 28, single, b. Richmond Co., s/o Griffin and Maria [A. Sanders] Saunders, to ETTA EDMONDS, age 22, single, b. Richmond Co., d/o George [A.] and Sarah [Ann Hall] Edmonds, *q.v.* Consent 27 DEC 1886 by bride, wit. by L.C. Saunders. R.N. Reamy. 30 DEC 1886. [C11, R:317, R1:68]

Saunders, Thomas (Col.) to Elizabeth Walker (Col.). THOMAS SAUNDERS, farming, age 23, single, b. Richmond Co., s/o John and Betsey Saunders, to ELIZABETH WALKER, age 17, single, b. Westmoreland Co., d/o Pearson Taylor and Amanda Walker. Consent 14 MAR 1887 by Thomas Sanders [sic] and Mandy Walker. George [his X mark] Laws. 17 MAR 1887 in Warsaw, Va. [C11, R:290, R1:69]

---

[1] Joseph F. Sanders and Mary M. Bowing were married by bond 21 MAR 1842 in Richmond Co.

Saunders, Thomas H. to Martha Ellen English.[1] THOMAS H. SAUNDERS, farmer, age 25, single, b. Richmond Co., s/o Henry S. and Margaret J. [Alderson] Saunders,[2] to MARTHA E. ENGLISH, age 18, single, b. Richmond Co., d/o Thomas and Matilda [Corey] English.[3] Consent 9 DEC 1859 by father Thomas English, wit. Thos. D. Ficklin. Robert Williamson, M.G. 11 DEC 1859. [C2, R:165, R1:8]

Saunders, William H.[4] to Julia Haynes. WILLIAM H. SAUNDERS, farmer, age 36, single, b. Richmond Co., s/o Henry S. and Margaret J. [Alderson] Saunders, to JULIA HAYNES, age 24, single, b. Richmond Co., d/o Austin B. and Catharine [Street] Haynes.[5] Consent 22 OCT 1866 by bride, no wit. Robert Williamson, M.G. 24 OCT 1866 at Farnham Church. [C4, R:272, R1:18]

Saunders, William H.[6] to Mrs. Elizabeth Marks. WILLIAM H. SAUNDERS,[7] farmer, age 26, single, b. Richmond Co., parents names omitted for "good cause," to ELIZABETH MARKS, age 24, widow, b. Richmond Co., d/o James C. and Sallie Saunders. Consent 29 DEC 1866 by bride Elizabeth [her X mark] Marks, wit. Abr. P. Wilson. John Pullen. 3 JAN 1867 at James C. Saunders'. [C4, R:273, R1:19]

Saunders, William O. to Catharine Jennings.[8] WILLIAM O. SAUNDERS, farmer, age about 25, widower, b. upper part of Richmond Co., s/o Thomas Sanders and wife Susan [Jones],[9] to CATHARINE JENNINGS, age about 22, single, b. upper part of Richmond Co., d/o James Jennings and wife Elizabeth. Consent 25 DEC 1855 by Catherine Jennings, wit. Zachariah Saunders. John Pullen, M.G. 1 JAN 1856 at the residence of Zacarrah [sic] Sanders. [C1, R, R1:3]

Saunders, William S. to Mary Mollie Bispham. WILLIAM S. SAUNDERS, farmer, age 21y9m, single, b. and res. Westmoreland Co., s/o John H. and Mary Saunders, to MOLLIE M. BISPHAM, age 19, single, b. Richmond Co., d/o Robert and Mary Jane [Jenkins] Bispham, *q.v.* Consent 23 SEP 1875 by bride, wit. Marion F. Hinson. R.N. Reamy. 23 SEP 1875 at M. Hinson's. [C7, R:262, R1:38]

Saunders, William T. to Emma Ambrose. WILLIAM T. SAUNDERS, oystering, age 35, single, b. and res. Westmoreland Co., s/o Lovel Saunders and Lista Mothershead, to EMMA AMBROSE, age 21y6m, single, b. Richmond Co., d/o Elijah and Delia [Cordelia A. Moss] Ambrose, *q.v.* Consent 4 JUN 1887 by bride, wit. by her parents. R.N. Reamy. 8 JUN 1887. [C11, R:292, R1:70]

Saunders, Winfield Scott[10] to Nannie K. Sisson. WINFIELD S. SAUNDERS, farmer, age 23, single, b. Richmond Co., s/o A.N. [Augustine], M.D. and Mary C. [Catharine Sands] Saunders, to

---

[1] Thomas H. Saunders (b. 20 FEB 1834) and wife Martha Ellen English (b. 26 MAY 1841, d. 29 DEC 1903), d/o Thomas and Matilda English, are bur. in Farnham Baptist Church cemetery.
[2] Margaret J. Saunders (b. 18 OCT 1819, d. 11 SEP 1895) is bur. in Farnham Baptist Church cemetery. Henry S. Saunders and Margaret J. Alderson were married by bond 7 JAN 1828 in Richmond Co.
[3] Thomas English and Matilda Corey were married by bond 5 DEC 1831 in Richmond Co.
[4] William H. Saunders (b. 1 FEB 1829, d. 28 DEC 1872) is bur. in Farnham Baptist Church cemetery.
[5] Austin B. Haynes and Catharine Street were married 28 FEB 1838 in Richmond Co. by Rev. Addison Hall.
[6] A William H. Saunders, b. MAY 1842, farmer, s/o Joseph Saunders, d. 22 JUL 1912 of pneumonia, bur. Welcome Grove.
[7] Recorded in the Register as Sanders.
[8] Consent gives William O. Sanders to Catherine Jenings.
[9] Thomas Sanders and Susannah Jones were married by bond 22 SEP 1819 in Richmond Co.
[10] Winfield Scott Saunders (b. 28 DEC 1858, d. 23 SEP 1930) is bur. at Roseland Cemetery, Reedville, Va.

NANNIE K. SISSON, age 21, single, b. Richmond Co., d/o Robert and Amanda Sisson. Consent 10 MAY 1883 by Nannie K. Sisson and Robert Sisson, wit. Henry J. Mills. R.N. Reamy. 15 MAY 1883. [C10, R:356, R1:59]

Sawyer, Edward to Emeline Rankins. EDWARD SAWYER, farmer, age 50, single, b. near Elizabeth City, N.C., s/o Malachi and Lavenia Sawyer, to EMELINE RANKINS, age 25, single, b. Richmond Co., d/o George and Sarah Rankins. William F. Bain. 7 JAN 1866 at Mr. A. Clark's in Warsaw, Va. [C4, R:270, R1:16]

Scates, Alfred to Ofela Jane Coates. ALFRED SCATES, farmer, age 23, single, b. Richmond Co., s/o Joseph and Lucy Scates, to AFELA JANE COATES, age 23, single, b. Richmond Co., d/o John A. and Elizabeth [Balderson] Coates. Consent 15 FEB 1859 by bride. John Pullen, M.G. 17 FEB 1859. [C2, R:165, R1:7]

Scates, James A. to Virginia A. Hinson. JAMES SCATES, miller, age 21y2m11d, single, b. Richmond Co., s/o Joseph and Lucy [Sanders] Scates,[1] to VIRGINIA A. HINSON, age 23, single, b. Richmond Co., d/o Daniel and Sophia [Newman] Hinson.[2] Consent 6 JUN 1864 by bride Virginia A. [her X mark] Hinson, wit. James H. Sanders. John Pullen. 12 JUN 1864 at Allen Sanders'. [C3, R:139, R1:13]

Scates, James Henry to Sarah J. Balderson. JAMES HENRY SCATES, farmer, age 19, single, b. Richmond Co., s/o Thomas and Susan [Sanders] Scates,[3] to SARAH J. BALDERSON, age 22, single, b. Richmond Co., d/o Henry and Frances [Balderson] Balderson.[4] Consent 1 FEB 1869 by Susan [her X mark] Scates, wit. T.N. Balderson, Jas. A.B. Sanders. Robert N. Reamy. 4 FEB 1869 at Mrs. Fanny Conily's [Connelly's]. [C5, R, R1:25]

Scates, James Henry to Mrs. Lucy A.C. Booker, widow of Augustus C. Boswell. JAMES H. SCATES, farming, age 30, widowed, b. Richmond Co., s/o Thomas and Susan [Sanders] Scates, to LUCY BOSWELL, age 28, widow, b. Richmond Co., d/o George and Mary Booker. Consent 29 DEC 1878 by bride, wit. Braxton Reynolds. A.B. Dunaway. 29 DEC 1878. [C8, R:312, R1:46]

Scates, James Madison to Cornelia Ann Balderson.[5] JAMES M. SCATES, farmer, age 29, widowed, b. Richmond Co., s/o John B. [Bartlett] and Elizabeth [Marks] Scates,[6] to CORNELIA A. BALDERSON, age 23, single, b. Richmond Co., d/o T.N. [Theoderick Noel] and Dorothea L. [Lane Sanders] Balderson [d. 23 FEB 1903]. John Pullen. 14 FEB 1867 at T.N. Balderson's. [C4, R:285, R1:20]

Scates, Joseph to Sarah A. Hinson. JOSEPH SCATES, fisherman, age 27, single, b. Richmond Co., s/o Joseph and Lucy [Sanders] Scates, to SARAH A. HINSON, age 20, single, b.

[1] Joseph Scates and Lucy Sanders were married by bond 15 FEB 1826 in Richmond Co.
[2] Daniel Hinson and Sophia Newman were married by bond 20 JAN 1840 in Richmond Co.
[3] Thomas Scates and Susan Sanders were married by bond 5 FEB 1838 in Richmond Co. by Rev. Thomas M. Washington.
[4] Henry Balderson and Frances Balderson were married by bond 18 DEC 1838 in Richmond Co.
[5] James M. Scates (b. 11 SEP 1836 at Newland, Va., d. 6 OCT 1884) and his second wife Cornelia A. Balderson (b. 1842, d. 20 APR 1915) are bur. in Rappahannock Baptist Church cemetery. He served as captain in Co. D, 40th Va. Inf., C.S.A. NN:1 APR 1881 notes the store of James M. Scates burned. NN:10 OCT 1884, obituary.
[6] John B. Scates and Betsy Marks were married by bond 10 MAR 1830 in Richmond Co.

Richmond Co., d/o Daniel and Sophia [Newman] Hinson. John Pullen. 21 MAR 1867 at res. of Daniel Hinson. [C4, R:286, R1:21]

Scates, Joseph to Mary Mathews. JOSEPH SCATES, farmer, age 23y10m9d, single, b. Richmond Co., s/o Richard and Mary Scates, to MARY MATHEWS, age 20, single, b. Richmond Co., d/o Eliza Mathews. Consent 9 NOV 1880 by mother Eliza [her X mark] Mathews, bride Mary [her X mark] Mathews, and groom Joseph [his X mark] Scates, wit. A.H. Saunders. R.N. Reamy. 18 NOV 1880. [C9, R:316, R1:51]

Scates, Richard Joseph[1] to Frances A. Coats. RICHARD J. SCATES, miller, age 23, single, b. Richmond Co., s/o Elijah and Louisa [A. Bartlett] Scates,[2] to FRANCES A. COATS, age 19, single, b. Richmond Co., d/o Henry and Fanny Coats. E.L. Williams. 8 FEB 1865 at the res. of George B. Scrimger. [C3, R:204, R1:14]

Scates, Richard Joseph[3] to Mary E. Douglas. RICHARD J. SCATES, sawyer, age 37, widowed, b. Richmond Co., s/o Elijah and L. [Louisa A. Bartlett] Scates, to MARY E. DOUGLAS, age 22, single, b. Richmond Co., d/o Samuel H. and [Lucy] Ann [Doggett] Douglas.[4] Consent 26 NOV 1878 by bride, no wit. J.B. DeBerry, Pastor Richmond Circuit. 26 NOV 1878 at the res. of the bride's father. [C8, R:312, R1:45]

Scates, Thomas Allen to Martha S. Bowen. THOMAS A. SCATES, farmer, age 19, single, b. Richmond Co., s/o Thomas and Susan [Sanders] Scates, to MARTHA S. BOWEN, age 21, single, b. Richmond Co., d/o Richard and Polly Bowen. John Pullen. 17 AUG 1865 at John Pullen's. [C3, R:204, R1:15]

Scates, Thomas Allen to Joanna Scates. THOMAS A. SCATES, farming, age 40, widowed,[5] b. Richmond Co., s/o Thomas and Susan [Sanders] Scates, to JOANNA SCATES, age 38, single, b. Richmond Co., d/o Joseph and Roberta [W. Butler] Scates.[6] Consent undated by bride Joanner [her X mark] Scates. Geo. M. Conley. 2 APR 1890 near Newland, Va. [C12, R:323a, R1:76]

Scates, Valentine James[7] to Mary Frances Jenkins. VALENTINE J. SCATES, fisherman, age 24, single, b. Richmond Co., s/o John [Bartlett] and Elizabeth [Marks] Scates, to MARY F. JENKINS, age 25, single, b. Richmond Co., d/o George and Mary F. Jenkins. R.N. Reamy. 16 FEB 1876 at L. Saunders'. [C7, R:304, R1:40]

Schools, Charles William to Bettie Woolard.[8] CHARLES WILLIAM SCHOOLS, farming, age 24, single, b. Richmond Co., s/o Alexander and Laura N. Schools, to BETTIE WOOLARD, age 17, single, b. Richmond Co., d/o [blank] and Bettie Woolard. Consent 22 DEC 1885 by bride's

---

[1] R.J. Scates (1843-1900) is bur. in Rappahannock Baptist Church cemetery. Richard J. Scates served in Co. K, 9th Va. Cav., C.S.A.

[2] Elijah Scates and Louisa A. Bartlett were married by bond 5 FEB 1827 in Richmond Co.

[3] Richard Joseph Scates (1854-1900) is bur. at Rappahannock Baptist Church cemetery.

[4] Samuel H. Douglass and Lucy Ann Doggett were married 1 JUN 1850 in Richmond Co. by Rev. John Godwin.

[5] Thomas A. Scates was previously married 17 AUG 1865 in Richmond Co. to Martha S. Bowen.

[6] Joseph Scates and Roberta W. Butler were married by bond 3 MAR 1845 in Richmond Co.

[7] Valentine J. Scates (b. 14 FEB 1848, d. 19 DEC 1902, was found dead in the wood near his home) is bur. in Rappahannock Baptist Church cemetery.

[8] Charles William Schools (b. 8 MAR1860, d. 8 OCT 1935) and wife Bettie Woolard (b. 17 OCT 1866, d. 8 MAY 1962) are bur. in Jerusalem Baptist Church cemetery.

mother, wit. Joseph A. Schools. G.H. Northam. 23 DEC 1885 at Mrs. Woolard's. [C11, NN:8 JAN 1886, R:318, R1:66]

Schools, John W. to Elton Jane Mealey,[1] b. 29 DEC 1849. JOHN W. SCHOOLS, farming, age 30, single, b. Richmond Co., s/o Alexander and Laura [N.] Schools, to ELTON JANE MEALEY, age 30, single, b. Richmond Co., d/o Jesse and Sarah [B. Harris] Mealey.[2] Consent 17 JAN 1881 by bride. G.H. Northam. 18 JAN 1881 at *West View.* [C9, R:335, R1:52]

Schools, Joseph A. to Lucy J. Rowe.[3] JOSEPH A. SCHOOLS, oysterman, age 27, single, b. Richmond Co., s/o Alexander and Laura [N.] Schools, to LUCY J. ROWE, age 21, single, b. Richmond Co., d/o John and Polly Rowe. Consent 7 JUN 1880 by bride, wit. James R. Fidler. G.H. Northam. 9 JUN 1880 at Jerusalem Baptist Church. [C9, R:315, R1:50]

Schools, Robert to Mrs. Virginia Thrift, widow of Wiley Schools. ROBERT SCHOOLS, farmer, age 42, widowed, b. King and Queen Co., s/o Jeremiah and Martha Schools, to VIRGINIA SCHOOLS, age 40, widow, b. Richmond Co., d/o William and Jane [Northen] Thrift. G.H. Northam. 28 JUN 1877 at Jerusalem Church. [C8, R:307, R1:43]

Schools, Robert Thomas to Edmonia Clarke.[4] ROBERT THOMAS SCHOOLS, sailor, age 29, single, b. King & Queen Co., s/o Robert Schools, to EDMONIA CLARKE, age 19, single, b. Richmond Co., d/o Cyrus Clarke and Sarah Jane his wife now Connelly. Consent 18 FEB 1887 by parties and Sarah Jane Conley [Connellee]. G.H. Northam. 3 MAR 1887 at res. of Mr. Connelly. [C11, R:290, R1:69]

Schools, Rufus[5] to Mahala Catharine "Kate" Mealey. RUFUS SCHOOLS, oysterman, age 29y6m, widowed, b. King and Queen Co., s/o Alexander and Sarah Schools, to MAHALA CATHARINE MALEY [sic], age 22y8m, single, b. Richmond Co., d/o Jesse and Sarah [B. Morris] Mealey. Oath to age of groom 7 APR 1876 at *Milton Wharf*, by Edward Clausen. G.H. Northam. 9 APR 1876. [C7, R:305, R1:40]

Schools, Wiley to Virginia Thrift.[6] WILEY SCHOOLS, farmer, age 22, single, b. King and Queen Co., s/o Jeremiah and Patsy Schools, to VIRGINIA THRIFT, age 24, single, b. Richmond Co., d/o William and Jane [Northen] Thrift.[7] E.L. Williams. 12 JAN 1861. [C3, R:123, R1:10]

Schools, William F. to Gertrude W. Tellis. WILLIAM F. SCHOOLS, farming, age 23, single, b. Richmond Co., s/o Wylie and Virginia [Thrift] Schools, *q.v.*, to GERTRUDE W. TELLIS, age 18, single, b. Richmond Co., d/o John C. and Ann Tellis. Consent 29 SEP 1885 by father J.C. Tellis, wit. B.A. Woollard. G.H. Northam. 30 SEP 1885 at *Walker's Hill.* [C10, NN:9 OCT 1885, R:317, R1:65]

---

[1] Elton Jane Mealey (b. 1 JAN 1851, d. 17 MAR 1919), wife of John W. Schools, is bur. in Jerusalem Baptist Church cemetery.
[2] Jesse Mealey and Sarah B. Harris were married 22 FEB 1844 in Richmond Co. by Rev. William N. Ward.
[3] Joseph A. Schools (1854-1922) and wife Lucy J. Rowe (1862-1921) are bur. in Jerusalem Baptist Church cemetery.
[4] Robert T. Schools (1856-1896) and wife Monia Clark (1867-) are bur. at Calvary United Methodist Church cemetery. Her death year is blank on the tombstone.
[5] Rufus Schools (b. 1845 in King and Queen Co., d. 4 JUL 1930) is bur. in Jerusalem Baptist Church cemetery.
[6] Wiley Schools (b. 1839, d. 21 NOV 1871) and his wife Virginia Thrift (1836-1903) are bur. in Jerusalem Baptist Church cemetery. He served as a private in Co. D, 47th Va. Inf., C.S.A., and was a prisoner at Point Lookout, Md.
[7] William Thrift and Jane Northen, d/o Katharine G. Northen, were married by bond 12 NOV 1818 in Richmond Co.

Scott, Anderson (Col.) to Winnie Maiden (Col.). ANDERSON SCOTT, farmer, age 60, widowed, b. Essex Co., s/o Joe and Winnie Scott, to WINNIE MAIDEN, age 32, single, b. Richmond Co., [names of parents not completed]. Consent 21 SEP 1874 by bride Winnie [her X mark] Maiden, wit. Thos. F. Kemp. Elder James A. Weaver. 24 SEP 1874 at the res. of Peter [P]uton. [C7, R:230, R1:37]

Scott, Buck (Col.) to Nettie Yerby (Col.). BUCK SCOTT, oysterman, age 21, single, b. Essex Co., s/o Dandridge and Martha Scott, to NETTIE YERBY, age 20, single, b. Richmond Co., d/o Samuel and Louisa Yerby (both dec'd.). Rev. W. Carter. 20 APR 1882 at the res. of Bal Caspillar. [C9, R:312, R1:56]

Scott, Frank Covington to Sallie V.B.T. Somers. FRANK COVINGTON SCOTT, farming, age 22, single, b. Richmond Co., s/o H.P. and Rebecca C. Scott, to SALLIE V.B.T. SOMERS, age 17, single, b. King George Co., d/o W.S. and E.A. Somers. Consent 15 OCT 1886 by parent W.S. Somers, wit. [M.]C. Scott. Robert Williamson. 26 OCT 1886 at Farnham, Va. [C11, R:316, R1:68]

Scott, Nelson (Col.) to Celia Cox (Col.). NELSON SCOTT, oystering, age 24, single, b. Essex Co., s/o Dandridge and Martha Scott, to CELIA COX, age 22, single, b. Richmond Co., d/o Mat and Sarah Cox. Rev. W. Carter. 6 FEB 1890 at the bride's home. [C12, R:323, R1:76]

Scrimger, George B. to Lelia Efford. GEORGE B. SCRIMGER, sailor, age 46, widowed, b. Richmond Co., s/o James and Sally [Sarah Fowler] Scrimger,[1] to LELIA EFFORD, age 38, single, b. Richmond Co., d/o William and Nancy Efford. Robert Williamson, M.G. 13 FEB 1867 at *Marleton*. [C4, R:285, R1:20]

Scrimger, James, to Susan Littrell. JAMES SCRIMGER, farmer, age 72, widowed, b. Westmoreland Co., s/o Walter J. and Charity Scrimger, to SUSAN LITTRELL, age 42, single, b. Richmond Co., d/o John D. and Elizabeth Littrell. Consent by bride. Elder James A. Weaver. 6 FEB 1861. [C3, R:123, R1:10]

Scrimger, Lombard Walter to Ella E. Newman.[2] WALTER LOMBARD SCRIMGER, oystering, age 23y7m21d, single, b. Richmond Co., s/o George B. and Susan Ann [Hill] Scrimger, to ELLA E. NEWMAN, age 21y7m26d, single, b. Richmond Co., d/o Henry and Elizabeth [Pugh] Newman, *q.v.* G.H. Northam. 26 JAN 1882. [C9, NN:3 FEB 1882, R:312, R1:55]

Self, Daniel to Maria Lewis. DANIEL SELF, farming, age 26, single, b. Northumberland Co., s/o Stephen and Mary Ann [Wilkins] Self, to MARIA LEWIS, age 24, single, b. Richmond Co., d/o Austin and Nancy Lewis. Consent 7 JAN 1880 by bride Maria [her X mark] Lewis, wit. Rd. [his X mark] Hale. G.H. Northam. 8 JAN 1880. [C9; R:314, R1:49]

Self, Fleet W. to Sarah Ann Efford. FLEET W. SELF, farmer, age 27, single, b. Richmond Co., s/o Stephen and Eliza Self, to SARAH ANN EFFORD, age 21, single, b. Richmond Co., d/o George W. and Elizabeth [W. Thrift] Efford.[3] Consent 22 DEC 1868 by bride, wits. Lewis L. Headley,

---

[1] James Scrimsher and Sarah Fowler, widow, were married by bond 7 JAN 1811 in Richmond Co.
[2] Lombard W. Scrimger (b. 15 SEP 1857, d. 28 JAN 1911) and wife Ella E. Newman (b. 15 SEP 1860, d. 28 JAN 1905) are bur. in Farnham Baptist Church cemetery.
[3] George W. Efford and Elizabeth W. Thrift were married by bond 24 DEC 1836 in Richmond Co.

Elizabeth W. Efford. Robert Williamson, M.G. 24 DEC 1868 at Mrs. Efford's. [C5, R:254, R1:24]

Self, Henry (Col.) to Mrs. Louisa Sorrell, widow of John Peterson (Col.). HENRY SELF, farmer, age 52, widowed, b. Westmoreland Co., res. *Milden Hall*, s/o Moses Self and Sarah Smith, to LOUISA PETERSON, age 28, widow, b. Richmond Co., res. *Milden Hall*, d/o David and Ellen Sorrell. Allen Brown, minister. 20 APR 1876 at *Milden Hall*.[1] [C7, R:305, R1:40]

Self, James to Mrs. Maria Wilkins Self. JAMES SELF, farmer, age 33, single, b. Northumberland Co., s/o Stephen and Mary Ann [Wilkins] Self,[2] to MARIA SELF, age 33, widow, b. Richmond Co., d/o Samuel and Mary Wilkins. Oath 11 APR 1889 from Farnham by J.W. Chinn as to ages of parties. Robert Williamson. 14 APR 1889 at *Woodford*. [C12, R:327, R1:74]

Self, John Robert to Mary Ida Luckham. JOHN ROBERT SELF, farmer, age 24, single, b. Richmond Co., s/o Zach and Martha Ann Self, to MARY IDA LUCKHAM, age 16, single, b. Richmond Co., d/o Thomas B. and Mary Ann [Brooks] Luckham, *q.v.* Consent 29 DEC 1881 by bride, wits. Richard H. Luckham, Thomas B. [his X mark] Luckham. F.W. Claybrook. 3 JAN 1882 at the res. of Thomas B. Luckham. [C9, R:312, R1:55]

Self, Joseph to Annie Dunaway. JOSEPH SELF, oystering, age 25, single, b. Northumberland Co., s/o Stephen and Mary [Ann Wilkins] Self, to ANNIE DUNAWAY, age 20, single, b. Richmond Co., d/o R.R. and Mary Jane Dunaway. Rev. Robert Williamson, Farnham, Va. 5 JAN 1888 at *Woodford*. [C11, R:315, R1:72]

Self, Judy (Col.) to Laura Thompson (Col.). JUDY SELF, hauling, age 20, single, b. Richmond Co., s/o Moses Self and Catherine Johnson now Gaskins, to LAURA THOMPSON, age 17, single, b. Richmond Co., d/o Robert and Frances Thompson. Consent 24 DEC 1888 by Frances [her X mark] Thompson and Catherine [her X mark] Gaskins, wit. Fred [his X mark] Gaskins. Edmond Rich. 26 DEC 1888 at the res. of the minister. [C12, R:317, R1:72]

Self, Moses Andrew to Lucy Ann Sydnor.[3] MOSES SELF, farmer, age 21, single, b. Richmond Co., s/o Peter and Mary [Purcell] Self, to LUCY SYDNOR. age 21. single, b. Richmond Co., d/o Robert and Lucy [Kent] Sydnor.[4] Consent 22 FEB 1858 by father Robert Sydnor, wits. Benj. Tucker, Harriet Tucker. James A. Weaver, minister of the Union Baptist Church. 25 FEB 1858. [C1, R:138, R1:6]

Self, Peter A. to Lizzie B. King. PETER A. SELF, farming, age 20y10m8d, single, b. Richmond Co., s/o Moses A. [Andrew] and Lucy [Ann Sydnor] Self, *q.v.*, to LIZZIE B. KING, age 19, single, b. Richmond Co., d/o William King (dec'd.) and Martha King. Consent by bride, also signed by Moses A. and Lucy Self. G.H. Northam. 18 APR 1883. [C10, R:356, R1:58]

Self, Robert L. to Mrs. Mary J. Haydon, widow of Ferdinand Dodson.[5] ROBERT Z. SELF, farming and oystering, age 27, single, b. Richmond Co., s/o Stephen and Mary [Ann Wilkins] Self, to

---

[1] Location also spelled *Milton Hall*. *Milden Hall* is known as the home of Col. William Peachey, and is located at Sharps, Va.
[2] Stephen Self and Mary Ann Wilkins were married 14 JAN 1853 in Richmond Co. by Rev. John Godwin.
[3] Moses A. Self (b. 23 JUN 1837, d. 27 AUG 1895 in Westmoreland Co.) and his wife Lucy A. Sydnor (b. 9 NOV 1841, d. 21 JAN 1908) are bur. at Totuskey Baptist Church cemetery. He served in Co. K, 9th Va. Cav., C.S.A.
[4] Robert Sydnor and Lucy Kent were married by bond 9 JUL 1838 in Richmond Co.
[5] Robert L. Self (1858-1906) and Mary J. Dodson (1857-1945) are bur. in Farnham Baptist Church cemetery.

MARY J. DODSON, age 30, widow, b. Richmond Co., d/o John T. and Jane Haydon. Consent 7 OCT 1887 by parties, wit. J.T. Hayden. Rev. A.D. Reynolds. 9 OCT 1887 at the res. of John Haydon. [C11, R:292, R1:70]

Self, Steptoe T. to Mahala Lewis. STEPTOE T. SELF, farming, age 23, single, b. Northumberland Co., s/o Stephen and Mary [Ann Wilkins] Self, to MAHALA LEWIS, age 25y9m, single, b. Northumberland Co., d/o Austin D. and Nancy [Hale] Lewis.[1] Consent 17 DEC 1879 by bride Mahala [her X mark] Lewis, wit. Z.M. [his X mark] Lewis. G.H. Northam. 18 DEC 1879 at the res. of Mr. Lewis. [C9, R:309, R1:48]

Settle, Frederick Alexander to Martha "Mattie" S. Omohundro.[2] FREDERICK SETTLE, farmer, age 66y1m17d, widowed, b. Richmond Co., s/o William and Mary ["Polly" Greenlaw] Settle, to MATTIE S. OMOHUNDRO, age 33y3d, single, b. Westmoreland Co., d/o Edward B. Omohundro and Sarah Ann Redman [Reamy].[3] E.P. Parham, M.E. Church South. 6 JAN 1887 at *Farmers Fork*. [C11, R:290, R1:69]

Settle, Frederick G. to Martha V. Haynes.[4] FREDERICK G. SETTLE, farming, age 22, single, b. Richmond Co., s/o Frederick and Diana T. [Claughton] Settle, to MARTHA V. HAYNES, age 19, single, b. Richmond Co., d/o William C. and Louisa [R. Harwood] Haynes.[5] Consent undated by William C. Haynes, wit. C.W. McKenney. F.B. Beale. 25 DEC 1879. [C9, R:309, R1:49]

Settle, Richard Henry[6] to Harriet E. Yeatman. RICHARD H. SETTLE, farmer and soldier, age 23, single, b. Richmond Co., s/o Frederick [Alexander] and Diana [Turner Claughton] Settle,[7] to HARRIET E. YEATMAN, age 24, single, b. Richmond Co., d/o Tho. J. and Susannah [Susan P. Hunter] Yeatman. Consent signed by parties, wit. R. Montgomery. William F. Bain. 1 JAN 1865 at the Methodist Parsonage in Warsaw. [C3[8], R:204, R1:14]

Shackleford, George Nelson[9] to Nanny Murren. GEORGE NELSON SHACKLEFORD, laborer, age 27, single, b. Richmond Co., s/o John and Martha Shackleford, to NANNY MURREN, age 22, single, b. Richmond Co., d/o [William] Thompson and Mary [McPherson] Murren.[10] Oath 24 APR 1879 by L.D. Warner, clerk, to age of bride. G.H. Northam. 24 APR 1879. [C8, R:307, R1:47]

Shackleford, George Nelson[11] to Mary Weathers. GEORGE N. SHACKLEFORD, farming, age 34, widowed, b. Richmond Co., s/o John and Martha Shackleford, to MARY WEATHERS, age 35,

---

[1] Austin Lewis and Nancy Hale were married by bond 28 DEC 1836 in Northumberland Co.

[2] Frederick Alexander Settle (b. 12 NOV 1819, d. 5 FEB 1905) and wife Martha are bur. in the Settle Family Cemetery at Hague, Va. He served in Co. E, 40th Reg., Va. Inf., C.S.A. Military record gives death as 11 FEB 1902 of heart trouble.

[3] Edward B. Omohundro and Sarah A. Reamy were married by bond 1 JUL 1839 in Westmoreland Co.

[4] Frederick G. Settle (b. 11 NOV 1857, d. 23 JUL 1929) and his wife Martha V. Haynes (b. 8 AUG 1860, d. 6 JAN 1929) are bur. in Menokin Baptist Church cem.

[5] William C. Haynes and Louisa R. Harwood were married 30 MAR 1848 in Richmond Co. by Rev. George Northam.

[6] Richard H. Settle (b. 8 JUL 1841, d. 2 MAR 1927) is bur. at Carmel United Methodist Church cemetery, Kinsale, Va. He served in Co. B, 40th Va. Inf., C.S.A., wounded in action at Bethesda Church.

[7] Diana T. Claughton Settle (b. 23 JUL 1820, d. 14 OCT 1883) is bur. at Menokin Baptist Church cemetery.

[8] License is signed by William D. Garland, J.P., in absence of the clerk [Francis W. Pendleton] who is in the hands of the enemy.

[9] A George Nelson Shackleford (b. 1849, d. in JAN 1923) is bur. in St. John's Episcopal Church cemetery.

[10] William T. Murren and Mary McPherson, ward of Benjamin Clark, of Fredericksburg, Va., were married 19 JAN 1826 by Rev. Henry Slicer.

[11] George N. Shackleford (1849-1923) is bur. at St. John's Episcopal Church cemetery.

single, b. Richmond Co., d/o James and Betsey [Elizabeth Sutton] Weathers.[1] G.H. Northam. 24 SEP 1885 at *Glenmore.* [C10, R:317, R1:65]

Shackleford, John J. to Martha Dameron. JOHN J. SHACKLEFORD, farmer, age 24, single, b. Richmond Co., s/o John and Martha B. Shackleford, to MARTHA DAMERON, age 21, single, b. Richmond Co., d/o John C. [Jr.] and Lucy [Jane Hall] Dameron.[2] G.H. Northam. 6 JUN 1867. [C4, R:286, R1:21]

Shackleford, Lewis (Col.) to Martha Veney (Col.). LEWIS SHACKLEFORD, farming, age 43, single, b. Richmond Co., d/o Lyne and Lucy Shackleford, to MARTHA VENEY, age 35, single, b. Richmond Co., d/o John and Rachel Veney. David Veney, M.G. 5 DEC 1884. [C10, R:355, R1:63]

Shaw, George (Col.) to Amelia Davis (Col.). GEORGE SHAW, waterman, age 22, single, b. Richmond Co., s/o Julia Davis, to AMELIA DAVIS, age 23, single, b. Richmond Co., d/o Thomas Davis and Winney Davis now Kennedy. Consent 9 JAN 1878 by bride Amealia [her X mark] Davis, wit. A.P. Wilson. George Laws. 10 JAN 1878 at *Mulberry Island.* [C8, R:310, R1:44]

Shaw, Gilbert to Frances E. Pope. Consent 26 MAY 1856 by bride, wit. F.B. Cobb, Jas. A. McKnight. No lice or minister return. [C1]

Shelton, Ezekiel (Col.) to Betsey Sorrell (Col.). EZEKIEL SHELTON, farming, age 31, single, b. Westmoreland Co., s/o John and Susan Shelton, to BETSEY SORRELL, age 21, single, b. Richmond Co., parents unknown. Edmond Rich. 29 NOV 1885 at the res. of the minister. [C10, R:318, R1:65]

Shelton, Joseph H. to Mrs. Etta M. Luckham Hinson.[3] JOSEPH H. SHELTON, oystering, age 21y3m, single, b. Lancaster Co., s/o John M. and Dorothea Ann Shelton, to ETTA M. HINSON, age 20, widow, b. Richmond Co., d/o Thomas B. and Mary A. [Ann Brooks] Luckam, *q.v.* Consent 12 NOV 1888 by bride. Robert Williamson. 12 NOV 1888 at the res. of Milton Douglass's near Ivanhoe, Va. [C11, R:316, R1:73]

Shelton, Major (Col.) to Juliette Ann Veney (Col.). MAJOR SHELTON, farmer, age 42, single, b. Caroline Co., s/o Isaac and Sarah Shelton, to JULIETTE ANN VENEY, age 30, single, b. Richmond Co., d/o Travers and Crissy Veney. Allen Brown, minister. 16 OCT 1874 at the bride's house. [C7, R:230, R1:37]

Shelton, William (Col.) to Martha Johnson (Col.). WILLIAM SHELTON, farmer, age 25, single, b. Westmoreland Co., s/o John and Susan Shelton, to MARTHA JOHNSON, age 18, single, b. Richmond Co., d/o Ann Johnson and unknown father. Consent 24 DEC 1873 signed by parties, wit. J.P. Delano. Elder James A. Weaver. 25 DEC 1873 at the res. of Joseph P. Delano. [C6, R:236, R1:35]

---

[1] James Weathers and Elizabeth Susson were married 7 JAN 1846 in Richmond Co. by Rev. Elijah L. Williams.
[2] John C. Dameron, Jr. and Lucy Jane Hall were married 12 JAN 1842 in Richmond Co. by Rev. William N. Ward.
[3] Joseph H. Shelton (b. 3 SEP 1868, d. 22 DEC 1947) and wife Etta M. Hinson (b. 6 MAR 1869, d. 24 DEC 1932) are bur. at White Stone United Methodist Church cemetery.

Shelton, William (Col.) to Novella Ball (Col.). WILLIAM SHELTON, farmer, age 31, widowed, b. Westmoreland Co., s/o John and Susan Shelton, to NOVELLA BALL, age 23, single, b. Richmond Co., d/o George Weathers and Lucy Ball. Consent 28 NOV 1881 by Noveller [her X mark] Ball, wit. Wm. [his X mark] Ball. Edmond Rich. 1 DEC 1881 at the res. of William Allison. [C9, R:338, R1:54]

Shelton, William T. to Maria J. Stevens. WILLIAM T. SHELTON, sailor, age 26y9m16d, single, b. Lancaster Co., s/o John P. and Sarah A. Shelton,[1] to MARIA J. STEVENS, age 16y3d, single, b. Dorchester Co., [Md.], d/o Wm. W. and Harriet Stevens. Consent 21 JUL 1863 by mother Harrit Stevens, wits. J.W. Scrimger, Wm. E. [his X mark] Sisson. E.L. Williams. 29 JUL 1863 at res. of Mrs. H. Stephens. [C3, R:160, R1:13]

Short, William C. to Bettie B. Mitchell. WILLIAM C. SHORT, merchant, age 24, single, b. Westmoreland Co., res. Fairfax Co., s/o Benjamin and Mary J. [Crabb] Short,[2] to BETTIE B. MITCHELL, age 21, single, b. Richmond Co., d/o William B. and Julia Mitchell. Consent 8 JUN 1874 by bride, no wit. G.H. Northam. 9 JUN 1874 at *Belmont*.[3] [C7, R:230, R1:36]

Simonson, John E. to Maria Louise Headley.[4] JOHN E. SIMONSON, farmer, age 37, single, b. Hudson Co., N.J., s/o Andrew P. and Matilda Simonson, to MARIA L. HEADLEY, age 22, single, b. Richmond Co., d/o [W.H. and] Mary Headley. Consent 21 DEC 1874 by bride, wit. Francis W. Mullin. G.H. Northam. 23 DEC 1874. [C7, R:231, R1:38]

Sipes, Alexander to Elizabeth Kennan. ALEXANDER SIPES, farmer, age 33, widowed, b. Pennsylvania, parents not known, to ELIZABETH KENNAN,[5] age 23, single, b. Lancaster Co., d/o James Kennan and Milet Winder. Consent 22 JUN 1857 by bride Elizabeth [her X mark] Kenem [sic], wit. John H. Williams, Jr. Barth. Dodson, Baptist parson. 2 JUL 1857. [C1, R:159, R1:5]

Sisson, George H. to Rebecca Ann Davis.[6] GEORGE H. SISSON, farmer, age 24, single, b. Richmond Co., s/o Hiram and Sarah [Littrell] Sisson,[7] to REBECCA ANN DAVIS, age 22, single, b. Richmond Co., d/o Luke W. and Mahala [B. Kennan] Davis.[8] G.H. Northam. 23 DEC 1873. [C6, R:236, R1:35]

Sisson, Hempsel Clark to Margaret Rebecca Lamkin.[9] HEMPSEL CLARK SISSON, farming, age 19, single, b. Richmond Co., s/o John T. [Taliaferro] and Ann Eliza [Clarke] Sisson, to REBECCA LAMPKIN,[10] age 22, single, b. Westmoreland Co., d/o Lewis A.L. and Margaret S. Lampkin. Consent 26 DEC 1884 by J.T. Sisson, H.C. Sisson and bride. W.W. Walker. 28 DEC 1884 at the groom's residence. [C10, N:24 APR 1885, R:356, R1:63]

---

[1] There is a bond 15 JAN 1823 in Lancaster Co. for the marriage of John P. Shelton and Sally M.C. George.

[2] Benjamin Short and Mary J.J. Crabb were married by bond 19 DEC 1848 in Westmoreland Co.

[3] Since there is no Belmont in Richmond Co. this is presumably Belle Mount.

[4] Maria Louise Headley (b. 26 DEC 1852, d. 18 SEP 1930 in Sharps, Va.), widow of John E. Simonson, and d/o W.H. Headley, is bur. in Milden Cemetery.

[5] Spelling various, Kenum, Kenna, Kenen, etc.

[6] George H. Sisson (b. 17 SEP 1848, d. 8 MAY 1916) and wife Rebecca Ann Davis (b. 3 JUL 1849, d. 26 DEC 1932) are bur. in Jerusalem Baptist Church cemetery.

[7] Hierome [Hiram] Sisson and Sally Littrell were married by bond 24 FEB 1840 in Richmond Co.

[8] Luke W. Davis and Mrs. Mahalah B. Kennan were married 13 APR 1843 in Richmond Co. by Rev. William N. Ward.

[9] Hempsel C. Sisson (b. 1864, d. 10 DEC 1936) and wife Rebecca Lamkin (b. 1860, d. 5 MAY 1927) are bur. at Totuskey Baptist Church cemetery.

[10] Surname also appears as Lamkin.

Sisson, Henry J. to Alverta Elizabeth Bell.[1] HENRY J. SISSON, farming, age 26, single, b. Richmond Co., s/o Henry and Lavalia Sisson, to ALVERTA E. BELL, age 23, single, b. Richmond Co., d/o Vincent R. and Mary A. [Ann Rock] Bell. Consent 21 DEC 1882 by bride, wit. S.R. Franklin. G.H. Northam. 26 DEC 1882. [C10, R:314, R1:57]

Sisson, John F.H. to Margaret Murphy.[2] JOHN F.H. SISSON, saloon keeper, agea 33, widowed, b. and res. Westmoreland Co., s/o J.T. and Anna E. Sisson, to MARGARET MURPHY, age 35, single, b. Westmoreland Co., d/o Margaret Murphy. J. Dorsey Berry. 7 JUL 1890 at J.H. Settle's. [C12, R:323a, R1:77]

Sisson, John Martin to Elizabeth Frances King.[3] JOHN M. SISSON, farmer, age 33, single, b. Richmond Co., s/o Randall and Frances [Ann Gordon] Sisson,[4] to ELIZABETH F. KING, age 19, single, b. Richmond Co., d/o Burgess and Elizabeth A. King. G.H. Northam. 14 FEB 1867. [C4, R:285, R1:20]

Sisson, John W. to Lou Ella Woollard.[5] JOHN W. SISSON, mechanic, age 24, single, b. Richmond Co., s/o Hiram and Sallie Sisson (both dec'd.), to LOUELLA WOLLARD [sic], age 20, single, b. Richmond Co., d/o John T. (dec'd.) and Elizabeth S. Woollard. Consent 20 JUN 1881 by mother Elizabeth S. [her X mark] Woollard, wit. T.E. Johnson. G.H. Northam. 26 JUN 1881. [C9, R:336, R1:53]

Sisson, Lewis H. to Willie Ann Webb. LEWIS H. SISSON, age 30, single, b. Richmond Co., s/o William H. and Elizabeth [Sandy] Sisson,[6] to WILLIE ANN WEBB, age 20, single, b. Richmond Co., d/o William B. and Ann Webb. G.H. Northam. 26 DEC 1866. [C4, R:273, R1:19]

Sisson, Richard Hugh to Charlotte McAdam Bell.[7] RICHARD H. SISSON, farmer, age 35, widowed, b. Richmond Co., s/o Randall and Frances [Ann Gordon] Sisson, to LOTTIE M. BELL, age 22, single, b. Northumberland Co., d/o William D. [Dew] and Sallie M. [Charlotte McAdam Nutt] Bell.[8] Consent 17 JAN 1869 by bride, wit. James S. [Hinson]. Robert Williamson, M.G. 21 JAN 1869 at Mrs. Sallie M. Bell's. [C5, R, R1:25]

Sisson, Thomas E. to Rosey B. Mozingo. THOMAS E. SISSON, farmer, age 26, single, b. Richmond Co., s/o Randal[l] and Frances Ann [Gordon] Sisson, to ROSEY B. MOZINGO, age 18, single, b. Northumberland Co., d/o J.B. [Jonathan] and Matilda [Efford] Mozingo. Consent by bride, oath by E.L. Mozingo. Elder James A. Weaver. 10 DEC 1873 at the Royal Oak Church.[9] [C6, R:236, R1:35]

---

[1] Alverta Elizabeth Bell Sisson (b. 1853, d. 11 OCT 1943) is bur. in Calvary United Methodist Church cemetery.
[2] Margaret M. Sisson (b. 19 AUG 1853, d. 21 DEC 1936) is bur. at Calvary United Methodist Church cemetery.
[3] John M. Sisson (1832-1884) and his wife Elizabeth F. King [Hale] (b. 11 MAY 1846, d. 26 JAN 1904) are bur. at Totuskey Baptist Church cemetery. He served in Cos. B and E, 40th Reg., Va. Inf., C.S.A., transferred to Co. G, 15th Va. Cav.
[4] Randall Sisson and Frances A. Gordon were married by bond 30 DEC 1829 in Richmond Co.
[5] John W. Sisson (1856-1932) and wife Louella Woollard (1860-1954) are bur. in Jerusalem Baptist Church cemetery.
[6] William H. Sisson and Elizabeth Sandy were married by bond 21 JUL 1834 in Westmoreland Co.
[7] Richard H. Sisson (b. 24 OCT 1833, d. 19 JUN 1896 of paralysis) and wife Charlotte Mc. Bell (b. 16 FEB 1847, d. 2 OCT 1943) are bur. in Totuskey Baptist Church cemetery. He served in Co. G, 15th Va. Cav., C.S.A.
[8] William D. Bell and Charlotte Nutt, ward of Thomas S. Sydnor, were married by bond 24 JAN 1837 in Northumberland Co.
[9] This was an early name for Jerusalem Baptist Church.

Smith, Albert Washington to Maria Jane Jackson.[1] ALBERT W. SMITH, farming, age 23, single, b. Richmond Co., s/o Peter [C.] and Virginia [Adams Douglas] Smith,[2] to MARIA JANEY JACKSON [sic], age 21y17d, single, b. Richmond Co., d/o Daniel S. and Millie Jackson. Consent 1 JAN 1883 [sic] by father Daniel S. [his X mark] Jackson. G.H. Northam. 2 JAN 1884 at J. Mozingo's. [C10, NN:25 JAN 1884, R:353, R1:61]

Smith, Benjamin Smith to Mary Ann Smith. BENJAMIN SMITH, farmer, age 26, single, b. Westmoreland Co., s/o William and Peggy Smith, to MARY ANN SMITH, age 16, single, b. Richmond Co., d/o James S. and Mary [B. Sisson] Smith.[3] Consent 2 JUN 1860 by parents Mary Ann Smith and James S. Smith, wit. William H. Donahan. 5 JUN 1860. [C2, R:153, R1:9]

Smith, Charles A. (Col.) to Florence Thompson (Col.). CHARLES A. SMITH, cook, age 34, single, b. Richmond Co., s/o Aaron and Jane Smith, to FLORENCE THOMPSON, age 23, single, b. Westmoreland Co., d/o Robert and Rose Thompson. Consent 26 DEC 1889 from Totuskey by bride Florence [his X mark] Thompson, wit. Jas. F. Garland. G.H. Northam. 27 DEC 1889 at the Totuskey Bridge.[4] [C12, R:329, R1:75]

Smith, Charles W. to Josephine Lemoine. CHARLES W. SMITH, farmer, age 52, widower, b. *Moratico Hall*, s/o Charles and Catharine Smith, to JOSEPHINE LEMOINE, age 21, single, b. Warsaw, Va., d/o Feriol [Jr.] and Ann M. [Maria Saunders] Lemoine.[5] Consent 22 JUN 1858 by mother Ann M. Lemoine. Edmund Withers, P.E. Church, 23 JUN 1858 at *Kitesville* (the house of Mrs. Lemoine). [C2, R:138, R1:6]

Smith, Elias P. to Elizabeth Smith. ELIAS P. SMITH, farmer, age 25, single, b. Westmoreland Co., s/o William and Peggy Smith, to ELIZABETH SMITH, age 24, single, b. Richmond Co., d/o James S. and Mary [B. Sisson] Smith. Consent 31 DEC 1859 by mother Elizabeth Smith and father James S. Smith, wit. William H. Donahan. 5 JAN 1860. [C2, R:153, R1:8]

Smith, Jacob to Malinda Sydnor. JACOB SMITH, farmer, age 21, bachelor, b. Gloucester Co., s/o John and Nancy Smith, to MALINDA SYDNOR, age 22, single, b. Richmond Co., d/o Martin and Matilda Sydnor. Consent by bride, wit. Jos. Dickenson. Robert Williamson, M.G. 22 SEP 1870 at Mount Zion Church. [C5, R:233, R1:28]

Smith, James C. to Lucy V. Scott. JAMES C. SMITH, farmer, age 27y7m, single, b. Richmond Co., s/o James S. and Mary B. [Hardwick] Smith, to LUCY V. SCOTT, age 21, single, b. Richmond Co., d/o James and Matilda A. [Scott] Scott.[6] G.H. Northam. 15 FEB 1877. [C8, R:306a, R1:42]

Smith, John W. to Susan C. Hale.[7] JOHN W. SMITH, farming, age 30, single, b. Richmond Co., s/o Peter and Virginia Smith, to SUSAN C. HALE, age 24, single, b. Richmond Co., d/o Sydnor

---

[1] Albert W. Smith (b. 2 JUN 1860, d. 18 MAR 1952 at Haynesville, Va.) and wife Maria J. Jackson (1867-1933) are bur. at Totuskey Baptist Church cemetery. Haynesville is a village east of Warsaw, Va. at the junction of Routes 619 and 661 and was named for William Haynes who was the first postmaster there.
[2] Peter C. Smith (b. 24 AUG 1833 in Westmoreland Co., d. 6 SEP 1895) and wife Virginia A. Douglas (b. 15 SEP 1839, d. 11 FEB 1922 at Haynesville, Va.) are bur. at Totuskey Baptist Church cemetery. He served in Co. K, 40th Va. Inf., C.S.A.
[3] James S. Smith and Mary B. Sisson were married by bond 27 OCT 1830 in Richmond Co.
[4] The Totuskey Bridge conveys Highway 3 across Totuskey Creek, about 3½ miles southeast of Warsaw, Va.
[5] Feriol Lemoine, Jr. and Ann Maria Saunders were married by bond 5 FEB 1833 in Richmond Co.
[6] James Scott and Matilda A. Scott were married 6 NOV 1853 in Richmond Co. by Rev. George Northam.
[7] John W. Smith (b. 1858, d. 8 NOV 1931) and wife Susan C. Hale (1859-1912) are bur. in Jerusalem Baptist Church cemetery.

[P.] and Virginia [Sydnor] Hale, *q.v.* Consent 2 JAN 1889 by bride. W.A. Crocker. 5 JAN 1889 at the res. of the bride's father. [C12, R:327, R1:74]

Smith, Robert (Col.) to Lucy Boyd (Col.). ROBERT SMITH, laborer, age 33, single, b. Northumberland Co., s/o Joshua and Susan Smith, to LUCY BOYD, age 27, single, b. Lancaster Co., d/o Stephen and Mary Boyd. Robert Williamson, M.G. 1 NOV 1866 at James Yerby's. [C4, R:272, R1:18]

Smith, Rowland (Col.) to Nellie Diggs (Col.). ROWLAND SMITH, oysterman, age 22, single, b. and res. Lancaster Co., s/o William and Harriet Smith, to NELLIE DIGGS, age 19, single, b. Richmond Co., d/o Nelson Diggs and Mary Ann Diggs now Mason. Consent 8 DEC 1880 at *Point Isabell* from bride, wit. Mary Ann Mason. Daniel Payne. 9 DEC 1880 at the res. of Willis Mason. [C9, R:316, R1:51]

Smith, William H. to Augusta Blueford.[1] WILLIAM SMITH, farmer, age 21y10m19d, single, b. Richmond Co., s/o James [L.] and Patsey [Clarke] Smith,[2] to AUGUSTA BLUEFORD, age 21y1m9d, single, b. Richmond Co., d/o Robert [G.] and Alice [Hudson] Blueford. Consent 9 SEP 1874 by parties. Elder James A. Weaver. 10 SEP 1874 at the res. of Presly Hudson. [C7, R:230, R1:37]

Smith, William H. to Eleanor Mozingo. WILLIAM H. SMITH, farmer, age 30, widowed, b. Richmond Co., s/o James and Patsey [Clarke] Smith, to ELEANOR MOZINGO, age 22, single, b. Richmond Co., d/o John and Lillie Mozingo. Consent undated by bride. G.H. Northam. 9 JAN 1884 at J. Mozingo's. [C10, R:353, R1:61]

Smoot, Barton B. to Mary J. Balderson. BARTON B. SMOOT, farmer, age 27, single, b. Caroline Co., res. Westmoreland Co., s/o Benj. F. and Lucy A. [Ann Mothershead] Smoot, to MARY J. BALDERSON, age 27, single, b. Richmond Co., d/o Theoderick N. and Dorothea L. [Lane Sanders] Balderson. Robert N. Reamy. 12 FEB 1868 at the res. of T.N. Balderson. [C4, R:253, R1:23]

Snyder, Dr. John M. to Sophia Cook Tayloe.[3] JOHN M. SNYDER, physician, age 27, single, b. Charlestown, Jefferson Co., Va., s/o Samuel C. and Ann G. Snyder, to SOPHIA COOK TAYLOE, age 23, single, b. at *Mount Airy*, parents blank [William Henry Tayloe and Henrietta Ogle]. Consent 28 MAY 1855 by father Wm. H. Tayloe. William H. Coffin, M.G. 12 JUN 1855 at *Mount Airy*. [C1, R:153, R1:2]

Sorrell, Aaron (Col.) to Kitty Maiden (Col.). AARON SORREL, oysterman, age 21, single, b. Richmond Co., s/o Solomon and Alice Sorrell, to KITTY MAIDEN, age 22, single, b. Richmond Co., parents names "omitted for good cause." Travis Corbin. 14 FEB 1867 at Suggett's Point. [C4, R:285, R1:20]

---

[1] William H. Smith (b. 1853, d. 7 FEB 1915) and his wife Augusta Blueford are bur. at Totuskey Baptist Church cemetery.
[2] James Smith and Patsy Clarke were married 21 JAN 1852 in Richmond Co. by Rev. E.L. Williams.
[3] Dr. John M. Snyder (b. 21 DEC 1828 in Charles Town, Va., d. 3 AUG 1863 in D.C. at his farm *Greenwood*) and his wife Sophia Cook Taylor (b. 31 OCT 1831 at *Mount Airy*, d. 26 MAR 1906, d/o William Henry Tayloe [1791-1871] and Henrietta Ogle [1800-1844]) are bur. in Oak Hill Cemetery, Georgetown, D.C.

Sorrel, Charles H. (Col.) to Matilda Jane Veney (Col.). CHARLES H. SORREL, hewner of ties, age 22, single, b. Richmond Co., s/o Solomon Sorrel and Hannah Sorrel now Veney, to MATILDA JANE VENEY, age 22, single, b. Richmond Co., d/o Washington and Fanny Veney. Consent 28 DEC 1881 by Faney [her X mark] Veney, wit. William H. Veney. Peter Blackwell. 29 DEC 1881 at Fannie Venie's. [C9, R:337, R1:55]

Sorrel, Dennis (Col.) to Frances Taylor (Col.). DENNIS SORREL, farming, age 24, single, b. Richmond Co., s/o James and Laura Sorrel, to FRANCES TAYLOR, age 23, single, b. Westmoreland Co., d/o Judy Taylor now Davis. Consent 21 JAN 1880 by bride, wit. Daniel Gordon. George Laws. 22 JAN 1880 at *Grove Mount*. [C9, R:314, R1:49]

Sorrel, Edmund (Col.) to Judy Venie (Col.). EDMUND SORREL, laborer, age 40, single, b. Richmond Co., s/o Frederick and Mollie Sorrel, to JUDY VENIE, age 30, single, b. Richmond Co., d/o Joseph and Judy Venie. Travis Corbin. 27 JAN 1867 at Joseph Veney's. [C4, R:285, R1:19]

Sorrel, Edward (Col.) to Caroline Cupit (Col.). EDWARD SORREL, farmer, age 22, single, b. Richmond Co., s/o Frederick and Nancy Sorrel, to CAROLINE CUPIT, age 20, single, b. Richmond Co., d/o Lewis and Nancy Cupit. Consent 21 DEC 1875 signed by Caroline Cupit, Lewis Cupit, Nancy Cupit, John Saunders, wit. John Saunders. George [his X mark] Laws. 23 DEC 1875 at *Grove Mount*. [C7, R:262, R1:39]

Sorrel, Henry (Col.) to Lucy A. Jackson (Col.). HENRY SORREL, laborer, age 21y3m, single, b. Richmond Co., s/o Robert and Clara Sorrel, to LUCY A. JACKSON, age 21y8m, single, b. Richmond Co., d/o Andrew and Hannah Jackson. Consent by bride Lucy A. [her X mark] Jackson who is over age 21. David Veney. 22 JAN 1885 at Totuskey.[1] [C10, R1:64]

Sorrell, Henry Lee (Col.) to Ida Veney (Col.). HENRY LEE SORRELL, oystering, age 24, single, b. Richmond Co., s/o Solomon and Hannah Sorrell, to IDA VENEY, age 23, single, b. Richmond Co., d/o Thomas Veney (dec'd.) and Lucy Veney now Bird. Rev. [Atkins]. 6 JUN 1886 at Mulberry Church. [C11, R:316, R1:68]

Sorrel, Simon (Col.) to Mary Frances Cook (Col.). SIMON SORREL, farming, age 31, single, b. Richmond Co., s/o Laura Sorrel, to MARY FRANCES COOK, age 21, single, b. Richmond Co., parents unknown. Consent 17 AUG 1888 by bride. George [his X mark] Laws. 18 AUG 1888 at *Grove Mount*. [C11, R:316, R1:73]

Sorrell, Solomon (Col.) to Mary Blackwell (Col.). SOLOMON SORRELL, farmer, age 40, single, s/o Alexander and Lucy Sorrell, to MARY BLACKWELL, age 37, single, b. Northumberland Co., d/o Thomas and Judy Blackwell. Travis Corbin. 20 DEC 1866 at *Edge Hill*. [C4, R:272, R1:18]

Sorrell, Square (Col.) to Mary Lewis (Col.). SQUARE SORREL, oysterman, age 28, single, b. Richmond Co., s/o Square and Maria Sorrel, to MARY LEWIS, age 20, single, b. Richmond Co., d/o Henry and Gilsey Lewis. Allen Brown, minister. 11 APR 1874 at the bride's house. [C7, R:230, R1:36]

---

[1] Totuskey is a locality about a mile northeast of Haynesville at the junction of Routes 661 and 662.

Sorrel, Squire (Col.) to Charlotte Carter (Col.). SQUIRE SORREL, laborer, age 22, single, b. Richmond Co., s/o Elic Sorrel and Sophronia Rich, to CHARLOTTE CARTER, age 21y3m5d, single, b. Richmond Co., d/o John and Ellen Carter. Consent 6 APR 1881 by bride Charlot [sic] [her X mark] Carter, wit. Kenner R. Cralle who sent in oath. Robert Williamson. 7 APR 1881. [C9, R:335, R1:53]

Sorrel, Thomas (Col.) to Sarah Tibbs (Col.). THOMAS SORREL, farmer, age 21, single, b. Richmond Co., s/o Frederick and Nancy Sorrel, to SARAH TIBBS, age 21, single, b. Richmond Co., d/o Jefferson and Malinda Tibbs. Consent 9 JAN 1877 by bride Sarah [her X mark] Tibbs, wit. A.P. Wilson. George [his X mark] Laws. 11 JAN 1877 at *Smoot's*. [C8, R:306a, R1:42]

Sorrell, William (Col.) to Georgeianna Roane (Col.). WILLIAM SORRELL, farmer, age 22, single, b. Richmond Co., s/o Frederick Sorrell and Nancy Johnson, to GEORGEIANNA ROANE, age 19, single, b. Richmond Co., d/o William and Mary Grey. Consent 4 JAN 1872 by mother Martha [her X mark] Kelsick of Stone Wall Township, wit. Thos. E. Pullen. George Laws. 5 JAN 1872 at Deans, Va. [C6, R:237, R1:31]

Sorrel, William (Col.) to Martha Johnson (Col.). WILLIAM SORREL, farmer, age 22, single, b. Richmond Co., d/o James and Laura Sorrel, to MARTHA JOHNSON, age 19, single, b. Richmond Co., d/o Elias and Susan Johnson. Consent 26 OCT 1880 by Elias [his X mark] Johnson, wit. T.N. Balderson, Nelson [his X mark] Cupit. George Laws. 28 OCT 1880 at [*Kinderoak* or *Finderkoak*]. [C9, R:316, R1:51]

Sorrel, William (Col.) to Elizabeth Johnson (Col.). WILLIAM SORREL, farming, age 37y10m, widowed, b. Richmond Co., s/o Frederick and Nancy Sorrel, to ELIZABETH JOHNSON, age 21y9m, single, b. Essex Co., d/o Henry and Mary Johnson. Consent 13 JAN 1885 by bride's two sisters Amy Corbin and Sallie A. Johnson. Rev. Robert Lewis. 14 JAN 1885. [C10, R:316, R1:64]

Sorrell, William (Col.) to Susan Gillys (Col.). WILLIAM SORRELL, farmer, age 26, widowed, b. Richmond Co., s/o Frederick and Nancy Sorrell, to SUSAN GILLYS, age 21, single, b. Richmond Co., d/o Cyrus and Judy Gillys. Consent 29 DEC 1875 by father Cyrus [his X mark] Gillys., wit. John Saunders. George [his X mark] Laws. 30 DEC 1875 at Bruce's. [C7, R:262, R1:39]

Spence, Edmond (Col.) to Martha Wallace (Col.). EDMOND SPENCER, farmer, age 21, single, b. Richmond Co., s/o Simon and Susan Spence, to MARTHA WALLACE, age 21, single, b. Richmond Co., d/o Thomas and Rachell Wallace. Consent 28 DEC 1868 by mother Rachell [her X mark] Wallace. Thomas G. Thomas. 29 DEC 1868. [C5, R:254, R1:25]

Spence, Richard D. (Col.) to Lucy Ann Thompson (Col.). RICHARD D. SPENCER, farming, age 24, single, b. Richmond Co., s/o Richard and Hannah Ann Spence, to LUCY ANN THOMPSON, age 21, single, b. Richmond Co., d/o Lucinda Ball. Consent 25 APR 1881 by Richard D. Spence and Lucy Ann [her X mark] Thompson, wit. John Middleton. John Wilkerson. 27 APR 1881 at *Pinena* [*Piney*] *Grove*. [C9, R:336, R1:53]

Spence, William (Col.) to Caroline Croxton (Col.). WILLIAM SPENCE, farmer, age 30, widowed, b. Richmond Co., s/o Isaac and Sukie Spence, to CAROLINE CROXTON, age 26, single, b.

Richmond Co., d/o Jerry and Mary Croxton. Consent 14 DEC 1874 by bride Caroline [her X mark] Croxton, no wit. Allen Brown, minister. 17 DEC 1874 at res. of the bride. [C7, R:230, R1:37]

Stansbury, William H.[1] to Sue A. Yeatman. WILLIAM H. STANSBURRY [sic], machinist, age 25, single, b. and res. Baltimore, Md., s/o Wm. T. and Mary A. Stansburry, to SUE A. YEATMAN, age 26, single, b. Richmond Co., d/o A.J. and E.J. Yeatman. Consent 23 JUN 1869 by bride, no wit.; oath to age. No minister return. 24 JUN 1869. [C5, R, R1:26]

Stephens, Charles E. to Bettie F. Douglas. CHARLES E. STEPHENS, farming, age 21y1d, single, b. and res. Westmoreland Co., s/o Henry H. Stephens and Bettie Oldham, to BETTIE F. DOUGLAS, age 22, single, b. Richmond Co., d/o George W. Douglas and Mary Ann Hayden. Consent 9 FEB 1883 by bride, sworn C.L. Thrift. G.H. Northam. 14 FEB 1883 at res. of G.H. Douglas. [C10, R:355, R1:58]

Stephens, Samuel W. (Col.) to Susie Goldman (Col.). SAMUEL W. STEPHENS, oystering, age 22, single, b. Kent Co., Md., s/o Samuel and Addie Stephens, to SUSIE GOLDMAN, age 21, single, b. Richmond Co., s/o Edmond Goldman and Judy Baynham. Consent 14 APR 1890 by mother Juddy [her X mark] Baynham, wit. Kenner R. Cralle. Rev. W. Carter. 15 APR 1890 at the bride's home. [C12, R:323a, R1:77]

Stevens, Thomas W. to Ellen J. Scrimger. THOMAS W. STEVENS, farmer, age 22, single, b. Somerset Co., Md., s/o William and Harriet Stevens, to ELLEN J. SCRIMGER, age 16, single, b. Richmond Co., d/o James and Lilly A. Scrimger. Consent by bride, wit. J.W. Scrimger. E.L. Williams. 6 FEB 1861. [C3, R:123, R1:10]

Stevens, William E. to Elizabeth Keyser. WILLIAM E. STEVENS, farmer, age 21, single, b. Richmond Co., s/o John and Polly Stevens, to ELIZABETH KEYSER, age 18, single, b. Richmond Co., d/o John and Eliza Keyser. Robert Williamson. 31 JAN 1862 at res. of John Keyser. [C3, R:140, R1:11]

Stewart, John to Minnie Wright. JOHN STEWART, farming, age 29, single, b. Westmoreland Co., res. Lancaster Co., s/o G. Henry and Sarah E. Stewart, to MINNIE WRIGHT, age 26, single, b. Richmond Co., d/o Alexander and Belle Wright. Consent 1 MAR 1886 by bride, no wit. R.H. Potts. 7 MAR 1886. [C11, R:315, R1:67]

Stewart, Richard B.[2] to Eva P. Cook. RICHARD B. STEWART, merchant, age 57, widowed, b. Anne Arundel Co., Md., s/o Thomas and Elizabeth Stewart, to EVA P. COOK, age 32, single, b. Warren Co., Pa., d/o William and Phebe Cook. W.A. Crocker. 28 NOV 1876 at the house of the bride's father. [C7, R:306, R1:41]

Stewart, Thomas [FB] to Mary Ann Jenkins [FB]. THOMAS STEWART, age 36, widower, b. Petersburg, Va., s/o Henry Stewart and Mariah Brown, to MARY ANN JENKINS, age 19, single, b. Westmoreland Co., d/o Frances Jenkins, father not known. Consent 28 OCT 1854 by mother

---

[1] William H. Stansbury (b. 11 APR 1844, d. 28 AUG 1904) is bur. in Loudouun Park cemetery, Baltimore, Md.
[2] Richard B. Stewart served in Co. K, 9th Va. Cav., C.S.A., and d. 11 MAR 1915 in Washington, D.C.

Frankey Jenkins, wit. S.F. Cooke. License notes parties are free mulattoes. William N. Ward, M.G. 29 OCT 1854 at res. of Rev. Wm. N. Ward. [C1, R, R1:1]

Stott, Joseph Oliver to Susan F. Bryant.[1] JOSEPH O. STOTT, farmer, age 24, single, b. Richmond Co., s/o Thaddeus C. and Elizabeth W. [Dale] Stott,[2] to SUSAN F. BRYANT, age 21, single, b. Richmond Co., d/o Joseph W. and Catherine Bryant. Consent 7 MAR 1870 by bride, no wit. Wm. H. Kirk. 9 MAR 1870 at the res. of Joseph Bryant. [C5, R:233, R1:27]

Stowell, Rufus to Martha Susan Davis. RUFUS STOWELL, lumber man, age 41, divorced, b. Oxford Co., Me., s/o Rufus and Sarah Stowell, to MARTHA SUSAN DAVIS, age 26, single, b. Richmond Co., d/o Henry H. and Mary E. Davis. Elder James A. Weaver. 13 JAN 1878 at *Spring Hill*, the res. of the parson. [C8, R:310, R1:44]

Stowers, Hiram (Col.) to Mary V. Willmore (Col.). HIRAM STOWERS, oystering, age 23y7m, single, b. Richmond, s/o William Dunaway and Louisa Stowers, to MARY V. WILLMORE, age 23, single, b. Kent Co., Md., d/o Perry and Bettie Willmore. Consent 19 OCT 1887 by bride Mary V. [her X mark] Willmore, wit. Moses Carter. Rev. Jacob Robinson, Pastor of Mt. Zion Baptist Church. 20 OCT 1887. [C11, R:292, R1:70]

Stowers, Redman (Col.) to Mrs. Juliet Thompson (Col.). REDMAN STOWERS, farming, ate 51, widowed, b. Northumberland Co., s/o Samuel and Polly Stowers, to JULIET THOMPSON, age 51, widow, b. Richmond Co., d/o Philip and Ailcey Thompson. Consent 12 NOV 1885 by bride. Rev. Jacob Robinson, Pastor of Mt. Zion Baptist Church. [C10, R:318, R1:65]

Straughan, John H. (Col.) to Milly Gordon (Col.). JOHN H. STRAUGHAN, farming, age 27y8m10d, single, b. and res. Northumberland Co., s/o George Straughan and Winnie Cralle, to MILLY GORDON, age 28, single, b. Richmond Co., d/o John Gordon and Elizabeth Bayley. Consent 23 JUL 1881 by groom and bride Milley [her X mark] Gordon, wit. Sigmund? [his X mark] Toms. John Wilkerson. 26 JUL 1881 at the Gordon farm. [C9, R:338, R1:53]

Sullenberger, Samuel to Octavia Eugenia Northen.[3] SAMUEL SULLENBERGER, farmer, age 45, widowed, b. and res. Pendleton Co., W.Va., s/o Samuel and Martha Sullenberger, to OCTAVIA E. NORTHEN, age 27, single, b. Richmond Co., d/o Wm. S. and Sarah [A. Davis] Northen.[4] J.H. Davis. 2 SEP 1869 at the res. of Wm. S. Northen. [C5, R, R1:26]

Sumuelle, Ezekiel (Col.) to Nelly Johnson (Col.). EZEKIEL SUMUELLE, laborer, age 21y3m, single, b. Richmond Co., s/o James and Suky Sumuelle, to NELLY JOHNSON, age 16, single, b. Westmoreland Co., d/o Elias and Susan Johnson. Consent 2 JAN 1878 by father Elias [his X mark] Johnson, wits. T.N. Balderson, Saml. Gordon. George Laws. 3 JAN 1878 at Mollie Kelly's. [C8, R:310, R1:44]

Sutton, Robert Vincent to Theodosia Harrison. ROBERT VINCENT SUTTON, farming, age 23, single, b. and res. Westmoreland Co., s/o John and Mary Sutton, to THEODOSIA HARRISON,

---

[1] Joseph O. Stott (b. 12 NOV 1845, d. 11 MAY 1880) and wife Susan F. Bryant (1849-1886) are bur. in Farnham Baptist Church cemetery.
[2] Thaddus [sic] C. Stott and Elizabeth W. Dale were married by bond 31 MAY 1834 in Richmond Co.
[3] Samuel Sullenberger (b. 23 JUL 1823, d. 28 DEC 1905) and wife Octavia E. Northen (b. 1840, d. 1928) are bur. in Monterey Cemetery in Highland Co.
[4] William S. Northen and Sarah A. Davis weere married by bond 20 DEC 1832 in Richmond Co.

age 17, single, b. Richmond Co., d/o John [C.] and Margaret B. Harrison.[1] R.N. Reamy. 5 FEB 1880 at John Harrison's. [C9, NN:13 FEB 1880, R:314, R1:49]

Sydnor, Addison to Caroline Hudson. ADDISON SYDNOR, farmer, age 24, single, b. Richmond Co., s/o Fortunatus and Martha [Hale] Sydnor, to CAROLINE HUDSON, age 22, single, b. Richmond Co., d/o Samuel and Nancy Hudson. Elder James A. Weaver. 14 MAR 1867 at the res. of Matthew Hudson. [C4, R:286, R1:20]

Sydnor, Dandridge to Mrs. Harriet Tucker. DANDRIDGE SYDNOR, farmer, age 28, widowed, b. Westmoreland Co., s/o William B. and Ann [Hale] Sydnor, to HARRIET TUCKER, age 35, widow, b. Richmond Co., d/o Mr. Thrift. Consent, undated, by bride Harriet [her X mark] Tucker, no wit. Elder James A. Weaver. 6 AUG 1869 at the res. of *wedder king* [sic]. [C5, R, R1:26]

Sydnor, Dandridge[2] to Ann Elizabeth Dameron. DANDRIDGE SYDNOR, farmer, age 22, single, b. Northumberland Co., s/o William B. and Ann [Hale] Sydnor, to ANN ELIZABETH DAMERON, age 24, single, b. Northumberland Co., d/o Leroy Dameron and Frances [Walker] Sydnor.[3] Consent 1 MAR 1862 by bride, wit. James B. Sydnor. James A. Weaver. 1 MAR 1862 at Robert Sydnor's. [C3, R:140, R1:11]

Sydnor, Dandridge to Maria E. Hudson, as his third wife. DANDRIDGE SYDNOR, farmer, age 33, widowed, b. Richmond Co., s/o William [B.] and Ann [Hale] Sydnor, to MARIA E. HUDSON, age 35, single, b. Richmond Co., d/o William and Sally [Brann] Hudson.[4] Consent 3 OCT 1873 by bride, no wit. Elder James A. Weaver. 3 OCT 1873 at the res. of the bridegroom. [C6, R:235, R1:34]

Sydnor, Fletcher (Col.) to Maria Gaskins (Col.). FLETCHER SYDNOR, farmer, age 24, single, b. Richmond Co., s/o Harry Palmer and Sophia Sydnor, to MARIA GASKINS, age 22, single, b. Westmoreland Co., d/o George and Juilet Gaskins. Consent 12 JAN 1871 by bride Maria E. [her X mark] Gaskins, wit. C.A. Purssell. David Veney. 12 JAN 1871 at the house of Redman Pursell. [C5, R:244, R1:29]

Sydnor, George H. to Elinor Pauline Smith.[5] GEORGE H. SYDNOR, farmer, age 30, single, b. Richmond Co., s/o Thomas [Henry] and Jane [Self] Sydnor,[6] to ELEANOR P. SMITH [sic], age 20y23d, single, b. Richmond Co., d/o Peter [C.] and Virginia [Adams Douglas] Smith. Consent 1 MAR 1887 by bride. G.H. Northam. 2 MAR 1887 at Mr. Smith's. [C11, R:290, R1:69]

Sydnor, George W. to Caroline A. Yeatman. GEORGE W. SYDNOR, in mercantile business, age 29, single, b. Westmoreland, res. Warsaw, Va., s/o Richard and Eliza Sydnor, to CAROLINE A. YEATMAN, age 28, single, b. Westmoreland Co., d/o Henry A. [Austin] and Mary S. Yeatman. Consent 23 AUG 1858 by bride. Wit. George W. Sydnor. W.W. Walker, M.G. 26 AUG 1858 at wife's father's. [C2, R:138, R1:6]

---

[1] John C. Harrison (b. 1821, d. 25 SEP 1882) and wife Margaret B. Richardson (b. 1826, d. 28 MAR 1889), who were married in Northumberland Co., are bur. in Gibeon Baptist Church cemetery.

[2] Dandridge Sydnor served in Co. E, 40th Reg., Va. Inf., C.S.A.

[3] Leroy Dameron and Frances Walker were married by bond 15 JUL 1820 in Northumberland Co.

[4] William Hudson and Sarah Brann were married by bond 12 DEC 1831 in Richmond Co.

[5] George H. Sydnor (b. 16 MAY 1856, d. 1 FEB 1922) and wife Elinor Pauline Smith (b. 13 FEB 1867, d. 25 MAR 1946) are bur. at Totuskey Baptist Church cemetery.

[6] Thomas Sydnor and Jane Self were married by bond 15 AUG 1834 in Richmond Co.

Sydnor, Henry (Col.) to Sarah Newton (Col.). HENRY SYDNOR, laborer, age 25, single, b. Richmond Co., s/o Portius and Sophia Sydnor, to SARAH NEWTON, age 20, single, b. Richmond Co., d/o Isaac and Polly Newton. Consent by bride's father and age of groom proved by oath of George Johnson. Robert Williamson, M.G. 27 MAY 1866 at Jerusalem Church. [C4, R:271, R1:17]

Sydnor, Henry H. to Celestial Rebecca Shackleford.[1] HENRY H. SYDNOR, farmer, age 25, widowed, b. Richmond Co., s/o Thomas [Henry] and Jane [Self] Sydnor, to CELESTIAL SHACKLEFORD, age 21, single, b. Richmond Co., d/o Richard and Sarah E. Shackleford. Consent 18 JAN 1873 by bride, wit. Daniel S. Jackson. Elder James A. Weaver. 20 FEB 1873 at the res. of William Sisson. [C6, R:235, R1:26]

Sydnor, Henry H.[2] to Caroline R. Sisson. HENRY H. SYDNOR, farmer, age 22, single, b. Richmond Co., s/o Thomas C. [sic] and Jane [Self] Sydnor, to CAROLINE R. SISSON, age 25, single, b. Richmond Co., d/o Randall and Frances [A. Gordon] Sisson.[3] James A. Weaver. 21 JUL 1869 at the res. of the bride. [C5, R, R1:33]

Sydnor, James B. to Mrs. Patsey Clark Smith. JAMES B. SYDNOR, farmer, age 20, single, b. Richmond Co., s/o Robert and Lucy [Kent] Sydnor, to PATSEY SMITH, age 25, widow, b. Richmond Co., d/o Meshack and Eliza [Elizabeth B. Clark] Clark.[4] Consent 6 JUN 1859 by bride Patsy [her X mark] Smith, consent by groom's father Robert [his X mark] Sydnor, wits. Benjamin Tucker, William B.C. Carter. James A. Weaver. 8 JUN 1859. [C2, R:165, R1:7]

Sydnor, John to Ann Lewis. JOHN SYDNOR, farmer, age 32, widower, b. Richmond Co., s/o John and Nancy Sydnor, to ANN LEWIS, age 23, single, b. Northumberland Co., d/o Austin and Nancy [Hale] Lewis. Consent 2 JUN 1860 by bride Ann [her X mark] Louis [sic], wit. Fortunatus [his X mark] Sydnor, Benja. Tucker. Elder James A. Weaver. 3 JUN 1860.[5] [C2, R:153, R1:8]

Sydnor, Judson D. to Sarah Rebecca Weathers [or Withers].[6] JUDSON SYDNOR, farming, age 23, single, b. Richmond Co., s/o Dandridge Sydnor and Ann Sydnor (dec'd.), to REBECCA WEATHERS, age 22, single, b. Richmond Co., d/o Joseph Weathers (dec'd.) and Nancy E. Weathers. Consent 6 APR 1887 by parties Judson [his X mark] Sydnor, Becca [her X mark] Withers [sic], wit. Nancy A. Wethers [sic], Napolean B. Sydnor. G.H. Northam. 7 APR 1887 at Mrs. Wethers'. [C11, R:291, R1:69]

Sydnor, Napoleon to Arretta Weathers. NAPOLEON SYDNOR, farmer, age 19, single, b. Richmond Co., s/o William B. and Ann Sydnor, to ARRETTA WEATHERS, age 18, single, b. Richmond Co., d/o Joseph and Nancy E. Weathers. Consent 7 APR 1881 by bride, wit. Joseph [his X mark] Weathers, Nancy [her X mark] E. Weathers, William [his X mark] B. Sydnor. G.H. Northam. 7 APR 1881. [C9, R:335, R1:52]

---

[1] Henry H. Sydnor (b. 13 SEP 1849, d. 13 JAN 1918) and his second wife Celestial R. Shackleford (b. 10 JAN 1857, d. 10 JUL 1908) are bur. at Totuskey Baptist Church cemetery.
[2] Henry H. Sydnor (b. 13 SEP 1849, d. 13 JAN 1918) is bur. with his second wife Celestial Rebecca Shackleford in Totuskey Baptist Church cemetery.
[3] Randall Sisson and Frances A. Gordon were married by bond 30 DEC 1829 in Richmond Co.
[4] Meshack Clark and Elizabeth B. Clark were married by bond 2 JAN 1824 in Richmond Co.
[5] Minister return notes date of marriage as 3 JUN 1860, while the license notes date 2 JUN 1860.
[6] Sarah R. Weathers (b. 15 MAR 1865, d. 6 JUN 1928), wife of Judson D. Sydnor (b. 1865, d. 3 JUL 1935), is bur. at Totuskey Baptist Church cemetery.

Sydnor, Perryman to Esther Gaskins. BERRYMAN SYDNOR, farmer, age 23, single, b. Richmond Co., s/o Harry and Sophia Palmer, to ESTHER GASKINS, age 22, single, b. Westmoreland Co., d/o Hiram and Julia Gaskins. Consent 28 DEC 1870 by bride Esther [her X mark] Gaskins, wits. C.A. Pursell, S.P. Pursell; age of bride sworn by George Johnson. Davy Veney. 29 DEC 1870 at *Whirlabout*. [C5, R:234, R1:28]

Sydnor, Robert to Mrs. Mary Packett. ROBERT SYDNOR, farmer, age 60, widowed, b. Richmond Co., s/o John and Nancy Sydnor, to MARY PACKETT, age 29, widow, b. Richmond Co., d/o Richard and Maria Reynolds. Consent 19 FEB 1866 by bride, wits. Thos. O. Vanlandingham, Benjn. Tucker. Elder James A. Weaver. 21 FEB 1866 at res. of Thos. O. Vanlandingham. [C4, R:270, R1:16]

Sydnor, Robert Washington to Sarah Rebecca Clark.[1] ROBERT W. SYDNOR, farmer, age 17, single, b. Richmond Co., s/o Robert and Lucy Sydnor, to SARAH R. CLARKE [sic], age 21, single, b. Richmond Co., d/o Meshack and Eliza [Elizabeth B. Clark] Clark.[2] Consent 6 DEC 1865 by bride, wit. William Tucker. Consent from father Robert [his X mark] Sydnor, wit. William Tucker. Elder James A. Weaver. 6 DEC 1865 at Meshack Clarke's. [C3, R:204, R1:15]

Sydnor, Samuel to Mary Barrick. SAMUEL SYDNOR, age 22, single, b. Richmond Co., s/o Thomas and Jane [Self] Sydnor, to MARY BARRICK, age 21, single, b. Richmond Co., d/o Thomas and Maria J. Barrick. Consent 25 APR 1865 by bride Mary [her X mark] Barrick, wit. D.S. Jackson. James A. Weaver. 25 APR 1865 at Milly Sydnor's. [C3, R:204, R1:15]

Sydnor, Samuel to Mrs. Mary J. Hudson, widow of William H. Hale. SAMUEL SYDNOR, farmer, 30, widowed, b. Richmond Co., s/o Thomas and Jane [Self] Sydnor, to MARY J. HALE, age 30, widow, b. Richmond Co., d/o Samuel and Nancy [Lewis] Hudson. Consent 20 JAN 1872 by bride and groom Samuel [his X mark] Sydnor, wit. Wm. P. Middleton. G.H. Northam. 21 JAN 1872. [C6, R:237, R1:31]

Sydnor, Thomas, Jr. to Mary E. Bell. THOMAS SYDNOR, farmer, age 36, widowed, b. Richmond Co., s/o Thomas Sydnor, Sr. and Jane [Self] Sydnor, to MARY E. BELL, age 18, single, b. Northumberland Co., d/o Vincent R. and Mary A. [Ann Rock] Bell.[3] Consent 26 AUG 1876 by bride and also signed by mother Mary A. Bell. J.A. Weaver. 27 AUG 1876. [C7, R:305, R1:41]

Sydnor, Thomas to Lucy Barrick. THOMAS SYDNOR, farmer, age 27, single, b. Richmond Co., s/o Thomas and Jane Sydnor, to LUCY BARRICK, age 21, single, b. Richmond Co., d/o Thomas and Maria Barrick. Consent 6 DEC 1866 by Thomas Sydnor and Maria [her X mark] Thrift, wit. Daniel [his X mark] Jackson. Elder James A. Weaver. 6 DEC 1866 at the res. of Daniel Jackson. [C4, R:272, R1:18]

Sydnor, William Ball to Sophiah Hudson. WILLIAM BALL SYDNOR, farmer, age 60, widower, b. Richmond Co., s/o John and Susan Sydnor, to SOPHIAH HUDSON, age 25, single, b.

---

[1] Robert W. Sydnor (b. 1848, d. 18 APR 1919 in Westmoreland Co.) and wife Sarah R. Clarke (b. 1845, d. 11 JAN 1921) are bur. at Totuskey Baptist Church cemetery. He served in the 15th Va. Cav., C.S.A.
[2] Meshack Clark and Elizabeth B. Clark were married by bond 2 JAN 1824 in Richmond Co.
[3] Vincent R. Bell (1823-1866) and his wife Mary Ann Rock (b. 1832, d. 19 FEB 1900) are bur. in Gibeon Baptist Church cemetery. Vincent R. Bell and Mary Ann Rock were married by bond 22 JUN 1848 in Northumberland Co.

Richmond Co., d/o Henry and Mary Hudson. Consent 4 JUN 1881 by William B. [his X mark] Sydnor, wit. Dan[dridge] Clark. G.H. Northam. 7 JUN 1881. [C9, R:336, R1:53]

T

Tallent, William C. to Mollie B. Sisson. WILLIAM C. TALLENT, mechanic, age 23, single, b. Richmond Co., s/o Geo. W.C. and M.A. Tallent, to MOLLIE B. SISSON, age 32, single, b. Richmond Co., s/o Henry C. and Elizabeth Sisson. J. Dorsey Berry. 7 AUG 1890 at Menokin Baptist Church. [C12, R:323a, R1:77]

Tapscott, Aulbin Delaney to Bettie Alice Lyell.[1] AULBIN D. TAPSCOTT, merchant, age 35, single, b. Lancaster Co., res. New York City, s/o Samuel C. and A.C. [Ann C. Moore] Tapscott, to BETTIE ALICE LYELL, age 28, single, b. Richmond Co., d/o R.H. [Richard] and Elizabeth T. [Tapscott] Lyell. Consent 29 OCT 1874 by father R.H. Lyell, wits. S.F. [Sarah Frances] Lyell, A.R. Pendleton. W.A. Crocker. 3 NOV 1874 at the res. of the bride's father. [C7, R:230, R1:37]

Tarlton, John T. to Sarah A. Thrift. JOHN T. TARLTON, farmer, age 27y8m20d, single, b. St. Mary's Co., Md., s/o Bazil Tarlton, to SARAH A. THRIFT, age 19y8m22d, single, b. Lancaster Co., d/o John F. and Eliza [Douglas] Thrift.[2] Robert Williamson, M.G. 3 FEB 1864 at John F. Thrift's. [C3, R:139, R1:13]

Tarlton, John T. to Frances Ann French.[3] JOHN T. TARLTON, farmer, age 41y9m, widowed, b. St. Mary's Co., Md., s/o B. and Eliza Tarlton who was Eliza Price, to FRANCES FRENCH, age 35, single, b. Northumberland Co., d/o Rhoda and Fanny French. Consent 9 FEB 1877 by bride, wit. James Lowry. J.B. DeBerry. 14 FEB 1877 at the res. of the bride's mother. [C8, R:306a, R1:42]

Tate, Charles (Col.) to Mary Susan Washington (Col.). CHARLES TATE, laborer, age 28, single, b. Westmoreland Co., s/o Aaron Tate and Julia Minor, to MARY SUSAN WASHINGTON, age 25, single, b. Richmond Co., d/o Robert Washington and Peggy Davis. Rev. Robert Lewis. 1 JAN 1884 at res. of Julia Minor. [C10, R:353, R1:61]

Tate, James Luther (Col.) to Florence Corbin (Col.). JAMES LUTHER TATE, laborer, age 23, single, b. Westmoreland Co., s/o Aaron Tate and Julia Minor formerly Tate, to FLORENCE CORBIN, age 24y11m16d, single, b. Richmond Co., d/o Henry and Betsey Corbin. Rev. Robert Lewis. 23 FEB 1882. [C9, R:312, R1:55]

Tate, John (Col.) to Mrs. Lucinda Corbin Coats (Col.). JOHN TATE, laborer, age 26, single, b. Westmoreland Co., s/o Aaron Tate and Julia Tate now Minor, to LUCINDA COATS, age 30, widow, b. Westmoreland Co., d/o William and Felicia Corbin. Consent 24 MAY 1877 by bride Lucinda [her X mark] Coats. Jeremiah Graham. 24 MAY 1877 at *Oak Farm*. [C8, R:307, R1:43]

---

[1] Lieut. Aulbin D. Tapscott (b. 17 JUN 1838, d. 10 JUN 1911) and wife Alice Lyell (b. 28 SEP 1845, d. 14 DEC 1920) are bur. in Fredericksburg Cemetery, Fredericksburg, Va. He served in Co. D, 9th Cav., C.S.A.
[2] John F. Thrift and Eliza Douglass were married by bond 4 JUN 1833 in Lancaster Co.
[3] Frances Ann French Tarlton (b. 30 OCT 1840, d. 27 MAY 1916) is bur. in Hopewell Methodist Church cemetery. Her tombstone is in error with maiden name France.

Tate, John (Col.) to Martha Ellen Newman (Col.). JOHN TATE, oystering, age 22, single, b. Richmond Co., s/o Lawson and Sarah Tate, to MARTHA ELLEN NEWMAN, age 19, single, b. Richmond Co., d/o Thomas and Winnie Newman. Consent 13 DEC 1890 by bride's parents. L. Marshall, Pastor. 14 DEC 1890 at the Second Baptist Church. [C12, R:324, R1:77]

Tate, Lawson (Col.) to Sarah Thompson (Col.). LAWRENCE TATE, farmer, age 22, single, b. Richmond Co., s/o Joe and Betsy Tate, to SARAH THOMPSON, age 21, single, b. Richmond Co., d/o Jane Thompson (father unknown). Consent 9 NOV 1863 by bride Sarah [her X mark] Thompson, wit. J.M. Stiff. Robert Williamson, M.G. 12 NOV 1863 at the bride's mother. [C3, R:160, R1:13]

Tate, Lawson (Col.) to Edmonia Bailor (Col.). LAWSON TATE, farming, age 40, widowed, b. Richmond Co., s/o Joseph and Betsey Tate, to EDMONIA BAILOR, age 28, single, b. Richmond Co., d/o John and Louisa Bailor. Rev. John Wilkerson. 11 NOV 1886 at [*Sabine*] *Hall*. [C11, R:316, R1:68]

Tate, Lewis (Col.) to Mary A. Rich (Col.). LEWIS TATE, farmer, age 24, single, b. Richmond Co., s/o Joseph and Betsy Tate, to MARY A. RICH, age 21, single, b. Richmond Co., d/o Linsey and Felicia Rich. No minister return. 4 NOV 1865. [R:204, R1:15, R1:46]

Tate, Lewis (Col.) to Millie Maiden (Col.). LEWIS TATE, farmer, age 42, divorced, b. Richmond Co., s/o Joe and Betsey Tate, to MILLIE MAIDEN, age 24, single, b. Richmond Co., d/o Del Maiden and Lucy Boyd. George [his X mark] Laws. 28 NOV 1878. [C8, R:312]

Tate, Lieutenant to Mary Susan Maiden [Madon], free persons of color. LIEUTENANT TATE, farmer, age 21, single, b. Westmoreland Co., s/o Lewis and Hannah Tate, to MARY SUSAN MAIDEN, age 17, single, b. Richmond Co., d/o Maria Maiden. Consent 11 FEB 1859 by Mariah [her X mark] Madon, wits. James Jones, John [his X mark] Madon. John Pullen, M.G. 18 FEB 1859. [C2, R:165, R1:7]

Tate, Robert Fox (Col.) to Lizzie Ball (Col.). ROBERT FOX TATE, farmer, age 22y10m, single, b. Richmond Co., s/o Lucinda Tate, to LIZZIE BALL, age 17, single, b. Richmond Co., d/o Alfred Niclas [sic] and Harriet Ball. Consent 2 JAN 1873 by Mary [her X mark] Ball, wit. F. Settle. George Laws. 3 JAN 1873 at Linsey Yeatman's. [C6, R:235, R1:33]

Tate, William to Ailcy Hinson. WILLIAM TATE, farmer, age about 40, widower, b. Westmoreland Co., s/o William Tate and wife Betsy, to AILCY HINSON, age about 30, single, b. Westmoreland Co., d/o Prestly Hinson and Catharine. Consent 12 JUN 1855 by bride Ailcy [her X mark] Hinson, wit. Charles L. [his X mark] Coats. John Pullen. 13 JUN 1855 at John Hinson's, upper parish, Richmond Co. [C1, R:153, R1:2]

Tate, William H. (Col.) to Mrs. Isadore Carrington (Col.). WILLIAM H. TATE, farmer, age 21, single, b. Westmoreland Co., s/o Lucinda Tate (father unknown), to ISADORE CARRINGTON, age 30, widow, b. Richmond Co., d/o Thomas G. and Winny Page. Thomas G. Thomas. 19 MAR 1868. [C4, R:253, R1:23]

Taylor, Dennis (Col.) to Mary King (Col.). DENNIS TAYLOR, farming, age 26, single, b. Westmoreland Co., s/o John and Julia Taylor, to MARY KING, age 25, single, b. Richmond Co., d/o Martha King. Rev. Robert Lewis. 2 MAR 1887 at the res. of Martha King. [C11, R:290, R1:69]

Taylor, George (Col.) to Georgeanna Dunaway (Col.). GEORGE TAYLOR, oystering, age 23, single, b. Richmond Co., s/o Peter Taylor and Margaret Taylor (dec'd.), to GEORGEANNA DUNAWAY, age 21, single, b. Richmond Co., d/o William and Jennie Dunaway. Consent 23 DEC 1889 by bride George Anna [her X mark] Dunaway. Rev. W. Carter. 26 DEC 1889 at the bride's home. [C12, R:328, R1:75]

Taylor, John (Col.) to Patsey Taylor (Col.). JOHN TAYLOR, farmer, age 30, single, b. Richmond Co., s/o Shedrick and Rachel Taylor, to PATSEY TAYLOR, age 22, single, b. Richmond Co., d/o Stephen and Lucy Taylor. Consent 15 SEP 1881 by Patsey [her X mark] Taylor, wit. Dennis Johnson. Allen Brown. 23 SEP 1881. [C9, R:338, R1:54]

Taylor, Joseph (Col.) to Molly Sorrel (Col.). JOSEPH TAYLOR, farming, age 29y10m, single, b. Richmond Co., s/o Ellie and Mary Taylor, to MOLLY SORREL, age 23, single, b. Richmond Co., d/o Edmond and Nancy Sorrel. George [his X mark] Laws. 22 JAN 1885 at the *Old Fork*. [C10, R:316, R1:64]

Taylor, Washington (Col.) to Ella Carrington (Col.). WASHINGTON TAYLOR, laborer, age 23y6m, single, b. Westmoreland Co., s/o John and Julia Taylor, to ELLA CARRINGTON, age 21y11m, single, b. Richmond Co., d/o Emily Carrington now Baily. Thomas G. Thomas. 24 APR 1879 at the minister's house. [C8, R:307, R1:47]

Taylor, William Henry (Col.) to Fanny Stewart (Col.). WILLIAM HENRY TAYLOR, age 24, single, b. Richmond Co., s/o Lewis and Mary Taylor, to FANNY STEWART, age 19, single, b. Richmond Co., d/o Henry and Hannah Stewart. Rev. Chauncey Leonard. 5 AUG 1871 at *Westview*. [C6, R:245, R1:30]

Tellis, Rev. John to Frances A. Harriss. JOHN TELLIS, Baptist parson, age 22, single, b. Richmond Co., s/o John C. Tellis and L. Thrift, to FRANCIS A. HARRISS, age 24, single, b. Richmond Co., d/o Henry Harriss and Frances Maley. Barth. Dodson. 27 DEC 1860. [C2, R:154, R1:9]

Thomas, Andrew B.[1] to Elizabeth B. Connellee. ANDREW B. THOMAS, farmer, age 31, single, b. Richmond Co., s/o Griffin and Nancy Thomas, to ELIZABETH B. CONNELLEE, age 21, single, b. Richmond Co., d/o Washington [T.] and [Mrs.] Betsy [Hundley] Connellee. Wm. H. Kirk. 30 JAN 1868 at res. of Washington Connellee. [C4, R:253, R1:23]

Thomas, Henry (Col.) to Betsy Veney (Col.). HENRY THOMAS, brick mason, age 35, single, b. Prince George's Co., Md., s/o George and Maria Thomas, to BETSY VENEY, age 21, single, b. Richmond Co., d/o Humphrey and Winny Veney. Isaiah Hankinson. 29 DEC 1867 at Mulberry Chapel. [C4, R:287, R1:22]

---

[1] Andrew B. Thomas served in Co. E, 40th Reg., Va. Inf., C.S.A.

Thomas, Joseph M. to Sarah Dunaway. JOSEPH M. THOMAS, farmer, age 22, widower, b. Northumberland Co., s/o Thomas S. and Harriet A. [Ann Booth] Thomas,[1] to SARAH DUNAWAY, age 21, single, b. Richmond Co., d/o John J. and Nancy A. Dunaway. Consent 8 MAR 1859 by bride, wit. J.W. Bryant. Robert Williamson. 15 MAR 1859. [C2, R:165, R1:5, R1:7]

Thomas, Joseph M. to Judith Newgent. JOSEPH M. THOMAS, age 21, single, b. Northumberland Co., s/o Thomas S. Thomas and Harriet [A.] Booth, to JUDITH NEWGENT, age 22, single, b. Richmond Co., d/o George Newgent and Sarah Nash. Consent 7 DEC 1857 by bride, wits. Wm. H. Davenport, Charles Barrick. Barth. Dodson, Baptist parson. 10 DEC 1857. [C1]

Thomas, Rev. Thomas G. (Col.), Rev. to Mrs. Mary Barber (Col.). THOMAS G. THOMAS, preaching, age 74y3m, widowed, b. Richmond Co., s/o Henry and Agnes Thomas, to MARY BARBER, age 56, widow, b. Richmond Co., d/o George and Rosetta Lomax. George Laws. 28 DEC 1886 at Clarksville Church. [C11, R:317, R1:68]

Thomas, William E. to Virginia A. Connelly.[2] WILLIAM E. THOMAS, farmer, age 25, single, b. Northumberland Co., res. Lancaster Co., s/o William and E.F. [Elizabeth F. Davenport] Thomas, to VIRGINIA A. CONNELLY, age 22, single, b. Richmond Co., d/o Washington [T.] and Elizabeth [G. Hundley] Connelly. Consent 18 FEB 1878 by bride, wit. Phillip Thomas. J.B. DeBerry, Pastor. 20 FEB 1878 at Hopewell M.E. Church South.[3] [C8, R:310, R1:44]

Thompson, Austin (Col.) to Betsey Thompson (Col.). AUSTIN THOMPSON, farming, age 20, single, b. Richmond Co., s/o Betsey Thompson, to BETSEY THOMPSON, age 18, single, b. Richmond Co., d/o Virginia Johnson. Consent 24 DEC 1890 by Virginia [her X mark] Johnson, wit. Jas. Thompson. Edmond Rich. 25 DEC 1890 at the res. of the minister. [C12, R:324, R1:78]

Thompson, Barzilla (Col.) to Nancy Croxton (Col.). BARZILLA THOMPSON, oysterman, age 24, single, b. Richmond Co., s/o John Thompson and Betsey Veney formerly Thompson, to NANCY CROXTON, age 20y4m, single, b. Richmond Co., d/o Jere and Mary Croxton. Consent 8 OCT 1873 by mother Mary [her X mark] Croxton, wit. Thos. English. Travis Corbin, D.D. 12 OCT 1873 at the home of the bride's mother. [C6, R:235, R1:34]

Thompson, Benjamin (Col.) to Hannah Ann Ball (Col.). BENJAMIN THOMPSON, laborer, age 24, single, b. Richmond Co., s/o Moses and Peggy Thompson, to HANNAH ANN BALL, age 21, single, b. Richmond Co., d/o Mary Ball [father unknown]. John G. Rowe, M.G. 24 DEC 1857 at Mrs. Ball's. [C1, R:160, R1:5]

Thompson, Benjamin (Col.) to Mrs. Frances Thompson (Col.). BENJAMIN THOMPSON, farming, age 40, widowed, b. Richmond Co., s/o Moses and Peggy Thompson, to FRANCES THOMPSON, age 30, widow, b. Westmoreland Co., d/o Ben Middleton and Nancy Burrel. Rev. John Wilkerson. 9 NOV 1882 at Thompson Town. [C9, R:313, R1:56]

---

[1] Thomas S. Thomas and Harriett Ann Booth, d/o Joseph Booth, were married 28 MAR 1831 in Northumberland Co.
[2] Virginia A. Connelly (1854-1932), wife of William E. Thomas, is bur. at Hopewell Methodist Church cemetery.
[3] Hopewell Church is located in the southeast corner of the county on Route 600, about 1 mile west of Route 611 and at Lara, Va. Lara was also called Davenport, Va. after Joseph Davenport who opened a store before 1882.

Thompson, Benjamin (Col.) to Margaret Thompson (Col.). BENJAMIN THOMPSON, farming, age 40, widowed, b. Richmond Co., s/o John and Betsey Thompson, to MARGARET THOMPSON, age 30, single, b. Richmond Co., d/o Charles and Millie Thompson. Edmond Rich. 24 JUN 1883 at his residence. [C10, R:356, R1:59]

Thompson, Charles (Col.) to Maggie Coats (Col.). CHARLES THOMPSON, farming, age 21, single, b. Richmond Co., s/o Harry and Jane Thompson, to MAGGIE COATS, age 18, single, b. Richmond Co., d/o Sandy and Lucinda Coats. Consent 14 OCT 1879 by mother Lucinda [her X mark] Costs, wit. Cornelius [his X mark] Coats. Robert [his X mark] Lewis. 15 OCT 1879 at John Tate's house. [C8, R:308, R1:48]

Thompson, Dungain and Malinda Burwell. Consent 16 JUL 1855 by bride Malinda [her X mark] Burwell, wits. Richard T. Oldham, Benj. Tucker. No license or minister return. [C1]

Thompson, Fairfax (Col.) to Sophia Cupit (Col.). FAIRFAX THOMPSON, farming, age 21, single, b. Richmond Co., s/o Harry and Jane Thompson, to SOPHIA CUPIT, age 19, single, b. Richmond Co., d/o Tasker and Louisa Cupit. Rev. Robert Lewis. 13 MAR 1884. [C10, R:354, R1:61]

Thompson, George (Col.) to Mary Alice Fauntleroy (Col.). THOMPSON GEORGE, farming, age 33, single, b. Richmond Co., s/o John and Betsey Thompson, to ALICE FAUNTLEROY, age 30, single, b. Richmond Co., d/o Henry Fauntleroy and Ann Williams. Consent 31 DEC 1887 by bride. Rev. Jacob Robinson. 4 JAN 1888 at the res. of the bride's father. [C11, R:315, R1:72]

Thompson, George, Jr. (Col.) to Rebecca Jane Veney (Col.). GEORGE THOMPSON, JR., farming and oystering, age 28, widowed, b. Richmond Co., s/o John and Betsey Thompson, to REBECCA JANE VENEY, age 25, single, b. Richmond Co., d/o Jack and Mary Veney. David Veney, Sr. 3 JUL 1887 at *Long Joe's*. [C11, R:292, R1:70]

Thompson, George W. to Donna Maria Jett.[1] GEORGE W. THOMPSON, farmer, age 22, single, b. King George Co., s/o William D. and Ellen [Moxley] Thompson,[2] to DONNA M. JETT, age 18y5m18d, b. King George Co., d/o Henry S. and Martha Ann [Jones] Jett.[3] A.B. Dunaway. 22 DEC 1874 at *Morattico Hall*.[4] [C7, R:231, R1:38]

Thompson, George W. (Col.) to Octavia Veney (Col.). GEORGE W. THOMPSON, oysterman, age 21, single, b. Richmond Co., s/o John Thompson (dec'd.) and Betsey Thompson now Veney, to OCTAVIA VENEY, age 21, single, b. Richmond Co., d/o John Veney (dec'd.) and Rachel Veney. Consent by bride Octavia [her X mark] Veney, wit. Arthur C. Pearson. Allen Brown, minister. 7 MAR 1879 at the [Bruce] home. [C8, R:307, R1:46]

Thompson, James Henry (Col.) to Polly Reed (Col.). JAMES HENRY THOMPSON, farming, age 24, single, b. Richmond Co., s/o William and Ellen Thompson, to POLLY REED, age 24, single,

---

[1] George W. Thompson (1852-1941) and wife Donna Maria Jett (b. 1 JUL 1856, d. 20 JAN 1942) are bur. in White Stone Baptist Church cemetery.
[2] William D. Thompson and Ellen Moxley were married 14 FEB 1850 in King George Co. by Rev. John McDaniel.
[3] Henry S. Jett and Martha Ann Jones were married 5 APR 1848 in King George Co. by Rev. Philip Montague.
[4] *Morattico Hall* is the home of the Grymes Family, and later the Oakley Family, and was located on Morattico Creek. The house was destroyed by erosion of the Rappahannock River bank.

b. Richmond Co., d/o Martha Ann Veney (dec'd.). John Wilkerson. 29 MAY 1887 at *Totuskey Farm*, Farnham, Va. [C11, R:292, R1:70]

Thompson, James W. (Col.) to Camomile Jones (Col.). JAMES T. THOMPSON, farming, age 36, single, b. Richmond Co., s/o Ben Thompson and Rebecca Weldon, to CAMOMILE JONES, age 27, single, b. Richmond Co., d/o Hannah Jones. Consent 13 NOV 1889 by bride Camomile [her X mark] Jones, wit. J.L. Hammack. Edmond Rich. 14 NOV 1889 at the res. of Hannah Jones. [C12, R:328, R1:75]

Thompson, John [FB] to Sophia Ann Newman [FB]. Consent 6 MAY 1854 by father John [his X mark] Newman, wit. Edman [his X mark] Rich. No license or minister return. [C1]

Thompson, John (Col.) to Sarah Johnson (Col.). JOHN THOMPSON, farmer, age 57, widowed, b. and res. Westmoreland Co., s/o James and Sally Thompson, to SARAH JOHNSON, age 50, single, b. Westmoreland Co., d/o Reuben Johnson. Consent 6 APR 1874 by bride. Elder James A. Weaver. 23 APR 1874 at the res. of the *parsons*.[1] [C7, R:230, R1:36]

Thompson, John (Col.) to Maria Burrel (Col.). JOHN THOMPSON, laborer, age 22, single, b. and res. Westmoreland Co., s/o Duncan and Malinda Thompson, to MARIA BURREL, age 23, single, b. Richmond Co., d/o Jennie Burrel. Edmond Rich. 28 JAN 1881 at the home of John Thompson. [C9, R:335, R1:52]

Thompson, John Henry (Col.) to Mary Brown (Col.). JOHN HENRY THOMPSON, farming, age 22y2m, single, b. Richmond Co., s/o Harry and Sally Thompson, to MARY BROWN, age 22y9m, single, b. Richmond Co., d/o Edward and Susan Brown. Consent undated by bride Mary [her X mark] Brown, wit. John C.G. [Charles Groom] Veazey. G.H. Northam. 28 MAR 1880. [C9, R:315, R1:50]

Thompson, John Henry (Col.) to Carrie E. Jackson (Col.). JOHN HENRY THOMPSON, sailing, age 26y10m, single, b. Richmond Co., s/o Peter Newton and Sally Rich, to CARRIE E. JACKSON, age 21, single, b. Richmond Co., Thomas and Louisa Jackson. Consent 1 MAR 1890 by father Thomas Jackson, wit. John W. Thompson. Rev. John Wilkerson. 2 MAR 1890 at her father's house. [C12, R:323a, R1:76]

Thompson, John W. (Col.) to Betsy Carter (Col.). JOHN W. THOMPSON, farmer, age 35, single, b. Richmond Co., s/o John and Betsy Thompson, to BETSY CARTER, age 24, single, b. Richmond Co., d/o Edward and Lucy Carter. Thomas G. Thomas. 1 JAN 1868. [C4, R:253, R1:23]

Thompson, Joseph (Col.) to Lizzie Tate (Col.). JOSEPH THOMPSON, farmer, age 28, single, b. Richmond Co., s/o Moses and Peggy Thompson, to LIZZIE TATE, age 28, single, b. Westmoreland Co., d/o Aaron Tate and Julia Tate now Minor. Edmond Rich. 8 AUG 1878 at the house of Joseph Thompson. [C8, R:311, R1:45]

Thompson, Joseph (Col.) to Bertha Mathews (Col.). JOSEPH THOMPSON, farming, age 55, widowed, b. Fredericksburg, Va., s/o Joseph Turner and Sally Thompson, to BERTHA

---

[1] It is presumed that "parsons" means the residence of the minister.

MATHEWS, age 31, single, b. Essex Co., d/o William Mathews and Betsey Saunders. Consent undated by bride, wit. Th. Saunders. George Laws. 30 DEC 1886. [C11, R:317, R1:68]

Thompson, Lewis to Mary E. Johnson. Consent undated signed by Louis Thomson [sic], Mary E. Johnson, Ruben Johnson, wit. Cephas [his X mark] Johnson. No license or minister return. [C1]

Thompson, Moses (Col.) to Elizabeth Ball (Col.). MOSES THOMPSON, farmer, age 20y8m, single, b. Richmond Co., s/o Daniel and Hannah Thompson, to ELIZABETH BALL, age 25, single, b. Richmond Co., d/o Sally Ball. Consent 8 MAR 1873 by father Daniel [his X mark] Thompson, wit. Chapman Page. Thomas G. Thomas. 9 MAR 1873 at Clarksville, Va. [C6, R:235, R1:33]

Thompson, Moses (Col.) to Bettie Churchwell (Col.). MOSES THOMPSON, farmer, age 28, widowed, b. Richmond Co., s/o Daniel and Hannah Thompson, to BETTIE CHURCHWELL, age 20, single, b. Richmond Co., d/o George and Fenton Churchwell. G.H. Northam. 18 DEC 1879 at George Churchwell's. [C9, R:309, R1:48]

Thompson, Moses (Col.) to Haynie Thompson (Col.). MOSES THOMPSON, farming, age 24, single, b. Richmond Co., s/o Benjamin and Hannah Thompson, to HAYNIE THOMPSON, age 22, single, b. Richmond Co., d/o Richard Newman and Nelly Thompson. Rev. John Wilkerson. 9 NOV 1882 at Thompson Town. [C9, R:313, R1:56]

Thompson, Phillip to Julia Lomax. PHILLIP THOMPSON, shoemaker, age 35, widowed, b. Richmond Co., s/o John and Laura Thompson, to JULIA LOMAX, age 25, single, b. Westmoreland Co., [names of parents blank]. Thomas G. Thomas. 26 JUN 1869 at James M. Harris'. [C5, R, R1:26]

Thompson, Richard Henry (Col.) to Henrietta Jones (Col.). RICHARD HENRY THOMPSON, oystering, age 26, single, b. Richmond Co., s/o John Thompson and Harriet Davis, to HENRIETTA JONES, age 21y4m, single, b. Westmoreland Co., d/o Patrick Jones and Julia Tarlton. Rev. W. Carter. 21 FEB 1889 at the bride's home. [C12, R:327, R1:74]

Thompson, Robert J. (Col.) to Mrs. Felicia Veney (Col.). ROBERT J. THOMPSON, farmer, age 48, widowed, b. Richmond Co., s/o Moses and Tena Thompson, to FELICIA VENEY, age 49, widow, place of birth not given, [names of parents not given], widow of Jesse Veney. Consent 8 JUL 1889 by bride and Joseph Thompson. Edmond Rich. 9 JUL 1889 at the res. of Lishia Veney. [C12, R:327, R1:74]

Thompson, Thomas Edward (Col.) to Harriet Lizzie Newman (Col.). THOMAS EDWARD THOMPSON, oysterman, age 27, single, b. Richmond Co., s/o John and Betsy Thompson, to HARRIET LIZZIE NEWMAN, age 18, single, b. Richmond Co., d/o Cephas and Dorcas Newman. Consent 6 JAN 1874 by mother Dorcas [her X mark] Newman from Emmerton, Va., wit. Thos. [N. Barnes]. Travis Corbin, minister. 8 JAN 1874 at res. of bride's mother. [C7, R:230, R1:36]

Thompson, Warren (Col.) to Climsy Ann Rich (Col.). WARREN THOMPSON, oysterman, age 21y6m, single, b. Richmond Co., s/o John Thompson and Harriet his wife, to CLIMSY ANN RICH, age 21y1m20d, single, b. Richmond Co., d/o Henry and Catherine Rich. Consent of

Henry Rich and Catherine Rich, signed by parties Warren [his X mark] Thompson and Climsy Ann [her X mark] Rich, wit. Redman Stowells. Peter Blackwell. 9 FEB 1879 at Mount Zion Church. [C8, R:307, R1:46]

Thompson, Warren (Col.) to Lavinia Wheeler (Col.). WARREN THOMPSON, age 22y4m, single, b. Richmond Co., s/o Joseph and Arretta Thompson, to LAVINIA WHEELER, age 16y12d, single, b. Richmond Co., d/o Daniel and Harriet Wheeler. Rev. Robert Lewis. 16 DEC 1880 at Mary Fisher's house. [C9, R:316, R1:51]

Thompson, Washington (Col.) to Roberta Venie (Col.). WASHINGTON THOMPSON, farmer, age 26, single, b. Richmond Co., s/o Tasker and Polly Thompson, to ROBERTA VENIE, age 23, single, b. Richmond Co., d/o Jef. and Rachel Venie. Consent 18 OCT 1878 by bride Robertha [her X mark] Venie, sworn by Hy. Campbell. J.B. DeBerry, Pastor Richmond Circuit. 24 OCT 1878 at Farnham Church. [C8, R:312, R1:45]

Thompson, William Anderson (Col.) to Anna Johnson (Col.). WILLIAM ANDERSON THOMPSON, farmer, age 24, single, b. Richmond Co., s/o Charlotte Veney, to ANNA JOHNSON, age 21, single, b. Richmond Co., d/o Kitty Johnson (parents are both dead). Consent 15 DEC 1875 by parties, wit. W.B. Scott. Allen [his X mark] Brown. 17 DEC 1875 at *Edge Hill*. [C7, R:262, R1:39]

Thrift, George W. to Lucy Frances Mealey.[1] GEORGE W. THRIFT, farmer, age 39, widowed, b. Richmond Co., s/o William and Jane [Northen] Thrift, to LUCY FRANCES MEALEY,[2] age 21, single, b. Lancaster Co., d/o John and Frances Mealey. Consent 14 JUL 1863 by bride. James A. Weaver. 14 JUL 1863 at Elizabeth Littrell's. [C3, R:160, R1:12]

Thrift, John Addison to Novella L. Hudson.[3] JOHN A. THRIFT, farming, age 34, widowed, b. Richmond Co., s/o Samuel B. and Mary A. [G. Webb] Thrift,[4] to NOVELLA L. HUDSON, age 23, single, b. Richmond Co., d/o P.J. [Presley James] and Sarah A. [Ann Balderson] Hudson, *q.v.* Consent 24 MAY 1887 from Village, Va. by parties, wit. H.S. Thrift. A. Judson Reamy. 25 MAY 1887 at the res. of Mr. P.J. Hudson. [C11, R:291, R1:71]

Thrift, John F. to Mrs. Mariah Thrift Berrick. JOHN F. THRIFT, farmer, age 52, widowed, b. Richmond Co., s/o John and Jane Thrift, to MARIAH BERRICK, age 38, widow, b. Richmond Co., d/o George and Mary Thrift. E.L. Williams. 15 JAN 1863 at R. Bryant's. [C3, R:160, R1:12]

Thrift, John W. to Nancy S. Headley. JOHN W. THRIFT, gentleman, farmer, age 27, single, b. Richmond Co., s/o John and Sally Thrift, to NANCY S. HEADLEY, lady, age 21, single, b. Richmond Co., d/o Lindsey and Eliza Headley. Consent 18 MAR 1856 signed by Lindsey Headley and Nancy [her X mark] Headley, wit. Wm. B. Hale. E.L. Williams, minister. 20 MAR 1856. [C1, R, R1:3]

---

[1] Lucy F. Thrift (b. 27 MAR 1842, d. 21 DEC 1926) is bur. at Jerusalem Baptist Church cemetery.
[2] Surname appears as Maley and Mealey, but her signature on the consent is Mealey.
[3] John A. Thrift and (b. 6 APR 1852, d. 30 NOV 1907) his second wife Novella L. Hudson (b. 4 SEP 1864, d. 18 DEC 1938) are bur. at Bethany Baptist Church cemetery.
[4] Samuel B. Thrift and Mary A.G. Webb were married by bone 4 MAY 1844 in Richmond Co.

Thrift, John W. to Sarah J. Beazley. JOHN W. THRIFT, farmer, age 51, widowed, b. Richmond Co., s/o John and Sarah Thrift, to SARAH J. BEAZLEY, age 36, single, b. Richmond Co., d/o Richard H. and Crelee Ann Beazley. Consent 10 MAY 1880 by parties, wit. John A. Thrift. W.A. Crocker. 12 MAY 1880. [C9, R:315, R1:50]

Thrift, Lawson Whitfield to Mary Ann Lewis.[1] LAWSON W. THRIFT, farmer, age 23, single, b. Richmond Co., s/o Richard T. and Alice Ann [Lewis] Thrift,[2] to MARY A. LEWIS, age 20, single, b. Richmond Co., d/o Thomas P. [Parker] and M.V. [Mary Virginia Stephens] Lewis. Consent 12 JUL 1881 by parties, wits. Joseph C. Thrift, Thomas P. Lewis. G.H. Northam. 17 JUL 1881 at the res. of Wm. Middleton. [C9, R:336, R1:53]

Thrift, Richard Addison to Anna Elizabeth Bryant.[3] RICHARD A. THRIFT, age 21, single, b. Richmond Co., s/o Richard T. and Alice A. [Ann Lewis] Thrift,[4] to ELIZABETH A. BRYANT, age 16, single, b. Richmond Co., d/o Reubin A. and Mary [Thrift] Bryant.[5] Consent 28 NOV 1865 by bride and her father Reubin A. [his X mark] Bryant, wit. Benjn. Tucker; Robert Hall, clerk, attests to father's consent. Elder James A. Weaver. 29 NOV 1865 at the res. of Reubin A. Bryant. [C3, R:204, R1:15]

Thrift, William H. to Ann Eliza Connellee. WILLIAM H. THRIFT, age 52, divorced, b. Richmond Co., s/o George and Jane [Neasom] Thrift, to ANN ELIZA CONNELLEE, age 24, single, b. Richmond Co., d/o James and Mary Connellee. F.B. Beale. 22 JUL 1879 at *The Island.* [C8, R:308, R1:47]

Tomlin, William to Jane Wheeler. WILLIAM TOMLIN, farmer, age 28, single, b. Richmond Co., s/o Peter and Eliza Tomlin, to JANE WHEELER, age 20, single, b. Richmond Co., d/o Thornton and Mary Wheeler. Allen Brown. 13 AUG 1868 at Dr. Motley's. [C5, R:254, R1:24]

Turner, George (Col.) to Susan Veney (Col.). GEORGE TURNER, farmer, age 22, single, b. Richmond Co., s/o Rachel Veney, to SUSAN VENEY, age 21, single, b. Richmond Co., d/o Charlotte Veney. Consent 8 NOV 1876 by bride Susan [her X mark] Veney, wit. J.M. Lemoine. Allen Brown, minister. 10 NOV 1876 at the bride's house. [C7, R:305, R1:41]

Tyler, James to Frances Keyser. JAMES TYLER, farmer, age 41, widowed, b. Henrico Co., s/o Thomas and Ellen Tyler, to FRANCES KEYSER, age 20, single, b. Richmond Co., d/o John and Eliza Keyser. Robert Williamson, M.G. 31 DEC 1865 at John Keyser's. [C3, R:205, R1:15]

Tyson, Harry T. to Mrs. Rosella Frances Winstead,[6] widow of Hiram Montague Sandy. HARRY TYSON, sailing, age 51, widowed, b. Denmark, res. Northumberland Co., s/o Erastus and Annie Tyson, to R.F. SANDY, age 42, widow, b. Richmond Co., d/o George L. and Martha [H.B.

---

[1] Lawson W. Thrift (b. 20 OCT 1857, d. 7 MAR 1911) and wife Mary A. Lewis (b. 4 MAR 1861, d. 13 DEC 1931) are bur. in Gibeon Baptist Church cemetery.
[2] Richard T. Thrift and Alice Ann Lewis, d/o Jeremiah Lewis, were married by bond 14 OCT 1841 in Richmond Co.
[3] Richard A. Thrift (b. 17 NOV 1844, d. 3 MAY 1911 in Village, Va.) and wife Anna E. Bryant (b. 1849, d. 1933 in Village, Va.) are bur. in Gibeon Baptist Church cemetery.
[4] Richard T. Thrift and Alice Ann Lewis, d/o Jeremiah Lewis, were married by bond 14 OCT 1841 in Richmond Co.
[5] Reuben Bryant and Mary Thrift were married 18 DEC 1845 in Richmond Co. by Rev. E.L. Williams.
[6] Harry T. Tyson (1833-1910) and his wife Rosella F. Winstead (b. 22 DEC 1845, d. 25 JUN 1942) are bur. at Henderson United Methodist Church cemetery, Hyacinth, Va.

Headley] Winstead.[1] Consent 17 OCT 1887 from Village, Va. by bride, wit. James O. Lowry. W.H. Edwards. 20 OCT 1887 at *The Village*. [C11, R:293, R1:70]

U

Urgums, Leroy (Col.) to Louisa Norris (Col.). LEROY URGUMS, oysterman, no age given, widowed, b. Richmond Co., s/o Jubiter Urgums, to LOUISA NORRIS, age 22, single, b. Richmond Co., d/o Cyrus Norris. Walker Carter. 9 SEP 1880 at the bride's home. [C9, R:316, R1:51]

V

Van Ness, Julius B. to Mary M. Porter. JULIUS B. VAN NESS, merchant, age 41, widower, b. Columbia, N.Y., s/o Benjamin and Delia Van Ness, to MARY M. PORTER, age 26, single, b. Westmoreland Co., d/o William and Amanda [C. Baber] Porter.[2] Consent 4 JUN 1855 by bride. B.H. Johnson, Minister of the Methodist Episcopal Church South, 5 JUN 1855 in Westmoreland Co. [C1, R:153, R1:2]

Veazey, Henry to Mittie Barnes. HENRY VEAZEY, sailing, age 21y6m14d, single, b. Wilmington, Del., res. Annapolis, Md., s/o Edward and Ann Veazey, to MITTIE BARNES, age 18, single, b. Richmond Co., d/o Thomas W.K. [William Keane] and Harriet [A. Elmore] Barnes. Consent 5 NOV 1890 by bride, wit. Thos. W.K. Barnes. W.A. Crocker. 10 NOV 1890 at the res. of B. Elmore. [C12, R:324, R1:77]

Veazey, John Charles Groom to Margaret Ann Gallagher.[3] JOHN CHARLES G. VEAZEY, farmer, age 39 on 27 JUN 1870, single, b. near Paradise, Lancaster Co., Pa., res. Farnham Parish, s/o [Dr.] Edward and Eliza [Fox] Veazey, to MARGARET ANN GALLAGHER, age 29 on 29 OCT 1870, single, b. at Hare's Corner, New Castle Co., Del., res. Farnham Parish, d/o William and Francina Gallagher. G.H. Northam. 8 NOV 1870 at the house of John C.G. Veazey. [C5, R:234, R1:28]

Veney, Alfred (Col.) to Fanny Veney (Col.). ALFRED VENEY, farming, age 23, single, b. Richmond Co., s/o Thomas and Mary Veney, to FANNY VENEY, age 19, single, b. Richmond Co., d/o Mary Veney (dec'd.) (name of father not provided). Consent 22 DEC 1882 from Emmerton, Va. by Charlotte [her X mark] Veney, wits. O.M. Lemoine, Geo. [his X mark] Turner. Davey Veney, M.G. 24 DEC 1882. [C10, R:314, R1:57]

Veney, Claiborne (Col.) to Adeline Tate (Col.). CLAIBORNE VENEY, age 30, single, b. Richmond Co., s/o Mollie Veney (name of father omitted "for good cause"), to ADELINE TATE, age 21, single, b. Richmond Co., d/o Robert and Maria Tate. Consent 27 JAN 1866 by mother Maria [her X mark] Tate, wit. Thomas [his X mark] Jackson. Andrew Fisher. 28 JAN 1866 in Warsaw, Va. [C4, R:270, R1:186]

Veney, Claiborne (Col.) to Catharine Veney (Col.). CLAIBORNE VENEY, farmer, age 35, widowed, b. Richmond Co., d/o Mollie Veney, to CATHARINE VENEY, age 21, single, b. Richmond Co.,

---

[1] George L. Winstead and Martha H.B. Headley, d/o Griffin Headley, were married by bond 8 NOV 1836 in Richmond Co.
[2] William Porter and Amanda C. Baber were married by bond 11 NOV 1823 in Westmoreland Co.
[3] John Charles Groom Veazey (b. 26 MAY 1831 in Lancaster Co., s/o Edward Veazey and Eliza Fox, d. 6 NOV 1911) and his wife M.G. Veazey (b. OCT 1841, d. JAN 1929) are bur. in North Farnham Episcopal Church cemetery, Farnham, Va.

d/o John and Mary Veney. Davy Veney, parson. 3 DEC 1878 at the res. of Jack Veney. [C8, R:312, R1:45]

Veney, Cornelius (Col.) to Sopha Reed (Col.). CORNELIUS VENEY, oysterman and farmer, age 21y5m, single, b. Richmond Co., s/o Robert and Mary Ann Veney, to SOPHA REED, age 22, single, b. Richmond Co., d/o Nelson and Martha Ann Reed. Note: "This is to Certifies the reason why the License was not return [sic], Sopha Reed Mother Died 5th of May 1880. Cornelius Veney." Rev. John Wilkerson. 20 MAY 1880 at Mulberry Baptist Church. [C9, R:315, R1:50]

Veney, Daniel (Col.) to Ariana Brown (Col.). DANIEL VENEY, farming, age 62, widowed, b. Richmond Co., s/o Robert Tayloe and Mollie Veney, to ARIANA BROWN, age 40, widow, b. Richmond Co., d/o Jere and Charlotte Veney. Consent 26 JAN 1887 from Ivanhoe by bride Ariana [her X mark] Brown, wit. Wm. Garland. Rev. W. Carter. 27 JAN 1887 at the res. of the bride. [C11, R:290, R1:69]

Veney, David (Col.) to Mrs. Charlotte Kelley (Col.). DAVID VENEY, miller, age about 55, widower, b. Richmond Co., s/o Humphrey and Milly Veney, to CHARLOTTE KELLEY, age 50, widow, b. Richmond Co., d/o Joseph and Judy Veney. Consent 6 APR 1885 from Emmerton, Va. by bride, wit. J.D. Connellee. Edmond Rich. 6 APR 1885. [C10, R:316, R1:64]

Veney, David, Jr. (Col.) to Hannah Thompson (Col.). DAVID VENEY, JR., farmer, age 26, single, b. Richmond Co., s/o David and Judy Veney, to HANNAH THOMPSON, age 25, single, b. Richmond Co., d/o Sally Thompson. David Veney. 7 JUL 1872 at the res. of the minister. [C6, R:238, R1:32]

Veney, David, Jr. (Col.) to Georgeanna Howard (Col.). DAVY VENEY, JR., farmer, age 27, widowed, b. Richmond Co., s/o David, Sr. and Judy Veney, to GEORGEANNA HOWARD, age 27, single, b. Va., d/o Sally Howard. Consent 8 DEC 1876 by bride Georgeanna [her X mark] Howard, wit. O.[M.] Lemoine. David Veney. 10 DEC 1876 at the res. of Davy Veney. [C7, R:306, R1:41]

Veney, Elias (Col.) to Mary Jane Thompson (Col.). ELIAS VENEY, farmer, age 21, single, b. Richmond Co., s/o Davy and Judy Veney, to MARY JANE THOMPSON, age 21, single, b. Richmond Co., d/o John and Betsy Thompson. Consent 5 DEC 1870 by bride Mary Jane [her X mark] Thompson, wit. M. Lemoine, Robert [his X mark] Veney. Thomas G. Thomas. 11 DEC 1870 at Mulberry Chapel. [C5, R:234, R1:28]

Veney, George (Col.) to Julia Ann Ficklin. GEORGE VENEY, oysterman, age 21, single, b. Richmond Co., s/o Humphrey and Susan Veney, to JULIA ANN FICKLIN, age 15, single, b. Richmond, d/o Washington and Emily Ficklin. Travis Corbin. 18 MAY 1867 at *Cabinet Hall*. [C4, R:286, R1:21]

Veney, George (Col.) to Cornelia Veney (Col.). GEORGE VENEY, farming, age 25, widowed, b. Richmond Co., s/o Travers and Annie Veney, to CORNELIA VENEY, age 22y24d, single, b. Richmond Co., s/o James D. and Rachel Veney. Consent 16 JAN 1883 by bride, also by H. Marks, wit. James B. McCarty. Charles Sparks. 17 JAN 1883 at James Veney's place. [C10, R:355, R1:58]

Veney, George Washington (Col.) to Lucinda Sorrell (Col.). GEORGE WASHINGTON VENEY, oysterman, age 24, single, b. Richmond Co., s/o Washington and Betsey Veney, to LUCINDA SORRELL, age 21, single, b. Richmond Co., d/o Solomon Sorrell and Hannah Veney. Consent 12 FEB 1880 by Hannah [her X mark] Veney, wit. O.M. Lemoine. Davy Veney, minister. 12 FEB 1880 at *Mountfickler's*. [C9, R:314, R1:49]

Veney, Griffin (Col.) to Catharine Veney (Col.). GRIFFIN VENEY, farmer, age 22, single, b. Richmond Co., s/o Davy and Judy Veney, to CATHARINE VENEY, age 23, single, b. Richmond Co., d/o Washington and Fanny Veney. Thomas G. Thomas. 2 JAN 1879 at the house of Niece Veney. [C8, R:307, R1:46]

Veney, Harry (Col.) to Judy Veney (Col.). HARRY VENEY, farmer, age 35, widower, b. Richmond Co., s/o Travis and Anna Veney, to JUDY VENEY, age 20, single, b. Richmond Co., d/o Jack and Mary Veney. David Veney, D.D. 2 AUG 1872 at house of Jack Veney. [C6, R:238, R1:32]

Veney, Harry P. (Col.) to Louisa Johnson (Col.). HARRY P. VENEY, farming, age 36, widowed, b. Richmond Co., s/o Travers and Anna Veney, to LOUISA JOHNSON, age 26, single, b. Richmond Co., d/o Benjamin and Fanny Johnson. David Veney, M.G. 25 NOV 1883 at the res. of Davy Jenkins. [C10, R:357, R1:59]

Veney, Henry Lawson (Col.) to Sarah Shelton (Col.). HENRY LAWSON VENEY, oystering, age 25, single, b. Richmond Co., s/o George W. and Betsey Veney, to SARAH SHELTON, age 15, single, b. Richmond Co., d/o Major and Julia Ann Shelton. Allen Brown. 30 MAR 1882 at the res. of the bride. [C9, R:312, R1:56]

Veney, Humphrey (Col.) to Betsey Rich (Col.). HUMPHREY VENEY, farmer, age 47, single, b. Richmond Co., s/o Humphrey and Milly Veney, to BETSEY RICH, age 40, single, b. Richmond Co., d/o David and Hannah Rich. David Veney. 10 MAY 1868 at Mulberry Chapel. [C4, R:253, R1:23]

Veney, Humphrey, Jr. (Col.) to Richardanna Campbell (Col.). HUMPHREY VENEY, JR., farming, age 25, single, b. Richmond Co., s/o Davy and Judy Veney, to RICHARDANNA CAMPBELL, age 21, single, b. Richmond Co., d/o Dick and Judy Campbell. Consent 21 MAY 1879 by bride Richardanna [her X mark] Campbell, wit. O.M. Lemoine. Allen Brown, minister. 5 JUN 1879 at the bride's home. [C8, R:308, R1:47]

Veney, James Adaniram (Col.) to Roxanna Reece (Col.). JAMES ADANIRAM VENEY, farmer, age 28, single, b. Richmond Co., s/o Jack and Mary Veney, to ROXANNA REECE, age 20, single, b. Richmond Co., d/o Allen and Peggy Reece. Robert Williamson, Farnham, Va. 5 MAY 1887 at Farnham. [C11, R:291, R1:71]

Veney, James H. (Col.) to Prisilla Veney (Col.).[1] JAMES H. VENEY, oysterman, age 23, single, b. Richmond Co., s/o Robert and Hannah Veney, to PRISCILLA VENEY, age 20, single, b. Richmond Co., d/o Washington and Fanny Veney. Consent undated by Fanny [her X mark] Veany, wit. W.H. Veney. John Wilkerson. 15 DEC 1881 at *Mounticlis*. [C9, R:337, R1:54]

---

[1] The surname is also spelled Veany.

Veney, James Henry (Col.) to Catherine Elizabeth Veney (Col.). JAMES HENRY VENEY, farmer, age 26, single, b. Richmond Co., s/o Washington and Mary Veney, to CATHERINE ELIZABETH VENEY, age 28, single, b. Richmond Co., d/o David Veney, Sr. and Judy Veney. Rev. Pymus Nutt. 31 OCT 1875 at home. [C7, R:262, R1:38]

Veney, James L. (Col.) to Virginia Veney (Col.). JAMES L. VENEY, oysterman, age 23, single, b. Richmond Co., s/o Washington and Betsey Veney, to VIRGINIA VENEY, age 18, single, b. Richmond Co., d/o George and Martha Ann Veney. Consent by George [his X mark] Veney, wit. Jesse [his X mark] Veney. Allen Brown, minister. 1 MAY 1882 at the bride's home. [C9, R:313, R1:56]

Veney, Jefferson (Col.) to Mrs. Aggy Rich Diggs (Col.). JEFFERSON VENEY, farmer, age 49, widow, b. Richmond Co., s/o Humphrey and Milly Veney, to AGGY DIGGS, age 48, widow, b. Richmond Co., d/o David and Hanna Rich. Thomas G. Thomas. 20 DEC 1866 at the house of Edward Webb. [C4, R:272, R1:18]

Veney, Jesse (Col.) to Judy Griffin (Col.). JESSE VENEY, farmer, age 23, single, b. Richmond Co., s/o Tom and Rachel Veney, to JUDY GRIFFIN, age 24, single, b. Richmond Co., d/o John Griffin and Sarah Veney. Davy Veney. 11 FEB 1871 at Harry Veney's. [C5, R:244, R1:29]

Veney, Joseph (B) to Sarah J. Veney (B). JOSEPH VENEY, farmer, age 23, single, b. Richmond Co., s/o Joseph and Fanny Veney, to SARAH J. VENEY, age 16, single, b. Richmond Co., d/o Louis and Adline Veney. Consent 17 OCT 1876 by Louis Veney, Adline Veney, wit. George Rich. David Veney. 19 OCT 1876 at Sanford's. [C7, R:305, R1:41]

Veney, Joseph (Col.) to Luemma Ball (Col.). JOSEPH VENEY, farmer, age 23, single, b. Richmond Co., s/o Jesse and Felicia Veney, to LUEMMA BALL, age 18, single, b. Richmond Co., d/o Luemma Ball (dec'd.) [name of father not given]. Davey Veaney [sic]. 7 SEP 1882 at [Valley?] farm. [C9, R:313, R1:56]

Veney, Major Humphrey (Col.) to Jane Loper (Col.). MAJOR HUMPHREY VENEY, laborer, age 46, single, b. Richmond Co., s/o Humphrey and Betsey Veney, to JANE LOPER, age 21, single, b. Richmond Co., d/o Edward Loper. G.H. Northam. 8 AUG 1890 at *Glenmore*. [C12, R:324, R1:77]

Veany, Moses to Ellen Veany. Consent 15 FEB 1854 by parties, wit. Lewis Thompson. No return. [C]

Veney, Richard Henry (Col.) to Cremore Veney (Col.). RICHARD HENRY VENEY, farming, age 21, single, b. Richmond Co., s/o Lewis Veney and Adeline Veney, to CREMORE VENEY, age 21, single, b. Richmond Co., d/o Jefferson and Agnes Veney. Consent 15 MAR 1888 by parties. Rev. John Wilkerson. 15 MAR 1888 at res. of Jefferson Veney, Farnham, Va. [C11, R:315, R1:72]

Veney, Samuel (Col.) to Sukey Veney (Col.). SAMUEL VENEY, farmer, age 26, single, b. Richmond Co., s/o Jack and Mary Veney, to SUKEY VENEY, age 22, single, b. Richmond Co., d/o James Thompson and Rachel Veney. Travis Corbin, minister. 13 FEB 1873 in Washington Township. [C6, R:235, R1:33]

Venie, Steptoe (B) to Eliza Lee (B). STEPTOE VENIE, oysterman, age 25, single, b. Richmond Co., s/o John and Rachel Venie, to ELIZA LEE, age 24, single, b. Richmond Co., d/o Nancy Curry (father not known). Consent 19 JUN 1880 by bride Eliser [her X mark] Lee, wit. George Thomson. Peter Blackwell. 20 JUN 1880 at [Ebenezer] Church. [C9[1], R:315, R1:50]

Veney, Thaddeus (Col.) to Mrs. Easter Bold (Col.). THADDEUS VENEY, farmer, age 60, widowed, b. Richmond Co., s/o Daniel and Sally Veney, to EASTER BOLD, age 50, widow, b. Essex Co., parents unknown. David Veney, Sr. 12 APR 1874 at Mulberry Church. [C7, R:230, R1:376]

Veney, Thomas (Col.) to Mrs. Frances Newton (Col.). THOMAS VENEY, farmer, age 21, single, b. Richmond Co., s/o Jefferson and Rachel Veney, to FRANCES NEWTON, age 24, widow, b. Richmond Co., d/o Isaac and Fanny Newton. Allen Brown. 14 MAR 1868 at res. of Jefferson Veney. [C4, R1:23]

Veney, Thomas (Col.) to Mary Ann Burrell (Col.). THOMAS VENEY, laborer, age 25, single, b. Richmond Co., s/o Dennis and Dorcas Veney, to MARY ANN BURRELL, age 19, single, b. Richmond Co., d/o Thomas and Alice Burrell. Consent by father Thomas Burrell and Alice Burrell. Elder James A. Weaver. 24 APR 1873 at the res. of the bride's parents. [C6, R:235, R1:34]

Veney, Thomas Burkley (Col.) to Georgiana Connor (Col.).[2] THOMAS BUBKLEY VENEY, oystering, age 23, single, b. Richmond Co., s/o James D. and Charlotte Veney, to GEORGIANA CONNOR, age 23, single, b. Richmond Co., d/o John and Susan Connor. Consent 10 MAR 1884 by Susan [her X mark] Connor and George Annah [her X mark] Connor. Robert Haynie. 16 MAR 1884 at Susan Connor's. [C10, R:354, R1:61]

Veney, Thornton to Catharine Jackson. THORNTON VENEY, laborer, age 32, widower, b. Richmond Co., s/o Beverly and Jane Veney, to CATHARINE JACKSON, age 18, single, b. Richmond Co., d/o Samuel and Martha Jackson. No minister return. 23 DEC 1858. [C2, R:138, R1:6]

Veney, Thornton to Maria Burrell. THORNTON VENEY, day laborer, age 32, widowed, b. Richmond Co., s/o Beverly Gouldman and Jane Veney, to MARIA BURRELL, age 23, single, birthplace not known, d/o George and Mary Burrell. Consent 24 SEP 1860 by bride Mariah [her X mark] Burrell, wit. Dandrige [his X mark] Burrell. No minister return. 26 SEP 1860. [C2, R:154, R1:9]

Veney, Travis (Col.) to Jinny Grant (Col.). TRAVIS VENEY, farmer, age 24, single, b. Richmond Co., s/o Joseph and Judy Veney, to JINNY GRANT, age 21, single, b. Richmond Co., d/o George Grant and Mary Campbell. Travis Corbin. 29 MAY 1867 at *Edge Hill*. [C4, R:286, R1:21]

Veny, Walter R. to Martha Adams. WALTER R. VENEY, farmer, age 22, single, b. Richmond Co., s/o Thaddeus and Evelina Veney, to MARTHA ADAMS, age 17, single, b. Richmond Co., d/o Thomas and Ann Adams. Consent 21 JUL 1863 by bride Martha [her X mark] Adams, wit. J.W.

[1] The consent is filmed out of sequence with March 1880 records.
[2] Consent is for George Annah Connnor to Phineas Veney.

Scrimger, oath by Lawson Tate. E.L. Williams. 22 JUL 1863 at Thaddeus Veney's.[1] [C3, R:160, R1:12]

Venie, Washington, to Frances Venie. Consent 23 MAR 1855 by Frances [her X mark] Venie, wit. Thornton [his X mark] Venie, attest W.H. Connellee. No license or minister return. [C1]

Veney, Washington (Col.) to Sophia Jackson (Col.). WASHINGTON VENEY, oysterman, age 29, single, b. Richmond Co., s/o Washington and Fannie Veney, to SOPHIA JACKSON, age 21, single, b. Richmond Co., d/o Griffen Veney and Susan Jackson. Consent by Sopfie [her X mark] Jackson. Rev. John Wilkerson. 7 APR 1887 at the house of Fannie Veney. [C11, R:291, R1:69]

Venie, William Henry (Col.) to Sarah Catherine Rich (Col.). WILLIAM HENRY VENIE, farmer, age 27y10m, single, b. Richmond Co., s/o Joseph and Fanny Venie, to SARAH CATHERINE RICH, age 21, single, b. Richmond Co., d/o Beverly and Mary Rich. Consent by parents of the bride Beverly [his X mark] Rich and Mary [her X mark] Rich, wit. C.V. Middleton. Robert Williamson. 13 APR 1871 at Durrettsville, Va. [C5, R:244, R1:29]

Veney, William Henry (Col.) to Masonria Hill (Col.). WILLIAM HENRY VENEY, oystering, age 23y9m, single, b. Richmond Co., s/o Jesse and Falicia Veney, to MASONRIA HILL, age 23, single, b. Richmond Co., d/o Annie Hill. Consent 9 DEC 1887 by bride. Edmond Rich. 29 DEC 1887 at the res. of Anny Hill. [C11, R:293, R1:71]

W

Walker, Alfred (Col.) to Lucinda Allen (Col.). ALFRED WALKER, farmer, age 30, widowed, b. Richmond Co., d/o Davy and Betsey Walker, to LUCINDA ALLEN, age 36, single, b. Richmond Co., d/o Judy Allen. Consent 16 NOV 1874 by bride Lucinda [her X mark] Allen, wit. Abra. [P.] Wilson. John Roy. 22 NOV 1874. [C7, R:230, R1:37]

Walker, Edward to Bettie Emsy Winstead. EDWARD WALKER, farmer, age 21, single, b. Richmond Co., s/o Eppa C. [Christopher] and Jane [Ann Dodson] Walker,[2] to BETTIE EMSY WINSTEAD, age 17, single, b. Northumberland Co., d/o William and Jane R. Winstead. Consent 13 NOV 1876 by mother Jane R. Winstead, wit. Leroy B. Dodson. R.J. Sanford. 21 NOV 1876. [C7, R:306, R1:41]

Walker, Eppa Sydnor to Nancy Albiny Lewis.[3] EPPA S. WALKER, farming, age 20, single, b. Richmond Co., s/o Eppa C. [Christopher] and Jane A. [Ann Dodson] Walker, to NANCY A. LEWIS, age 19, single, b. Richmond Co., d/o John T. and Rachel Lewis. Consent 26 NOV 1886 by bride, wits. John T. Lewis, Eppy C. Walker. Charles N. Betts. 28 NOV 1886 at Maon [sic] Baptist Church. [C11, R:316, R1:68]

---

[1] The license gives place of marriage at Thaddeus Veney's, while the return gives the residence of Hannah Tate.
[2] Eppa Walkker and Jane A. Dodson were married by bond 11 MAY 1847 in Richmond Co. by Rev. Bartholomew Dodson.
[3] Eppa S. Walker (b. 12 APR 1866, d. 26 JUN 1940) and wife Nancy A. Lewis (b. 1867, d. 19 JAN 1949) are bur. in Oakland United Methodist Church cemetery.

Walker, James Christopher to Olivia Nutt Dodson.[1] JAMES C. WALKER, farmer, age 20, single, b. Richmond Co., s/o Eppa C. [Christopher] and Jane A. [Ann Dodson] Walker,[2] to OLIVIA N. DODSON, age 16, single, b. Richmond Co., d/o Alexander and Catharine D. [Bryant] Dodson.[3] B. Dodson. Consent 21 MAR 1868 by bride Olivia N. [her X mark] Dodson, wit. Eppa C. Walker. 24 MAR 1868 at Mrs. Dodson's. [C4, C5, R:253, R1:23]

Walker, John W. to Virginia A. Lewis. JOHN W. WALKER, farmer, age 19y11m, single, b. Richmond Co., s/o Eppa C. [Christopher] and Jane A. [Ann Dodson] Walker, to VIRGINIA A. LEWIS, age 16, single, b. Richmond Co., d/o John B. and Alice A. Lewis. Consent by groom and Eppa C. Walker, wit. John B. Lewis. James F. Brannin. 31 MAR 1880 at the house of John B. Lewis. [C9, R:315, R1:50]

Walker, Willie (Col.) to Bettie Saunders (Col.). WILLIE WALKER, laborer, age 21y3m, single, b. Westmoreland Co., s/o Alfred and Sally Walker, to BETTIE SAUNDERS, age 21, single, b. Richmond Co., d/o Robert and Betsey Saunders. Consent 12 DEC 1883 by bride, no wit. George Laws. 16 DEC 1883 at *Doctor's Hall*. [C10, R:357, R1:60]

Wallace, Benjamin Godfrey to Willie Ann Phillips.[4] BENJAMIN G. WALLACE, farmer, age 30, single, b. Dorchester Co., Md., s/o Aaron P. and Mary Wallace, to WILLIE A. PHILLIPS, age 23, single, b. Richmond Co., d/o John W. and Maria L. [Fogg] Phillips. Robert Williamson, M.G. 26 MAY 1868 at Capt. J.W. Phillips. [C4, R:254, R1:24]

Wallace, Benjamin Godfrey to Ida B. Daniels. BENJAMIN G. WALLACE, farmer, age 37, widowed, b. Dorchester Co., Md., s/o A.P. [Aaron] and Mary Wallace, to IDA B. DANIELS, age 21, single, b. Middlesex Co., d/o George and Mary Daniels. Letter from Ida Daniels. G.H. Northam. 28 FEB 1877. [C8, R:306a, R1:42]

Wallace, William Garland to Lucilla A. Clarke. WILLIAM G. WALLACE, farmer, age 24, single, b. Richmond Co., s/o Joseph and Willie A. [Williann E. Garland] Wallace,[5] to LUCILLA A. CLARKE, age 23, single, b. Richmond Co., d/o Atterson and Caroline [McClanahan] Clarke.[6] G.H. Northam. 20 MAY 1869. [C5, R, R1:26]

Waple, John T. to Maria A. Bowen. JOHN T. WAPLE, farmer, age 21, single, b. Richmond Co., s/o John and Maria Waple, to MARIA A. BOWEN, age 21, single, b. Richmond Co., d/o William H. and Nancy Bowen. Age of husband proved by oath of W.H. Burgess. Consent 22 JUN 1866 by mother of bride Nancy [her X mark] Bowen, wit. W.H. Burgess. John Pullen. 24 JUN 1866 at Nancy Bowen's. [C4, R:271, R1:17]

Waple, John T. to Olivia A. Bowen. JOHN T. WAPLE, farmer, age 29, widowed, b. Richmond Co., s/o [John and] Maria Waple, to OLIVIA A. BOWEN, age 26, single, b. Richmond Co., d/o Richard and Mary Bowen. Consent 29 JAN 1874 by parties John T. [his X mark] Waple and

---

[1] James C. Walker (b. 15 MAR 1848, d. 25 FEB 1924) and his wife Olivia N. Dodson (b. 17 SEP 1851, d. 29 DEC 1898) are bur. at Corrottoman Baptist Church cemetery, Ottoman, Va.
[2] Eppa C. Walker (b. 15 MAR 1823, d. 23 DEC 1895) and wife Jane A. Dodson (b. 2 AUG 1828, d. 17 FEB 1908) are bur. in Oakland United Methodist Church cemetery.
[3] Alexander Dodson and Catharine Bryant were married by bond 3 FEB 1848 in Northumberland Co., Va.
[4] Willie Ann Phillips Wallace (b. 1844, d. 19 FEB 1875) is bur. at Jerusalem Baptist Church cemetery.
[5] Joseph Wallace and Williann E. Garland were married by bond 24 MAY 1843 in Richmond Co.
[6] Atterson Clarke and Caroline McClanahan, d/o Jeremiah Webb and Apphia Northen, wid/o Vincent M. McClanahan, were married by bond 20 MAY 1837 in Richmond Co.

Olivia A. [her X mark] Bowen, wits. Thos. E. Pullen, Sr., Thos. Jenkins. H.H. Fones. 3 FEB 1874. [C7, R:230, R1:36]

Ward, Cornelius (Col.) to Patsy Jackson (Col.). CORNELIUS WARD, farmer, age 38, single, b. Richmond Co., s/o Ralph and Eliza Ward, to PATSY JACKSON, age 24, single, b. Prince William Co., parents names omitted "for good cause." Thomas G. Thomas. 8 DEC 1866 at *Mount Airy*. [C4, R:272, R1:18]

Waring, Walter (Col.) to Maria Sorrell (Col.). WALTER WARING, oystering, age 26y3m21d, single, b. Richmond Co., s/o Julia Ann Veney née Rich, to MARIA SORRELL, age 21, single, b. Richmond Co., d/o Aaron and Eliza Sorrell. Consent 4 JUN 1885 by bride, no wit. Charles Sparks. 4 JUN 1885 at the parents' residence. [C10, R:317, R:64]

Warner, Loren D. to Lucie E. Jeffries. LOREN D. WARNER, teacher, age 30, single, b. Worcester Co., Mass., s/o Luke and Louisa Warner, to LUCIE E. JEFFRIES, age 23, single, b. Richmond Co., d/o John F.B. and Matilda A. Jeffries. Andrew Fisher, of Episcopal Church. 28 AUG 1860. [C2, R:153, R1:9]

Warner, Loren D. to Lucy B. Sturman. LOREN D. WARNER, clerk of courts,[1] age 50y1m16d, widowed, b. Worcester Co., Mass., s/o Luke and Louisa Warner, to LUCY B. STURMAN, age 36y8m8d, single, b. Richmond Co., d/o William Y. [Young][2] and Clementina [Webb] Sturman.[3] Consent in MAY 1880 by bride. Peter Ainslie. 13 MAY 1880 at Laurel Brooke Church. [C9, NN:14 MAY 1880, R:315, R1:50]

Warner, Waldo to Frances Myrteen Payton. WALDO WARNER, farming, age 63, single, b. and res. Harvard, Mass., s/o Calvin and Lydia Warner, to FRANCES MYRTEEN PAYTON, age 21, single, b. Richmond Co., d/o William H. and Frances R. Payton. Arthur B. Kinsolving. 24 OCT 1889 at *Menokin*. [C12, R:328, R1:74]

Warwick, John B.[4] to Martha J. Connollee. JOHN B. WARWICK, carpenter, age 23, single, b. and res. Lancaster Co., s/o James and Mary Warwick, to MARTHA J. CONNOLLEE, age 21, single, b. Richmond Co., d/o Washington and Elizabeth Connollee. Edmund Withers, minister of the P.E. Church. 15 DEC 1857 at res. of W. Connollee. [C1, R:160, R1:5]

Washington, Adam (Col.) to Mrs. Ann Brown (Col.). ADAM WASHINGTON, farming, age 21y7m, single, b. Richmond Co., s/o Cyrus and Celia Washington, to ANN BROWN, age 36, widow, b. Richmond Co., d/o Joseph and Ellen Palmer. Rev. Thomas G. Thomas. 15 JAN 1880 at the house of Frank Spinlar, Jr. [C9, R:314, R1:49]

Washington, Cyrus (Col.) to Mrs. Laura Sorrel (Col.). CYRUS WASHINGTON, mechanic, age 70, widowed, b. Richmond Co., s/o William Smith and [blank] Washington, to LAURA SORREL, age 40, widow, b. Richmond Co., d/o Denis Cupit and Gessilla Gordon. Consent by bride Laura [her

---

[1] L.D. Warner was clerk of Richmond County Court, 1868-1870 and 1871-1901, with William A. Brockenbrough seated 1870-1871.
[2] William Y. Sturman was Commonwealth's Attorney for Richmond County, 1828-1848.
[3] William Y. Sturman and Mrs. Clementina Jeffries were married 2 DEC 1841 in Richmond Co. by Rev. William N. Ward. See King., p. 198, for genealogy. She was the d/o Jeremiah and Apphia (Northen) Webb, and the wid/o Thomas H. Jeffries. Also is found in Richmond, Va. newspapers the following: "Married [c. DEC 1841] at Warsaw, Richmond Co., by Rev. Wm. N. Ward, Wm. Y. Sturman, Esq. to Mrs. Clementina Jeffries.
[4] A John B. Warwick (b. 1832, d. 1909 in Lancaster Co.) served in Co. E, 40th Reg., Va. Inf., C.S.A.

X mark] Sorrel, widow of James Sorrel. George [his X mark] Laws. 12 MAY 1881 at *Grove Mount*. [C9, R:336, R1:53]

Washington, David (Col.) to Laura Gray (Col.). DAVID WASHINGTON, farming, age 21, single, b. Richmond Co., s/o John and Martha Washington, to LAURA GRAY, age 21, single, b. Westmoreland Co., d/o John and Emily Gray. Rev. Robert Lewis at [Galle] Church in Westmoreland Co. 3 APR 1881. [C9, R:335, R1:52]

Washington, George (Col.) to Sally Nelson Goode (Col.). GEORGE WASHINGTON, farmer, age 25, bachelor, b. Richmond Co., s/o Robert and Pine Key Washington, to SALLY NELSON GOODE, age 17, single, b. Richmond Co., d/o James Goode and Minny Bowser. Thomas G. Thomas. 28 APR 1870 at the house of William Nelson. [C5, R:233, R1:27]

Washington, Henry (Col.) to Fanny Landon (Col.). HENRY WASHINGTON, farmer, age 22, single, b. Richmond Co., s/o Robert and Pinkey Washington, to FANNY LANDON, age 22, single, b. Richmond Co., d/o Richard and Peggy Landon. Thomas G. Thomas. 12 MAR 1874 at the house of Richard Landon. [C7, R:230, R1:36]

Washington, Presley (Col.) to Ida Laws (Col.). PRESLEY WASHINGTON, farming, age 28, widowed, b. Richmond Co., s/o James and Ann Washington, to IDA LAWS, age 20, single, b. Richmond Co., d/o Taylor and Betsey Laws. Rev. W. Carter. 23 MAR 1888 at the res. of the minister in Ivanhoe, Va. [C11, R:315, R1:72]

Washington, Robert (Col.) to Mrs. Mary Bailor (Col.). ROBERT WASHINGTON, laborer, age 53, widowed, b. Richmond Co., s/o George and Grace Washington, to MARY BAILOR, age 56, widow, b. Essex Co., names of parents left blank. Thomas G. Thomas. 9 APR 1871 at Clarksville Church. [C5, R:244, R1:29]

Washington, Samuel (Col.) to Louisa Newton (Col.). SAMUEL WASHINGTON, laborer, age 22, single, b. Northumberland Co., s/o James and Harriet Washington, to LOUISA NEWTON, age 16, single, b. Richmond Co., d/o Thomas Saunders and Martha Newton. Consent 26 DEC 1866 by mother Martha [her X mark] Bailey, wit. Jas. [his X mark] Bailey. Travis Corbin. 27 DEC 1866 at Durrettsville, Va. [C4, R:273, R1:189]

Waterfield, Ellyson Creddy to Susan Ann Hutt.[1] E. CREDDY WATERFIELD,[2] farmer, age 21, single, b. Richmond Co., s/o John and Rachel Waterfield, to SUSAN HUTT, age 23, single, b. Westmoreland Co., "given names of parents not known, she is a Hutt." Consent 7 APR 1884 by bride and Saban Hutt, wit. [Daniel Clark]. G.H. Northam. 8 APR 1884 at Mr. D. Clark's. [C10, R:354, R1:62]

Waterfield, John Thomas to Rachel Clark. JOHN THOMAS WATERFIELD, farmer, age 24, single, b. Accomack Co., s/o John and Sarah Ann Waterfield, to RACHEL CLARK, age 18, single, b. Richmond Co., d/o John B. and Lucinda Clark. E.L. Williams, minister. 19 DEC 1855. [C1, R, R1:3]

---

[1] Ellyson C. Waterfield (1865-1923) and wife Susan A. Hutt (1860-1933) are bur. at Totuskey Baptist Church cemetery.
[2] The surname also appears as Warterfield.

Waterfield, John Thomas to Mrs. Elizabeth Ann Douglas. JOHN T. WATTERFIELD [sic], farmer and sailor, age 35, widowed, b. Accomack Co., s/o John and Sarah Ann Waterfield, to ELIZABETH ANN DOUGLAS, age 25, widow, b. Richmond Co., d/o of Mr. and Mrs. Dameron. Consent 17 MAY 1877 by bride, wit. Richard C. Lewis. J.B. DeBerry, P.C. 20 MAY 1877 at *Oakland.* [C8, R:307, R1:42]

Watkins, Lewis (Col.) to Mrs. Nancy Johnson (Col.). LEWIS WATKINS, laborer, age 45, widowed, b. Essex Co., s/o Nelson and Sarga Watkins, to NANCY JOHNSON, age 40, widow, b. Richmond Co., d/o Humphrey and Lina Veney. Consent 19 SEP 1877 by bride Nancy [her X mark] Johnson, wit. Aren Sorel. Allen Brown, minister. 26 SEP 1877 at the res. of the bride. [C8, R:307, R1:43]

Weadon, James to Mary E. Bulger. JAMES WEADON, farming, age 60, widowed, b. Richmond Co., s/o Thomas and Elizabeth [Bowing] Weadon,[1] to MARY E. BULGER, age 27, single, b. Richmond Co., d/o John and Julia Ann [Hinson] Bulger.[2] Consent 27 NOV 1885 by bride Mary E. [her X mark] Bulger. R.N. Reamy. 1 DEC 1885. [C11, R:319, R1:66]

Weathers, Andrew to Mary D. Clark. ANDREW WEATHERS, farming, age 25, single, b. Richmond Co., res. Northumberland Co., s/o George W. and Frances A. Weathers, to MARY D. CLARK, age 20y9m20d, single, b. Northumberland Co., d/o William J. and Mary Jane Clark. Consent 12 APR 1887 by bride's father William J. Clark, wit. Oliver R. [his X mark] Weathers. Rev. A. Judson Reamy. 14 APR 1887 at the home of the bride. [C11, R:291, R1:71]

Weathers, George to Frances Dameron. GEORGE WETHERS [sic], farming, age 23, single, b. Richmond Co., s/o William Weathers, to FRANCES DAMERON, age 18, single, b. Richmond Co., d/o [blank].[3] A. Dulaney, minister. 4 SEP 1856. [C1, R:159, R1:4]

Weathers, George, Jr. to Emma A. Thrift. GEORGE WEATHERS, JR., farming, age 26, single, b. Richmond, s/o George W. [Sr.] and Frances [A.] Weathers, to EMMA A. THRIFT, age 18, single, b. Richmond Co., d/o Robert H. [Henry] and Mary J. [Jane King] Thrift.[4] Consent 17 MAR 1888 from Village, Va. by Robert H. [his X mark], Mary J. Thrift, the bride, and Lawson [his X mark] Thrift. Rev. A.D. Reynolds. 21 MAR 1888 at the res. of the bride's parents. [C11, R:315, R1:72]

Weathers, Joseph and Elizabeth Clarke. Consent 18 DEC 1855 by bride Elizabeth [her X mark] Clarke, wits. John Boyle, Benjamin Tucker. License 18 DEC 1855 by F.W. Pendleton, clerk. No license or minister return.[5] [C1, C2, R:153, R1:2]

Weathers, Joseph to Emily Clarke. JOSEPH WEATHERS,[6] farmer, age 30, widowed, b. Richmond Co., s/o William Wethers, to EMILY CLARKE, age 18, single, b. Richmond Co., d/o Meshack Clarke. Consent 28 JUL 1857 by father Meshack [his X mark] Clarke, wit. Joseph Clarke. A. Dulaney, minister. 28 JUL 1857. [C1, R:159, R1:5]

---

[1] Thomas Weeden and Elizabeth Bowing were married by bond 4 JUN 1805 in Richmond Co.
[2] John Bulger and Julia Ann Hinson were married 24 JAN 1850 in Richmond Co. by Rev. John Pullen.
[3] The license provides parent Frances Wethers [sic], presumably in error, while the Register is blank.
[4] Robert H. Thrift (b. 8 JAN 1849, d. 28 MAR 1935) and his wife Mary Jane King (b. 6 JAN 1850 at *Hyacinth*, Northumberland Co., d. 5 MAY 1921) are bur. in the Thrift Family Cemetery.
[5] The Register assigns minister William C. Haynes, although most of the information blanks are incomplete.
[6] Spelling varies, Wethers, Weathers, etc.

Weaver, Lawson A. to Sarah Anne Oldham.[1] LAWSON A. WEAVER, merchant, age 30, b. Westmoreland Co., s/o James A. and Susan Weaver, to SARAH A. OLDHAM, age 24, single, b. Richmond Co., d/o William C. and Virginia [Ficklin] Oldham.[2] Consent 26 NOV 1874 by bride, wit. R.[L.] Reynolds. G.H. Northam. 1 DEC 1874. [C7, R:230, R1:37]

Weaver, William (Col.) to Laura Lewis (Col.). WILLIAM WEAVER, farming, age 28, single, b. Richmond Co., s/o Samuel and Betsey Weaver, to LAURA LEWIS, age 28, single, b. Richmond Co., d/o Benjamin and Maria Lewis. Consent 23 DEC 1886 from Farnham, Va. by bride. Robert Williamson. 23 DEC 1886 at Farnham Church. [C11, R:317, R1:68]

Weaver, William to Mary M. Bispham. WILLIAM WEAVER, farming, age about 31, single, b. Westmoreland Co., s/o Henry Weaver and wife Ann, to MARY M. BISPHAM, age about 29, single, b. Richmond Co., d/o William Bispham and wife Mary. Consent 13 DEC 1855 by bride, wit. Robert Bispham. John Pullen, M.G. 18 DEC 1855 at the residence of Robert Bispham. [C1, R, R1:23]

Weaver, William Henry to Mrs. Mary Elizabeth Bowen Mozingo. WILLIAM HENRY WEAVER, farming, age 23, single, b. Richmond Co., s/o Betsy Weaver (name of father not known), to MARY ELIZABETH MOZINGO, age 24, widow, b. Richmond Co., d/o Frederick and Mary Bowen. Consent by bride Mary Elizabeth [her X mark] Mozingo, wit. Redman [his X mark] Ambrose. D.M. Wharton. 7 MAR 1883 at the res. of the minister in Westmoreland Co. [C10, R:355, R1:58]

Webb, Austin (Col.) to Amelia Ann Jissup (Col.). AUSTIN WEBB, farmer, age 28, single, b. Richmond Co., s/o Edward and Fanny Webb, to AMELIA ANN JISSUP, age 22, single, b. Richmond Co., d/o Moses and Alice Jissup. Travis Corbin. 20 FEB 1868 at Farnham House. [C4, R:253, R1:23]

Webb, George S. to Sarah E. Courtney. GEORGE S. WEBB, mechanic, age 25, single, b. Richmond Co., s/o William B. and Ann E. Webb, to SARAH E. COURTNEY, age 23, single, b. Richmond Co., d/o William and Mary Ann Courtney. G.H. Northam. 18 DEC 1882. [C10, R:314, R1:57]

Webb, Richard E. to Louisa Frances Richards. RICHARD E. WEBB, farmer, age 23, single, b. Richmond Co., s/o William B. and Nancy [Reynolds] Webb, to LOUISA FRANCES RICHARDS, age nearly 19y10m, single, b. Richmond Co., d/o Austin N. and Martha C. [Drake] Richards. G.H. Northam. 9 JAN 1877. [C8, R:306a, R1:42]

Webb, Richard E. to Mary Susan Franklin.[3] RICHARD E. WEBB, farmer, age 27, single, b. Richmond Co., s/o William B. and Nancy [Reynolds] Webb, to MARY SUSAN FRANKLIN, age 24, single, b. Richmond Co., d/o Samuel R. and Susan S. [Sisson] Franklin.[4] G.H. Northam. 24 MAR 1881. [C9; R:335, R1:52]

---

[1] Lawson A. Weaver (1843-1924) and wife Sarah Anne Oldham (1848-1917) are bur. in Jerusalem Baptist Church cemetery. He served as private in Co. D, 15th Va. Cav., C.S.A., living in Baltimore, Md. in 1894.
[2] William C. Oldham and Virginia Ficklin were married by bond 8 AUG 1843 in Richmond Co. by Rev. Nathan Healy.
[3] Richard E. Webb (b. 31 JUL 1853, d. 22 NOV 1932) and his wife Mary Susan Franklin (b. 13 MAY 1856, d. 14 JUL 1932) are bur. at Menokin Baptist Church cemetery.
[4] Samuel R. Franklin and Susan S. Sisson were married by bond 24 FEB 1841 in Richmond Co., with consent by William H. Sisson.

Webb, Richard R. to Frances A. Yeatman. Rev. George Northam. 4 JAN 1854. No license. [C]

Webb, William S. to Elizabeth Sutton. WILLIAM S. WEBB, mechanic, age 21, single, b. Richmond Co., s/o William B. and Nancy [Reynolds] Webb, to ELIZABETH SUTTON, age 21y11m, single, b. Westmoreland Co., d/o John and Martha [Elizabeth Mothershead] Sutton. G.H. Northam. 13 JUN 1872. [C6, R:237, R1:32]

Weitzell, William to Sophia Moore. WILLIAM WEITZELL, miller, age 21, single, b. Baltimore, Md., s/o John and Elizabeth Weitzell, to SOPHIA MOORE, age 21, single, b. Richmond Co., d/o Joseph G. and Betsy Moore. Consent 29 JAN 1863 by bride Miss Sophey [her X mark] Moore, wit. James [his X mark] Gallagher. James S. Porter, M.G. 29 JAN 1863. [C3, R:160, R1:12]

White, Robert Gustavus to Virginia A. Balderson.[1] ROBERT G. WHITE, farmer, age 21, single, b. Westmoreland Co., s/o Granville and Leanah [Mothershead] White,[2] to VIRGINIA BALDERSON, age 17, single, b. Richmond Co., d/o Theoderick N.[3] and Dorothea L. [Lane Sanders] Balderson.[4] Consent by father of bride, age of groom proved by oath of T.N. Balderson. John Pullen. 3 JUN 1866 at res. of T.N. Balderson. [C4, R:271, R1:17]

Wilcox, James Henry to Susan Malvina Schools.[5] JAMES H. WILCOX, farming, age 23, single, b. Richmond Co., s/o Alexander and Fanny Wilcox, to SUSIA M. SCHOOLS, age 21, single, b. Richmond Co., d/o Robert and Laura Schools. Consent 28 APR 1884 by bride. G.H. Northam. 29 APR 1884. [C10, NN:2 MAY 1884, R:354, R1:62]

Wilder, Nathan S. to Menora Hammock. NATHAN S. WILDER, sailor, age 23, single, b. Portsmouth, Va., res. Baltimore, Md., s/o John D. and Rebecca Wilder, to MENORA HAMMOCK, age 25, single, b. Richmond Co., parents unknown. Elder James A. Weaver. 17 DEC 1872 at the res. of James Gallagher. [C6, R:238, R1:32]

Wilkerson, J.B. to Araminta B. Reamy. J.B. WILKERSON, farmer, age 30, single, b. King George Co., res. Essex Co., s/o J.A. [Joseph] and S.A. [Sidney A. Clark] Wilkerson,[6] to ARAMINTA B. REAMY, age 23, single, b. Richmond Co., d/o William J. and Jane E. Reamy. Consent undated by father Wm. J. Reamy, wit. W.J.C. Walker. H.H. Fones. 2 MAY 1887. [C11, R:291, R1:71]

Wilkerson, John Pullen to Susan Erminie Reamy.[7] JOHN P. WILKERSON, farmer, age 20y8m, single, b. King George Co., s/o Joseph A. and S.A. [Sidney A. Clarke] Wilkerson, to SUSAN E. REAMY, age 21, single, b. Richmond Co., d/o Samuel T. and Susan C. [Fones] Reamy. Consent by Joseph A. Wilkerson and parties, wit. J.A. Pullen. Henry H. Fones. 2 OCT 1873 at *Foneswood*. [C6, R:235, R1:34]

---

[1] Robert Gustavus White (bl 26 DEC 1844, d. 18 MAR 1908) and wife Virginia A. Balderson (b. 26 NOV 1848, d. 31 OCT 1931) are bur. in the White Family Cemetery off of Route 3 near Lerty, Va. He served in Co. C, 47th Va. Inf., C.S.A.
[2] Granville White and Leannah Mothershead, d/o Sarah Mothershead, were married by bond 3 MAR 1838 in Westmoreland Co.
[3] Library of Virginia, Bible Records, Saunders Family Bible Record, 1782-1903, "Theoderick Noel Balderson departed this life December 23, 1890 in the 75th year of his age."
[4] Ibid., "Dorothea [sometimes Dorethia, or Doretha] Lane Sanders Balderson, wife of T. Noel Balderson, departed this life February 23, 1903 in the 84th year of her age." Also, "Doretha Lane Sanders, Daughter of Daniel Sanders and Mary his wife was Born December the 31st in the year of our Lord 1821."
[5] James Henry Wilcox (b. 10 AUG 1859, d. 3 NOV 1912) and wife Susan Malvina Schools (b. 27 JUL 1863, d. 2 SEP 1929) are bur. in Jerusalem Baptist Church cemetery.
[6] Joseph A. Wilkerson and Sidney A. Clark were married 14 JUL 1848 in King George Co. by Rev. James S. Petty.
[7] John P. Wilkerson (b. 23 JAN 1853, d. 13 JUL 1929) and wife Susan E. Reamy (b. 17 DEC 1852, d. 6 MAY 1915) are bur. in Ephesus Baptist Church cemetery, Dunnsville, Essex Co.

Wilkerson, John, Rev. (Col.) to Elizabeth "Lizzie" E. Rich (Col.) . JOHN WILKERSON, preacher, age 50, widowed, b. Richmond Co., s/o Solomon and Lucy Wilkerson, to ELIZABETH E. RICH, age 33, single, b. Richmond Co., d/o James and Kitty Rich. Consent 12 SEP 1888 by mother Kitty Rich. Rev. T.G. Thomas. 16 SEP 1888 at the house of Kitty Rich. [C11, R:316, R1:723]

Wilkins, George W. to Elizabeth Ann Lewis. GEORGE W. WILKINS, farmer, age 23, single, b. Westmoreland Co., s/o Susan Wilkins, to ELIZABETH ANN LEWIS, age 14, single, b. Richmond Co., d/o Middleton and Sarah Lewis. Consent 10 MAY 1881 by mother Sarah [her X mark] Lewis. G.H. Northam. 12 MAY 1881. [C9, R:336, R1:53]

Wilkins, Smith (Col.) to Malinda Blair (Col.). SMITH WILKINS, farming, age 28, single, b. Gloucester Co., s/o Jeremiah and Millie Ann Wilkins, to MALINDA BLAIR, age 28, single, b. Richmond Co., d/o Joseph and Peggy Blair. Rev. Thomas G. Thomas. 19 FEB 1880 at the house of the minister. [C9, R:314, R1:49]

Wilkins, William to Mrs. Margaret A. Jones. WILLIAM WILKINS, farming, age 35, widowed, b. Richmond Co., s/o Samuel and Jane Wilkins, to MARGARET A. JONES, age 30, widow, b. Richmond Co., d/o Frances Jones (name of father not given). Consent 21 DEC 1881 by bride Margret [sic] A. [her X mark] Jones, wits. Richard C. [his X mark] Rock, George Wilkins. G.H. Northam. 23 DEC 1881. [C9, R:337, R1:55]

Willey, Robert Wesley to Lelia E. Thompson.[1] ROBERT WESLEY WILLEY, mariner, age 26, single, b. Wicomico Co., Md., res. Lancaster Co., s/o John F. and Sarah A. Willey, to LELIA E. THOMPSON, age 18, single, b. King George Co., d/o William D. Thompson and Ellen [Moxley] Thompson[2] now Jett. Robert Williamson. 18 OCT 1881 at *Indian Banks*. [C9, NN:21 OCT 1881, R:338, R1:54]

Williams, Daniel (Col.) to Mahala Smith (Col.). DANIEL WILLIAMS, oysterman, age 26, single, b. Richmond Co., s/o Squire and Milly Williams, to MAHALA SMITH, age 22, single, b. Richmond Co., d/o Robert and Mary Smith. Consent 7 APR 1880 by bride Mahala [her X mark] Smith, wit. F.J. Comodore, sworn D. [his X mark] Williams. Rev. Walker Carter. 8 APR 1880 at the bride's home. [C9, R:315, R1:50]

Williams, Elijah (Col.) to Gustella Corbin (Col.). ELIJAH WILLIAMS, farmer, age 38, widowed, b. Richmond Co., s/o Lewis and Lucy Williams, to GUSTELLA CORBIN, age 25, single, b. Richmond Co., d/o Goin and Matilda Corbin. Travis Corbin. 13 FEB 1868 at Sign House. [C4, R:253, R1:23]

Williams, Elijah (Col.) to Mrs. Susan Foushee Mason (Col.). ELIJAH WILLIAMS, oysterman, age 49, widowed, b. Richmond Co., s/o Lewis and Lucy Williams, to SUSAN MASON, age [3]0, widow, b. Richmond Co., d/o John ~~Deshield~~ and Winney Foushee. Allen Brown, minister. 25 JUN 1876 at the res. of the bride. [C7, R:305, R1:40]

Williams, Henry (Col.) to Nancy Jenkins (Col.). HENRY WILLIAMS, laborer, age 21y6m, single, b. Westmoreland Co., s/o Robert and Maria Williams, to NANCY JENKINS, age 21y5m, single,

---

[1] Robert W. Willey (b. 28 JAN 1854, d. 15 AUG 1933) and wife Lelia E. (b. 6 DEC 1863, d. 3 MAR 1896) are buried at Irvington Baptist Church cemetery.
[2] William D. Thompson and Ellen Moxley were married 14 FEB 1850 in King George Co. by Rev. John McDaniel.

b. Richmond Co., d/o Davy and Polly Jenkins. Consent 1 JAN 1881 by bride Nancy [her X mark] Jenkins, wit. Geo. J. Northam, Ro. [his X mark] Williams. G.H. Northam. 4 JAN 1881 at *Glenmore.* [C9, R:335, R1:52]

Williams, John H., Jr. to Sarah E. Reynolds. Consent 14 JUL 1854 by bride, wit. F.W. Mozingo. No license or minister return. [C1]

Williams, Thomas G. to Betsey C. Duff.[1] THOMAS G. WILLIAMS, farmer, age 35, widowed, b. Westmoreland Co., s/o E.L. [Elijah] and Julia [McKildoe] Williams,[2] to BETSEY C. DUFF, age 19, single, b. and res. Essex Co., d/o Peter T. and Olivia D. [Dunn] Duff.[3] Peter Ainslie. 6 APR 1869 at the res. of Peter T. Duff in Essex Co. [C5, R, R1:25]

Williamson, Rev. Robert O. to Matoaca Dickenson.[4] ROBERT WILLIAMSON, minister of gospel, age 33, single, b. Princess Anne Co., s/o Abel and Polly Williamson, to MATOACA DICKENSON, age 20, single, b. King and Queen Co., d/o James and Sarah Dickenson. Consent 4 SEP 1862 by father James Dickinson, wit. James S. Mothershead. G.H. Northam. 11 SEP 1862 at *Sion House.* [C3, R:140, R1:12]

Wilson, Abraham P. to Elizabeth C. Croxton. ABRAHAM P. WILSON, farmer, age 57 on 1 JAN 1870, widowed, b. King and Queen Co., s/o Samuel and Fanny Wilson, to ELIZABETH C. CROXTON, age 37, single, b. Richmond Co., d/o Carter Croxton. Consent 2 DEC 1869 by bride, wit. G.W.C. Tallent. M. Beale, Baptist Church. 19 DEC 1869 at res. of L. Lampkin in Westmoreland Co. [C5, NN:8 OCT 1880, R, R1:27]

Wilson, Charles (Col.) to Mrs. Bettie Smith, widow of Ralph Elms (Col.). CHARLES WILSON, oysterman, age 36, widower, b. and res. St. Mary's Co., Md., s/o Jacob and Betsey Wilson, to BETTIE ELMS, age 27, widow, b. Richmond Co., d/o James and Sarah Smith. Allen Brown, minister. 20 MAY 1872 at *Shandy Hall.* [C6, R:237, R1:31]

Wilson, James to Catharine Bowen. JAMES WILSON, farmer, age 63, widowed, b. Richmond Co., s/o James and Sally Wilson, to CATHARINE BOWEN, age 62, single, b. Richmond Co., d/o Joshua and Mary Bowen. John Pullen. 10 NOV 1864 at the groom's residence. [C3, R:139, R1:14]

Wilson, James to Mary Jenkins. JAMES WILSON, farmer, age 50, widowed, b. Richmond Co., s/o James and Sallie Wilson, to MARY JENKINS, age 40, widow, b. Richmond Co., d/o James and Franky Jenkins. John Pullen. 22 AUG 1867 at James Wilson's. [C4, R:287, R1:21]

Wilson, James H. to Mrs. Jane Thrift Luttrell. JAMES H. WILSON, age 25, single, b. Westmoreland Co., s/o Henry and Lucy Wilson, to JANE LUTTRELL, age 34, widow, b. Richmond Co., d/o William and Virginia Thrift. Consent 18 DEC 1866 by bride Jane [her X mark] Luttrell, wit. T.H. Northen. Robert Williamson, M.G. 19 DEC 1866 at Mrs. Luttrell's. [C3, C4, R:272, R1:18]

---

[1] T.G. Williams (1830-1900) and wife Betsey "Bettie" C. Duff (1850-1885) are bur. in Jerusalem Baptist Church cemetery.
[2] Elijah Williams and Juliana McKildoe were married by bond 16 SEP 1826 in Westmoreland Co.
[3] Peter Duff and Olivia Dunn, d/o James Dunn, were married 19 JUN 1838 in Essex Co.
[4] Rev. Robert Williamson (b. 10 DEC 1828, d. 2 OCT 1910) and his wife Matoaca Dickenson (b. 25 NOV 1842, d. 27 JUL 1890) are bur. at Farnham Baptist Church cemetery.

Wilson, Robert H. to Elizabeth M. Reynolds. ROBERT H. WILSON, farmer, age 24, single, b. Richmond Co., s/o Allen and Winny [Winifred Reynolds] Wilson,[1] to ELIZABETH M. REYNOLDS, age 23, single, b. Westmoreland Co., d/o Henry and Luzetta Reynolds. Robert Williamson, M.G. Consent 24 MAR 1866 by bride, wit. E.R. Pullin. 25 MAR 1866 at A. Bryant's. [C4, R:271, R1:17]

Wilson, William to Susan Oliff. WILLIAM WILSON, farmer, age 24 in August, single, b. Richmond Co., s/o James and Susan Wilson, to SUSAN OLIFF, age 21 on 30 JUN 1860, single, b. Richmond Co., d/o James S. and Lucinda Oliff. Consent 25 APR 1860 by Wm. Carter, guardian of bride, wit. Lovell Sanders. John Pullen. 1 or 3 MAY 1860[2] at Robert W. Ramey's. [C2, R:153, R1:8]

Wilson, William A. to Mary J. Cralle. WILLIAM A. WILSON, farmer, age 25, single, b. and res. Northumberland Co., s/o William H. and Ann M.F. Wilson, to MARY J. CRALLE, age 21, single, b. Richmond Co., d/o Samuel [Jr.] and Frances [M. Belfield] Cralle.[3] Robert N. Reamy. 12 FEB 1867 at Mrs. Cralle's. [C4, R:286, R1:20]

Wilson, William H. to Lavinia M. Dodson. WILLIAM H. WILSON, farmer, age 22, single, b. Upson Co., Ga., s/o Samuel M. and Cynthia Wilson, to LAVINIA M. DODSON, age 17, single, b. Richmond Co., d/o Alexander and Catharine [Bryant] Dodson.[4] Barth. Dodson, Parson. 23 DEC 1866 at house of [Mr.] Jones. [C4, R:273, R1:19]

Wingate, Napoleon B.[5] to Elizabeth F. Hazzard. NAPOLEON B. WINGATE, farmer, age 23, single, b. Northumberland Co., res. Lancaster Co., s/o William B. and Jane Ann [Lewis] Wingate, to ELIZABETH F. HAZZARD, age 28, single, b. Richmond Co., d/o William H. and Frances Hazzard. William F. Bain. 20 MAR 1867 at the house of Mrs. Hazzard. [C4, R:286, R1:20]

Winstead, John Taylor to Octavia Delilia Oldham.[6] JOHN T. WINSTEAD, farmer, age 27, single, b. Richmond Co., s/o George L. [Lunsford] and Martha B. [Hall Beacham Headley] Winstead,[7] to OCTAVIA D. OLDHAM, age 22, single, b. Westmoreland Co., d/o John T. and Elizabeth [Morris] Oldham.[8] Consent 19 JUN 1867 by bride, wit. Lindsey Headley. W.W. Walker. 22 JAN 1867 at the house of Mr. Straughan. [C3, C4, R:285, R1:19]

Winters, Humphrey (Col.) to Lucy Rich (Col.). HUMPHREY WINTERS, steward, age 32, divorced, b. Westmoreland Co., s/o William and Rebecca Winters, to LUCY RICH, age 18, single, b. Richmond Co., d/o George and Sarah Rich. Rev. John Wilkerson. 17 JUN 1888 at *Oak Hill.*[9] [C11, R:316, R1:72]

Winters, William (Col.) to Ann Johnson (Col.). WILLIAM WINTERS, laborer, age 70, widowed, b. Westmoreland Co., s/o George and Kezia Winters, to ANN JOHNSON, age 42, single, b.

---

[1] Allen Willson and Winifred Reynolds were married by bond 23 JAN 1826 in Richmond Co.
[2] Minister return gives date of marriage 1 MAY 1860, while the license notes date 3 MAY 1860.
[3] Samuel Cralle, Jr. and Frances M. Belfield, d/o Joseph Belfield, were married by bond 10 SEP 1832 in Richmond Co.
[4] Alexander Dodson and Catharine Bryant were married 3 FEB 1848 in Richmond Co. by Rev. Bartholomew Dodson.
[5] Napoleon B. Wingate (1843-1920) is bur. at Bethel United Methodist Church cemetery at Lively, Va.
[6] John T. Winstead (b. 30 JUN 1839, d. 30 JUL 1922) and wife Octavia D. Oldham (b. 13 FEB 1844, d. 4 MAR 1912) are bur. in Henderson United Methodist Church cemetery, Hyacinth, Va. He served in Co. G, 15th Va. Cav., C.S.A.
[7] George L. Winstead and Martha H.B. Headley, d/o Griffin Headley, were married by bond 8 NOV 1836 in Richmond Co.
[8] John T. Oldham and Elizabeth Morris were married by bond 31 MAY 1825 in Westmoreland Co.
[9] *Oak Hill* was the name Williamson Ball Tomlin gave to his tract called *Bloomsbury.* Located in Cobham Park Neck.

Richmond Co., d/o Ben and Fanny Johnson. Consent 14 OCT 1881 by parties William [his X mark] Winters, and Ann [her X mark] Johnson, wit. William [his X mark] Self. Edmond Rich. 13 OCT 1881 at *Belleville*. [C9, R:338, R1:54]

Wise, Joseph W. to Sarah A. Dobyns. Consent 12 JUL 1855 by bride Sarah [her X mark] Dobyns, wit. H. Coates. No license or minister return. [C1]

Withers, Henry to Lucy J. Self. HENRY WITHERS, farming, age 23, single, b. Richmond Co., s/o Joseph and Emily Withers, to LUCY J. SELF, age 15y11m, single, b. Northumberland Co., d/o Moses A. and Lucy A. Self. Consent 11 APR 1882 by bride's parents. M.A. and Lucy A. Self, wit. J.F. Sisson. G.H. Northam. 13 APR 1882. [C9, R:312, R1:56]

Wood, Charles H. (Col.) to Mrs. Mary Sorrel (Col.).[1] CHARLES H. WOOD, oysterman, age 27, single, b. Lancaster Co., s/o James Wood and Jane Wood (dec'd.), to MARY SORREL, age 25, widow, b. Richmond Co., d/o Henry and Delcie Lewis. Allen Brown, minister. 28 APR 1881 at the bride's home. [C9, R:336, R1:53]

Wood, Robert (Col.) to Catherine Glasco (Col.). ROBERT WOOD, laborer, age 23, single, b. Richmond Co., s/o William and Martha Wood, to CATHERINE GLASCO, age 19y10m, single, b. Richmond Co., d/o Thomas and Amy Glasco. Consent 1 NOV 1881 by bride's parents Thomas [his X mark] Glasco and Amy [her X mark] Glasco, wits. Nacy [his X mark] Glasco and H.C. Curtis. Nelson Atkins. 2 NOV 1881 at Ebenezer Baptist Church. [C9; R:338, R1:54]

Wood, Robert (Col.) to Laura Bailey (Col.). ROBERT WOOD, farming, age 31, widowed,[2] b. Richmond Co., s/o William and Martha Wood, to LAURA BAILEY, age 23y8m14d, single, b. Richmond Co., d/o Stephen and Maria Bailey. Rev. L. Harrod, Pastor, Mulberry Baptist Church. 24 APR 1890 at the res. of the parents. [C12, R:323a, R1:77]

Wood, Thomas (Col.) to Willie Anne Malory (Col.). THOMAS WOOD, laborer, age 43, widowed, b. Essex Co., s/o Reuben and Hannah Wood, to WILLIE ANNE MALORY, age 25, single, b. King and Queen Co., names of parents incomplete. Thomas G. Thomas. 3 JAN 1877 at the res. of the bride's parents. [C8, R:306a, R1:42]

Woodey, Albert (Col.) to Mrs. Wincy Carlton (Col.). ALBERT WOODEY, farmer, age 22, single, b. Richmond Co., s/o Lewis and Polly Woodey, to WINCY CARLTON, age 30, widow, b. Richmond Co., d/o John and Mincy Newman. George Laws. 3 SEP 1868 at John Newman's. [C5, R1:24]

Woods, Edward L. to Georgie A. Hardwick. EDWARD L. WOODS, shoemaker, age 30, single, b. Baltimore, Md., res. *Nominy Grove*, Westmoreland Co., s/o Edward and Ellen B. Woods, to GEORGIE A. HARDWICK, age 24, single, b. Richmond Co., d/o John and Mary M. Hardwick. J.H. Davis. 15 MAY 1867 at the res. of the bride's mother. [C4, R:286, R1:21]

Woody, Lewis (Col.) to Lucinda Beverly (Col.). LEWIS WOODY, farmer, age 19, single, b. Richmond Co., s/o Lewis and Polly Woody, to LUCINDA BEVERLY, age 24, single, b. Caroline

---

[1] Her first husband Squire Sorrel died 27 JUN 1877 when Mary was about 25 years of age.
[2] Robert Wood was previously married 2 NOV 1881 in Richmond Co. to Catherine Glasco.

Co., parents names blank. George Laws. 24 JUL 1868 at Robert Jackson's. [C5, R:254, R1:24]

Woody, Robert (Col.) to Winney Robinson (Col.). ROBERT WOODY, farmer, age 22, single, b. Richmond Co., s/o Lewis and Polly Woody, to WINNEY ROBINSON, age 26, single, b. and res. Essex Co., d/o Rebecca Robinson. George Laws. 26 DEC 1869 at Robert Jackson's. [C5, R, R1:27]

Woollard, Alpheus to Lydia A. Tucker. ALPHEUS WOOLLARD, farmer, age 22, single, b. Richmond Co., s/o Thomas W. and Mary E. [Elizabeth Williams] Woollard,[1] to LYDIA A. TUCKER, age 17, single, b. Richmond Co., d/o Benjamin F. and Harriet R. [Thrift] Tucker.[2] Elder James A. Weaver. 14 FEB 1867 at the res. of the bride. [C4, R:285, R1:20]

Woollard, Benjamin A. to Susannah P. Mealey. BENJAMIN A. WOOLLARD, farmer, age 25, single, b. Richmond Co., s/o Sydnor F. and Ann Woollard, to SUSANNAH P. MEALEY, age 18, single, b. Richmond Co., d/o Jesse and Sarah [B. Harris] Mealey.[3] Consent 4 AUG 1875 by William N. Harris, guardian, wit. William Allison. W.A. Crocker. 5 AUG 1875 at Jerusalem Church. [C7, R:262, R1:38]

Woolard, David Henry to Roberta O. Balderson.[4] DAVID WOOLLARD [sic], farmer, age 24, single, b. Richmond Co., s/o Thomas [William] Woolard [and Elizabeth Nutt Bell],[5] to ROBERTA BALDERSON, age 21, single, b. Northumberland Co., d/o Randall and Jemima [Lewis] Balderson. Consent 6 FEB 1878 by parties, wit. Thomas [A.] Lewis. R.N. Reamy. 6 FEB 1878 at Wm. Middleton's. [C8, R:310, R1:44]

Woollard, James to Julia Ann Rust. JAMES WOOLLARD, farmer, age 22, single, b. Richmond Co., s/o John T. and Mary Woollard, to JULIA A. RUST, age 21, single, b. Richmond Co., d/o Elizabeth Rust (father's name unknown). Robert Williamson, M.G. 23 DEC 1860 at res. of Richard Davis. [C2, R:154, R1:9]

Woollard, James G. to Mrs. Melissa S. Rust. JAMES G. WOOLLARD, farmer, age 26, widowed, b. Richmond Co., s/o John T. and Mary Woollard, to MELISSA S. RUST, age 21, widow, b. Richmond Co., d/o Robert G. and Matilda [Woollard] Lewis.[6] Robert Williamson, M.G. 1 DEC 1864 at res. of George Hanks. [C3, R:139, R1:14]

Woollard, James G. to Elizabeth S. Sisson. JAMES G. WOOLLARD, farmer, age 32, widowed, b. Richmond Co., parents names blank [John T. and Mary Woollard], to ELIZABETH S. SISSON, age 23, single, b. Richmond Co., d/o Hiram and Sarah [Littrell] Sisson.[7] Consent 4 JUN 1870 by bride, wit. Thomas [H.] Barns. Charles E. Watts. 4 JUN 1870 at Jerusalem Church. [C5, R:233, R1:28]

---

[1] Thomas W. Woollard and Mary Elizabeth Williams, d/o E.L. Williams, were married 20 JAN 1847 in Richmond Co. by Rev. Addison Hall.
[2] Benjamin Tucker and Harriet Thrift were married by bond 21 DEC 1840 in Richmond Co. by Rev. Nathan Healy.
[3] Jesse Mealey and Sarah B. Harris were married 22 FEB 1844 in Richmond Co. by Rev. William N. Ward.
[4] David H. Woolard (b. 26 NOV 1866, d. 1 JUN 1941) and wife Roberta O. Balderson (b. 26 OCT 1862, d. 27 SEP 1938) are bur. in Gibeon Baptist Church cemetery.
[5] Thomas W. Woolard (b. 1824, d. 1899 in Haynesville, Va.) and his second wife Eliza Nutt Bell (1844-1899) are bur. in Totuskey Baptist Church cemetery.
[6] Robert Lewis and Matilda Woollard were married by bond 27 APR 1835 in Richmond Co.
[7] Heirome [Hiram] Sisson and Sally Littrell were married by bond 24 FEB 1840 in Richmond Co.

Woolard, John J. to Nannie Hale. JOHN J. WOOLARD, farming, age 24, single, b. Richmond Co., s/o James G. and Julia A. Woolard, to NANNIE HALE, age 15, single, b. Richmond Co., d/o Roystin R. and Winnie Hale. Consent 31 DEC 1885 by father Roystin R. Hale, wits. Thos. F. Hammack, Jas. L. Hammack. G.H. Northam. 3 JAN 1886 at William Hale's. [C11, HH:15 JAN 1886 gives bride's surname as Hall, R:315, R1:67]

Woollard, John T. to Elizabeth S. Thrift. Consent 15 JAN 1857 by Elizabeth [her X mark] Thrift, wit. A. Bryant. No license or minister return. [C1]

Woollard, John William[1] to Catharine J. "Kate" Lawrence. JOHN WILLIAM WOOLLARD, farming, age 21y9m, single, b. Richmond Co., s/o John T. and Elizabeth [S. Thrift] Woollard, to CATHARINE J. LAWRENCE, age 17, single, b. New Jersey, d/o Andrew and Catharine Lawrence. Consent 6 DEC 1882 by parents Andrew and Katie J. Lawrence, wit. J.E. Northen. G.H. Northam. 9 DEC 1882. [C9, R:314, R1:57]

Woolard, Lemuel L. to Laura Smith Northen.[2] LEMUEL L. WOOLLARD [sic], farmer, age 27, single, b. Lancaster Co., s/o Lemuel L. and Apphia [T. Tune] Woolard,[3] to LAURA S. NORTHEN, age 22, single, b. Richmond Co., d/o Edward J. [Jr.] and Catharine [M. Northen] Northen.[4] Consent 20 MAY 1868 by bride, no wit. G.H. Northam. 21 MAY 1868. [C4, C5, R:253, R1:23]

Woolard, Richard L. to Mary "Mollie" A. Roe.[5] RICHARD L. WOOLLARD [sic], farming, age 25, single, b. Richmond Co., s/o John and Elizabeth Woolard, to MOLLIE A. ROE, age 33, single, b. Richmond Co., d/o Samuel B. and Winnie [Winnefred Woollard] Roe.[6] Consent 12 FEB 1890 by bride, wit. John W. Roe. Rev. J. Manning Dunaway. 12 FEB 1890 at the bride's residence. [C12, R:323, R1:76]

Woolard, Thomas William to Elizabeth Nutt Bell.[7] THOMAS W. WOOLLARD [sic], farmer, age 42, widowed, b. Richmond Co., s/o Lemuel L. and Apphia [T. Tune] Woollard, to ELIZA N. BELL, age 22, single, b. Northumberland Co., d/o William D. [Dew] and Charlotte [McAdams Nutt] Bell.[8] Consent 19 DEC 1866 by parties. Robert Williamson, M.G. 20 DEC 1866 at Mrs. Charlotte Bell's. [C4, R:272, R1:18]

Wormbley, James to Martha Burrell. JAMES WORMBLEY, farmer, age 70, widower, b. and res. Westmoreland Co., s/o William and Silvey Thompson, to MARTHA BURRELL, age 16, single, b. Richmond Co., d/o James and Mary Burrell. Elder James A. Weaver. 29 DEC 1867 at the res. of Albert D. Reynolds. [C4, R:287, R1:22]

---

[1] J.W. Woolard (b. 2 MAR 1862, d. 30 MAR 1944) and his wife Kate J. Woolard (b. 4 APR 1865, d. 27 JUL 1936) are bur. in Jerusalem Baptist Church cemetery.
[2] Lemuel L. Woolard (b. 5 AUG 1840, d. 14 DEC 1916) and wife Laura Smith Northen (b. 21 JAN 1845, d. 10 MAY 1928) are bur. in Jerusalem Baptist Church cemetery. Her served as a private in Co. D, 47th Va. Cav., C.S.A.
[3] Lemuel L. Woollard and Apphia T. Tune were married by bond 20 JAN 1824 in Richmond Co.
[4] Edward J. Northen, Jr. and Catharine M. Northen were married by bond 7 DEC 1832 in Richmond Co.
[5] Richard L. Woolard (1863-1945) and wife Mary A. Roe (1856-1935) are bur. in Jerusalem Baptist Church cemetery.
[6] Samuel B. Roe and Winnefred Woollard were married by bond 29 MAR 1848 in Richmond Co.
[7] Thomas W. Woolard (b. 1824, d. 1899 in Haynesville, Va.) and his second wife Elizabeth Nutt Bell (b. 1844, d. 1899 in Haynesville, Va.) are bur. at Totuskey Baptist Church cemetery.
[8] William D. Bell and Charlotte Nutt, ward of Thomas S. Sydnor, were married by bond 24 JAN 1827 in Richmond Co.

Wormeley, Alexander (Col.) to Julia Page (Col.). ALEXANDER WORMELEY, laborer, age 36, widowed, b. Richmond Co., s/o George and Catherine Wormeley, to JULIA PAGE, age 18, single, b. Richmond Co., d/o Chapman and Virginia Page. Consent 4 JUL 1890 by Chapman [his X mark] Page, Alexander [his X mark] Wormeley. Letter 13 FEB 1890 from Louisa Tate. Rev. T.G. Thomas. 6 JUL 1890 at the house of Chapman Page. [C12, R:323a, R1:77]

Wormley, Elick (Col.) to Virginia Tate (Col.). ELICK WORMLEY, miller, age 24, single, b. Richmond Co., s/o George and Kitty Wormley, to VIRGINIA TATE, age 20, single, b. Westmoreland Co., d/o Campbell and Mary Ann Tate. Consent by Frederick Hubbard, guardian, unsigned. Thomas G. Thomas. 28 NOV 1872 at George Wormley's house. [C6, R:238, R1:32]

Wormsey, Charles (Col.) to Etta Sorrel (Col.). CHARLES WORMSEY, laborer, age 23, single, b. King and Queen Co., s/o Ralph and Lucy Wormsey, to ETTA SORREL, age 21, single, b. King and Queen Co., d/o William and Delia Tunstall. Elijah L. Williams. 17 MAY 1866. [C4, R:271, R1:187]

Wright, Alexander M. to Frances A.A. Parry. Consent 20 MAR 1854 by father J.H. Parry, wit. H.B. Scott. No return. [C]

Wright, Alexander M. to Mrs. Adithia A. Hanks, widow of Peter S. Northen. ALEXANDER M. WRIGHT, farmer, age 42, widowed, b. Richmond Co., [names of parents incomplete], to ADITHIA A. NORTHEN, age 27, widow, b. Richmond Co., d/o Joseph [T.] and Judy [Judith P. Hanks] Hanks.[1] Consent 1 NOV 1879 by bride, wit. R.H. Forester; consent 10 NOV 1879 by groom, wit. R.H. Forester. G.H. Northam. 18 NOV 1879. [C8, R:309, R1:48]

Wright, Edward A. to Willie A. Newman. EDWARD A. WRIGHT, farming, age 26, single, b. Richmond Co., s/o Andrew and Cornelia Wright, to WILLIE A. NEWMAN, age 24, single, b. Richmond Co., d/o Henry and Elizabeth Newman. Robert Williamson. 26 DEC 1888 at *Indian Banks*. [C12, R:317, R1:723]

Wright, Edwin Theopolis to Maria Isabella Lamkin.[2] EDWIN T. WRIGHT, farmer, age 27, single, b. and res. Westmoreland Co., s/o Mottram M. [Middleton] and Malinda A. [Lamkin] Wright,[3] to MARIA I. LAMKIN,[4] age 19, single, b. Northumberland Co., d/o James L. and Judith [Sampson] Lamkin.[5] No minister return. 15 DEC 1859. [C2, R:165, R1:7]

Wright, George H.[6] to Catharine Headley. GEORGE H. WRIGHT, farmer, age 29, single, b. Westmoreland Co., s/o George M. and Catharine M.P. Wright, to CATHARINE HEADLEY, age 45, single, b. Northumberland Co., d/o James and Betty Headley. Consent 24 NOV 1860 by bride, wit. William English. Robert Williamson, M.G. 29 NOV 1860. [C2, R:154, R1:9]

---

[1] Joseph T. Hanks and Judith P. Hanks were married by bond 12 SEP 1837 in Richmond Co.
[2] Edwin T. Wright (b. 15 MAY 1832, d. 3 FEB 1892) and wife Maria Isabella Lamkin (b. 20 NOV 1840, d. 29 AUG 1890) are bur. in the Wright Family Cemetery at Oldhams, Va. Served in Co. K, 40th Reg., Va. Inf., C.S.A., wounded in forearm, made ambulance driver.
[3] Mottram M. Wright (b. 1800, d. 10 NOV 1858) and his wife Malinda A. Lamkin (b. 1809, d. 8 MAR 1868) are bur. in the Wright Family Cemetery at Oldhams, Va. Mottrom M. Wright and Malinda Lamkin were married by bond 6 APR 1830 in Richmond Co.
[4] The surname also appears as Lampkin.
[5] James L. Lamkin and Judith Sampson were married by bond 19 SEP 1828 in Northumberland Co.
[6] George H. Wright served in Co. D, 47th Reg., Va. Inf., C.S.A.

Wright, John M. to Medora Middleton. JOHN M. WRIGHT, merchant, age 33, widowed, b. Richmond Co., s/o George M. and Catharine M.P. Wright, to MEDORA MIDDLETON, age 22, single, b. Northumberland Co., d/o William and Mary E. Middleton. Robert Williamson, M.G. 3 OCT 1861 at *Edge Hill.* [C3, R:124, R1:11]

Wright, John M. to Virginia S. Parry. JOHN M. WRIGHT, age 38, widowed, b. Richmond Co., s/o George M. and Catharine M.P. Wright, to VIRGINIA S. PARRY, age 22, single, b. Essex Co., d/o John H. and Virginia Parry. Consent 3 MAR 1865 by bride, wit. Andrew Wright. Robert Williamson, M.G. 3 APR 1865 at Farnham Church. [C3, R:204, R1:14]

Wright, Rawleigh W. (Col.) to Millie Corbin (Col.). RAWLEIGH W. WRIGHT, age 21, single, b. Northumberland Co., s/o Henry and Violet Wright, to MILLIE CORBIN, age 17, single, b. Richmond Co., d/o Henry and Betsy Corbin. Consent 26 DEC 1866 by mother Betsy [her X mark] Corbin. Thomas G. Thomas. 10 JAN 1867 at house of Eben Jeffries. [C4, R:285 (twice), R1:19 and 20]

Y

Yates, Grant (Col.) to Roxanna Mason (Col.). GRANT YATES, oystering, age 27y11m, single, b. Richmond Co., s/o Walter J. Yates and Ella Williams, to ROXANNA MASON, age 21y3m, single, b. Richmond Co., d/o Oscar Mason and Susan Williams. Consent 17 DEC 1890 by bride and Mrs. Susan Williams, wit. Andrew Fisher, Gr. Cralle. Rev. L. Harrod, Pastor of Ebenezer and Mulberry Baptist Churches. 18 DEC 1890 at Mt. Zion Baptist Church. [C12, R:324, R1:78]

Yeatman, Charles Warren to Augusta Ella Nash.[1] CHARLES W. YEATMAN, farming, age 27, single, b. Richmond Co., s/o Levi and Mary [Beverton] Yeatman,[2] to AUGUSTA E. NASH, age 20, single, b. Richmond Co., d/o Zachariah and Susan A. Nash. Consent 11 JAN 1882 by Susan A. Nash and bride Augusta E. [her X mark] Nash, wit. T.C. [his X mark] Barrett.[3] R.N. Reamy. 12 JAN 1882 at res. of Zachariah Nash. [C9, R:312, R1:55]

Yeatman, George Washington to Harriet Isabella Bryant.[4] GEORGE W. YEATMAN, mechanic, age 25, single, b. Richmond Co., res. Northumberland Co., s/o Matthew and Mary Elizabeth Yeatman, to HARRIET ISABELLA BRYANT, age 21, single, b. Richmond Co., d/o Reuben and Mary [Ann Thrift] Bryant. G.H. Northam. 27 JAN 1876. [C7, R:304, R1:40]

Yeatman, James H. to Alice [or Alcey] J. Belfield. JAMES H. YEATMAN, farming, age 31 on 7 JUN 1854, single, b. Richmond Co., s/o Mathew Yeatman and Nelly, to ALICE J. BELFIELD, age 27 on 7 MAR 1854, single, b. Richmond Co., d/o Joseph Belfield and Jane. Consent 14 JAN 1854 by bride, wit. George H. Belfield. Return by Rev. John Pullen, at Wm. B. Belfield's in Richmond Co. 18 JAN 1854. [C, R, R1:1]

---

[1] Charles W. Yeatman (1854-1921) and his wife Augusta E. Nash Yeatman (1861-1935) are bur. in Rappahannock Baptist Church cemetery.
[2] Levi Yeatman and Mary Beverton were married 7 MAR 1850 in Richmond Co. by Rev. George Northam.
[3] Tuncil C. Barrett is bur. at Welcome Grove Baptist Church cemetery. He was married to Mary Susan Marks.
[4] George W. Yeatman (b. 1 JAN 1848, d. 27 JUL 1916) and wife Harriet I. Bryant (b. 15 FEB 1854, d. 1 AUG 1926) are bur. at Totuskey Baptist Church cemetery.

Yeatman, John E. to Mrs. Mary M. Bispham, widow of William S. Saunders. JOHN E. YEATMAN, farming, age 25y4m20d, single, b. Richmond Co., s/o James H. and Alice Jane Yeatman, to MARY M. SAUNDERS, age 25, widow, b. Richmond Co., d/o W. Robert Bispham and Jane Bispham now Hinson. Consent undated by bride Mary M. [her X mark] Saunders, wit. Benjamin B. Belfield. D.M. Wharton. 12 AUG 1885 at the res. of M. Hinson. [C10, R:317, R1:65]

Yeatman, Mathew Vincent to Julia Ann Hall.[1] MATHEW VINCENT YEATMAN, farmer, age 33, single, b. Richmond Co., s/o Mathew and Elizabeth [Figett] Yeatman,[2] to JULIA ANN HALL, age 26, single, b. Richmond Co., d/o James and Nancy Hall. G.H. Northam. 28 DEC 1870 at Mrs. Hall's. [C5, R:234, R1:28]

Yeatman, Milton Henry[3] to Catharine Biscoe Crabb. MILTON H. YEATMAN, engineer, age 25, single, b. Richmond Co., s/o Henry A. and Ann W. [Reynolds] Yeatman,[4] to CATHARINE [B.] CRABB, age 26, single, b. Richmond Co., s/o William M.M. and A. [Ann] T. [Peck] Crabb.[5] G.H. Northam. 21 FEB 1867 at *Pittsville*. [C4, R:285, R1:20]

Yerby, Addison O. to Mrs. Cordelia B. Chinn. ADDISON O. YERBY, in 37th year, widower, b. Fauquier Co., s/o William G. Yerby [and Fanny Pullin],[6] to CORDELIA B. CHINN, in 35th year, widow, b. Richmond Co., d/o William D. and [Margaret] Frances [Yerby] McCarty.[7] William N. Ward, M.G. 25 APR 1854 at Mrs. Cordelia B. Chinn's. [C1, R, R1:1]

Yerby, Henry H. (Col.) to Frances Ball (Col.). HENRY H. YERBY, oystering, age 27y9m, single, b. Richmond Co., s/o Shadrack and Nancy Yerby, to FRANCES BALL, age21y2m13d, single, b. Lancaster Co., d/o Julia Ball (name of father not given). Consent by bride Frances [her X mark] Ball, wit. J.H. Lemoine. Rev. W. Carter. 22 DEC 1881 at the res. of Moses Carter. [C9, R:337, R1:55]

Yerby, John to Mrs. Mary Veny. JOHN YERBY, farmer, age 27, single, b. Lancaster Co., s/o Shedrick and Nancy Yerby, to MARY VENY, age 26, widow, b. Middlesex Co., d/o Loudoun and Fanny West. Consent 13 JAN 1869 by bride Mary [her X mark] Veny, wit. M.E. Hill. Robert Williamson, M.G. 14 JAN 1869 at *Morattico*. [C5, R, R1:25]

Young, Benjamin (Col.) to Margaret Alfred (Col.). BENJAMIN YOUNG, oysterman, age 22, single, b. Essex Co., s/o Isaac and Handie Young, to MARGARET ALFRED, age 21, single, b. Richmond Co., names of parents blank. Consent 12 APR 1880 by bride Margaret [her X mark] Alfred, wit. George [his X mark] Dunaway. Rev. Walker Carter. 15 APR 1880 at the bride's home. [C9, R:315, R1:50]

---

[1] Mathew V. Yeatman (b. 7 OCT 1837, d. 12 AUG 1912) and wife Julia A. Hall (b. 25 AUG 1842, d. 30 AUG 1925) are bur. in Nomini Baptist Church cemetery. He served in Co. B and D, 40th Va. Inf., C.S.A., court-marshaled.
[2] Mathew Yeatman, Jr. and Elizabeth Figett were married by bond 13 DEC 1826 in Richmond Co.
[3] Milton H. Yeatman (b. 24 FEB 1842, d. 20 SEP 1921) is bur. at Warsaw United Methodist Church cemetery. The grave of his wife Catherine B. Crabbe is not found. He served in Co. B, 40th Reg., Va. Inf., detailed as wagon master, and Co. K, 9th Va. Cav., C.S.A.
[4] Henry A. Yeatman, of Westmoreland Co., and Nancy W. Reynolds, were married by bond 8 JUL 1833 in Richmond Co.
[5] William M.M. Crabb, of Westmoreland Co., and Ann T. Peck, were married 22 FEB 1838 in Richmond Co. by Rev. Lovell Marders.
[6] William G. Yerby and Fanny Pullin were married by bond 18 JUL 1815 in Richmond Co.
[7] William D. McCarty and Margaret F. Yerby were married by bond 7 DEC 1813 in Richmond Co.

BIBLIOGRAPHY

In addition to original and microfilm copy court records, the publications listed below have been consulted.

Booker, James Motley, *A Booker Family of Virginia: Gloucester and Essex Counties and the Northern Neck, With Some of the Descendants and Related Families* (Heathsville, Va.: The Northumberland County Historical Society, 1994)

Derieux, Susanne P. and Wesley E. Pippenger, *Essex County, Virginia Marriage Records: Transcripts of Consents, Affidavits, Minister Returns, and Marriage Licenses, Volume 1: 1850-1872* (Tappahannock, Va.: Barbour Printing Services, Inc., 2011)

Derieux, Susanne P. and Wesley E. Pippenger, *Essex County, Virginia Cemeteries: Volume I – County Church Cemeteries* (Tappahannock, Va.: Barbour Printing Services, Inc., 2011)

Fisher, Therese, *Marriages of Caroline County, Virginia, 1777-1853* (Bowie, Md.: Heritage Books, Inc., 1998)

Fortier, John, *15th Virginia Cavalry* (Lynchburg, Va.: H.E. Howard, Inc., 1993)

The Genealogical Society of the Northern Neck, *The Shepherd's Fold: Cemetery Records of Northumberland County, Virginia Churches* (Athens, Ga.: New Papyrus Publishing Company, 2012)

Hill, Margaret Lester and Clyde H. Ratcliffe, *In Remembrance: Gravestone Inscriptions and Burials of Lancaster County, Virginia* (White Stone, Va.: By the Compilers, 2002)

King, George Harrison Sanford, *Marriages of Richmond County, Virginia, 1668-1863* (Fredericksburg, Va.: By the Author, 1964)

King George County Historical Society, *Cemeteries of King George County, Virginia, Volume II - Private Cemeteries* (King George, Va.: By the Society, 2005)

Knorr, Catherine L., *Marriages of Fredericksburg, Virginia, 1782-1850* (Pine Bluff, Ark.: Duplicating Service, The Purdue Co., 1954)

Krick, Robert E.L., *40th Virginia Infantry* (Lynchburg, Va.: H.E. Howard, Inc., 1985)

Krick, Robert K., *9th Virginia Cavalry*, 4th Ed. (Lynchburg, Va.: H.E. Howard, Inc., 1982)

Lee, Elizabeth Nuckols, *King George County, Virginia Marriages: Volume I, Marriage Bonds Book 1, 1786-1850 [including ministers' returns]* (Athens, Ga.: Iberian Publishing Co., 1995)

Lee, Ida J., *Lancaster County, Virginia Marriage Bonds, 1862-1850* (Baltimore, Md.: Genealogical Publishing Co., 1972)

Malory, Dalton W., *Westmoreland County, Virginia Cemeteries: Volume One* (Athens, Ga.: New Papyrus Publishing, 2009)

Miller, Thomas Michael, *Alexandria & Alexandria (Arlington) Couunty, Virginia Minister Returns & Marriage Bonds – 1801-1852* (Bowie, Md.: Heritage Books, Inc., 1987)

Nottingham, Stratton, *The Marriage License Bonds of Lancaster County, Virginia, From 1701 to 1848* (Onancock, Va.: By the Author, 1927; reprint Baltimore, Va.: Clearfield Co., Inc., 1992)

Nottingham, Stratton, *The Marriage License Bonds of Northumberland County, Virginia, From 1783 to 1850* (Onancock, Va.: By the Author, 1929; reprint Blatimore, Md.: Genealogical Publishing Co., Inc., 1976)

Nottingham, Stratton, *The Marriage License Bonds of Westmoreland County, Virginia, From1786 to 1850* (Onancock, Va.: By the Author, 1928; reprint Baltimore, Md.: Genealogical Publishing Co., Inc., 1975)

Pippenger, Wesley E., *District of Columbia Marriage Licenses, Register 1, 1811-1858* (Westminster, Md.: Family Line Publications, 1994)

Pippenger, Wesley E., *Death Notices from Richmond, Virginia Newspapers, 1841-1853* (Richmond, Va.: The Virginia Genealogical Society, 2002)

Pippenger, Wesley E., *John Alexander: A Northern Neck Proprietor, His Family, Friends and Kin* (Baltimore, Md.: Gateway Press, Inc., 1990)

Ruby, Ann Todd, Florence Isabelle Stacy and Herbert Ridgeway Collins, *Speaking of Families: The Tod(d)s of Caroline County, Virginia and Their Kin* (Columbia, Mo.: Artcraft Press, 1960)

Ryland, Elizabeth Lowell, ed., *Richmond County, Virgilnia: A Review Commemorating The Bicentennial* (Warsaw, Va.: Richmond County Board of Supervisors, 1976)

Virginia Genealogical Society, *Marriages of Middlesex County, Virginia, 1740-1852* (Richmond, Va.: By the Society, 1965)

Wilkerson, Eva Eubank, *Index to Marriages of Old Rappahannock and Essex Counties, Virginia, 1665-1900* (Richmond, Va.: Whittet & Shepperson, 1953)

233

240

241

243

253

254

256

275

283

285

287

291

293

301

304

306

311

Heritage Books by Wesley E. Pippenger:

Alexander Family: Migrations from Maryland

Alexandria (Arlington) County, Virginia Death Records, 1853–1896

Alexandria City and Arlington County, Virginia Records Index: Vol. 1

Alexandria City and Arlington County, Virginia Records Index: Vol. 2

Alexandria County, Virginia Marriage Records, 1853–1895

Alexandria Virginia Marriage Index, January 10, 1893 to August 31, 1905

Alexandria, Virginia Marriages, 1870–1892

Alexandria, Virginia Town Lots, 1749–1801
Together with the Proceedings of the Board of Trustees, 1749–1780

Alexandria, Virginia Wills, Administrations and Guardianships, 1786–1800

Alexandria, Virginia 1808 Census (Wards 1, 2, 3, and 4)

Alexandria, Virginia Death Records, 1863–1896

Alexandria, Virginia Hustings Court Orders, Volume 1, 1780–1787

Connections and Separations: Divorce, Name Change and Other
Genealogical Tidbits from the Acts of the Virginia General Assembly

Daily National Intelligencer *Index to Deaths, 1855–1870*

Daily National Intelligencer, *Washington, District of Columbia*
Marriages and Deaths Notices (January 1, 1851 to December 30, 1854)

Dead People on the Move: Reconstruction of the Georgetown Presbyterian
Burying Ground, Holmead's (Western) Burying Ground, and
Other Removals in the District of Columbia

Death Notices from Richmond, Virginia Newspapers, 1841–1853

District of Columbia Ancestors,
A Guide to Records of the District of Columbia

District of Columbia Death Records: August 1, 1874–July 31, 1879

District of Columbia Foreign Deaths, 1888–1923

District of Columbia Guardianship Index, 1802–1928

District of Columbia Interments (Index to Deaths)
January 1, 1855 to July 31, 1874

District of Columbia Marriage Licenses, Register 1: 1811–1858

District of Columbia Marriage Licenses, Register 2: 1858–1870

District of Columbia Marriage Records Index
June 28, 1877 to October 19, 1885: Marriage Record Books 11 to 20
Wesley E. Pippenger and Dorothy S. Provine

District of Columbia Marriage Records Index
October 20, 1885 to January 20, 1892: Marriage Record Books 21 to 30

District of Columbia Marriage Records Index
January 20, 1892 to August 30, 1896: Marriage Record Books 31 to 40

District of Columbia Marriage Records Index
August 31, 1896 to December 17, 1900: Marriage Record Books 41 to 65

District of Columbia Probate Records, 1801–1852

District of Columbia: Original Land Owners, 1791–1800

Early Church Records of Alexandria City and Fairfax County, Virginia

Essex County, Virginia Guardianship and Orphans Records, 1707–1888: A Descriptive Index

Essex County, Virginia Marriage Bonds, 1804–1850, Annotated

Essex County, Virginia Newspaper Notices, 1738–1938